The Condition of Education 2013

MAY 2013

Susan Aud
National Center for Education Statistics

Sidney Wilkinson-Flicker
Paul Kristapovich
Amy Rathbun
Xiaolei Wang
Jijun Zhang
American Institutes for Research

Liz Notter
Production Manager
Synergy Enterprises, Inc.

Thomas Nachazel
Senior Editor
Allison Dziuba
Editor
American Institutes for Research

NCES 2013-037
U.S. DEPARTMENT OF EDUCATION

ies NATIONAL CENTER FOR EDUCATION STATISTICS
Institute of Education Sciences

U.S. Department of Education
Arne Duncan
Secretary

Institute of Education Sciences
John Q. Easton
Director

National Center for Education Statistics
Jack Buckley
Commissioner

The National Center for Education Statistics (NCES) is the primary federal entity for collecting, analyzing, and reporting data related to education in the United States and other nations. It fulfills a congressional mandate to collect, collate, analyze, and report full and complete statistics on the condition of education in the United States; conduct and publish reports and specialized analyses of the meaning and significance of such statistics; assist state and local education agencies in improving their statistical systems; and review and report on education activities in foreign countries.

NCES activities are designed to address high-priority education data needs; provide consistent, reliable, complete, and accurate indicators of education status and trends; and report timely, useful, and high-quality data to the U.S. Department of Education, the Congress, the states, other education policymakers, practitioners, data users, and the general public. Unless specifically noted all information contained herein is in the public domain.

We strive to make our products available in a variety of formats and in language that is appropriate to a variety of audiences. You, as our customer, are the best judge of our success in communicating information effectively. If you have any comments or suggestions about this or any other NCES product or report, we would like to hear from you. Please direct your comments to

    NCES, IES, U.S. Department of Education
    1990 K Street NW
    Washington, DC 20006-5651

May 2013

The NCES Home Page address is http://nces.ed.gov.
The NCES Publications and Products address is http://nces.ed.gov/pubsearch.

This report was prepared for the National Center for Education Statistics under Contract No. ED-IES-12-000176 with American Institutes for Research. Mention of trade names, commercial products, or organizations does not imply endorsement by the U.S. Government.

Suggested Citation
Aud, S., Wilkinson-Flicker, S., Kristapovich, P., Rathbun, A., Wang, X., and Zhang, J. (2013). *The Condition of Education 2013* (NCES 2013-037). U.S. Department of Education, National Center for Education Statistics. Washington, DC. Retrieved [date] from http://nces.ed.gov/pubsearch.

Content Contact
Susan Aud
(202) 219-7013
susan.aud@ed.gov

ISBN: 978-1-60175-897-2

Letter From the
Commissioner of the
National Center for Education Statistics

May 2013

To help inform policymakers and the public about the progress of education in the United States, Congress has mandated that the National Center for Education Statistics (NCES) produce an annual report, *The Condition of Education*. This year's report presents 42 indicators of important developments and trends in U.S. education. These indicators focus on population characteristics, participation in education, elementary and secondary education, and postsecondary education.

As this year's *Condition* shows, in 2012, about 90 percent of young adults ages 25 to 29 had a high school diploma, or its equivalent, and 33 percent had a bachelor's degree or higher. As in previous years, annual median earnings in 2011 were higher for those with higher levels of education—for example, 25- to 34-year-olds with a college degree earned over twice as much as high school dropouts.

In 2011, almost two-thirds of 3- to 5-year-olds were enrolled in preschool, and nearly 60 percent of these children were in full-day programs. At the elementary and secondary level, there were about 50 million public school students in 2011, a number that is expected to grow to 53 million in the next decade. Of these students, nearly 2 million attended charter schools. Postsecondary enrollment in 2011 was at 21 million students, including 18 million undergraduate and 3 million graduate students.

NCES's newest data on elementary and secondary schools show that about one in five public schools was considered high poverty in 2011—meaning that 75 percent or more of their enrolled students qualified for free or reduced-price lunch—up from about to one in eight in 2000. In school year 2009–10, some 3.1 million public high school students, or 78.2 percent, graduated on time with a regular diploma. And, in 2011, about 68 percent of recent high school completers were enrolled in college the following fall. Meanwhile, the status dropout rate, or the percentage of 16- to 24-year-olds who are not enrolled in school and do not have a high school diploma or its equivalent, declined from 12 percent in 1990 to 7 percent in 2011.

At 4-year colleges in 2011, nearly 90 percent of full-time students at public and private nonprofit institutions were under the age of 25. However, only about 29 percent of full-time students at private for-profit colleges were, while 39 percent were between the ages of 25 to 34 and another 32 percent were 35 and older. About 56 percent of male students and 61 percent of female students who began their bachelor's degree in the fall of 2005, and did not transfer, had completed their degree by 2011. In that year, there were 1.7 million bachelor's degrees and over 700,000 master's degrees awarded.

The Condition of Education 2013 includes the latest data available on these and more key indicators. As new data are released, the indicators will be updated and made available. Along with these indicators, NCES produces a wide range of reports and data to help inform policymakers and the American public about trends and conditions in U.S. education.

Jack Buckley
Commissioner
National Center for Education Statistics

This page intentionally left blank.

Reader's Guide

The Condition of Education is available in three forms: this print volume for 2013; on the National Center for Education Statistics (NCES) website as a full pdf, as individual pdfs, and in html; and on our mobile website. All reference tables are hyperlinked within the pdf and html versions, as are the sources for each of the graphics. The reference tables can be found in other NCES publications—primarily the *Digest of Education Statistics*. A pdf that contains all of the reference tables used in *The Condition of Education 2013* is available on the NCES website.

Data Sources and Estimates

The data in these indicators were obtained from many different sources—including students and teachers, state education agencies, local elementary and secondary schools, and colleges and universities—using surveys and compilations of administrative records. Users should be cautious when comparing data from different sources. Differences in aspects such as procedures, timing, question phrasing, and interviewer training can affect the comparability of results across data sources.

Most indicators summarize data from surveys conducted by NCES or by the Census Bureau with support from NCES. Brief explanations of the major NCES surveys used in these indicators can be found in the Guide to Sources (http://nces.ed.gov/programs/coe/sources.asp). More detailed explanations can be obtained on the NCES website (http://nces.ed.gov) under "Surveys and Programs."

The Guide to Sources also includes information on non-NCES sources used to compile indicators, such as the American Community Survey (ACS) and the Current Population Survey (CPS). These are Census Bureau surveys used extensively in the indicators. For further details on the ACS, see http://www.census.gov/acs/www/. For further details on the CPS, see http://www.census.gov/cps/.

Data for indicators are obtained primarily from two types of surveys: universe surveys and sample surveys. In universe surveys, information is collected from every member of the population. For example, in a survey regarding certain expenditures of public elementary and secondary schools, data would be obtained from each school district in the United States. When data from an entire population are available, estimates of the total population or a subpopulation are made by simply summing the units in the population or subpopulation. As a result, there is no sampling error, and observed differences are reported as true.

Since a universe survey is often expensive and time consuming, many surveys collect data from a sample of the population of interest (sample survey). For example, the National Assessment of Educational Progress (NAEP) assesses a representative sample of students rather than the entire population of students. When a sample survey is used, statistical uncertainty is introduced, because the data come from only a portion of the entire population. This statistical uncertainty must be considered when reporting estimates and making comparisons.

Various types of statistics derived from universe and sample surveys are reported in the indicators. Many indicators report the size of a population or a subpopulation, and often the size of a subpopulation is expressed as a percentage of the total population. In addition, the average (or *mean*) value of some characteristic of the population or subpopulation may be reported. The average is obtained by summing the values for all members of the population and dividing the sum by the size of the population. An example is the annual average salaries of full-time instructional faculty at degree-granting postsecondary institutions. Another measure that is sometimes used is the *median*. The median is the midpoint value of a characteristic at or *above* which 50 percent of the population is estimated to fall, and at or *below* which 50 percent of the population is estimated to fall. An example is the median annual earnings of young adults who are full-time, full-year wage and salary workers.

Standard Errors

Using estimates calculated from data based on a sample of the population requires consideration of several factors before the estimates become meaningful. When using data from a sample, some *margin of error* will always be present in estimations of characteristics of the total population or subpopulation because the data are available from only a portion of the total population. Consequently, data from samples can provide only an approximation of the true or actual value. The margin of error of an estimate, or the range of potential true or actual values, depends on several factors such as the amount of variation in the responses, the size and representativeness of the sample, and the size of the subgroup for which the estimate is computed. The magnitude of this margin of error is measured by what statisticians call the "standard error" of an estimate.

When data from sample surveys are reported, the standard error is calculated for each estimate. The standard errors for all estimated totals, means, medians, or percentages are reported in the reference tables.

In order to caution the reader when interpreting findings in the indicators, estimates from sample surveys are flagged with a "!" when the standard error is between 30 and 50 percent of the estimate, and suppressed with a "‡" when the standard error is 50 percent of the estimate or greater.

Data Analysis and Interpretation

When estimates are from a sample, caution is warranted when drawing conclusions about one estimate in comparison to another, or about whether a time series of estimates is increasing, decreasing, or staying the same. Although one estimate may appear to be larger than another, a statistical test may find that the apparent difference between them is not reliably measurable due to the uncertainty around the estimates. In this case, the estimates will be described as having *no measurable difference*, meaning that the difference between them is not statistically significant.

Whether differences in means or percentages are statistically significant can be determined using the standard errors of the estimates. In these indicators and other reports produced by NCES, when differences are statistically significant, the probability that the difference occurred by chance is less than 5 percent, according to NCES standards.

Data presented in the indicators do not investigate more complex hypotheses, account for interrelationships among variables, or support causal inferences. We encourage readers who are interested in more complex questions and in-depth analysis to explore other NCES resources, including publications, online data tools, and public- and restricted-use datasets at http://nces.ed.gov.

For all indicators that report estimates based on samples, differences between estimates (including increases and decreases) are stated only when they are statistically significant. To determine whether differences reported are statistically significant, two-tailed t tests at the .05 level are typically used. The t test formula for determining statistical significance is adjusted when the samples being compared are dependent. The t test formula is not adjusted for multiple comparisons, with the exception of statistical tests conducted using the NAEP Data Explorer (http://nces.ed.gov/nationsreportcard/tdw/database/data_tool.asp). When the variables to be tested are postulated to form a trend, the relationship may be tested using linear regression, logistic regression, or ANOVA trend analysis instead of a series of t tests. These alternate methods of analysis test for specific relationships (e.g., linear, quadratic, or cubic) among variables. For more information on data analysis, please see the NCES Statistical Standards, Standard 5-1, available at http://nces.ed.gov/statprog/2002/std5_1.asp.

A number of considerations influence the ultimate selection of the data years to feature in the indicators. To make analyses as timely as possible, the latest year of available data is shown. The choice of comparison years is often also based on the need to show the earliest available survey year, as in the case of the NAEP and the international assessment surveys. In the case of surveys with long time frames, such as surveys measuring enrollment, the decade's beginning year (e.g., 1980 or 1990) often starts the trend line. In the figures and tables of the indicators, intervening years are selected in increments in order to show the general trend. The narrative for the indicators typically compares the most current year's data with those from the initial year and then with those from a more recent period. Where applicable, the narrative may also note years in which the data begin to diverge from previous trends.

Rounding and Other Considerations

All calculations within the indicators are based on unrounded estimates. Therefore, the reader may find that a calculation, such as a difference or a percentage change, cited in the text or figure may not be identical to the calculation obtained by using the rounded values shown in the accompanying tables. Although values reported in the supplemental tables are generally rounded to one decimal place (e.g., 76.5 percent), values reported in each are generally rounded to whole numbers (with any value of 0.50 or above rounded to the next highest whole number). Due to rounding, cumulative percentages may sometimes equal 99 or 101 percent rather than 100 percent.

Race and Ethnicity

The Office of Management and Budget (OMB) is responsible for the standards that govern the categories used to collect and present federal data on race and ethnicity. The OMB revised the guidelines on racial/ethnic categories used by the federal government in October 1997, with a January 2003 deadline for implementation (Office of Management and Budget 1997). The revised standards require a minimum of these five categories for data on race: American Indian or Alaska Native, Asian, Black or African American, Native Hawaiian or Other Pacific Islander, and White. The standards also require the collection of data on the ethnicity categories Hispanic or Latino and Not Hispanic or Latino. It is important to note that Hispanic origin is an ethnicity rather than a race, and therefore persons of Hispanic origin may be of any race. Origin can be viewed as the heritage, nationality group, lineage, or country of birth of the person or the person's parents or ancestors before their arrival in the United States. The race categories White, Black, Asian, Native Hawaiian or Other Pacific Islander, and American Indian or Alaska Native, as presented in these indicators, exclude persons of Hispanic origin unless noted otherwise.

The categories are defined as follows:

- *American Indian or Alaska Native:* A person having origins in any of the original peoples of North and South America (including Central America) and maintaining tribal affiliation or community attachment.

- *Asian:* A person having origins in any of the original peoples of the Far East, Southeast Asia, or the Indian subcontinent, including, for example, Cambodia, China, India, Japan, Korea, Malaysia, Pakistan, the Philippine Islands, Thailand, and Vietnam.

- *Black or African American:* A person having origins in any of the black racial groups of Africa.

- *Native Hawaiian or Other Pacific Islander:* A person having origins in any of the original peoples of Hawaii, Guam, Samoa, or other Pacific Islands.

- *White:* A person having origins in any of the original peoples of Europe, the Middle East, or North Africa.

- *Hispanic or Latino:* A person of Mexican, Puerto Rican, Cuban, South or Central American, or other Spanish culture or origin, regardless of race.

Within these indicators, some of the category labels have been shortened in the text, tables, and figures. American Indian or Alaska Native is denoted as American Indian/Alaska Native (except when separate estimates are available for American Indians alone or Alaska Natives alone); Black or African American is shortened to Black; and Hispanic or Latino is shortened to Hispanic. When discussed separately from Asian estimates, Native Hawaiian or Other Pacific Islander is shortened to Native Hawaiian/Pacific Islander.

The indicators draw from a number of different sources. Many are federal surveys that collect data using the OMB standards for racial/ethnic classification described above; however, some sources have not fully adopted the standards, and some indicators include data collected prior to the adoption of the OMB standards. This report focuses on the six categories that are the most common among the various data sources used: White, Black, Hispanic, Asian, Native Hawaiian/Pacific Islander, and American Indian/Alaska Native. Asians and Native Hawaiians/Pacific Islanders are combined into one category in indicators for which the data were not collected separately for the two groups.

Some of the surveys from which data are presented in these indicators give respondents the option of selecting either an "other" race category, a "Two or more races" or "multiracial" category, or both. Where possible, indicators present data on the "Two or more races" category; however, in some cases this category may not be separately shown because the information was not collected or due to other data issues. The "other" category is not separately shown. Any comparisons made between persons of one racial/ethnic group to "all other racial/ethnic groups" include only the racial/ethnic groups shown in the indicator. In some surveys, respondents are not given the option to select more than one race. In these surveys, respondents of two or more races must select a single race category. Any comparisons between data from surveys that give the option to select more than one race and surveys that do not offer such an option should take into account the fact that there is a potential for bias if members of one racial group are more likely than members of the others to identify themselves as "Two or more races."[1] For postsecondary data, foreign students are counted separately and are therefore not included in any racial/ethnic category.

The American Community Survey (ACS), conducted by the U.S. Census Bureau, collects information regarding specific racial/ethnic ancestry. Selected indicators include Hispanic ancestry subgroups (such as Mexican, Puerto Rican, Cuban, Dominican, Salvadoran, Other Central American, and South American) and Asian ancestry subgroups (such as Asian Indian, Chinese, Filipino, Japanese, Korean, and Vietnamese). In addition, selected indicators include "Two or more races" subgroups (such as White and Black, White and Asian, and White and American Indian/Alaska Native).

For more information on the ACS, see the Guide to Sources (http://nces.ed.gov/programs/coe/sources.asp). For more information on race/ethnicity, see the Glossary (http://nces.ed.gov/programs/coe/glossary.asp).

Limitations of the Data

The relatively small sizes of the American Indian/Alaska Native and Native Hawaiian/Pacific Islander populations pose many measurement difficulties when conducting statistical analysis. Even in larger surveys, the numbers of American Indians/Alaska Natives and Native Hawaiians/Pacific Islanders included in a sample are often small. Researchers studying data on these two populations often face small sample sizes that reduce the reliability of results. Survey data for American Indians/Alaska Natives often have somewhat higher standard errors than data for other racial/ethnic groups. Due to large standard errors, differences that seem substantial are often not statistically

---

[1] Such bias was found by a National Center for Health Statistics study that examined race/ethnicity responses to the 2000 Census. This study found, for example, that as the percentage of multiple-race respondents in a county increased, the likelihood of respondents stating Black as their primary race increased among Black/White respondents but decreased among American Indian or Alaska Native/Black respondents. See Parker, J. et al. (2004). Bridging Between Two Standards for Collecting Information on Race and Ethnicity: An Application to Census 2000 and Vital Rates. *Public Health Reports, 119*(2): 192–205. Available through http://www.pubmedcentral.nih.gov/articlerender.fcgi?artid=1497618.

significant and, therefore, not cited in the text.

Data on American Indians/Alaska Natives are often subject to inaccuracies that can result from respondents self-identifying their race/ethnicity. Research on the collection of race/ethnicity data suggests that the categorization of American Indian and Alaska Native is the least stable self-identification (U.S. Department of Labor, Bureau of Labor Statistics [BLS] 1995). The racial/ethnic categories presented to a respondent, and the way in which the question is asked, can influence the response, especially for individuals who consider themselves of mixed race or ethnicity. These data limitations should be kept in mind when reading this report.

As mentioned above, Asians and Native Hawaiians/Pacific Islanders are combined into one category in indicators for which the data were not collected separately for the two groups. The combined category can sometimes mask significant differences between subgroups. For example, prior to 2011, the National Assessment of Educational Progress (NAEP) collected data that did not allow for separate reporting of estimates for Asians and Native Hawaiians/Pacific Islanders. Information from the *Digest of Education Statistics, 2011* (table 21), based on the Census Bureau Current Population Reports, indicates that 96 percent of all Asian/Pacific Islander 5- to 24-year-olds are Asian. This combined category for Asians/Pacific Islanders is more representative of Asians than Native Hawaiians/Pacific Islanders.

Symbols

In accordance with the NCES Statistical Standards, many tables in this volume use a series of symbols to alert the reader to special statistical notes. These symbols, and their meanings, are as follows:

— Not available.

† Not applicable.

Rounds to zero.

! Interpret data with caution. The coefficient of variation (CV) for this estimate is between 30 and 50 percent.

‡ Reporting standards not met. Either there are too few cases for a reliable estimate or the coefficient of variation (CV) for this estimate is 50 percent or greater.

* $p < .05$ Significance level.

Contents

	Page
Letter from the Commissioner of the National Center for Education Statistics	iii
Reader's Guide	v

Spotlight on Economic Outcomes

Trends in Employment Rates by Educational Attainment 2

    Figure 1. Employment to population ratios, by age group and educational attainment: 2012 3

    Figure 2. Employment to population ratios, by age group, educational attainment, and sex: 2012 4

    Figure 3. Employment to population ratios of persons 20 to 24 years old, by sex and educational attainment: Selected years, 1990 through 2012 5

    Figure 4. Employment to population ratios of persons 25 to 64 years old, by sex and educational attainment: Selected years, 1990 through 2012 6

    Figure 5. Employment to population ratios of persons 25 to 34 years old, by sex and educational attainment: Selected years, 1990 through 2012 7

Attainment

1   Educational Attainment 8

    Figure 1. Percentage of 25- to 29-year-olds who completed bachelor's and master's degrees, by sex: Selected years, 1990–2012 8

    Figure 2. Percentage of 25- to 29-year-olds who completed at least a high school diploma or its equivalent, by race/ethnicity: Selected years, 1990–2012 9

    Figure 3. Percentage of 25- to 29-year-olds with a bachelor's degree or higher, by race/ethnicity: Selected years, 1990–2012 10

2   International Educational Attainment 12

    Figure 1. Percentage of the population 25 to 64 years old in Organisation for Economic Co-operation and Development (OECD) countries who attained selected levels of education, by age group: 2010 12

    Figure 2. Percentage of the population 25 to 64 years old in Organisation for Economic Co-operation and Development (OECD) countries who attained selected levels of education: Selected years, 2001, 2005, and 2010 13

Economic Outcomes

3   Annual Earnings of Young Adults 16

    Figure 1. Median annual earnings of full-time, full-year wage and salary workers ages 25–34, by educational attainment: 2011 16

    Figure 2. Median annual earnings of full-time, full-year wage and salary workers ages 25–34, by educational attainment: 1995–2011 17

    Figure 3. Median annual earnings of full-time, full-year wage and salary workers ages 25–34, by educational attainment and sex: 2011 18

4   Labor Force Participation and Unemployment Rates by Educational Attainment 20

    Figure 1. Unemployment rates, by age group and educational attainment: 2012 20

    Figure 2. Unemployment rates of persons 20 to 24 years old, by sex and educational attainment: Selected years, 1990 through 2012 21

    Figure 3. Unemployment rates of persons 25 to 64 years old, by sex and educational attainment: Selected years, 1990 through 2012 22

    Figure 4. Unemployment rates of persons 25 to 34 years old, by sex and educational attainment: Selected years, 1990 through 2012 23

Demographics

5   Children Living in Poverty 26
     Figure 1.   Percentage of 5- to 17-year-olds in families living in poverty, by region: 1990, 2000, and 2011 26
     Figure 2.   Percentage of 5- to 17-year-olds in families living in poverty, by state: 2011 27
     Figure 3.   Percentage of children under age 18 living in poverty, by race/ethnicity and family type: 2011 28

Spotlight on Preprimary Education

Kindergarten Entry Status: On-Time, Delayed-Entry, and Repeating Kindergartners 32
     Figure 1.   Percentage distribution of kindergarten students, by age at the time child first started kindergarten and race/ethnicity: Fall 2010 32
     Figure 2.   Percentage distribution of kindergarten students, by parents' highest level of education and poverty status: School year 2010–11 33
     Figure 3.   Percentage distribution of kindergarten students, by kindergarten entry status: Fall 2010 34
     Figure 4.   Percentage of kindergarten students, by kindergarten entry status and race/ethnicity: Fall 2010 35
     Figure 5.   Percentage of kindergarten students, by kindergarten entry status and parents' highest level of education: Fall 2010 36
     Figure 6.   Percentage of kindergarten students, by kindergarten entry status and poverty status: Fall 2010 37
     Figure 7.   Kindergartners' mean reading scale scores, by time of assessment and kindergarten entry status: School year 2010–11 38
     Figure 8.   Kindergartners' mean mathematics scale scores, by time of assessment and kindergarten entry status: School year 2010–11 39
     Figure 9.   Kindergartners' mean approaches to learning scale scores, by time of assessment and kindergarten entry status: School year 2010–11 40

All Ages

6   Enrollment Trends by Age 42
     Figure 1.   Percentage of the population ages 3–34 enrolled in school, by education level and age group: October 1970–2011 42
     Figure 2.   Percentage of the population ages 3–34 enrolled in school, by age group: October 2011 43

Preprimary Education

7   Early Education and Child Care Arrangements of Young Children 44
     Figure 1.   Percentage of 3-, 4-, and 5-year-old children enrolled in full-day preprimary programs: Selected years, 1980 through 2011 44
     Figure 2.   Percentage of 3-, 4-, and 5-year-old children enrolled in preprimary programs, by parents' educational attainment and attendance status: October 2011 45

Elementary/Secondary Enrollment

8   Public School Enrollment 46
     Figure 1.   Actual and projected public school enrollment in grades prekindergarten (preK) through 12, by grade level: School years 1970–71 through 2021–22 46
     Figure 2.   Projected percent change in public school enrollment in grades prekindergarten (preK) through 12, by state or jurisdiction: Between school years 2010–11 and 2021–22 47

9   Charter School Enrollment 48
     Figure 1.   Number of students enrolled in public charter schools: Selected school years, 1999–2000 through 2010–11 48
     Figure 2.   Percentage of all public school students enrolled in charter schools, by state or jurisdiction: School year 2010–11 49

10 Private School Enrollment 50

    Figure 1.   Number of private school students in prekindergarten through grade 12, by school type: Various school years, 1995–96 through 2009–10 50

    Figure 2.   Percent distribution of private school enrollment, by school type and level: 2009–10 51

11 Racial/Ethnic Enrollment in Public Schools 52

    Figure 1.   Percentage distribution of U.S. public school students enrolled in prekindergarten through 12th grade, by race/ethnicity: Selected years, fall 2000–fall 2021 52

    Figure 2.   Number of U.S. public school students enrolled in prekindergarten through 12th grade, by region and race/ethnicity: Fall 2000–fall 2010 53

12 English Language Learners 54

    Figure 1.   Percentage of public school students who are English language learners (ELL), by state: School year 2010–11 54

    Figure 2.   Average reading scores of 4th-grade students, by English language learner (ELL) status: Selected years, 2002–11 55

    Figure 3.   Average reading scores of 8th-grade students, by English language learner (ELL) status: Selected years, 2002–11 55

13 Children and Youth With Disabilities 58

    Figure 1.   Percentage distribution of children ages 3–21 served under the Individuals with Disabilities Education Act (IDEA), Part B, by disability type: School year 2010–11 58

    Figure 2.   Percentage of students ages 6–21 served under the Individuals with Disabilities Education Act (IDEA), Part B, placed in a regular public school environment, by amount of time spent inside general classes: Selected school years 1990–91 through 2010–11 59

Postsecondary Enrollment

14 Undergraduate Enrollment 60

    Figure 1.   Actual and projected undergraduate enrollment in degree-granting postsecondary institutions, by sex: Fall 1970–2021 60

    Figure 2.   Actual and projected undergraduate enrollment in degree-granting postsecondary institutions, by attendance status: Fall 1970–2021 61

    Figure 3.   Actual and projected undergraduate enrollment in degree-granting postsecondary institutions, by control of institution: Fall 1970–2021 62

    Figure 4.   Actual and projected undergraduate enrollment in degree-granting postsecondary institutions, by level of institution: Fall 1970–2021 63

15 Postbaccalaureate Enrollment 64

    Figure 1.   Actual and projected postbaccalaureate enrollment in degree-granting postsecondary institutions, by sex: Fall 1970–2021 64

    Figure 2.   Actual and projected postbaccalaureate enrollment in degree-granting postsecondary institutions, by attendance status: Fall 1970–2021 65

    Figure 3.   Full-time postbaccalaureate enrollment in degree-granting postsecondary institutions, by control of institution: Fall 1970–2011 66

Spotlight on School Characteristics and Climate

The Status of Rural Education 70

    Figure 1.   Percentage distribution of public elementary and secondary students, schools, and districts, by locale: School year 2010–11 70

    Figure 2.   Percentage distribution of public elementary and secondary students, by locale and race/ethnicity: Fall 2010 71

    Figure 3.   Percentage of 5- to 17-year-olds in families living in poverty, by district locale and region: 2010 72

    Figure 4.   Percentage distribution of public elementary and secondary students, by locale and percentage of students in school eligible for free or reduced-price lunch (FRPL): Fall 2010 73

    Figure 5a.   Percentage distribution of 4th-grade public school students across National Assessment of Educational Progress (NAEP) reading achievement levels, by locale: 2011 74

    Figure 5b.   Percentage distribution of 8th-grade public school students across National Assessment of Educational Progress (NAEP) reading achievement levels, by locale: 2011 74

    Figure 6a.   Percentage distribution of 4th-grade public school students across National Assessment of Educational Progress (NAEP) mathematics achievement levels, by locale: 2011 75

    Figure 6b.   Percentage distribution of 8th-grade public school students across National Assessment of Educational Progress (NAEP) mathematics achievement levels, by locale: 2011 75

    Figure 7.   Averaged freshman graduation rate (AFGR) for public high school students, by locale: School year 2008–09 76

School Characteristics and Climate

16 Characteristics of Public Elementary and Secondary Schools 78

    Figure 1.   Percentage distribution of public schools, by school control and enrollment size: School years 1999–2000 and 2010–11 78

    Figure 2.   Percentage distribution of public schools, by school locale, region, and control: School year 2010–11 79

17 Concentration of Public School Students Eligible for Free or Reduced-Price Lunch 80

    Figure 1.   Percentage distribution of public school students, by school poverty level: School years 1999–2000 and 2010–11 80

    Figure 2.   Percentage distribution of public school students, by school locale and school poverty level: School year 2010–11 81

18 Rates of School Crime 82

    Figure 1.   Rate of total nonfatal victimizations against students ages 12–18 per 1,000 students, by location: 1992–2011 82

    Figure 2.   Rate of thefts against students ages 12–18 per 1,000 students, by location: 1992–2011 83

    Figure 3.   Rate of violent victimizations against students ages 12–18 per 1,000 students, by location: 1992–2011 84

    Figure 4.   Rate of serious violent victimizations against students ages 12–18 per 1,000 students, by location: 1992–2011 84

    Figure 5.   Rate of nonfatal victimizations against students ages 12–18 at and away from school per 1,000 students, by type of victimization and age: 2011 85

    Figure 6.   Rate of nonfatal victimizations against students ages 12–18 at and away from school per 1,000 students, by type of victimization and sex: 2011 86

19 Teachers and Pupil/Teacher Ratios 88

    Figure 1.   Teachers as a percentage of staff in public elementary and secondary school systems, by state or jurisdiction: fall 2010 88

    Figure 2.   Public and private elementary and secondary school pupil/teacher ratios: Selected years, fall 1955 through fall 2010 89

Finance

20 Public School Revenue Sources 90

    Figure 1.   Total revenues for public elementary and secondary schools, by revenue source: School years 1990–91 through 2009–10 90

    Figure 2.   Primary source of revenue as a percentage of total public elementary and secondary school revenue, by state: School year 2009–10 91

    Figure 3.   Property tax revenue for public elementary and secondary schools as a percentage of total school revenue, by state: School year 2009–10 92

21 Public School Expenditures 94

    Figure 1.   Total expenditures per student in fall enrollment in public elementary and secondary schools, in constant 2011–12 dollars, by type of total expenditures: 1999–2000, 2005–06, and 2009–10 94

    Figure 2.   Current expenditures per student in fall enrollment in public elementary and secondary schools, in constant 2011–12 dollars, by function of current expenditures: 1999–2000, 2005–06, and 2009–10 95

    Figure 3.   Percentage of current expenditures per student in fall enrollment in public elementary and secondary schools, by object of current expenditures: 1999–2000, 2005–06, and 2009–10 96

22 Education Expenditures by Country 98

    Figure 1.   Annual expenditures per full-time-equivalent student for elementary and secondary education in selected Organisation for Economic Co-operation and Development (OECD) countries, by gross domestic product (GDP) per capita: 2009 99

    Figure 2.   Annual expenditures per full-time-equivalent student for postsecondary education in selected Organisation for Economic Co-operation and Development (OECD) countries, by gross domestic product (GDP) per capita: 2009 99

Assessments

23 Reading Performance 102

    Figure 1.   Average reading scale scores of 4th-, 8th-, and 12th-grade students: Selected years, 1992–2011 102

    Figure 2.   Percentage distribution of 4th- and 8th-grade students across National Assessment of Educational Progress (NAEP) reading achievement levels: Selected years, 1992–2011 103

24 Mathematics Performance 104

    Figure 1.   Average mathematics scale scores of 4th- and 8th-grade students: Selected years, 1990–2011 104

    Figure 2.   Percentage distribution of 4th- and 8th-grade students across National Assessment of Educational Progress (NAEP) mathematics achievement levels: Selected years, 1990–2011 105

25 Reading and Mathematics Score Trends 106

    Figure 1.   Average reading scale scores on the long-term trend National Assessment of Educational Progress (NAEP), by age: Selected years, 1971 through 2008 106

    Figure 2.   Average mathematics scale scores on the long-term trend National Assessment of Educational Progress (NAEP), by age: Selected years, 1973 through 2008 107

26 International Assessments 110

    Table 1.   Average TIMSS mathematics assessment scale scores of 4th-grade students, by education system: 2011 111

    Table 2.   Average TIMSS science assessment scale scores of 4th-grade students, by education system: 2011 112

    Table 3.   Average TIMSS mathematics assessment scale scores of 8th-grade students, by education system: 2011 113

Table 4.	Average TIMSS science assessment scale scores of 8th-grade students, by education system: 2011	114
Figure 1.	Number of instructional hours per year for 4th-grade students, by country or education system and subject: 2011	115
Figure 2.	Number of instructional hours per year for 8th-grade students, by country or education system and subject: 2011	117
Table 5.	Average PIRLS reading literacy assessment scale scores of 4th-grade students, by education system: 2011	119

Student Effort, Persistence and Progress

27 High School Coursetaking		120
Figure 1.	Percentage of high school graduates who completed selected mathematics and science courses in high school: 1990 and 2009	120
Figure 2.	Average National Assessment of Educational Progress (NAEP) 12th-grade mathematics scale scores of high school graduates, by highest mathematics course taken and race/ethnicity: 2009	121
28 Public High School Graduation Rates		124
Figure 1.	Averaged Freshman Graduation Rate (AFGR) for public high school students: School years 1990–91 through 2009–10	124
Figure 2.	Averaged Freshman Graduation Rate (AFGR) for public high school students, by race/ethnicity: School year 2009–10	125
Figure 3.	Averaged Freshman Graduation Rate (AFGR) for public high school students, by state or jurisdiction: School year 2009–10	126
29 Status Dropout Rates		128
Figure 1.	Status dropout rates of 16- through 24-year-olds, by race/ethnicity: 1990 through 2011	128
Figure 2.	Status dropout rates of 16- through 24-year-olds, by number of years of school completed: Selected years, 1990 through 2011	129
Figure 3.	Status dropout rates of 16- through 24-year-olds in the noninstitutionalized group quarters and household population, by nativity and race/ethnicity: American Community Survey (ACS) 2010	130

Transition to College

30 Immediate Transition to College		132
Figure 1.	Percentage of high school completers who were enrolled in 2- or 4-year colleges by the October immediately following high school completion, by family income: 1975–2011	132
Figure 2.	Percentage of high school completers who were enrolled in 2- or 4-year colleges by the October immediately following high school completion, by level of institution: 1975–2011	133

Spotlight on Finance and Resources

Financing Postsecondary Education in the United States		136
Figure 1.	Total fall enrollment in degree-granting postsecondary institutions: Academic years 2000–01 through 2010–11	136
Figure 2.	Total expenditures of postsecondary degree-granting institutions in constant 2011–12 dollars: Fiscal years 2000–01 through 2011–12	137
Figure 3.	Total annual disbursements of grants and student loans by the federal government, in constant 2011–12 dollars: Fiscal years 2000–01 through 2010–11	138
Figure 4.	Total outstanding balance of student loans owned by the federal government, in constant 2011 dollars: October 2000 through October 2012	139
Figure 5.	Total outstanding student loan debt held by consumers, in constant 2011 dollars: Third quarter 2003 through third quarter 2012	139

Figure 6. Postsecondary federal student loan 2-year cohort default rates: Fiscal years October 2000 through October 2010 140

Figure 7. Percentage of total outstanding student loan debt held by consumers that is 90 or more days delinquent: First quarter 2003 though third quarter 2012 141

Characteristics of Postsecondary Students

31 Characteristics of Postsecondary Institutions 142

Figure 1. Number of degree-granting institutions with first-year undergraduates, by level and control of institution: 2000–01 and 2011–12 142

Figure 2. Percentage distribution of 4-year degree-granting institutions with first-year undergraduates, by application acceptance rate and control of institution: 2011–12 143

Figure 3. Percentage distribution of 2-year degree-granting institutions with first-year undergraduates, by application acceptance rate and control of institution: 2011–12 144

Figure 4. Percentage of 4-year degree-granting institutions with first-year undergraduates, by admissions requirement and control of institution: 2011–12 144

Figure 5. Percentage of 2-year degree-granting institutions with first-year undergraduates, by admissions requirement and control of institution: 2011–12 145

32 Characteristics of Postsecondary Students 146

Figure 1. Percentage distribution of full-time undergraduate enrollment in degree-granting institutions, by institutional level and control and student age: Fall 2011 146

Figure 2. Percentage distribution of part-time undergraduate enrollment in degree-granting institutions, by institutional level and control and student age: Fall 2011 147

Figure 3. Percentage distribution of total undergraduate enrollment in degree-granting institutions, by institutional level and control and race/ethnicity of student: Fall 2011 148

Figure 4. Percentage distribution of total postbaccalaureate enrollment in degree-granting institutions, by institutional control and race/ethnicity of student: Fall 2011 149

Figure 5. Percentage of undergraduate college students 16 to 24 years old who were employed, by attendance status, hours worked per week, and institutional level: October 2011 150

Figure 6. Percentage of college students 16 to 24 years old who were employed, by attendance status and hours worked per week: October 2000 through October 2011 151

Programs and Courses

33 Undergraduate Fields of Study 152

Figure 1. Number of associate's degrees awarded by degree-granting institutions in selected fields of study: Academic years 2000–01 and 2010–11 152

Figure 2. Number of bachelor's degrees awarded by degree-granting institutions in selected fields of study: Academic years 2000–01 and 2010–11 153

34 Graduate Fields of Study 154

Figure 1. Number of master's degrees awarded by degree-granting institutions in selected fields of study: Academic years 2000–01 and 2010–11 154

Figure 2. Number of doctor's degrees awarded by degree-granting institutions in selected fields of study: Academic years 2000–01 and 2010–11 155

Finance and Resources

35 Price of Attending an Undergraduate Institution 156

Figure 1. Average total cost of attending degree-granting institutions for first-time, full-time students, by level and control of institution and living arrangement: Academic year 2011–12 156

Figure 2. Average total price, net price, and grants and scholarship aid for first-time, full-time students paying in-state tuition and receiving aid at public 4-year institutions, by income level: Academic year 2010–11 157

Figure 3. Average total price, net price, and grants and scholarship aid for first-time, full-time students receiving aid at private for-profit 4-year institutions, by income level: Academic year 2010–11 158

Figure 4. Average total price, net price, and grants and scholarship aid for first-time, full-time students receiving aid at private nonprofit 4-year institutions, by income level: Academic year 2010–11 159

36 Grants and Loan Aid to Undergraduate Students 160

Figure 1. Percentage of first-time, full-time undergraduate students in degree-granting institutions receiving any financial aid, by level and control of institution: Academic years 2006–07 through 2010–11 160

Figure 2. Percentage of first-time, full-time undergraduate students receiving financial aid at 4-year degree-granting institutions, by type of aid and institutional control: Academic year 2010–11 161

Figure 3. Percentage of first-time, full-time undergraduate students receiving financial aid at 2-year degree-granting institutions, by type of aid and institutional control: Academic year 2010–11 162

Figure 4. Average amount of student aid awarded to first-time, full-time undergraduate students receiving aid at 4-year degree-granting institutions, by institutional control and type of financial aid: Academic year 2010–11 163

Figure 5. Average amount of student aid awarded to first-time, full-time undergraduate students receiving aid at 2-year degree-granting institutions, by institutional control and type of financial aid: Academic year 2010–11 164

37 Postsecondary Revenues by Source 166

Figure 1. Percentage distribution of total revenues at postsecondary degree-granting institutions, by institution level, institution control, and source of funds: 2010–11 166

Figure 2. Revenues per full-time-equivalent (FTE) student from tuition and fees for postsecondary degree-granting institutions, by institution control and level: 2005–06 and 2010–11 167

Figure 3. Revenue per full-time-equivalent (FTE) student from government grants, contracts, and appropriations for postsecondary degree-granting institutions, by type of revenue and institution control and level: 2005–06 and 2010–11 168

38 Expenses of Postsecondary Institutions 170

Figure 1. Percentage of total expenses at degree-granting postsecondary institutions, by purpose of expenses and control of institution: 2010–11 170

Figure 2. Expenses per full-time-equivalent (FTE) student at degree-granting postsecondary institutions, by purpose of expenses and control of institution: 2010–11 171

Figure 3. Instructional expenses per full-time-equivalent (FTE) student for instruction at 2-year and 4-year degree-granting postsecondary institutions, by control of institution: 2005–06 and 2010–11 172

39 Characteristics of Postsecondary Faculty 174

Figure 1. Number of faculty in degree-granting institutions, by employment status: Selected years, fall 1991 through fall 2011 174

Figure 2. Percentage of full-time faculty whose race/ethnicity was known, in degree-granting institutions, by academic rank, selected race/ethnicity, and sex: Fall 2011 175

Figure 3. Average salary of full-time instructional faculty on 9-month contracts in degree-granting institutions, by control and level of institution: 2011–12 176

40 Student Loan Volume and Default Rates 178

Figure 1. Average tuition and fees and average loan amounts for first-time, full-time students with loans at postsecondary degree-granting institutions, by level and control of institution: 2010–11 178

Figure 2. Two-year student loan cohort default rates at postsecondary degree-granting institutions, by level and control of institution: Fiscal years (FY) 2007 through 2010 179

Completions

41 Institutional Retention and Graduation Rates for Undergraduate Students 182

    Figure 1.   Percentage of students seeking a bachelor's degree at 4-year degree-granting institutions who completed a bachelor's degree within 6 years, by control of institution and sex: Starting cohort year 2005 182

    Figure 2.   Percentage of students seeking a certificate or degree at 2-year degree-granting institutions who completed a credential within 150 percent of the normal time required to do so (for example, 3 years for a 2-year degree), by control of institution and sex: Starting cohort year 2008 183

    Figure 3.   Percentage of students seeking a bachelor's degree at 4-year degree-granting institutions who completed a bachelor's degree within 6 years, by applicant acceptance rate: Starting cohort year 2005 184

    Figure 4.   Annual full-time student retention rates at 2- and 4-year degree-granting institutions, by institution level, acceptance rate, and institution control: 2011 185

42 Degrees Conferred by Public and Private Institutions 186

    Table 1.   Number of degrees conferred by Title IV institutions and percent change, by control of institution and level of degree: Academic years 2000–01 and 2010–11 186

    Figure 1.   Number of certificates and associate's degrees conferred by Title IV institutions: Academic years 2000–01, 2005–06, and 2010–11 187

    Figure 2.   Number of bachelor's and master's degrees conferred by Title IV institutions, by level of degree: Academic years 2000–01, 2005–06, and 2010–11 188

Guide to Sources 190

Glossary 210

The indicators in this chapter of *The Condition of Education* report on educational attainment and economic outcomes for the United States as a whole. The level of education attained by an individual has implications for his or her median earnings and other labor outcomes, such as unemployment. Comparisons at the national level to other industrialized nations provides insight into our global competitiveness. In addition, this chapter contains indicators on key demographic characteristics, such as poverty.

Chapter 1

Population Characteristics

Spotlight on Economic Outcomes
Trends in Employment Rates by Educational Attainment 2

Attainment
Indicator 1.   Educational Attainment 8
Indicator 2.   International Educational Attainment 12

Economic Outcomes
Indicator 3.   Annual Earnings of Young Adults 16
Indicator 4.   Labor Force Participation and Unemployment Rates
              by Educational Attainment 20

Demographics
Indicator 5.   Children Living in Poverty 26

Spotlight

Trends in Employment Rates by Educational Attainment

The employment to population ratio, also referred to as the employment rate, represents the proportion of the civilian population that is employed, and it is used as a measure of labor market conditions and the economy's ability to provide jobs for a growing population. In 2012, the employment rate was 69 percent for young adults (those ages 20–24) and 73 percent for 25- to 34-year-olds. Between 1990 and 2012, employment rates for adults with at least a bachelor's degree were higher than employment rates for adults without a bachelor's degree. This pattern was consistently observed for young adults, 25- to 64-year-olds, and 25- to 34-year-olds (a subset of 25- to 64-year-olds).

The *employment to population ratio*, also referred to as the employment rate, represents the proportion of the civilian population that is employed, and it is used as a measure of labor market conditions and the economy's ability to provide jobs for a growing population. In this indicator, *employment to population ratio* and *employment rate* are used interchangeably. The employment to population ratio and unemployment rate are related. Movements in the unemployment rate reflect net changes in the number of people who are looking for work but are unable to find it, while movements in the employment to population ratio reflect whether the economy is generating jobs fast enough to provide employment for a constant proportion of the population. Further, changes in the employment to population ratio for a particular subgroup (e.g., male high school dropouts) indicate the economy's performance in providing jobs for that particular group.

This spotlight examines employment rates between 1990 and 2012 for three age groups: young adults (those ages 20–24), 25- to 34-year-olds, and 25- to 64-year-olds. In 2012, the employment rate was 69 percent for young adults and 73 percent for 25- to 34-year-olds (see *Digest of Education Statistics 2012*, table 431). The employment rate for 25- to 64-year-olds overall (71 percent) was higher than the employment rate for young adults, but lower than the employment rate for 25- to 34-year-olds. This indicator also examines employment rates by *educational attainment*, which refers to the highest level of education achieved (i.e., less than high school completion, high school completion, some college, or a bachelor's degree or higher).

For more information, see the Reader's Guide and the Guide to Sources.

Chapter: 1/Population Characteristics
Section: Spotlight

Figure 1. Employment to population ratios, by age group and educational attainment: 2012

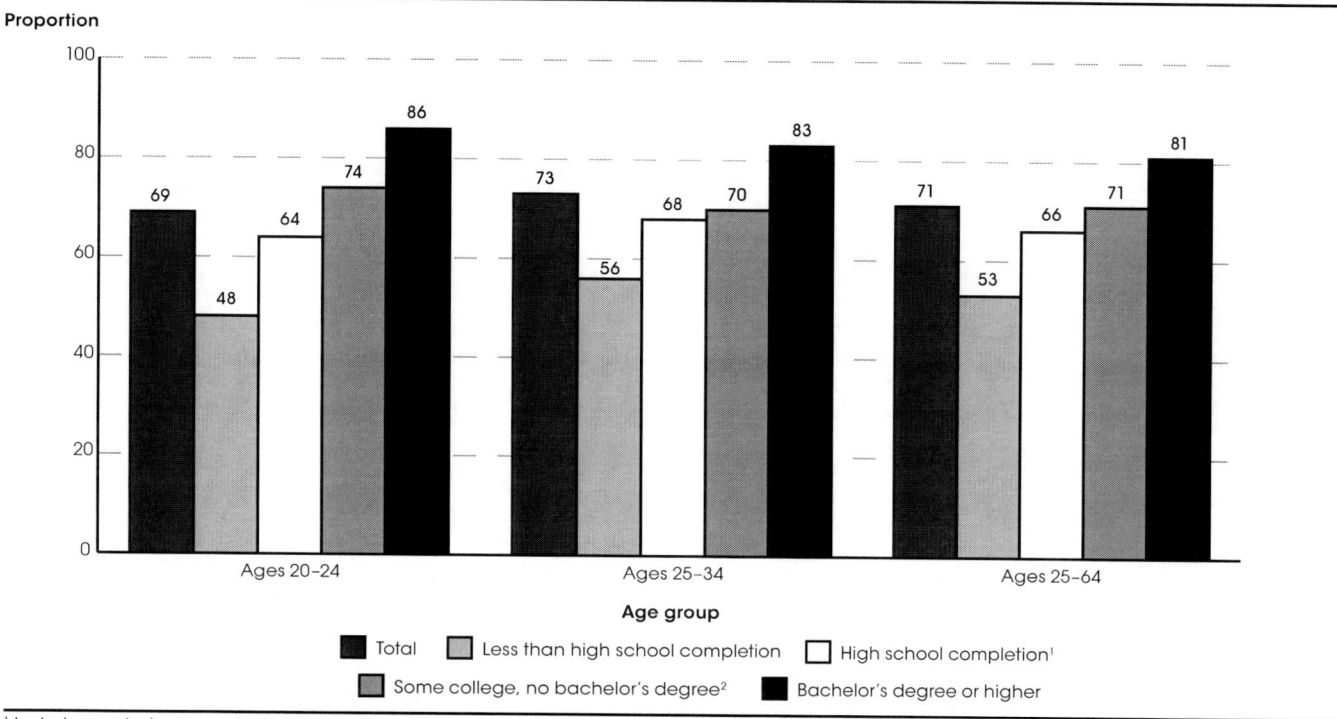

Proportion

Age group	Total	Less than high school completion	High school completion[1]	Some college, no bachelor's degree[2]	Bachelor's degree or higher
Ages 20–24	69	48	64	74	86
Ages 25–34	73	56	68	70	83
Ages 25–64	71	53	66	71	81

[1] Includes equivalency credentials, such as the General Educational Development (GED) credential.
[2] Includes persons with no college degree as well as those with an associate's degree.
NOTE: The employment to population ratio is defined as the proportion of the civilian population that is employed. Educational attainment refers to the highest level of education achieved (i.e., less than high school completion, high school completion, some college, or a bachelor's degree or higher). Data for 20- to 24-year-olds exclude persons enrolled in school.
SOURCE: U.S. Department of Labor, Bureau of Labor Statistics, Office of Employment and Unemployment Statistics, unpublished annual average data from the Current Population Survey (CPS), 2012. See *Digest of Education Statistics 2012*, table 431.

Between 1990 and 2012, employment rates for adults with at least a bachelor's degree were generally higher than employment rates for adults without a bachelor's degree. This pattern was consistently observed for young adults, 25- to 34-year-olds, and 25- to 64-year-olds. In 2012, for example, the employment rate for young adults was 86 percent for those with at least a bachelor's degree, compared with 74 percent for those whose educational attainment was some college, 64 percent for high school completers, and 48 percent for those who did not complete high school. The employment rate for 25- to 34-year-olds was higher for those with at least a bachelor's degree (83 percent) than for those with some college education (70 percent), those who were high school completers (68 percent), and those who did not complete high school (56 percent). This pattern of higher employment rates corresponding with higher levels of educational attainment also generally held across males and females for each age group from 1990 to 2012 (see *Digest of Education Statistics 2012*, tables 432 and 433).

For more information, see the Reader's Guide and the Guide to Sources.

Chapter: 1/Population Characteristics
Section: Spotlight

Figure 2. Employment to population ratios, by age group, educational attainment, and sex: 2012

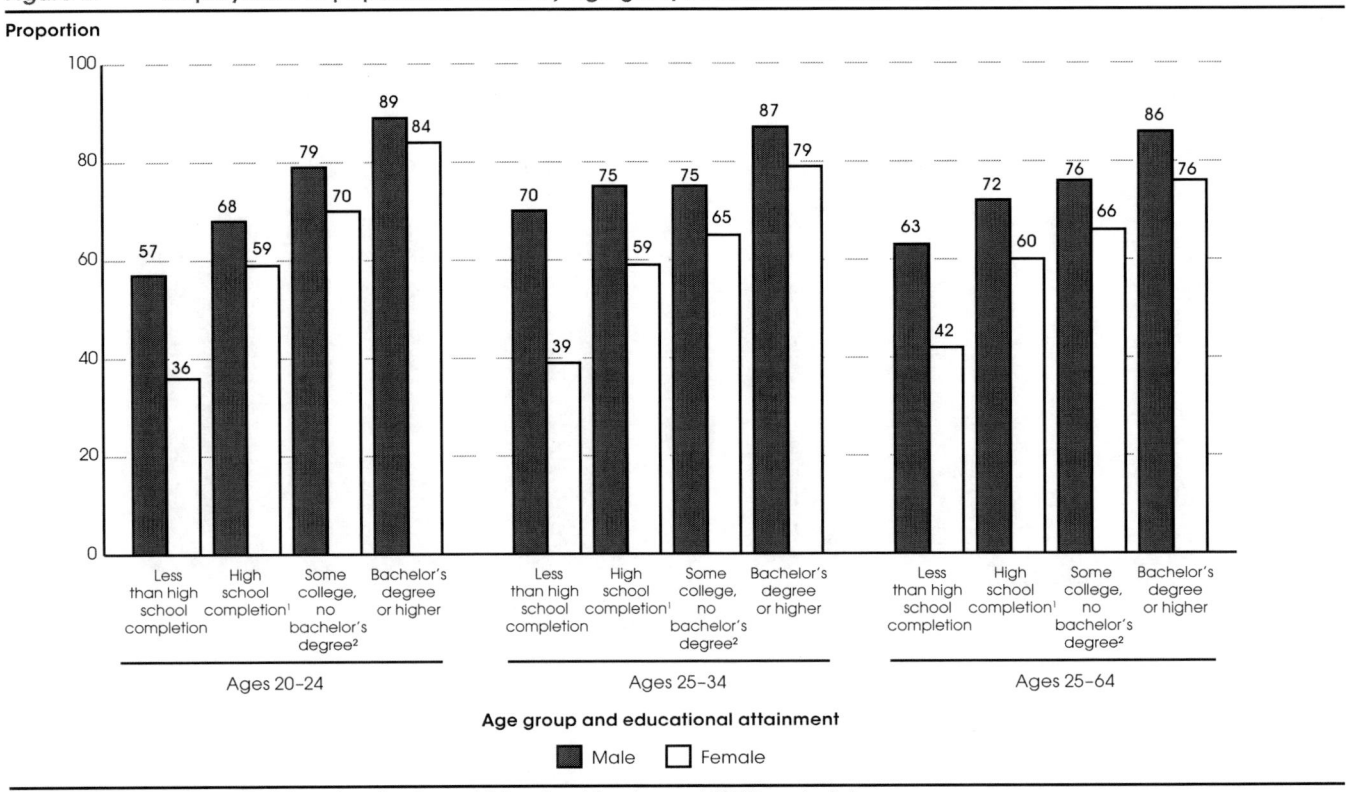

Proportion

Ages 20–24
- Less than high school completion: Male 57, Female 36
- High school completion[1]: Male 68, Female 59
- Some college, no bachelor's degree[2]: Male 79, Female 70
- Bachelor's degree or higher: Male 89, Female 84

Ages 25–34
- Less than high school completion: Male 70, Female 39
- High school completion[1]: Male 75, Female 59
- Some college, no bachelor's degree[2]: Male 75, Female 65
- Bachelor's degree or higher: Male 87, Female 79

Ages 25–64
- Less than high school completion: Male 63, Female 42
- High school completion[1]: Male 72, Female 60
- Some college, no bachelor's degree[2]: Male 76, Female 66
- Bachelor's degree or higher: Male 86, Female 76

Age group and educational attainment

■ Male □ Female

[1] Includes equivalency credentials, such as the General Educational Development (GED) credential.
[2] Includes persons with no college degree as well as those with an associate's degree.
NOTE: The employment to population ratio is defined as the proportion of the civilian population that is employed. Educational attainment refers to the highest level of education achieved (i.e., less than high school completion, high school completion, some college, or a bachelor's degree or higher). Data for 20- to 24-year-olds exclude persons enrolled in school.
SOURCE: U.S. Department of Labor, Bureau of Labor Statistics, Office of Employment and Unemployment Statistics, unpublished 2012 annual average data from the Current Population Survey (CPS). See *Digest of Education Statistics 2012*, tables 432 and 433.

Among young adults, males without a bachelor's degree generally had higher employment rates than their female counterparts between 1990 and 2012. In 2012, for example, the employment rate for young adults whose educational attainment was less than high school was 57 percent for males and 36 percent for females, and the employment rate for young adults whose educational attainment was high school completion was 68 percent for males and 59 percent for females. The employment rate for male young adults with some college education was 79 percent in 2012, while it was 70 percent for their female counterparts. In most years during the period, however, employment rates for female and male young adults who had at least a bachelor's degree were not measurably different. In 2011, for example, there was no measurable difference in the employment rate for young adults by sex for those with at least a bachelor's degree. In 2012, however, the employment rate for young adults with at least a bachelor's degree differed by sex: males had a higher employment rate than females (89 vs. 84 percent). For 25- to 64-year-olds, as well as for its subset population of 25- to 34-year-olds, the employment rate for females was lower than that for males at each level of educational attainment between 1990 and 2012. For example, in 2012 the employment rate was 39 percent for female 25- to 34-year-olds who did not complete high school, compared with 70 percent for their male counterparts.

When there was a male-female gap in employment rates, it was generally wider for those who completed high school, as well as those who did not, than for those who attained at least a bachelor's degree. This pattern was observed for every age group examined between 1990 and 2012. For example, for 25- to 34-year-olds, the male-female gaps in 2012 were 31 percentage points for those who did not complete high school and 16 percentage points for high school completers, compared with an 8-percentage-point gap for those who had at least a bachelor's degree. For 25- to 64-year-olds, the male-female gaps were 21 percentage points for those who did not complete high school and 12 percentage points for high school completers, while the gap was 9 percentage points for those who had at least a bachelor's degree.

During the most recent economic recession (as determined by the National Bureau of Economic Research to be the period beginning in December 2007 and continuing through June 2009, see http://www.nber.org/cycles/sept2010.html), employment rates generally declined across age groups and educational attainment levels. The magnitude of change in employment rates varied by sex and by educational attainment. The recession had a less marked effect on the employment rate of males with at least a bachelor's degree than on the rate of males with less than a bachelor's. For females, the magnitude of change

For more information, see the Reader's Guide and the Guide to Sources.

Chapter: 1/Population Characteristics
Section: Spotlight

in the employment rate was not measurably different across educational levels. And although the economy was recovering in 2010, the employment rate for females, in general, did not change measurably from 2010 to 2012. Compared with the employment rate in 2008, the employment rate in 2012 was either lower or not measurably different for both males and females across the age groups and educational achievement levels examined.

Figure 3. Employment to population ratios of persons 20 to 24 years old, by sex and educational attainment: Selected years, 1990 through 2012

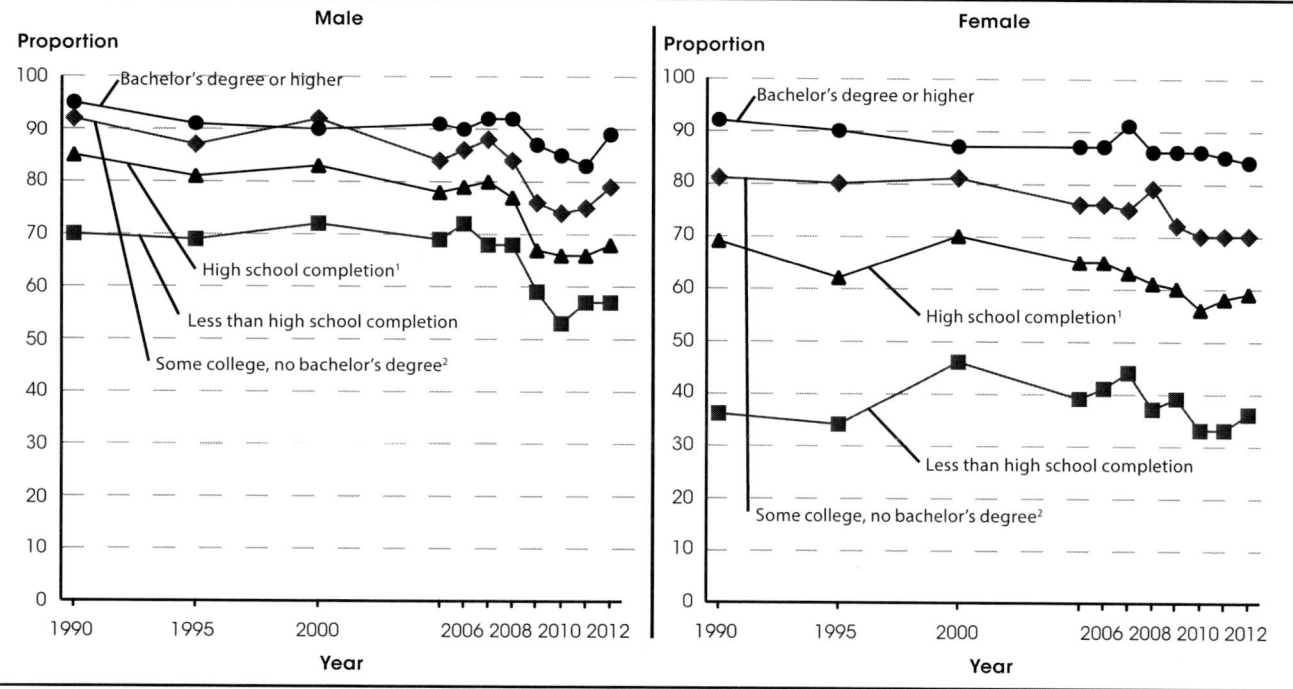

[1] Includes equivalency credentials, such as the General Educational Development (GED) credential.
[2] Includes persons with no college degree as well as those with an associate's degree.
NOTE: The employment to population ratio is defined as the proportion of the civilian population that is employed. Educational attainment refers to the highest level of education achieved (i.e., less than high school completion, high school completion, some college, or a bachelor's degree or higher). Data for 20- to 24-year-olds exclude persons enrolled in school.
SOURCE: U.S. Department of Labor, Bureau of Labor Statistics, Office of Employment and Unemployment Statistics, unpublished 1990, 1995, 2000, and 2005 through 2012 annual average data from the Current Population Survey (CPS). See *Digest of Education Statistics 2012*, tables 432 and 433.

The employment rate for young adult male 20- to 24-year-olds was lower in 2010 than in 2008 at each level of educational attainment. However, from 2008 to 2010, the 7-percentage-point decrease (from 92 to 85 percent) for males who had at least a bachelor's degree was smaller than the 15-percentage-point decrease (from 68 to 53 percent) for males who did not complete high school. For female 20- to 24-year-olds, the employment rate declined from 2008 to 2010 for those with some college education (from 79 to 70 percent) and for high school completers (from 61 to 56 percent).

Though the economy was recovering from 2010 to 2012, the employment rate did not change measurably for either male or female 20- to 24-year-olds at any level of educational attainment except for the rate for males who had some college education (which increased from 74 percent in 2010 to 79 percent in 2012).

Over the entire four year period from 2008 to 2012, the employment rate decreased for male young adults who did not attain a bachelor's degree: for those who had some college education, the employment rate was 79 percent in 2012 vs. 84 percent in 2008; for high school completers, it was 68 percent in 2012 vs. 77 percent in 2008; and for those who did not complete high school, it was 57 percent in 2012 vs. 68 percent in 2008. The employment rate for young adult males with at least a bachelor's degree in 2012, however, was not measurably different from that in 2008. The 2012 employment rate for young adult females with some college education (70 percent) was lower than the corresponding 2008 employment rate (79 percent). However, employment rates in 2012 were not measurably different from those in 2008 for female young adults at any of the other three levels of educational attainment examined.

For more information, see the Reader's Guide and the Guide to Sources.

Chapter: 1/Population Characteristics
Section: Spotlight

Figure 4. Employment to population ratios of persons 25 to 64 years old, by sex and educational attainment: Selected years, 1990 through 2012

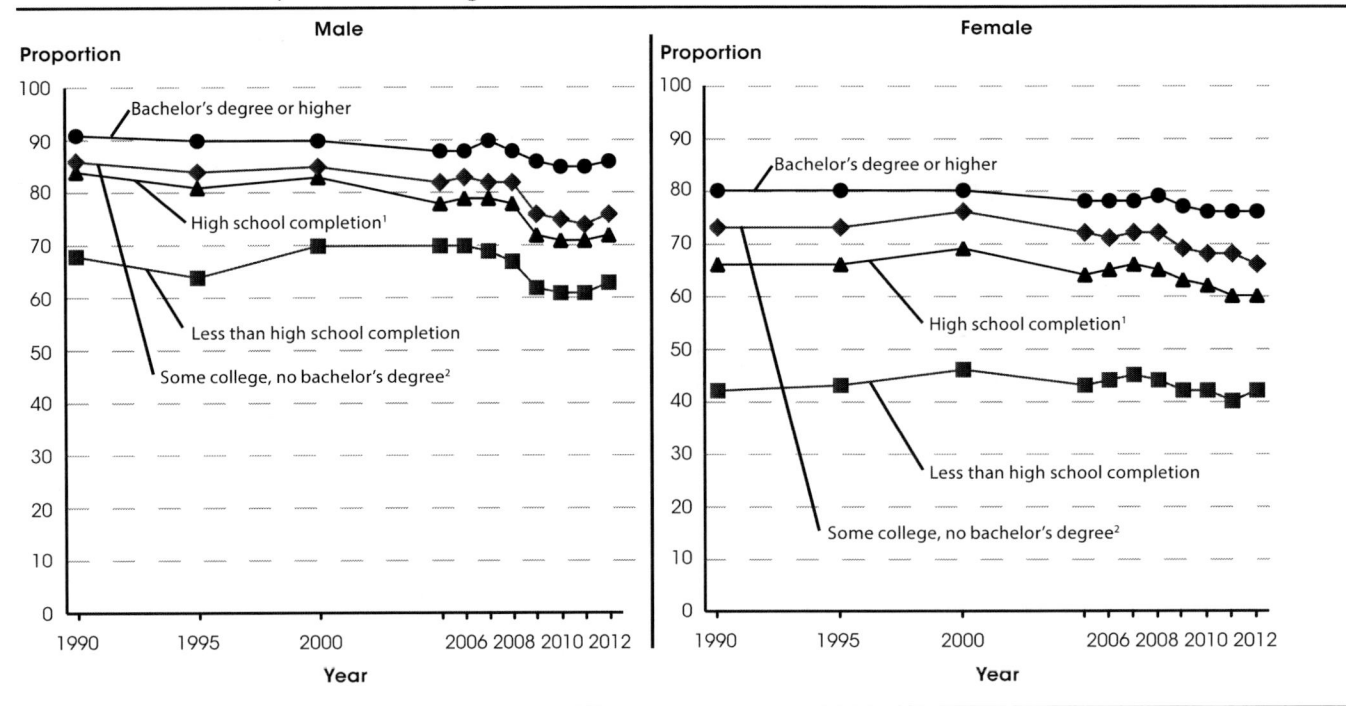

[1] Includes equivalency credentials, such as the General Educational Development (GED) credential.
[2] Includes persons with no college degree as well as those with an associate's degree.
NOTE: The employment to population ratio is defined as the proportion of the civilian population that is employed. Educational attainment refers to the highest level of education achieved (i.e., less than high school completion, high school completion, some college, or a bachelor's degree or higher).
SOURCE: U.S. Department of Labor, Bureau of Labor Statistics, Office of Employment and Unemployment Statistics, unpublished 1990, 1995, 2000, and 2005 through 2012 annual average data from the Current Population Survey (CPS). See *Digest of Education Statistics 2012*, tables 432 and 433.

For 25- to 64-year-olds, male and female employment rates decreased from 2008 to 2010 at each level of educational attainment examined (see *Digest of Education Statistics 2012*, tables 432 and 433). In addition, the 3-percentage-point decrease (from 88 to 85 percent) for males with at least a bachelor's degree was smaller than the 6-percentage-point decrease (from 82 to 75 percent) for males with some college education and the 6-percentage-point decrease (from 78 percent to 71 percent) for male high school completers. Although the employment rate declined for female high school completers (from 65 to 62 percent), females with some college education (from 72 to 68 percent), and females with at least a bachelor's degree (from 79 to 76 percent) during this period, the magnitudes of decrease were not measurably different between these levels of educational attainment.

From 2010 to 2012, the employment rate did not change measurably, generally speaking, for either males or females at any of the levels of educational attainment examined, with the exception that the employment rate continued to decline for female high school completers (from 62 to 60 percent) and females with some college education (from 68 to 66 percent).

Over the entire four year period, employment rates for both male and female 25- to 64-year-olds were generally lower in 2012 than in 2008 at each level of educational attainment.

For more information, see the Reader's Guide and the Guide to Sources.

Chapter: 1/Population Characteristics
Section: Spotlight

Figure 5. Employment to population ratios of persons 25 to 34 years old, by sex and educational attainment: Selected years, 1990 through 2012

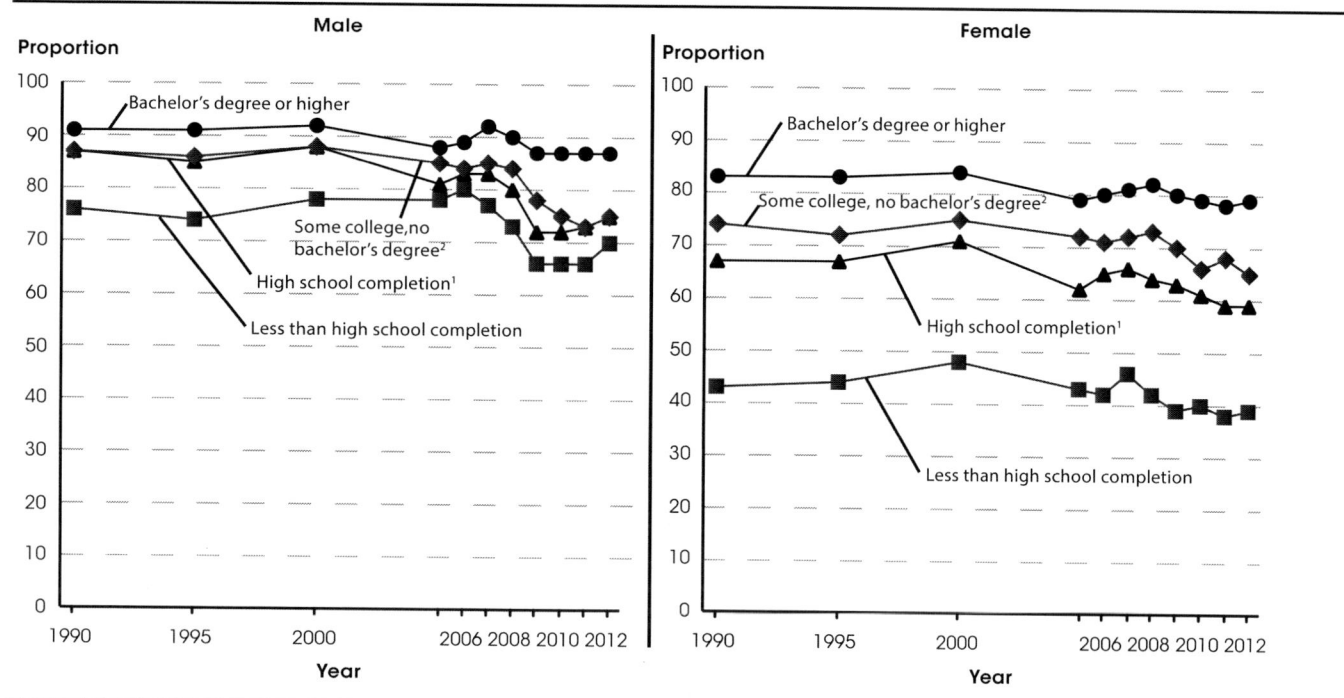

[1] Includes equivalency credentials, such as the General Educational Development (GED) credential.
[2] Includes persons with no college degree as well as those with an associate's degree.
NOTE: The employment to population ratio is defined as the proportion of the civilian population that is employed. Educational attainment refers to the highest level of education achieved (i.e., less than high school completion, high school completion, some college, or a bachelor's degree or higher).
SOURCE: U.S. Department of Labor, Bureau of Labor Statistics, Office of Employment and Unemployment Statistics, unpublished 1990, 1995, 2000, and 2005 through 2012 annual average data from the Current Population Survey (CPS). See *Digest of Education Statistics 2012,* tables 432 and 433.

Regarding the 25- to 34-year-old age group, male employment rates were lower in 2010 than in 2008 at each level of educational attainment. From 2008 to 2010, the employment rate decrease was 3 percentage points (from 90 to 87 percent) for males with at least a bachelor's degree, compared with 8 percentage points (from 84 to 75 percent) for males with some college education, 8 percentage points (from 80 to 72 percent) for male high school completers, and 7 percentage points (from 73 percent to 66 percent) for males who did not complete high school. The female employment rate in 2010 was lower than in 2008 for those with at least a bachelor's degree (79 vs. 82 percent) and for those whose educational attainment was some college (66 vs. 73 percent). Between 2010 and 2012, the employment rate did not measurably change for females at any level of educational attainment, and the employment rate only changed for males who were high school completers—their employment rate was higher in 2012 (75 percent) than in 2010 (72 percent). For both males and females, the 2012 employment rates remained lower than they were in 2008 at each level of educational attainment except for those who did not complete high school. For both males and females who did not complete high school, the seemingly lower employment rates in 2012 were not statistically different from the rates in 2008 due to relatively large sampling errors.

Reference tables: *Digest of Education Statistics 2012,* tables 431, 432, 433

Glossary: Bachelor's degree, Educational attainment, High school completer

For more information, see the Reader's Guide and the Guide to Sources.

Chapter: 1/Population Characteristics
Section: Attainment

Indicator 1
Educational Attainment

In 2012, some 33 percent of 25- to 29-year-olds had completed a bachelor's degree or higher credential. The size of the White-Black gap at this educational level in 2012 was not measurably different from that in 1990, while the White-Hispanic gap widened from 18 to 25 percentage points.

In this indicator, *educational attainment* represents the achievement of at least the cited credential (i.e., a high school diploma or equivalency certificate, a bachelor's degree, or a master's degree). Between 1990 and 2012, educational attainment among 25- to 29-year-olds increased: the percentage who had received at least a high school diploma or its equivalent increased from 86 to 90 percent, and the percentage who had completed a bachelor's degree or higher increased from 23 to 33 percent. In 2012, some 7 percent of 25- to 29-year-olds had completed a master's degree or higher, a 3 percentage-point increase from 1995.

Figure 1. Percentage of 25- to 29-year-olds who completed bachelor's and master's degrees, by sex: Selected years, 1990–2012

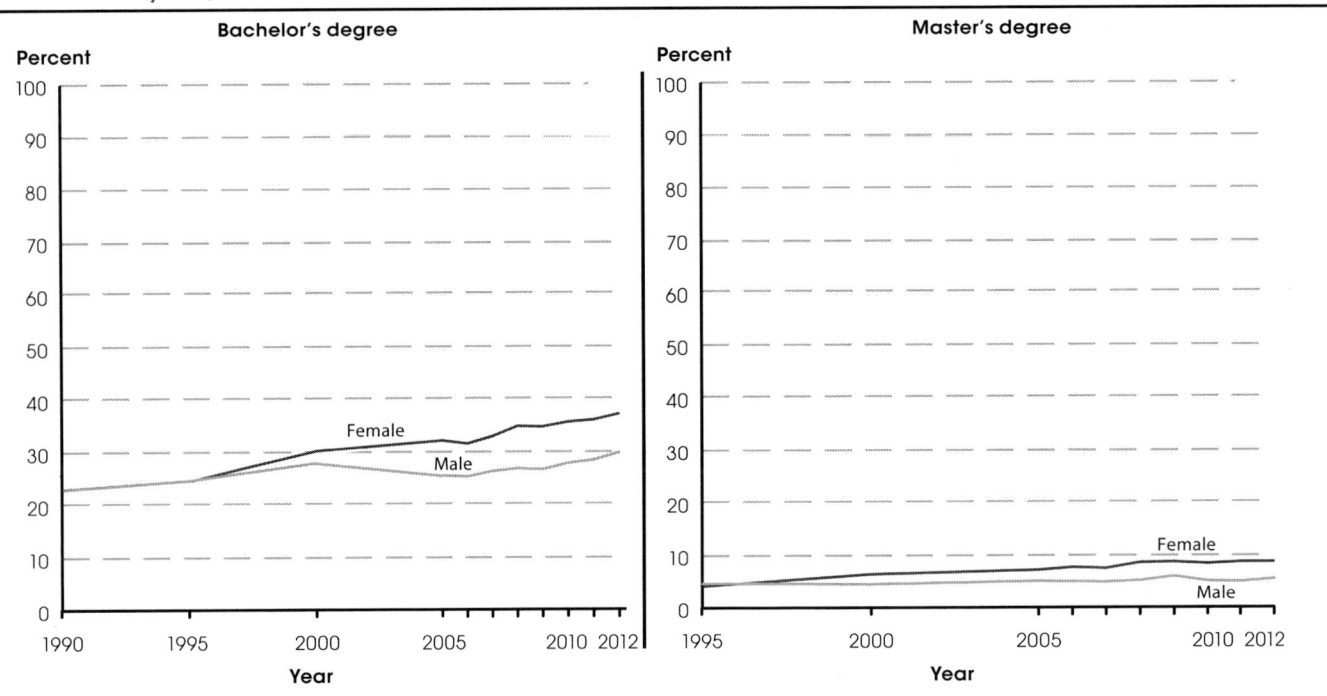

NOTE: Prior to 1995, data on attainment of a master's degree were not available.
SOURCE: U.S. Department of Commerce, Census Bureau, Current Population Survey (CPS), "Annual Social and Economic Supplement," selected years, 1990–2012. See *Digest of Education Statistics 2012*, table 9.

Differences in educational attainment by sex have shifted over the past few decades, with female attainment rates now higher than male attainment rates at each education level. For example, in 1990 the percentages of male and female 25- to 29-year-olds who had completed a bachelor's degree or higher were not measurably different, but in 2012 the percentage of females (37 percent) attaining this level was 7 points higher than the percentage of males doing so (30 percent). Similarly, in 1995 the percentages of males and females who had completed a master's degree or higher were not measurably different, but in 2012 the percentage of females (9 percent) was 3 points higher than the percentage of males (6 percent).

For more information, see the Reader's Guide and the Guide to Sources.

Chapter: 1/Population Characteristics
Section: Attainment

Figure 2. Percentage of 25- to 29-year-olds who completed at least a high school diploma or its equivalent, by race/ethnicity: Selected years, 1990–2012

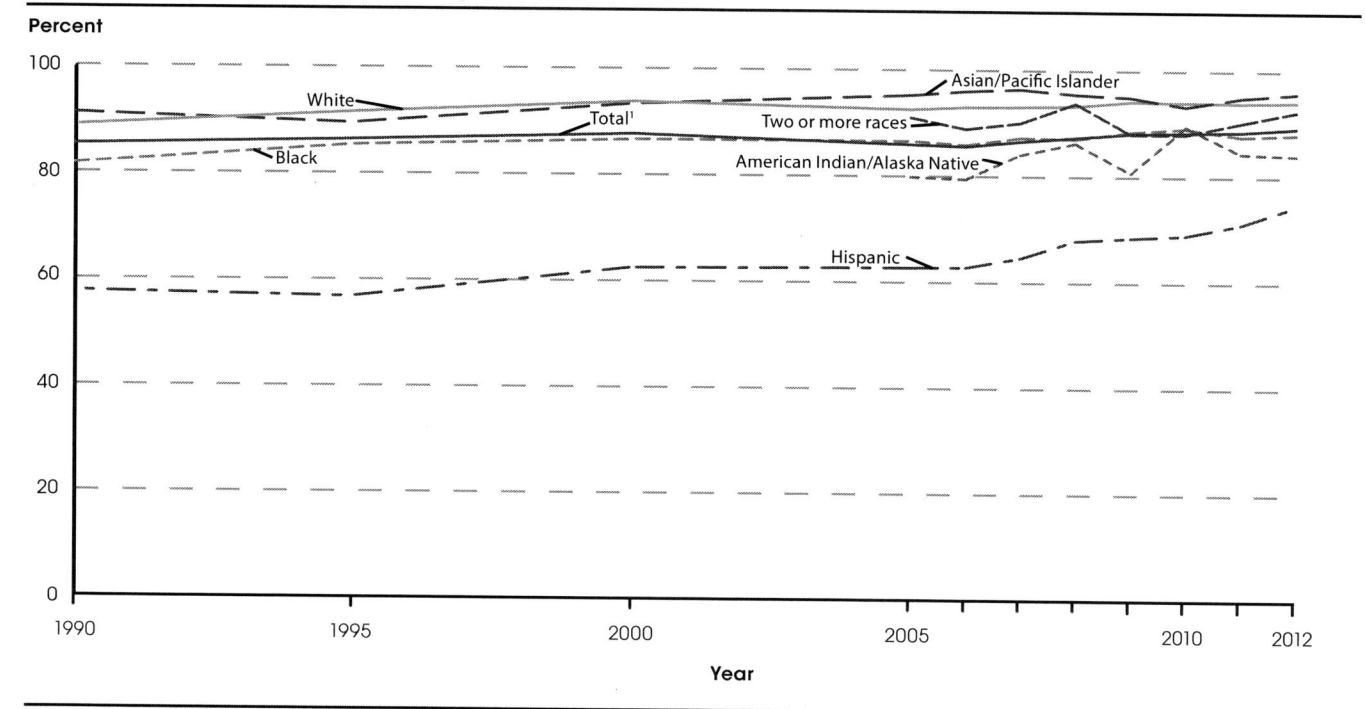

[1] Included in the total, but not shown separately, are estimates for persons from other racial/ethnic groups.
NOTE: Race categories exclude persons of Hispanic ethnicity. Prior to 2005, data on American Indians/Alaska Natives and persons of two or more races were not available.
SOURCE: U.S. Department of Commerce, Census Bureau, Current Population Survey (CPS), "Annual Social and Economic Supplement," selected years, 1990–2012. See *Digest of Education Statistics 2012*, table 9.

Between 1990 and 2012, the educational attainment rate of 25- to 29-year-olds who received at least a high school diploma or its equivalent increased for Whites (from 90 to 95 percent), Blacks (from 82 to 89 percent), Hispanics (from 58 to 75 percent), and Asians/Pacific Islanders (from 92 to 96 percent). The percentage of Whites who received at least a high school diploma or its equivalent remained higher than that of Blacks and Hispanics. The size of the White-Black gap at this educational level in 2012 was not measurably different from that in 1990, while the White-Hispanic gap narrowed from 32 to 20 percentage points.

For more information, see the Reader's Guide and the Guide to Sources.

Chapter: 1/Population Characteristics
Section: Attainment

Figure 3. Percentage of 25- to 29-year-olds with a bachelor's degree or higher, by race/ethnicity: Selected years, 1990–2012

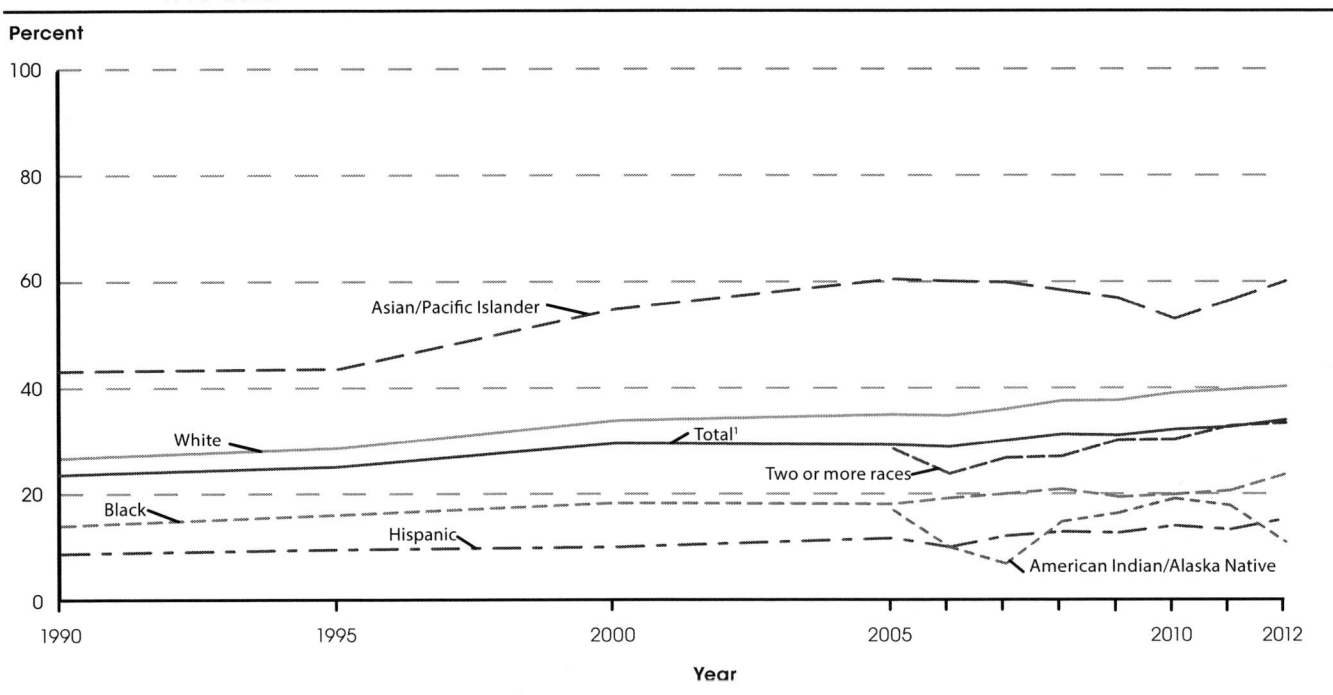

[1] Included in the total, but not shown separately, are estimates for persons from other racial/ethnic groups.
NOTE: Race categories exclude persons of Hispanic ethnicity. Prior to 2005, data on American Indians/Alaska Natives and persons of two or more races were not available.
SOURCE: U.S. Department of Commerce, Census Bureau, Current Population Survey (CPS), "Annual Social and Economic Supplement," selected years, 1990–2012. See *Digest of Education Statistics 2012*, table 9.

From 1990 to 2012, the percentage of 25- to 29-year-olds who attained a bachelor's degree or higher increased from 26 to 40 percent for Whites, from 13 to 23 percent for Blacks, and from 8 to 15 percent for Hispanics. For Asians/Pacific Islanders, the educational attainment rate of at least a bachelor's degree in 2012 (60 percent) was higher than the rate in 1990 (43 percent). Between 1990 and 2012, the gap in the attainment rate between Whites and Hispanics at the level of bachelor's degree or higher widened from 18 to 25 percentage points. The apparent difference in the White-Black gap between 1990 (13 percentage points) and 2012 (17 percentage points) was not statistically significant. However, from 1990 to 2011, there was a widening in the gap.

From 1995 to 2012, the percentage of 25- to 29-year-olds who attained a master's degree or higher increased for Whites (from 5 to 8 percent) and Blacks (from 2 to 5 percent). For Asians/Pacific Islanders, the attainment rate of a master's degree or higher in 2012 (18 percent) was higher than the rate in 1995 (11 percent). The gap in the attainment of a master's degree or higher between Blacks and Whites in 2012 was not measurably different from that in 1995, while the White-Hispanic gap in 2012 (5 percentage points) was wider than in 1995 (4 percentage points).

Reference table: *Digest of Education Statistics 2012*, table 9

Glossary: Educational attainment

For more information, see the Reader's Guide and the Guide to Sources.

This page intentionally left blank.

Chapter: 1/Population Characteristics
Section: Attainment

Indicator 2
International Educational Attainment

Across OECD countries, the percentage of 25- to 64-year-olds who had earned a college degree was higher in 2010 (22 percent) than in 2001 (15 percent). The percentage of the U.S. adult population with a bachelor's or higher degree was 32 percent in 2010, compared with 28 percent in 2001.

The Organisation for Economic Co-operation and Development (OECD) is an organization of 34 countries whose purpose is to promote trade and economic growth. This indicator presents data on high school and bachelor's degree completion rates for the adult population (ages 25 to 64) of OECD member countries. Attainment data in this indicator refer to comparable levels of degrees, as classified by the International Standard Classification of Education (ISCED).

In 2010, some 26 out of 33 OECD countries reported that 70 percent or more of their adult populations had completed high school. Among all OECD countries, the percentages of high school completers ranged from under 40 percent in Turkey, Portugal, and Mexico, to over 90 percent in the Slovak Republic and the Czech Republic. Additionally, some 21 OECD countries reported that 20 percent or more of their adult populations had completed a bachelor's or higher degree. Among all OECD countries, the percentages of bachelor's degree completers ranged from under 15 percent in Austria, Slovenia, Turkey, and Italy, to over 30 percent in Israel, the United States, and Norway.

Figure 1. Percentage of the population 25 to 64 years old in Organisation for Economic Co-operation and Development (OECD) countries who attained selected levels of education, by age group: 2010

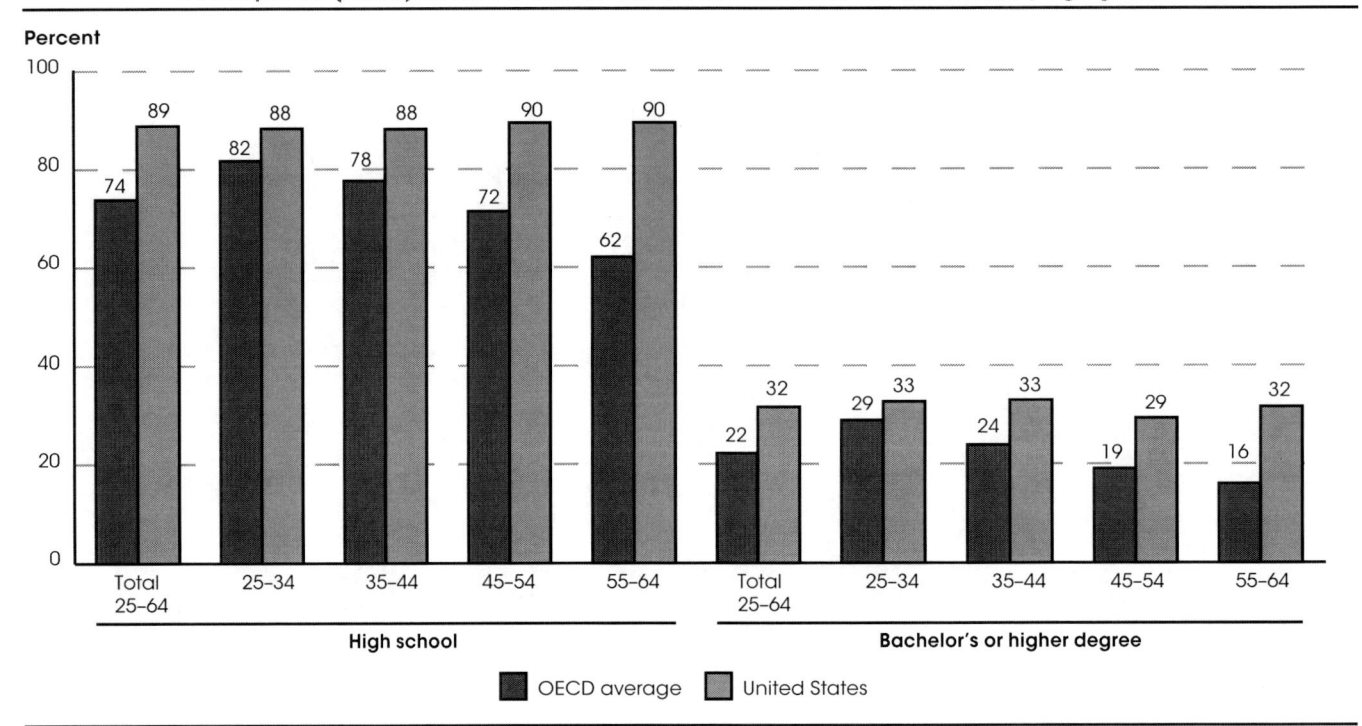

NOTE: Educational attainment data in this figure refer to degrees classified by the OECD as International Standard Classification of Education (ISCED) level 3 for high school and level 5A or 6 for bachelor's or higher degree. The OECD average refers to the mean of the data values for all reporting OECD countries, to which each country reporting data contributes equally.
SOURCE: Organisation for Economic Co-operation and Development (OECD), *Education at a Glance*, 2002, 2007, and 2012. See *Digest of Education Statistics 2012*, tables 467 and 469.

For more information, see the Reader's Guide and the Guide to Sources.

Chapter: 1/Population Characteristics
Section: Attainment

In 2010, on average, higher percentages of the youngest age group had completed high school compared with the oldest age group in most OECD countries. For example, the average percentage of 25- to 34-year-olds completing high school across OECD countries was 20 percentage points higher than the average percentage of 55- to 64-year-olds completing high school (82 vs. 62 percent, respectively). The United States was one of two countries, along with Estonia, for which there was no measurable difference between the percentage of 25- to 34-year-olds completing high school and the percentage of 55- to 64-year-olds completing high school: in 2010, some 90 percent of both U.S. 25- to 34-year-olds and 55- to 64-year olds had completed high school. The only other countries where 80 percent or more of 55- to 64-year-olds had completed high school were the Czech Republic, Estonia, the Slovak Republic, Germany, Canada, and Switzerland.

The same general pattern of higher percentages of the youngest age groups attaining higher levels of education also applied to the attainment of bachelor's degrees in 2010. In all OECD countries, a higher percentage of 25- to 34-year-olds than of 55- to 64-year-olds had attained a bachelor's or higher degree in 2010. On average, 29 percent of 25- to 34-year-olds had a bachelor's degree in 2010, compared with 16 percent of 55- to 64-year-olds. In the United States, 33 percent of 25- to 34-year-olds and 32 percent of 55- to 64-year-olds had a bachelor's or higher degree. The United States was the only country where at least 30 percent of 55- to 64-year-olds had attained at least a bachelor's degree in 2010.

Figure 2. Percentage of the population 25 to 64 years old in Organisation for Economic Co-operation and Development (OECD) countries who attained selected levels of education: Selected years, 2001, 2005, and 2010

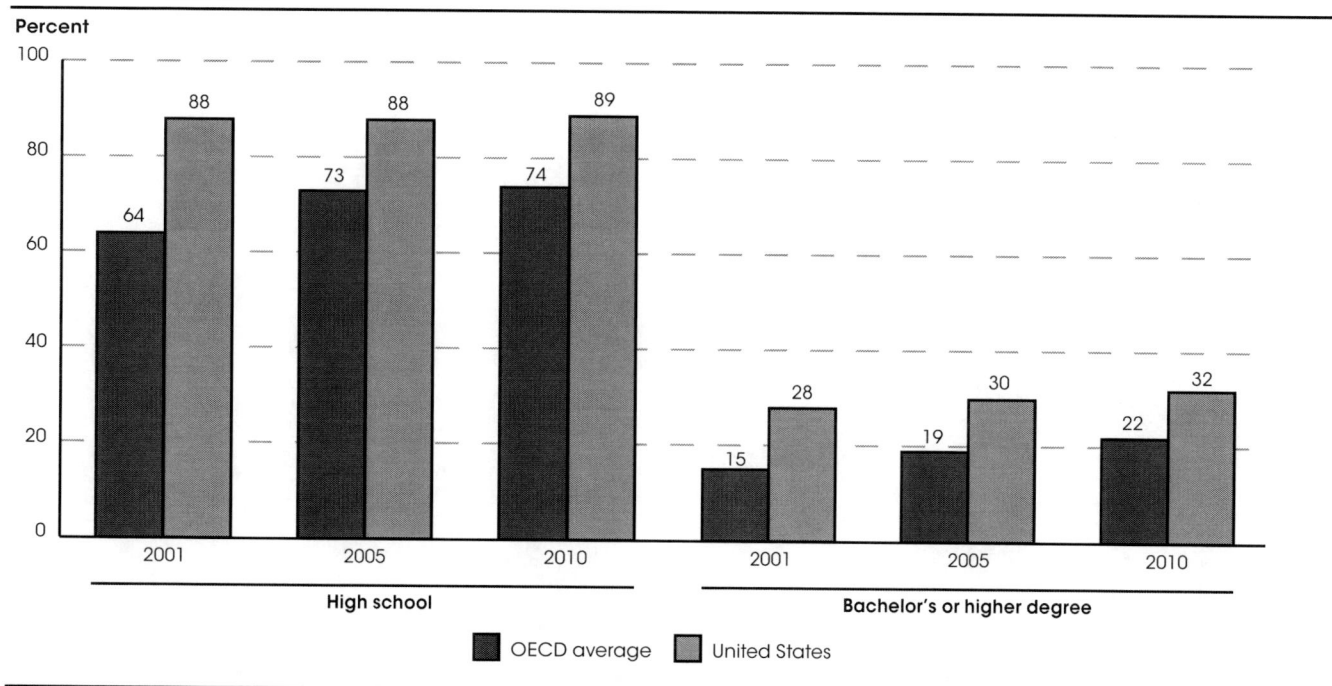

NOTE: Educational attainment data in this figure refer to degrees classified by the OECD as International Standard Classification of Education (ISCED) level 3 for high school and level 5A or 6 for bachelor's or higher degree. The OECD average refers to the mean of the data values for all reporting OECD countries, to which each country reporting data contributes equally.
SOURCE: Organisation for Economic Co-operation and Development (OECD), *Education at a Glance*, 2012. See *Digest of Education Statistics 2012*, tables 467 and 468.

Most OECD countries reported that the percentages of 25- to 64-year-olds who had completed a high school education or attained a bachelor's or higher degree were higher in 2010 than they were in 2001. Across OECD countries, the average percentage of the adult population completing a high school education increased 10 percentage points, from 64 percent in 2001 to 74 percent in 2010. The percentage of adults in the United States who had completed high school increased 1 percentage point during this period, from 88 to 89 percent. The OECD percentage of 25- to 34-year-olds with a high school education increased 8 percentage points, from 74 percent in 2001 to 82 percent in 2010. In comparison, there was no measurable change in the percentage of U.S. young adults with a high school education (88 percent) during that period.

The OECD average percentage of the adult population with a bachelor's or higher degree increased 7 percentage points between 2001 and 2010, from 15 percent to 22 percent. During the same period, the percentage of U.S. adults with a bachelor's or higher degree increased 4 percentage points, from 28 percent to 32 percent. Similarly, the OECD percentage of 25- to 34-year-olds with a bachelor's or higher degree rose from 18 percent in 2001 to 29 percent in 2010, an increase of 11 percentage points. The comparable percentage for young adults in

For more information, see the Reader's Guide and the Guide to Sources.

Chapter: 1/Population Characteristics
Section: Attainment

the United States increased 3 percentage points, from 30 percent to 33 percent. Thus, the relatively larger increases in the bachelor's or higher degree attainment rates for young adults in many OECD countries compared with the United States were reflected by a decreasing difference between OECD average and U.S. attainment rates.

In 2001, there was a 12 percentage point gap between the OECD average and the United States in the rate of attainment of a bachelor's or higher degree among 25- to 34-year-olds; by 2010, this gap had decreased to 4 percentage points.

Reference tables: *Digest of Education Statistics 2012,* tables 467, 468, 469

Glossary: Bachelor's degree, Educational attainment, High school completion, International Standard Classification of Education (ISCED), Organisation for Economic Co-operation and Development (OECD)

For more information, see the Reader's Guide and the Guide to Sources.

This page intentionally left blank.

Indicator 3
Annual Earnings of Young Adults

Chapter: 1/Population Characteristics
Section: Economic Outcomes

In 2011, young adults with a bachelor's degree earned almost twice as much as those without a high school diploma or its equivalent (97 percent more), 50 percent more than young adult high school completers, and 21 percent more than young adults with an associate's degree.

This indicator examines the annual earnings of young adults ages 25–34, many of whom have recently completed their education and constitute the youngest group of the general working-age population. In 2011, some 63 percent of young adults ages 25–34 who were in the labor force worked *full time* (i.e., 35 or more hours per week) and *full year* (i.e., 50 or more weeks per year). The percentage of young adults working full time throughout a full year was generally higher for those with higher levels of educational attainment. For example, 71 percent of young adults with a bachelor's degree or higher were full-time, full-year workers in 2011, compared with 59 percent of young adult high school completers (those with a high school diploma or its equivalent).

For young adults ages 25–34 who worked full time throughout a full year, higher educational attainment was associated with higher median earnings. This pattern of higher median earnings corresponding with higher levels of educational attainment was consistent for selected years 1995, 2000, and 2005–2011. For example, young adults with a bachelor's degree consistently had higher median earnings than those with less education. During this period, this pattern also held across sex and selected racial/ethnic subgroups (White, Black, Hispanic, and Asian).

Figure 1. Median annual earnings of full-time, full-year wage and salary workers ages 25–34, by educational attainment: 2011

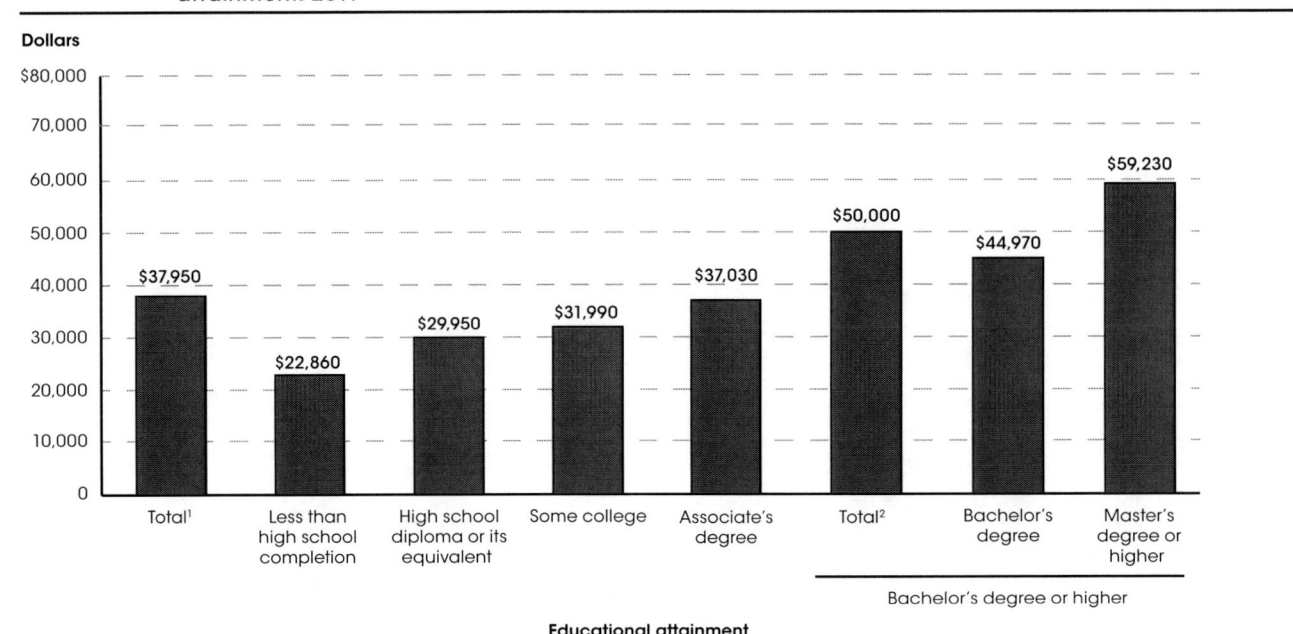

Educational attainment	Dollars
Total[1]	$37,950
Less than high school completion	$22,860
High school diploma or its equivalent	$29,950
Some college	$31,990
Associate's degree	$37,030
Total[2] (Bachelor's degree or higher)	$50,000
Bachelor's degree	$44,970
Master's degree or higher	$59,230

[1] Total represents median annual earnings of all full-time, full-year wage and salary workers ages 25–34.
[2] Total represents median annual earnings of young adults with a bachelor's degree or higher.
NOTE: *Full-year workers* refers to those who were employed 50 or more weeks during the previous year; *full-time workers* refers to those who were usually employed 35 or more hours per week.
SOURCE: U.S. Department of Commerce, Census Bureau, Current Population Survey (CPS), "Annual Social and Economic Supplement," 2012. See *Digest of Education Statistics 2012*, table 439.

For more information, see the Reader's Guide and the Guide to Sources.

Chapter: 1/Population Characteristics
Section: Economic Outcomes

In 2011, the median of earnings for young adults with a bachelor's degree was $45,000, while the median was $22,900 for those without a high school diploma or its equivalent, $30,000 for those with a high school diploma or its equivalent, and $37,000 for those with an associate's degree. In other words, young adults with a bachelor's degree earned almost twice as much as those without a high school diploma or its equivalent (97 percent more), 50 percent more than young adult high school completers, and 21 percent more than young adults with an associate's degree. Additionally, in 2011 the median of earnings for young adults with a master's degree or higher was $59,200, some 32 percent more than the median for young adults with a bachelor's degree.

Figure 2. Median annual earnings of full-time, full-year wage and salary workers ages 25–34, by educational attainment: 1995–2011

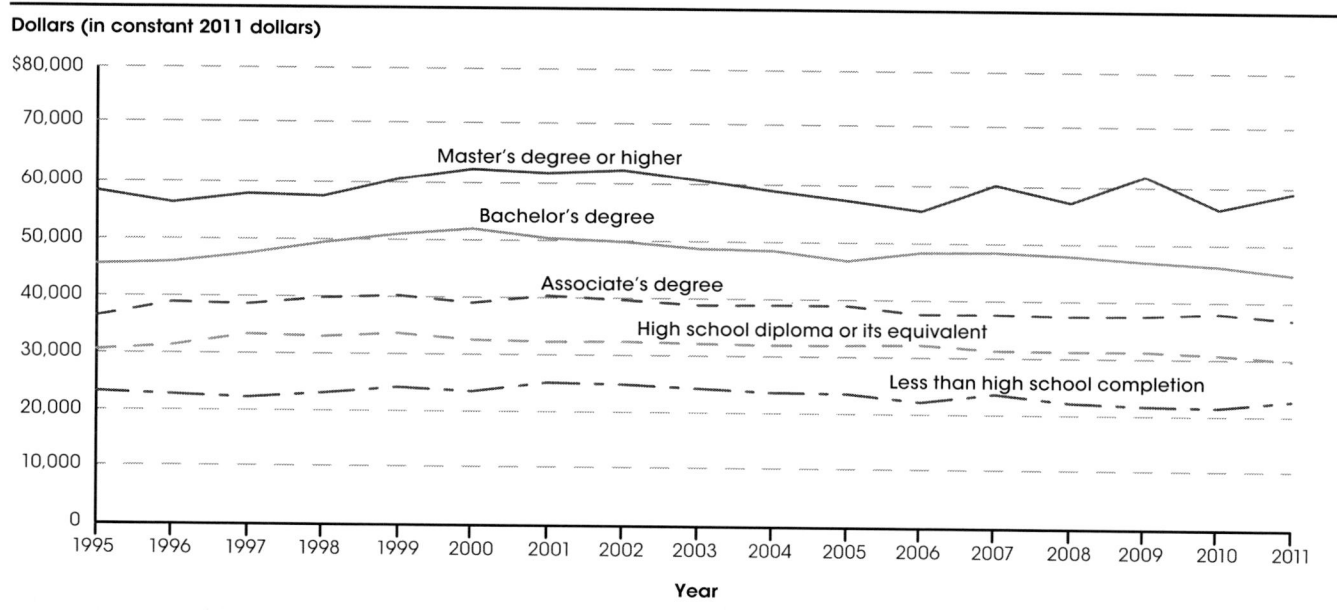

NOTE: Earnings are presented in constant dollars, based on the Consumer Price Index (CPI), to eliminate inflationary factors and to allow for direct comparison across years. *Full-year workers* refers to those who were employed 50 or more weeks during the previous year; *full-time workers* refers to those who were usually employed 35 or more hours per week.
SOURCE: U.S. Department of Commerce, Census Bureau, Current Population Survey (CPS), "Annual Social and Economic Supplement," 1996–2012. See *Digest of Education Statistics 2012*, table 439.

Median earnings (in constant 2011 dollars) for young adults with different levels of educational attainment exhibited different patterns of change over time. Between 2000 and 2011, the median earnings of young adult high school completers declined 8 percent from $32,700 to $30,000, and the median earnings for those with a bachelor's degree decreased by 14 percent from $52,100 to $45,000. The median earnings for young adults without a high school diploma or its equivalent and for those with a master's degree or higher did not change measurably between 2000 and 2011.

The difference (in constant 2011 dollars) in median earnings between those with a bachelor's degree or higher and those without a high school diploma or its equivalent widened between 1995 and 2009 and then narrowed between 2009 and 2011. In 1995, the median of earnings for young adults with a bachelor's degree or higher was $25,300 greater than the median for those without a high school diploma or its equivalent; in 2009, this earnings differential was $30,400; but in 2011, this earnings differential was $27,100. Though there were no patterns of increase or decrease in the earnings differential between those with a bachelor's degree or higher and high school completers between 1995 and 2011, the earnings differential was greater in 2011 ($20,000) than in 1995 ($18,000). There was no measurable difference, however, between the 2011 median earnings differential and the 1995 median earnings differential of those with a master's degree or higher over those with a bachelor's degree.

For more information, see the Reader's Guide and the Guide to Sources.

Chapter: 1/Population Characteristics
Section: Economic Outcomes

Figure 3. Median annual earnings of full-time, full-year wage and salary workers ages 25–34, by educational attainment and sex: 2011

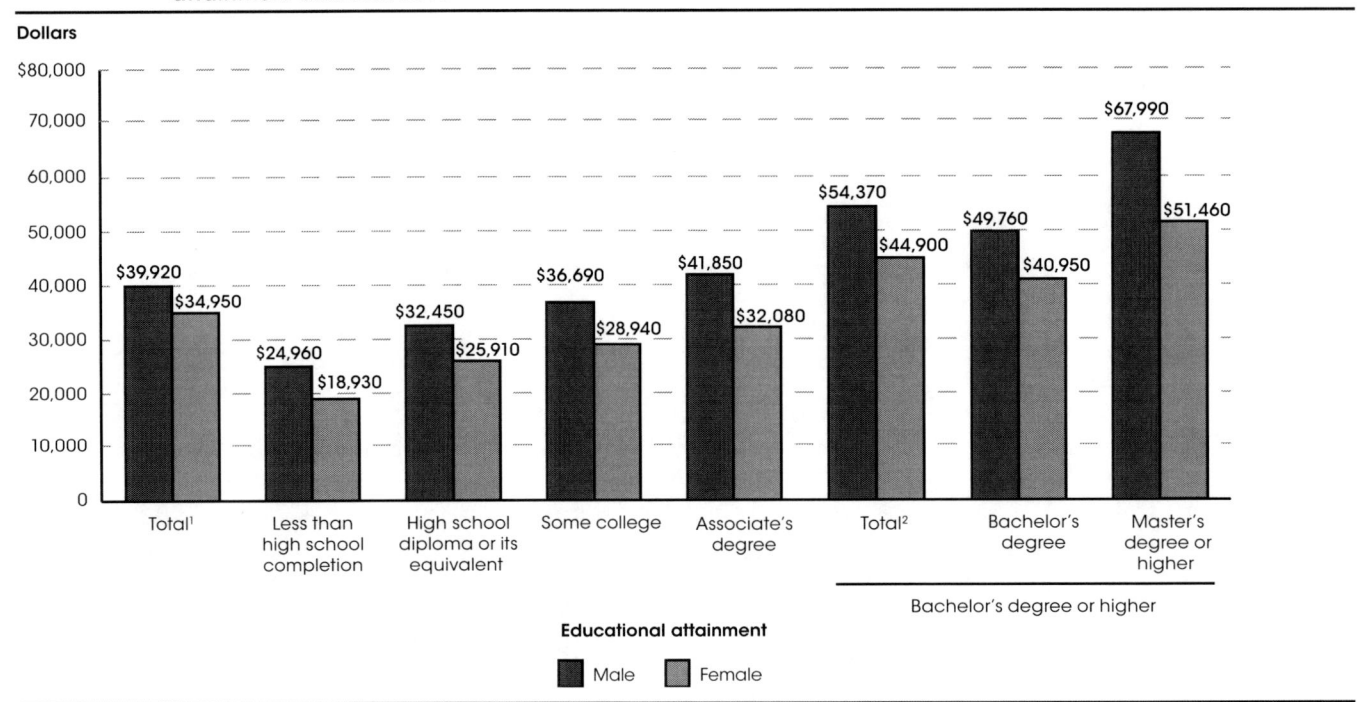

[Bar chart showing median annual earnings in dollars by educational attainment and sex]

Educational attainment	Male	Female
Total[1]	$39,920	$34,950
Less than high school completion	$24,960	$18,930
High school diploma or its equivalent	$32,450	$25,910
Some college	$36,690	$28,940
Associate's degree	$41,850	$32,080
Total[2] (Bachelor's degree or higher)	$54,370	$44,900
Bachelor's degree	$49,760	$40,950
Master's degree or higher	$67,990	$51,460

[1] Total represents median annual earnings of all full-time, full-year wage and salary workers ages 25–34.
[2] Total represents median annual earnings of young adults with a bachelor's degree or higher.
NOTE: *Full-year workers* refers to those who were employed 50 or more weeks during the previous year; *full-time workers* refers to those who were usually employed 35 or more hours per week.
SOURCE: U.S. Department of Commerce, Census Bureau, Current Population Survey (CPS), "Annual Social and Economic Supplement," 2012. See *Digest of Education Statistics 2012*, table 439.

In 2011, the median of earnings for young adult males was higher than the median for young adult females at every education level. For example, in 2011 young adult males with a bachelor's degree earned $49,800, while their female counterparts earned $40,900. In the same year, the median of earnings by education level for White young adults exceeded the corresponding medians for Black and Hispanic young adults. Asian young adults with a bachelor's degree or with a master's degree or higher had higher median earnings than did their Black and Hispanic counterparts in 2011; in addition, Asian young adults with at least a master's degree also had higher median earnings than did their White peers. For example, the median of earnings in 2011 for young adults with at least a master's degree was $73,200 for Asians, $58,700 for Whites, $50,900 for Hispanics, and $50,000 for Blacks.

Reference tables: *Digest of Education Statistics 2012*, table 439

Glossary: Bachelor's degree, Constant dollars, Consumer Price Index (CPI), Educational attainment, High school completer, Master's degree

For more information, see the Reader's Guide and the Guide to Sources.

This page intentionally left blank.

Chapter: 1/Population Characteristics
Section: Economic Outcomes

Indicator 4

Labor Force Participation and Unemployment Rates by Educational Attainment

In 2012, the unemployment rate for those with at least a bachelor's degree was lower than the rates for those with lower levels of educational attainment. During the most recent economic recession (December 2007 through June 2009), the unemployment rate increased less for those who had at least a bachelor's degree than for those who had less than a bachelor's degree.

In 2012, some 15.5 percent of young adults ages 20–24 were unemployed, as were 9.2 percent of 25- to 34-year-olds. The unemployment rates for both of these younger age cohorts were higher than the unemployment rate for 25- to 64-year-olds (7.4 percent), which included the subset of 25- to 34-year-olds. This pattern was consistent across several levels of educational attainment in 2012, such as the attainment levels of high school completion and of some college education. Educational attainment in this indicator refers to the highest level of education achieved (i.e., less than high school completion, high school completion, some college education, or a bachelor's degree or higher). In this indicator, the unemployment rate is defined as the percentage of persons in the civilian labor force who are not working *and who made specific efforts to find employment* during the prior 4 weeks. The civilian labor force refers to the civilian population who are employed or seeking employment.

Figure 1. Unemployment rates, by age group and educational attainment: 2012

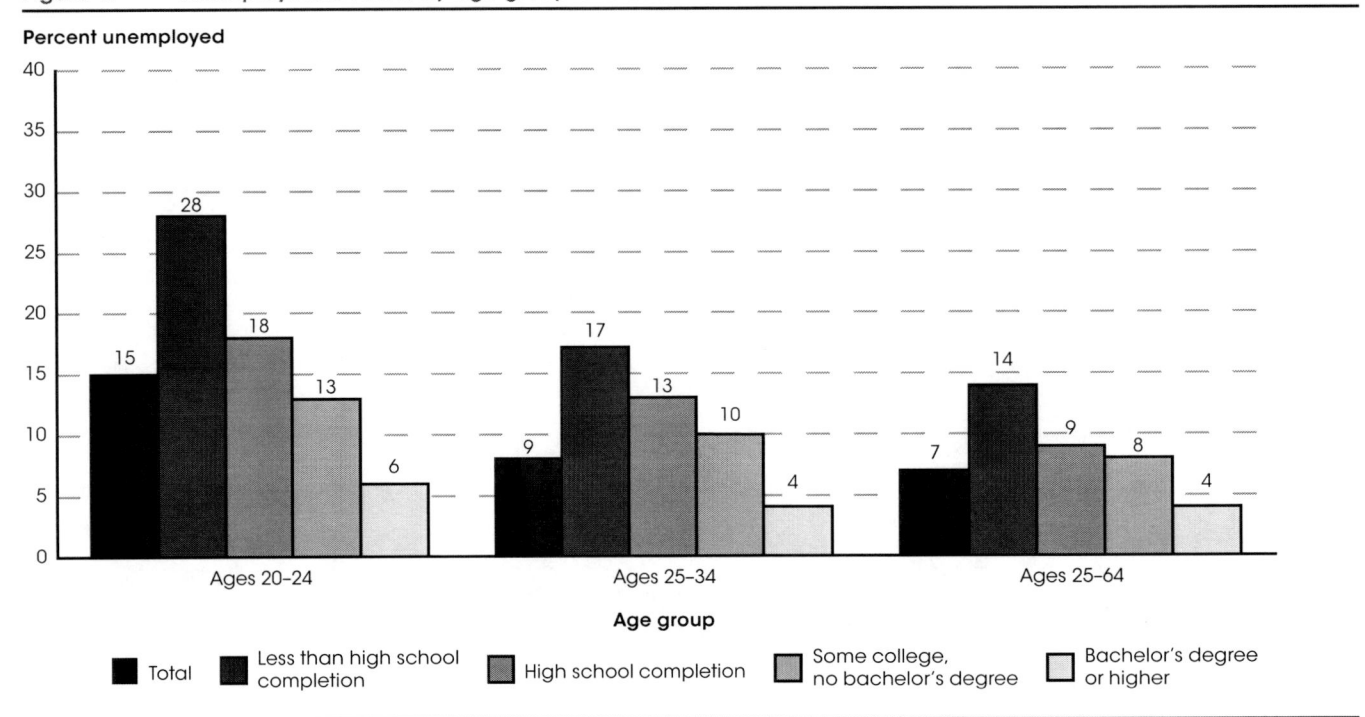

Percent unemployed

Age group	Total	Less than high school completion	High school completion	Some college, no bachelor's degree	Bachelor's degree or higher
Ages 20–24	15	28	18	13	6
Ages 25–34	9	17	13	10	4
Ages 25–64	7	14	9	8	4

NOTE: The unemployment rate is the percentage of persons in the civilian labor force who are not working and who made specific efforts to find employment sometime during the prior 4 weeks. The civilian labor force consists of all civilians who are employed or seeking employment. Data for 20- to 24-year-olds exclude persons enrolled in school. High school completion includes equivalency credentials, such as the General Educational Development (GED) credential.
SOURCE: U.S. Department of Labor, Bureau of Labor Statistics, Office of Employment and Unemployment Statistics, unpublished annual average data from the Current Population Survey (CPS), 2012. See *Digest of Education Statistics 2012*, table 434.

For more information, see the Reader's Guide and the Guide to Sources.

Chapter: 1/Population Characteristics
Section: Economic Outcomes

Between 1990 and 2012, the unemployment rate for individuals without a bachelor's degree was generally higher than the rate for their peers with at least a bachelor's degree. This pattern was consistent for young adults (ages 20–24), 25- to 34-year-olds, and 25- to 64-year-olds. In 2012, for example, the unemployment rate for young adults (ages 20–24) was 27.6 percent for those who did not complete high school, 18.3 percent for those whose highest level of education was high school completion, and 12.7 percent for those with some college education, compared with an unemployment rate of 6.0 percent for those with at least a bachelor's degree. For 25- to 34-year-olds, the unemployment rates for those with some college education (10.1 percent), high school completers (12.8 percent), and those who did not complete high school (16.8 percent) were also higher than the unemployment rate for those with a bachelor's degree or higher (4.1 percent). This pattern of higher unemployment rates corresponding with lower levels of educational attainment also generally held across males and females for each age group from 1990 to 2012.

In 2012, for young adults ages 20–24, the unemployment rates of males and females were not measurably different at each level of educational attainment examined, although the overall unemployment rate was higher for males (16.6 percent) than for females (14.1 percent). For 25- to 64-year-olds, the unemployment rate overall as well as that for high school completers was higher for males (8.0 and 10.1 percent, respectively) than for females (6.8 and 8.1 percent, respectively). For individuals ages 25–34, the overall male unemployment rate and the rate for males with some college education (10.0 and 11.1 percent, respectively) were higher than the corresponding female unemployment rates (8.2 and 9.1 percent, respectively). However, the unemployment rate for males who did not complete high school (14.3 percent) was lower than that for their female counterparts (22.0 percent). For individuals ages 25–34 whose educational attainment was high school completion and for those with at least a bachelor's degree, the employment rates for males and females were not measurably different.

Figure 2. Unemployment rates of persons 20 to 24 years old, by sex and educational attainment: Selected years, 1990 through 2012

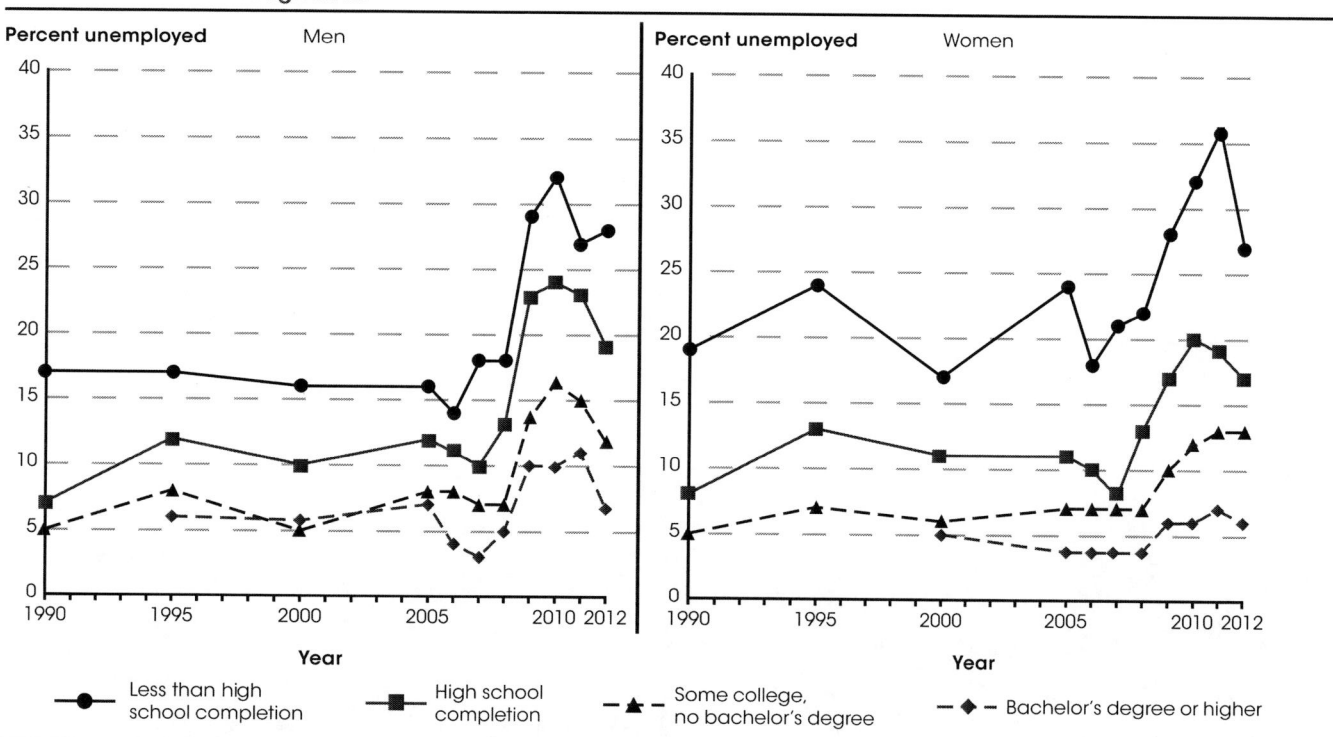

NOTE: The unemployment rate is the percentage of persons in the civilian labor force who are not working and who made specific efforts to find employment sometime during the prior 4 weeks. The civilian labor force consists of all civilians who are employed or seeking employment. Data for 20- to 24-year-olds exclude persons enrolled in school. High school completion includes equivalency credentials, such as the General Educational Development (GED) credential. The unemployment rates for males and females with a bachelor's degree or higher in 1990 as well as for females with a bachelor's degree or higher in 1995 were suppressed because reporting standards were not met.
SOURCE: U.S. Department of Labor, Bureau of Labor Statistics, Office of Employment and Unemployment Statistics, unpublished annual average data from the Current Population Survey (CPS), selected years, 1990 through 2012. See *Digest of Education Statistics 2012*, tables 435 and 436.

For more information, see the Reader's Guide and the Guide to Sources.

Chapter: 1/Population Characteristics
Section: Economic Outcomes

During the recent economic recession and recovery from 2008 to 2012, the magnitude of change in unemployment rates varied by educational attainment. In general, compared with high school completers and those who did not complete high school, individuals with at least a bachelor's degree were affected to a lesser extent by the recession in terms of unemployment. For young adults ages 20–24, the unemployment rates for males and females generally increased from 2008 to 2010 at each level of educational attainment. From 2008 to 2010, the 14.3-percentage-point increase (from 18.2 to 32.4 percent) in the unemployment rate for males who did not complete high school and the 10.5-percentage-point increase (from 13.3 to 23.7 percent) for male high school completers were higher than the 5.1-percentage-point increase (from 4.7 to 9.8 percent) for males with at least a bachelor's degree. For female young adults, the unemployment rate for those who had at least a bachelor's degree did not change measurably between 2008 and 2010. Although the unemployment rate for female young adults increased from 2008 to 2010 for those with some college education (from 6.5 to 12.1 percent), for those who were high school completers (from 12.5 to 19.9 percent), and for those who did not complete high school (from 21.6 to 32.2 percent), these unemployment rate increases across educational attainment levels were not measurably different from each other.

As the economy was recovering from 2010 to 2012, unemployment rates for young adults ages 20–24 did not change measurably within any of the educational attainment levels for females or males, with the exceptions of males with some college education and male high school completers. The unemployment rates for both males with some college education and male high school completers were lower in 2012 (12.0 and 19.0 percent, respectively) than in 2010 (16.4 and 23.7 percent, respectively). Compared with 2008, when the recession started, the unemployment rates for both male and female young adult high school completers as well as both males and females with some college education remained higher in 2012. The unemployment rate for male young adults who did not complete high school also remained higher in 2012: some 27.8 percent were unemployed in 2012, compared with 18.2 percent in 2008. However, for male and female young adults with a bachelor's degree or higher, the 2012 unemployment rate was not measurably different from the rate in 2008. In addition, the 2012 unemployment rate for female young adults who did not complete high school was not measurably different from the 2008 rate.

Figure 3. Unemployment rates of persons 25 to 64 years old, by sex and educational attainment: Selected years, 1990 through 2012

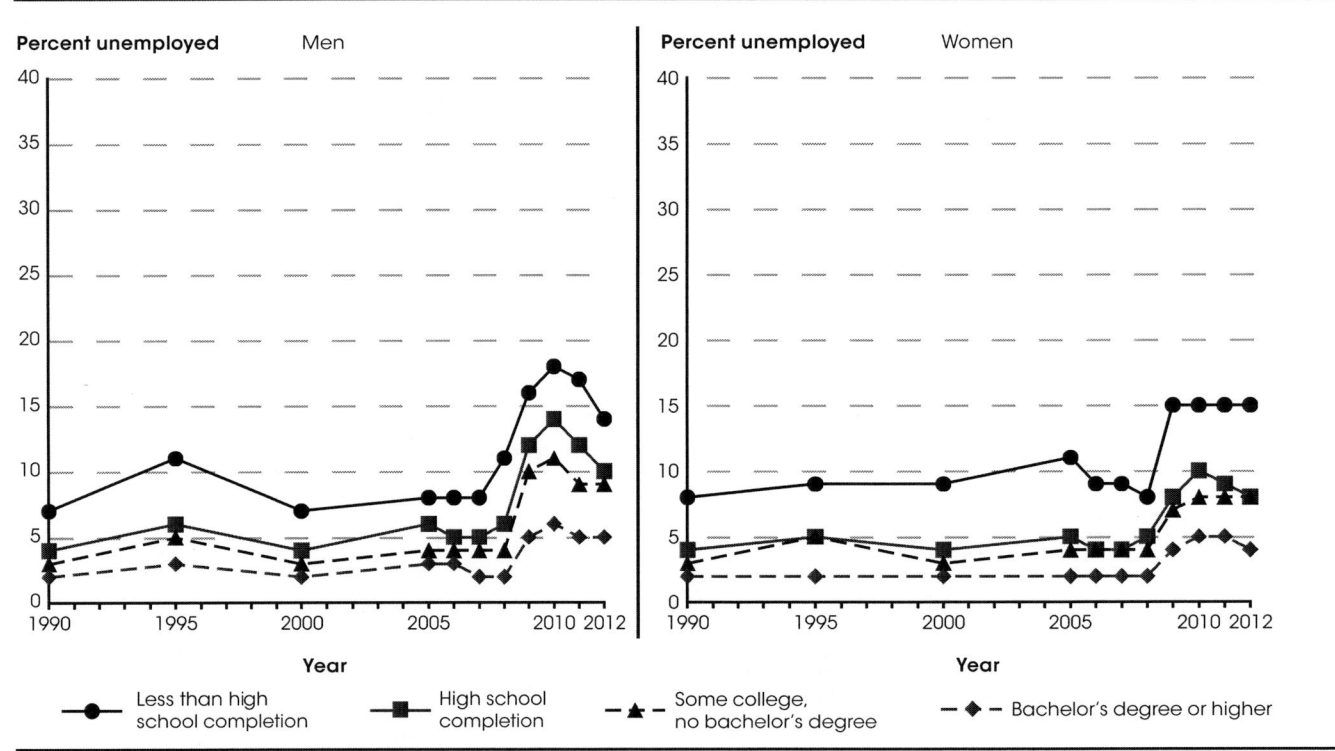

NOTE: The unemployment rate is the percentage of persons in the civilian labor force who are not working and who made specific efforts to find employment sometime during the prior 4 weeks. The civilian labor force consists of all civilians who are employed or seeking employment. High school completion includes equivalency credentials, such as the General Educational Development (GED) credential.
SOURCE: U.S. Department of Labor, Bureau of Labor Statistics, Office of Employment and Unemployment Statistics, unpublished annual average data from the Current Population Survey (CPS), selected years, 1990 through 2012. See *Digest of Education Statistics 2012*, tables 435 and 436.

For more information, see the Reader's Guide and the Guide to Sources.

Chapter: 1/Population Characteristics
Section: Economic Outcomes

As was the case for male young adults ages 20–24, unemployment rates for both male and female 25- to 64-year-olds also increased from 2008 to 2010 at each level of educational attainment. The increase in the unemployment rate from 2008 to 2010 was higher for both males and females who did not complete high school, who did complete high school, and who had some college education than for both males and females who had at least a bachelor's degree. From 2008 to 2010, for 25- to 64-year-olds, the unemployment rate increased 6.9 percentage points (from 10.9 to 17.8 percent) for males who did not complete high school, 7.5 percentage points (from 6.3 to 13.8 percent) for male high school completers, and 6.0 percentage points (from 4.2 to 10.2 percent) for males with some college education, whereas it increased 3.1 percentage points (from 2.0 to 5.1 percent) for males with at least a bachelor's degree. During the same period, the unemployment rate increases were 6.5 percentage points (from 8.5 to 15.0 percent) for females who did not complete high school, 4.8 percentage points (from 5.1 to 9.8 percent) for female high school completers, and 3.3 percentage points (from 4.2 to 7.5 percent) for females with some college education, compared with an increase of 2.2 percentage points (from 2.1 to 4.3 percent) for females with at least a bachelor's degree. From 2010 to 2012, unemployment rates for 25- to 64-year-old males decreased at each level of educational attainment: the decreases were 0.8 percentage points (from 5.1 to 4.3 percent) for males with at least a bachelor's degree, 2.0 percentage points (from 10.2 to 8.2 percent) for males with some college education, 3.8 percentage points (from 13.8 to 10.1 percent) for male high school completers, and 4.2 percentage points (from 17.8 to 13.6 percent) for males who did not complete high school. The unemployment rate for female high school completers also decreased from 2010 to 2012 (from 9.8 to 8.1 percent). Nevertheless, for both male and female 25- to 64-year-olds at each level of educational attainment unemployment rates in 2012 remained higher than they had been in 2008.

Figure 4. Unemployment rates of persons 25 to 34 years old, by sex and educational attainment: Selected years, 1990 through 2012

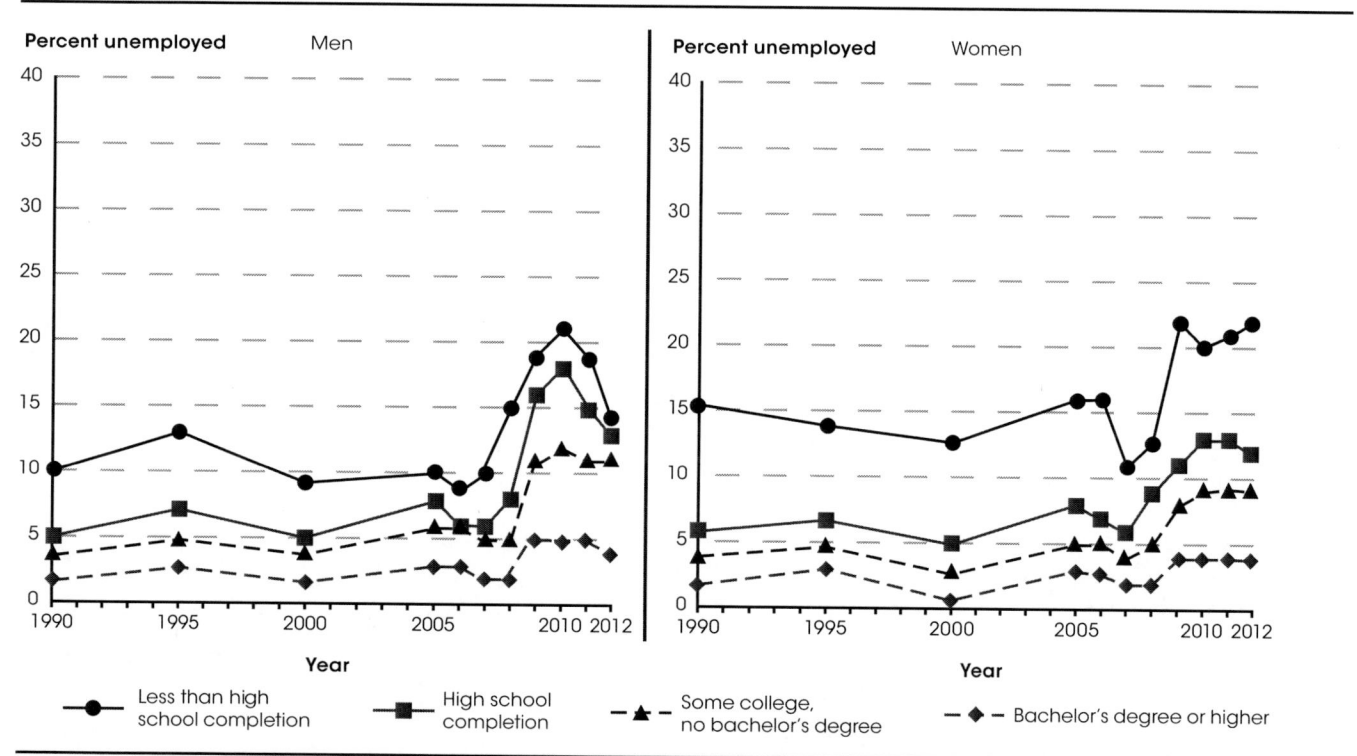

NOTE: The unemployment rate is the percentage of persons in the civilian labor force who are not working and who made specific efforts to find employment sometime during the prior 4 weeks. The civilian labor force consists of all civilians who are employed or seeking employment. High school completion includes equivalency credentials, such as the General Educational Development (GED) credential.
SOURCE: U.S. Department of Labor, Bureau of Labor Statistics, Office of Employment and Unemployment Statistics, unpublished annual average data from the Current Population Survey (CPS), selected years, 1990 through 2012. See *Digest of Education Statistics 2012*, tables 435 and 436.

For more information, see the Reader's Guide and the Guide to Sources.

Chapter: 1/Population Characteristics
Section: Economic Outcomes

For 25- to 34-year-olds, the change in unemployment rates from 2008 to 2010 followed a pattern similar to that of the change in unemployment rates for 25- to 64-year-olds. For example, from 2008 to 2010 the unemployment rate increases were 9.3 percentage points (from 8.5 to 17.8 percent) for male high school completers and 6.8 percentage points (from 5.0 to 11.8 percent) for males with some college education, compared with a 2.7-percentage-point increase (from 2.1 to 4.8 percent) for males with at least a bachelor's degree. For females, from 2008 to 2010 the unemployment rates increased 4.3 percentage points (from 5.1 to 9.3 percent) for those with some college education and 6.7 percentage points (from 12.8 to 19.5 percent) for those who did not complete high school, compared with a 2.0-percentage-point increase (from 2.3 to 4.3 percent) for those with at least a bachelor's degree. Between 2010 and 2012, the unemployment rate did not change measurably for females ages 25–34 overall or at any level of educational attainment. The unemployment rate for males, however, was lower in 2012 than in 2010 for those who did not complete high school (14.3 vs. 20.7 percent) and for high school completers (13.5 vs. 17.8 percent). For both male and female 25- to 34-year-olds, the unemployment rate remained higher in 2012 than in 2008, except in the case of males who did not complete high school.

Reference tables: *Digest of Education Statistics 2012,* tables 434, 435, 436

Glossary: Bachelor's degree, Educational attainment, High school completer

For more information, see the Reader's Guide and the Guide to Sources.

This page intentionally left blank.

Chapter: 1/Population Characteristics
Section: Demographics

Indicator 5
Children Living in Poverty

In 2011, approximately 21 percent of school-age children in the United States were in families living in poverty. The percentage of school-age children living in poverty ranged across the United States from 9 percent in North Dakota to 30 percent in the District of Columbia.

In 2011, approximately 10.9 million school-age children, or children 5 to 17 years old, were in families living in poverty. In this indicator, data on household income and the number of people living in the household are combined with the poverty threshold, published by the Census Bureau, to determine the poverty status of children. It includes all families in which children are related to the householder by birth or adoption, or through marriage. In 2011, the poverty threshold for a family of four was $22,811. The householder is the person (or one of the people) who owns or rents (maintains) the housing unit. Over the past two decades, the percentage of school-age children in the United States living in poverty has increased. Following a decrease from 1990 (17 percent) to 2000 (15 percent), the poverty rate for school-age children increased to 21 percent in 2011. Overall, between 1990 and 2011 the percentage of school-age children living in families in poverty increased by 4 percentage points.

Figure 1. Percentage of 5- to 17-year-olds in families living in poverty, by region: 1990, 2000, and 2011

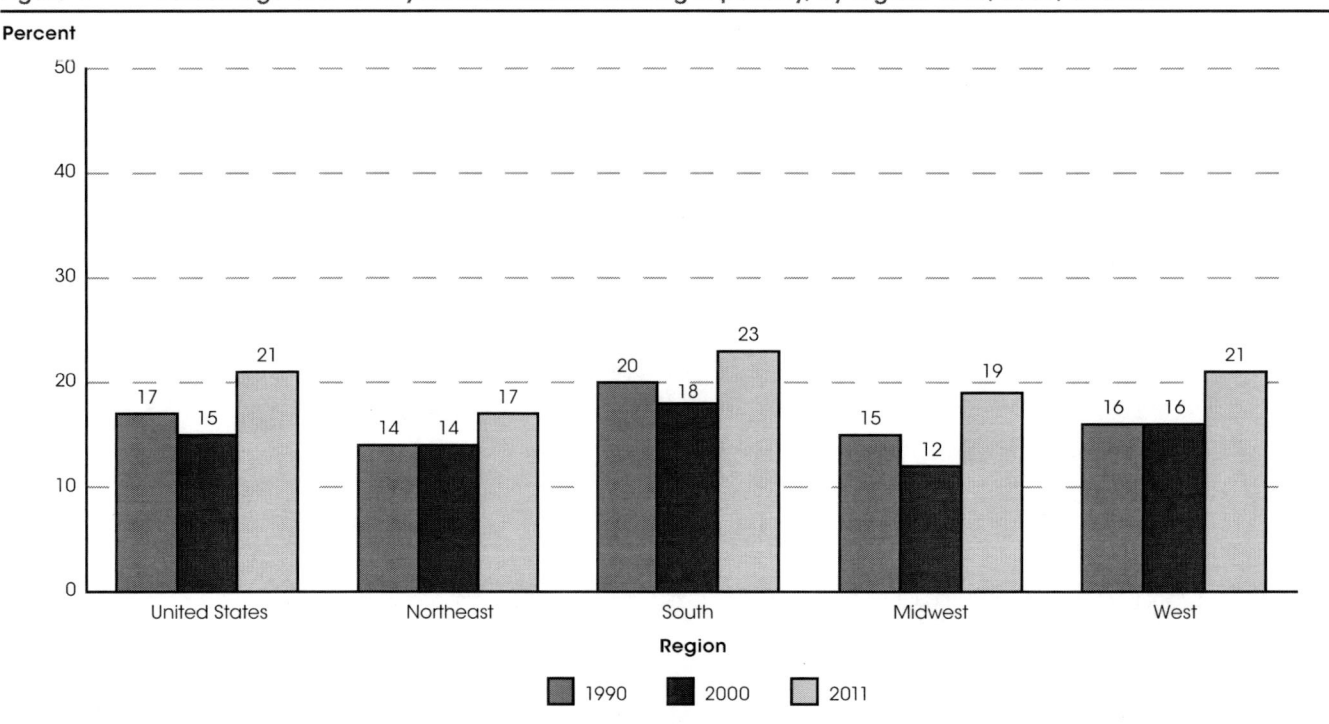

Region	1990	2000	2011
United States	17	15	21
Northeast	14	14	17
South	20	18	23
Midwest	15	12	19
West	16	16	21

NOTE: The measure of child poverty includes families in which all children are related to the householder by birth, marriage, or adoption. The 1990 data are based on 1989 incomes and family sizes collected in the 1990 census, and 2000 data are based on 1999 incomes and family sizes collected in the 2000 census. Both years may differ from Current Population Survey data that are shown in other tables.
SOURCE: U.S. Department of Commerce, Census Bureau, 1990 Summary Tape File 3 (STF 3), "Median Household Income in 1989" and "Poverty Status in 1989 by Family Type and Age"; Decennial Census, 1990, Minority Economic Profiles, unpublished data; Decennial Census, 2000, Summary Social, Economic, and Housing Characteristics; Census 2000 Summary File 4 (SF 4), "Poverty Status in 1999 of Related Children Under 18 Years by Family Type and Age"; and American Community Survey (ACS), 2011. See *Digest of Education Statistics 2012*, table 25.

Across the United States, all regions (Northeast, South, Midwest, and West) had higher poverty rates for school-age children in 2011 than in 1990. From 1990 to 2000, both the South and the Midwest experienced a decrease in the poverty rate for school-age children (from 20 to 18 percent and from 15 to 12 percent, respectively), while the Northeast and the West did not show measurable changes. From 2000 to 2011, all regions experienced an increase in the percentage of school-age children living in poverty. In 2011, the South had the highest rate of poverty for school-age children (23 percent), followed by the West (21 percent), Midwest (19 percent), and Northeast (17 percent).

For more information, see the Reader's Guide and the Guide to Sources.

Chapter: 1/Population Characteristics
Section: Demographics

Figure 2. Percentage of 5- to 17-year-olds in families living in poverty, by state: 2011

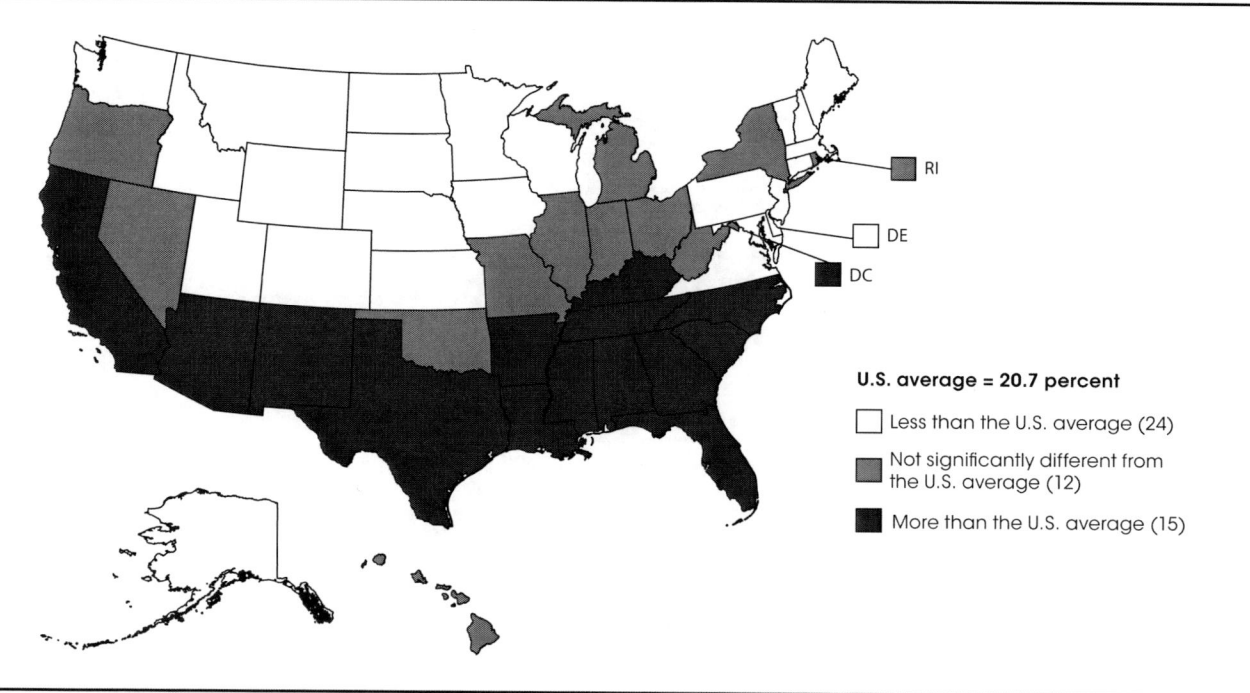

U.S. average = 20.7 percent

☐ Less than the U.S. average (24)

▨ Not significantly different from the U.S. average (12)

■ More than the U.S. average (15)

NOTE: The measure of child poverty includes families in which all children are related to the householder by birth, marriage, or adoption.
SOURCE: U.S. Department of Commerce, Census Bureau, American Community Survey (ACS), 2011. See *Digest of Education Statistics 2012*, table 25.

In 2011, some 37 states had higher poverty rates for school-age children than in 1990, while 9 states plus the District of Columbia had poverty rates for school-age children that were not measurably different from those in 1990. In four states, the percentage of school-age children living in poverty was lower in 2011 than in 1990: Louisiana, Mississippi, North Dakota, and South Dakota. From 1990 to 2000, the poverty rate for school-age children decreased in 38 states, while it increased in 6 states plus the District of Columbia. From 2000 to 2011, the poverty rate for school-age children was higher in 41 states. North Dakota was the only state with a rate that was lower (12 percent in 2000 vs. 9 percent in 2011). The remaining eight states (Alaska, Louisiana, Montana, Rhode Island, South Dakota, Vermont, West Virginia, and Wyoming) plus the District of Columbia had rates in 2011 that were not measurably different from those in 2000. In 2011, within the United States, the percentage of school-age children living in poverty ranged from 9 percent (North Dakota) to 30 percent (District of Columbia). In that same year, the national average poverty rate for school-age children was 21 percent; some 24 states had poverty rates for school-age children that were below the national average, 14 states plus the District of Columbia had rates that were above the national average, and 12 states had rates that were not measurably different from the national average. Of the 15 jurisdictions (14 states and the District of Columbia) that had poverty rates above the national average, 12 were located in the South.

For more information, see the Reader's Guide and the Guide to Sources.

Chapter: 1/Population Characteristics
Section: Demographics

Figure 3. Percentage of children under age 18 living in poverty, by race/ethnicity and family type: 2011

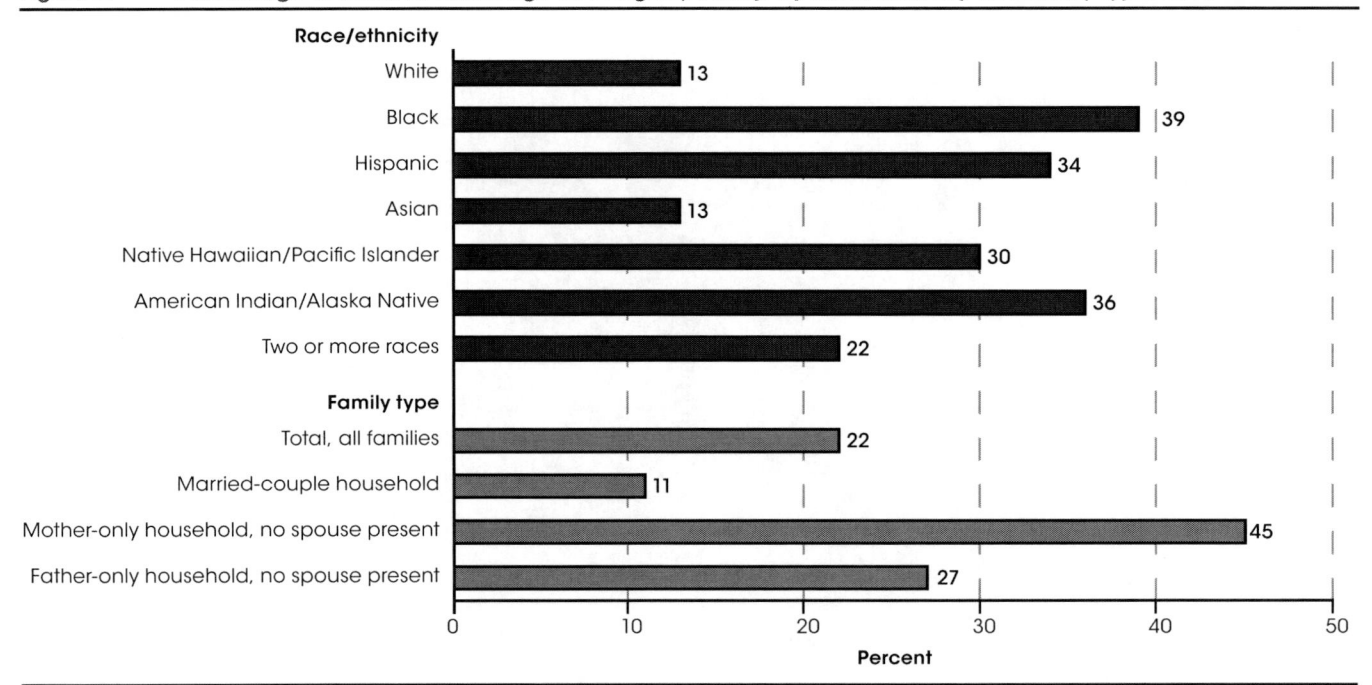

Race/ethnicity
- White: 13
- Black: 39
- Hispanic: 34
- Asian: 13
- Native Hawaiian/Pacific Islander: 30
- American Indian/Alaska Native: 36
- Two or more races: 22

Family type
- Total, all families: 22
- Married-couple household: 11
- Mother-only household, no spouse present: 45
- Father-only household, no spouse present: 27

NOTE: The measure of child poverty includes families in which all children are related to the householder by birth, marriage, or adoption. Race categories exclude persons of Hispanic ethnicity.
SOURCE: U.S. Department of Commerce, Census Bureau, American Community Survey (ACS), 2011. See *Digest of Education Statistics 2012*, table 27.

In 2011, approximately 15.9 million, or 22 percent, of all children under the age of 18 were in families living in poverty; this population includes the 10.9 million 5- to 17-year-olds living in poverty. The percentage of children living in poverty varied across racial/ethnic groups. In 2011, the percentage was highest for Black children (39 percent), followed by American Indian/Alaska Native children (36 percent) and Hispanic children (34 percent), Native Hawaiian/Pacific Islander children (30 percent), and children of two or more races (22 percent). The poverty rate was lowest for White children (13 percent) and Asian children (12 percent). Among children under age 18 living in poverty in 2011, those living in a mother-only household had the highest rate of poverty (45 percent), followed by those living in a father-only household (27 percent). Children living in a married-couple household had the lowest rate of poverty, at 11 percent.

Reference tables: *Digest of Education Statistics 2012*, tables 25, 27

Glossary: Poverty, Racial/ethnic group

For more information, see the Reader's Guide and the Guide to Sources.

This page intentionally left blank.

The indicators in this section of *The Condition of Education* report trends in enrollments across all levels of education. Enrollment is a key indicator of the scope of and access to educational opportunities and functions as a basic descriptor of American education. Changes in enrollment have implications for the demand for educational resources such as qualified teachers, physical facilities, and funding levels, all of which are required to provide high-quality education for our nation's students.

The indicators in this section include information on enrollment rates reported by age group, as well as enrollment by level of the education system. These levels are preprimary education, elementary and secondary education, undergraduate education, graduate and professional education, and adult education. Some of the indicators in this section provide information about the characteristics of the students who are enrolled in formal education and, in some cases, how enrollment rates of different types of students vary across schools.

Indicators on participation in education from previous editions of *The Condition of Education* not included in this volume are available at http://nces.ed.gov/programs/coe.

Chapter 2

Participation in Education

Spotlight on Preprimary Education
Kindergarten Entry Status: On-Time, Delayed-Entry, and Repeating Kindergartners 32

All Ages
Indicator 6.   Enrollment Trends by Age 42

Preprimary Education
Indicator 7.   Early Education and Child Care Arrangements of Young Children 44

Elementary/Secondary Enrollment
Indicator 8.   Public School Enrollment 46
Indicator 9.   Charter School Enrollment 48
Indicator 10. Private School Enrollment 50
Indicator 11. Racial/Ethnic Enrollment in Public Schools 52
Indicator 12. English Language Learners 54
Indicator 13. Children and Youth With Disabilities 58

Postsecondary Enrollment
Indicator 14. Undergraduate Enrollment 60
Indicator 15. Postbaccalaureate Enrollment 64

Chapter: 2/Participation in Education
Section: Spotlight

Spotlight

Kindergarten Entry Status: On-Time, Delayed-Entry, and Repeating Kindergartners

In the fall of 2010, reading scores were higher, on average, for delayed-entry kindergartners (36 points) and repeating kindergartners (37 points) than for on-time kindergartners (35 points). In the spring of 2011, however, reading scores were higher for delayed-entry kindergartners and on-time kindergartners (51 and 50 points, respectively) than for repeating kindergartners (48 points).

As of May 2011, 42 states and the District of Columbia required their school districts to offer kindergarten programs, and 15 states and the District of Columbia required children to attend kindergarten (see *Digest of Education Statistics 2012,* table 197). In the 2010–11 school year, about 4 million students were enrolled in kindergarten in the United States (see *Digest of Education Statistics 2012,* table 136). About 89 percent of the kindergartners attended public schools and 11 percent attended private schools.

Figure 1. Percentage distribution of kindergarten students, by age at the time child first started kindergarten and race/ethnicity: Fall 2010

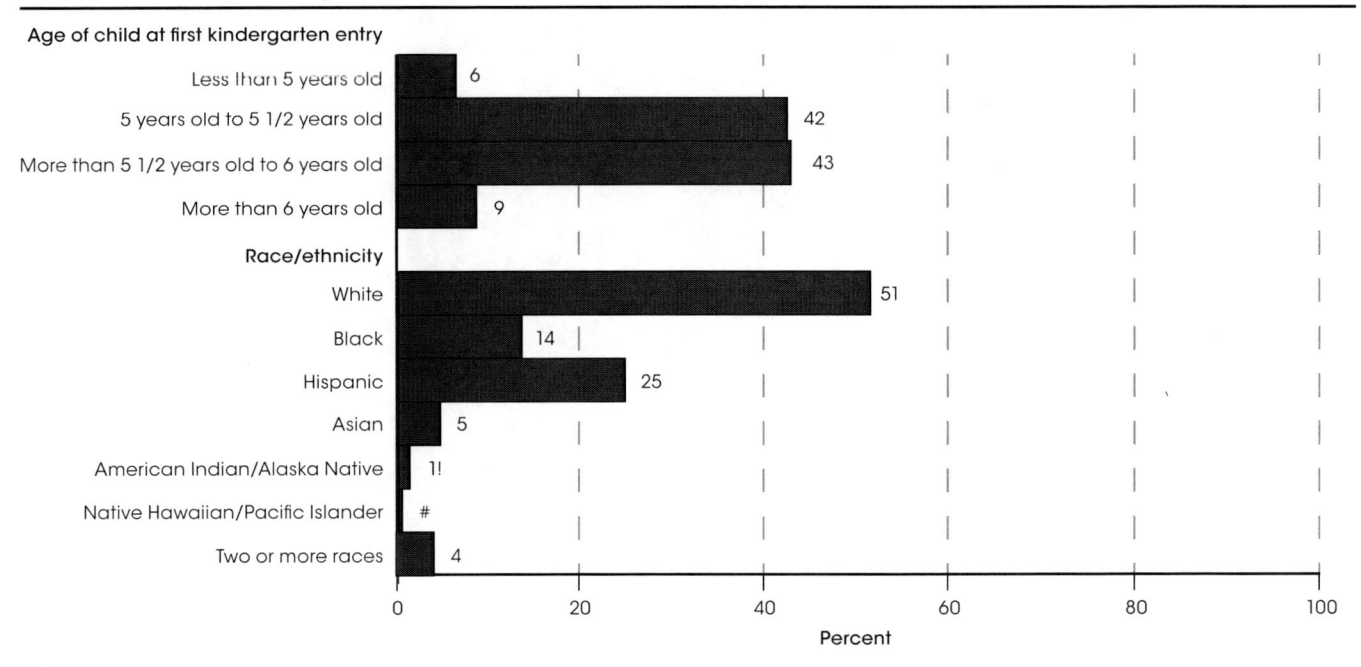

Age of child at first kindergarten entry
- Less than 5 years old: 6
- 5 years old to 5 1/2 years old: 42
- More than 5 1/2 years old to 6 years old: 43
- More than 6 years old: 9

Race/ethnicity
- White: 51
- Black: 14
- Hispanic: 25
- Asian: 5
- American Indian/Alaska Native: 1!
- Native Hawaiian/Pacific Islander: #
- Two or more races: 4

Rounds to zero.
! Interpret data with caution. The coefficient of variation (CV) for this estimate is between 30 and 50 percent.
NOTE: Most of the children first entered kindergarten in 2010–11, but the children who were repeating kindergarten in 2010–11 had first entered kindergarten in an earlier school year. Race categories exclude persons of Hispanic ethnicity. Detail may not sum to totals because of rounding and survey item nonresponse.
SOURCE: U.S. Department of Education, National Center for Education Statistics, Early Childhood Longitudinal Study, Kindergarten Class of 2010–11 (ECLS-K:2011), Preliminary Restricted-Use Data File. See *Digest of Education Statistics 2012,* table 136.

The kindergarten class of 2010–11 was diverse with respect to characteristics of individual children and their families. Six percent of kindergartners started their first year of kindergarten before they turned 5 years old, while 42 percent started when they were between 5 and 5½ years old, 43 percent started when they were more than 5½ years old to 6 years old, and 9 percent started after they turned 6 years old. Some 51 percent of kindergartners were White, 25 percent were Hispanic, 14 percent were Black, 5 percent were Asian, 4 percent were of two or more races, 1 percent were American Indian or Alaska Native, and less than 1 percent were Native Hawaiian or other Pacific Islander. Fifty-five percent had attended center-based care as their primary care arrangement in the year prior to kindergarten.

For more information, see the Reader's Guide and the Guide to Sources.

Chapter: 2/Participation in Education
Section: Spotlight

Figure 2. Percentage distribution of kindergarten students, by parents' highest level of education and poverty status: School year 2010–11

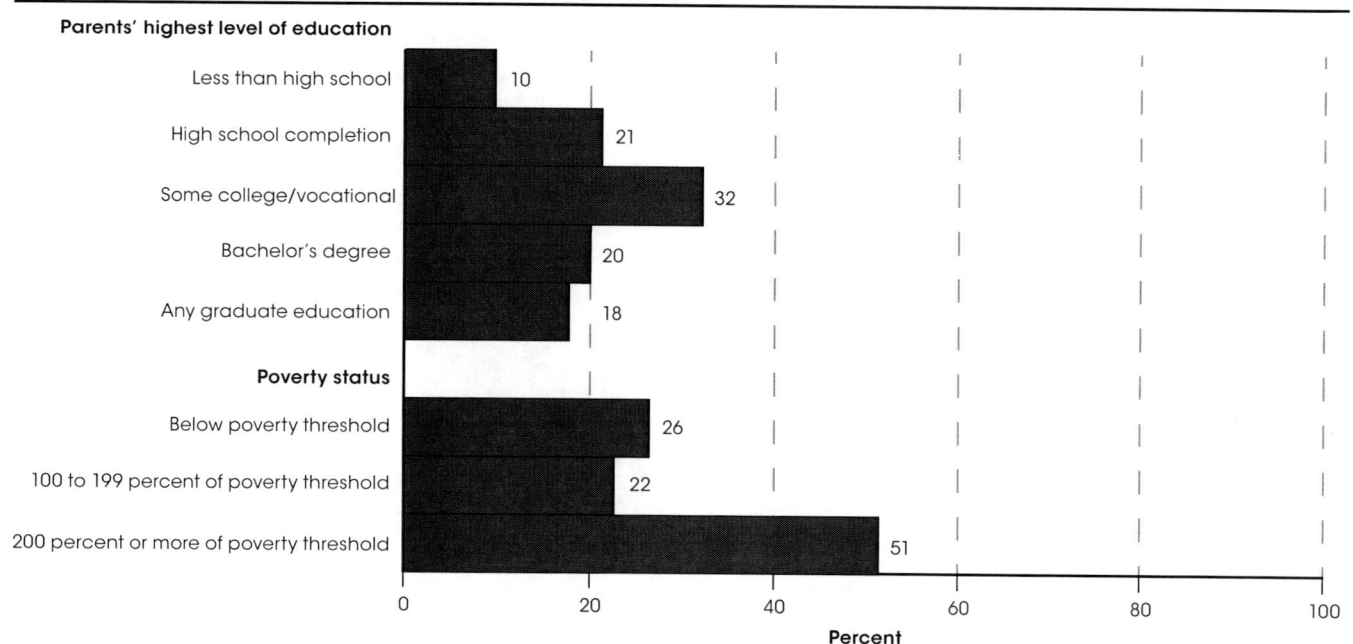

Parents' highest level of education

Category	Percent
Less than high school	10
High school completion	21
Some college/vocational	32
Bachelor's degree	20
Any graduate education	18

Poverty status

Category	Percent
Below poverty threshold	26
100 to 199 percent of poverty threshold	22
200 percent or more of poverty threshold	51

NOTE: Parents' highest level of education is the highest level of education achieved by either of the parents or guardians in a two-parent household, by the only parent in a single-parent household, or by any guardian in a household with no parents. Poverty status is based on preliminary U.S. Census income thresholds for 2010, which identify incomes determined to meet household needs, given family size and composition. For example, a family of three with one child was below the poverty threshold if its income was less than $17,552 in 2010. Detail may not sum to totals because of rounding and survey item nonresponse.
SOURCE: U.S. Department of Education, National Center for Education Statistics, Early Childhood Longitudinal Study, Kindergarten Class of 2010–11 (ECLS-K:2011), Preliminary Restricted-Use Data File. See *Digest of Education Statistics 2012,* table 136.

In the 2010–11 school year, about 10 percent of kindergartners lived in a household where no parent had completed high school; 21 percent lived in a household where the highest education level of any parent was a high school diploma or its equivalent; 32 percent lived in a household where the highest education level of any parent was completion of some college or a vocational degree; and 37 percent lived in a household where at least one parent had a bachelor's degree or any graduate education. Twenty-six percent of kindergartners lived in households that were below the federal poverty threshold, 22 percent lived in households that were from 100 to 199 percent of the poverty threshold, and 51 percent lived in households that were at 200 percent or more of the poverty threshold. Sixteen percent of kindergartners lived in a household where English was not the primary language, and 23 percent lived in single-parent households (i.e., 21 percent in mother-only households and 2 percent in father-only households).

For more information, see the Reader's Guide and the Guide to Sources.

Chapter: 2/Participation in Education
Section: Spotlight

Figure 3. Percentage distribution of kindergarten students, by kindergarten entry status: Fall 2010

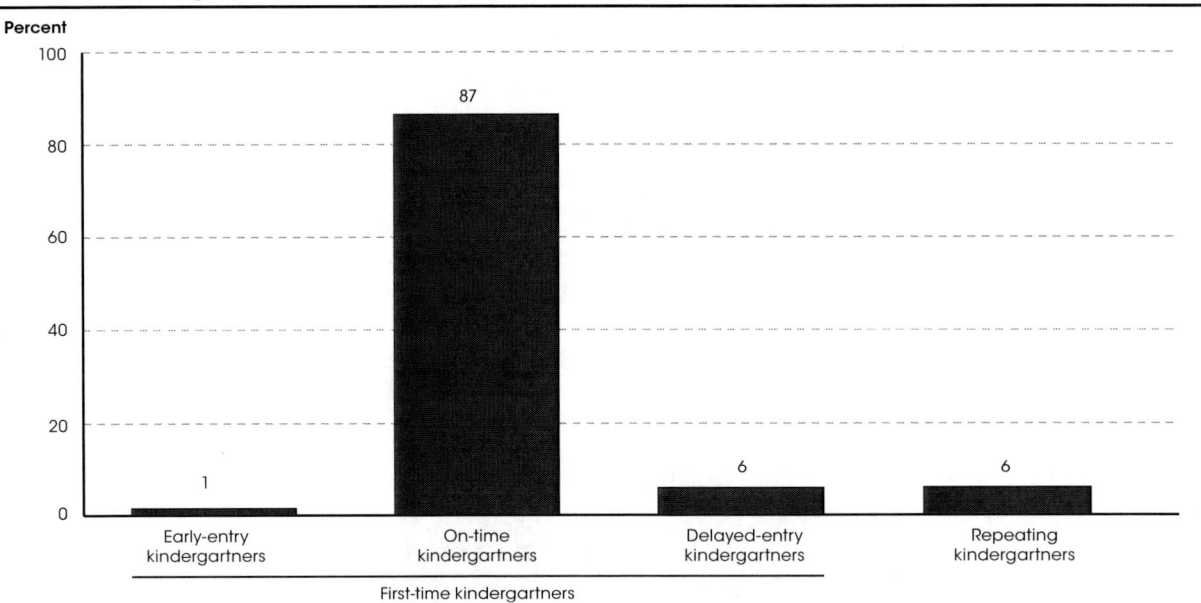

```
Percent
100
 80
 60
 40
 20            87
  0    1              6           6
     Early-entry  On-time  Delayed-entry  Repeating
     kindergartners  kindergartners  kindergartners  kindergartners
                First-time kindergartners
                 Kindergarten entry status
```

NOTE: A child who enrolled in kindergarten for the first time in 2010–11 is classified as an early, on-time, or delayed kindergarten entrant depending on whether the parent reported enrolling the child early, enrolling the child when he or she was old enough, or waiting until the child was older relative to school guidelines about when children can start school based on their birth date. A child is classified as a kindergarten repeater if the parent reported that 2010–11 was the child's second (or third or more) year of kindergarten. Excludes students with missing kindergarten enrollment status information. Detail may not sum to totals because of rounding and survey item nonresponse.
SOURCE: U.S. Department of Education, National Center for Education Statistics, Early Childhood Longitudinal Study, Kindergarten Class of 2010–11 (ECLS-K:2011), Preliminary Restricted-Use Data File. See *Digest of Education Statistics 2012*, table 136.

Over the years, policies and practices have emerged that are intended to improve children's early school experiences by giving them more time to develop and mature (e.g., changes to age of entry requirements and use of transitional grades and readiness testing). One such enrollment strategy is to purposefully delay a child's entrance into kindergarten, a practice known as "academic redshirting."[1] Parents or school staff may decide to wait a year to enroll a child in kindergarten if the child's birthday is close to the school system's cutoff date for kindergarten age requirements. Redshirting may occur if parents do not wish their child to be among the youngest in their kindergarten class, or if there is concern that the child exhibits less mature academic, social, or physical skills than their peers of the same age. A second strategy is to retain kindergartners who did not achieve the same level of academic or social skills as their peers in their first year of school and to have them repeat kindergarten. In the fall of 2010, about 94 percent of kindergartners were attending their first year of kindergarten: 87 percent were on-time kindergartners who started kindergarten within the age requirements set by their school system, while 6 percent were delayed-entry kindergartners and 1 percent were early-entry kindergartners, based on school system age requirements. In addition, about 6 percent of fall 2010 kindergartners were repeating kindergarten.

[1] Katz, L.G. (2000). *Redshirting and Young Children*. Champaign, IL: ERIC Clearinghouse on Elementary and Early Childhood Education. (ERIC ED447951)

For more information, see the Reader's Guide and the Guide to Sources.

Chapter: 2/Participation in Education
Section: Spotlight

Figure 4. Percentage of kindergarten students, by kindergarten entry status and race/ethnicity: Fall 2010

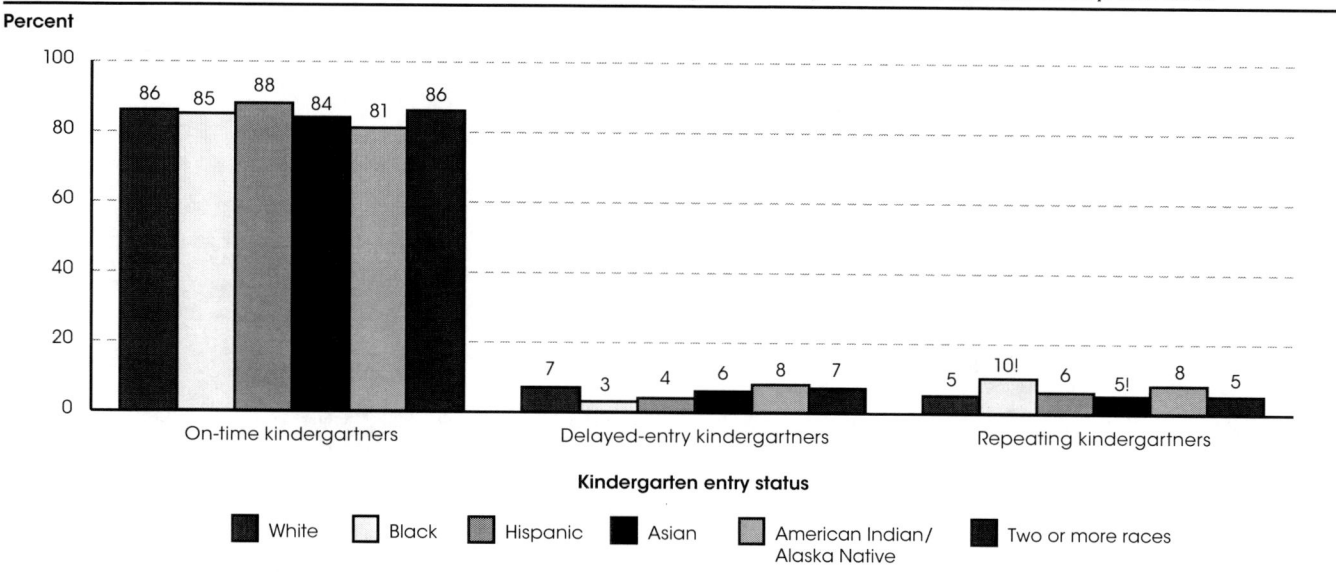

Kindergarten entry status	White	Black	Hispanic	Asian	American Indian/Alaska Native	Two or more races
On-time kindergartners	86	85	88	84	81	86
Delayed-entry kindergartners	7	3	4	6	8	7
Repeating kindergartners	5	10!	6	5!	8	5

! Interpret data with caution. The coefficient of variation (CV) for this estimate is between 30 and 50 percent.
NOTE: A child who enrolled in kindergarten for the first time in 2010–11 is classified as an early, on-time, or delayed kindergarten entrant depending on whether the parent reported enrolling the child early, enrolling the child when he or she was old enough, or waiting until the child was older relative to school guidelines about when children can start school based on their birth date. A child is classified as a kindergarten repeater if the parent reported that 2010–11 was the child's second (or third or more) year of kindergarten. Excludes students with missing kindergarten enrollment status information and students whose parents reported that they entered kindergarten at an earlier age than the criteria set by the school district. Reporting standards for Native Hawaiian/Pacific Islander kindergartners were not met; therefore, data for this group are not shown in the figure. Race categories exclude persons of Hispanic ethnicity.
SOURCE: U.S. Department of Education, National Center for Education Statistics, Early Childhood Longitudinal Study, Kindergarten Class of 2010–11 (ECLS-K:2011), Preliminary Restricted-Use Data File. See *Digest of Education Statistics 2012*, table 136.

In fall 2010, about 6 percent of all kindergartners were delayed entrants. Higher percentages of American Indians/Alaska Natives (8 percent), Whites (7 percent), and students of two or more races (7 percent) than of Hispanics (4 percent) or Blacks (3 percent) were delayed-entry kindergartners. Also, a higher percentage of Asian students than of Black students (6 vs. 3 percent) were delayed-entry kindergartners. No measurable differences were observed in the percentages of repeating kindergartners across different racial/ethnic groups. Comparisons could not be made for early-entry kindergartners due to the small number of children in the sample.

For more information, see the Reader's Guide and the Guide to Sources.

Chapter: 2/Participation in Education
Section: Spotlight

Figure 5. Percentage of kindergarten students, by kindergarten entry status and parents' highest level of education: Fall 2010

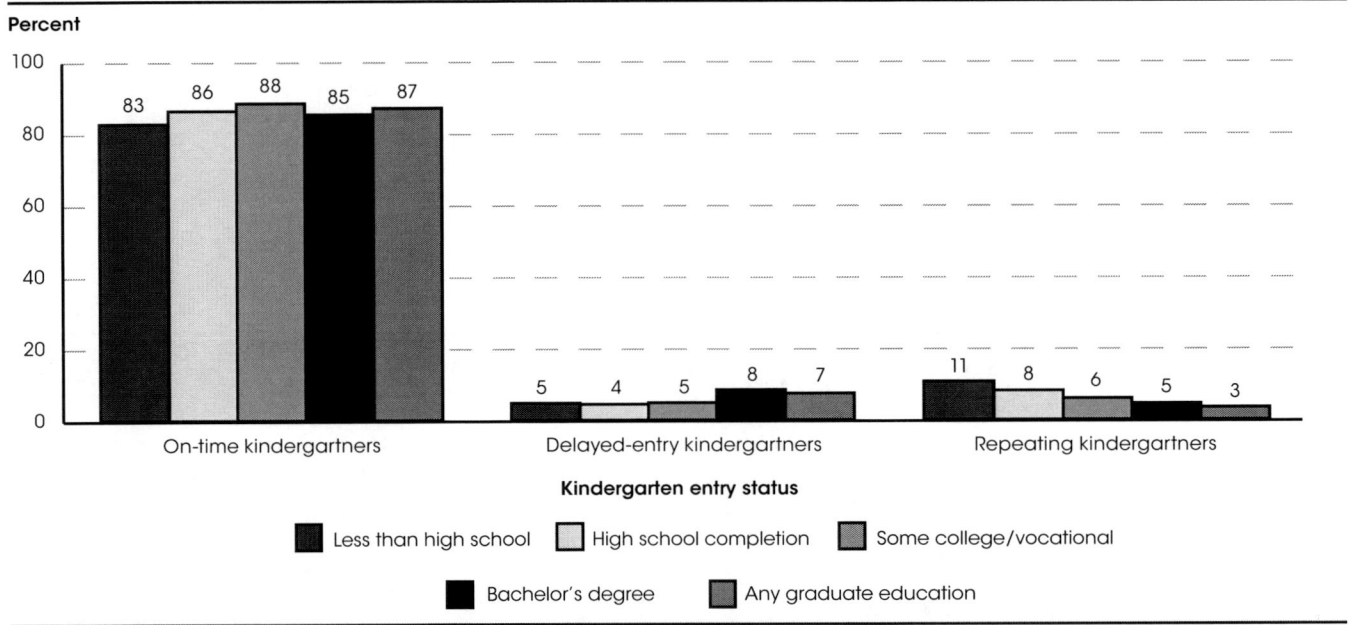

Kindergarten entry status	Less than high school	High school completion	Some college/vocational	Bachelor's degree	Any graduate education
On-time kindergartners	83	86	88	85	87
Delayed-entry kindergartners	5	4	5	8	7
Repeating kindergartners	11	8	6	5	3

NOTE: A child who enrolled in kindergarten for the first time in 2010–11 is classified as an early, on-time, or delayed kindergarten entrant depending on whether the parent reported enrolling the child early, enrolling the child when he or she was old enough, or waiting until the child was older relative to school guidelines about when children can start school based on their birth date. A child is classified as a kindergarten repeater if the parent reported that 2010–11 was the child's second (or third or more) year of kindergarten. Excludes students with missing kindergarten enrollment status information and students whose parents reported that they entered kindergarten at an earlier age than the criteria set by the school district. Parents' highest level of education is the highest level of education achieved by either of the parents or guardians in a two-parent household, by the only parent in a single-parent household, or by any guardian in a household with no parents.
SOURCE: U.S. Department of Education, National Center for Education Statistics, Early Childhood Longitudinal Study, Kindergarten Class of 2010–11 (ECLS-K:2011), Preliminary Restricted-Use Data File. See *Digest of Education Statistics 2012*, table 136.

The percentages of delayed-entry kindergartners were higher for students living in households where at least one parent had completed a bachelor's degree (8 percent) or some graduate education (7 percent) than for students whose parents had lower levels of educational attainment (4 to 5 percent). Conversely, the percentages of repeating kindergartners were higher for students who did not have any parent completing high school (11 percent) and for students whose parents' highest education level was a high school diploma or equivalent (8 percent) than for students who had at least one parent completing a bachelor's degree (5 percent) or some graduate education (3 percent).

For more information, see the Reader's Guide and the Guide to Sources.

Chapter: 2/Participation in Education
Section: Spotlight

Figure 6. Percentage of kindergarten students, by kindergarten entry status and poverty status: Fall 2010

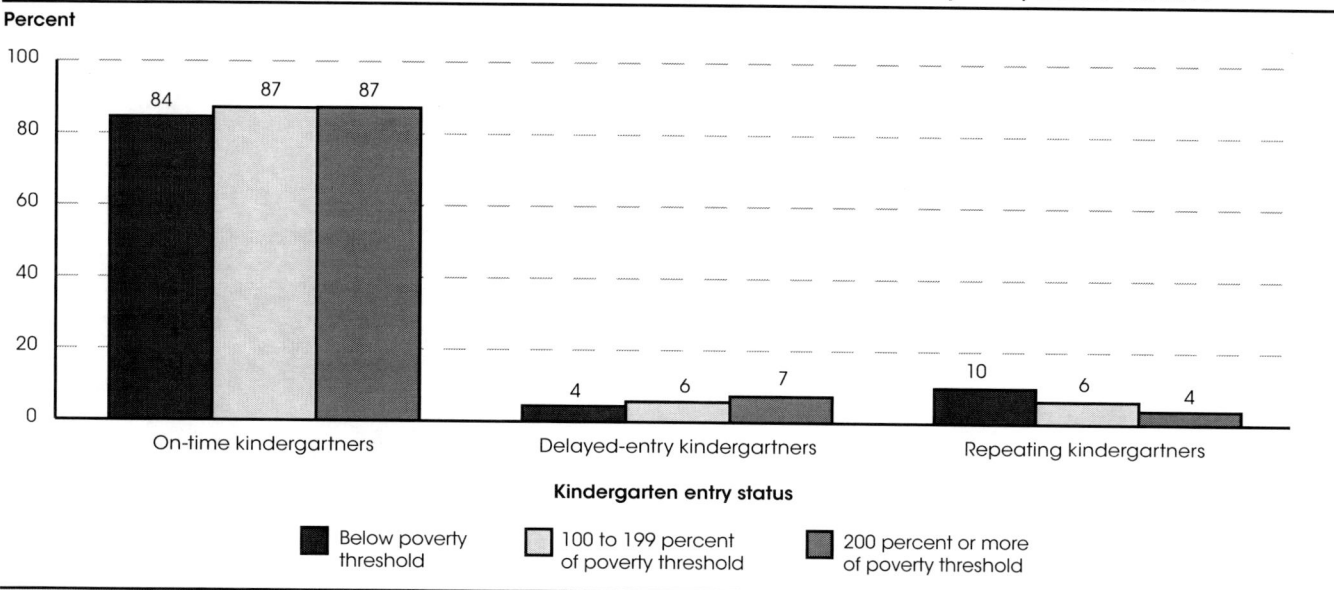

Kindergarten entry status	Below poverty threshold	100 to 199 percent of poverty threshold	200 percent or more of poverty threshold
On-time kindergartners	84	87	87
Delayed-entry kindergartners	4	6	7
Repeating kindergartners	10	6	4

NOTE: A child who enrolled in kindergarten for the first time in 2010–11 is classified as an early, on-time, or delayed kindergarten entrant depending on whether the parent reported enrolling the child early, enrolling the child when he or she was old enough, or waiting until the child was older relative to school guidelines about when children can start school based on their birth date. A child is classified as a kindergarten repeater if the parent reported that 2010–11 was the child's second (or third or more) year of kindergarten. Excludes students with missing kindergarten enrollment status information and students whose parents reported that they entered kindergarten at an earlier age than the criteria set by the school district. Poverty status is based on preliminary U.S. Census income thresholds for 2010, which identify incomes determined to meet household needs, given family size and composition. For example, a family of three with one child was below the poverty threshold if its income was less than $17,552 in 2010.
SOURCE: U.S. Department of Education, National Center for Education Statistics, Early Childhood Longitudinal Study, Kindergarten Class of 2010–11 (ECLS-K:2011), Preliminary Restricted-Use Data File. See *Digest of Education Statistics 2012*, table 136.

In fall 2010, the percentages of delayed-entry kindergartners were higher for students living in households that were at 200 percent or more of the federal poverty threshold (7 percent) than for students living below the poverty threshold (4 percent). In contrast, the percentages of repeating kindergartners were higher for students living below the poverty threshold (10 percent) or for those living between 100 percent and 199 percent of the poverty threshold (6 percent) than for students living in households that were at 200 percent or more of the poverty threshold (4 percent).

For more information, see the Reader's Guide and the Guide to Sources.

Chapter: 2/Participation in Education
Section: Spotlight

Figure 7. Kindergartners' mean reading scale scores, by time of assessment and kindergarten entry status: School year 2010–11

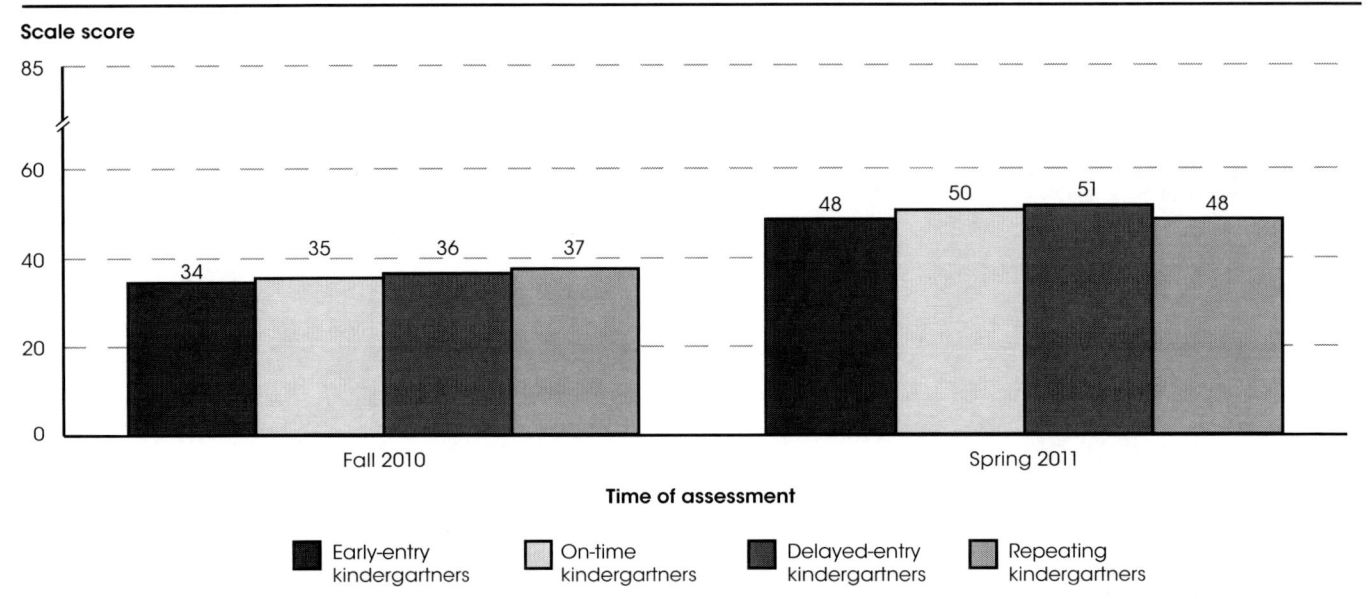

Scale score

Time of assessment	Early-entry	On-time	Delayed-entry	Repeating
Fall 2010	34	35	36	37
Spring 2011	48	50	51	48

NOTE: A child who enrolled in kindergarten for the first time in 2010–11 is classified as an early, on-time, or delayed kindergarten entrant depending on whether the parent reported enrolling the child early, enrolling the child when he or she was old enough, or waiting until the child was older relative to school guidelines about when children can start school based on their birth date. A child is classified as a kindergarten repeater if the parent reported that 2010–11 was the child's second (or third or more) year of kindergarten. Excludes students with missing kindergarten enrollment status information. Actual reading scores range from 6 to 83.
SOURCE: U.S. Department of Education, National Center for Education Statistics, Early Childhood Longitudinal Study, Kindergarten Class of 2010–11 (ECLS-K:2011), Preliminary Restricted-Use Data File. See *Digest of Education Statistics 2012*, table 137.

For the most part, delayed-entry kindergartners tended to outscore on-time and repeating kindergartners in reading, mathematics, and science in the 2010–11 school year. In reading, for instance, the fall scores were higher, on average, for delayed-entry kindergartners (36 points) and repeating kindergartners (37 points) than for on-time kindergartners (35 points) (see *Digest of Education Statistics 2012*, table 137). In the spring, however, reading scores were higher for delayed-entry kindergartners and on-time kindergartners (51 and 50 points, respectively) than for repeating kindergartners (48 points).

For more information, see the Reader's Guide and the Guide to Sources.

Chapter: 2/Participation in Education
Section: Spotlight

Figure 8. Kindergartners' mean mathematics scale scores, by time of assessment and kindergarten entry status: School year 2010–11

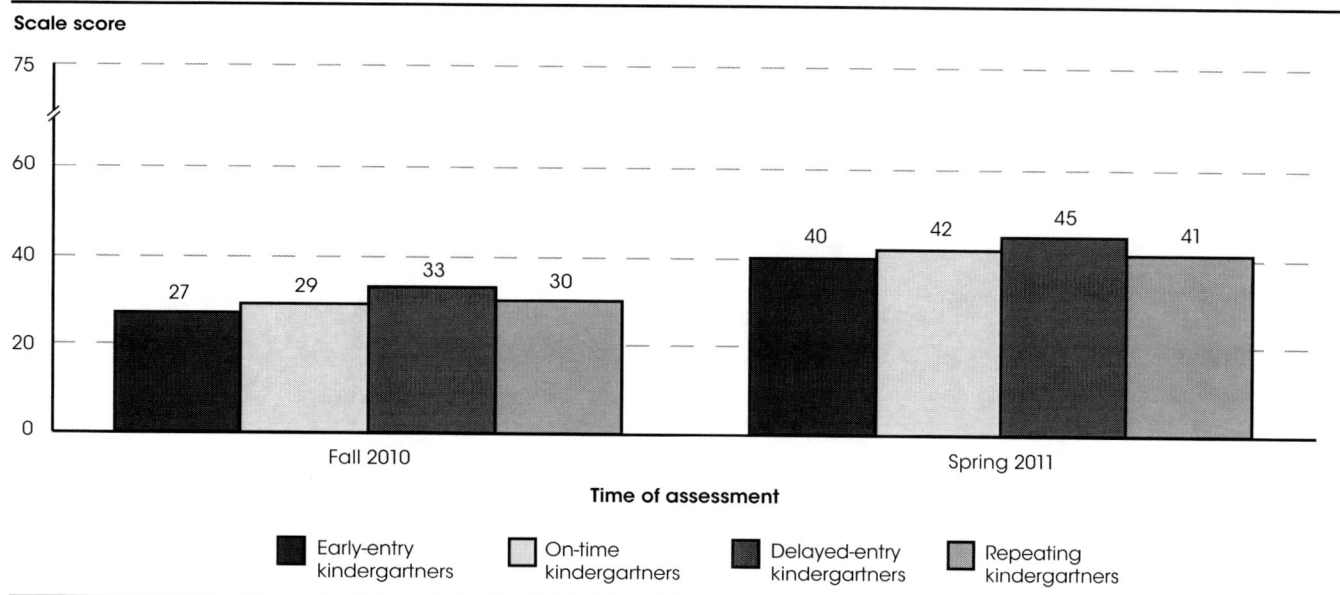

Scale score

	Fall 2010	Spring 2011
Early-entry kindergartners	27	40
On-time kindergartners	29	42
Delayed-entry kindergartners	33	45
Repeating kindergartners	30	41

NOTE: A child who enrolled in kindergarten for the first time in 2010–11 is classified as an early, on-time, or delayed kindergarten entrant depending on whether the parent reported enrolling the child early, enrolling the child when he or she was old enough, or waiting until the child was older relative to school guidelines about when children can start school based on their birth date. A child is classified as a kindergarten repeater if the parent reported that 2010–11 was the child's second (or third or more) year of kindergarten. Excludes students with missing kindergarten enrollment status information. Actual mathematics scores range from 5 to 75.
SOURCE: U.S. Department of Education, National Center for Education Statistics, Early Childhood Longitudinal Study, Kindergarten Class of 2010–11 (ECLS-K:2011), Preliminary Restricted-Use Data File. See *Digest of Education Statistics 2012*, table 137.

In mathematics, the fall 2010 scores were higher for delayed-entry kindergartners (33 points) than for on-time kindergartners (29 points) and repeating kindergartners (30 points). This pattern was also observed in the spring of 2011: delayed-entry kindergartners had an average mathematics score of 45 points, compared with an average score of 42 points for on-time kindergartners and an average score of 41 points for repeating kindergartners. Kindergartners were also assessed in science in the spring of 2011. The science assessment reflects student performance on questions about physical sciences, life sciences, environmental sciences, and scientific inquiry. For that assessment, scores were higher, on average, for delayed-entry kindergartners (12.1 points) than for on-time kindergartners (11.4 points) and repeating kindergartners (11.0 points).

For more information, see the Reader's Guide and the Guide to Sources.

Chapter: 2/Participation in Education
Section: Spotlight

Figure 9. Kindergartners' mean approaches to learning scale scores, by time of assessment and kindergarten entry status: School year 2010–11

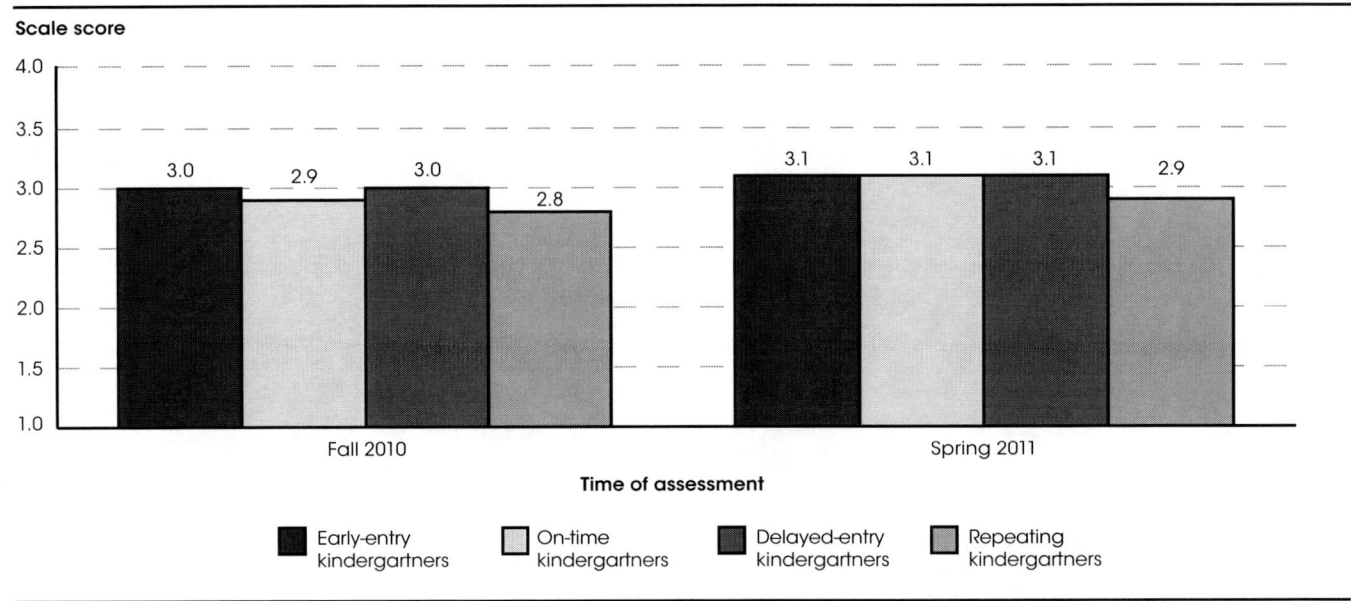

Time of assessment	Early-entry kindergartners	On-time kindergartners	Delayed-entry kindergartners	Repeating kindergartners
Fall 2010	3.0	2.9	3.0	2.8
Spring 2011	3.1	3.1	3.1	2.9

NOTE: A child who enrolled in kindergarten for the first time in 2010–11 is classified as an early, on-time, or delayed kindergarten entrant depending on whether the parent reported enrolling the child early, enrolling the child when he or she was old enough, or waiting until the child was older relative to school guidelines about when children can start school based on their birth date. A child is classified as a kindergarten repeater if the parent reported that 2010–11 was the child's second (or third or more) year of kindergarten. Excludes students with missing kindergarten enrollment status information. The approaches to learning scale is based on teachers' reports on how students rate in seven areas: attentiveness, task persistence, eagerness to learn, learning independence, flexibility, organization, and ability to follow classroom rules. Actual scores range from 1 to 4, with higher scores indicating that a child exhibits positive learning behaviors more often.
SOURCE: U.S. Department of Education, National Center for Education Statistics, Early Childhood Longitudinal Study, Kindergarten Class of 2010–11 (ECLS-K:2011), Preliminary Restricted-Use Data File. See *Digest of Education Statistics 2012*, table 137.

In the fall of 2010 and the spring of 2011, kindergarten teachers were asked to rate their students on a set of seven approaches to learning behaviors: attentiveness, task persistence, eagerness to learn, learning independence, flexibility, organization, and ability to follow classroom rules. Scores ranged from 1 to 4, with higher scores indicating that a child exhibited positive learning behaviors more often. In both the fall and spring of the kindergarten year, delayed-entry and on-time kindergartners had higher scores on the approaches to learning scale than repeating kindergartners. In the spring, for example, delayed-entry and on-time kindergartners both had average scores of 3.1 points on the 4-point scale, while repeating kindergartners had an average score of 2.9 points.

Reference tables: *Digest of Education Statistics 2012*, tables 136, 137, 197

Glossary: Educational attainment, Poverty, Racial/ethnic group

For more information, see the Reader's Guide and the Guide to Sources.

This page intentionally left blank.

Chapter: 2/Participation in Education
Section: All Ages

Indicator 6
Enrollment Trends by Age

Between 2000 and 2011, enrollment rates increased for age groups between 18 and 34; students in these age groups are typically enrolled in college or graduate school.

Changes in the number of students enrolled can stem from fluctuations in population size or shifts in enrollment rates. Enrollment rates may reflect changes in state compulsory attendance requirements, the prevalence of homeschooling, the perceived value of education, particularly for preschoolers and college students, and the time taken to complete a degree. For most age groups from 3 to 34, the total school enrollment rate was higher in 2011 than in the 1970s. The only exceptions were for youth ages 7–13 and 14–15, whose enrollments rates fluctuated between 97 and 99 percent over the past four decades. The slight decline for youth ages 7–13, from 99 percent in 1970 to 98 percent in 2011, reflects an increase in the rate of homeschooling.

Figure 1. Percentage of the population ages 3–34 enrolled in school, by education level and age group: October 1970–2011

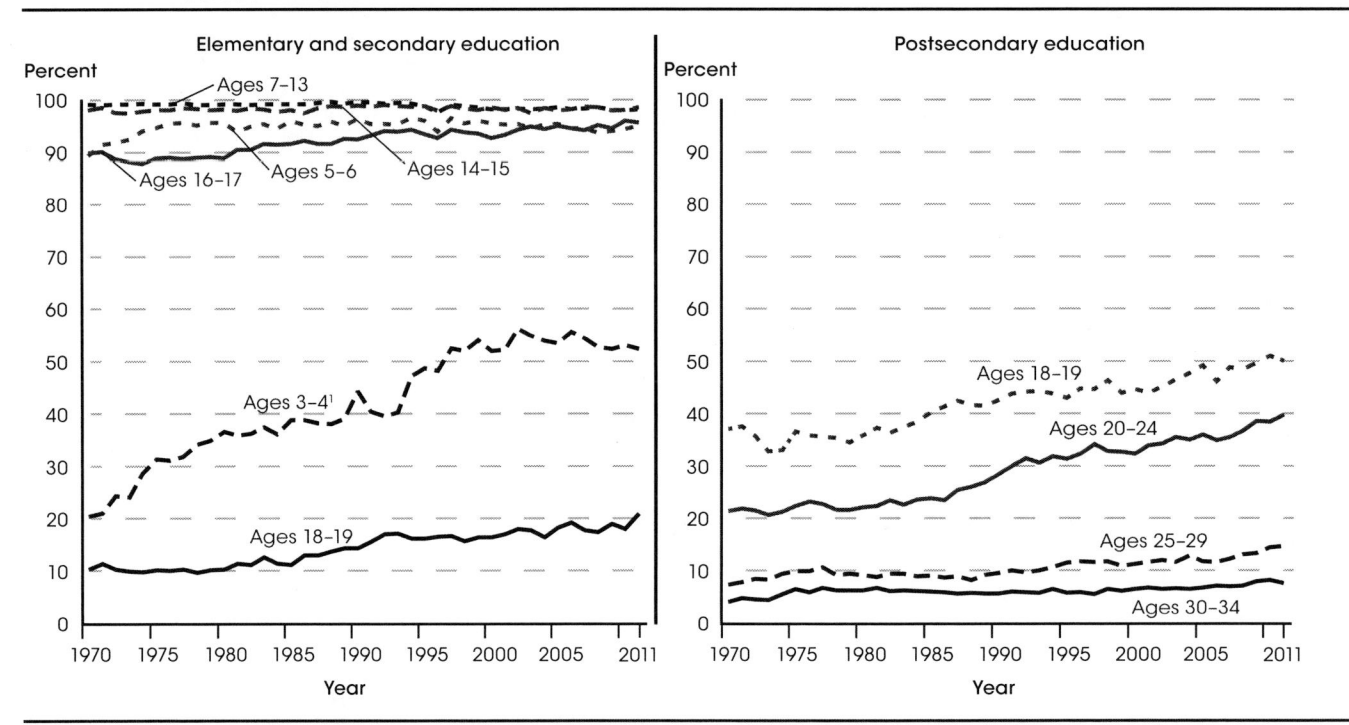

[1] Beginning in 1994, new procedures were used to collect enrollment data on children ages 3–4. As a result, pre-1994 data may not be comparable to data from 1994 or later.
SOURCE: U.S. Department of Commerce, Census Bureau, Current Population Survey (CPS), October Supplement, 1970–2011. See *Digest of Education Statistics 2012*, table 7.

Between 1970 and 2011, the enrollment rate for children ages 3–4 (the ages at which children are typically enrolled in nursery or preschool) increased from 20 to 52 percent. For children ages 5–6, the biggest increase in the enrollment rate was between 1970 and 1974, when it rose from 90 percent to 94 percent. The enrollment rate has varied between 94 percent and 97 percent from 1974 to 2011. There were no measurable differences in the enrollment rates for children ages 3–4 or for children ages 5–6 between 2000 and 2011.

The enrollment rates for 7- to 13-year-olds and 14- to 15-year-olds were generally higher than the rate for 16- to 17-year-olds from 1970 to 2011, but the rate for 16- to 17-year-olds did increase from 90 percent in 1970 to 96 percent in 2011. Between 2000 and 2011, enrollment rates were not measurably different for either 7- to 13-year-olds or 14- to 15-year-olds, while for 16- to 17-year-olds, the rate increased from 93 to 96 percent.

Young adults at ages 18–19 are typically transitioning into either college education or the workforce. Between 1970 and 2011, the overall enrollment rate (i.e., enrollment at both the secondary level and the college level) for young adults ages 18–19 increased from 48 to 71 percent. During this period, the enrollment rate for 18- and 19-year-olds at the secondary level increased from 10 to 21 percent, while the rate at the college level

For more information, see the Reader's Guide and the Guide to Sources.

rose from 37 to 50 percent. Between 2000 and 2011, the overall enrollment rate increased from 61 to 71 percent, the secondary enrollment rate increased from 16 to 21 percent, and the college enrollment rate increased from 45 to 50 percent.

Enrolled adults ages 20–34 are usually in college or graduate school. Between 1970 and 2011, the enrollment rate for adults ages 20–24 increased from 22 to 40 percent, and the rate for adults ages 25–29 increased from 8 to 15 percent. The enrollment rate for adults ages 30–34 increased from 4 percent in 1970 to 8 percent in 2011. Between 2000 and 2011, the enrollment rate for adults ages 20–24 increased from 32 to 40 percent, for adults ages 25–29, it increased from 11 to 15 percent, and for adults ages 30–34, it increased from 7 to 8 percent.

Figure 2. Percentage of the population ages 3–34 enrolled in school, by age group: October 2011

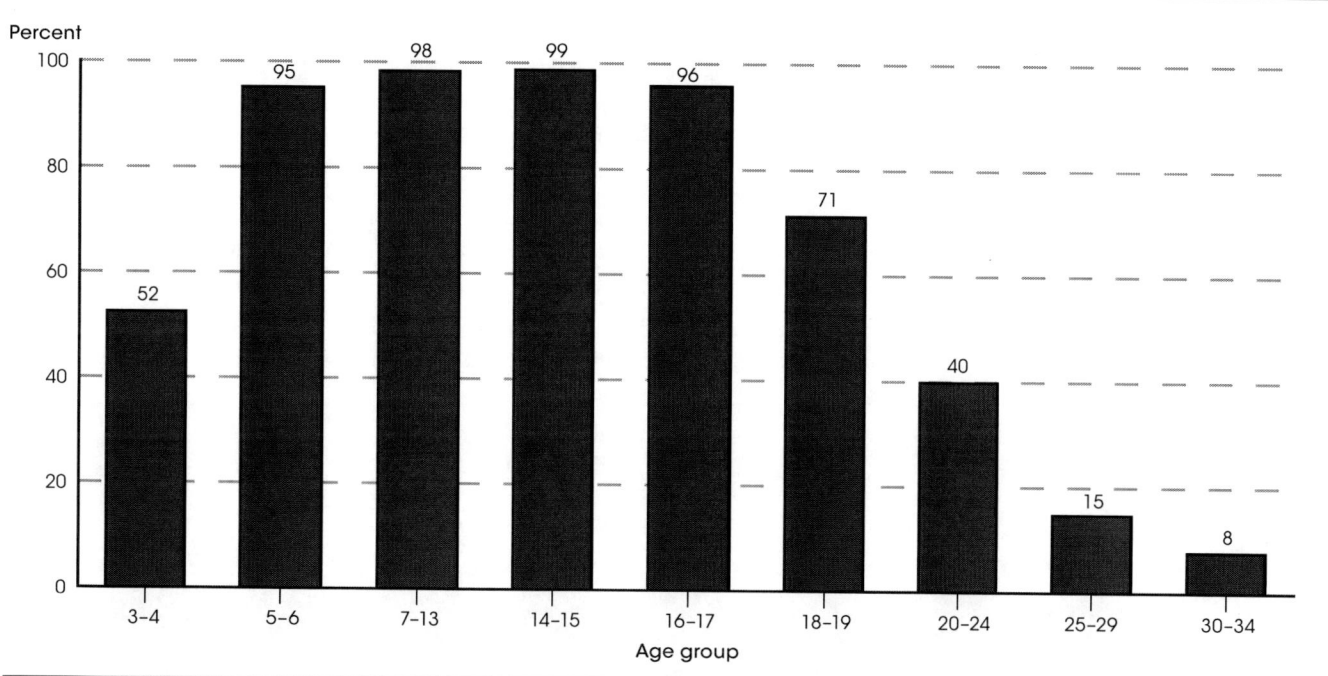

Age group	Percent
3–4	52
5–6	95
7–13	98
14–15	99
16–17	96
18–19	71
20–24	40
25–29	15
30–34	8

NOTE: The enrollment rate for those ages 18–19 includes enrollment at both the secondary level and the college level.
SOURCE: U.S. Department of Commerce, Census Bureau, Current Population Survey (CPS), October Supplement, 2011. See *Digest of Education Statistics 2012*, table 7.

Reference table: *Digest of Education Statistics 2012*, table 7   **Glossary:** College, Secondary school

For more information, see the Reader's Guide and the Guide to Sources.

Indicator 7

Early Education and Child Care Arrangements of Young Children

From 1980 to 2011, the percentage of 3- to 5-year-olds enrolled in preprimary programs increased from 53 percent to 64 percent. The percentage of these children who attended full-day programs increased from 32 percent to 59 percent during this time period.

Preprimary programs are groups or classes that are organized to provide educational experiences for children and include kindergarten, preschool, and nursery school programs. From 1980 to 2011, the percentage of 3- to 5-year-olds enrolled in preprimary programs increased from 53 percent to 64 percent, with most of the growth occurring between 1980 and 2000. From 1980 to 2000, the percentage of children enrolled in preprimary programs increased from 27 to 39 percent for 3-year-olds and from 46 to 65 percent for 4-year-olds. The enrollment rate for 5-year-olds was higher in 2000 than in 1980 (88 percent vs. 85 percent). However, the percentages enrolled in preprimary programs were not measurably different in 2000 compared to 2011 for any of the age groups.

Figure 1. Percentage of 3-, 4-, and 5-year-old children enrolled in full-day preprimary programs: Selected years, 1980 through 2011

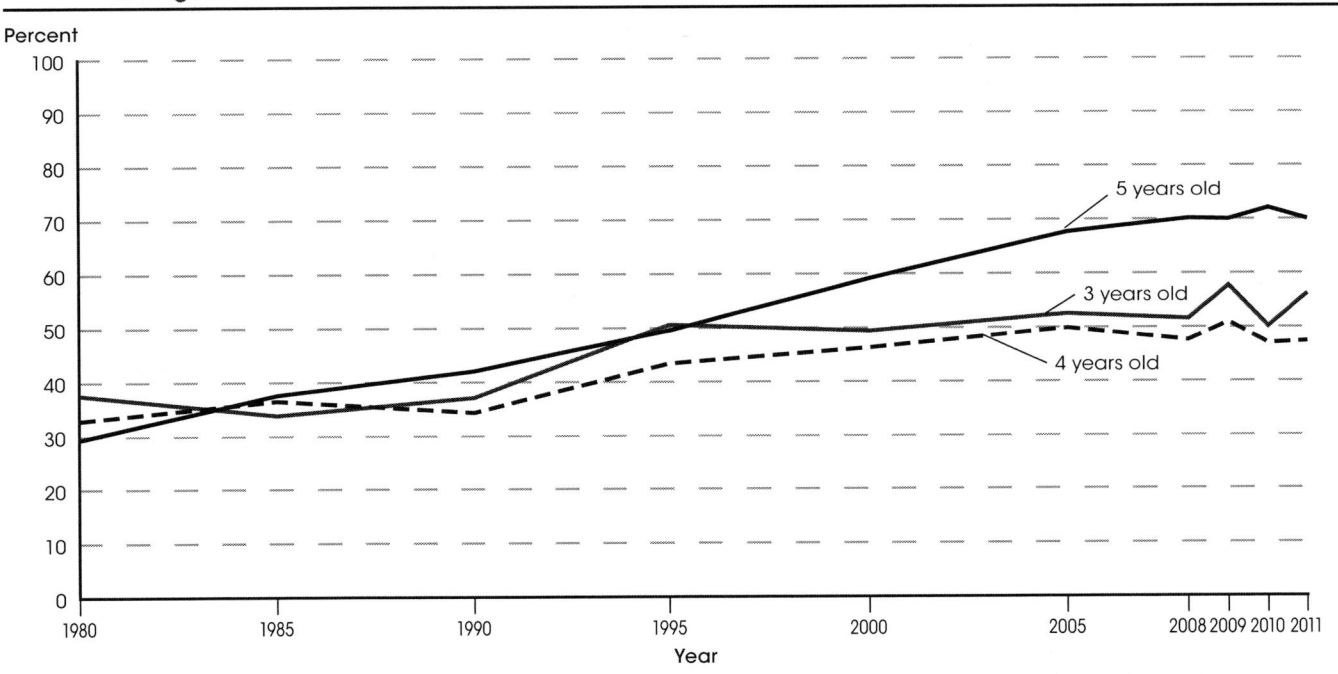

NOTE: *Preprimary programs* are groups or classes that are organized to provide educational experiences for children and include kindergarten, preschool, and nursery school programs. Enrollment data for 5-year-olds include only those students in preprimary programs and do not include those enrolled in primary programs. Beginning in 1995, new procedures were used in the CPS to collect preprimary enrollment data. As a result, pre-1995 data may not be comparable to data from 1995 or later. Data are based on sample surveys of the civilian noninstitutional population.
SOURCE: U.S. Department of Commerce, Census Bureau, Current Population Survey (CPS), October 1980 through 2011. See *Digest of Education Statistics 2012*, table 53.

The percentage of 3- to 5-year-olds in preprimary programs who attended full-day programs increased from 32 percent in 1980 to 59 percent in 2011. In addition to the overall increase, the full-day attendance percentage increased for each age group during this period. The enrollment rate for 3-year-olds was higher in 2000 than in 1980 (49 percent vs. 37 percent). From 1980 to 2000, the percentage of 4-year-olds enrolled in full-day preprimary programs increased from 33 to 46 percent, and the percentage of 5-year-olds increased from 29 to 59 percent. The full-day enrollment rates were also higher in 2011 than in 2000 for 3-year-olds (56 percent vs. 49 percent) and 5-year-olds (70 percent vs. 59 percent), but not measurably different for 4-year-olds.

For more information, see the Reader's Guide and the Guide to Sources.

Chapter: 2/Participation in Education
Section: Preprimary Education

Differences by age in enrollment in full-day preprimary programs have shifted over the past few decades. For example, in 1980, the percentage of 5-year-olds enrolled in full-day preprimary programs was 8 points lower than the percentage of 3-year-olds (29 percent vs. 37 percent), and not measurably different from the percentage of 4-year-olds (33 percent); but in 2011, the percentage of 5-year-olds was 14 points higher than the percentage of 3-year-olds (70 percent vs. 56 percent), and 23 points higher than the percentage of 4-year-olds (47 percent).

Figure 2. Percentage of 3-, 4-, and 5-year-old children enrolled in preprimary programs, by parents' educational attainment and attendance status: October 2011

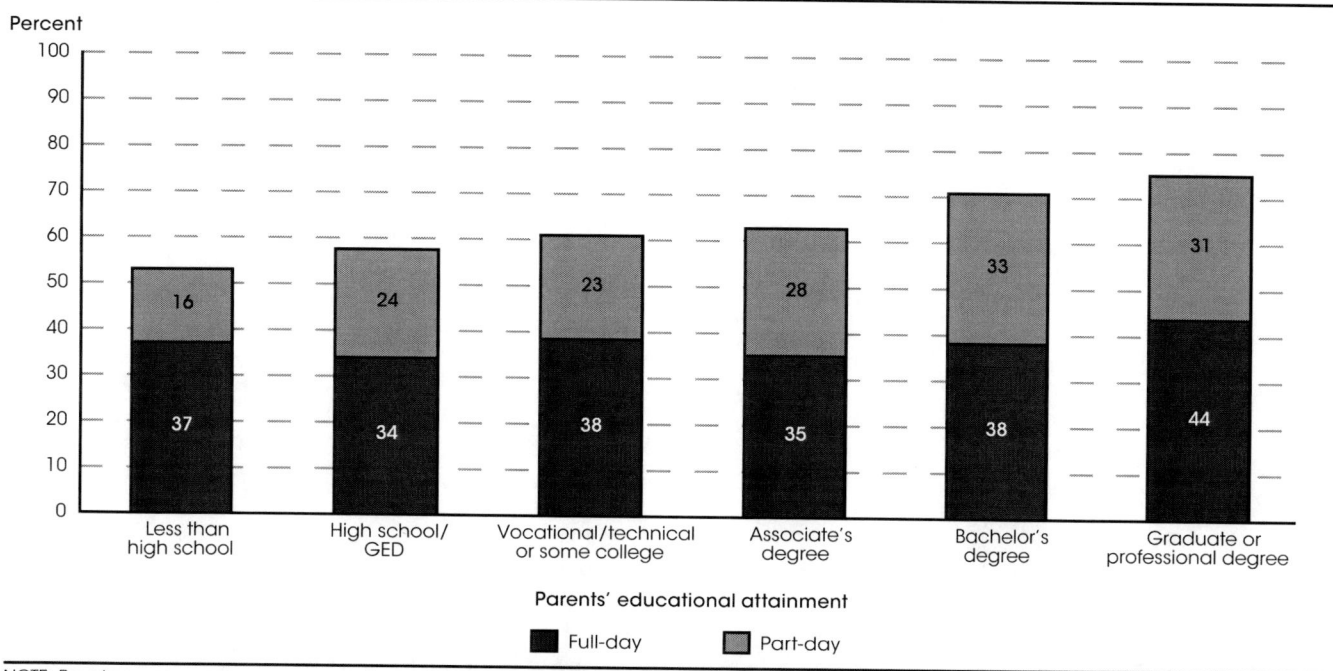

Parents' educational attainment	Full-day	Part-day
Less than high school	37	16
High school/GED	34	24
Vocational/technical or some college	38	23
Associate's degree	35	28
Bachelor's degree	38	33
Graduate or professional degree	44	31

NOTE: *Preprimary programs* are groups or classes that are organized to provide educational experiences for children and include kindergarten, preschool, and nursery school programs. Enrollment data for 5-year-olds include only those students in preprimary programs and do not include those enrolled in primary programs. Highest level of education is defined as the diploma attained by the most educated parent. Data are based on sample surveys of the civilian noninstitutional population.
SOURCE: U.S. Department of Commerce, Census Bureau, Current Population Survey (CPS), October, 2011. See *Digest of Education Statisitcs 2012*, table 53.5.

Enrollment in preprimary programs varied by parents' highest level of education, defined as the diploma attained by the most educated parent. In 2011, higher percentages of 3- to 5-year-olds whose parents had either a graduate or professional degree (75 percent) or a bachelor's degree (71 percent) were enrolled in preprimary programs than children of parents with any other level of educational attainment. For instance, 53 percent of children whose parents had less than a high school degree and 58 percent of children whose parents had a high school credential were enrolled in preprimary programs. Enrollment in full-day and part-day preprimary programs also differed by the highest educational attainment of parents or guardians. Forty-four percent of 3- to 5-year-olds whose parents had a graduate or professional degree were enrolled in full-day preprimary programs, an enrollment rate that was generally higher than for children whose parents had any other level of educational attainment, except for those whose parents had attended a vocational/technical program or some college. Children whose parents had a graduate or professional degree (31 percent) or a bachelor's degree (33 percent) were also enrolled in part-day preprimary programs at higher percentages than those of children whose parents had less than a high school degree (16 percent) or a high school credential (24 percent).

Reference tables: *Digest of Education Statistics 2012*, tables 53, 53.5

Glossary: Nursery school

For more information, see the Reader's Guide and the Guide to Sources.

Chapter: 2/Participation in Education
Section: Elementary/Secondary Enrollment

Indicator 8
Public School Enrollment

From school years 2010–11 through 2021–22, public elementary and secondary school enrollment is projected to increase by 7 percent from 49.5 to 53.1 million students, but with changes across states ranging from an increase of 22 percent in Alaska to a decrease of 15 percent in the District of Columbia.

In school year 2010–11, some 49.5 million students were enrolled in public elementary and secondary schools. Of these students, 34.6 million were enrolled in prekindergarten (preK) through grade 8, and 14.9 million were enrolled in grades 9 through 12.

Public school enrollment declined during the 1970s and early 1980s and rose in the latter part of the 1980s. Enrollment continued to increase throughout the 1990s and early 2000s. By school year 1997–98, public school enrollment had reached 46.1 million students and had surpassed its early 1970s peak. Between 2000–01 and 2006–07, public school enrollment increased by 2.1 million students, reaching 49.3 million students in school year 2006–07 where it remained until 2008–09. Total public school enrollment reached 49.5 million in 2010–11. From 2010–11 to 2021–22, total public school enrollment is projected to increase by 7 percent to 53.1 million (2021–22 is the last year for which projected data are available).

Enrollment trends in grades preK–8 and 9–12 have differed over time as successive cohorts of students have moved through the public school system. For example, enrollment in grades preK–8 decreased throughout the 1970s and early 1980s, while enrollment in grades 9–12 generally decreased in the late 1970s and throughout the 1980s. Enrollment in grades preK–8 increased from 1985–86 through 2003–04 and fluctuated between 34.2 million and 34.6 million between 2003–04 and 2010–11. Public school enrollment in grades preK–8 is projected to increase from 34.6 million in 2010–11 to an estimated 37.6 million in 2021–22, reflecting an increase of 9 percent in 2021–22. Public school enrollment in grades

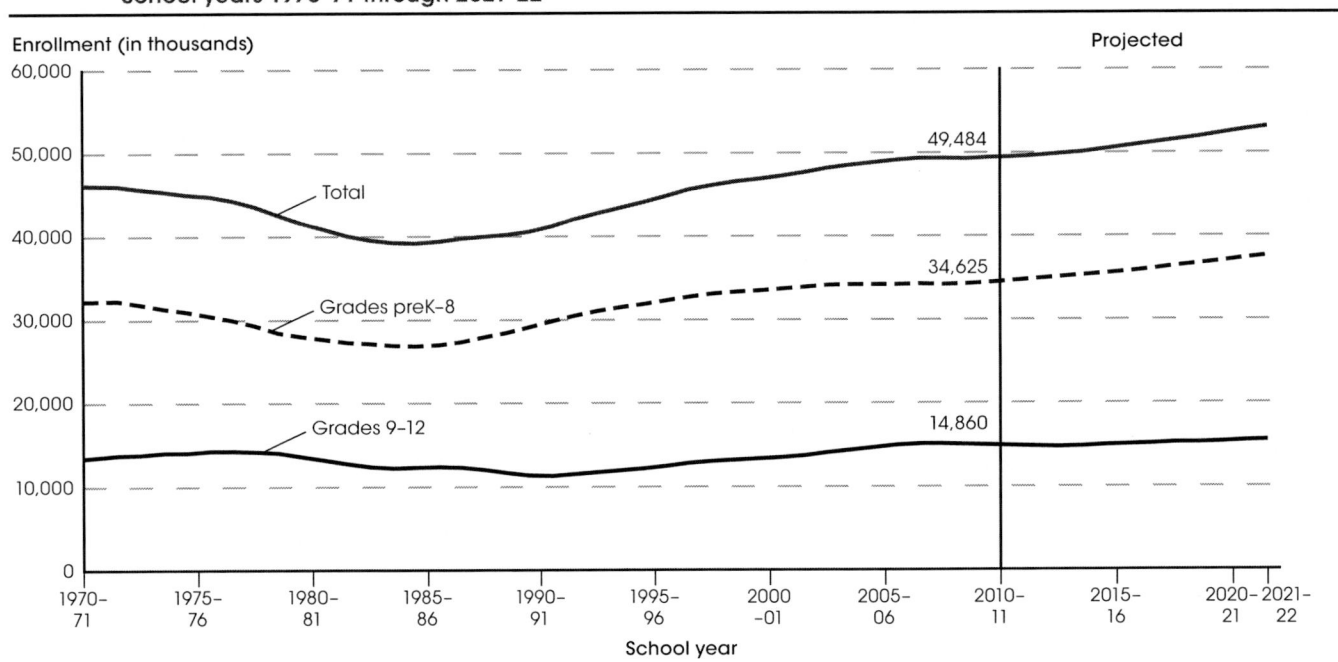

Figure 1. Actual and projected public school enrollment in grades prekindergarten (preK) through 12, by grade level: School years 1970–71 through 2021–22

SOURCE: U.S. Department of Education, National Center for Education Statistics, Statistics of Public Elementary and Secondary Day Schools, 1970–71 through 1984–85; Common Core of Data (CCD), "State Nonfiscal Survey of Public Elementary/Secondary Education," 1985–86 through 2010–11, and National Elementary and Secondary Enrollment Model, 1972–2010; Projections of Education Statistics to 2021. See *Digest of Education Statistics 2012*, table 36.

For more information, see the Reader's Guide and the Guide to Sources.

Chapter: 2/Participation in Education
Section: Elementary/Secondary Enrollment

9–12 increased from 1991–92 through 2007–08, but declined through 2010–11 and is projected to continue declining through 2012–13. From 2013–14 through 2021–22, enrollment in grades 9–12 is projected to increase, and it is projected to surpass its 2007–08 level by 2021–22. Overall, public school enrollment in grades 9–12 is projected to increase 4 percent between 2010–11 and 2021–22.

Figure 2. Projected percent change in public school enrollment in grades prekindergarten (preK) through 12, by state or jurisdiction: Between school years 2010–11 and 2021–22

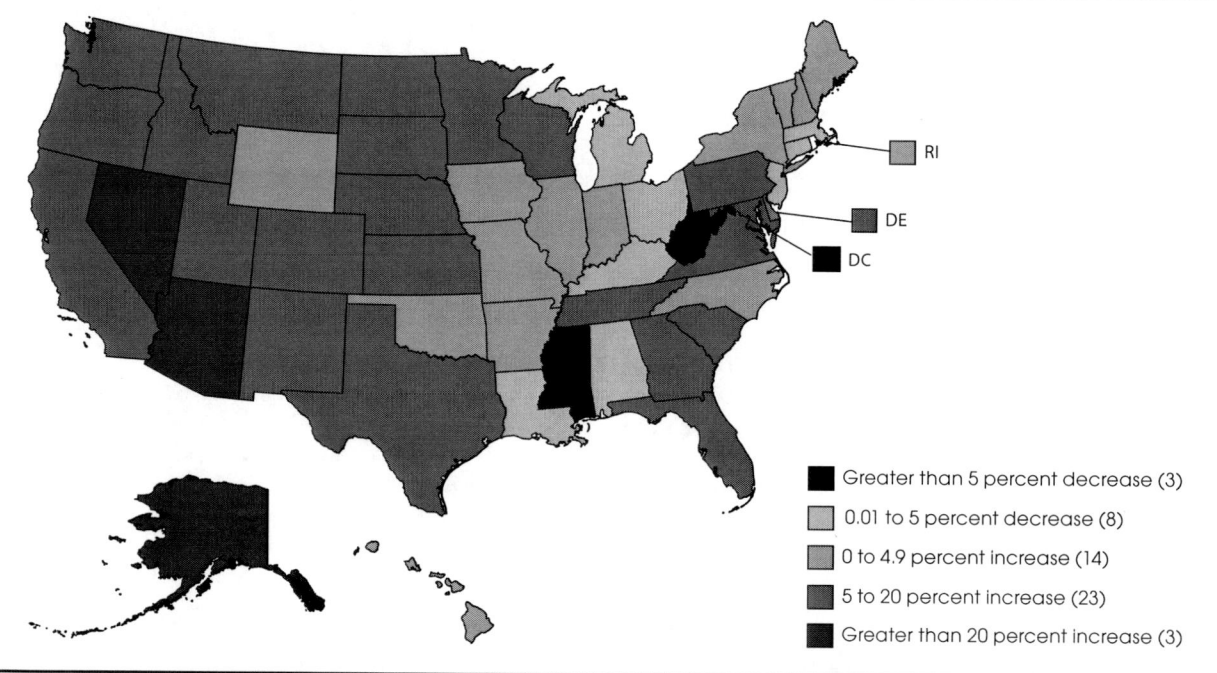

■ Greater than 5 percent decrease (3)
▨ 0.01 to 5 percent decrease (8)
□ 0 to 4.9 percent increase (14)
▨ 5 to 20 percent increase (23)
■ Greater than 20 percent increase (3)

SOURCE: U.S. Department of Education, National Center for Education Statistics, Common Core of Data (CCD), "State Nonfiscal Survey of Public Elementary/Secondary Education," 2010–11; and Public State Elementary and Secondary Enrollment Model, 1980–2010. Projections of Education Statistics to 2021. See *Digest of Education Statistics 2012*, table 36.

Public school enrollment in grades preK–12 increased in 41 states from 1989–90 to 2010–11, with the greatest increases occurring in Nevada and Arizona (134 and 76 percent, respectively). During that period, total enrollment declined in nine states and the District of Columbia. From 2010–11 to 2021–22, Alaska, Nevada, and Arizona are projected to see the greatest percentage increases in total enrollment (22, 21, and 20, respectively). The District of Columbia is projected to see the largest percentage decrease in total enrollment over the same time period (15 percent).

From 2010–11 to 2021–22, the changes in public elementary and secondary enrollments are projected to differ among the states. Reflecting the larger national enrollment increase expected at the preK–8 than at the grade 9–12 level, 43 states are expected to have enrollment increases at the preK–8 level between 2009–10 to 2021–22, while 36 states are expected to have increases at the grade 9–12 level. In grades preK–8, enrollment is projected to increase by more than 20 percent in Alaska, Nevada, Arizona, and Washington but decrease by 11 and 13 percent, respectively, in the District of Columbia and West Virginia. Enrollment in grades 9–12 in Texas is expected to increase by more than 20 percent, while enrollment in these grades in the District of Columbia is projected to decrease by 20 percent or more.

Reference table: *Digest of Education Statistics 2012*, table 36

Glossary: Elementary school, Secondary school, Prekindergarten, Public school

For more information, see the Reader's Guide and the Guide to Sources.

Chapter: 2/Participation in Education
Section: Elementary/Secondary Enrollment

Indicator 9
Charter School Enrollment

From school year 1999–2000 to 2010–11, the number of students enrolled in public charter schools increased from 0.3 million to 1.8 million students. During this period, the percentage of all public schools that were public charter schools increased from 2 to 5 percent, comprising 5,300 schools in 2010–11.

A *public charter school* is a publicly funded school that is typically governed by a group or organization under a legislative contract or charter with the state or jurisdiction. The charter exempts the school from selected state or local rules and regulations. In return for funding and autonomy, the charter school must meet the accountability standards articulated in its charter. A school's charter is reviewed periodically (typically every 3 to 5 years) by the group or jurisdiction that granted its charter and can be revoked if guidelines on curriculum and management are not followed or if the standards are not met. The first law allowing the establishment of charter schools was passed in Minnesota in 1991. In school year 2010–11, charter schools legislation had been passed in 41 states and the District of Columbia.

In Maine, no charter schools were operational in 2010–11, even though the establishment of them had been approved. In the following states, charter school legislation has not been passed: Alabama, Kentucky, Montana, Nebraska, North Dakota, South Dakota, Vermont, Washington, and West Virginia.

From 1999–2000 to 2010–11, the number of students enrolled in public charter schools increased from 0.3 million to 1.8 million students. During this period, the percentage of all public schools that were public charter schools, based on schools that reported enrollment, increased from 2 to 5 percent, comprising 5,300 schools in 2010–11.

Figure 1. Number of students enrolled in public charter schools: Selected school years, 1999–2000 through 2010–11

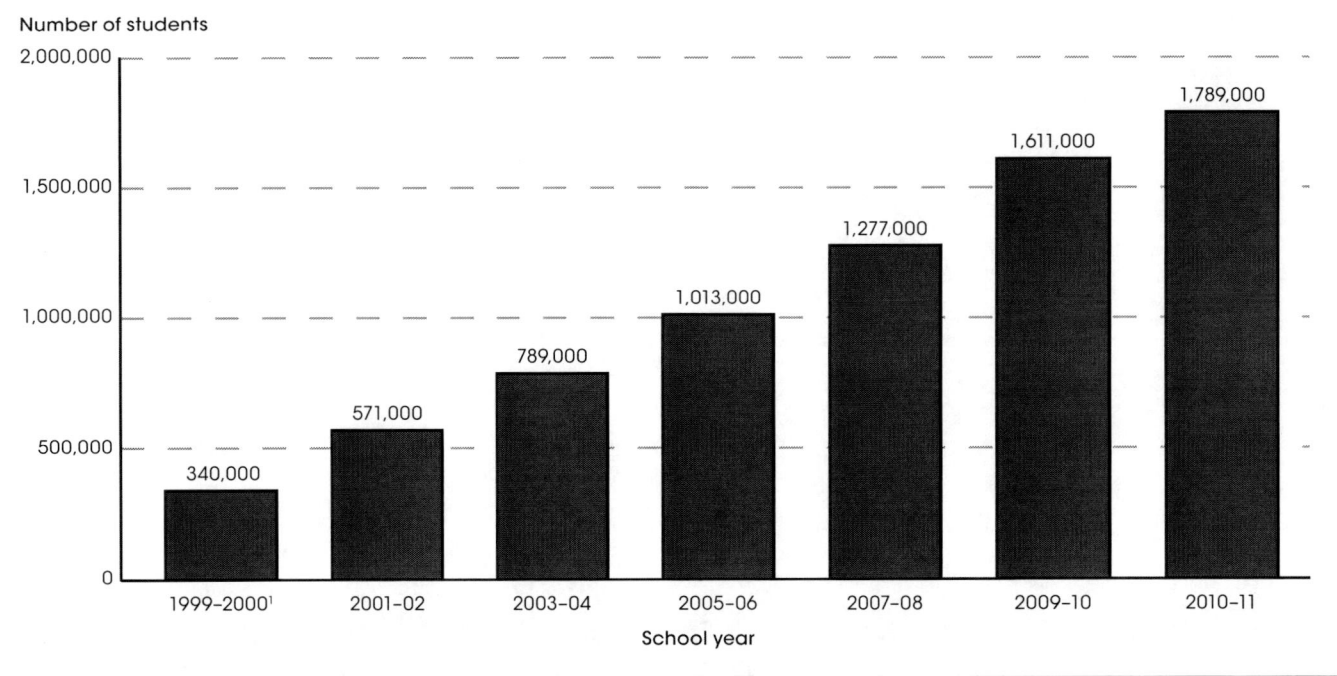

School year	Number of students
1999–2000[1]	340,000
2001–02	571,000
2003–04	789,000
2005–06	1,013,000
2007–08	1,277,000
2009–10	1,611,000
2010–11	1,789,000

[1] Data for New Jersey were not available and therefore are not included in the estimates.
NOTE: Data are for schools reporting student membership. Student membership is defined as an annual headcount of students enrolled in school on October 1 or the school day closest to that date. The Common Core of Data (CCD) allows a student to be reported for only a single school or agency. For example, a virtual school (identified as a "shared time" school) may provide classes to students from other schools and report no membership of its own.
SOURCE: U.S. Department of Education, National Center for Education Statistics, Common Core of Data (CCD), "Public Elementary/Secondary School Universe Survey," 1999–2000 through 2010–11. See *Digest of Education Statistics 2012*, table 116.

For more information, see the Reader's Guide and the Guide to Sources.

Chapter: 2/Participation in Education
Section: Elementary/Secondary Enrollment

In addition to the increase in the number of charter schools, the enrollment size of charter schools has grown over time. The percentage of charter schools with enrollments under 300 students decreased from 77 percent in 1999–2000 to 59 percent in 2010–11. The percentage of charter schools with enrollments of 300–499 students increased from 12 to 22 percent during this period; the percentage with 500–999 students increased from 9 to 15 percent; and the percentage with 1,000 students or more increased from 2 to 4 percent.

Figure 2. Percentage of all public school students enrolled in charter schools, by state or jurisdiction: School year 2010–11

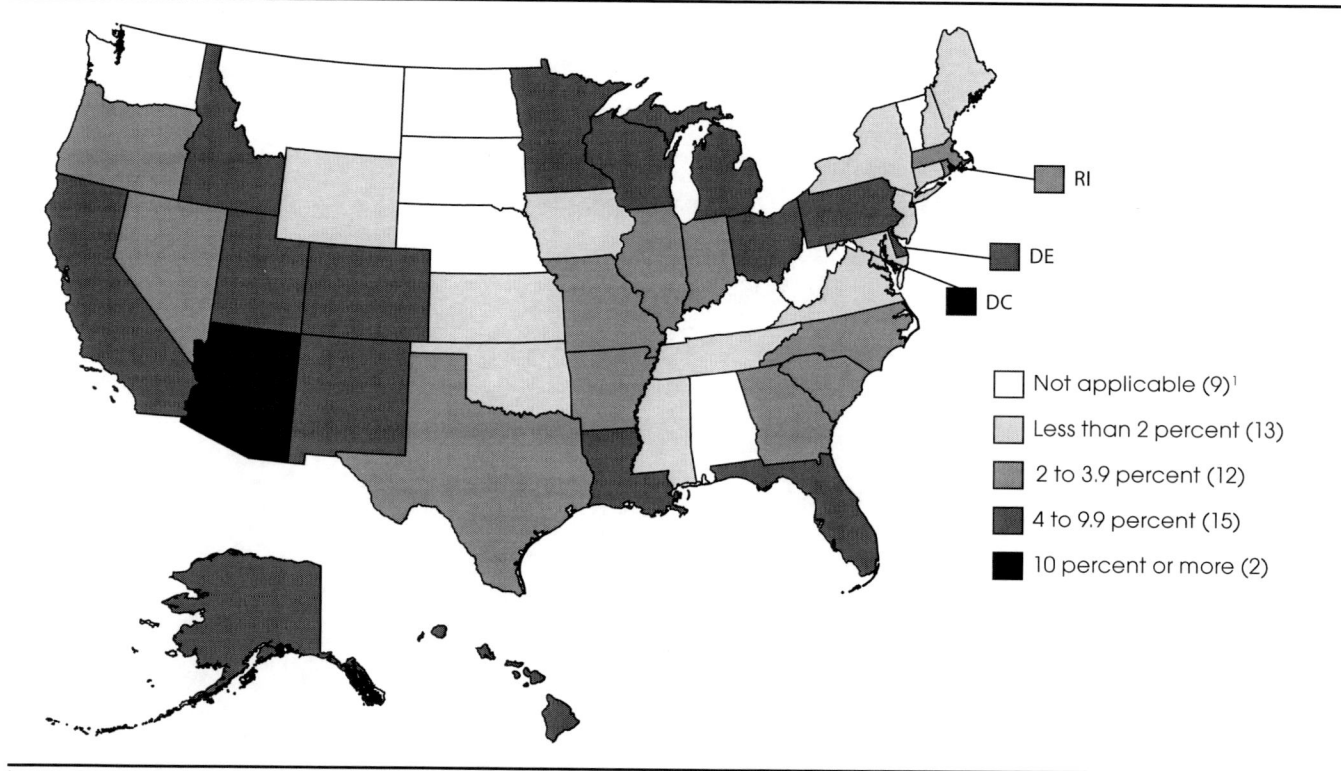

[1] Not applicable. State has not passed a charter school law.
NOTE: Data are for schools reporting student membership. Student membership is defined as an annual headcount of students enrolled in school on October 1 or the school day closest to that date. The Common Core of Data (CCD) allows a student to be reported for only a single school or agency. For example, a virtual school (identified as a "shared time" school) may provide classes to students from other schools and report no membership of its own.
SOURCE: U.S. Department of Education, National Center for Education Statistics, Common Core of Data (CCD), "Public Elementary/Secondary School Universe Survey," 2010–11 (version 1a). See *Digest of Education Statistics 2012*, table 117.

In 2010–11, California enrolled the most students in charter schools (364,000), and the District of Columbia enrolled the highest percentage of public school students in charter schools (38 percent), representing 27,000 students. In that same year, more than 10 percent of public school students in Arizona were enrolled in charter schools. In 15 additional states, between 4 and 9.9 percent of public school students were enrolled in charter schools. Of the states with 4 percent or more public school students enrolled in charter schools, eight were in the West; three, plus the District of Columbia, were in the South; four were in the Midwest; and one was in the Northeast.

Reference table: *Digest of Education Statistics 2012*, tables 116, 117

Glossary: National School Lunch Program, Charter school, Student membership, Traditional public school, Free or reduced-price lunch, Elementary school, Secondary school, Combined school

For more information, see the Reader's Guide and the Guide to Sources.

Indicator 10
Private School Enrollment

Private school enrollment in prekindergarten through grade 12 increased from 5.9 million in 1995–96 to 6.3 million in 2001–02 then decreased to 5.5 million in 2009–10. Some 10 percent of all elementary and secondary school students were in private schools in 2009–10.

Private school enrollment in prekindergarten through grade 12 increased from 5.9 million in 1995–96 to 6.3 million in 2001–02 then decreased to 5.5 million in 2009–10, excluding prekindergarten students who were enrolled in private schools that did not offer at least one grade of kindergarten or higher. Some 10 percent of all elementary and secondary school students were in private schools in 2009–10, which was lower than the percentage in 1995–96 (12 percent).

Figure 1. Number of private school students in prekindergarten through grade 12, by school type: Various school years, 1995–96 through 2009–10

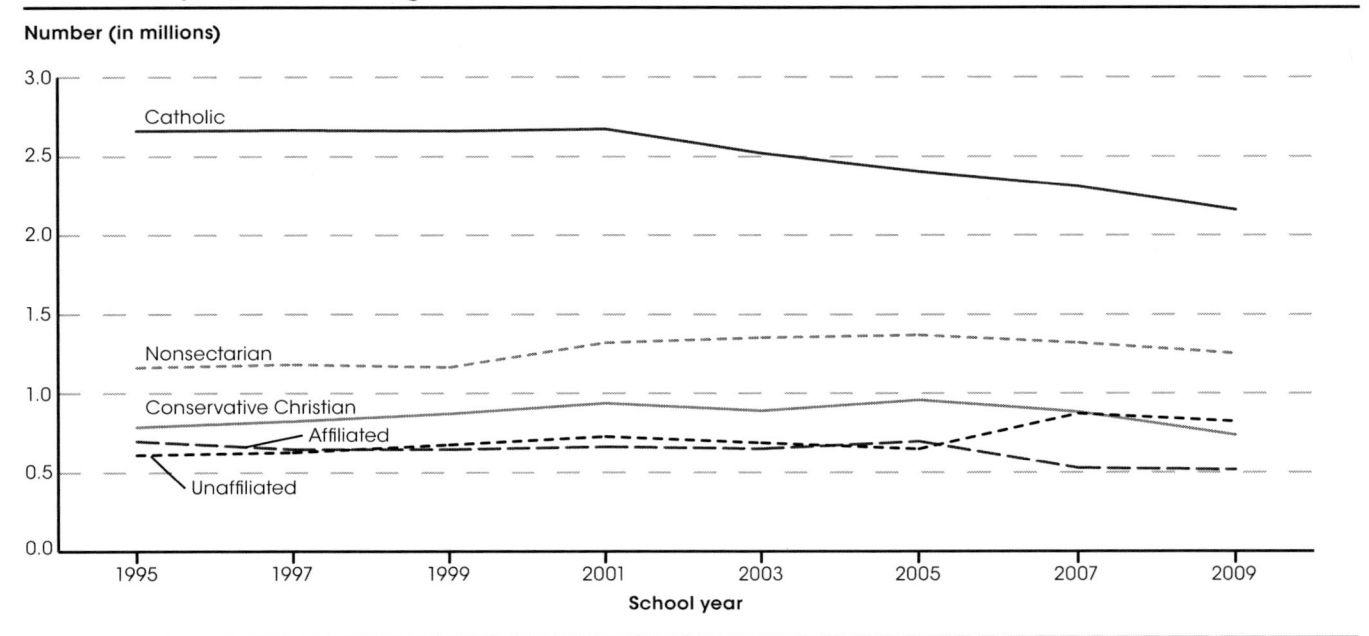

NOTE: Prekindergarten students who are enrolled in private schools that do not offer kindergarten or higher grades are not included in this analysis. *Catholic schools* include parochial, diocesan, and private Catholic schools. *Affiliated religious schools* have a specific religious orientation or purpose but are not Catholic. *Unaffiliated schools* have a more general religious orientation or purpose but are not classified as Conservative Christian or affiliated with a specific religion. *Nonsectarian schools* do not have a religious orientation or purpose.
SOURCE: U.S. Department of Education, National Center for Education Statistics, Private School Universe Survey (PSS), various years, 1995–96 through 2009–10. See *Digest of Education Statistics 2012*, table 68.

Between 1995–96 and 2005–06, Catholic schools maintained the largest share of total private school enrollment. However, the percentage of all private school students enrolled in Catholic schools decreased from 45 percent in 1995–96 to 39 percent in 2009–10. The number of students enrolled in Catholic schools in 2009–10 was higher than the number of students enrolled in other religious schools. The decrease in Catholic school enrollment was due to a decline in the number of students enrolled in parochial schools (those run by a parish, not by a diocese or independently). The numbers of students enrolled in Conservative Christian (schools with membership in at least one of four associations: Accelerated Christian Education, American Association of Christian Schools, Association of Christian Schools International, or Oral Roberts University Education Fellowship) and Affiliated ("Other religious" schools not classified as Conservative Christian with membership in at least 1 of 11 associations) schools also were lower in 2009 than in 1995. In contrast, the number of students enrolled in Unaffiliated schools, meaning schools that have a more general religious orientation or purpose but are not classified as Conservative Christian or affiliated with a specific religion, increased 35 percent from 611 million in 1995–96 to 823 million in 2009–10.

For more information, see the Reader's Guide and the Guide to Sources.

Chapter: 2/Participation in Education
Section: Elementary/Secondary

Figure 2. Percent distribution of private school enrollment, by school type and level: 2009–10

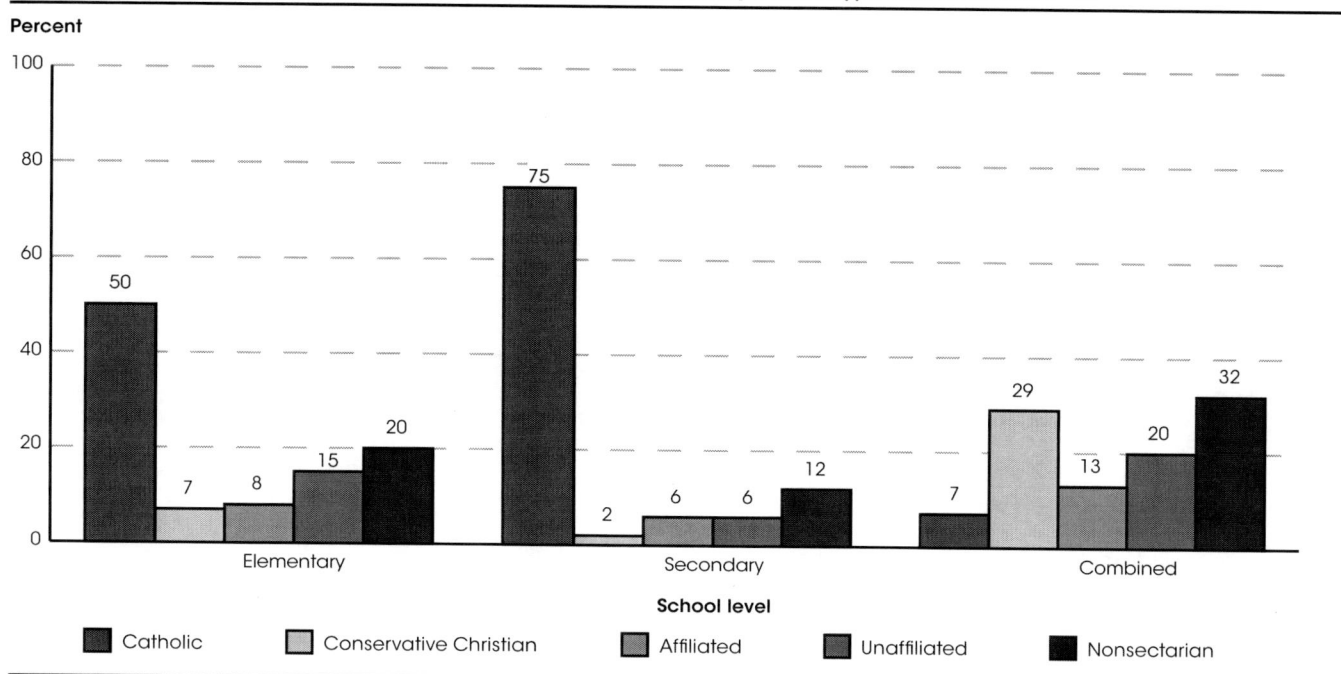

School level	Catholic	Conservative Christian	Affiliated	Unaffiliated	Nonsectarian
Elementary	50	7	8	15	20
Secondary	75	2	6	6	12
Combined	7	29	13	20	32

NOTE: Prekindergarten students who are enrolled in private schools that do not offer kindergarten or higher grades are not included in this analysis. *Elementary schools* are schools classified as elementary by state and local practice and composed of any span of grades not above grade 8. *Combined schools* are schools that encompass instruction at both the elementary and the secondary levels; includes schools starting with grade 6 or below and ending with grade 9 or above. *Secondary schools* are schools comprising any span of grades beginning with the next grade following an elementary or middle school (usually 7, 8, or 9) and ending with or below grade 12. Both junior high schools and senior high schools are included. *Catholic schools* include parochial, diocesan, and private Catholic schools. *Affiliated religious schools* have a specific religious orientation or purpose but are not Catholic. *Unaffiliated schools* have a more general religious orientation or purpose but are not classified as Conservative Christian or affiliated with a specific religion. *Nonsectarian schools* do not have a religious orientation or purpose. Ungraded students are prorated into preK–8 and 9–12 enrollment totals. Detail may not sum to totals because of rounding.
SOURCE: U.S. Department of Education, National Center for Education Statistics, Private School Universe Survey (PSS), 2009–10. See *Digest of Education Statistics 2012*, table 69.

In 2009–10, most private secondary school students were enrolled in Catholic schools (75 percent). Of the remaining students, 2 percent were enrolled in Conservative Christian schools, 6 percent each were enrolled in Affiliated and Unaffiliated religious schools, and 12 percent were enrolled in Nonsectarian, or non-religious, schools. Similarly, more private elementary school students were enrolled in Catholic schools than in any other school type (50 percent). In contrast to the large percentage of private school students enrolled in Catholic secondary and elementary schools, Catholic students made up the minority of private school students enrolled in combined schools, at only 7 percent.

In 2009–10, the percentage of all students who were enrolled in private schools was higher in the Northeast (14 percent) than in the Midwest (11 percent), the South (9 percent), and the West (8 percent). The percentage of students enrolled in private schools was lower in 2009–10 than in 1995–96 in all four regions.

There were differences in attendance by school type within racial/ethnic groups. Hispanic, Asian, and American Indian/Alaska Native students and students of two or more races all had higher percentages of students attending Catholic schools than other religious or nonsectarian schools. In contrast, there was a higher percentage of Black students attending other religious schools than attending Catholic schools. White and Pacific Islander groups had higher percentages of students attending Catholic schools than nonsectarian schools. However, the percentages of White and Pacific Islander students attending Catholic schools were not measurably different from the percentages attending other religious schools.

Reference table: *Digest of Education Statistics 2012*, tables 67, 68, 69

Glossary: Prekindergarten, Private schools

For more information, see the Reader's Guide and the Guide to Sources.

Chapter: 2/Participation in Education
Section: Elementary/Secondary Education

Indicator 11
Racial/Ethnic Enrollment in Public Schools

From fall 2000 through fall 2010, the number of White students enrolled in prekindergarten through 12th grade in U.S. public schools decreased from 28.9 million to 25.9 million, and their share of enrollment decreased from 61 to 52 percent. In contrast, Hispanic public school enrollment during this period increased from 7.7 to 11.4 million students, and the percentage of public school students who were Hispanic increased from 16 to 23 percent.

Figure 1. Percentage distribution of U.S. public school students enrolled in prekindergarten through 12th grade, by race/ethnicity: Selected years, fall 2000–fall 2021

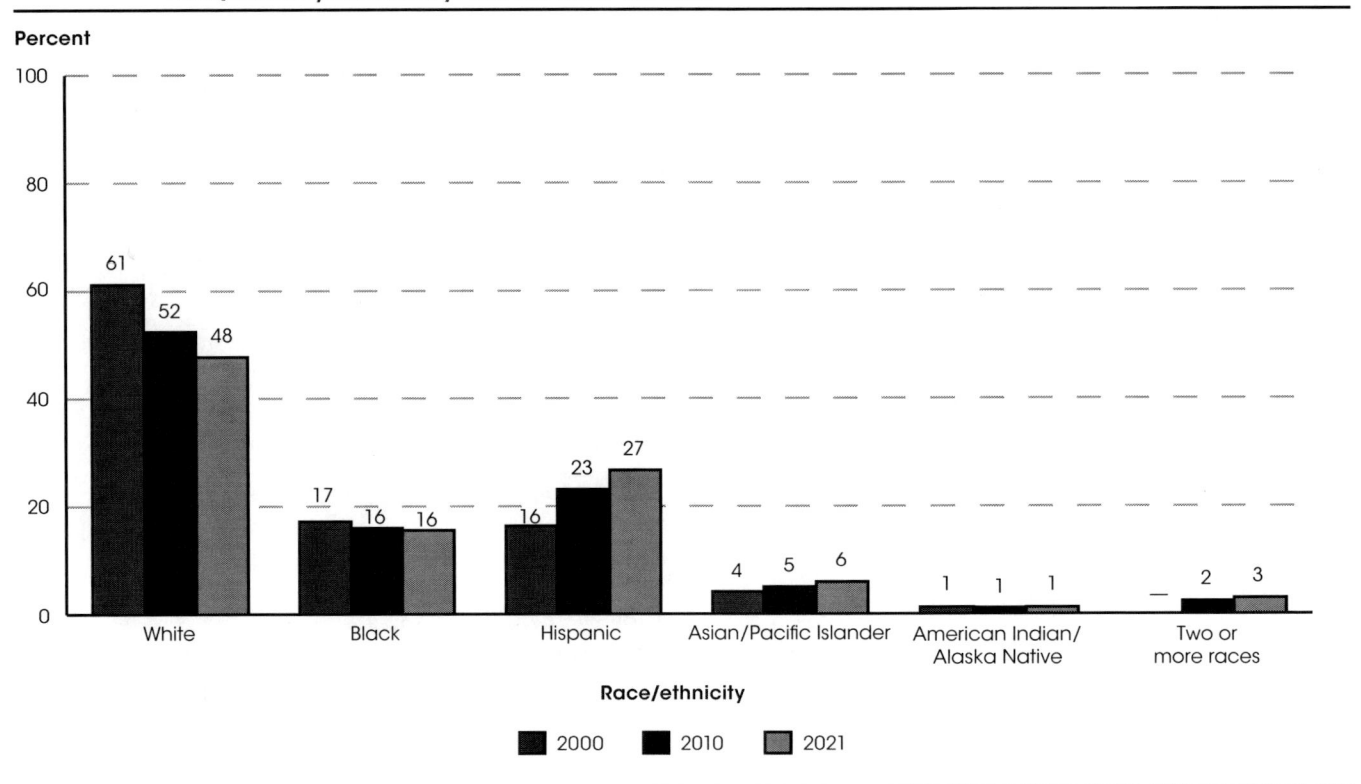

Race/ethnicity	2000	2010	2021
White	61	52	48
Black	17	16	16
Hispanic	16	23	27
Asian/Pacific Islander	4	5	6
American Indian/Alaska Native	1	1	1
Two or more races	—	2	3

— Data not available.
NOTE: Detail may not sum to totals because of rounding. Data for 2021 are projected.
SOURCE: U.S. Department of Education, National Center for Education Statistics, *Projections of Education Statistics to 2021;* and Common Core of Data (CCD), "State Nonfiscal Survey of Public Elementary and Secondary Education," selected years, 2000–01 through 2010–11. See *Digest of Education Statistics 2012,* table 44.

From fall 2000 through fall 2010, the number of White students enrolled in prekindergarten through 12th grade in U.S. public schools decreased from 28.9 million to 25.9 million, and their share of enrollment decreased from 61 to 52 percent. In contrast, Hispanic public school enrollment during this period increased from 7.7 to 11.4 million students, and the percentage of public school students who were Hispanic increased from 16 to 23 percent. While the total number of Black students fluctuated between 7.9 million and 8.4 million, their share of enrollment decreased from 17 to 16 percent. In 2002, the percentage of public school students who were Hispanic exceeded the percentage of those who were Black and has remained higher than the Black share of enrollment in each subsequent year through 2010.

For more information, see the Reader's Guide and the Guide to Sources.

Chapter: 2/Participation in Education
Section: Elementary/Secondary Education

Figure 2. Number of U.S. public school students enrolled in prekindergarten through 12th grade, by region and race/ethnicity: Fall 2000–fall 2010

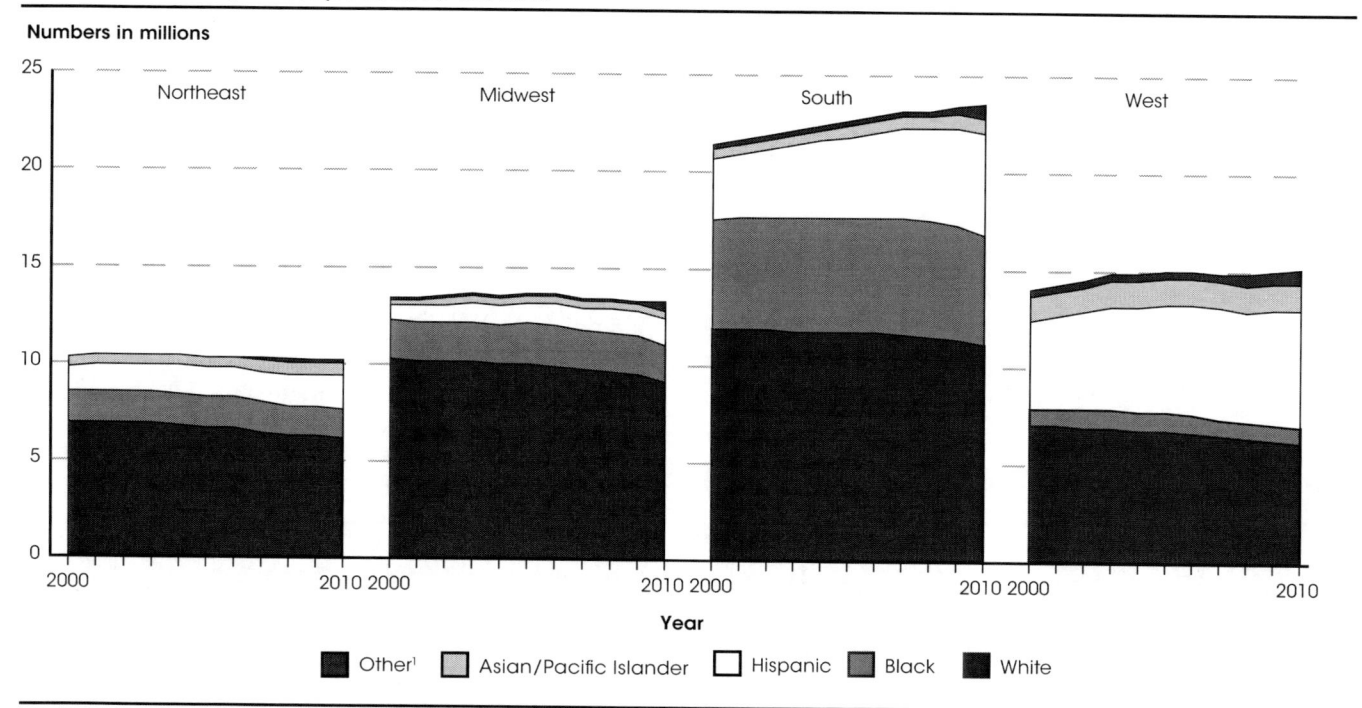

[1] Other includes all students who identified themselves as American Indian/Alaska Native or two or more races.
NOTE: Prior to 2008, data on students of two or more races were not collected. In 2008 and 2009, data on students of two or more races were reported by only a small number of states.
SOURCE: U.S. Department of Education, National Center for Education Statistics, Common Core of Data (CCD), "State Nonfiscal Survey of Public Elementary and Secondary Education," 2000–01 through 2010–11. See *Digest of Education Statistics 2012*, table 44.

The change in racial/ethnic distribution of public school enrollment differed by region. From fall 2000 through fall 2010, the number and percentage enrollment of White students decreased in all regions, with the largest percentage decrease in the West (9 percentage points). The number of Hispanic students and their share of enrollment increased in all four regions, with the largest increase in the South (8 percentage points). From 2000 through 2010, the number of Black students fluctuated in all regions with the exception of the Northeast, where the number decreased. The enrollment percentage of Black students fluctuated in the Midwest and decreased in the Northeast, West, and South. The number and percentage enrollment of Asian/Pacific Islander students increased in all regions, with the largest increase in the Northeast (2 percentage points). There was minimal change among other racial/ethnic groups during this period.

Racial/ethnic distribution of public school enrollment differed by region in fall 2010. As a result of the regional shifts in White and Hispanic enrollment, there was less than a 1 percentage point gap in the share of enrollment between White and Hispanic groups in the West (both approximately 40 percent). However, for all other regions the percentage share of White students was at least 20 percentage points greater than that of Hispanics in 2010. Black enrollment was within 2 percentage points of the overall U.S. percentage distribution (16 percent) in the Northeast and Midwest, while accounting for 24 percent of student enrollment in the South and 6 percent in the West. American Indian/Alaska Native students represented 2 percent or less of student enrollment in all regions of the United States. In 2010, students of two or more races made up 3 percent of enrollment each in the West and Midwest, 2 percent in the South, and 1 percent in the Northeast.

Between fall 2011 and fall 2021 (2021 is the last year for which projected data are available), the number of White students enrolled in U.S. public schools is projected to continue decreasing, from 25.9 million to 25.3 million, and their share of enrollment is expected to decline to 48 percent. The number of Hispanic public school students is projected to increase from 11.7 million in 2011 to 14.2 million in 2021, representing a 27 percent share of enrollment. The total number of Black students is expected to increase from 7.9 million in 2011 to 8.3 million in 2021, but their share of enrollment is expected to remain at approximately 16 percent. According to the projections, beginning in 2016 and continuing through 2021 the percentage of public school students who are White will be less than 50 percent. The decrease in their share is partly due to the increases in Hispanic and Asian enrollment.

Reference table: *Digest of Education Statistics 2012*, table 44 **Glossary:** Public school

For more information, see the Reader's Guide and the Guide to Sources.

Chapter: 2/Participation in Education
Section: Elementary/Secondary Enrollment

Indicator 12
English Language Learners

The percentage of public school students in the United States who were English language learners (ELL) was higher in 2010–11 (10 percent) than in 2002–03 (9 percent). In 2011, the achievement gaps between ELL and non-ELL students in the NAEP reading assessment were 36 points at the 4th-grade level and 44 points at the 8th-grade level.

English language learner (ELL) refers to students being served in appropriate programs of language assistance (e.g., English as a Second Language, High Intensity Language Training, bilingual education). The percentage of public school students in the United States who were English language learners was higher in 2010–11 (10 percent, or an estimated 4.7 million students) than in 2002–03 (9 percent, or an estimated 4.1 million students).

Figure 1. Percentage of public school students who are English language learners (ELL), by state: School year 2010–11

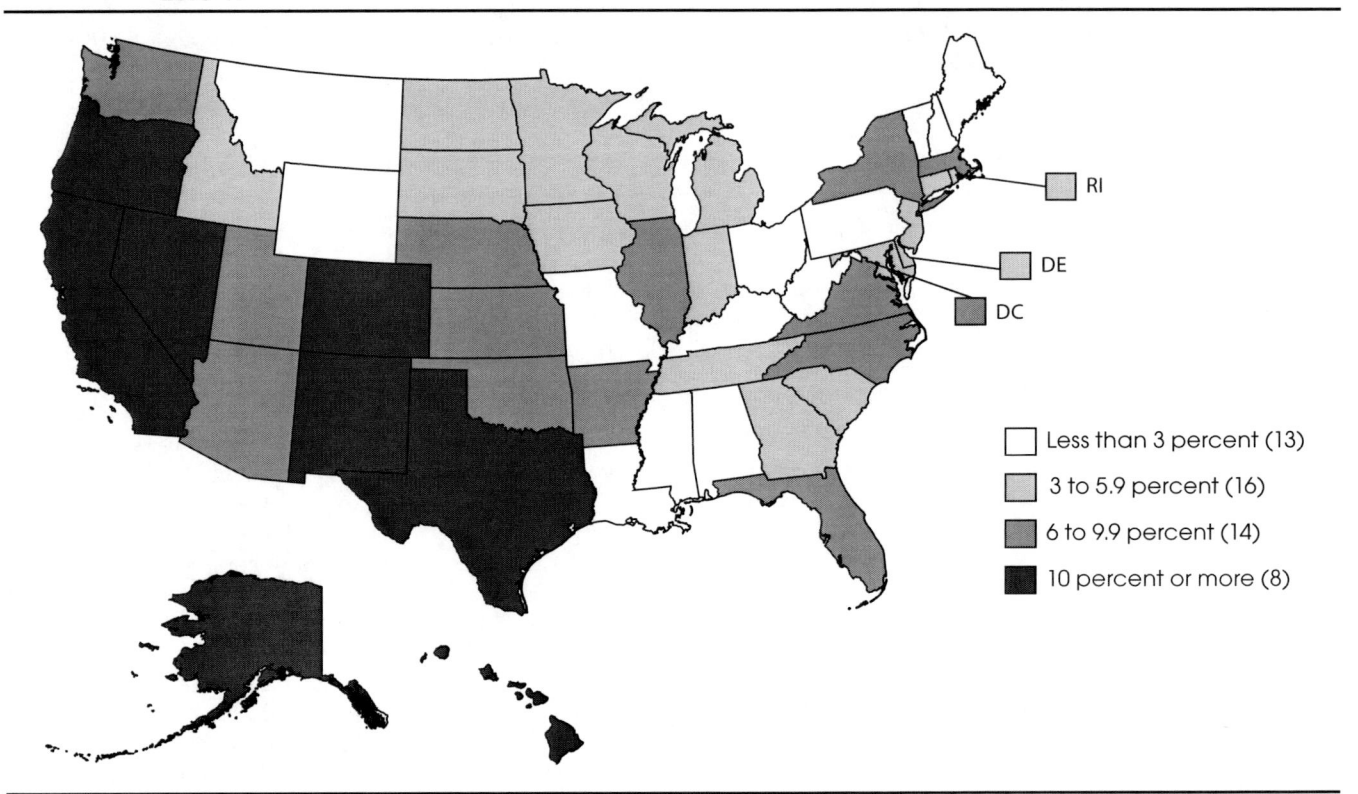

Legend:
- Less than 3 percent (13)
- 3 to 5.9 percent (16)
- 6 to 9.9 percent (14)
- 10 percent or more (8)

SOURCE: U.S. Department of Education, National Center for Education Statistics, Common Core of Data (CCD), "Local Education Agency School Universe Survey," 2010–11. See *Digest of Education Statistics 2012*, table 47.

In 2010–11, states in the West had the highest percentages of ELL students in their public schools. In 8 states, 10 percent or more of public school students were English language learners—Oregon, Hawaii, Alaska, Colorado, Texas, New Mexico, Nevada, and California (California data were imputed from 2009–10 data)—with ELL students constituting 29 percent of public school enrollment in California. Thirteen states and the District of Columbia had percentages of ELL public school enrollment between 6 and 9.9 percent. In addition to the District of Columbia, these states were Oklahoma, Arkansas, Massachusetts, Nebraska, North Carolina, Virginia, Arizona, Utah, New York, Kansas, Illinois, Washington, and Florida. The percentage of ELL students in public schools was less than 3 percent in 13 states; this percentage was between 3 and 5.9 percent in 16 states.

The percentage of ELL students in public schools was higher in 2010–11 than in 2002–03 in all but 12 states, with the largest percentage-point increases occurring in Kansas, South Carolina, Hawaii, and Nevada (all with 4 percentage points) and the largest percentage-point decreases occurring in Arizona (8 percentage points) and

For more information, see the Reader's Guide and the Guide to Sources.

Chapter: 2/Participation in Education
Section: Elementary/Secondary Enrollment

New Mexico (6 percentage points). The percentage of ELL students in public schools was higher in 2010–11 than in 2009–10 in just over half of the states (28 states), with the largest increase in percentage points occurring in Nevada (3 percentage points) and the largest decrease in percentage points occurring in Minnesota (2 percentage points).

In 2011 and in all previous assessment years since 2002, the National Assessment of Educational Progress (NAEP) reading scale scores for non-ELL 4th- and 8th-graders were higher than their ELL peers' scores. This disparity is known as an achievement gap—in NAEP reading scores, the achievement gap is seen by the differences between the average scores of two student

Figure 2. Average reading scores of 4th-grade students, by English language learner (ELL) status: Selected years, 2002–11

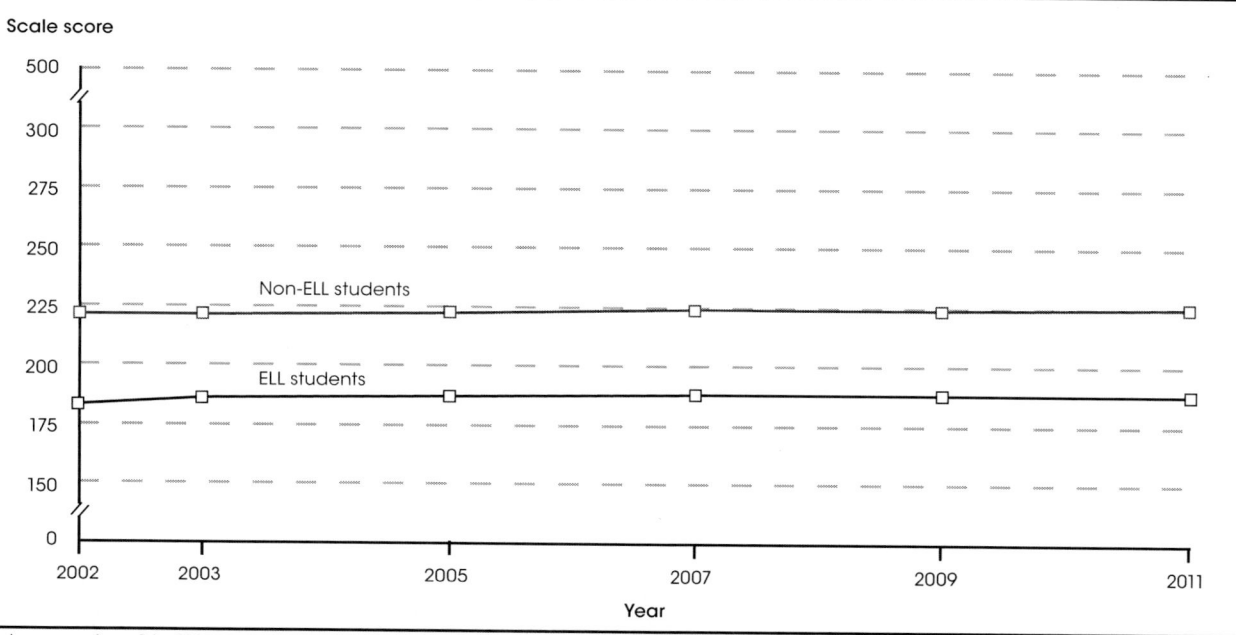

NOTE: Scale ranges from 0 to 500.
SOURCE: U.S. Department of Education, National Center for Education Statistics, National Assessment of Educational Progress (NAEP), selected years, 2002–11 Reading Assessments, NAEP Data Explorer. See *Digest of Education Statistics 2012*, table 142.

Figure 3. Average reading scores of 8th-grade students, by English language learner (ELL) status: Selected years, 2002–11

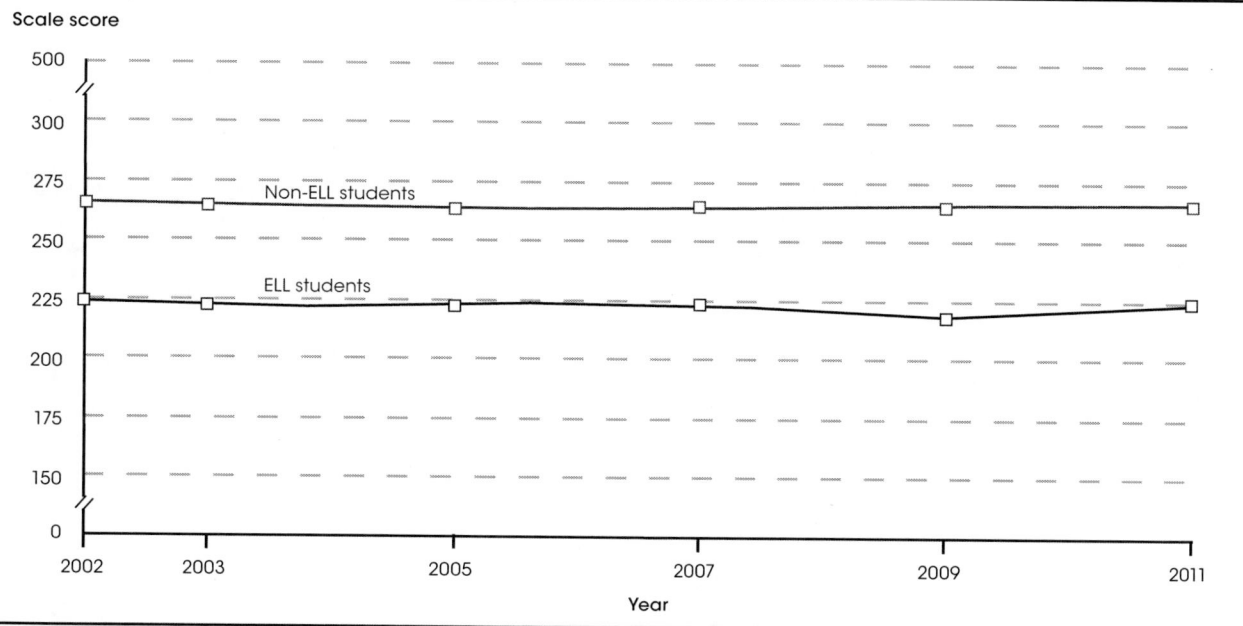

NOTE: Scale ranges from 0 to 500.
SOURCE: U.S. Department of Education, National Center for Education Statistics, National Assessment of Educational Progress (NAEP), selected years, 2002–11 Reading Assessments, NAEP Data Explorer. See *Digest of Education Statistics 2012*, table 142.

For more information, see the Reader's Guide and the Guide to Sources.

subgroups on the standardized assessment. In 2011, the achievement gap between non-ELL and ELL students was 36 points at the 4th-grade level and 44 points at the 8th-grade level. At grade 4, this achievement gap was not measurably different from that in any assessment year since 2002. At grade 8, the achievement gap between non-ELL and ELL students in reading scores was 3 points smaller in 2011 than in 2009 (47 points), but not measurably different from the achievement gap in 2002.

Reference table: *Digest of Education Statistics 2012*, tables 47, 142

Glossary: Achievement gap, English language learner, Public school

For more information, see the Reader's Guide and the Guide to Sources.

This page intentionally left blank.

Indicator 13
Children and Youth With Disabilities

The number of children and youth ages 3–21 receiving special education services was 6.4 million in 2010–11, or about 13 percent of all public school students. Some 37 percent of the students receiving special education services had specific learning disabilities.

Enacted in 1975, the Individuals with Disabilities Education Act (IDEA), formerly known as The Education for All Handicapped Children Act (EAHCA), mandates the provision of a free and appropriate public school education for eligible children and youth ages 3–21. Eligible children and youth are those identified by a team of professionals as having a disability that adversely affects academic performance and as being in need of special education and related services. Data collection activities to monitor compliance with IDEA began in 1976. From school years 1980–81 through 2004–05, the number of children and youth ages 3–21 who received special education services increased, as did their percentage of total public school students. The number and percentage of children and youth served under IDEA have declined each year from 2005–06 through 2010–11. In 1980–81, some 4.1 million children and youth ages 3–21 received special education services. The number of children and youth served under IDEA increased to 6.7 million in 2004–05, or about 14 percent of total public school enrollment. By 2010–11, the number of children and youth receiving services declined to 6.4 million, corresponding to 13 percent of total public school enrollment.

A greater percentage of children and youth ages 3–21 received special education services under IDEA for specific learning disabilities than for any other type of disability in 2010–11. A specific learning disability is a disorder in one or more of the basic psychological processes involved in understanding or using language, spoken or written, that may manifest itself in an imperfect ability to listen, think, speak, read, write, spell, or do mathematical calculations. In 2010–11, some 37 percent of all children and youth receiving special education services had specific learning disabilities, 22 percent

Figure 1. Percentage distribution of children ages 3–21 served under the Individuals with Disabilities Education Act (IDEA), Part B, by disability type: School year 2010–11

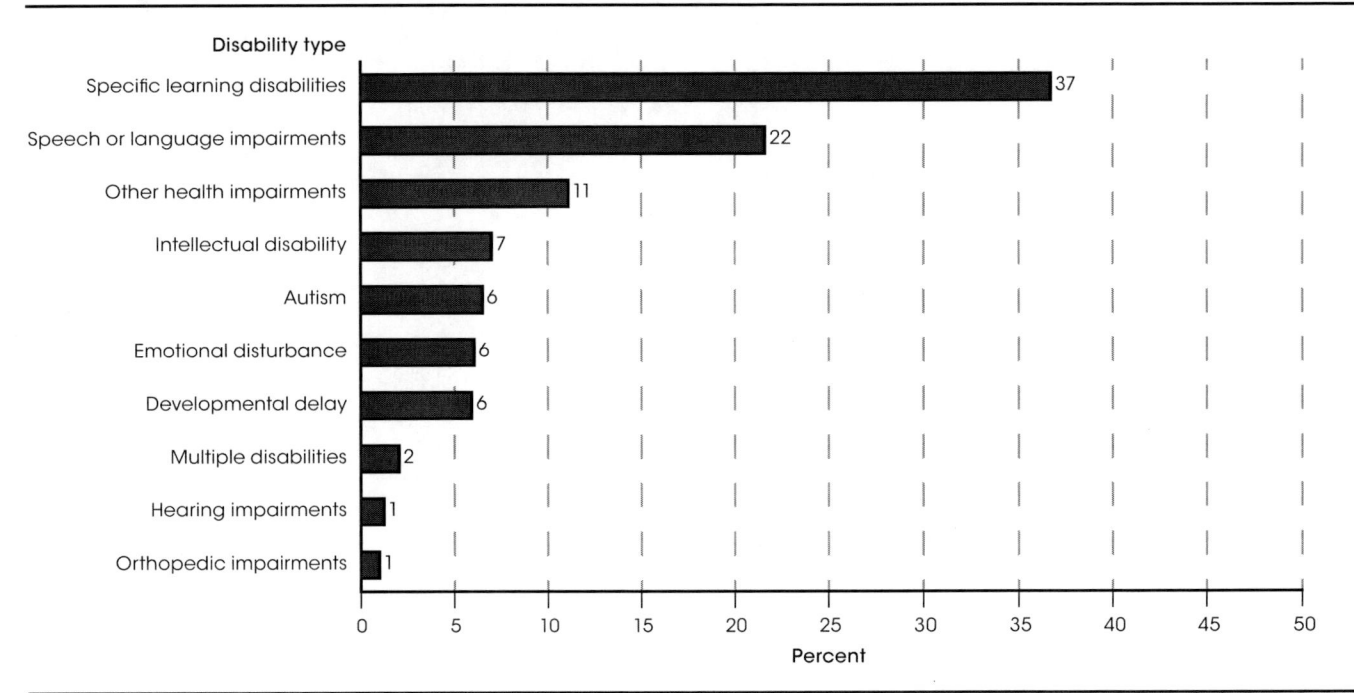

Disability type	Percent
Specific learning disabilities	37
Speech or language impairments	22
Other health impairments	11
Intellectual disability	7
Autism	6
Emotional disturbance	6
Developmental delay	6
Multiple disabilities	2
Hearing impairments	1
Orthopedic impairments	1

NOTE: Deaf-blindness, traumatic brain injury, and visual impairments are not shown because they each account for less than 1 percent of children served under IDEA. Due to categories not shown, detail does not sum to total.
SOURCE: U.S. Department of Education, Office of Special Education Programs, Individuals with Disabilities Education Act (IDEA) database, retrieved from https://www.ideadata.org/DACAnalyticTool/Intro_2.asp. See *Digest of Education Statistics 2012*, table 48.

For more information, see the Reader's Guide and the Guide to Sources.

Chapter: 2/Participation in Education
Section: Elementary/Secondary Enrollment

had speech or language impairments, and 11 percent had other health impairments (includes having limited strength, vitality, or alertness due to chronic or acute health problems such as a heart condition, tuberculosis, rheumatic fever, nephritis, asthma, sickle cell anemia, hemophilia, epilepsy, lead poisoning, leukemia, or diabetes). Students with disabilities such as intellectual disabilities, emotional disturbances, developmental delay, and autism each accounted for between 6 and 7 percent of children and youth served under IDEA. Children and youth with multiple disabilities; hearing impairments, orthopedic impairments, and visual impairments; traumatic brain injury; and deaf-blindness each accounted for 2 percent or less of children served under IDEA.

About 95 percent of school-age children and youth ages 6–21 who were served under IDEA in school year 2010–11 were enrolled in regular schools. Three percent of children and youth ages 6–21 who were served under IDEA were enrolled in separate schools (public or private) for students with disabilities; 1 percent were placed by their parents in regular private schools; and less than 1 percent each were in separate residential facilities (public and private), homebound or in hospitals, or in correctional facilities.

Figure 2. Percentage of students ages 6–21 served under the Individuals with Disabilities Education Act (IDEA), Part B, placed in a regular public school environment, by amount of time spent inside general classes: Selected school years 1990–91 through 2010–11

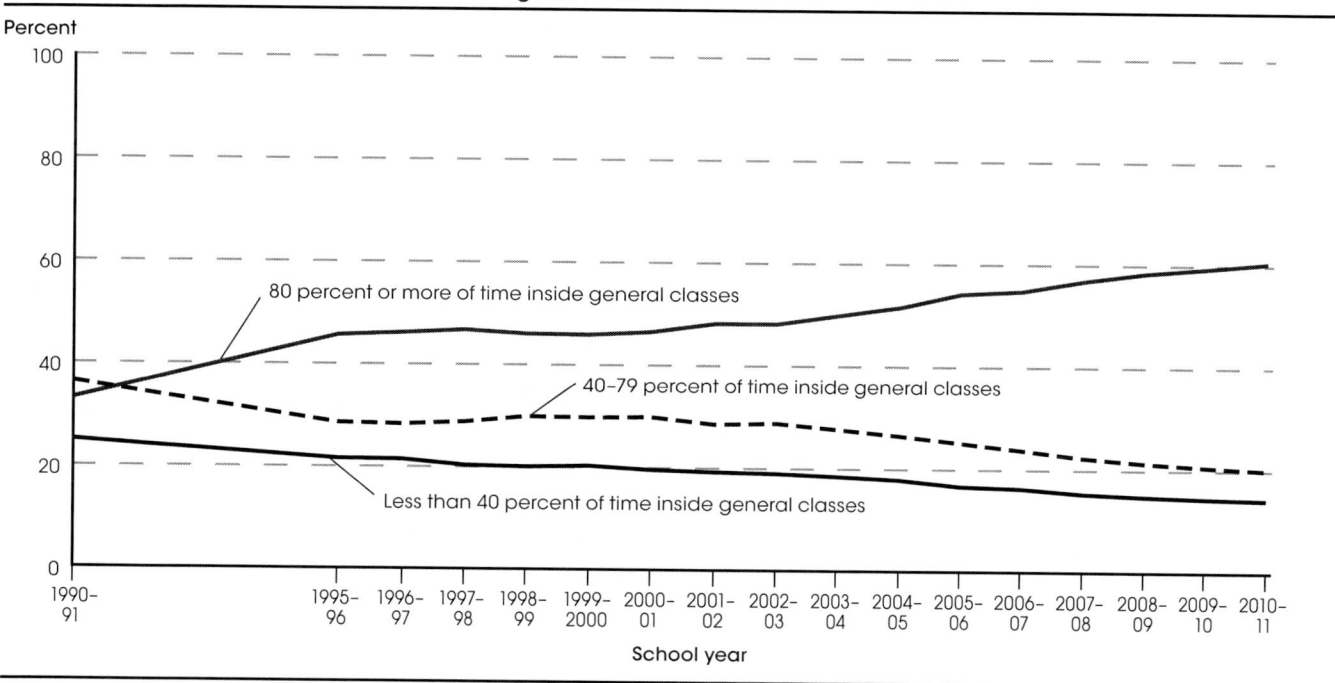

NOTE: Detail may not sum to totals because of rounding.
SOURCE: U.S. Department of Education, Office of Special Education Programs, Annual Report to Congress on the Implementation of the Individuals with Disabilities Education Act (IDEA), selected years, 1990–2009; and IDEA database, retrieved from http://www.ideadata.org/PartBdata.asp. See *Digest of Education Statistics 2012*, table 50.

Among all children and youth ages 6–21 who were served by IDEA and enrolled in regular schools, the percentage of children and youth who spent most of their school day in general classes (80 percent or more inside their general class) was highest in 2010–11. For example, in 2010–11, some 61 percent of these children and youth spent most of their school day in general class, compared to 46 percent in 1995–96 and 47 percent in 2000–01. In 2010–11, the percentage of students served under IDEA who spent most of their school day in general classes was highest for students with speech or language impairments (86 percent). Sixty-five percent each of students with specific learning disabilities and 64 percent of students with visual impairments spent most of their school day in general classes. In contrast, 18 percent of students with intellectual disabilities and 13 percent of students with multiple disabilities spent most of the school day in general classes.

Reference table: *Digest of Education Statistics 2012*, tables 48, 50

Glossary: Disabilities, Individuals with Disabilities Education Act (IDEA), Regular school

For more information, see the Reader's Guide and the Guide to Sources.

Indicator 14
Undergraduate Enrollment

Chapter: 2/Participation in Education
Section: Postsecondary Enrollment

Total undergraduate enrollment in degree-granting postsecondary institutions increased by 37 percent in the most recent decade, from 13.2 million students in fall 2000 to 17.6 million in fall 2009. By 2011, some 18.1 million undergraduate students were enrolled, a decrease of less than 1 percent from 2010.

In the most recent decade, total undergraduate enrollment in degree-granting postsecondary institutions increased from 13.2 million students in fall 2000 to 17.6 million in fall 2009. Undergraduate enrollment increased at a faster rate between 2000 and 2009 (34 percent) than during the 1980s (12 percent) and the 1990s (7 percent); during the 1970s, the rate of growth was 36 percent. During the two most recent survey years, 2010 and 2011, undergraduate enrollment decreased by less than 1 percent. Between 2011 and 2021, undergraduate enrollment is expected to increase to 20.3 million students. This will reflect a slower rate of increase (12 percent) than during the early 2000s.

Figure 1. Actual and projected undergraduate enrollment in degree-granting postsecondary institutions, by sex: Fall 1970–2021

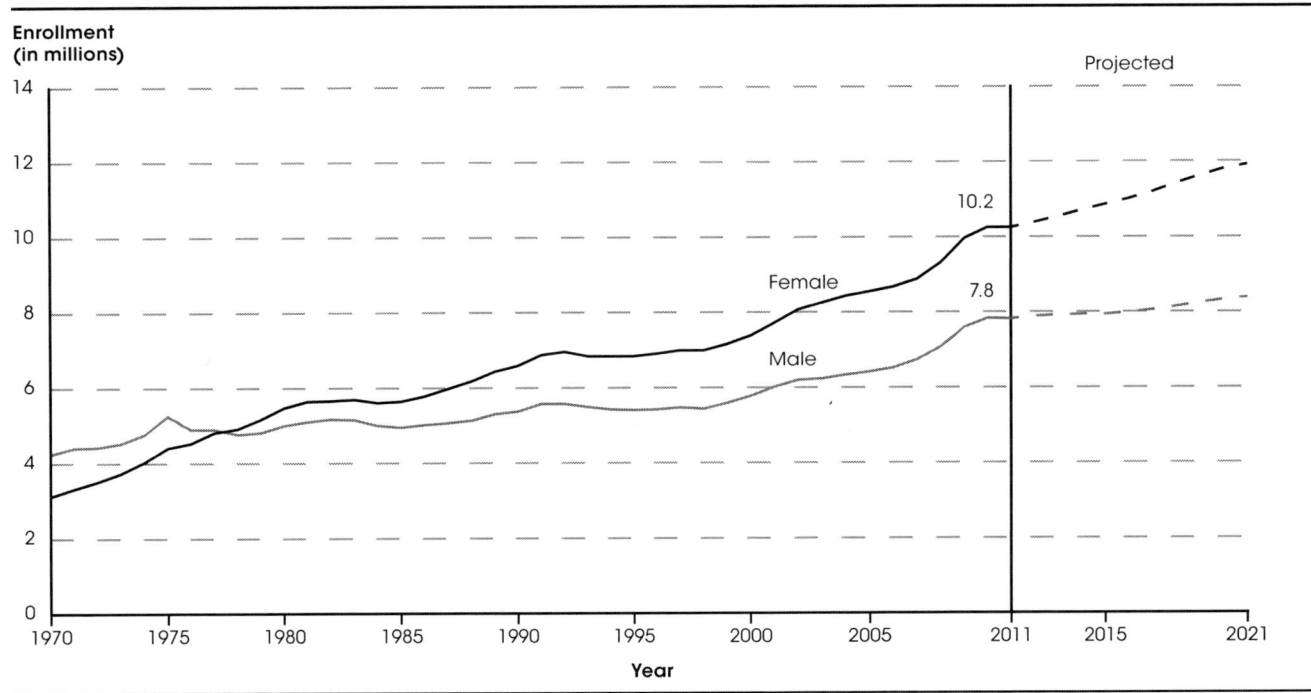

NOTE: Projections are based on data through 2011. Data include unclassified undergraduate students. Data through 1995 are for institutions of higher education, while later data are for degree-granting institutions. Degree-granting institutions grant associate's or higher degrees and participate in Title IV federal financial aid programs. The degree-granting classification is very similar to the earlier higher education classification, but it includes more 2-year colleges and excludes a few higher education institutions that did not grant degrees. Some data have been revised from previously published figures.
SOURCE: U.S. Department of Education, National Center for Education Statistics, Higher Education General Information Survey (HEGIS), "Fall Enrollment in Colleges and Universities" surveys, 1970 through 1985; Integrated Postsecondary Education Data System (IPEDS), "Fall Enrollment Survey" (IPEDS-EF:86–99); and IPEDS Spring 2001 through Spring 2012, Enrollment component. See *Digest of Education Statistics 2012*, tables 2 and 240 and *Digest of Education Statistics 2011*, table 214.

In 2011, there were 10.2 million female undergraduate students (57 percent of total enrollment) and 7.8 million male undergraduate students (43 percent). From 1970 to 1979, female enrollment increased by 66 percent, while male enrollment increased by 13 percent. The larger increase in the number of female students resulted in females accounting for the majority of undergraduate enrollment beginning in 1978. In more recent years, the increases in enrollment for female and male students have been more similar. Between 2000 and 2009, female enrollment increased by 35 percent, while male enrollment increased by 31 percent. Female enrollment is expected to increase by 16 percent (from 10.2 to 11.9 million students) between 2011 and 2021, while male enrollment is expected to increase by 7 percent (from 7.8 to 8.4 million students).

For more information, see the Reader's Guide and the Guide to Sources.

Chapter: 2/Participation in Education
Section: Postsecondary Enrollment

Figure 2. Actual and projected undergraduate enrollment in degree-granting postsecondary institutions, by attendance status: Fall 1970–2021

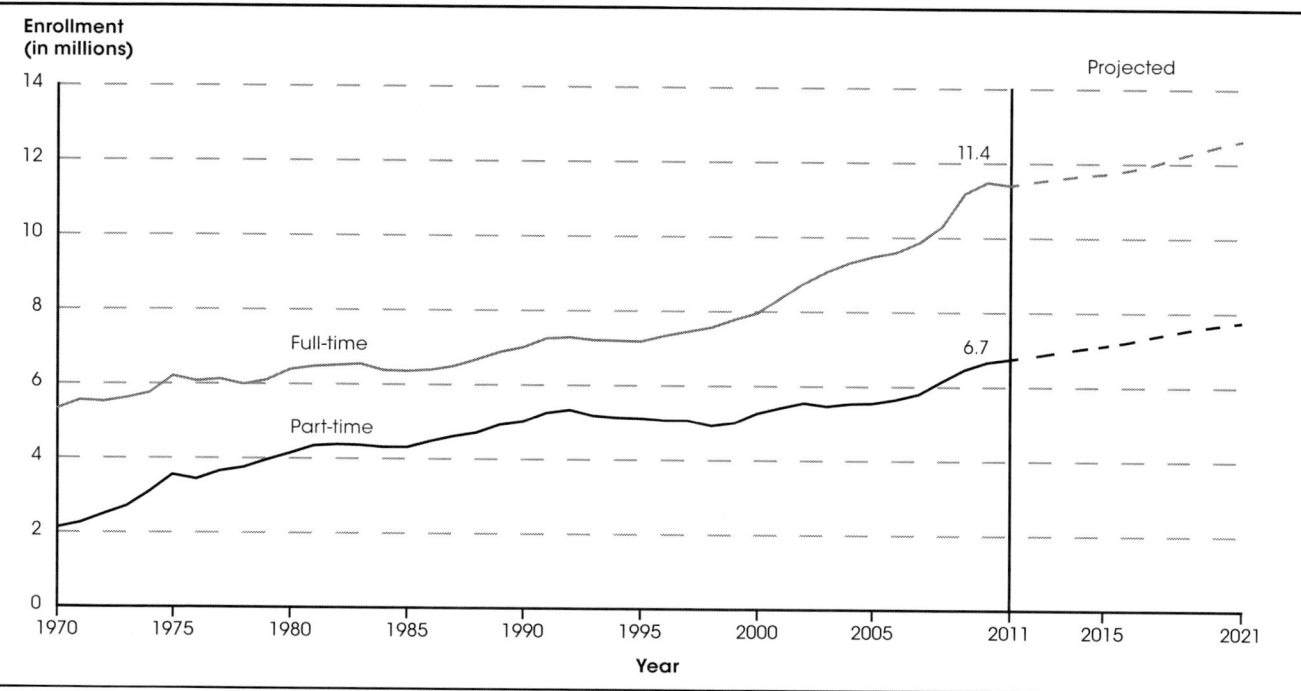

NOTE: Projections are based on data through 2011. Data include unclassified undergraduate students. Data through 1995 are for institutions of higher education, while later data are for degree-granting institutions. Degree-granting institutions grant associate's or higher degrees and participate in Title IV federal financial aid programs. The degree-granting classification is very similar to the earlier higher education classification, but it includes more 2-year colleges and excludes a few higher education institutions that did not grant degrees. Some data have been revised from previously published figures.
SOURCE: U.S. Department of Education, National Center for Education Statistics, Higher Education General Information Survey (HEGIS), "Fall Enrollment in Colleges and Universities" surveys, 1970 through 1985; Integrated Postsecondary Education Data System (IPEDS), "Fall Enrollment Survey" (IPEDS-EF:86-99); and IPEDS Spring 2001 through Spring 2012, Enrollment component. See *Digest of Education Statistics 2012*, tables 2 and 240 and *Digest of Education Statistics 2011*, table 214.

In 2011, there were 11.4 million full-time undergraduate students and 6.7 million part-time undergraduate students. From fall 1970 to fall 2011, the number of full-time undergraduate students in postsecondary degree-granting institutions more than doubled, and the number of part-time students more than tripled. However, the patterns of increase shifted over this period: During the 1970s, full-time undergraduate enrollment increased by 15 percent, while part-time undergraduate enrollment increased by 88 percent. During the 1980s, part-time undergraduate enrollment also experienced a larger percentage increase (19 percent) than did full-time undergraduate enrollment (8 percent). Since that period, full-time undergraduate enrollment has increased more rapidly than part-time undergraduate enrollment.

During the 1990s, full-time undergraduate enrollment increased by 11 percent, compared with a less than 1 percent increase for part-time undergraduate enrollment. Between 2000 and 2009, full-time undergraduate enrollment increased by 41 percent, compared with 23 percent for part-time undergraduate enrollment. Between the two most recent survey years, 2010 and 2011, full-time undergraduate enrollment decreased by 1 percent, while part-time undergraduate enrollment increased by 1 percent. Between 2011 and 2021, part-time undergraduate enrollment is projected to increase by 15 percent (from 6.7 to 7.7 million students), faster than full-time undergraduate enrollment is projected to increase (11 percent, from 11.4 to 12.6 million students).

For more information, see the Reader's Guide and the Guide to Sources.

Chapter: 2/Participation in Education
Section: Postsecondary Enrollment

Figure 3. Actual and projected undergraduate enrollment in degree-granting postsecondary institutions, by control of institution: Fall 1970–2021

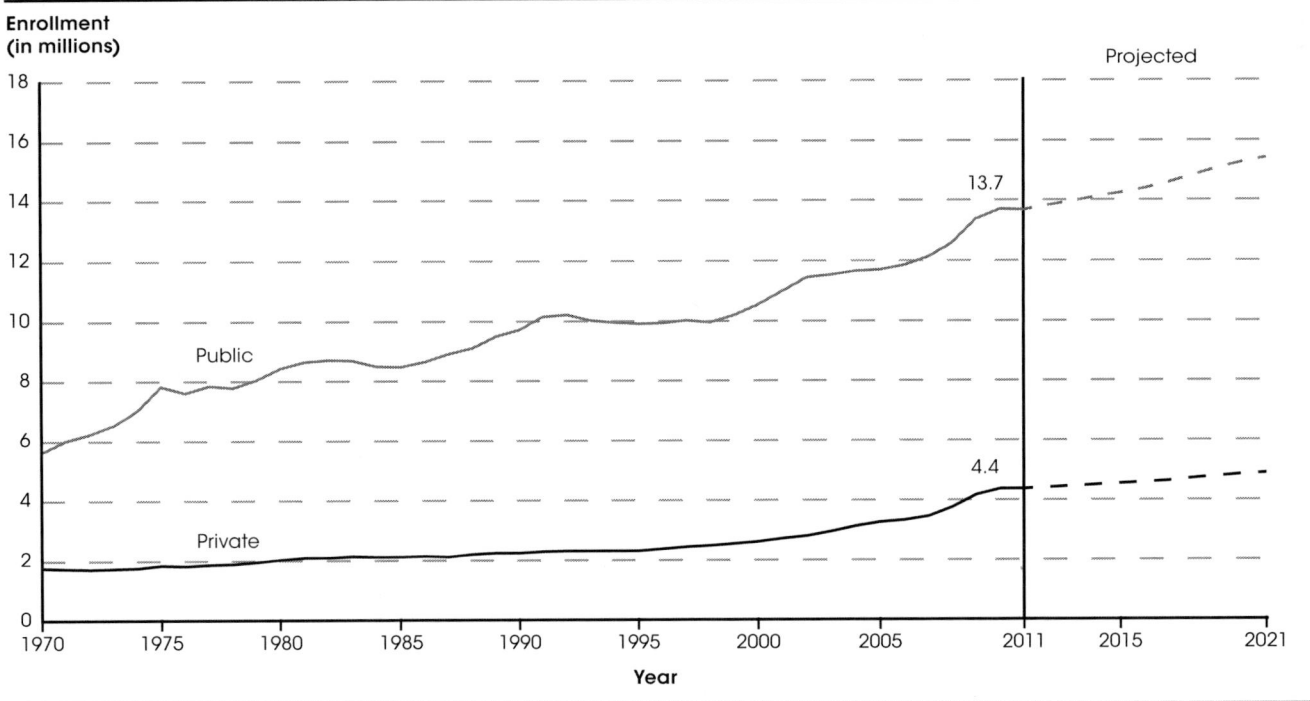

NOTE: Projections are based on data through 2011. Data include unclassified undergraduate students. Data through 1995 are for institutions of higher education, while later data are for degree-granting institutions. Degree-granting institutions grant associate's or higher degrees and participate in Title IV federal financial aid programs. The degree-granting classification is very similar to the earlier higher education classification, but it includes more 2-year colleges and excludes a few higher education institutions that did not grant degrees. Some data have been revised from previously published figures.
SOURCE: U.S. Department of Education, National Center for Education Statistics, Higher Education General Information Survey (HEGIS), "Fall Enrollment in Colleges and Universities" surveys, 1970 through 1985; Integrated Postsecondary Education Data System (IPEDS), "Fall Enrollment Survey" (IPEDS-EF:86–99); and IPEDS Spring 2001 through Spring 2012, Enrollment component. See *Digest of Education Statistics 2012*, tables 2 and 240 and *Digest of Education Statistics 2011*, table 214.

Between fall 1970 and fall 2011, undergraduate enrollment at private nonprofit institutions increased by a lower percentage (57 percent) than at public institutions (144 percent). During this period, undergraduate enrollment at private nonprofit institutions increased from 1.7 to 2.7 million students, and undergraduate enrollment at public institutions increased from 5.6 to 13.7 million students. Undergraduate enrollment at private for-profit institutions increased by a large percentage between 1970 and 2011 compared with increases at private nonprofit and public institutions, but there were a relatively small number of undergraduate students enrolled at private for-profit institutions in 1970. Undergraduate enrollment at private for-profit institutions increased from 18,000 students in 1970 to 1.7 million in 2011. Most of this growth in the number of students occurred between 2000 and 2009; undergraduate enrollment at private for-profit institutions increased by 293 percent (from 0.4 to 1.6 million students). During the same period, undergraduate enrollment at private nonprofit institutions increased by 17 percent, and undergraduate enrollment at public institutions increased by 27 percent. As a result of these different rates of undergraduate enrollment growth, the proportion of all undergraduate students enrolled at private for-profit institutions increased from 3 percent in 2000 to 9 percent in 2009, while the proportion of all undergraduate students enrolled at private nonprofit institutions and public institutions decreased from 17 to 15 percent and from 80 to 76 percent, respectively. The distribution of undergraduate students remained the same in 2011 as that in 2009. More recently, the pattern of rapid undergraduate enrollment increases at private for-profit institutions compared with other types of institutions changed. Between the two most recent survey years, 2010 and 2011, undergraduate enrollment at private for-profit institutions decreased by 4 percent, while enrollment at private nonprofit institutions increased by 2 percent. At public institutions, undergraduate enrollment decreased by one-tenth of a percentage point.

For more information, see the Reader's Guide and the Guide to Sources.

Chapter: 2/Participation in Education
Section: Postsecondary Enrollment

Figure 4. Actual and projected undergraduate enrollment in degree-granting postsecondary institutions, by level of institution: Fall 1970–2021

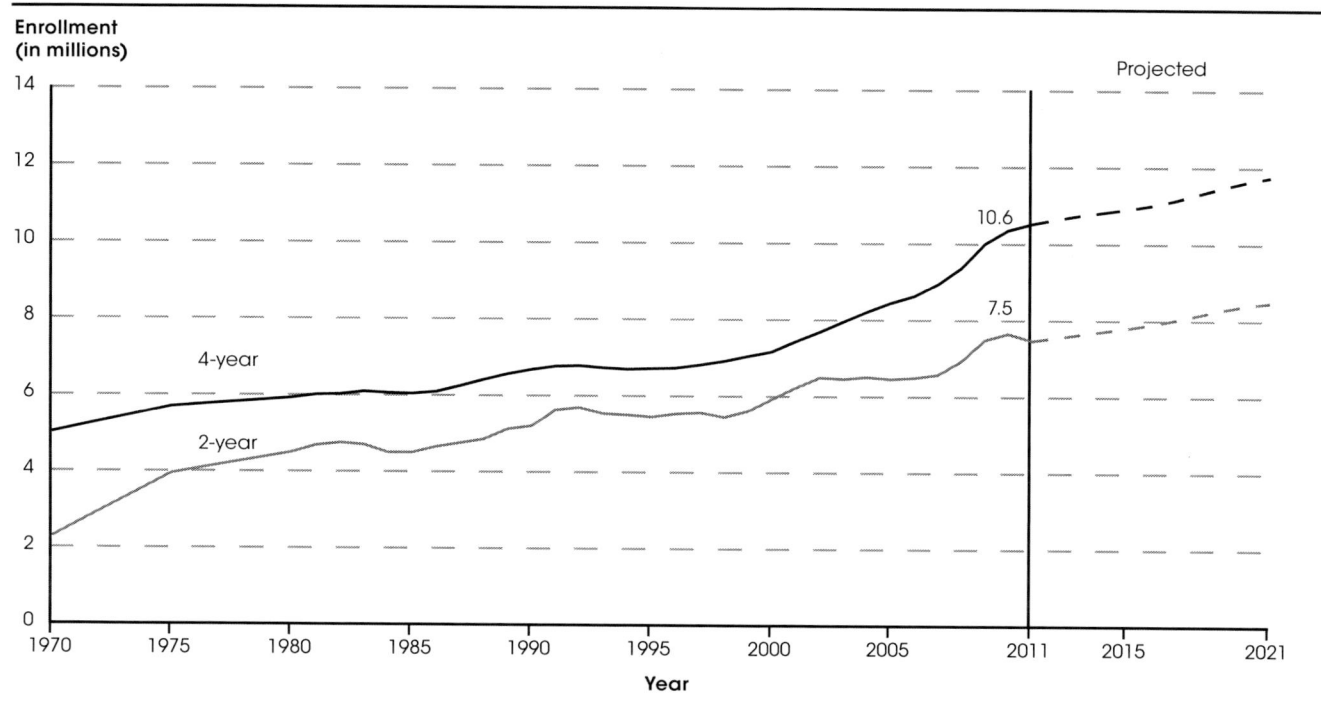

NOTE: Projections are based on data through 2011. Data include unclassified undergraduate students. Data through 1995 are for institutions of higher education, while later data are for degree-granting institutions. Degree-granting institutions grant associate's or higher degrees and participate in Title IV federal financial aid programs. The degree-granting classification is very similar to the earlier higher education classification, but it includes more 2-year colleges and excludes a few higher education institutions that did not grant degrees. Some data have been revised from previously published figures.
SOURCE: U.S. Department of Education, National Center for Education Statistics, Higher Education General Information Survey (HEGIS), "Fall Enrollment in Colleges and Universities" surveys, 1970 through 1985; Integrated Postsecondary Education Data System (IPEDS), "Fall Enrollment Survey" (IPEDS-EF:86–99); and IPEDS Spring 2001 through Spring 2012, Enrollment component. See *Digest of Education Statistics 2012*, tables 2 and 240.

From 1970 to 1980, undergraduate enrollment at 2-year institutions increased at a faster rate (95 percent, from 2.3 to 4.5 million students) than at 4-year institutions (18 percent, from 5.0 to 5.9 million students). The growth rate of undergraduate enrollment at 2-year institutions continued to outpace the rate at 4-year institutions during the 1980s and the 1990s. However, the pattern shifted between 2000 and 2009, when 4-year institutions had a larger percentage increase in undergraduate enrollment (39 percent, from 7.2 to 10.0 million students) than did 2-year institutions (26 percent, from 5.9 to 7.5 million students). Between 2000 and 2009, private for-profit 4-year institutions had the highest percentage increase in undergraduate enrollment among all types of institutions (470 percent, from 0.2 to 1.2 million students). Undergraduate enrollment increased by 30 percent at public 4-year institutions (from 4.8 to 6.3 million students) and by 19 percent at private nonprofit 4-year institutions (from 2.2 to 2.6 million students). Private for-profit 2-year institutions had the second largest increase in undergraduate enrollment (100 percent, from 0.2 to 0.4 million students) among all types of institutions after private for-profit 4-year institutions. Undergraduate enrollment increased by 25 percent at public 2-year institutions (from 5.7 to 7.1 million students). In contrast, undergraduate enrollment at private nonprofit 2-year institutions decreased by 41 percent, from 59,000 to 35,000 students, during the same period. Between the two most recent survey years, 2010 and 2011, only private nonprofit 2-year institutions experienced an increase in undergraduate enrollment (6 percent). Private for-profit 2-year institutions experienced the largest decrease during this period (10 percent, from 430,000 to 385,000 students). Overall in 2011, some 58 percent of undergraduate students were enrolled at 4-year institutions (10.6 million students), compared with 42 percent at 2-year institutions (7.5 million students).

Reference tables: *Digest of Education Statistics 2012*, tables 2, 240; *Digest of Education Statistics 2011*, table 214

Glossary: 2-year institution, 4-year institution, For-profit institution, Full-time enrollment, Higher education institutions, Nonprofit institution, Part-time enrollment, Private institution, Public school or institution, Undergraduate students

For more information, see the Reader's Guide and the Guide to Sources.

Chapter: 2/Participation in Education
Section: Postsecondary Enrollment

Indicator 15
Postbaccalaureate Enrollment

Total enrollment in postbaccalaureate degree programs increased from 2.2 million students in fall 2000 to 2.8 million in fall 2009, the largest percent increase (33 percent) of any decade since the 1970s. By fall 2011, some 2.9 million students were enrolled in postbaccalaureate degree programs.

In fall 2011, some 2.9 million students were enrolled in postbaccalaureate degree programs. Postbaccalaureate degree programs include master's and doctoral programs as well as programs formerly classified as first-professional, such as law, medicine, and dentistry. Postbaccalaureate enrollment increased at a faster rate (33 percent) between fall 2000 and fall 2009 than in any decade since the 1970s. Enrollment increased by 30 percent in the 1970s; it also increased throughout the 1980s and 1990s, but at slower rates (11 and 13 percent, respectively). Between 2010 and 2011, the two most recent survey years, postbaccalaureate enrollment decreased by less than 1 percent. Between fall 2011 and fall 2021, postbaccalaureate enrollment is projected to increase to 3.5 million, resulting in a slower rate of increase (18 percent) than during the early 2000s.

Figure 1. Actual and projected postbaccalaureate enrollment in degree-granting postsecondary institutions, by sex: Fall 1970–2021

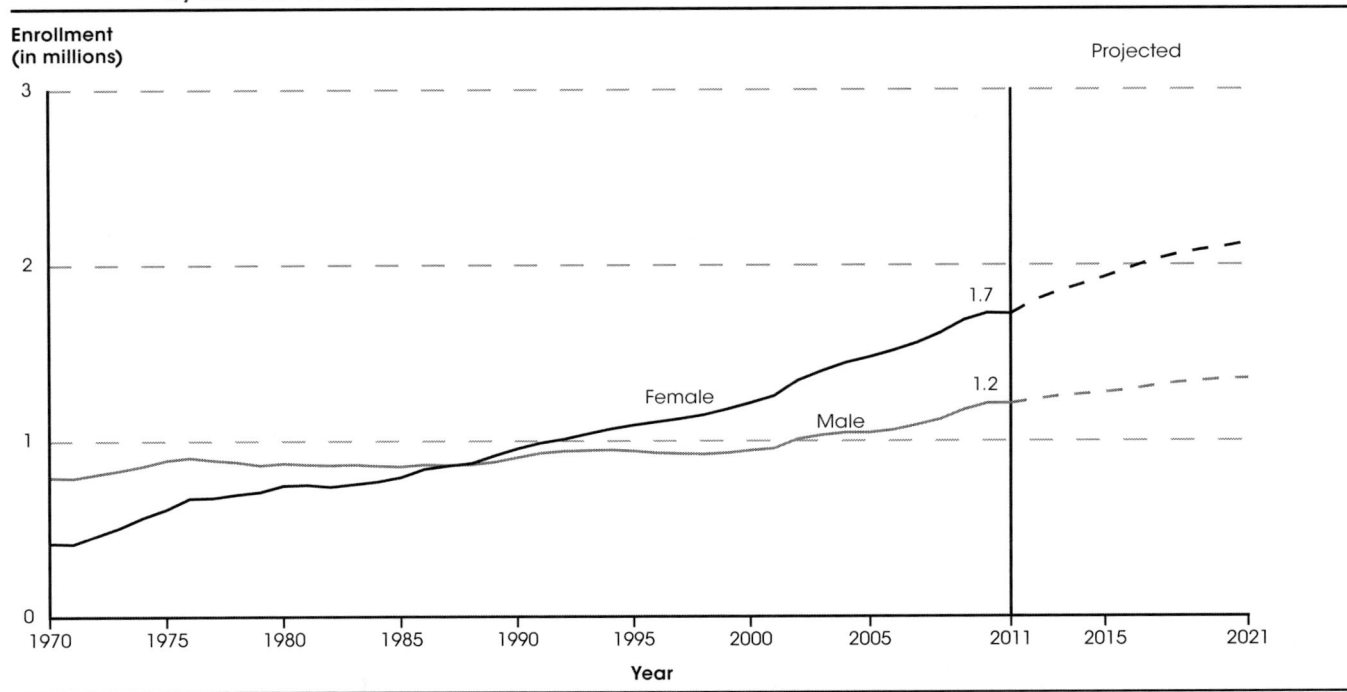

NOTE: Projections are based on data through 2011. Data include students in postbaccalaureate degree programs and unclassified graduate students. Data through 1995 are for institutions of higher education, while later data are for degree-granting institutions. Degree-granting institutions grant associate's or higher degrees and participate in Title IV federal financial aid programs. The degree-granting classification is very similar to the earlier higher education classification, but it includes more 2-year colleges and excludes a few higher education institutions that did not grant degrees.
SOURCE: U.S. Department of Education, National Center for Education Statistics, Higher Education General Information Survey (HEGIS), "Fall Enrollment in Colleges and Universities" surveys, 1970 through 1985; Integrated Postsecondary Education Data System (IPEDS), "Fall Enrollment Survey" (IPEDS-EF:86–99); and IPEDS Spring 2001 through Spring 2012, Enrollment component. See *Digest of Education Statistics 2012*, tables 2 and 241.

In fall 2011, some 1.7 million postbaccalaureate students were female (59 percent of enrollment) and 1.2 million were male (41 percent). By comparison, in fall 1975 females accounted for 41 percent of enrollment and males accounted for 59 percent. From fall 1970 to fall 1989, female enrollment more than doubled, while male enrollment increased by 11 percent. The larger increase in the number of female students resulted in females accounting for 50 percent of postbaccalaureate enrollment beginning in 1988, with 875,000 female students out of a total enrollment of 1.7 million students. In more recent years, female enrollment has continued to increase at a faster rate than male enrollment. Between fall 2000 and fall 2009, female enrollment increased by 39 percent, and male enrollment increased by 24 percent. Between 2010 and 2011, both female and male postbaccalaureate enrollment decreased by less than 1 percent. Female enrollment is projected to increase by 22 percent between fall 2011 and fall 2021, from 1.7 to 2.1 million students, while male enrollment is expected to increase by 12 percent, from 1.2 to 1.4 million students.

For more information, see the Reader's Guide and the Guide to Sources.

Chapter: 2/Participation in Education
Section: Postsecondary Enrollment

Figure 2. Actual and projected postbaccalaureate enrollment in degree-granting postsecondary institutions, by attendance status: Fall 1970–2021

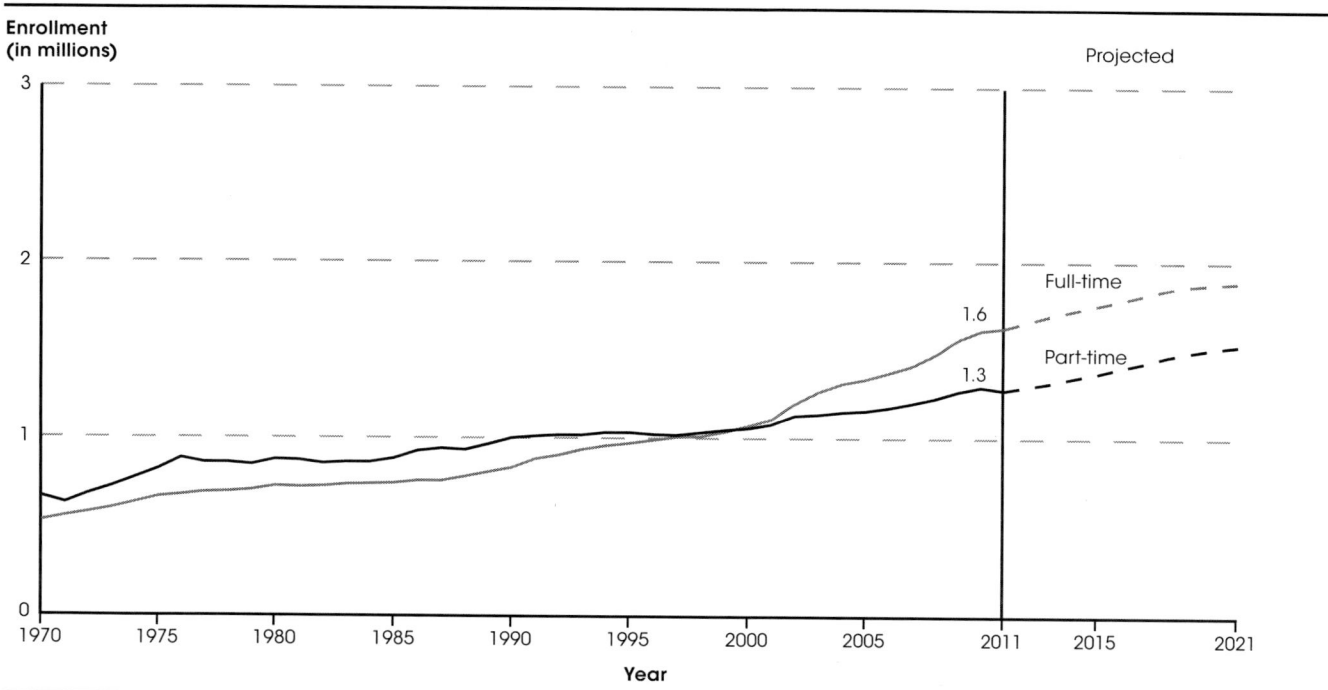

NOTE: Projections are based on data through 2011. Data include students in postbaccalaureate degree programs and unclassified graduate students. Data through 1995 are for institutions of higher education, while later data are for degree-granting institutions. Degree-granting institutions grant associate's or higher degrees and participate in Title IV federal financial aid programs. The degree-granting classification is very similar to the earlier higher education classification, but it includes more 2-year colleges and excludes a few higher education institutions that did not grant degrees.
SOURCE: U.S. Department of Education, National Center for Education Statistics, Higher Education General Information Survey (HEGIS), "Fall Enrollment in Colleges and Universities" surveys, 1970 through 1985; Integrated Postsecondary Education Data System (IPEDS), "Fall Enrollment Survey" (IPEDS-EF:86-99); and IPEDS Spring 2001 through Spring 2012, Enrollment component. See *Digest of Education Statistics 2012*, tables 2 and 241.

In fall 2011, there were 1.6 million full-time students and 1.3 million part-time students. From fall 1970 through fall 2011, the number of full-time postbaccalaureate students more than tripled, and the number of part-time postbaccalaureate students almost doubled. Since fall 1970, full-time enrollment has consistently increased at a faster rate than part-time enrollment. During the 1970s, full-time enrollment increased by 33 percent, while part-time enrollment increased by 27 percent. During the 1980s, full-time enrollment also increased by a larger percentage (11 percent) than part-time enrollment (10 percent). During the 1990s, full-time enrollment increased by 24 percent, while part-time enrollment increased by 5 percent. Between fall 2000 and fall 2009, full-time enrollment increased by 45 percent, while part-time enrollment increased by 20 percent. Most recently, full-time enrollment increased by 1 percent, while part-time enrollment decreased by 1 percent between fall 2010 and fall 2011. This pattern of larger percent increases in full-time enrollment is not expected to continue between fall 2011 and fall 2021, with full-time enrollment projected to increase by 16 percent and part-time enrollment projected to increase by 20 percent.

For more information, see the Reader's Guide and the Guide to Sources.

Participation in Education

Chapter: 2/Participation in Education
Section: Postsecondary Enrollment

Figure 3. Full-time postbaccalaureate enrollment in degree-granting postsecondary institutions, by control of institution: Fall 1970–2011

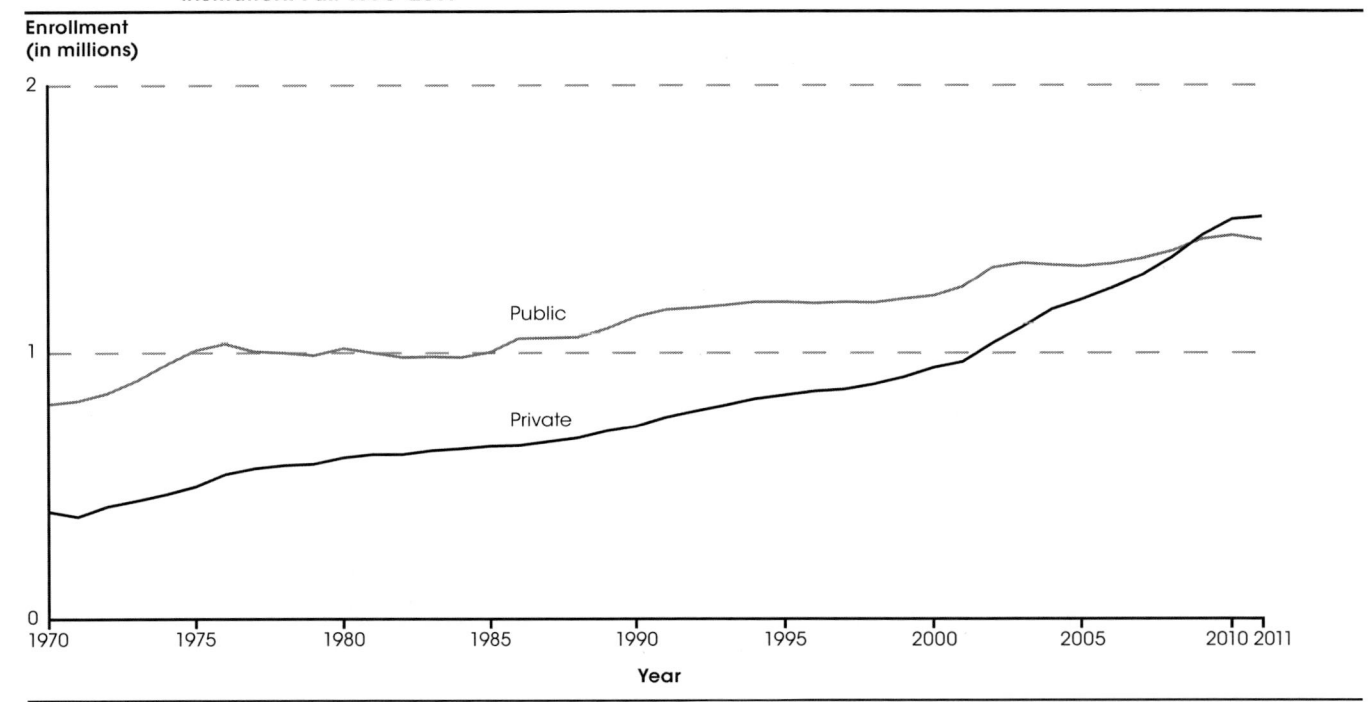

NOTE: Data include students in postbaccalaureate degree programs and unclassified graduate students. Data through 1995 are for institutions of higher education, while later data are for degree-granting institutions. Degree-granting institutions grant associate's or higher degrees and participate in Title IV federal financial aid programs. The degree-granting classification is very similar to the earlier higher education classification, but it includes more 2-year colleges and excludes a few higher education institutions that did not grant degrees.
SOURCE: U.S. Department of Education, National Center for Education Statistics, Higher Education General Information Survey (HEGIS), "Fall Enrollment in Colleges and Universities" surveys, 1970 through 1985; Integrated Postsecondary Education Data System (IPEDS), "Fall Enrollment Survey" (IPEDS-EF:86-99); and IPEDS Spring 2001 through Spring 2012, Enrollment component. See *Digest of Education Statistics 2012*, table 241.

Between fall 1970 and fall 2011, postbaccalaureate degree enrollment at private institutions nearly quadrupled, while the enrollment at public institutions increased by 76 percent. During this period, enrollment at private institutions increased from 0.4 to 1.5 million students, and enrollment at public institutions increased from 0.8 to 1.4 million. Since fall 1970, enrollment at private institutions has grown at a faster rate than at public institutions. During the 1970s, enrollment at private institutions increased by 44 percent, while enrollment at public institutions increased by 23 percent. During the 1980s, enrollment at private institutions also increased by a larger percentage (16 percent) than did enrollment at public institutions (7 percent). During the 1990s, enrollment at private institutions increased by 25 percent, compared with a 6 percent increase at public institutions. Between fall 2000 and fall 2009, enrollment at private institutions experienced its fastest rate of growth (52 percent), while enrollment at public institutions increased by 17 percent. In fall 2008, for the first time, private and public institutions each constituted 50 percent of total postbaccalaureate degree enrollment. From fall 2008 to fall 2011, enrollment at private institutions increased by 11 percent, and enrollment at public institutions increased by 3 percent. In fall 2011, some 52 percent of students were enrolled at private institutions, and 48 percent were enrolled at public institutions.

Reference tables: *Digest of Education Statistics 2012*, tables 2, 241

Glossary: For-profit institution, Full-time enrollment, Nonprofit institution, Part-time enrollment, Postbaccalaureate enrollment, Private institution, Public school or institution

For more information, see the Reader's Guide and the Guide to Sources.

This page intentionally left blank.

The indicators in this section of *The Condition of Education* measure aspects of elementary and secondary education in the United States. The indicators examine school characteristics and climate; principals, teachers and staff; elementary and secondary financial resources; student assessments; and other measures of the progress students make as they move through the education system, such as graduation rates.

In this section, particular attention is given to how various subgroups in the population proceed through school and attain different levels of education, as well as the factors that are associated with their progress along the way. The indicators on student achievement illustrate how students are performing on assessments in reading, mathematics, science, and other academic subject areas. Others examine aspects of the context of learning in elementary and secondary schools.

Indicators on elementary and secondary education and outcomes from previous editions of *The Condition of Education* not included in this volume are available at http://nces.ed.gov/programs/coe.

Chapter 3

Elementary and Secondary Education

Spotlight on School Characteristics and Climate
The Status of Rural Education 70

School Characteristics and Climate
Indicator 16. Characteristics of Public Elementary and Secondary Schools 78
Indicator 17. Concentration of Public School Students Eligible for Free or
 Reduced-Price Lunch 80
Indicator 18. Rates of School Crime 82
Indicator 19. Teachers and Pupil/Teacher Ratios 88

Finance
Indicator 20. Public School Revenue Sources... 90
Indicator 21. Public School Expenditures 94
Indicator 22. Education Expenditures by Country.. 98

Assessments
Indicator 23. Reading Performance 102
Indicator 24. Mathematics Performance 104
Indicator 25. Reading and Mathematics Score Trend 106
Indicator 26. International Assessments... 110

Student Effort, Persistence, and Progress
Indicator 27. High School Coursetaking 120
Indicator 28. Public High School Graduation Rates 124
Indicator 29. Status Dropout Rates 128

Transition to College
Indicator 30. Immediate Transition to College 132

Spotlight
The Status of Rural Education

In school year 2010–11, over half of all operating regular school districts and about one-third of all public schools were in rural areas, while about one-quarter of all public school students were enrolled in rural schools.

The National Center for Education Statistics (NCES) revised its definitions of school locale types in 2006 after working with the Census Bureau to create a new locale classification system. This urban-centric classification system has four major locale categories—city, suburban, town, and rural—each of which is divided into three subcategories. Cities and suburbs are subdivided into the categories *small, midsize,* or *large;* towns and rural areas are subdivided by their proximity to an urbanized area into the categories *fringe, distant,* or *remote.* Unlike the previous classification system, which differentiated towns on the basis of population size, this system differentiates towns and rural areas on the basis of their proximity to larger urban centers. This key feature allows NCES to identify and differentiate rural schools and school districts in relatively remote areas from those that may be located just outside an urban center.

In school year 2010–11, some 99,000 public elementary and secondary schools, located in 14,000 school districts, served over 49 million students in the United States (see NCES Rural Education in America website, tables A.1.a.-1, A.1.a.-2, and A.1.a.-3). The distribution of districts, schools, and students across locales highlights some key differences in the size and nature of education in rural America, compared with towns, suburbs, and cities.

In 2010–11, more than half of all operating regular school districts were located in rural areas (57 percent), while 20 percent of districts were located in suburban areas, 18 percent in towns, and 5 percent in cities.

Figure 1. Percentage distribution of public elementary and secondary students, schools, and districts, by locale: School year 2010–11

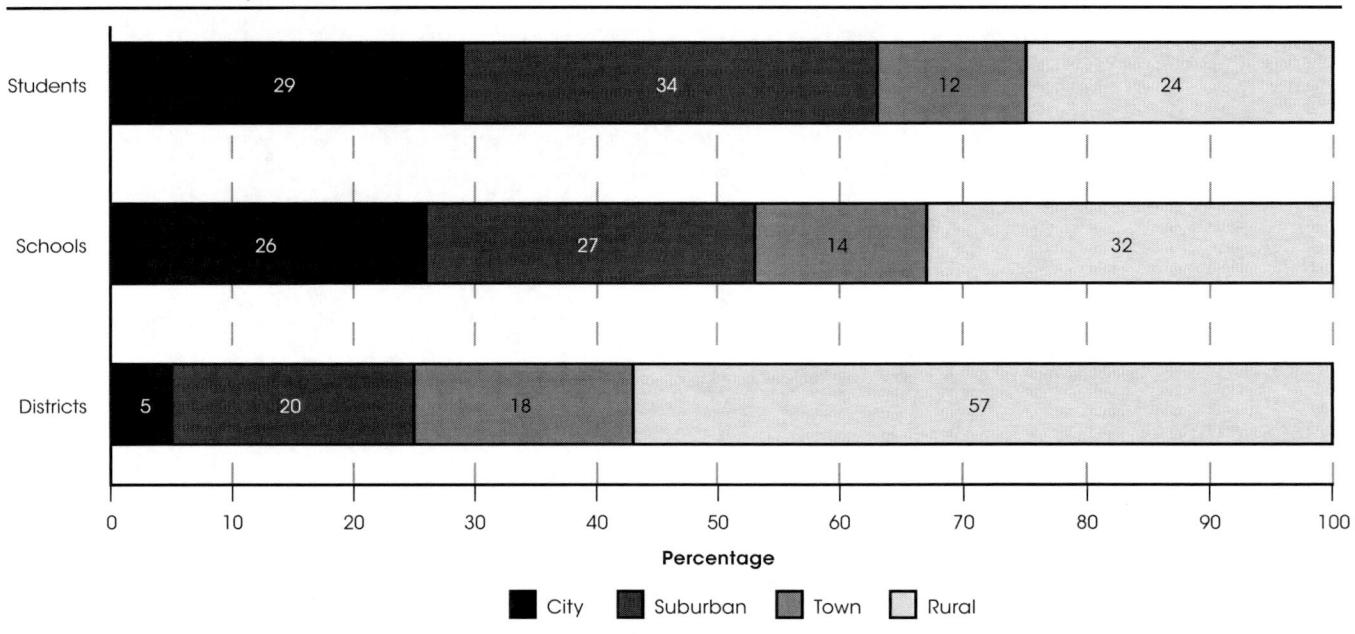

Category	City	Suburban	Town	Rural
Students	29	34	12	24
Schools	26	27	14	32
Districts	5	20	18	57

NOTE: Regular districts exclude regional education service agencies and supervisory union administrative centers, state-operated agencies, federally operated agencies, and other types of local education agencies, such as independent charter schools. Schools with no reported enrollment are included in school totals but excluded from student totals. Detail may not sum to totals because of rounding.
SOURCE: U.S. Department of Education, National Center for Education Statistics, Common Core of Data (CCD), "Local Education Agency Universe Survey," 2010–11 (versions 1a and 1b); "Public Elementary/Secondary School Universe Survey," 2010–11 (version 2a). See tables A.1.a.-1, A.1.a.-2, and A.1.a.-3 at http://nces.ed.gov/surveys/ruraled/.

For more information, see the Reader's Guide and the Guide to Sources.

Chapter: 3/Elementary and Secondary Education
Section: Spotlight

About one-third of the approximately 100,000 public schools in the United States in 2010–11 were located in rural areas (32,000), more than in suburbs (27,000), cities (26,000), or towns (14,000). Fewer students, however, were enrolled in public schools in rural areas than in suburbs and cities. Public schools in rural areas enrolled 12 million students, representing 24 percent of total enrollment, compared with 17 million in suburban areas (34 percent of enrollment) and 14 million in cities (29 percent of enrollment). The smallest share of enrollment in 2010–11 was in towns, which enrolled 6 million students, or 12 percent of total enrollment.

Rural public school systems differ from those in other locales in terms of the population they serve. In the 2010–11 school year, 52 percent of all public elementary and secondary school students were White, 16 percent were Black, 23 percent were Hispanic, 5 percent were Asian/Pacific Islander, 1 percent were American Indian/Alaska Native, and 2 percent were of two or more races (see NCES Rural Education in America website, table B.1.b.-1). In rural areas, 71 percent of public school students were White, 10 percent were Black, 13 percent were Hispanic, 2 percent were Asian/Pacific Islander, 2 percent were American Indian/Alaska Native, and 2 percent were of two or more races. These data do not include students in Bureau of Indian Education (BIE) schools.

Figure 2.   Percentage distribution of public elementary and secondary students, by locale and race/ethnicity: Fall 2010

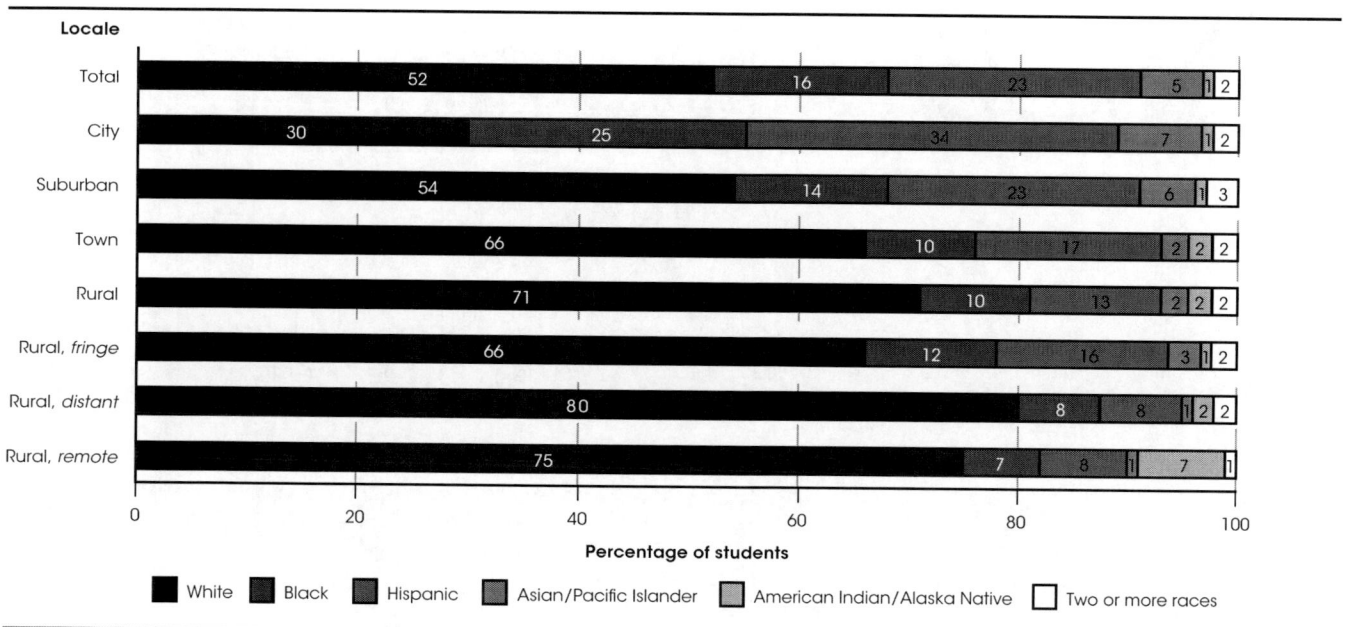

Locale	White	Black	Hispanic	Asian/Pacific Islander	American Indian/Alaska Native	Two or more races
Total	52	16	23	5	1	2
City	30	25	34	7	1	2
Suburban	54	14	23	6	1	3
Town	66	10	17	2	2	2
Rural	71	10	13	2	2	2
Rural, fringe	66	12	16	3	1	2
Rural, distant	80	8	8	1	2	2
Rural, remote	75	7	8	1	7	1

NOTE: Race/ethnicity information was not reported for 58,721 students. Race categories exclude persons of Hispanic ethnicity. Detail may not sum to totals because of rounding. Asian students and Pacific Islander students are shown separately in the reference table, but were combined into a single category for the purpose of this Spotlight. Students who identified as both Asian and Pacific Islander would be part of the "Two or more races" group.
SOURCE: U.S. Department of Education, National Center for Education Statistics, Common Core of Data (CCD), "Public Elementary/Secondary School Universe Survey," 2010–11 (version 1a). See table B.1.b.-1 at http://nces.ed.gov/surveys/ruraled/.

The percentage of students in public elementary and secondary schools who were White was higher in rural areas (71 percent) than in cities (30 percent), suburban areas (54 percent), and towns (66 percent). Conversely, the percentages of these students in rural areas who were Black, Hispanic, and Asian/Pacific Islander were lower than the corresponding percentages in cities and suburban areas. A higher percentage of students in rural areas and towns were American Indian/Alaska Native (2 percent each) than in cities and suburbs (1 percent each).

Within rural areas, a lower percentage of students in fringe rural areas were White (66 percent) than in remote rural (75 percent) and distant rural (80 percent). A greater proportion of students attending public schools in fringe rural areas were Black (12 percent), Hispanic (16 percent), and Asian/Pacific Islander (3 percent) than in distant rural and remote rural areas. However, 7 percent of students attending schools in remote rural areas were American Indian/Alaska Native, compared with 1 percent in fringe rural areas and 2 percent in distant rural areas.

A smaller percentage of school-age children in rural areas live below the poverty threshold than those in cities or towns. Using annual household income data collected by the American Community Survey (ACS), households in poverty are defined as those with an annual income below the poverty threshold. In 2009, that poverty threshold for a family of four was $22,050. In 2010, some 19 percent of children between the ages of 5 and 17 were living in families below the poverty threshold (see NCES Rural Education in America website, table A.1.a.-6). The percentage of children ages 5 to 17 in rural areas who were living in families in poverty (19 percent) was smaller than in cities and towns (25 and 21 percent, respectively).

For more information, see the Reader's Guide and the Guide to Sources.

However, a larger percentage of rural children lived in poverty than suburban children (19 vs. 15 percent). There were regional differences in the percentages of rural children living in poverty in 2010. The percentage of rural children living in poverty was highest in the South, at 22 percent, followed by the West (20 percent), Midwest (15 percent), and Northeast (12 percent).

Figure 3. Percentage of 5- to 17-year-olds in families living in poverty, by district locale and region: 2010

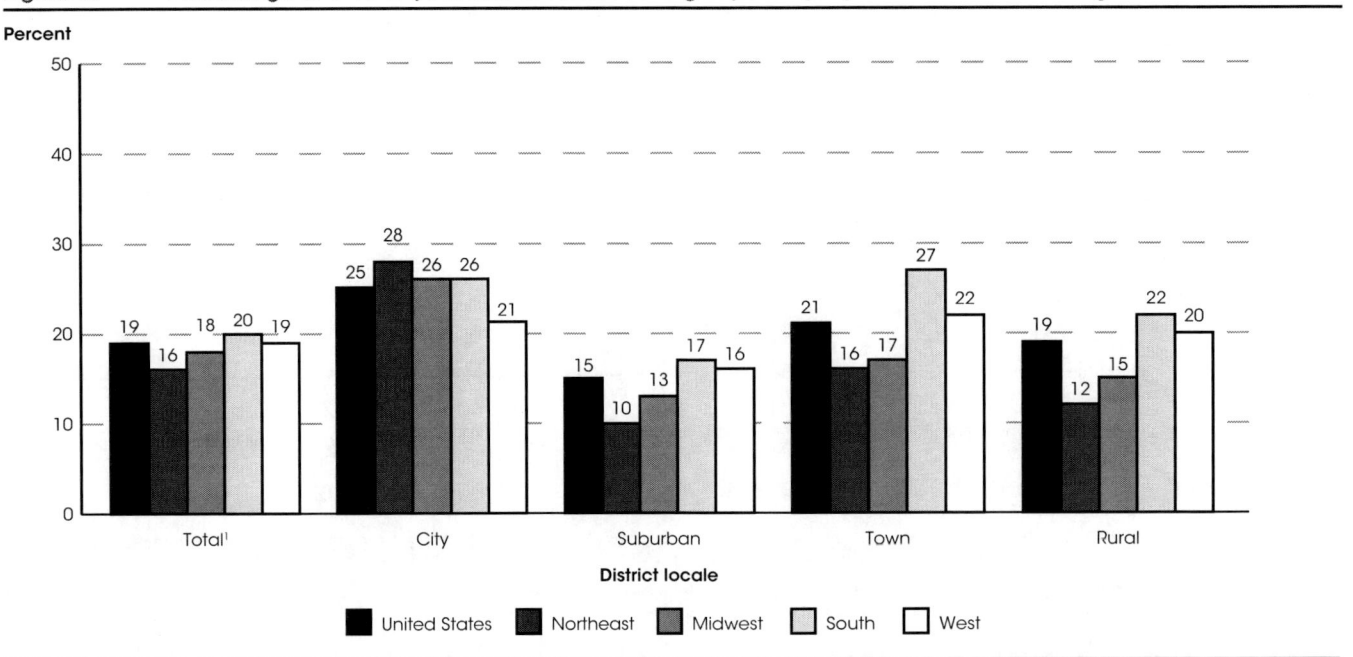

[1] Total includes data for children in Local Education Agencies that do not have urbanicity designations.
NOTE: Households in poverty are defined as those with an annual income below the poverty threshold. In 2009, that poverty threshold for a family of four was $22,050.
SOURCE: U.S. Department of Commerce, Census Bureau, "Small Area Income and Poverty Estimates." LEA dataset 2010; and U.S. Department of Education, National Center for Education Statistics, Common Core of Data, 2009–10, version 2a. See table A.1.a.-6 at http://nces.ed.gov/surveys/ruraled/.

A smaller percentage of rural students attended high-poverty schools than students in other locale types. During the 2010–11 school year, 48 percent of public elementary and secondary students nationwide were eligible for free or reduced-price lunch under the National School Lunch Program (see NCES Rural Education in America website, table B.1.e.-1). Using the percentage of students eligible for free or reduced-price lunch as a proxy for the poverty level within a school, high-poverty schools are defined, for the purposes of this analysis, as schools in which more than 75 percent of the students are eligible. The percentage of students in rural areas attending high-poverty schools (10 percent) was lower than the national percentage (20 percent). The percentage of students attending these schools was also lower than the percentage in cities (38 percent), suburbs (14 percent), and towns (15 percent).

For more information, see the Reader's Guide and the Guide to Sources.

Chapter: 3/Elementary and Secondary Education
Section: Spotlight

Figure 4. Percentage distribution of public elementary and secondary students, by locale and percentage of students in school eligible for free or reduced-price lunch (FRPL): Fall 2010

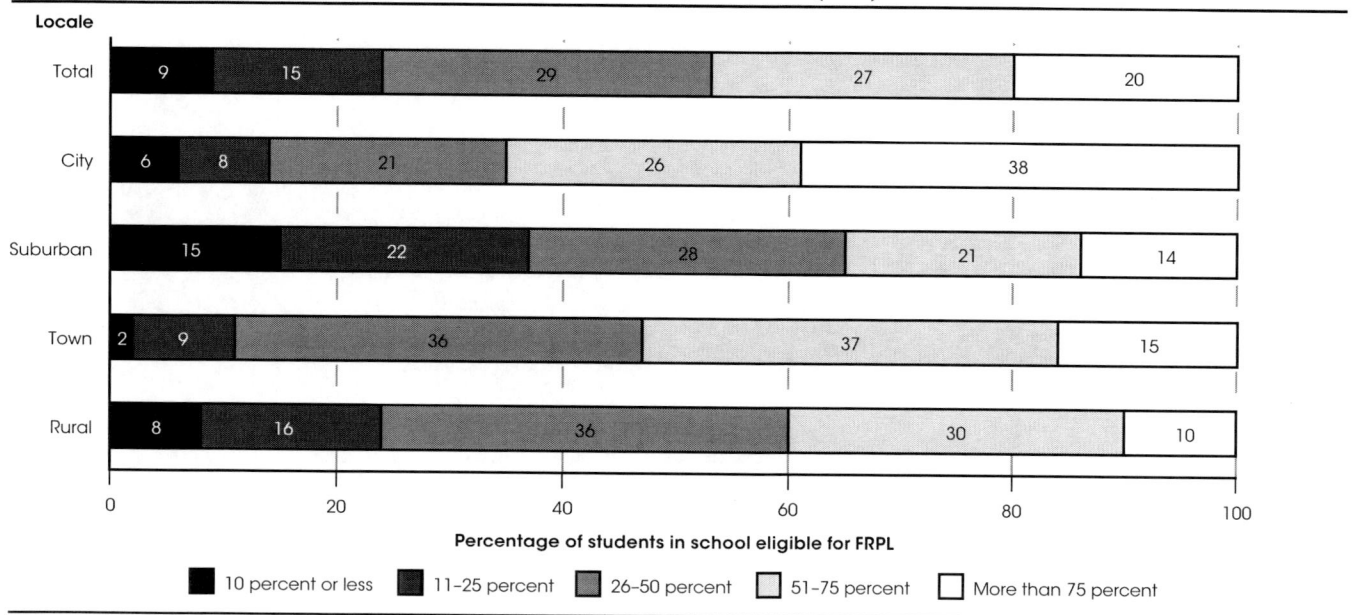

Locale	10 percent or less	11–25 percent	26–50 percent	51–75 percent	More than 75 percent
Total	9	15	29	27	20
City	6	8	21	26	38
Suburban	15	22	28	21	14
Town	2	9	36	37	15
Rural	8	16	36	30	10

NOTE: The National School Lunch Program is a federally assisted meal program. To be eligible, a student must be from a household with an income at or below 130 percent of the poverty threshold for free lunch or between 130 percent and 185 percent of the poverty threshold for reduced-price lunch. In total, 666 public schools with student enrollment did not report information on the number of students eligible for free or reduced-price lunch. Detail may not sum to totals because of rounding and missing data.
SOURCE: U.S. Department of Education, National Center for Education Statistics, Common Core of Data (CCD), "Public Elementary/Secondary School Universe Survey," 2010–11 (version 1a). See table B.1.e.-1 at http://nces.ed.gov/surveys/ruraled/.

Within the detailed rural locales, 19 percent of rural students in remote areas attended high-poverty schools in 2010–11, as did 11 percent in distant rural areas and 8 percent in fringe rural areas. Further, more than half of American Indian/Alaska Native and Black students (57 and 59 percent, respectively) in remote rural areas attended high-poverty schools, compared with 10 percent of White students, 29 percent of Hispanic students, 19 percent of Asian/Pacific Islander students, and 21 percent of students of two or more races.[2]

On average, public school students in rural areas perform better on the National Assessment of Educational Progress (NAEP) than their peers in cities and towns but generally not as well as their peers in suburban areas. Nationwide, 32 percent of 4th-grade public school students scored at or above the *Proficient* level on the 2011 NAEP reading assessment (see NCES Rural Education in America website, table B.2.a.-1). The percentage of 4th-graders in rural areas scoring at this achievement level (35 percent) was larger than in cities (26 percent) and towns (29 percent), but smaller than in suburban areas (37 percent). The pattern for 8th-grade public school students who scored at or above *Proficient* in reading was similar to that for 4th-graders, with 32 percent of 8th-graders in the United States scoring at this level overall. The percentage of 8th-graders in rural areas scoring at or above *Proficient* (33 percent) was larger than in cities (26 percent) and towns (30 percent) but smaller than in suburban areas (36 percent).

[2] Asian students and Pacific Islander students are shown separately in the reference table, but were combined into a single category for the purpose of this Spotlight. Students who identified as both Asian and Pacific Islander would be part of the "Two or more races" group.

For more information, see the Reader's Guide and the Guide to Sources.

Chapter: 3/Elementary and Secondary Education
Section: Spotlight

Figure 5a. Percentage distribution of 4th-grade public school students across National Assessment of Educational Progress (NAEP) reading achievement levels, by locale: 2011

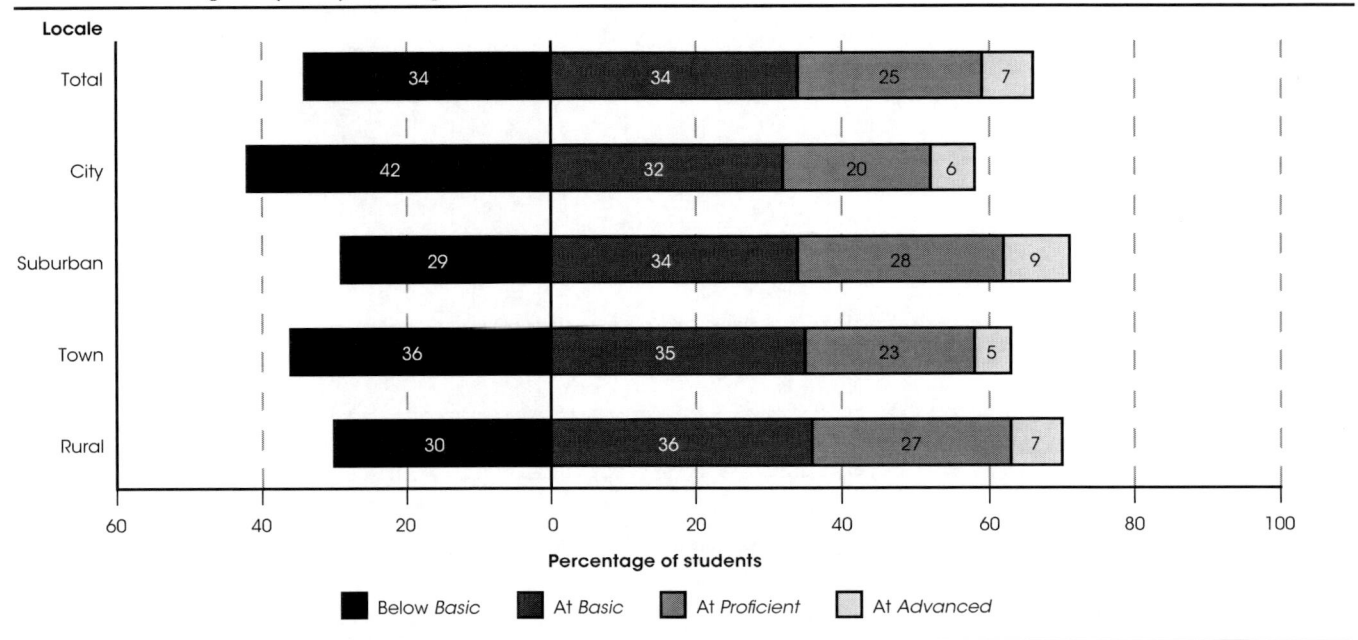

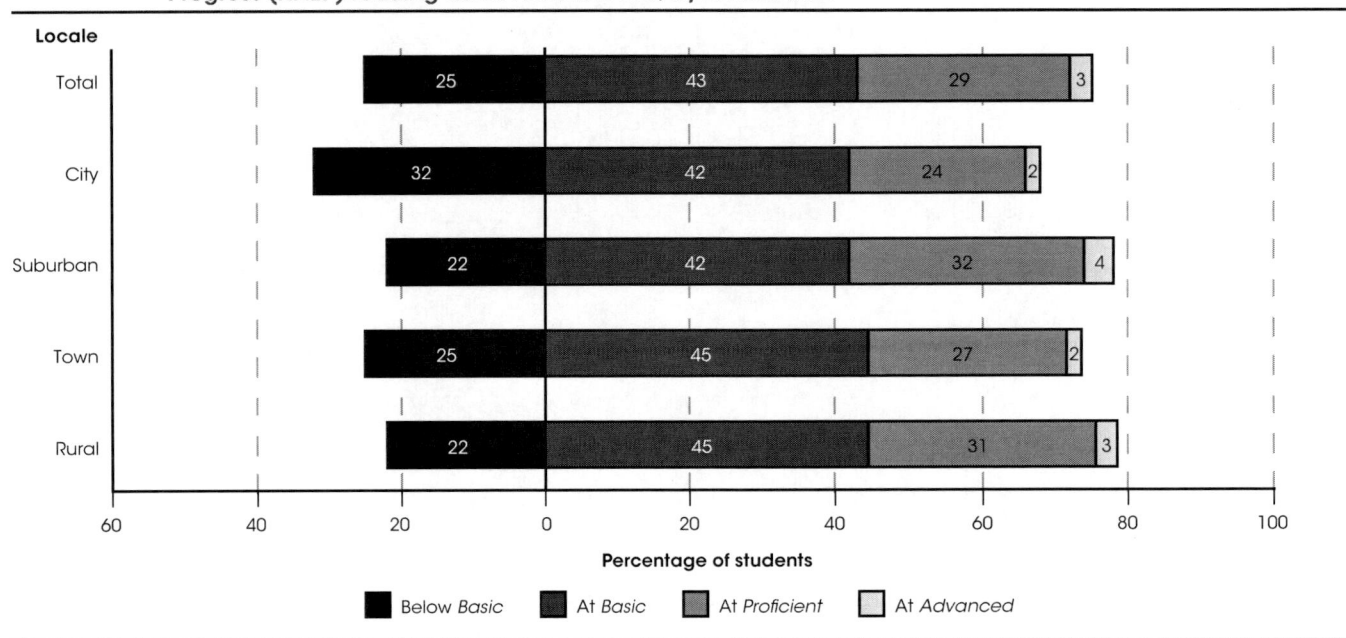

Locale	Below Basic	At Basic	At Proficient	At Advanced
Total	34	34	25	7
City	42	32	20	6
Suburban	29	34	28	9
Town	36	35	23	5
Rural	30	36	27	7

NOTE: Detail may not sum to totals because of rounding.
SOURCE: U.S. Department of Education, National Center for Education Statistics, National Assessment of Educational Progress (NAEP), 2011 Reading Assessment. See table B.2.a.-1 at http://nces.ed.gov/surveys/ruraled/.

Figure 5b. Percentage distribution of 8th-grade public school students across National Assessment of Educational Progress (NAEP) reading achievement levels, by locale: 2011

Locale	Below Basic	At Basic	At Proficient	At Advanced
Total	25	43	29	3
City	32	42	24	2
Suburban	22	42	32	4
Town	25	45	27	2
Rural	22	45	31	3

NOTE: Detail may not sum to totals because of rounding.
SOURCE: U.S. Department of Education, National Center for Education Statistics, National Assessment of Educational Progress (NAEP), 2011 Reading Assessment. See table B.2.a.-1 at http://nces.ed.gov/surveys/ruraled/.

For more information, see the Reader's Guide and the Guide to Sources.

Chapter: 3/Elementary and Secondary Education
Section: Spotlight

Nationwide, 40 percent of 4th-grade public school students scored at or above the *Proficient* level on the 2011 NAEP mathematics assessment. The percentage of 4th-graders in rural areas scoring at this achievement level (42 percent) was larger than in cities (33 percent) and towns (35 percent) but smaller than in suburban areas (45 percent) (see NCES Rural Education in America website, table B.2.a.-2). The pattern for 8th-grade public school students who scored at or above *Proficient* in mathematics was similar to that for 4th-graders, with 34 percent of 8th-graders in the United States scoring at this level overall. The percentage of 8th-graders in rural areas scoring at or above *Proficient* (35 percent) was larger than in cities (29 percent) and towns (31 percent) but smaller than in suburban areas (37 percent).

Figure 6a. Percentage distribution of 4th-grade public school students across National Assessment of Educational Progress (NAEP) mathematics achievement levels, by locale: 2011

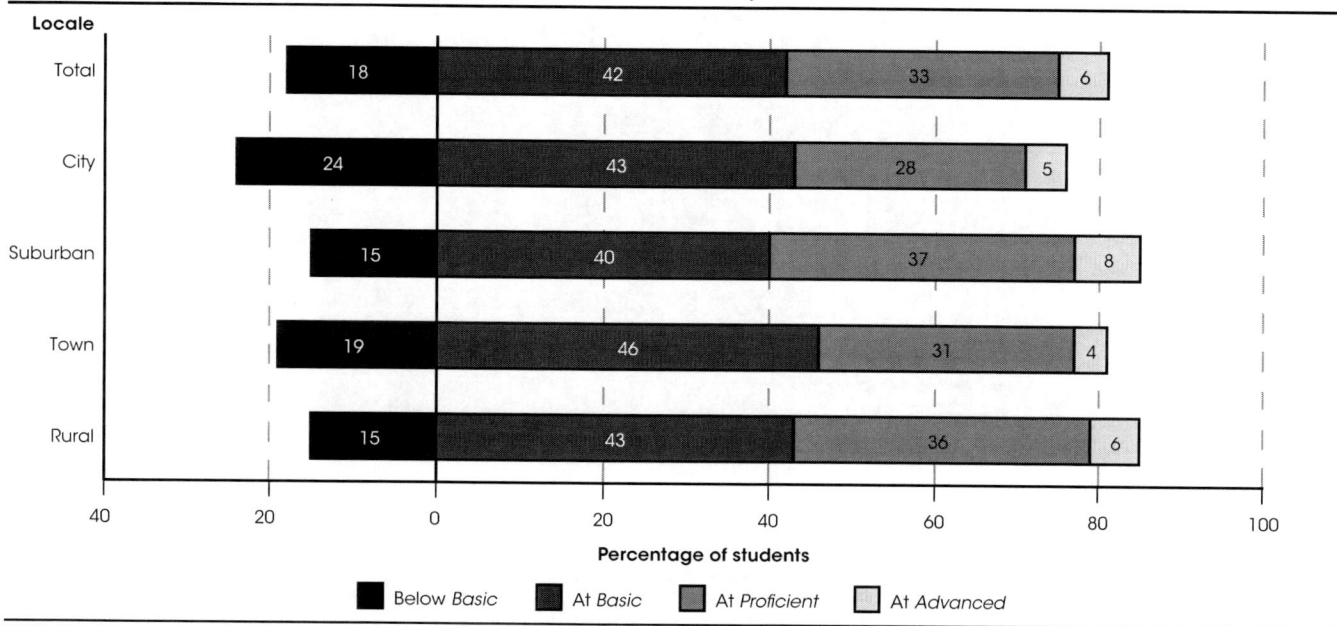

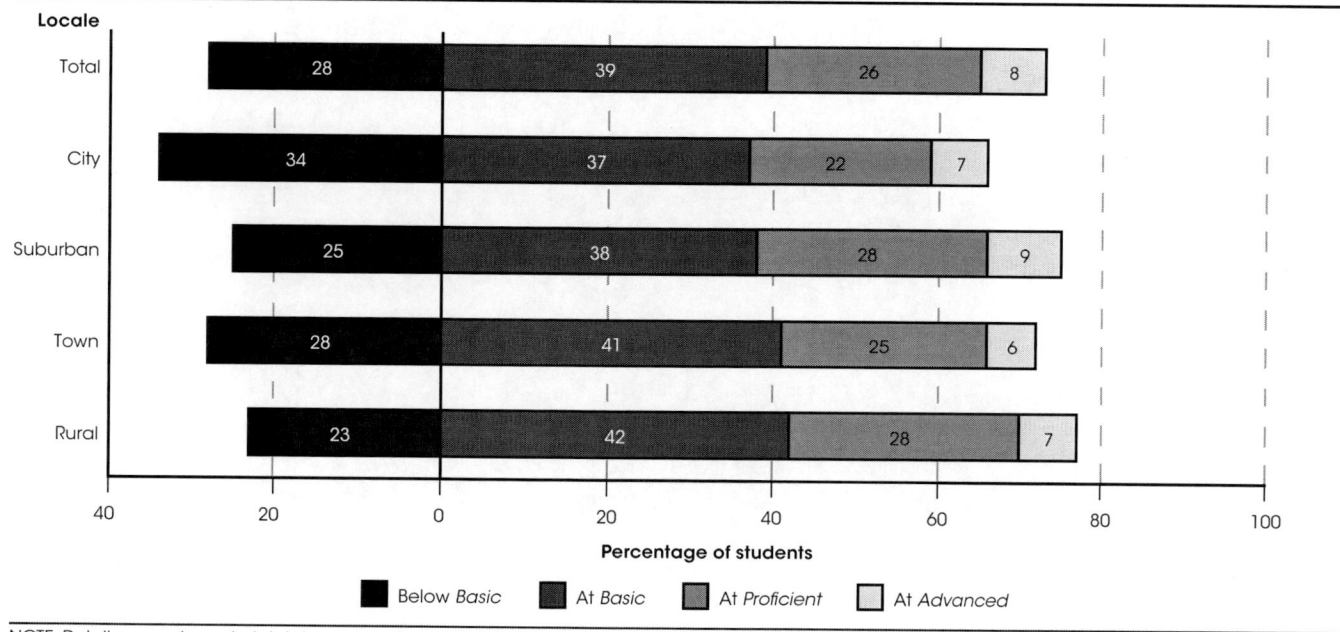

Locale	Below Basic	At Basic	At Proficient	At Advanced
Total	18	42	33	6
City	24	43	28	5
Suburban	15	40	37	8
Town	19	46	31	4
Rural	15	43	36	6

NOTE: Detail may not sum to totals because of rounding.
SOURCE: U.S. Department of Education, National Center for Education Statistics, National Assessment of Educational Progress (NAEP), 2011 Mathematics Assessment. See table B.2.a.-2 at http://nces.ed.gov/surveys/ruraled/.

Figure 6b. Percentage distribution of 8th-grade public school students across National Assessment of Educational Progress (NAEP) mathematics achievement levels, by locale: 2011

Locale	Below Basic	At Basic	At Proficient	At Advanced
Total	28	39	26	8
City	34	37	22	7
Suburban	25	38	28	9
Town	28	41	25	6
Rural	23	42	28	7

NOTE: Detail may not sum to totals because of rounding.
SOURCE: U.S. Department of Education, National Center for Education Statistics, National Assessment of Educational Progress (NAEP), 2011 Mathematics Assessment. See table B.2.a.-2 at http://nces.ed.gov/surveys/ruraled/.

For more information, see the Reader's Guide and the Guide to Sources.

Students in rural districts experienced higher graduation rates than their peers in districts in cities and towns. Nationally, during the 2008–09 school year (the latest year for which these data are available), the averaged freshman graduation rate (AFGR) for the 47 states that reported data (California, Nevada, and Vermont did not) and the District of Columbia was 77 percent (see NCES Rural Education in America website, table B.3.a.-1). The rate was higher in rural areas (80 percent) than across the 47 reporting states and the District of Columbia. The rate was also higher in rural areas than in cities (68 percent) and towns (79 percent) but was lower than the rate in suburban areas (81 percent).

Figure 7. Averaged freshman graduation rate (AFGR) for public high school students, by locale: School year 2008–09

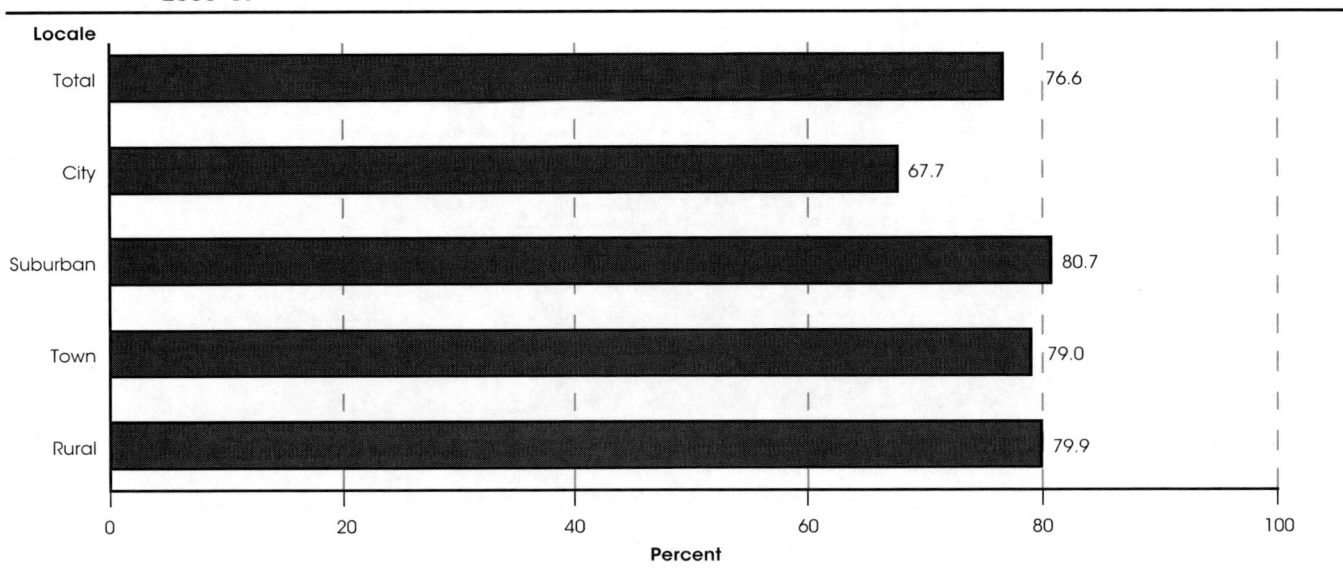

Locale	Percent
Total	76.6
City	67.7
Suburban	80.7
Town	79.0
Rural	79.9

NOTE: The analysis is limited to 47 states and the District of Columbia. California, Nevada, and Vermont are not included because completion data are not available. School districts with missing data on the number of diplomas or total enrollment base or locale code are excluded. Geographic districts in New York City are combined as one school district. High school students are students attending a school offering the final years of high school work necessary for graduation.
SOURCE: U.S. Department of Education, National Center for Education Statistics, Common Core of Data, Local Education Agency Universe Survey Dropout and Completion Restricted-Use Data File, School Year 2008–09 (version 1a) (NCES 2011-314). See table B.3.a.-1 at http://nces.ed.gov/surveys/ruraled/.

Reference tables: NCES Rural Education in America website, tables A.1.a.-1, A.1.a.-2, A.1.a.-3, A.1.a.-6, B.1.b.-1, B.1.e.-1, B.2.a.-1, B.2.a.-2, B.3.a.-1

Glossary: Achievement levels, Averaged Freshman Graduation Rate (AFGR), Elementary school, Free or reduced-price lunch, National School Lunch Program, Poverty, Public school, Secondary school

For more information, see the Reader's Guide and the Guide to Sources.

This page intentionally left blank.

Indicator 16

Characteristics of Public Elementary and Secondary Schools

In school year 2010–11, about 33 percent of traditional public schools were in rural areas, compared with 16 percent of charter schools. In contrast, 25 percent of traditional public schools were in cities, compared with 55 percent of charter schools.

In school year 2010–11, there were 98,817 public schools in the United States, including 93,543 traditional public schools and 5,274 charter schools. These numbers have increased from school year 1999–2000. In 1999–2000, there were a total of 92,012 public schools, with 90,488 traditional public schools and 1,524 charter schools. Over two-thirds of traditional public schools (69 percent) were elementary schools in 2010–11, compared with 54 percent of charter schools. By contrast, 19 percent of charter schools in that year were combined schools, meaning that they began with grade 6 or below and extended to grade 9 or above, compared with just 5 percent of traditional public schools.

Figure 1. Percentage distribution of public schools, by school control and enrollment size: School years 1999–2000 and 2010–11

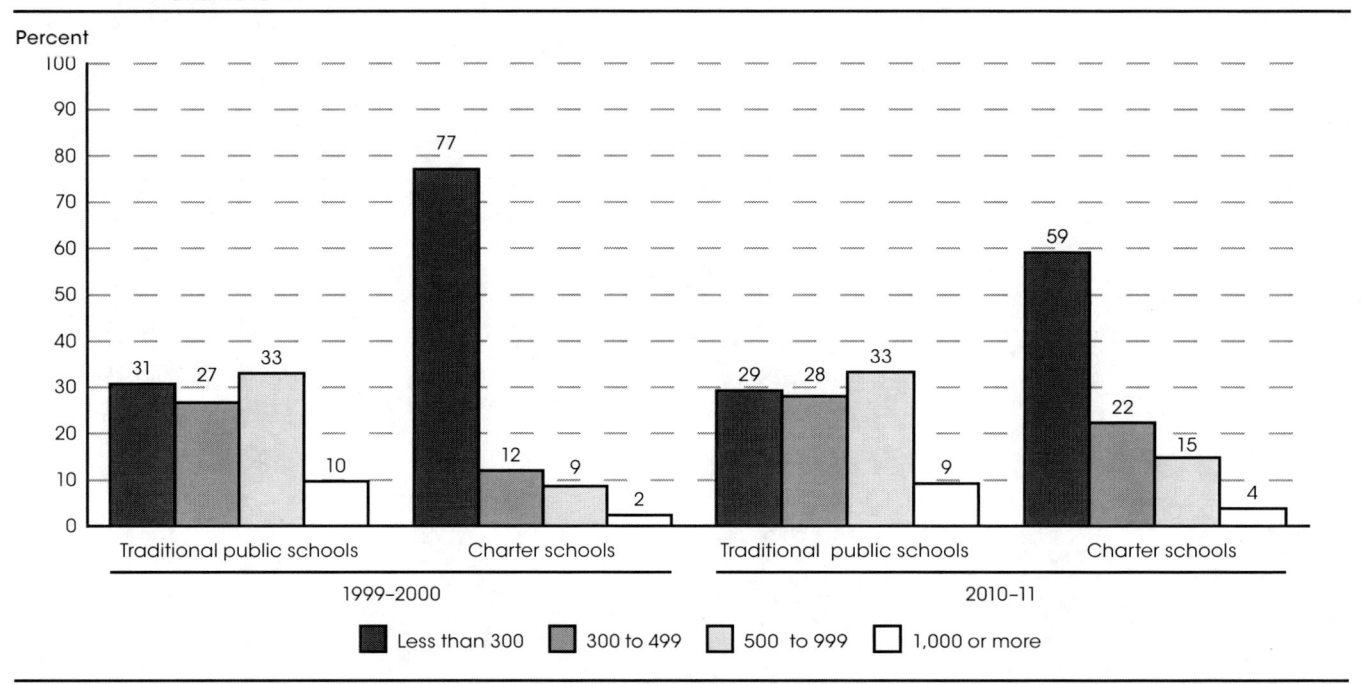

School type	Year	Less than 300	300 to 499	500 to 999	1,000 or more
Traditional public schools	1999–2000	31	27	33	10
Charter schools	1999–2000	77	12	9	2
Traditional public schools	2010–11	29	28	33	9
Charter schools	2010–11	59	22	15	4

SOURCE: U.S. Department of Education, National Center for Education Statistics, Common Core of Data (CCD), "Public Elementary/Secondary School Universe Survey," 1999–2000 and 2010–11. See *Digest of Education Statistics 2012*, table 116.

Charter schools tend to be smaller, in terms of enrollment, than traditional public schools. In 2010–11, some 29 percent of traditional public schools were small (enrollment of fewer than 300 students), compared with 59 percent of charter schools. In that same year, 9 percent of traditional public schools were large (1,000 or more students), compared with 4 percent of charter schools.

In 2010–11, some 60 percent of all public schools had enrollment in which more than half of the students were White, while 11 percent of public schools had enrollment in which more than half of the students were Black, and 14 percent of public schools had enrollment in which more than half of the students were Hispanic. Looking at charter schools only, 38 percent had more than 50 percent White enrollment, 25 percent had more than 50 percent Black enrollment, and 21 percent had more than 50 percent Hispanic enrollment.

High-poverty schools, in which more than 75 percent of the students qualify for free or reduced-price lunch (FRPL) under the National School Lunch Program

For more information, see the Reader's Guide and the Guide to Sources.

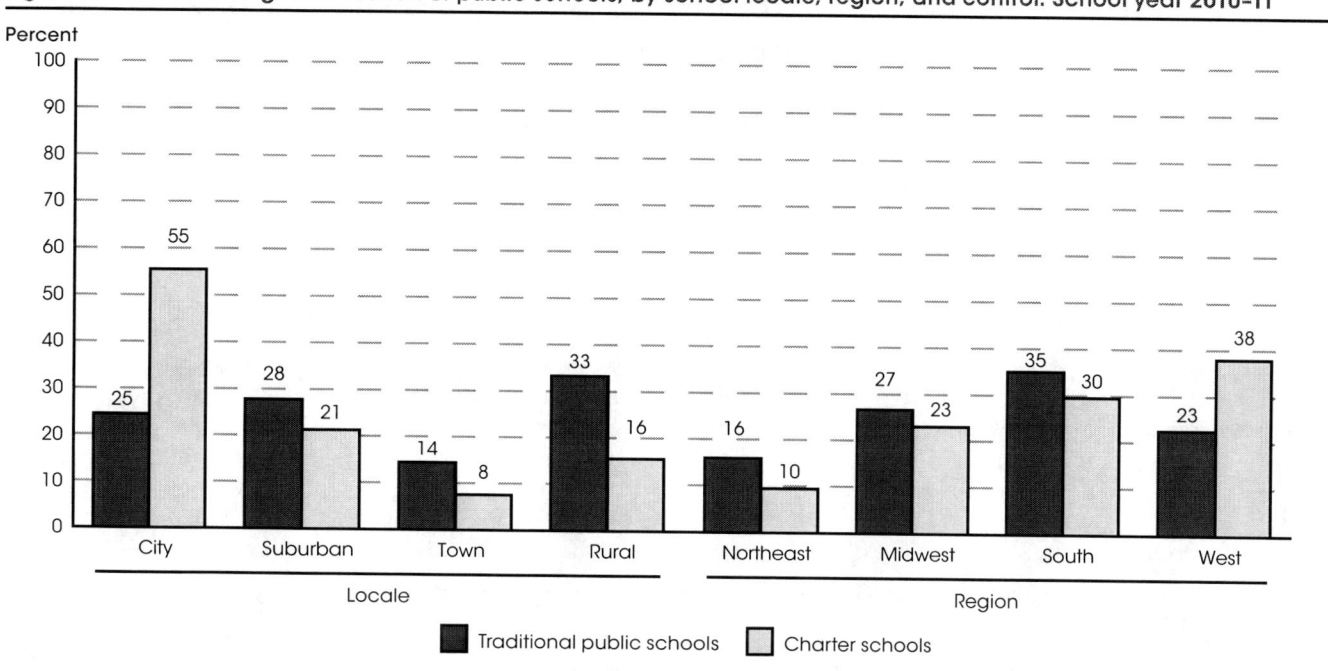

Chapter: 3/Elementary and Secondary Education
Section: School Characteristics and Climate

Figure 2. Percentage distribution of public schools, by school locale, region, and control: School year 2010–11

Locale / Region	Traditional public schools	Charter schools
City	25	55
Suburban	28	21
Town	14	8
Rural	33	16
Northeast	16	10
Midwest	27	23
South	35	30
West	23	38

SOURCE: U.S. Department of Education, National Center for Education Statistics, Common Core of Data (CCD), "Public Elementary/Secondary School Universe Survey," 1999–2000 and 2010–11. See *Digest of Education Statistics 2012*, table 116.

(NSLP), comprised 21 percent of all public schools in 2010–11, compared with 12 percent in 1999–2000. In 2010–11, some 21 percent of traditional public schools were high poverty, compared with 33 percent of charter schools.

In 2010–11, about 33 percent of traditional public schools were in rural areas, compared with 16 percent of charter schools. In contrast, 25 percent of traditional public schools were in cities, compared with 55 percent of charter schools.

Regionally, the highest percentage of traditional public schools was in the South (35 percent) in 2010–11, followed by the Midwest (27 percent), the West (23 percent), and the Northeast (16 percent). Charter schools followed a different pattern. In 2010–11, some 38 percent of charter schools were in the West, 30 percent were in the South, 23 percent were in the Midwest, and 10 percent were in the Northeast.

Reference table: *Digest of Education Statistics 2012*, table 116

Glossary: Traditional public school, Charter school, Private school, Elementary school, Secondary school, Combined school, National School Lunch Program, Free or reduced-price lunch

For more information, see the Reader's Guide and the Guide to Sources.

Indicator 17

Chapter: 3/Elementary and Secondary Education
Section: School Characteristics and Climate

Concentration of Public School Students Eligible for Free or Reduced-Price Lunch

In school year 2010–11, some 20 percent of public school students attended a high-poverty school, compared with 12 percent in 1999–2000. In 2010–11, some 24 percent of public school students attended a low-poverty school, compared with 45 percent in 1999–2000.

The percentage of students eligible for free or reduced-price lunch (FRPL) under the National School Lunch Program provides a proxy measure for the concentration of low-income students within a school. Children from families at or below 130 percent of the poverty level are eligible for free meals. Those from families with incomes that are above 130 and up to 185 percent of the poverty level are eligible for reduced-price meals. In this indicator, public schools (traditional and charter) are divided into categories by FRPL eligibility. A low-poverty school is defined as a public school where less than 25 percent of the students are eligible for the program and a high-poverty school is defined as a school where more than 75 percent of the students are eligible.

Figure 1. Percentage distribution of public school students, by school poverty level: School years 1999–2000 and 2010–11

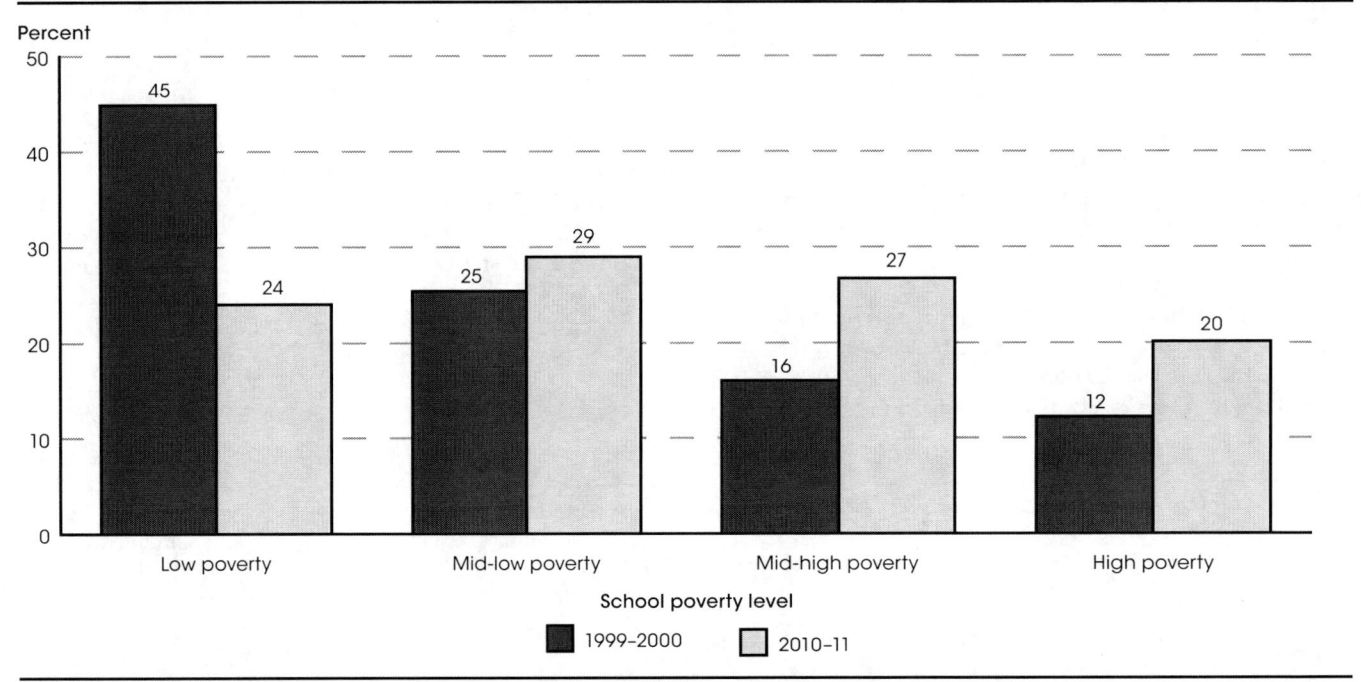

School poverty level	1999–2000	2010–11
Low poverty	45	24
Mid-low poverty	25	29
Mid-high poverty	16	27
High poverty	12	20

NOTE: This figure does not include schools for which information on free or reduced-price lunch (FRPL) is missing and schools that did not participate in the National Student Lunch Program (NSLP). High-poverty schools are defined as public schools where more than 75 percent of the students are eligible for the free or reduced-price lunch (FRPL) program, and mid-high poverty schools are those schools where 51 to 75 percent of students are eligible. Low-poverty schools are defined as public schools where 25 percent or fewer students are eligible for FRPL, and mid-low poverty schools are those schools where 26 to 50 percent of students are eligible for FRPL. Detail may not sum to totals because of rounding.
SOURCE: U.S. Department of Education, National Center for Education Statistics, Common Core of Data (CCD), "Public Elementary/Secondary School Universe Survey," 1999–2000 and 2010–11. See *Digest of Education Statistics 2012*, table 116.

A greater percentage of public school students attended a high-poverty school in 2010–11 than did a decade earlier. In school year 1999–2000, some 12 percent of public school students attended a high-poverty school, compared with 20 percent in 2010–11. The increase in the percentage of children who are eligible to participate may have been influenced by a number of factors, including more systematic identification of children who are eligible, as well as an increase in the actual rates of child poverty. In 2010, some 22 percent of children under the age of 18 were living in poverty, compared with 17 percent in 1999. In 2010–11, some 24 percent of public school students attended a low-poverty school, compared with 45 percent in 1999–2000.

For more information, see the Reader's Guide and the Guide to Sources.

Chapter: 3/Elementary and Secondary Education
Section: School Characteristics and Climate

Figure 2. Percentage distribution of public school students, by school locale and school poverty level: School year 2010–11

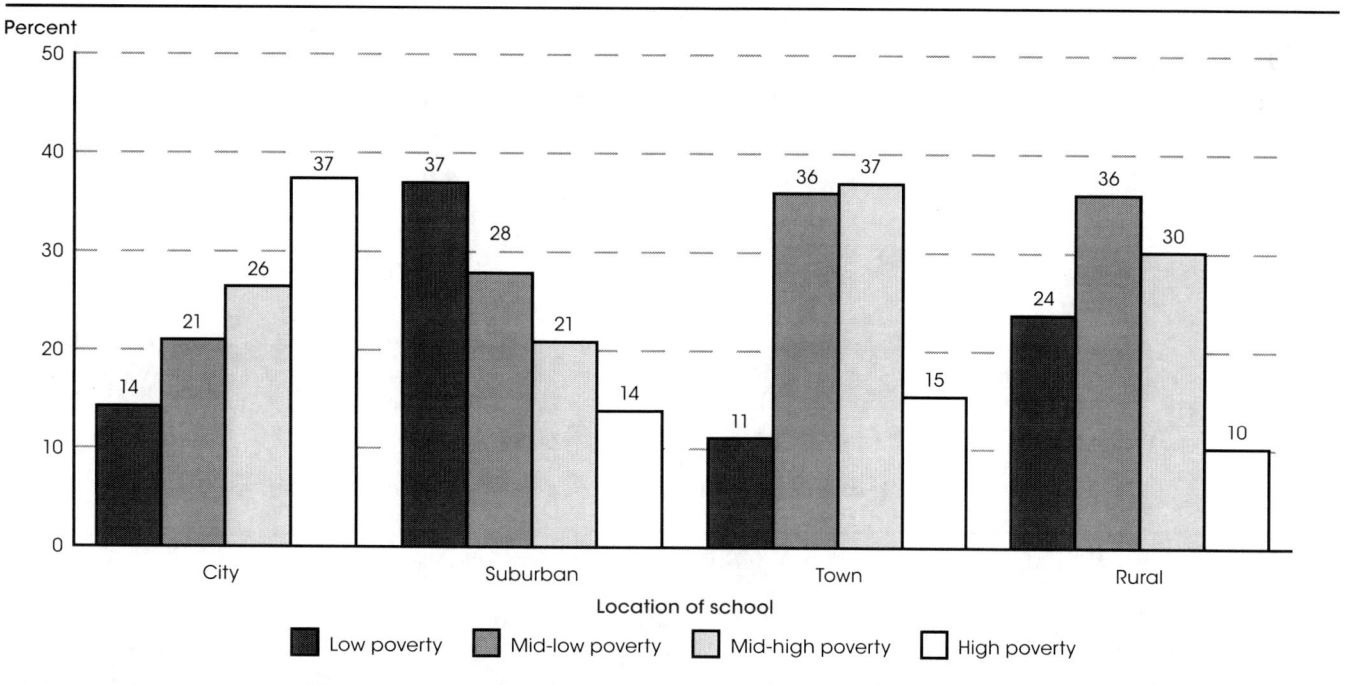

Location of school	Low poverty	Mid-low poverty	Mid-high poverty	High poverty
City	14	21	26	37
Suburban	37	28	21	14
Town	11	36	37	15
Rural	24	36	30	10

NOTE: This figure does not include schools for which information on free or reduced-price lunch (FRPL) is missing and schools that did not participate in the National Student Lunch Program (NSLP). High-poverty schools are defined as public schools where more than 75 percent of the students are eligible for the free or reduced-price lunch (FRPL) program, and mid-high poverty schools are those schools where 51 to 75 percent of students are eligible. Low-poverty schools are defined as public schools where 25 percent or fewer students are eligible for FRPL, and mid-low poverty schools are those schools where 26 to 50 percent of students are eligible for FRPL. Detail may not sum to totals because of rounding.
SOURCE: U.S. Department of Education, National Center for Education Statistics, Common Core of Data (CCD), "Public Elementary/Secondary School Universe Survey," 2010–11. See *Digest of Education Statistics 2012*, table 112.

The distribution of schools across poverty concentration varies by locale, e.g., city, suburbs, towns, and rural areas. In school year 2010–11, over one-third, or 37 percent, of students in city schools were enrolled in a high-poverty school, compared with 10 percent of students in rural schools, 14 percent of those in suburban schools, and 15 percent of those in town schools. On the other hand, the percentage of students in suburban schools who attended a low-poverty school (37 percent) was more than twice as large as the percentages of students in city schools and in town schools who attended a low-poverty school (14 and 11 percent, respectively). The percentage of students in suburban schools who attended a low-poverty school was also higher than the corresponding percentage of students in rural schools (24 percent).

Reference tables: *Digest of Education Statistics 2012*, tables 26, 112, 116

Glossary: National School Lunch Program, Public school, Free or reduced-price lunch

For more information, see the Reader's Guide and the Guide to Sources.

Indicator 18
Rates of School Crime

Following nearly two decades of steady decline, the total nonfatal victimization rate at school increased from 35 to 49 victimizations per 1,000 students for students ages 12–18 years old between 2010 and 2011. The victimization rate away from school increased from 27 to 38 victimizations per 1,000 students over the same period.

Between 1992 and 2011, the total nonfatal victimization rate for students ages 12–18 generally declined both at school (including inside the school building, on school property, or on the way to or from school) and away from school. Nonfatal victimizations include theft and all violent crime; violent crime includes serious violent crime (rape, sexual assault, robbery, and aggravated assault) and simple assault.

Figure 1. Rate of total nonfatal victimizations against students ages 12-18 per 1,000 students, by location: 1992-2011

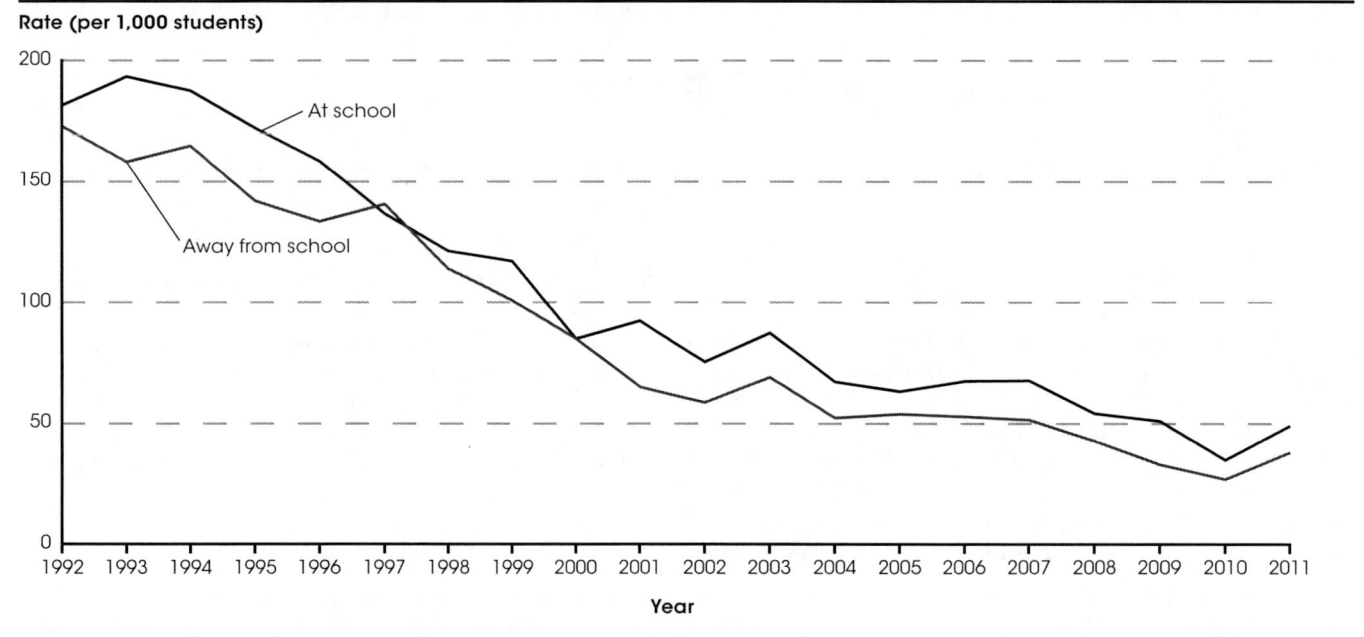

NOTE: Due to methodological changes, use caution when comparing 2006 estimates to other years. "Total victimization" includes violent crimes and theft. "At school" includes inside the school building, on school property, or on the way to or from school.
SOURCE: U.S. Department of Justice, Bureau of Justice Statistics, National Crime Victimization Survey (NCVS), 1992-2011. See *Indicators of School Crime and Safety 2012*, table 2.1.

In 2011, students ages 12–18 reported more nonfatal victimizations at school than away from school. Students ages 12–18 experienced 1,246,000 nonfatal victimizations (theft and violent crime) at school, compared with 965,200 nonfatal victimizations away from school. These data represent total crime victimization rates of 49 crimes per 1,000 students at school and 38 per 1,000 students away from school. Between the two most recent survey years, 2010 and 2011, the total nonfatal victimization rate against students ages 12–18 increased from 35 to 49 victimizations per 1,000 students at school and from 27 to 38 victimizations per 1,000 students away from school. From 1992 to 2011, the rate of nonfatal crime against students declined from 181 to 49 crimes per 1,000 students at school, or from nearly 1 in 5 students in 1992 to about 1 in 20 students in 2011; away from school, the rate of nonfatal crime against students also declined from 173 to 38 crimes per 1,000 students.

For more information, see the Reader's Guide and the Guide to Sources.

Chapter: 3/Elementary and Secondary Education
Section: School Characteristics and Climate

Figure 2. Rate of thefts against students ages 12-18 per 1,000 students, by location: 1992-2011

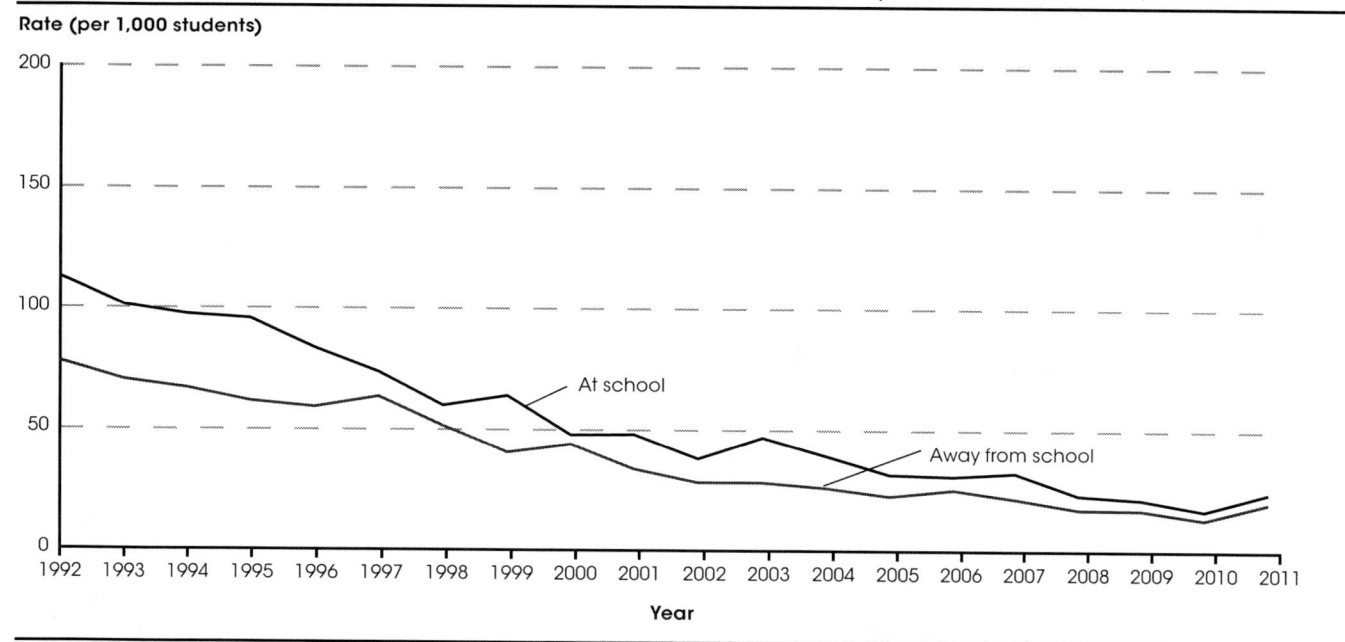

NOTE: Due to methodological changes, use caution when comparing 2006 estimates to other years. "Theft" includes purse-snatching, pickpocketing, and all attempted and completed thefts, with the exception of motor vehicle thefts. Theft does not include robbery in which threat or use of force is involved. Robbery is classified as a violent crime. "At school" includes inside the school building, on school property, or on the way to or from school.
SOURCE: U.S. Department of Justice, Bureau of Justice Statistics, National Crime Victimization Survey (NCVS), 1992-2011. See *Indicators of School Crime and Safety 2012*, table 2.1.

Theft also declined both at and away from school between 1992 and 2011. During this period, theft rates declined from 114 to 26 thefts per 1,000 students at school and from 79 to 21 thefts per 1,000 students away from school. Between 1992 and 2011, the difference in theft rates between at school and away from school narrowed (35 more thefts per 1,000 students at school than away from school in 1992 vs. no measurable difference in the rate of thefts at school and away from school in 2011). In the most recent period between 2010 and 2011, the rate of theft increased from 18 to 26 per 1,000 students at school and from 15 to 21 per 1,000 students away from school.

For more information, see the Reader's Guide and the Guide to Sources.

Chapter: 3/Elementary and Secondary Education
Section: School Characteristics and Climate

Figure 3. Rate of violent victimizations against students ages 12–18 per 1,000 students, by location: 1992–2011

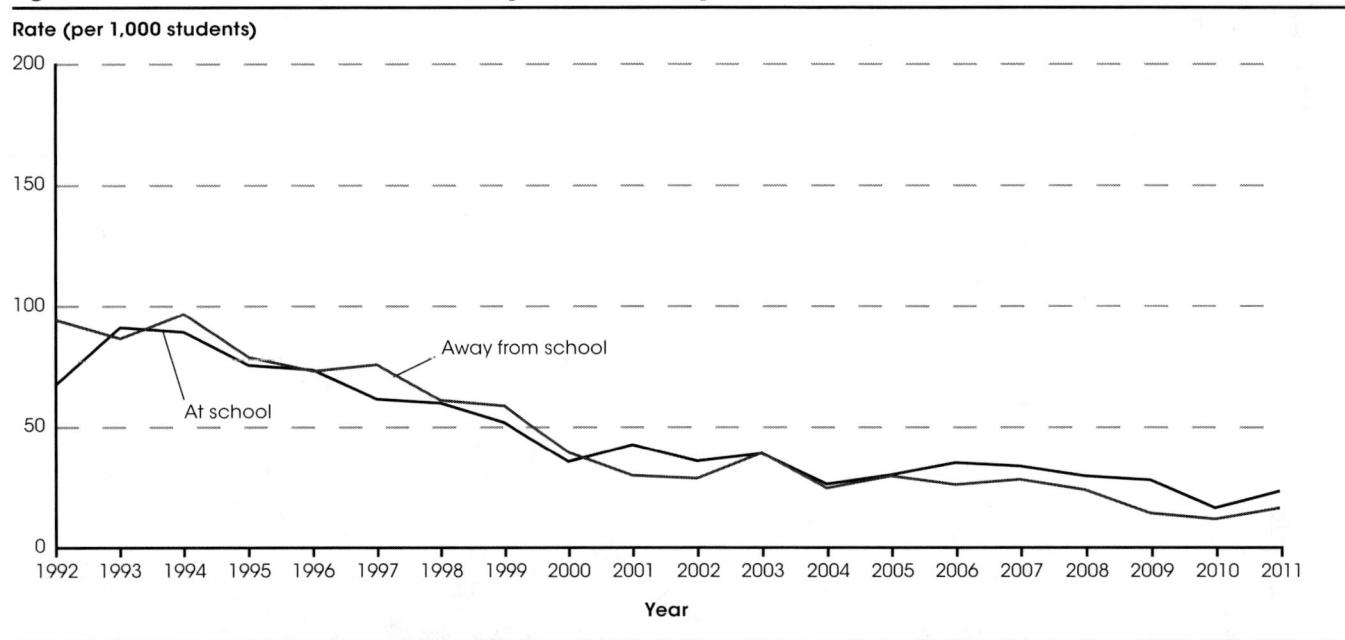

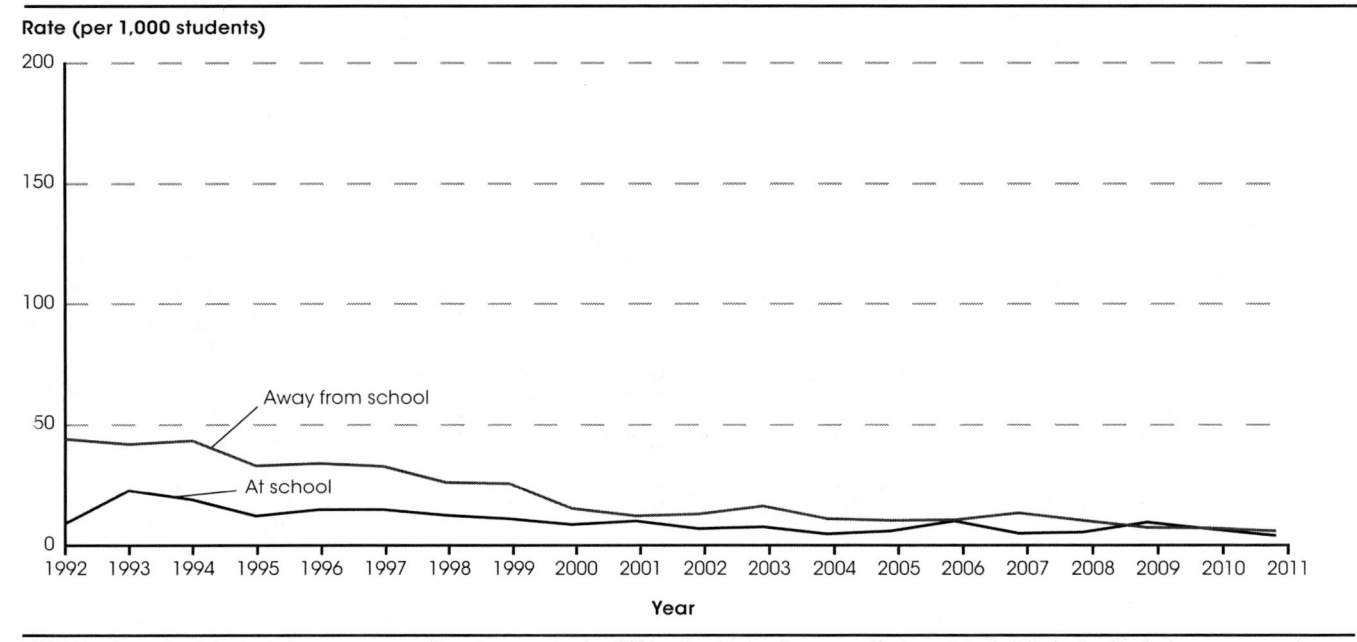

NOTE: Due to methodological changes, use caution when comparing 2006 estimates to other years. "Serious violent victimization" includes rape, sexual assault, robbery, and aggravated assault. "Violent victimization" includes serious violent crimes and simple assault. Robbery is classified as a violent crime. "At school" includes inside the school building, on school property, or on the way to or from school.
SOURCE: U.S. Department of Justice, Bureau of Justice Statistics, National Crime Victimization Survey (NCVS), 1992–2011. See *Indicators of School Crime and Safety 2012*, table 2.1.

Violent victimization rates also decreased both at and away from school between 1992 and 2011. During this period, violent victimization rates declined from 68 to 24 violent victimizations per 1,000 students at school and from 94 to 17 violent victimizations per 1,000 students away from school. In 1992, more violent victimizations occurred away from school (94 per 1,000) than at school (68 per 1,000); while in 2011, more violent victimizations occurred at school (24 per 1,000) than away from school (17 per 1,000). Between 2010 and 2011, the rate of violent victimization against students increased from 17 to 24 violent victimizations per 1,000 students at school; the rate away from school did not change measurably.

Figure 4. Rate of serious violent victimizations against students ages 12–18 per 1,000 students, by location: 1992–2011

NOTE: Due to methodological changes, use caution when comparing 2006 estimates to other years. "Serious violent victimization" includes rape, sexual assault, robbery, and aggravated assault. "Violent victimization" includes serious violent crimes and simple assault. Robbery is classified as a violent crime. "At school" includes inside the school building, on school property, or on the way to or from school.
SOURCE: U.S. Department of Justice, Bureau of Justice Statistics, National Crime Victimization Survey (NCVS), 1992–2011. See *Indicators of School Crime and Safety 2012*, table 2.1.

For more information, see the Reader's Guide and the Guide to Sources.

Chapter: 3/Elementary and Secondary Education
Section: School Characteristics and Climate

Serious violent victimization rates also decreased both at and away from school between 1992 and 2011. During this period, serious violent crime rates declined from a peak of 22 serious violent crimes per 1,000 students at school in 1993 to 4 serious violent crimes per 1,000 students at school in 2011. Serious violent crime rates away from school decreased from 43 to 5 serious violent crimes per 1,000 students between 1992 and 2011. Between 1992 and 2011, the difference in serious violent crime rates between at school and away from school narrowed (35 more serious violent crimes per 1,000 students away from school than at school in 1992 vs. no measurable difference in the rate of serious violent victimization at school and away from school in 2011).

There was no measurable difference in the rate of serious violent victimization against students at school or away from school between 2010 and 2011.

The victimization rates at school and away from school differed by type of crime. For example, in most years between 1992 and 2008 the rate of theft at school was generally higher than the rate away from school, while the rate of serious violent victimization at school was generally lower than the rate occurring away from school. Since 2009, there have been no measurable differences between at school and away from school in either victimization rate.

Figure 5. Rate of nonfatal victimizations against students ages 12–18 at and away from school per 1,000 students, by type of victimization and age: 2011

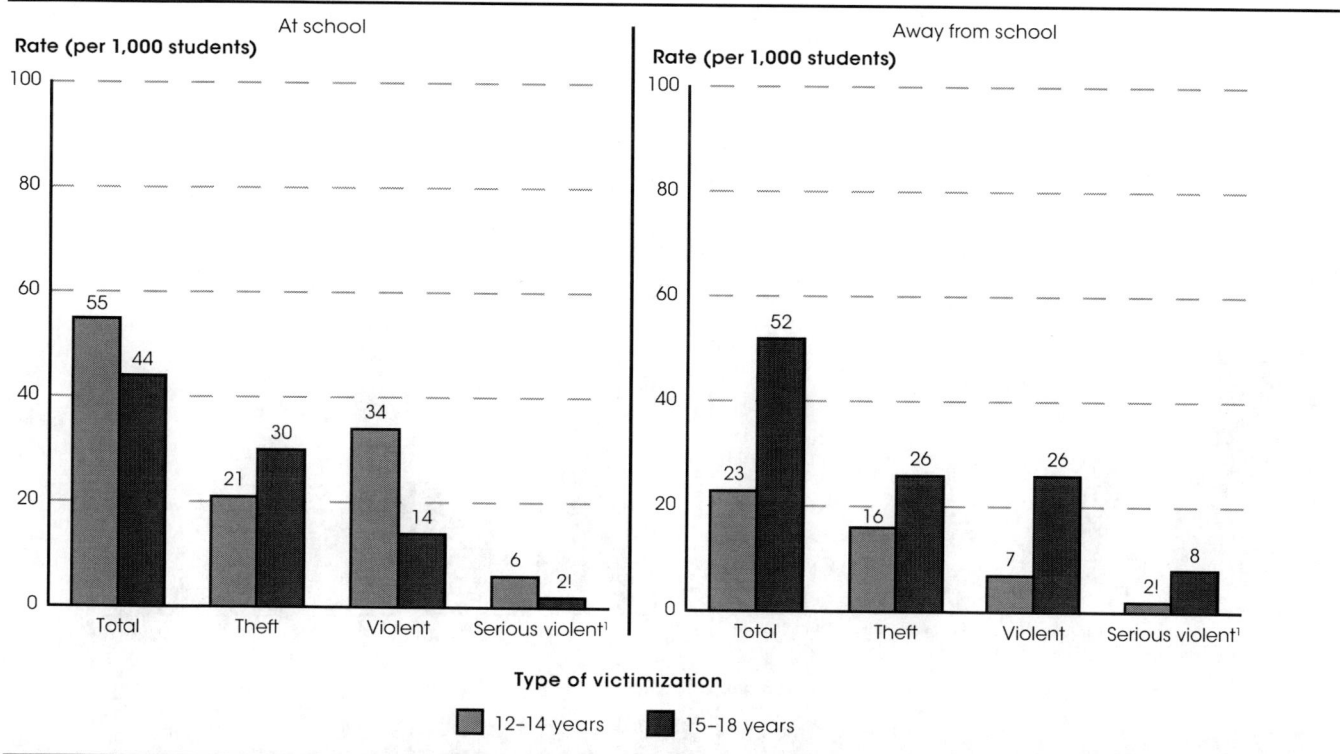

At school

Type of victimization	12–14 years	15–18 years
Total	55	44
Theft	21	30
Violent	34	14
Serious violent[1]	6	2!

Away from school

Type of victimization	12–14 years	15–18 years
Total	23	52
Theft	16	26
Violent	7	26
Serious violent[1]	2!	8

! Interpret with caution. The coefficient of variation (CV) for this estimate is between 30 and 50 percent.
[1] Serious violent victimization is also included in violent victimization.
NOTE: "Serious violent victimization" includes rape, sexual assault, robbery, and aggravated assault. "Violent victimization" includes serious violent crimes and simple assault. "Theft" includes purse-snatching, pickpocketing, and all attempted and completed thefts, with the exception of motor vehicle thefts. Theft does not include robbery in which threat or use of force is involved. Robbery is classified as a violent crime. "Total victimization" includes violent crimes and theft. "At school" includes inside the school building, on school property, or on the way to or from school. Detail may not sum to totals because of rounding.
SOURCE: U.S. Department of Justice, Bureau of Justice Statistics, National Crime Victimization Survey (NCVS), 2011. See *Indicators of School Crime and Safety 2012*, tables 2.2 and 2.3.

For more information, see the Reader's Guide and the Guide to Sources.

Chapter: 3/Elementary and Secondary Education
Section: School Characteristics and Climate

Victimization rates for students in 2011 varied according to student characteristics. For example, the rate of theft at school was lower for younger students than for older students: 21 per 1,000 students ages 12–14 were victims of theft, compared with 30 per 1,000 students ages 15–18. In contrast, the rate of violent victimization at school was higher for younger students than for older students: 34 per 1,000 students ages 12–14, compared with 14 per 1,000 students ages 15–18. No measurable differences were found by age group (i.e., students ages 12–14 vs. students ages 15–18) in the rates of total victimization or of serious violent victimization at school.

Away from school, the rates of total victimization, theft, violent victimization, and serious violent victimization were higher for older students (ages 15–18) than for younger students (ages 12–14). The total victimization rate away from school was 23 per 1,000 students ages 12–14, compared with 52 per 1,000 students ages 15–18. The rate of theft away from school was 16 per 1,000 students ages 12–14, compared with 26 per 1,000 students ages 15–18. The violent victimization rate away from school was 7 per 1,000 students ages 12–14, compared with 26 per 1,000 students ages 15–18. The serious violent victimization rate away from school was 2 per 1,000 students ages 12–14, compared with 8 per 1,000 students ages 15–18.

Figure 6. Rate of nonfatal victimizations against students ages 12–18 at and away from school per 1,000 students, by type of victimization and sex: 2011

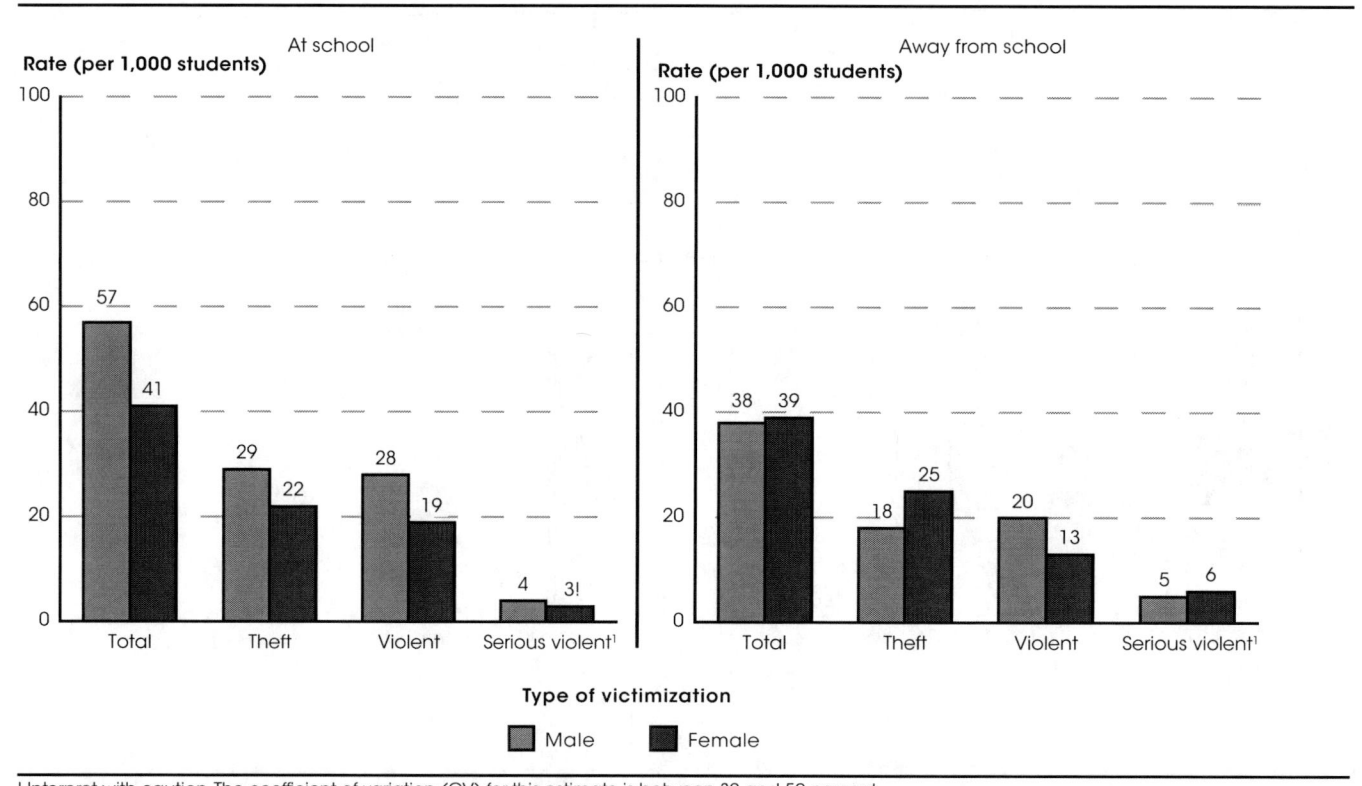

At school (Rate per 1,000 students)
- Total: Male 57, Female 41
- Theft: Male 29, Female 22
- Violent: Male 28, Female 19
- Serious violent[1]: Male 4, Female 3!

Away from school (Rate per 1,000 students)
- Total: Male 38, Female 39
- Theft: Male 18, Female 25
- Violent: Male 20, Female 13
- Serious violent[1]: Male 5, Female 6

Type of victimization — Male / Female

! Interpret with caution. The coefficient of variation (CV) for this estimate is between 30 and 50 percent.
[1] Serious violent victimization is also included in violent victimization.
NOTE: "Serious violent victimization" includes rape, sexual assault, robbery, and aggravated assault. "Violent victimization" includes serious violent crimes and simple assault. "Theft" includes purse-snatching, pickpocketing, and all attempted and completed thefts, with the exception of motor vehicle thefts. Theft does not include robbery in which threat or use of force is involved. Robbery is classified as a violent crime. "Total victimization" includes violent crimes and theft. "At school" includes inside the school building, on school property, or on the way to or from school. Detail may not sum to totals because of rounding.
SOURCE: U.S. Department of Justice, Bureau of Justice Statistics, National Crime Victimization Survey (NCVS), 2011. See *Indicators of School Crime and Safety 2012*, tables 2.2 and 2.3.

At school, the rate of violent victimization was lower for females (19 per 1,000) than for males (28 per 1,000) in 2011. There were no measurable differences between male and female rates of theft at school. Away from school, the rate of theft was higher for females (25 per 1,000) than for males (18 per 1,000) in 2011. No measurable differences were detected by sex for the rates of total and violent victimization away from school.

Reference tables: *Indicators of School Crime and Safety 2012*, tables 2.1, 2.2, 2.3, S2.1, S2.2, S2.3

For more information, see the Reader's Guide and the Guide to Sources.

This page intentionally left blank.

Indicator 19
Teachers and Pupil/Teacher Ratios

Chapter: 3/Elementary and Secondary Education
Section: School Characteristics and Climate

Of the 6.2 million staff members in public elementary and secondary schools in fall 2010, some 3.1 million, or half, were teachers.

Of the 6.2 million staff members in public elementary and secondary schools in fall 2010, some 3.1 million, or half, were teachers. In addition, there were 0.7 million instructional aides, who made up about 12 percent of the total staff. The 2010 percentage of teachers reflects a slight decrease from the fall 2000 ratio, when 52 percent of staff were teachers. The decrease in the ratio of teachers as a percentage of staff coincided with an increase, from 11 to 12 percent, in instructional aides as a percentage of staff. By comparison, in fall 1969 teachers represented 60 percent of public school staff, and instructional aides represented 2 percent of public school staff.

Figure 1. Teachers as a percentage of staff in public elementary and secondary school systems, by state or jurisdiction: fall 2010

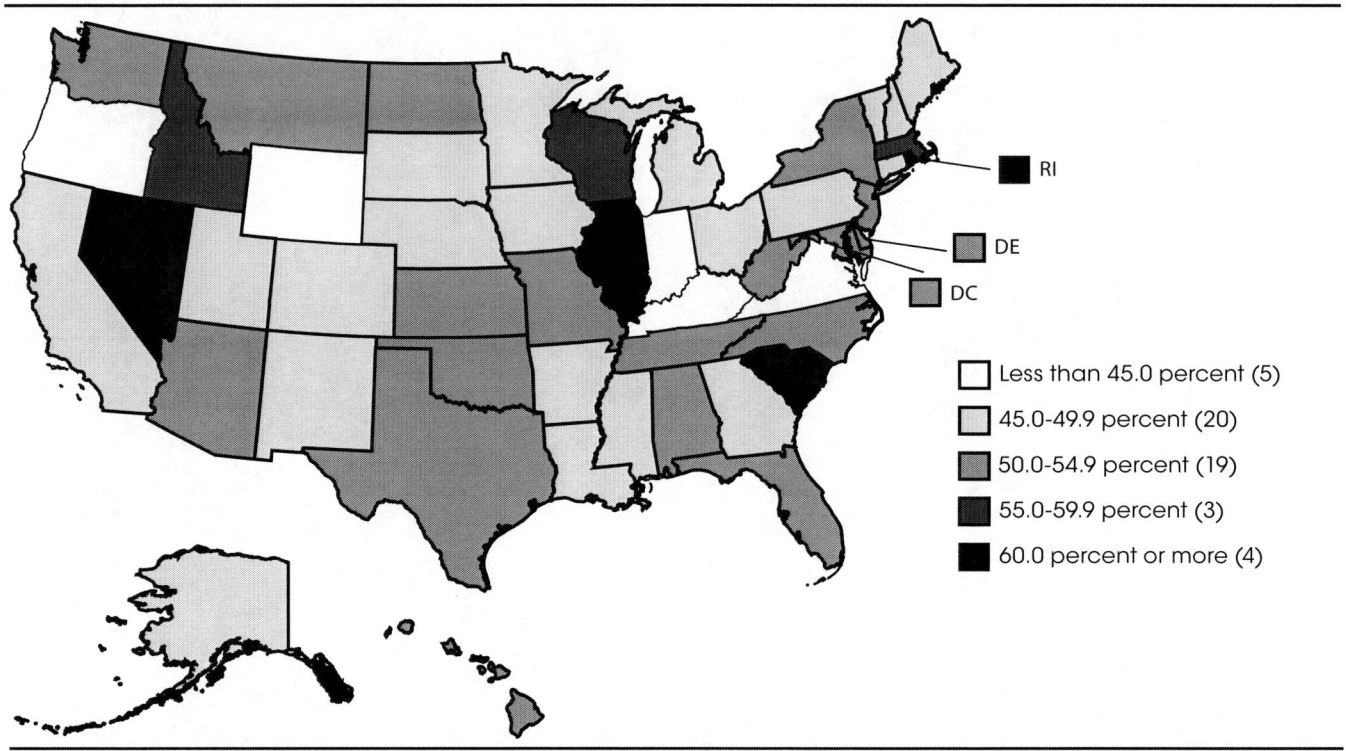

- Less than 45.0 percent (5)
- 45.0–49.9 percent (20)
- 50.0–54.9 percent (19)
- 55.0–59.9 percent (3)
- 60.0 percent or more (4)

SOURCE: U.S. Department of Education, National Center for Education Statistics, Common Core of Data (CCD), "State Nonfiscal Survey of Public Elementary/Secondary Education," 2010–11. See *Digest of Education Statistics 2012*, table 95.

In most states, between 45 and 55 percent of public school staff were teachers in 2010. There are five states where teachers make up less than 45 percent of the staff (Virginia, Indiana, Kentucky, Wyoming, and Oregon) and seven states where they make up more than 55 percent of the staff (Wisconsin, Massachusetts, Idaho, Rhode Island, Illinois, Nevada, and South Carolina).

For more information, see the Reader's Guide and the Guide to Sources.

Chapter: 3/Elementary and Secondary Education
Section: School Characteristics and Climate

Figure 2. Public and private elementary and secondary school pupil/teacher ratios: Selected years, fall 1955 through fall 2010

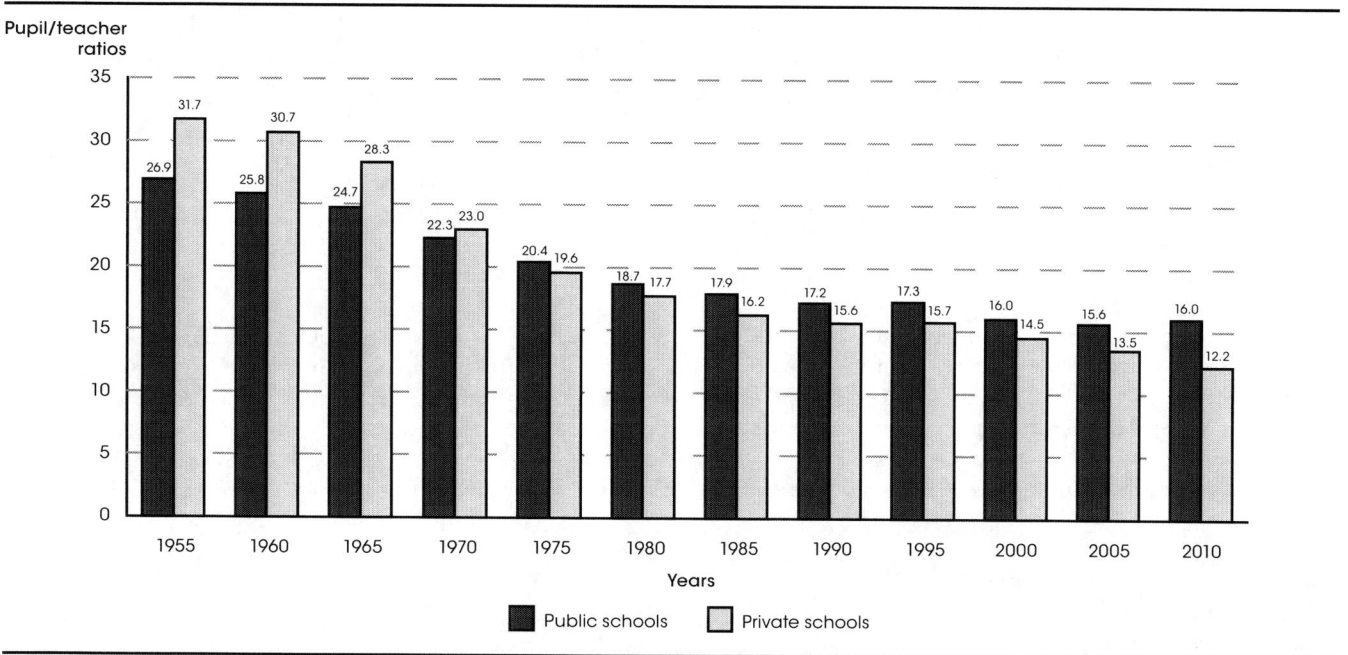

Year	Public schools	Private schools
1955	26.9	31.7
1960	25.8	30.7
1965	24.7	28.3
1970	22.3	23.0
1975	20.4	19.6
1980	18.7	17.7
1985	17.9	16.2
1990	17.2	15.6
1995	17.3	15.7
2000	16.0	14.5
2005	15.6	13.5
2010	16.0	12.2

NOTE: Data for private schools include prekindergarten through grade 12 in schools offering kindergarten or higher grades. Data for public schools include prekindergarten through grade 12. The pupil/teacher ratio includes teachers for students with disabilities and other special teachers. Ratios for public schools reflect totals reported by states and differ from totals reported for schools or school districts. Some data have been revised from previously published figures.
SOURCE: U.S. Department of Education, National Center for Education Statistics, Statistics of Public Elementary and Secondary Day Schools, 1955–56 through 1980–81; Common Core of Data (CCD), "State Nonfiscal Survey of Public Elementary/Secondary Education," 1981–82 through 2010–11; Private School Universe Survey (PSS), 1989–90 through 2009–10. See *Digest of Education Statistics 2012*, table 76.

The number of students per teacher, or the pupil/teacher ratio, has been decreasing for more than 50 years. In fall 1955, there were 1.1 million public and 145,000 private elementary and secondary school teachers in the United States. By fall 2010, these numbers had nearly tripled for public school teachers (to 3.1 million) and more than tripled for private school teachers (to 443,000). However, proportional increases in school enrollment were smaller over this time period: from 31 million public school students to 49 million (a 61 percent increase) and from 4.6 million private school students to 5.4 million (a 17 percent increase). The resulting decline in pupil/teacher ratios was concentrated in the period between 1955 and 1985 for public schools. During this period, public school pupil/teacher ratios fell from 26.9 to 17.9, or approximately 33 percent. Over the next 23 years, the public school pupil/teacher ratio declined by two additional students per teacher to 15.3 in 2008. There were slight increases in 2009 (15.4) and in 2010 (16.0). Private school pupil/teacher ratios decreased more steeply over this period, from 31.7 in 1955 to 12.2 in 2010. As a result, pupil/teacher ratios have been lower in private schools than in public schools since 1972.

Reference tables: *Digest of Education Statistics 2012,* tables 76, 92, 95

Indicator 20
Public School Revenue Sources

From school years 2000–01 through 2009–10, total elementary and secondary public school revenues increased from $522 billion to $627 billion (in constant 2011–12 dollars), a 20 percent increase, adjusting for inflation. From school years 2008–09 through 2009–10, total revenues for public elementary and secondary schools decreased by about $1 billion, or less than 1 percent.

From school years 2000–01 through 2009–10, total elementary and secondary public school revenues increased from $522 billion to $627 billion (in constant 2011–12 dollars), a 20 percent increase, adjusting for inflation using the Consumer Price Index (CPI). During this period, the total amounts from each revenue source (federal, state, and local) increased, but the percentage of increase differed by revenue source. Federal revenues, the smallest of the three revenue sources, increased by 111 percent, compared with increases of 22 percent for local revenues and 5 percent for state revenues. Federal revenues peaked in 2009–10 at $80 billion, while local revenues peaked in 2008–09 at $275 billion, and state revenues peaked in 2007–08 at $304 billion.

Figure 1. Total revenues for public elementary and secondary schools, by revenue source: School years 1990–91 through 2009–10

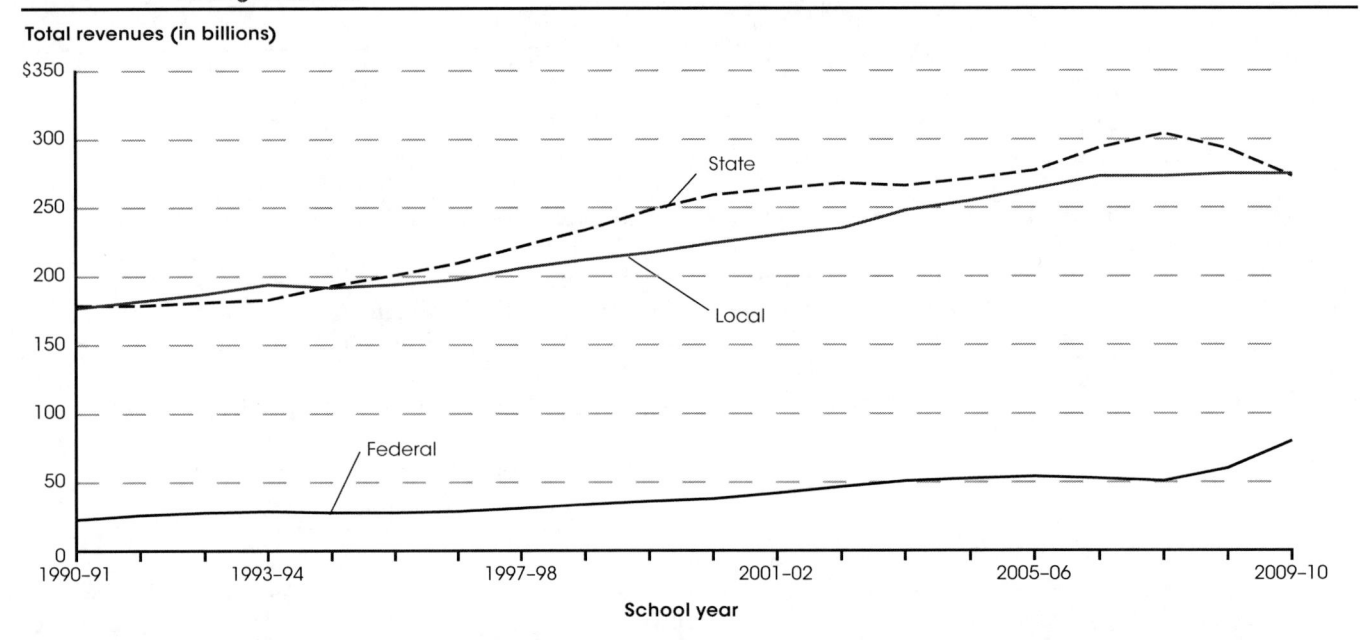

NOTE: Revenues are in constant 2011–12 dollars, adjusted using the Consumer Price Index (CPI).
SOURCE: U.S. Department of Education, National Center for Education Statistics, Common Core of Data (CCD), "National Public Education Financial Survey," 1990–91 through 2009–10. See *Digest of Education Statistics 2012*, table 202.

The percentage of total revenues for public elementary and secondary education that came from federal sources increased from 7 percent in school year 2000–01 to 13 percent in 2009–10. The American Recovery and Reinvestment Act[3] directed spending toward education and contributed to the increase in revenues during school years 2008–09 and 2009–10. The percentage coming from local sources fluctuated during this period: 43 percent in 2000–01, compared with 44 percent in 2009–10. The percentage of total revenues from state sources decreased from 50 percent in school year 2000–01 to 44 percent in school year 2009–10.

From school years 2008–09 through 2009–10, total revenues for public elementary and secondary schools decreased by about $1 billion in constant 2011–12 dollars (0.1 percent). During this period, state revenues declined by $20 billion, or 7 percent. Total local revenues declined by $0.1 billion (0.02 percent), despite the increase in the revenues from local property taxes ($3 billion, or 1 percent). In 2009–10, local property taxes constituted 81 percent of total local revenues and 35 percent of total revenues for elementary and secondary schools. Federal revenues were the only other source that increased from 2008–09 through 2009–10 (by $20 billion, or 33 percent).

[3] For more information on the American Recovery and Reinvestment Act, please go to http://www.ed.gov/recovery.

For more information, see the Reader's Guide and the Guide to Sources.

Chapter: 3/Elementary and Secondary Education
Section: Finance

Figure 2. Primary source of revenue as a percentage of total public elementary and secondary school revenue, by state: School year 2009–10

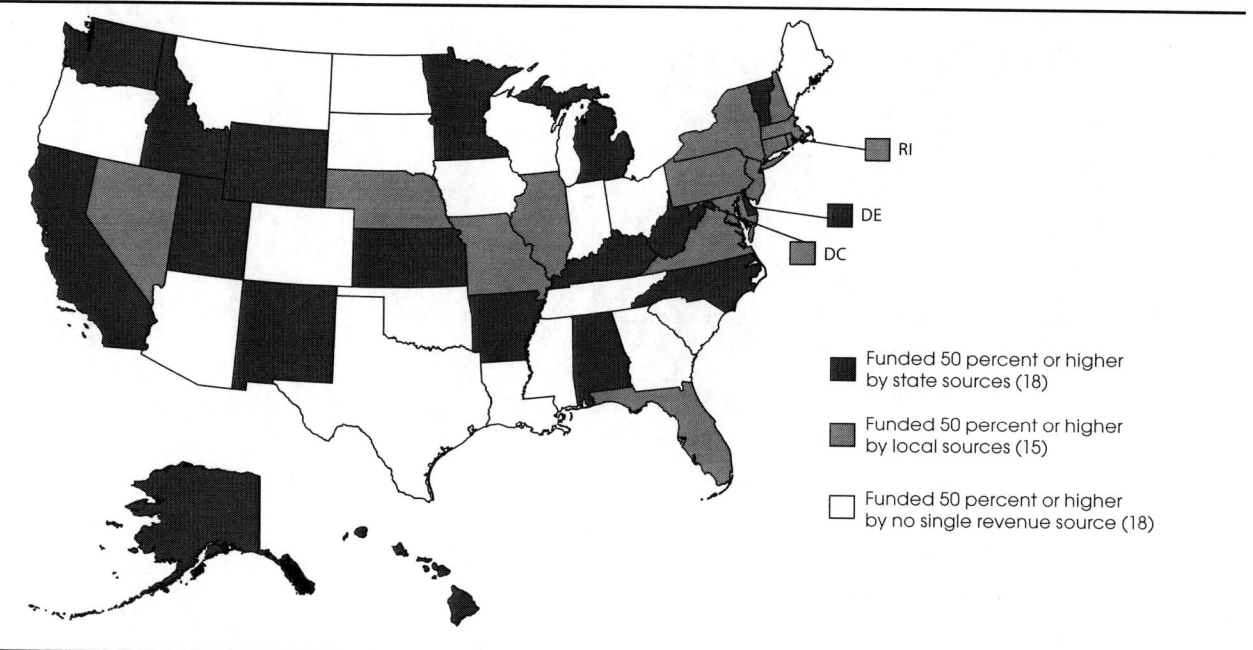

■ Funded 50 percent or higher by state sources (18)
▨ Funded 50 percent or higher by local sources (15)
□ Funded 50 percent or higher by no single revenue source (18)

NOTE: The District of Columbia and Hawaii have only one school district each; therefore, neither is comparable to the other states.
SOURCE: U.S. Department of Education, National Center for Education Statistics, Common Core of Data (CCD), "National Public Education Financial Survey," 2009–10. See *Digest of Education Statistics 2012*, table 203.

In school year 2009–10, there were significant variations across the states in the percentages of public school revenues coming from each revenue source. In 18 states, half or more of education revenues came from state governments, while in 14 states and the District of Columbia half or more came from local revenues. In the remaining 18 states, no single revenue source made up more than half of education revenues.

In school year 2009–10, the percentage of revenues coming from state sources was highest in Hawaii and Vermont (82 percent each). The percentage of revenues coming from state sources was lowest in Missouri and Illinois (29 and 28 percent, respectively). The District of Columbia does not receive any state revenue; in 2009–10, most of its revenues were from local sources (91 percent). The percentage of revenues coming from federal sources was highest in North Dakota (22 percent), followed by Mississippi, New Mexico, and Idaho (21 percent each); the percentage was lowest in Wyoming (7 percent), followed by Massachusetts, Maryland, and Colorado (8 percent each). Among all states, the percentage of revenues coming from local sources was highest in Illinois and Nevada (59 percent each) and lowest in Vermont and Hawaii (8 and 3 percent, respectively).

For more information, see the Reader's Guide and the Guide to Sources.

Chapter: 3/Elementary and Secondary Education
Section: Finance

Figure 3. Property tax revenue for public elementary and secondary schools as a percentage of total school revenue, by state: School year 2009–10

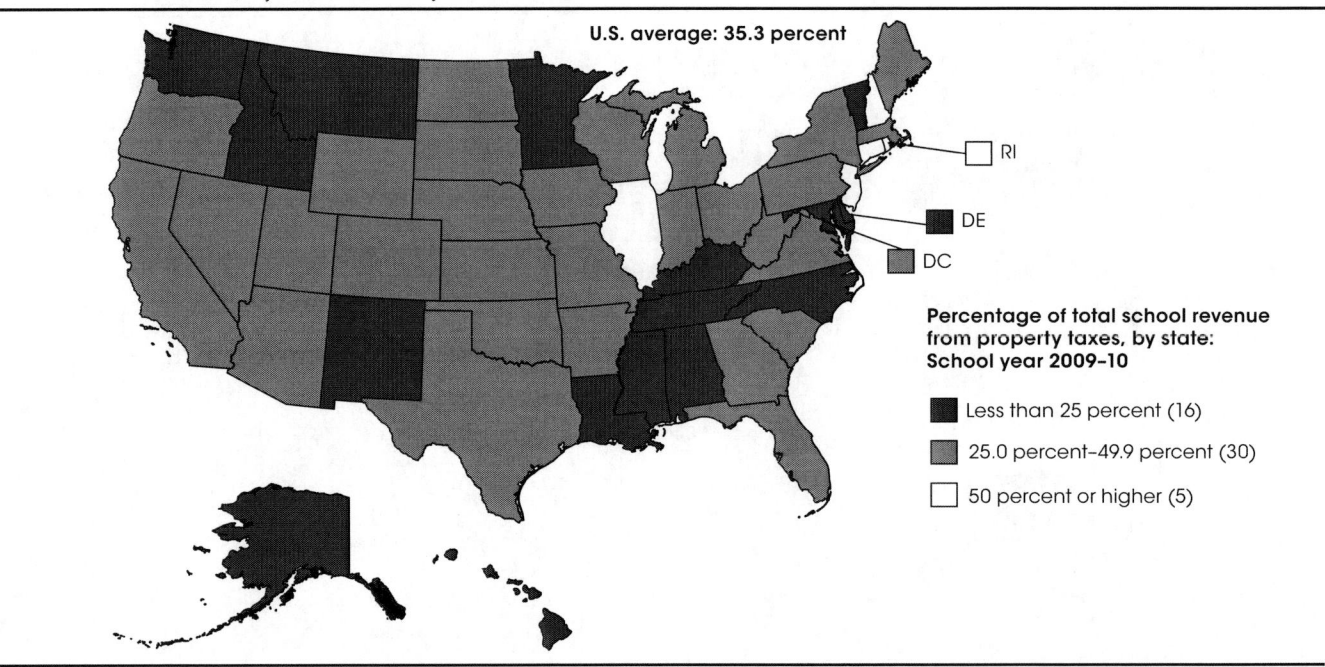

U.S. average: 35.3 percent

Percentage of total school revenue from property taxes, by state: School year 2009–10

- Less than 25 percent (16)
- 25.0 percent–49.9 percent (30)
- 50 percent or higher (5)

NOTE: The District of Columbia and Hawaii have only one school district each; therefore, neither is comparable to the other states. National average includes the District of Columbia.
SOURCE: U.S. Department of Education, National Center for Education Statistics, Common Core of Data (CCD), "National Public Education Financial Survey," 2009–10. See *Digest of Education Statistics 2012*, table 203.

In school year 2009–10, the percentages of local revenue from property taxes also differed by state. Connecticut had the highest percentage of local revenue from property taxes, at 55 percent. Four other states had percentages of local revenue from property taxes of 50 percent or more: New Hampshire, Rhode Island, Illinois, and New Jersey. Vermont and Hawaii[4] had the lowest percentages of local revenue from property taxes (0.2 percent and 0 percent, respectively). In 14 other states, property taxes made up less than 25 percent of education revenues (in descending order): Mississippi, Delaware, Washington, Maryland, Montana, Kentucky, North Carolina, Tennessee, Minnesota, Idaho, Louisiana, Alabama, New Mexico, and Alaska.

[4] Hawaii has only one school district, which has no funding from property taxes.

Reference tables: *Digest of Education Statistics 2012*, tables 202, 203

Glossary: Consumer Price Index (CPI), Elementary school, Property tax, Public school or institution, Revenue, Secondary school

For more information, see the Reader's Guide and the Guide to Sources.

This page intentionally left blank.

Indicator 21
Public School Expenditures

From 1999–2000 through 2009–10, current expenditures per student enrolled in the fall in public elementary and secondary schools increased by 20 percent, after adjusting for inflation. The relative increase in expenditures per student for instruction (19 percent) was greater than that for administration (15 percent) but smaller than that for student services (35 percent).

Total expenditures for public elementary and secondary schools in the United States amounted to $638 billion in 2009–10, or about $12,743 per public school student. These expenditures include $11,184 per student in current expenditures for operation of schools; $1,182 for capital outlay (i.e., expenditures for property and for buildings and alterations completed by school district staff or contractors); and $376 for interest on school debt. Expenditures are reported in constant 2011–12 dollars, based on the Consumer Price Index (CPI).

Figure 1. Total expenditures per student in fall enrollment in public elementary and secondary schools, in constant 2011–12 dollars, by type of total expenditures: 1999–2000, 2005–06, and 2009–10

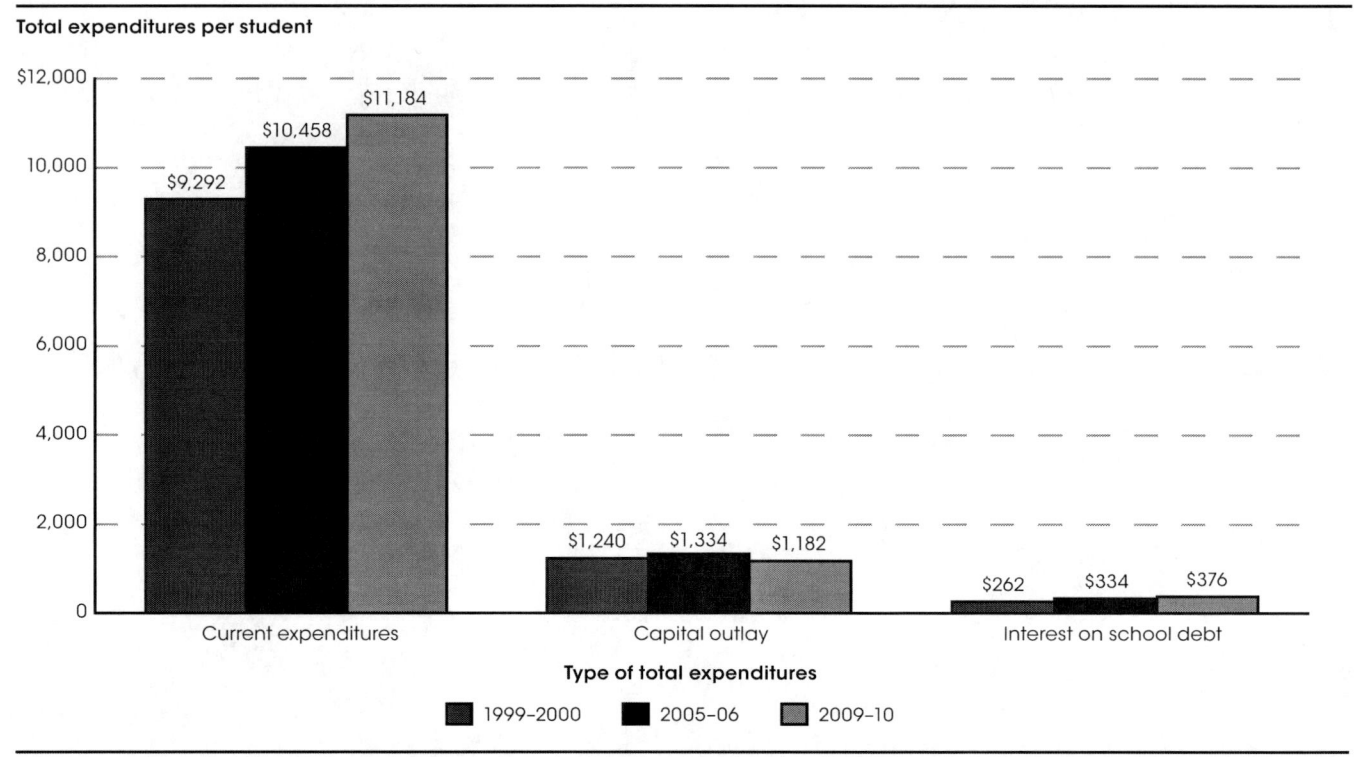

Total expenditures per student

Type of total expenditures	1999–2000	2005–06	2009–10
Current expenditures	$9,292	$10,458	$11,184
Capital outlay	$1,240	$1,334	$1,182
Interest on school debt	$262	$334	$376

NOTE: "Current expenditures," "Capital outlay," and "Interest on school debt" are subcategories of "Total expenditures." "Capital outlay" includes expenditures for property and for buildings and alterations completed by school district staff or contractors. Expenditures are reported in constant 2011–12 dollars, based on the Consumer Price Index (CPI).
SOURCE: U.S. Department of Education, National Center for Education Statistics, Common Core of Data (CCD), "National Public Education Financial Survey," 1999–2000, 2005–06, and 2009–10. See *Digest of Education Statistics 2012*, table 214.

From 1999–2000 to 2009–10, current expenditures per student enrolled in the fall increased by 20 percent, compared with a 44 percent increase for interest on school debt per student in fall enrollment. Much of the increase in current expenditures occurred during the early part of the period, with current expenditures per student increasing by 1 percent from 2007–08 to 2009–10. There was a 5 percent decrease in capital outlay expenditures per student overall from 1999–2000 to 2009–10. Over that period, however, these expenditures actually increased until 2007–08 (when they reached $1,449 in constant 2011–12 dollars), after which they began to decrease, ending up at $1,182 in 2009–10.

For more information, see the Reader's Guide and the Guide to Sources.

Chapter: 3/Elementary and Secondary Education
Section: Finance

Figure 2. Current expenditures per student in fall enrollment in public elementary and secondary schools, in constant 2011-12 dollars, by function of current expenditures: 1999–2000, 2005–06, and 2009–10

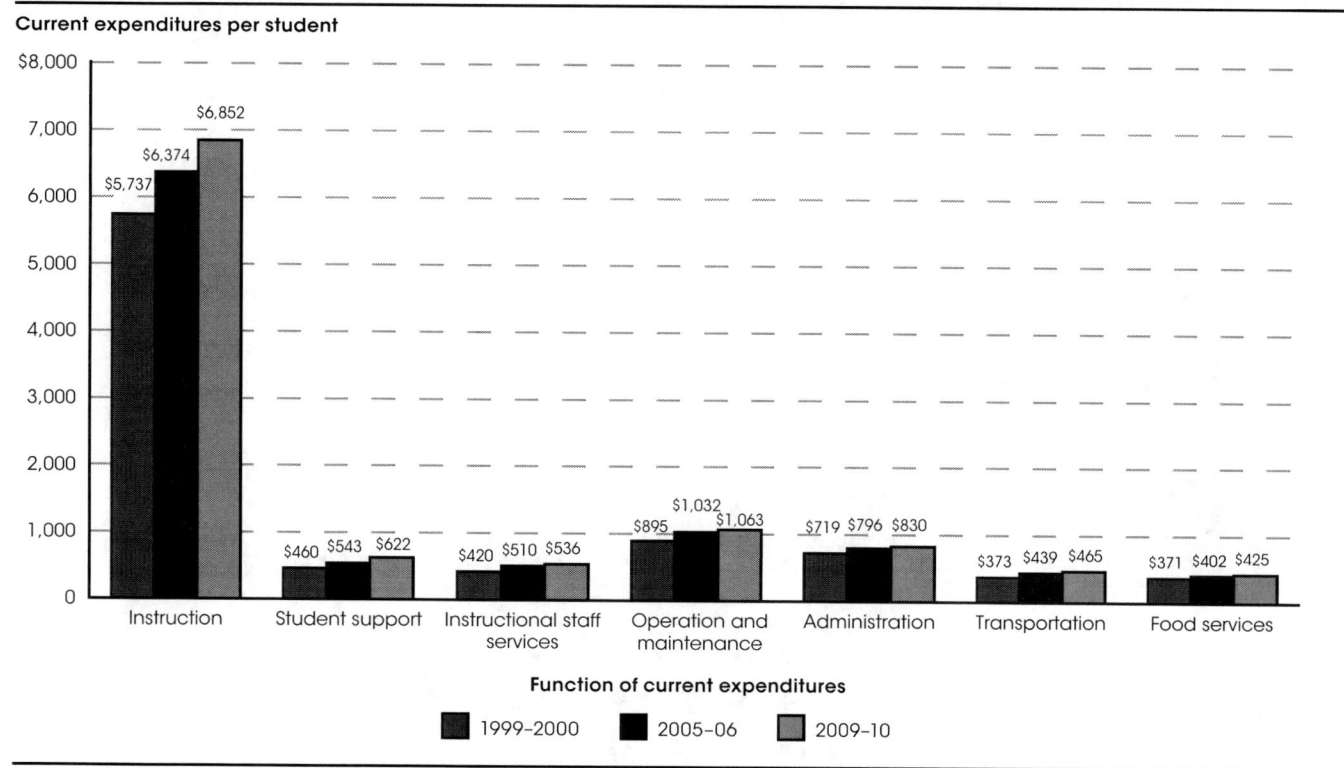

[Bar chart showing current expenditures per student by function:
- Instruction: $5,737 (1999–2000), $6,374 (2005–06), $6,852 (2009–10)
- Student support: $460, $543, $622
- Instructional staff services: $420, $510, $536
- Operation and maintenance: $895, $1,032, $1,063
- Administration: $719, $796, $830
- Transportation: $373, $439, $465
- Food services: $371, $402, $425]

NOTE: "Instruction," "Student support," "Instructional staff services," "Operation and maintenance," "Administration," "Transportation," and "Food services" are subcategories of "Current expenditures." "Student support" includes expenditures for guidance, health, attendance, and speech pathology services. "Instructional staff services" includes expenditures for curriculum development, staff training, libraries, and media and computer centers. Expenditures are reported in constant 2011-12 dollars, based on the Consumer Price Index (CPI).
SOURCE: U.S. Department of Education, National Center for Education Statistics, Common Core of Data (CCD), "National Public Education Financial Survey," selected years, 1999–2000, 2005–06, and 2009–10. See *Digest of Education Statistics 2012*, table 214.

The single largest component of current expenditures was instruction, amounting to about 61 percent of the total, or $6,852 per student in 2009–10. These expenditures include salaries and benefits of teachers and teaching assistants, as well as costs for instructional materials and instructional services provided under contract. Between 1999–2000 and 2009–10, expenditures for instruction per student increased by 19 percent. Expenditures for some major school activities increased more rapidly than this. For example, expenditures for student support services, such as for guidance and health personnel, increased by 35 percent, from $460 to $622. Expenditures per student for instructional staff services, including curriculum development, staff training, libraries, and media and computer centers, increased by 28 percent, reaching $536 in 2009–10. Also, transportation costs per student increased by 25 percent during this period, reaching $465 per student. In contrast, some categories of expenditure increased at a slower rate than instruction. School and general administrative costs per student and food services expenditures per student both increased by 15 percent, reaching $830 and $425, respectively, in 2009–10. Expenditures per student for operation and maintenance of schools increased by the same percentage as instruction costs (19 percent) and reached $1,063 per student in 2009–10.

For more information, see the Reader's Guide and the Guide to Sources.

Chapter: 3/Elementary and Secondary Education
Section: Finance

Figure 3. Percentage of current expenditures per student in fall enrollment in public elementary and secondary schools, by object of current expenditures: 1999–2000, 2005–06, and 2009–10

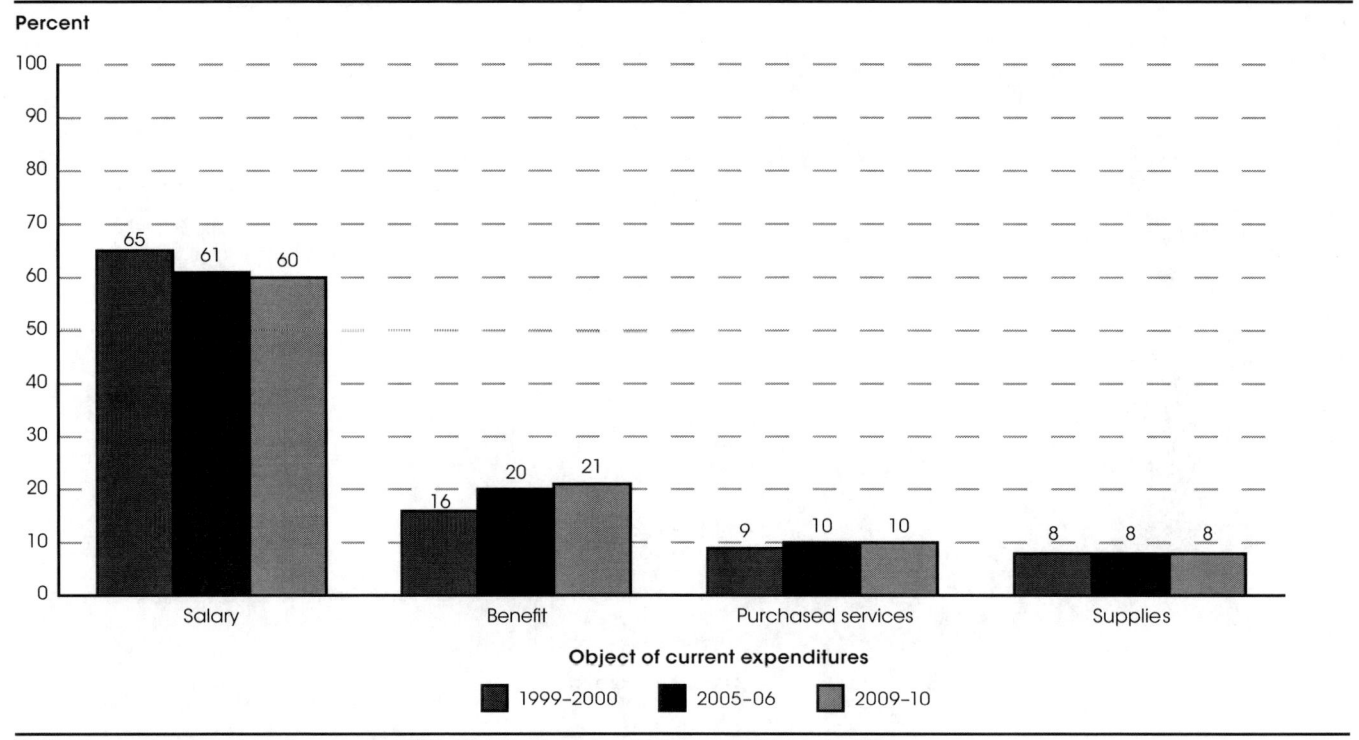

Object of current expenditures	1999–2000	2005–06	2009–10
Salary	65	61	60
Benefit	16	20	21
Purchased services	9	10	10
Supplies	8	8	8

NOTE: All percentages are based on constant 2011-12 dollars, based on the Consumer Price Index (CPI).
SOURCE: U.S. Department of Education, National Center for Education Statistics, Common Core of Data (CCD), "National Public Education Financial Survey," 1999-2000, 2005-06, and 2009-10. See *Digest of Education Statistics 2012*, table 214.

Current expenditures can also be expressed in terms of the percentage going toward salaries and benefits for all staff or for supplies for all activities. In 2009–10, about 81 percent of current expenditures were for salaries and benefits for staff. About 10 percent of current expenditures were for purchased services, which include a wide variety of items, such as contracts for food, transportation, or janitorial services, or for professional development for teachers. Another 8 percent of school expenditures were for supplies, ranging from books to heating oil. This expenditure distribution has shifted only slightly from 1999–2000 to 2009–10, when expenditures for purchased services increased from 9 to 10 percent and expenditures in other categories changed less than a percentage point. However, there has been a shift within the labor costs for staff. The proportion of school budgets for staff salaries decreased from 65 percent in 1999–2000 to 60 percent in 2009–10. In contrast, the proportion of school budgets for staff benefits increased from 16 to 21 percent during this period.

Reference tables: *Digest of Education Statistics 2012*, tables 205, 213, 214

Glossary: Consumer Price Index (CPI), Current expenditures (elementary/secondary), Expenditures, Public school or institution, Salary

For more information, see the Reader's Guide and the Guide to Sources.

This page intentionally left blank.

Chapter: 3/Elementary and Secondary Education
Section: Finance

Indicator 22
Education Expenditures by Country

In 2009, the United States spent $11,831 per full-time-equivalent (FTE) student on elementary and secondary education, an amount 38 percent higher than the OECD average of $8,595. At the postsecondary level, U.S. expenditures per FTE student were $29,201, more than twice as high as the OECD average of $13,461.

The Organisation for Economic Co-operation and Development (OECD) is an organization of 34 countries whose purpose is to promote trade and economic growth. This indicator uses material from the OECD report *Education at a Glance 2012* to compare countries' expenditures on education using the measures *expenditures per full-time-equivalent (FTE) student from both public and private sources* and *total education expenditures as a percentage of gross domestic product (GDP)*. The latter measure allows a comparison of countries' expenditures relative to their ability to finance education. Education expenditures are from public revenue sources (governments) and private revenue sources, and include current and capital expenditures. Private sources include payments from households for school-based expenses such as tuition, transportation fees, book rentals, or food services, as well as funds raised by institutions through endowments or returns on investments. Purchasing power parity (PPP) indexes are used to convert other currencies to U.S. dollars (i.e., absolute terms).

Expenditures per FTE student varied widely across OECD countries. At the elementary and secondary level, expenditures per FTE student in 2009 ranged from $2,339 for Mexico and $2,635 for Chile to $18,018 for Luxembourg. Expenditures per FTE student for the United States were $11,831, an amount 38 percent higher than the average of $8,595 for OECD member countries reporting data. U.S. expenditures were also higher than the Group of Eight (G8) countries of Canada, France, Germany, Italy, Japan, and the United Kingdom. In the G8, OECD countries other than the United States, expenditures per FTE student at the elementary and secondary level ranged from $8,502 for Japan to $9,602 for the United Kingdom.

At the postsecondary level, expenditures per FTE student in 2009 ranged from $6,071 for Chile and $6,373 for Estonia to $29,201 for the United States. U.S. expenditures per FTE student were more than twice as high as the OECD average of $13,461, and were the highest of the G8, OECD countries. In the G8, OECD countries other than the United States, expenditures per FTE student at the postsecondary level ranged from $9,562 in Italy to $16,338 in the United Kingdom.

Among the OECD countries reporting data in 2009, the five countries spending the highest percentage of GDP on total education expenditures for all education levels combined were Iceland (8.1 percent), Republic of Korea (8.0 percent), Denmark (7.9 percent), New Zealand (7.4 percent), and the United States (7.3 percent). In terms of countries' expenditures by education level, the percentage of GDP the United States spent on elementary and secondary education (4.3 percent) was higher than the OECD average percentage of GDP spent on elementary and secondary education (4.0 percent). Compared with the United States, 8 OECD countries spent a higher percentage and 20 spent a lower percentage. Iceland and New Zealand were the OECD countries that spent the highest percentage (both 5.2 percent) of GDP on elementary and secondary education. At the postsecondary level, spending as a percentage of GDP for the United States (2.6 percent) was higher than the OECD average (1.5 percent) and higher than spending as a percentage of GDP for any other OECD country reporting data except the Republic of Korea (2.6 percent).

For more information, see the Reader's Guide and the Guide to Sources.

Chapter: 3/Elementary and Secondary Education
Section: Finance

Figure 1. Annual expenditures per full-time-equivalent student for elementary and secondary education in selected Organisation for Economic Co-operation and Development (OECD) countries, by gross domestic product (GDP) per capita: 2009

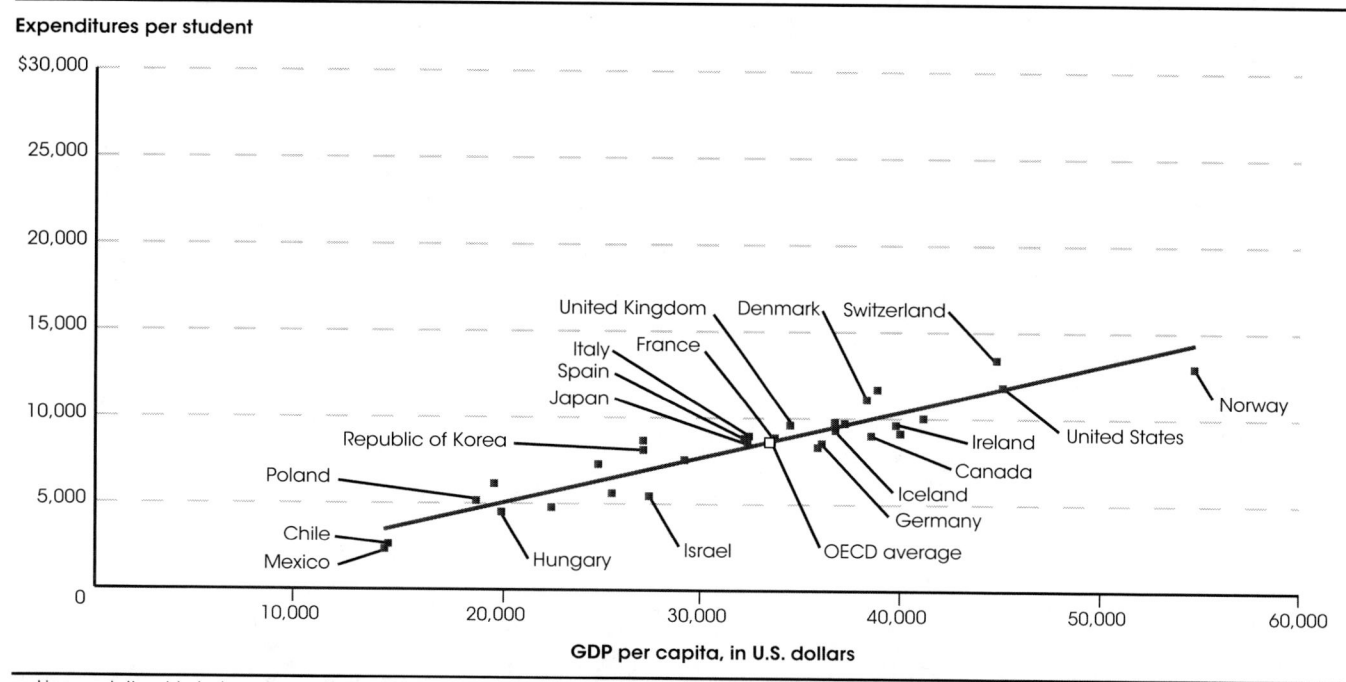

— Linear relationship between spending and country wealth for 31 OECD countries reporting data (elementary/secondary): $r^2 = .87$; slope = .27; intercept = -399.
NOTE: Data for Luxembourg are excluded because of anomalies in that country's Gross Domestic Product (GDP) per capita data. (Large revenues from international finance institutions distort the wealth of the population.) Data for Greece are excluded because expenditure data are not available for 2009 or 2008. Expenditure and GDP data for Canada are for 2008. Expenditures in this figure generally include postsecondary nontertiary (International Standard Classification of Education level 4) education expenditures, except for expenditures for Canada, France, Greece, Italy, Luxembourg, Portugal, and the United States.
SOURCE: Organisation for Economic Co-operation and Development (OECD), Center for Educational Research and Innovation. (2012). *Education at a Glance, 2012.* See *Digest of Education Statistics 2012,* table 476.

Figure 2. Annual expenditures per full-time-equivalent student for postsecondary education in selected Organisation for Economic Co-operation and Development (OECD) countries, by gross domestic product (GDP) per capita: 2009

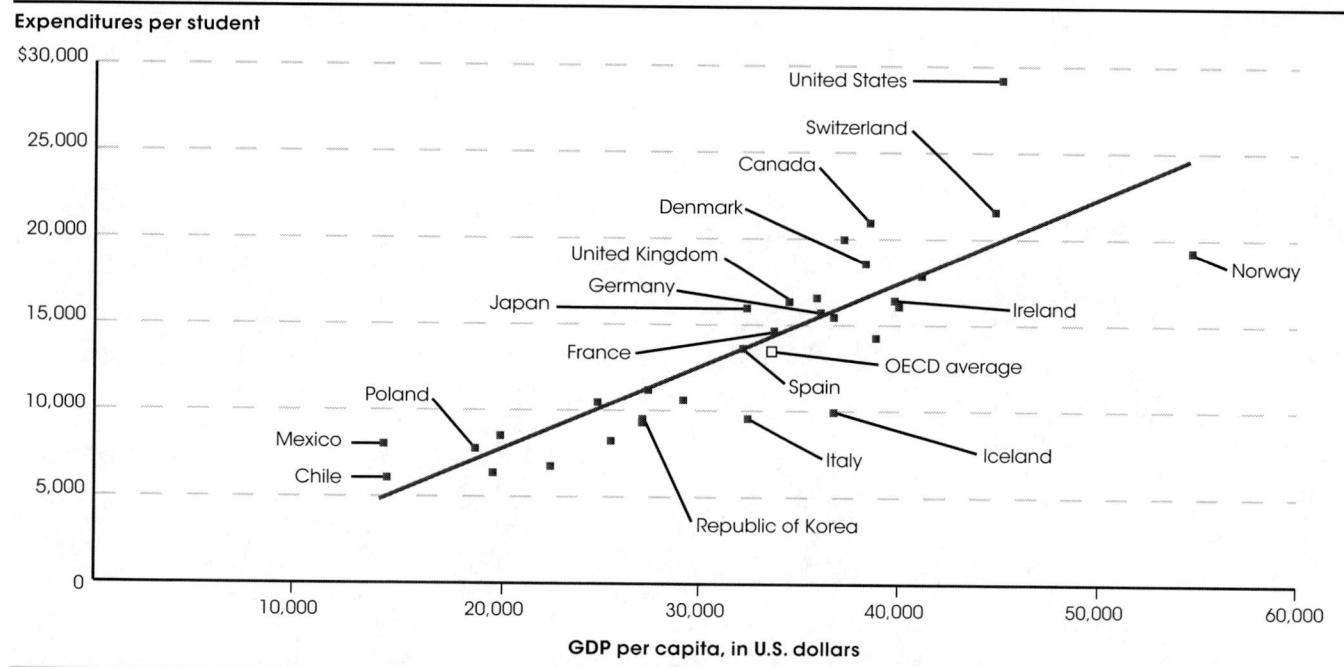

— Linear relationship between spending and country wealth for 31 OECD countries reporting data (postsecondary): $r^2 = .71$; slope = .49; intercept = -2,113.
NOTE: Data for Luxembourg are excluded because that country does not report expenditure data for postsecondary institutions. Data for Greece are excluded because expenditure data are not available for 2009. Expenditure and GDP data for Canada are for 2008.
SOURCE: Organisation for Economic Co-operation and Development (OECD), Center for Educational Research and Innovation. (2012). *Education at a Glance, 2012.* See *Digest of Education Statistics 2012,* table 476.

For more information, see the Reader's Guide and the Guide to Sources.

A country's wealth (defined as GDP per capita) is positively associated with expenditures per FTE student on education at the elementary and secondary level as well as at the postsecondary level. For example, education expenditures per FTE student (both elementary and secondary and postsecondary) for 9 of the OECD countries with the highest GDP per capita in 2009 were higher than the OECD average expenditures per FTE student. The expenditures per FTE student for the 10 OECD countries with the lowest GDP per capita were generally below the OECD average at both the elementary and secondary level and at the postsecondary level.

Reference tables: *Digest of Education Statistics 2012,* tables 476, 477

Glossary: Expenditures per pupil, Full-time-equivalent (FTE) enrollment, Gross domestic product (GDP), Organisation for Economic Co-operation and Development (OECD), Postsecondary education, Purchasing Power Parity (PPP) indexes

This page intentionally left blank.

Indicator 23
Reading Performance

The average grade 4 reading score in 2011 was not measurably different from that in 2009. The average grade 8 score, however, was 1 point higher in 2011 than in 2009.

Chapter: 3/Elementary and Secondary Education
Section: Assessments

The National Assessment of Educational Progress (NAEP) assesses student performance in reading at grades 4, 8, and 12. NAEP reading scores range from 0 to 500. NAEP achievement levels define what students should know and be able to do: *Basic* indicates partial mastery of fundamental skills; *Proficient* indicates demonstrated competency over challenging subject matter; and *Advanced* indicates superior performance. This indicator presents data on NAEP reading achievement levels for various student subgroups. NAEP reading assessments are administered periodically: the most recent reading assessment data were collected at grades 4 and 8 in 2011 and at grade 12 in 2009.

Figure 1. Average reading scale scores of 4th-, 8th-, and 12th-grade students: Selected years, 1992–2011

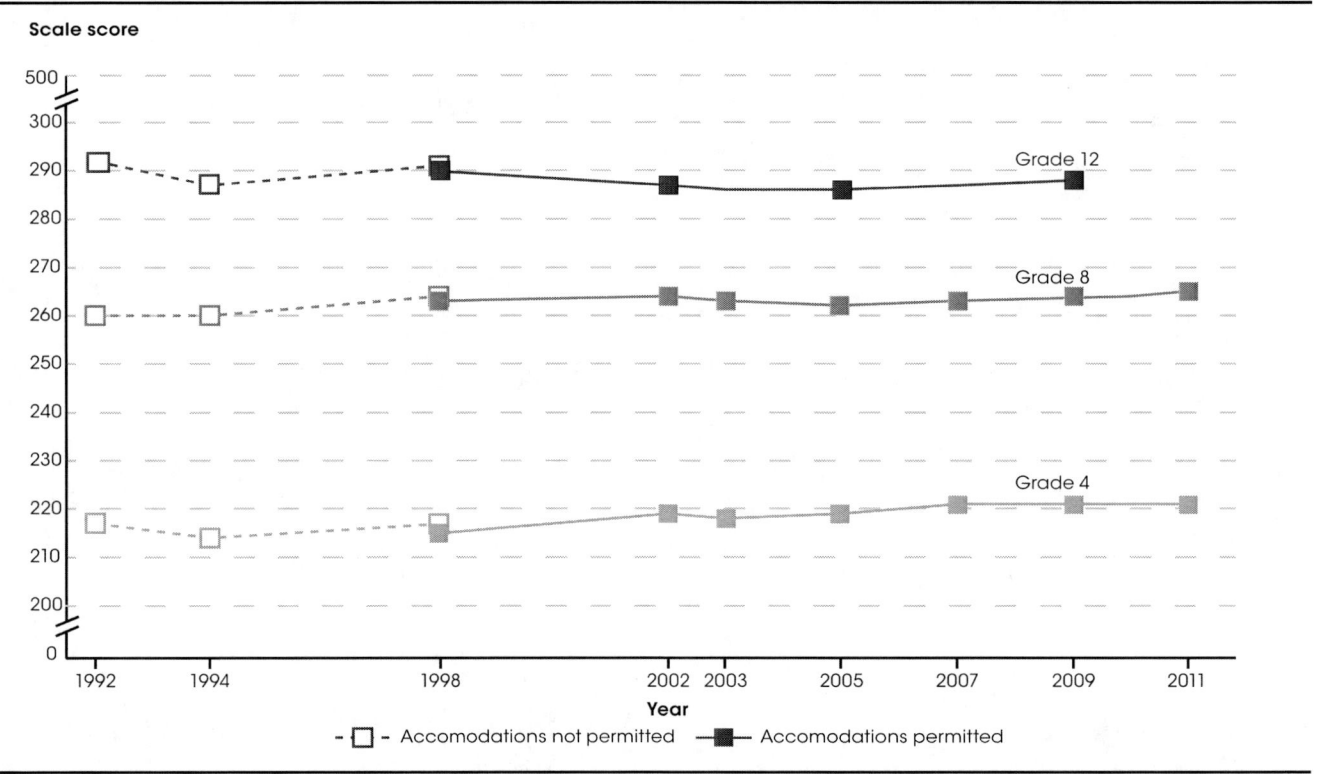

NOTE: The National Assessment of Educational Progress (NAEP) reading scale ranges from 0 to 500. Student assessments are not designed to permit comparisons across subjects or grades. Testing accommodations (e.g., extended time, small group testing) for children with disabilities and English language learners were not permitted in 1992 and 1994; students were tested with and without accommodations in 1998. The 12th-grade NAEP reading assessment was not administered in 2003, 2007, or 2011.
SOURCE: U.S. Department of Education, National Center for Education Statistics, National Assessment of Educational Progress (NAEP), selected years, 1992–2011 Reading Assessments, NAEP Data Explorer. See *Digest of Education Statistics 2012*, table 142.

In 2011, the average reading score for 4th-grade students (221) was not measurably different from the 2009 score (221), but it was higher than the scores on assessments between 1992 (217) and 2005 (219). For 8th-grade students, the average reading score in 2011 (265) was 1 point higher than in 2009 (264) and 5 points higher than in 1992 (260), but was not always measurably different from scores on assessments given in other years. In 2009, the average reading score for 12th-grade students (288) was 2 points higher than in 2005 (286) but 4 points lower than in 1992 (292).

For more information, see the Reader's Guide and the Guide to Sources.

Chapter: 3/Elementary and Secondary Education
Section: Assessments

Figure 2. Percentage distribution of 4th- and 8th-grade students across National Assessment of Educational Progress (NAEP) reading achievement levels: Selected years, 1992–2011

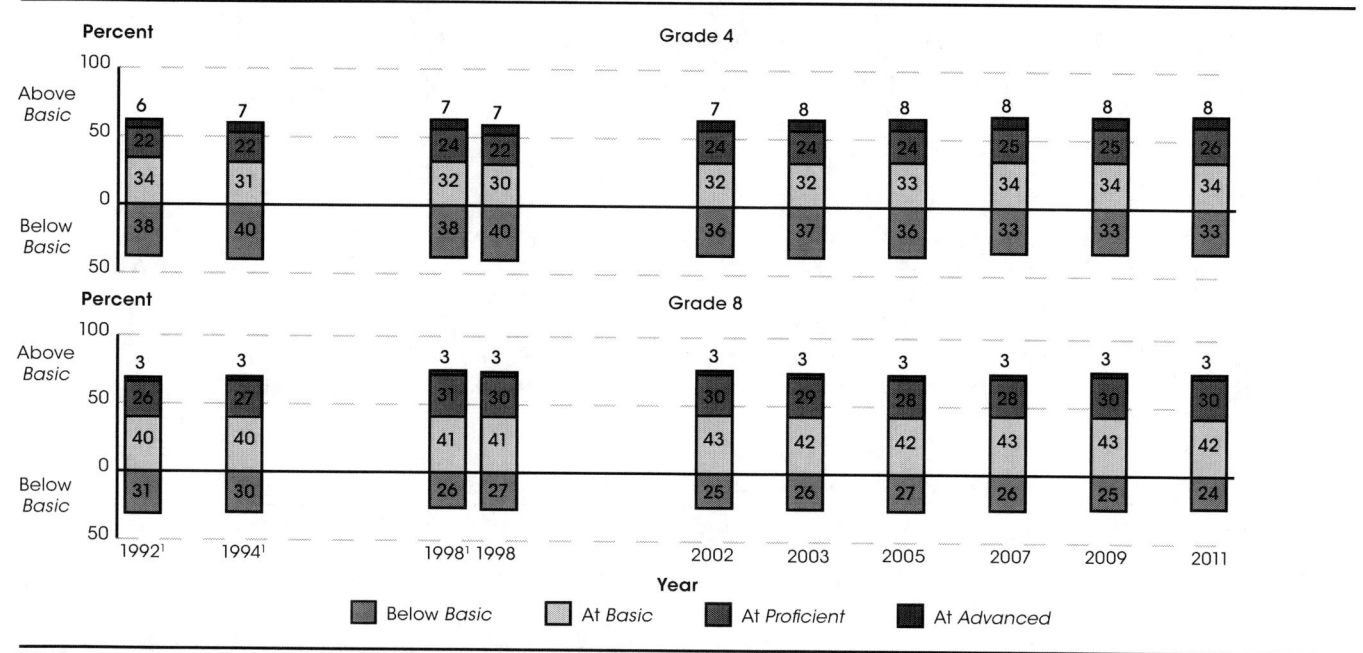

[1] Testing accommodations (e.g., extended time, small group testing) for children with disabilities and English language learners were not permitted during these assessments. Students were tested with and without accommodations in 1998.
NOTE: Achievement levels define what students should know and be able to do: *Basic* indicates partial mastery of fundamental skills, *Proficient* indicates demonstrated competency over challenging subject matter, and *Advanced* indicates superior performance. Detail may not sum to totals because of rounding.
SOURCE: U.S. Department of Education, National Center for Education Statistics, National Assessment of Educational Progress (NAEP), selected years, 1992–2011 Reading Assessments, NAEP Data Explorer. See *Digest of Education Statistics 2012*, table 143.

In 2011, the percentages of 4th-grade students performing at or above the *Basic* (67 percent), at or above the *Proficient* (34 percent), and at the *Advanced* (8 percent) achievement levels in reading showed no measurable change from 2009, but were higher than in 1992. Among 8th-grade students, the percentage performing at or above *Basic* in 2011 (76 percent) was not measurably different from that in 2009 (75 percent) but was higher than the percentage in 1992 (69 percent). A higher percentage of 8th-grade students performed at or above *Proficient* in 2011 (34 percent) than in 2009 (32 percent) and 1992 (29 percent). The percentage at the *Advanced* level in 2011 (3.4 percent) was half a percentage point higher than the percentage performing at *Advanced* in 2009 (2.8 percent) but was not measurably different from the percentage in 1992 (2.9 percent). Among 12th-grade students, the percentage performing at or above *Basic* (74 percent) in 2009 was not significantly different from the percentage in 2005 (73 percent), but was lower than the percentage in 1992 (80 percent). The percentage at or above *Proficient* was higher in 2009 (38 percent) than in 2005 (35 percent) but not significantly different from the percentage in 1992 (40 percent). There was no measurable change in the percentage of 12th-graders performing at *Advanced* from 2005 to 2009 (5 percent each), although the 2009 percentage was 1 percentage point higher than that in 1992.

At grade 4, the average reading scores in 2011 for White, Black, Hispanic, Asian/Pacific Islander, and American Indian/Alaska Native students were not measurably different from their scores in 2009. The 2011 grade 4 reading scores for White, Black, Hispanic, and Asian/Pacific Islander students were, however, higher than their scores in 1992. At grade 8, average reading scores for White, Black, and Hispanic students were higher in 2011 than their scores in any of the previous assessment years. At grade 12, average scores showed no measurable differences from 1992 to 2009 for White, Black, Hispanic, Asian/Pacific Islander, and American Indian/Alaska Native students.

NAEP results also permit state-level comparisons of the reading abilities of 4th- and 8th-grade students in public schools. While there was no measurable change from 2009 to 2011 in the overall average score for 4th-grade public school students in the nation, average scores were higher in 2011 than in 2009 in Alabama, Hawaii, Maryland, and Massachusetts, and scores were lower in 2011 in Missouri and South Dakota. At grade 8, although the average score for public school students in the nation was 2 points higher in 2011 than in 2009, only ten states had higher scores in 2011 than in 2009. These states were Colorado, Connecticut, Hawaii, Idaho, Maryland, Michigan, Montana, Nevada, North Carolina, and Rhode Island. In the remaining states and the District of Columbia, scores showed no measurable change.

Reference tables: *Digest of Education Statistics 2012*, tables 142, 143, 147, 148

Glossary: Achievement levels

For more information, see the Reader's Guide and the Guide to Sources.

Indicator 24
Mathematics Performance

At grades 4 and 8, the average mathematics scores in 2011 were higher than the average scores for those grades in all previous assessment years.

The National Assessment of Educational Progress (NAEP) assesses student performance in mathematics at grades 4, 8, and 12. NAEP mathematics scores range from 0 to 500 for grades 4 and 8. The framework for the 12th-grade mathematics assessment was revised in 2005; as a result, the 2005 and 2009 results cannot be compared with those from previous years. At grade 12, mathematics scores on the revised assessment range from 0 to 300.

NAEP achievement levels define what students should know and be able to do: *Basic* indicates partial mastery of fundamental skills; *Proficient* indicates demonstrated competency over challenging subject matter; and *Advanced* indicates superior performance. This indicator presents data on NAEP mathematics achievement levels. The most recent mathematics assessment data were collected at grades 4 and 8 in 2011 and at grade 12 in 2009.

Figure 1. Average mathematics scale scores of 4th- and 8th-grade students: Selected years, 1990–2011

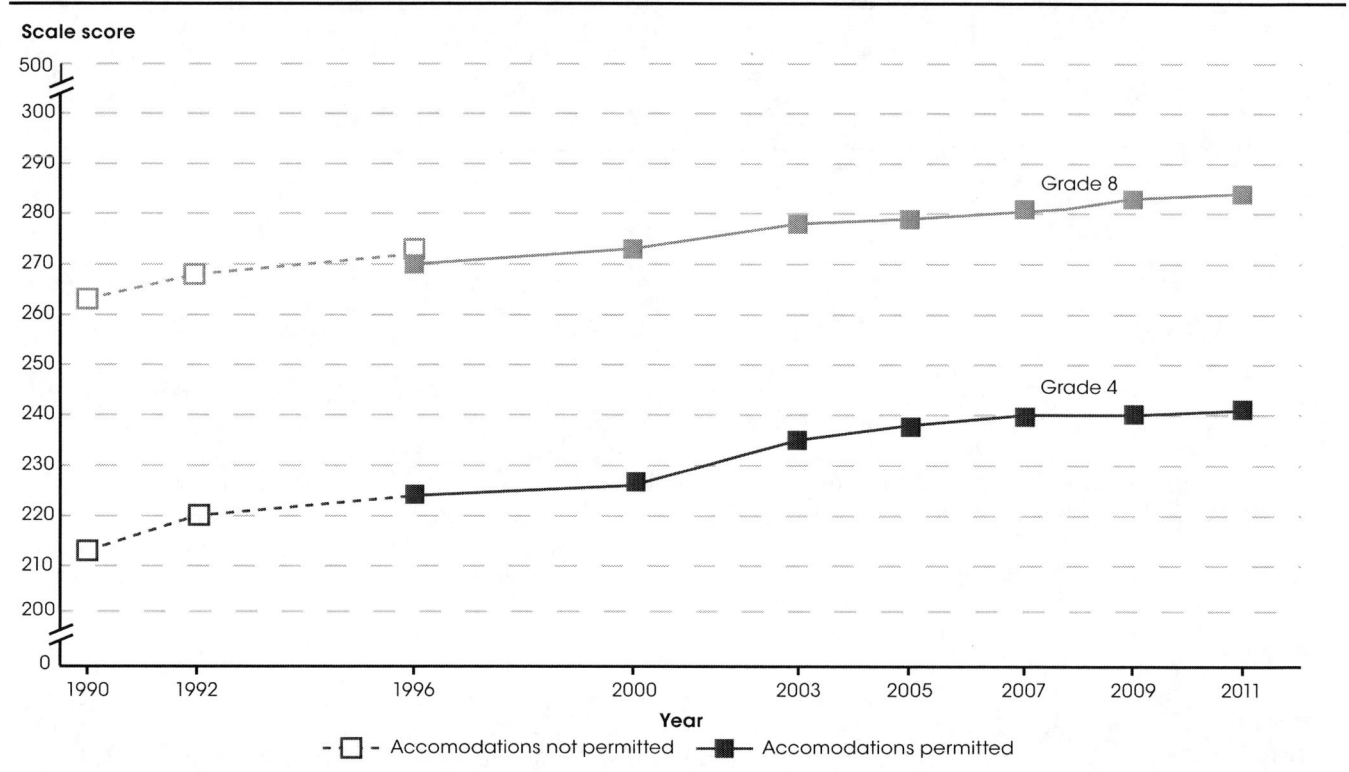

NOTE: At grades 4 and 8, the National Assessment of Educational Progress (NAEP) mathematics scale ranges from 0 to 500. Testing accommodations (e.g., extended time, small group testing) for children with disabilities and English language learners were not permitted in 1990 and 1992; students were tested with and without accommodations in 1996.
SOURCE: U.S. Department of Education, National Center for Education Statistics, National Assessment of Educational Progress (NAEP), selected years, 1990–2011 Mathematics Assessments, NAEP Data Explorer. See *Digest of Education Statistics 2012*, table 160.

In 2011, the average NAEP mathematics scores for 4th-grade and 8th-grade students were higher than their average scores in all previous assessment years. From 1990 to 2011, the average 4th-grade NAEP mathematics score increased by 28 points, from 213 to 241. During that same period, the average 8th-grade score increased by 21 points, from 263 to 284. Twelfth-graders were most recently assessed in 2009; in that year, the average 12th-grade mathematics score was 3 points higher than in 2005, the first year that the revised assessment was administered.

For more information, see the Reader's Guide and the Guide to Sources.

Chapter: 3/Elementary and Secondary Education
Section: Assessments

Figure 2. Percentage distribution of 4th- and 8th-grade students across National Assessment of Educational Progress (NAEP) mathematics achievement levels: Selected years, 1990–2011

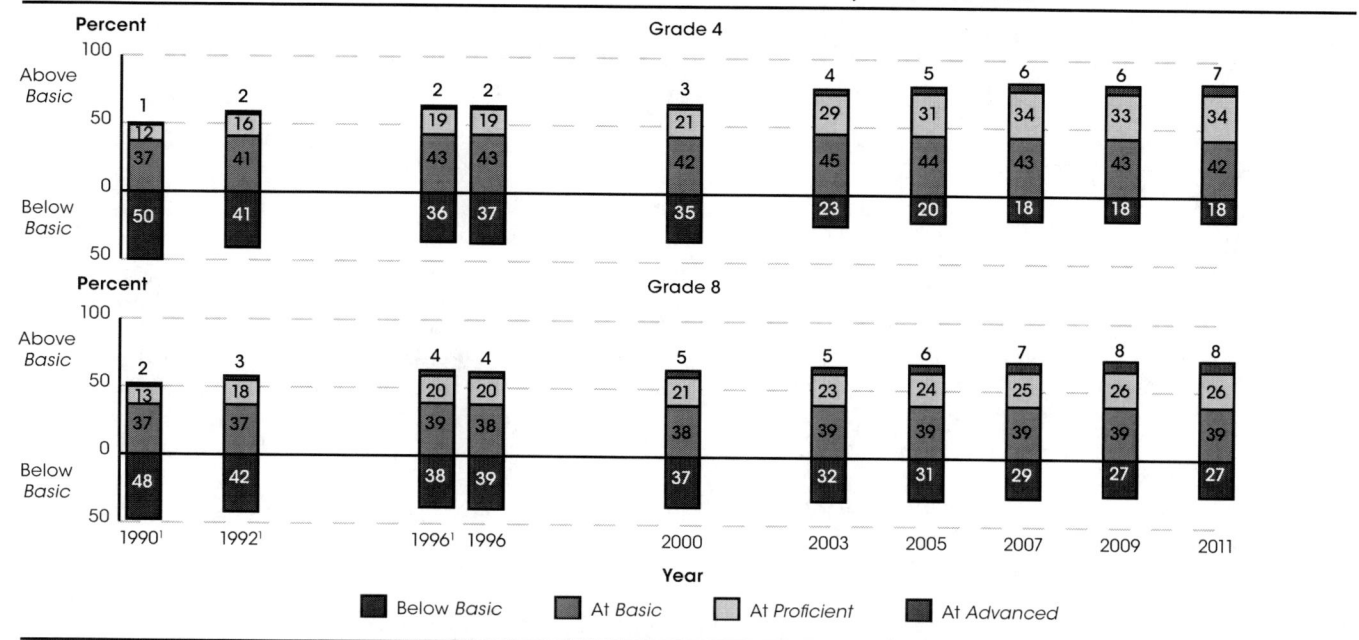

Grade 4	1990[1]	1992[1]	1996[1]	1996	2000	2003	2005	2007	2009	2011
At Advanced	1	2	2	2	3	4	5	6	6	7
At Proficient	12	16	19	19	21	29	31	34	33	34
At Basic	37	41	43	43	42	45	44	43	43	42
Below Basic	50	41	36	37	35	23	20	18	18	18

Grade 8	1990[1]	1992[1]	1996[1]	1996	2000	2003	2005	2007	2009	2011
At Advanced	2	3	4	4	5	5	6	7	8	8
At Proficient	13	18	20	20	21	23	24	25	26	26
At Basic	37	37	39	38	38	39	39	39	39	39
Below Basic	48	42	38	39	37	32	31	29	27	27

■ Below Basic ■ At Basic ■ At Proficient ■ At Advanced

[1] Testing accommodations (e.g., extended time, small group testing) for children with disabilities and English language learners were not permitted during these assessments. Students were tested with and without accommodations in 1996.
NOTE: Achievement levels define what students should know and be able to do: *Basic* indicates partial mastery of fundamental skills; *Proficient* indicates demonstrated competency over challenging subject matter; and *Advanced* indicates superior performance. Detail may not sum to totals because of rounding.
SOURCE: U.S. Department of Education, National Center for Education Statistics, National Assessment of Educational Progress (NAEP), selected years, 1990–2011 Mathematics Assessments, NAEP Data Explorer. See *Digest of Education Statistics 2012*, table 161.

In 2011, some 82 percent of 4th-grade students performed at or above the *Basic* achievement level, 40 percent performed at or above the *Proficient* level, and 7 percent performed at the *Advanced* level. While the percentage of students at or above the *Basic* level in 2011 was not measurably different from that in 2009 or 2007 (both 82 percent), it was higher than the percentage in 1990 (50 percent). Higher percentages of 4th-grade students performed at or above *Proficient* and at *Advanced* in 2011 than in all previous assessment years. In 2011, some 73 percent of 8th-grade students performed at or above *Basic*, 35 percent performed at or above *Proficient*, and 8 percent performed at *Advanced*. The percentage of 8th-grade students performing at or above *Proficient* increased by 1 percentage point from 2009 to 2011. The percentages at or above *Basic* and at *Advanced* in 2011 showed no measurable change from 2009, but were higher than the percentages in all assessment years prior to 2009. The percentages of 12th-grade students performing at or above *Basic* (64 percent) and at or above *Proficient* (26 percent) were each 3 percentage points higher in 2009 than in 2005. The percentages performing at the *Advanced* level in 2005 and 2009 were not measurably different (2 and 3 percent, respectively).

At grade 4, the average mathematics scores in 2011 for White (249), Black (224), and Hispanic students (229) were higher than their scores in both 2009 and 1990. The 2011 score for Asian/Pacific Islander 4th-graders (256) was not measurably different from the 2009 score (255), but was higher than the score in 1990. At grade 8, the average mathematics score for Hispanic students was 4 points higher in 2011 (270) than in 2009 (266), but the scores for White, Black, and Asian/Pacific Islander students did not measurably change. The 2011 scores for these four groups were, however, higher than their scores in 1990. The 2011 score for American Indian/Alaska Native 8th-grade students was not measurably different from their score in 2009. At grade 12, average mathematics scores were higher in 2009 than in 2005 for all racial/ethnic groups. For example, the average score for Asian/Pacific Islander 12th-grade students increased by 13 points, and the average score for American Indian/Alaska Native students increased by 10 points.

NAEP results also permit state-level comparisons of the mathematics achievement of 4th- and 8th-grade students in public schools. The average mathematics scores for 4th-grade public school students increased from 2009 to 2011 in eight states (Alabama, Arizona, Georgia, Hawaii, Maryland, New Mexico, Rhode Island, and Wyoming) and the District of Columbia and decreased in New York. At grade 8, scores were higher in 2011 than in 2009 in 12 states (Arkansas, Colorado, Hawaii, Maine, Mississippi, Nevada, New Mexico, Ohio, Oklahoma, Rhode Island, Texas, and West Virginia) and the District of Columbia. The average 8th-grade score in Missouri decreased.

Reference tables: *Digest of Education Statistics 2012*, tables 160, 161, 164, 165

Glossary: Achievement levels

For more information, see the Reader's Guide and the Guide to Sources.

Indicator 25
Reading and Mathematics Score Trends

Chapter: 3/Elementary and Secondary Education
Section: Assessments

The average reading and mathematics scores on the long-term trend National Assessment of Educational Progress were higher in 2008 than in the early 1970s for 9- and 13-year-olds; however, scores for 17-year-olds were not measurably different from the early 1970s.

The long-term trend National Assessment of Educational Progress (NAEP) provides information on the reading and mathematics achievement of 9-, 13-, and 17-year-olds enrolled in both public and private schools in the United States. Data have been collected every 2 to 5 years since 1971 for reading and since 1973 for mathematics. Long-term trend NAEP results may differ from the main NAEP results presented in other National Center for Education Statistics (NCES) publications since the long-term trend assessment measures a consistent body of knowledge and skills over an extended period, while the main NAEP undergoes changes periodically to reflect current curricula and emerging standards. Several administrative changes were initiated in the 2004 long-term trend assessment that have been carried forward to 2008, including allowing accommodations for students with disabilities and for English language learners. All comparisons referring to 2004 are based on the revised assessment scores.

Figure 1. Average reading scale scores on the long-term trend National Assessment of Educational Progress (NAEP), by age: Selected years, 1971 through 2008

NOTE: Includes public and private schools. NAEP scores range from 0 to 500. Several administrative changes were initiated in the 2004 long-term trend assessment that have been carried forward to 2008, including allowing accommodations for students with disabilities and for English language learners. To ensure that any changes in scores were due to actual changes in student performance and not due to changes in the assessment itself, two assessments were conducted in 2004—one based on the previous assessment and one based on the modified assessment. In 2008, only the modified assessment was used. Scores from both assessments are shown for 2004; the results for all assessments prior to 2004 are labeled as the original assessment. The results for the modified 2004 and 2008 assessments are labeled as the revised assessment.
SOURCE: Rampey, B.D., Dion, G.S., and Donahue, P.L. (2009). *NAEP 2008 Trends in Academic Progress in Reading and Mathematics* (NCES 2009-479). National Center for Education Statistics, Institute of Education Sciences, U.S. Department of Education, Washington, DC. See *Digest of Education Statistics 2012*, table 140.

For more information, see the Reader's Guide and the Guide to Sources.

Chapter: 3/Elementary and Secondary Education
Section: Assessments

Figure 2. Average mathematics scale scores on the long-term trend National Assessment of Educational Progress (NAEP), by age: Selected years, 1973 through 2008

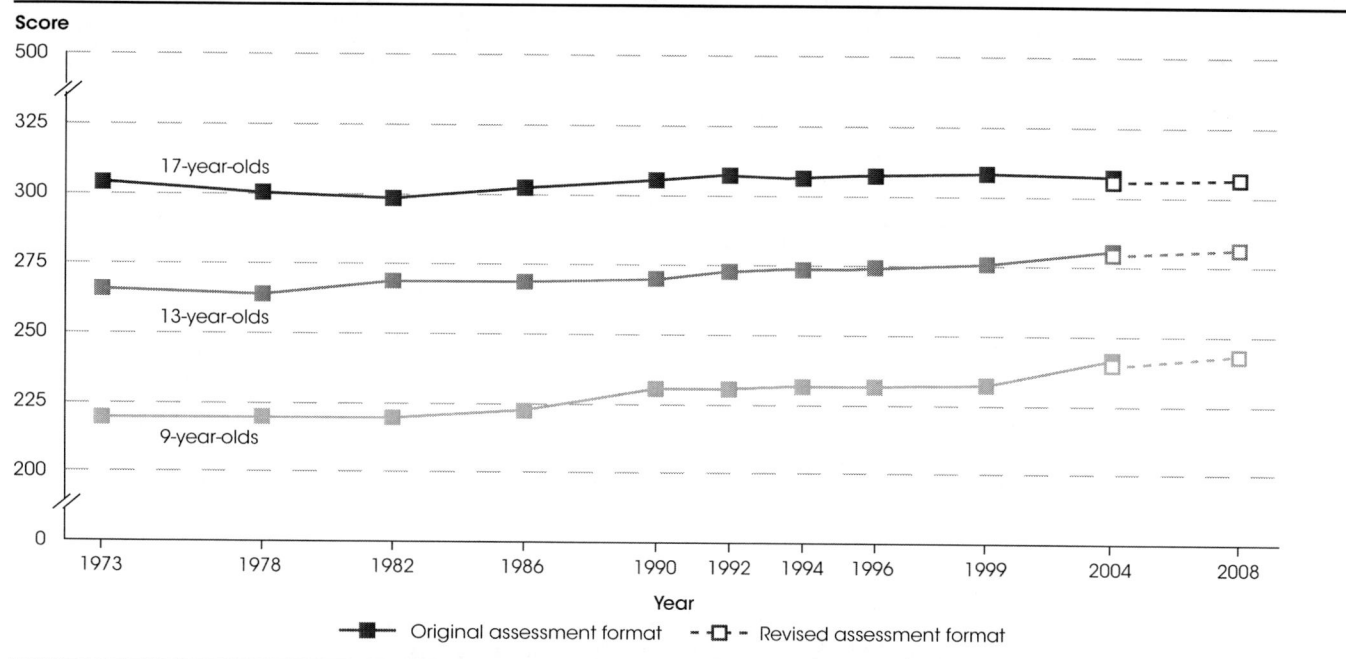

NOTE: Includes public and private schools. NAEP scores range from 0 to 500. Several administrative changes were initiated in the 2004 long-term trend assessment that have been carried forward to 2008, including allowing accommodations for students with disabilities and for English language learners. To ensure that any changes in scores were due to actual changes in student performance and not due to changes in the assessment itself, two assessments were conducted in 2004—one based on the previous assessment and one based on the modified assessment. In 2008, only the modified assessment was used. Scores from both assessments are shown for 2004; the results for all assessments prior to 2004 are labeled as the original assessment. The results for the modified 2004 and 2008 assessments are labeled as the revised assessment.
SOURCE: Rampey, B.D., Dion, G.S., and Donahue, P.L. (2009). *NAEP 2008 Trends in Academic Progress in Reading and Mathematics* (NCES 2009-479). National Center for Education Statistics, Institute of Education Sciences, U.S. Department of Education, Washington, DC. See *Digest of Education Statistics 2012*, table 157.

NAEP long-term trend results indicate that the average reading and mathematics achievement of 9- and 13-year-olds improved between the early 1970s and 2008. In reading, 9-year-olds scored higher in 2008 than in any previous assessment year, scoring 4 points higher than in 2004 and 12 points higher than in 1971. The average reading score for 13-year-olds was higher in 2008 than in both 2004 and 1971, but the 2008 score was not significantly different from the scores in 1980, 1988, and any test years from 1992 through 1999. In mathematics, the average scores for 9- and 13-year-olds were higher in 2008 than in all previous assessment years. The 2008 average mathematics score for 9-year-olds showed a 4-point increase over the 2004 score and a 24-point increase over the 1973 score. Thirteen-year-olds scored 3 points higher in 2008 than in 2004 and 15 points higher in 2008 than in 1973 in mathematics.

The average performance of 17-year-olds on the 2008 reading and mathematics assessments was not measurably different from their performance in the early 1970s. The average reading score for 17-year-olds was higher in 2008 than in 2004 but was not significantly different from the score in 1971. In mathematics, the average score for 17-year-olds in 2008 was not significantly different from the scores in either 2004 or 1973.

White, Black, and Hispanic 9-year-olds had higher average reading scores in 2008 than they had in previous assessments. The average reading score for White 9-year-old students was 14 points higher in 2008 than in 1971, the reading score for Black 9-year-old students was 34 points higher in 2008 than in 1971, and the reading score for Hispanic 9-year-old students was 25 points higher in 2008 than in 1975. Between 1971 and 2008, White 13-year-olds had a 7-point gain, and Black students showed a 25-point gain. Between 1971 and 2008, White 17-year-old students showed a gain of 4 points, while Black students showed a gain of 28 points. At ages 13 and 17, Hispanic student scores were higher in 2008 than in 1975. Scores for Hispanics increased between 1975 and 2008 by 10 points at age 13 and by 17 points at age 17.

Between 2004 and 2008, average reading scores increased for 9-year-olds across racial/ethnic groups. The average reading score for White 9-year-olds was 4 points higher in 2008 than in 2004, the reading score for Black 9-year-old students was 7 points higher in 2008 than in 2004, and the reading score for Hispanic 9-year-old students was 8 points higher in 2008 than in 2004. Between 2004 and 2008, White 13-year-olds had a 4-point gain, and Black students showed an 8-point gain. At age 17, only White students showed a significant increase (7 points) during this period.

For more information, see the Reader's Guide and the Guide to Sources.

Elementary and Secondary Education 107

In comparison to average mathematics scores in 1973, mathematics scores for 9-year-olds in 2008 were 25 points higher for White students, 34 points higher for Black students, and 32 points higher for Hispanic students. Between 1973 and 2008, White 13-year-olds gained 16 points, compared with a 34-point gain for Black 13-year-olds and a 29-point gain for Hispanic 13-year-olds. Similarly, the score for White 17-year-olds increased 4 points between 1973 and 2008, the score for Black students increased 17 points, and the score for Hispanic students increased 16 points.

In contrast to the increases in mathematics scores noted over the longer period from 1971 to 2008, only White 9-year-olds showed a significant increase (5 points) between 2004 and 2008.

Reference tables: *Digest of Education Statistics 2012*, tables 140, 157

This page intentionally left blank.

Indicator 26
International Assessments

At grade 4, the United States was among the top 15 and 10 participating education systems, respectively, in mathematics and science. At grade 8, the United States was among the top 24 and 23 participating education systems, respectively, in mathematics and science.

The United States participates in several international assessments that allow for cross-national comparisons of subject matter results, including the Trends in International Mathematics and Science Study (TIMSS) and the Progress in International Reading Literacy Study (PIRLS). Both assessments are coordinated by the TIMSS & PIRLS International Study Center at Boston College, under the auspices of the International Association for the Evaluation of Educational Achievement (IEA), an international organization of national research institutions and governmental research agencies. TIMSS assesses mathematics and science knowledge and skills at grades 4 and 8, and PIRLS assesses reading literacy at grade 4.

In 2011, there were 57 education systems that had TIMSS mathematics and science data at grade 4 and 56 education systems that had these data at grade 8. Education systems include countries (complete, independent, and political entities) and other benchmarking education systems (portions of a country, nation, kingdom, or emirate, or other non-national entities). These benchmarking systems are able to participate in TIMSS even though they may not be members of the IEA. Participating allows them the opportunity to assess their students' achievement and to view their curricula in an international context. In addition to participating in the U.S. national sample, several U.S. states participated individually and are included as education systems. At the 4th-grade level, two U.S. states (Florida-USA and North Carolina-USA) participated; at the 8th-grade level, nine U.S. states (Alabama-USA, California-USA, Colorado-USA, Connecticut-USA, Florida-USA, Indiana-USA, Massachusetts-USA, Minnesota-USA, and North Carolina-USA) participated.

For more information, see the Reader's Guide and the Guide to Sources.

Chapter: 3/Elementary and Secondary Education
Section: Assessments

Table 1. Average TIMSS mathematics assessment scale scores of 4th-grade students, by education system: 2011

Education system (Grade 4)	Average score	Education system (Grade 4)	Average score
TIMSS scale average	500	New Zealand	486 ▼
Singapore[1]	606 △	Spain	482 ▼
Korea, Rep. of	605 △	Romania	482 ▼
Hong Kong-CHN[1]	602 △	Poland	481 ▼
Chinese Taipei-CHN	591 △	Turkey	469 ▼
Japan	585 △	Azerbaijan[1,5]	463 ▼
Northern Ireland-GBR[2]	562 △	Chile	462 ▼
Belgium (Flemish)-BEL	549 △	Thailand	458 ▼
Finland	545	Armenia	452 ▼
England-GBR	542	Georgia[3,5]	450 ▼
Russian Federation	542	Bahrain	436 ▼
United States[1]	**541**	United Arab Emirates	434 ▼
Netherlands[2]	540	Iran, Islamic Rep. of	431 ▼
Denmark[1]	537	Qatar[1]	413 ▼
Lithuania[1,3]	534 ▼	Saudi Arabia	410 ▼
Portugal	532 ▼	Oman[6]	385 ▼
Germany	528 ▼	Tunisia[6]	359 ▼
Ireland	527 ▼	Kuwait[3,7]	342 ▼
Serbia[1]	516 ▼	Morocco[7]	335 ▼
Australia	516 ▼	Yemen[7]	248 ▼
Hungary	515 ▼		
Slovenia	513 ▼	**Benchmarking education systems**	
Czech Republic	511 ▼		
Austria	508 ▼	North Carolina-USA[1,3]	554 △
Italy	508 ▼	Florida-USA[3,8]	545
Slovak Republic	507 ▼	Quebec-CAN	533 ▼
Sweden	504 ▼	Ontario-CAN	518 ▼
Kazakhstan[1]	501 ▼	Alberta-CAN[1]	507 ▼
Malta	496 ▼	Dubai-UAE	468 ▼
Norway[4]	495 ▼	Abu Dhabi-UAE	417 ▼
Croatia[1]	490 ▼		

△ Average score is higher than U.S. average score.
▼ Average score is lower than U.S. average score.
[1] National Defined Population covers 90 to 95 percent of National Target Population defined by TIMSS.
[2] Met guidelines for sample participation rates only after replacement schools were included.
[3] National Target Population does not include all of the International Target Population defined by TIMSS.
[4] Nearly satisfied guidelines for sample participation rates after replacement schools were included.
[5] Exclusion rates for Azerbaijan and Georgia are slightly underestimated as some conflict zones were not covered and no official statistics were available.
[6] The TIMSS International Study Center has reservations about the reliability of the average achievement score because the percentage of students with achievement too low for estimation exceeds 15 percent, though it is less than 25 percent.
[7] The TIMSS International Study Center has reservations about the reliability of the average achievement score because the percentage of students with achievement too low for estimation exceeds 25 percent.
[8] National Defined Population covers less than 90 percent, but at least 77 percent, of National Target Population defined by TIMSS.
NOTE: Education systems are ordered by 2011 average score. Italics indicate participants identified and counted in this report as an education system and not as a separate country. Trends in International Mathematics and Science Study (TIMSS) scores are reported on a scale from 0 to 1,000, with the scale average set at 500 and the standard deviation set at 100. The TIMSS average includes only education systems that are members of the International Association for the Evaluation of Educational Achievement (IEA), which develops and implements TIMSS at the international level. "Benchmarking" education systems are not members of the IEA and are therefore not included in the average. All U.S. state data are based on public school students only.
SOURCE: Provasnik, S., Kastberg, D., Ferraro, D., Lemanski, N., Roey, S., and Jenkins, F. (2012). *Highlights From TIMSS 2011: Mathematics and Science Achievement of U.S. Fourth- and Eighth-Grade Students in an International Context* (NCES 2013-009), table 3, data from the International Association for the Evaluation of Educational Achievement (IEA), Trends in International Mathematics and Science Study (TIMSS), 2011. See *Digest of Education Statistics 2012*, table 460.

At grade 4, the U.S. average mathematics score (541) in 2011 was higher than the TIMSS scale average (500). The United States was among the top 15 education systems in mathematics (8 education systems had higher average scores, and 6 had scores that were not measurably different), and the United States scored higher, on average, than 42 education systems. Seven education systems with average mathematics scores above the U.S. score were Belgium (Flemish)-BEL, Chinese Taipei-CHN, Hong Kong-CHN, Japan, Northern Ireland-GBR, the Republic of Korea, and Singapore. Among the U.S. states that participated at grade 4, both North Carolina-USA and Florida-USA had average mathematics scores above the TIMSS scale average. North Carolina-USA's score was higher than the U.S. national average; however, Florida-USA's score was not measurably different from the U.S. national average in mathematics.

For more information, see the Reader's Guide and the Guide to Sources.

Chapter: 3/Elementary and Secondary Education
Section: Assessments

Table 2. Average TIMSS science assessment scale scores of 4th-grade students, by education system: 2011

Education system	Average score	Education system	Average score
TIMSS scale average	500	New Zealand	497 ▼
Korea, Rep. of	587 ▲	Kazakhstan[1]	495 ▼
Singapore[1]	583 ▲	Norway[4]	494 ▼
Finland	570 ▲	Chile	480 ▼
Japan	559 ▲	Thailand	472 ▼
Russian Federation	552 ▲	Turkey	463 ▼
Chinese Taipei-CHN	552 ▲	Georgia[3,5]	455 ▼
United States[1]	**544**	Iran, Islamic Rep. of	453 ▼
Czech Republic	536 ▼	Bahrain	449 ▼
Hong Kong-CHN[1]	535 ▼	Malta	446 ▼
Hungary	534 ▼	Azerbaijan[1,5]	438 ▼
Sweden	533 ▼	Saudi Arabia	429 ▼
Slovak Republic	532 ▼	United Arab Emirates	428 ▼
Austria	532 ▼	Armenia	416 ▼
Netherlands[2]	531 ▼	Qatar[1]	394 ▼
England-GBR	529 ▼	Oman	377 ▼
Denmark[1]	528 ▼	Kuwait[3,6]	347 ▼
Germany	528 ▼	Tunisia[6]	346 ▼
Italy	524 ▼	Morocco[7]	264 ▼
Portugal	522 ▼	Yemen[7]	209 ▼
Slovenia	520 ▼		
Northern Ireland-GBR[2]	517 ▼	**Benchmarking education systems**	
Ireland	516 ▼	*Florida-USA[3,8]*	545
Croatia[1]	516 ▼	*Alberta-CAN[1]*	541
Australia	516 ▼	*North Carolina-USA[1,3]*	538
Serbia[1]	516 ▼	*Ontario-CAN*	528 ▼
Lithuania[1,3]	515 ▼	*Quebec-CAN*	516 ▼
Belgium (Flemish)-BEL	509 ▼	*Dubai-UAE*	461 ▼
Romania	505 ▼	*Abu Dhabi-UAE*	411 ▼
Spain	505 ▼		
Poland	505 ▼		

▲ Average score is higher than U.S. average score.
▼ Average score is lower than U.S. average score.
[1] National Defined Population covers 90 to 95 percent of National Target Population defined by TIMSS.
[2] Met guidelines for sample participation rates only after replacement schools were included.
[3] National Target Population does not include all of the International Target Population defined by TIMSS.
[4] Nearly satisfied guidelines for sample participation rates after replacement schools were included.
[5] Exclusion rates for Azerbaijan and Georgia are slightly underestimated as some conflict zones were not covered and no official statistics were available.
[6] The TIMSS International Study Center has reservations about the reliability of the average achievement score because the percentage of students with achievement too low for estimation exceeds 15 percent, though it is less than 25 percent.
[7] The TIMSS International Study Center has reservations about the reliability of the average achievement score because the percentage of students with achievement too low for estimation exceeds 25 percent.
[8] National Defined Population covers less than 90 percent, but at least 77 percent, of National Target Population defined by TIMSS.
NOTE: Education systems are ordered by 2011 average score. Italics indicate participants identified and counted in this report as an education system and not as a separate country. Trends in International Mathematics and Science Study (TIMSS) scores are reported on a scale from 0 to 1,000, with the scale average set at 500 and the standard deviation set at 100. The TIMSS average includes only education systems that are members of the International Association for the Evaluation of Educational Achievement (IEA), which develops and implements TIMSS at the international level. "Benchmarking" education systems are not members of the IEA and are therefore not included in the average. All U.S. state data are based on public school students only.
SOURCE: Provasnik, S., Kastberg, D., Ferraro, D., Lemanski, N., Roey, S., and Jenkins, F. (2012). *Highlights From TIMSS 2011: Mathematics and Science Achievement of U.S. Fourth- and Eighth-Grade Students in an International Context* (NCES 2013-009), table 26, data from the International Association for the Evaluation of Educational Achievement (IEA), Trends in International Mathematics and Science Study (TIMSS), 2011. See *Digest of Education Statistics 2012*, table 460.

At grade 4, the U.S. average science score (544) was higher than the TIMSS scale average of 500. The United States was among the top 10 education systems in science (6 education systems had higher average science scores, and 3 had scores that were not measurably different). The United States also scored higher, on average, than 47 education systems in 2011. The six education systems with average science scores above the U.S. score were Chinese Taipei-CHN, Finland, Japan, the Republic of Korea, the Russian Federation, and Singapore. Of the participating education systems within the United States, both Florida-USA and North Carolina-USA scored above the TIMSS scale average, but their science scores were not measurably different from the U.S. national average.

For more information, see the Reader's Guide and the Guide to Sources.

Chapter: 3/Elementary and Secondary Education
Section: Assessments

Table 3. Average TIMSS mathematics assessment scale scores of 8th-grade students, by education system: 2011

Education system (Grade 8)	Average score	Education system (Grade 8)	Average score
TIMSS scale average	500	Chile	416 ▼
Korea, Rep. of	613 ▲	Iran, Islamic Rep. of[6]	415 ▼
Singapore[1]	611 ▲	Qatar[6]	410 ▼
Chinese Taipei-CHN	609 ▲	Bahrain[6]	409 ▼
Hong Kong-CHN	586 ▲	Jordan[6]	406 ▼
Japan	570 ▲	*Palestinian Nat'l Auth.*[6]	404 ▼
Russian Federation[1]	539 ▲	Saudi Arabia[6]	394 ▼
Israel[2]	516	Indonesia[6]	386 ▼
Finland	514	Syrian Arab Republic[6]	380 ▼
United States[1]	**509**	Morocco[7]	371 ▼
England-GBR[3]	507	Oman[6]	366 ▼
Hungary	505	Ghana[7]	331 ▼
Australia	505		
Slovenia	505	**Benchmarking education systems**	
Lithuania[4]	502		
Italy	498 ▼	*Massachusetts-USA*[1,4]	561 ▲
New Zealand	488 ▼	*Minnesota-USA*[4]	545 ▲
Kazakhstan	487 ▼	*North Carolina-USA*[2,4]	537 ▲
Sweden	484 ▼	*Quebec-CAN*	532 ▲
Ukraine	479 ▼	*Indiana-USA*[1,4]	522 ▲
Norway	475 ▼	*Colorado-USA*[4]	518
Armenia	467 ▼	*Connecticut-USA*[1,4]	518
Romania	458 ▼	*Florida-USA*[1,4]	513
United Arab Emirates	456 ▼	*Ontario-CAN*[1]	512
Turkey	452 ▼	*Alberta-CAN*[1]	505
Lebanon	449 ▼	*California-USA*[1,4]	493 ▼
Malaysia	440 ▼	*Dubai-UAE*	478 ▼
Georgia[4,5]	431 ▼	*Alabama-USA*[4]	466 ▼
Thailand	427 ▼	*Abu Dhabi-UAE*	449 ▼
Macedonia, Rep. of[6]	426 ▼		
Tunisia	425 ▼		

▲ Average score is higher than U.S. average score.
▼ Average score is lower than U.S. average score.
[1] National Defined Population covers 90 to 95 percent of National Target Population defined by TIMSS.
[2] National Defined Population covers less than 90 percent, but at least 77 percent, of National Target Population defined by TIMSS.
[3] Nearly satisfied guidelines for sample participation rates after replacement schools were included.
[4] National Target Population does not include all of the International Target Population defined by TIMSS.
[5] Exclusion rates for Georgia are slightly underestimated as some conflict zones were not covered and no official statistics were available.
[6] The TIMSS International Study Center has reservations about the reliability of the average achievement score because the percentage of students with achievement too low for estimation exceeds 15 percent, though it is less than 25 percent.
[7] The TIMSS International Study Center has reservations about the reliability of the average achievement score because the percentage of students with achievement too low for estimation exceeds 25 percent.
NOTE: Education systems are ordered by 2011 average score. Italics indicate participants identified and counted in this report as an education system and not as a separate country. Trends in International Mathematics and Science Study (TIMSS) scores are reported on a scale from 0 to 1,000, with the scale average set at 500 and the standard deviation set at 100. The TIMSS average includes only education systems that are members of the International Association for the Evaluation of Educational Achievement (IEA), which develops and implements TIMSS at the international level. "Benchmarking" education systems are not members of the IEA and are therefore not included in the average. All U.S. state data are based on public school students only.
SOURCE: Provasnik, S., Kastberg, D., Ferraro, K., Lemanski, N., Roey, S., and Jenkins, F. (2012). *Highlights From TIMSS 2011: Mathematics and Science Achievement of U.S. Fourth- and Eighth-Grade Students in an International Context* (NCES 2013-009), table 4, data from the International Association for the Evaluation of Educational Achievement (IEA), Trends in International Mathematics and Science Study (TIMSS), 2011. See *Digest of Education Statistics 2012*, table 461.

At grade 8, the U.S. average mathematics score (509) was higher than the TIMSS scale average of 500. The United States was among the top 24 education systems in mathematics in 2011 (11 education systems had higher average scores, and 12 had scores that were not measurably different). In addition, the United States scored higher, on average, than 32 education systems. The 11 education systems with average mathematics scores above the U.S. score were Chinese Taipei-CHN, Hong Kong-CHN, Japan, Quebec-CAN, the Republic of Korea, the Russian Federation, Singapore, and, within the United States, Indiana-USA, Massachusetts-USA, Minnesota-USA, and North Carolina-USA.

In addition to scoring above the U.S. average in 8th-grade mathematics, Indiana-USA, Massachusetts-USA, Minnesota-USA, and North Carolina-USA also scored above the TIMSS scale average. Colorado-USA, Connecticut-USA, and Florida-USA scored above the TIMSS scale average, but their scores were not measurably different from the U.S. national average. California-USA's score was not measurably different from the TIMSS scale average, but it was below the U.S. national average; Alabama-USA scored below both the TIMSS scale average and the U.S. national average in mathematics.

For more information, see the Reader's Guide and the Guide to Sources.

Chapter: 3/Elementary and Secondary Education
Section: Assessments

Table 4.　　Average TIMSS science assessment scale scores of 8th-grade students, by education system: 2011

Education system (Grade 8)	Average score	Education system (Grade 8)	Average score
TIMSS scale average	500	Saudi Arabia	436 ▼
Singapore[1]	590 ▲	Malaysia	426 ▼
Chinese Taipei-CHN	564 ▲	Syrian Arab Republic	426 ▼
Korea, Rep. of	560 ▲	*Palestinian Nat'l Auth.*	420 ▼
Japan	558 ▲	Georgia[4,5]	420 ▼
Finland	552 ▲	Oman	420 ▼
Slovenia	543 ▲	Qatar	419 ▼
Russian Federation[1]	542 ▲	Macedonia, Rep. of	407 ▼
Hong Kong-CHN	535 ▲	Lebanon	406 ▼
England-GBR[2]	533	Indonesia	406 ▼
United States[1]	**525**	Morocco	376 ▼
Hungary	522	Ghana[6]	306 ▼
Australia	519		
Israel[3]	516	**Benchmarking education systems**	
Lithuania[4]	514 ▼		
New Zealand	512 ▼	*Massachusetts-USA*[1,4]	567 ▲
Sweden	509 ▼	*Minnesota-USA*[4]	553 ▲
Italy	501 ▼	*Alberta-CAN*[1]	546 ▲
Ukraine	501 ▼	*Colorado-USA*[4]	542 ▲
Norway	494 ▼	*Indiana-USA*[1,4]	533
Kazakhstan	490 ▼	*Connecticut-USA*[1,4]	532
Turkey	483 ▼	*North Carolina-USA*[3,4]	532
Iran, Islamic Rep. of	474 ▼	*Florida-USA*[1,4]	530
Romania	465 ▼	*Ontario-CAN*[1]	521
United Arab Emirates	465 ▼	*Quebec-CAN*	520
Chile	461 ▼	*California-USA*[1,4]	499 ▼
Bahrain	452 ▼	*Alabama-USA*[4]	485 ▼
Thailand	451 ▼	*Dubai-UAE*	485 ▼
Jordan	449 ▼	*Abu Dhabi-UAE*	461 ▼
Tunisia	439 ▼		
Armenia	437 ▼		

▲ Average score is higher than U.S. average score.
▼ Average score is lower than U.S. average score.
[1] National Defined Population covers 90 to 95 percent of National Target Population defined by TIMSS.
[2] Nearly satisfied guidelines for sample participation rates after replacement schools were included.
[3] National Defined Population covers less than 90 percent, but at least 77 percent, of National Target Population defined by TIMSS.
[4] National Target Population does not include all of the International Target Population defined by TIMSS.
[5] Exclusion rates for Georgia are slightly underestimated as some conflict zones were not covered and no official statistics were available.
[6] The TIMSS International Study Center has reservations about the reliability of the average achievement score because the percentage of students with achievement too low for estimation exceeds 15 percent, though it is less than 25 percent.
NOTE: Education systems are ordered by 2011 average score. Italics indicate participants identified and counted in this report as an education system and not as a separate country. Trends in International Mathematics and Science Study (TIMSS) scores are reported on a scale from 0 to 1,000, with the scale average set at 500 and the standard deviation set at 100. The TIMSS average includes only education systems that are members of the International Association for the Evaluation of Educational Achievement (IEA), which develops and implements TIMSS at the international level. "Benchmarking" education systems are not members of the IEA and are therefore not included in the average. All U.S. state data are based on public school students only.
SOURCE: Provasnik, S., Kastberg, D., Ferraro, D., Lemanski, N., Roey, S., and Jenkins, F. (2012). *Highlights From TIMSS 2011: Mathematics and Science Achievement of U.S. Fourth- and Eighth-Grade Students in an International Context* (NCES 2013-009), table 27, data from the International Association for the Evaluation of Educational Achievement (IEA), Trends in International Mathematics and Science Study (TIMSS), 2011. See *Digest of Education Statistics 2012*, table 461.

At grade 8, the U.S. average science score (525) was higher than the TIMSS scale average of 500. The United States was among the top 23 education systems in science in 2011 (12 education systems had higher average scores, and 10 had scores that were not measurably different). The United States scored higher, on average, than 33 education systems. The 12 education systems with average science scores above the U.S. score were Alberta-CAN, Chinese Taipei-CHN, Finland, Hong Kong-CHN, Japan, the Republic of Korea, the Russian Federation, Singapore, Slovenia, and, within the United States, Colorado-USA, Massachusetts-USA, and Minnesota-USA.

Aside from scoring above the U.S. average in 8th-grade science, Colorado-USA, Massachusetts-USA, and Minnesota-USA also scored above the TIMSS scale average of 500. Connecticut-USA, Florida-USA, Indiana-USA, and North Carolina-USA scored above the TIMSS scale average, but their scores were not measurably different from the U.S. national average. California-USA's score was not measurably different from the TIMSS scale average, but it was below the U.S. national average; Alabama-USA scored below both the TIMSS scale average and the U.S. national average in science.

For more information, see the Reader's Guide and the Guide to Sources.

Chapter: 3/Elementary and Secondary Education
Section: Assessments

Figure 1. Number of instructional hours per year for 4th-grade students, by country or education system and subject: 2011

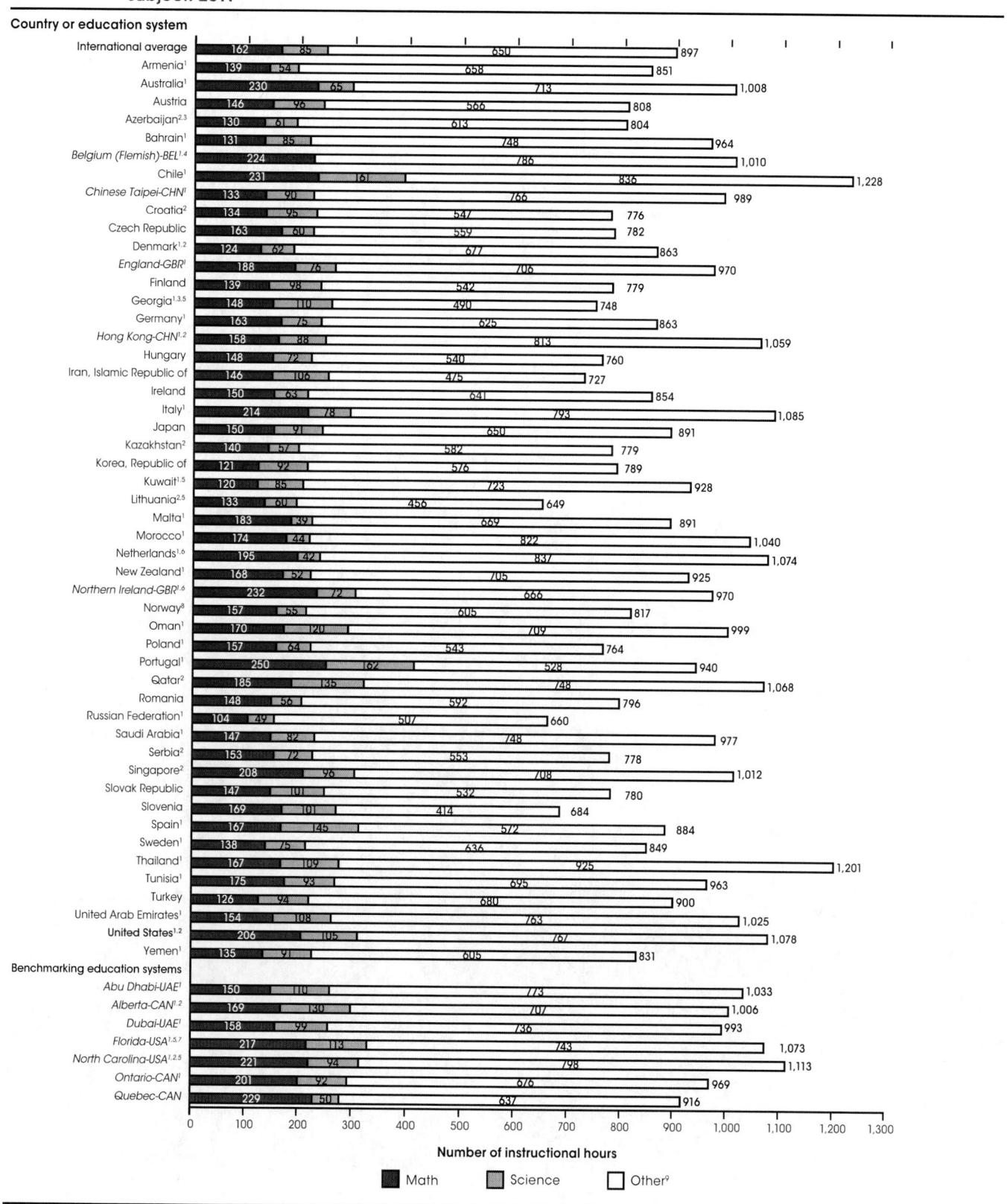

Country or education system	Math	Science	Other	Total
International average	162	85	650	897
Armenia[1]	139	54	658	851
Australia[1]	230	65	713	1,008
Austria	146	96	566	808
Azerbaijan[2,3]	130	61	613	804
Bahrain[1]	131	85	748	964
Belgium (Flemish)-BEL[1,4]	224	—	786	1,010
Chile[1]	231	161	836	1,228
Chinese Taipei-CHN[1]	133	90	766	989
Croatia[2]	134	95	547	776
Czech Republic	163	60	559	782
Denmark[1,2]	124	62	677	863
England-GBR[1]	188	76	706	970
Finland	139	98	542	779
Georgia[1,3,5]	148	110	490	748
Germany[1]	163	75	625	863
Hong Kong-CHN[1,2]	158	88	813	1,059
Hungary	148	72	540	760
Iran, Islamic Republic of	146	106	475	727
Ireland	150	63	641	854
Italy[1]	214	78	793	1,085
Japan	150	91	650	891
Kazakhstan[2]	140	57	582	779
Korea, Republic of	121	92	576	789
Kuwait[1,5]	120	85	723	928
Lithuania[2,5]	133	60	456	649
Malta[1]	183	39	669	891
Morocco[1]	174	44	822	1,040
Netherlands[1,6]	195	42	837	1,074
New Zealand[1]	168	52	705	925
Northern Ireland-GBR[1,6]	232	72	666	970
Norway[8]	157	55	605	817
Oman[1]	170	120	709	999
Poland[1]	157	64	543	764
Portugal[1]	250	162	528	940
Qatar[2]	185	135	748	1,068
Romania	148	56	592	796
Russian Federation[1]	104	49	507	660
Saudi Arabia[1]	147	82	748	977
Serbia[2]	153	72	553	778
Singapore[2]	208	96	708	1,012
Slovak Republic	147	101	532	780
Slovenia	169	101	414	684
Spain[1]	167	145	572	884
Sweden[1]	138	75	636	849
Thailand[1]	167	109	925	1,201
Tunisia[1]	175	93	695	963
Turkey	126	94	680	900
United Arab Emirates[1]	154	108	763	1,025
United States[1,2]	206	105	767	1,078
Yemen[1]	135	91	605	831
Benchmarking education systems				
Abu Dhabi-UAE[1]	150	110	773	1,033
Alberta-CAN[1,2]	169	130	707	1,006
Dubai-UAE[1]	158	99	736	993
Florida-USA[1,5,7]	217	113	743	1,073
North Carolina-USA[1,2,5]	221	94	798	1,113
Ontario-CAN[1]	201	92	676	969
Quebec-CAN	229	50	637	916

Number of instructional hours

■ Math ▨ Science ☐ Other[9]

See notes on next page.

For more information, see the Reader's Guide and the Guide to Sources.

Elementary and Secondary Education 115

Chapter: 3/Elementary and Secondary Education
Section: Assessments

[1] Data for number of math, science, and/or total instructional hours are available for at least 50 percent but less than 85 percent of students.
[2] National Defined Population covers 90 to 95 percent of National Target Population defined by TIMSS.
[3] Exclusion rates for Azerbaijan and Georgia are slightly underestimated as some conflict zones were not covered and no official statistics were available.
[4] Data for instructional hours in science are not available. Other instructional hours calculated by subtracting instruction hours in mathematics from total instructional hours.
[5] National Target Population does not include all of the International Target Population defined by TIMSS.
[6] Met guidelines for sample participation rates only after replacement schools were included.
[7] National Defined Population covers less than 90 percent, but at least 77 percent, of National Target Population defined by TIMSS.
[8] Nearly satisfied guidelines for sample participation rates only after replacement schools were included.
[9] Other instructional hours calculated by adding instructional hours in mathematics to instructional hours in science and then subtracting from total instructional hours.
NOTE: Italics indicate participants identified and counted in this report as an education system and not as a separate country. Instructional times shown in this figure are actual or implemented times (as opposed to intended times prescribed by the curriculum). Principals reported total instructional hours per day and school days per year. Total instructional hours per year were calculated by multiplying the number of school days per year by the number of instructional hours per day. Teachers reported instructional hours per week in mathematics and science. Instructional hours per year in mathematics and science were calculated by dividing weekly instructional hours by the number of school days per week and then multiplying by the number of school days per year. International average instructional hours includes only education systems that are members of the International Association for the Evaluation of Educational Achievement (IEA), which develops and implements TIMSS at the international level. "Benchmarking" education systems are not members of the IEA and are therefore not included in the average. All U.S. state data are based on public school students only.
SOURCE: Mullis, I.V.S., Martin, M.O., Foy, P., and Arora, A. (2012). *TIMSS 2011 International Results in Mathematics*, exhibit 8.6, and Martin, M.O., Mullis, I.V.S., Foy, P., and Stanco, G.M. (2012). *TIMSS 2011 International Results in Science*, exhibit 8.6. See *Digest of Education Statistics 2012*, table 460.

In addition to assessing achievement in mathematics and science, TIMSS collects information from principals on the total number of annual instructional hours in school. TIMSS also collects information from teachers on the number of annual instructional hours spent on mathematics and science instruction at grades 4 and 8. In 2011, education systems (excluding the benchmarking participants) participating in TIMSS at grade 4 spent an average of 897 total hours on instructional time, of which an average of 162 hours (18 percent) were spent on mathematics instruction and 85 hours (10 percent) were spent on science instruction. In 2011, the average number of total instructional hours (1,078 hours) spent in the United States at grade 4 was higher than the international average (897 hours). The average numbers of instructional hours spent on grade 4 mathematics instruction (206 hours) and science instruction (105 hours) in the United States were also higher than the international averages (162 and 85 hours, respectively).

For more information, see the Reader's Guide and the Guide to Sources.

Chapter: 3/Elementary and Secondary Education
Section: Assessments

Figure 2. Number of instructional hours per year for 8th-grade students, by country or education system and subject: 2011

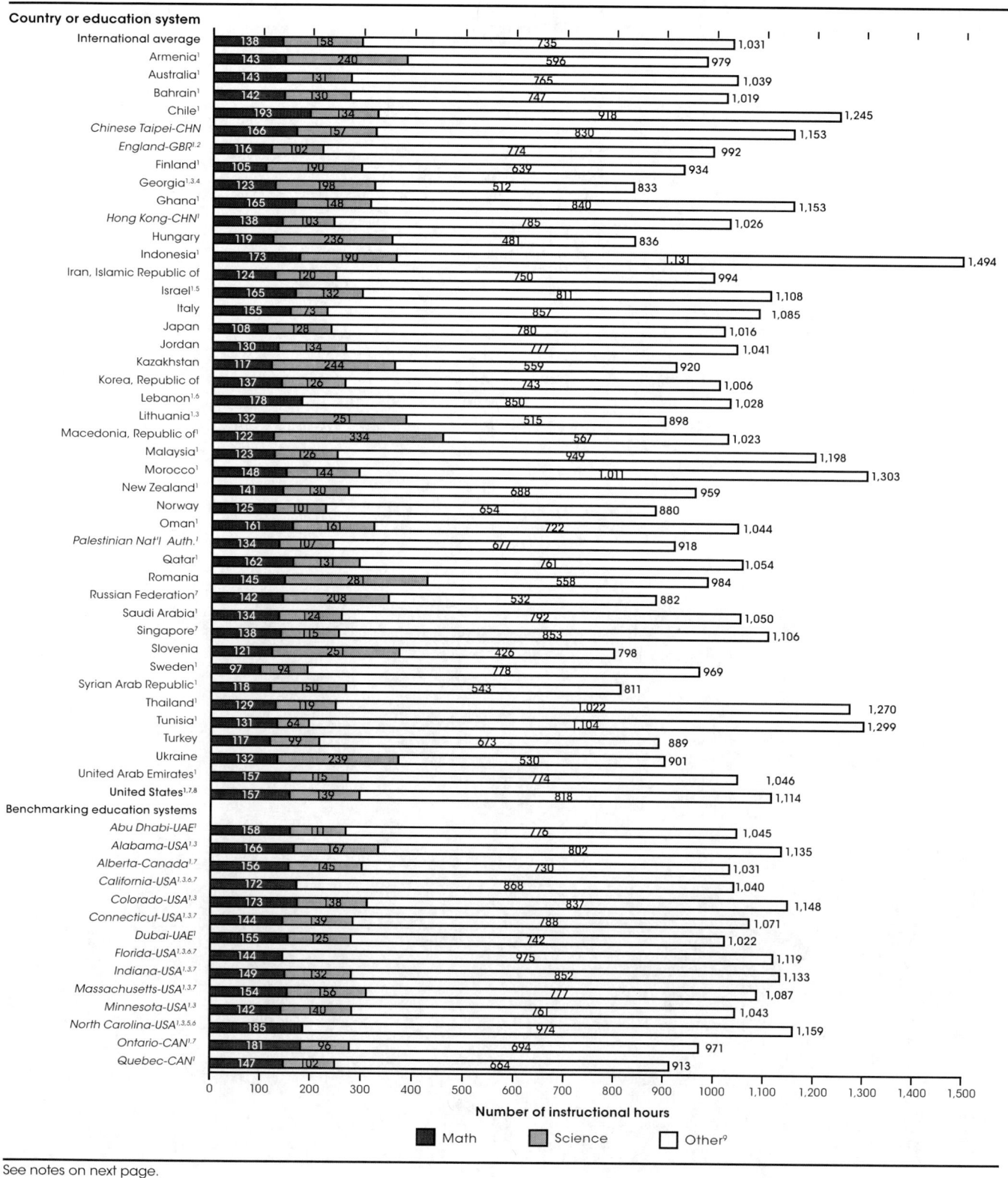

Country or education system	Math	Science	Other	Total
International average	138	158	735	1,031
Armenia[1]	143	240	596	979
Australia[1]	143	131	765	1,039
Bahrain[1]	142	130	747	1,019
Chile[1]	193	134	918	1,245
Chinese Taipei-CHN	166	157	830	1,153
England-GBR[1,2]	116	102	774	992
Finland[1]	105	190	639	934
Georgia[1,3,4]	123	198	512	833
Ghana[1]	165	148	840	1,153
Hong Kong-CHN[1]	138	103	785	1,026
Hungary	119	236	481	836
Indonesia[1]	173	190	1,131	1,494
Iran, Islamic Republic of	124	120	750	994
Israel[1,5]	165	132	811	1,108
Italy	155	73	857	1,085
Japan	108	128	780	1,016
Jordan	130	134	777	1,041
Kazakhstan	117	244	559	920
Korea, Republic of	137	126	743	1,006
Lebanon[1,6]	178	—	850	1,028
Lithuania[1,3]	132	251	515	898
Macedonia, Republic of[1]	122	334	567	1,023
Malaysia[1]	123	126	949	1,198
Morocco[1]	148	144	1,011	1,303
New Zealand[1]	141	130	688	959
Norway	125	101	654	880
Oman[1]	161	161	722	1,044
Palestinian Nat'l Auth.[1]	134	107	677	918
Qatar[1]	162	131	761	1,054
Romania	145	281	558	984
Russian Federation[7]	142	208	532	882
Saudi Arabia[1]	134	124	792	1,050
Singapore[7]	138	115	853	1,106
Slovenia	121	251	426	798
Sweden[1]	97	94	778	969
Syrian Arab Republic[1]	118	150	543	811
Thailand[1]	129	119	1,022	1,270
Tunisia[1]	131	64	1,104	1,299
Turkey	117	99	673	889
Ukraine	132	239	530	901
United Arab Emirates[1]	157	115	774	1,046
United States[1,7,8]	157	139	818	1,114
Benchmarking education systems				
Abu Dhabi-UAE[1]	158	111	776	1,045
Alabama-USA[1,3]	166	167	802	1,135
Alberta-Canada[1,7]	156	145	730	1,031
California-USA[1,3,6,7]	172	—	868	1,040
Colorado-USA[1,3]	173	138	837	1,148
Connecticut-USA[1,3,7]	144	139	788	1,071
Dubai-UAE[1]	155	125	742	1,022
Florida-USA[1,3,6,7]	144	—	975	1,119
Indiana-USA[1,3,7]	149	132	852	1,133
Massachusetts-USA[1,3,7]	154	156	777	1,087
Minnesota-USA[1,3]	142	140	761	1,043
North Carolina-USA[1,3,5,6]	185	—	974	1,159
Ontario-CAN[1,7]	181	96	694	971
Quebec-CAN[1]	147	102	664	913

Number of instructional hours: ■ Math ▨ Science □ Other[9]

See notes on next page.

For more information, see the Reader's Guide and the Guide to Sources.

Elementary and Secondary Education 117

[1] Data for number of math and/or science instructional hours are available for at least 50 percent but less than 85 percent of students.
[2] Nearly satisfied guidelines for sample participation rate after replacement schools were included.
[3] National Target Population does not include all of the International Target Population defined by TIMSS.
[4] Exclusion rates for Georgia are slightly underestimated as some conflict zones were not covered and no official statistics were available.
[5] National Defined Population covers less than 90 percent, but at least 77 percent, of National Target Population defined by TIMSS.
[6] Data for instructional hours in science were not available. Other instructional hours calculated by subtracting instruction hours in mathematics from total instructional hours.
[7] National Defined Population covers 90 to 95 percent of National Target Population defined by TIMSS.
[8] Data for science are for 2007 and are from TIMSS 2007 International Results in Science. Met guidelines for sample participation rates only after substitute schools were included. Data for number of math instructional hours are available for at least 50 percent but less than 70 percent of students.
[9] Other instructional hours calculated by adding instructional hours in mathematics to instructional hours in science and then subtracting from total instructional hours.
NOTE: Instructional times shown in this figure are actual or implemented times (as opposed to intended times prescribed by the curriculum). Principals reported total instructional hours per day and school days per year. Total instructional hours per year were calculated by multiplying the number of school days per year by the number of instructional hours per day. Teachers reported instructional hours per week in mathematics and science. Instructional hours per year in mathematics and science were calculated by dividing weekly instructional hours by the number of school days per week and then multiplying by the number of school days per year. International average instructional hours includes only education systems that are members of the International Association for the Evaluation of Educational Achievement (IEA), which develops and implements TIMSS at the international level. "Benchmarking" education systems are not members of the IEA and are therefore not included in the average. All U.S. state data are based on public school students only.
SOURCE: Mullis, I.V.S., Martin, M.O., Foy, P., and Arora, A. (2012). *TIMSS 2011 International Results in Mathematics*, exhibit 8.7, and Martin, M.O., Mullis, I.V.S., Foy, P., and Stanco, G.M. (2012). *TIMSS 2011 International Results in Science*, exhibit 8.7. See *Digest of Education Statistics 2012*, table 461.

At grade 8, education systems (excluding the benchmarking participants) participating in TIMSS spent an average of 1,031 total annual hours on instructional time in 2011, of which 138 hours (14 percent) were spent on mathematics instruction and 158 hours (11 percent) were spent on science instruction. Similar to the findings at grade 4, the United States' average number of total instructional hours at grade 8 (1,114 hours) was higher than the international average (1,031 hours). The average hours spent on grade 8 mathematics instruction (157 hours) in the United States was also higher than the international average (138 hours).

For more information, see the Reader's Guide and the Guide to Sources.

Chapter: 3/Elementary and Secondary Education
Section: Assessments

Table 5. Average PIRLS reading literacy assessment scale scores of 4th-grade students, by education system: 2011

Education system	Overall reading average scale score	Education system	Overall reading average scale score
PIRLS scale average	500	PIRLS scale average	500
Hong Kong-CHN[1]	571 ▲	France	
Russian Federation	568 ▲	Spain	
Finland	568 ▲	Norway[5]	
Singapore[2]	567 ▲	Belgium (French)-BEL[2,3]	
Northern Ireland-GBR[3]	558	Romania	502 ▼
United States[2]	**556**	Georgia[4,6]	488 ▼
Denmark[2]	554	Malta	477 ▼
Croatia[2]	553	Trinidad and Tobago	471 ▼
Chinese Taipei-CHN	553	Azerbaijan[2,6]	462 ▼
Ireland	552	Iran, Islamic Rep. of	457 ▼
England-GBR[3]	552	Colombia	448 ▼
Canada[2]	548 ▼	United Arab Emirates	439 ▼
Netherlands[3]	546 ▼	Saudi Arabia	430 ▼
Czech Republic	545 ▼	Indonesia	428 ▼
Sweden	542 ▼	Qatar[2]	425 ▼
Italy	541 ▼	Oman[7]	391 ▼
Germany	541 ▼	Morocco[8]	310 ▼
Israel[1]	541 ▼		
Portugal	541 ▼	**Benchmarking education systems**	
Hungary	539 ▼	Florida-USA[1,4]	569 ▲
Slovak Republic	535 ▼	Ontario-CAN[2]	552
Bulgaria	532 ▼	Alberta-CAN[2]	548 ▼
New Zealand	531 ▼	Quebec-CAN	538 ▼
Slovenia	530 ▼	Andalusia-ESP	515 ▼
Austria	529 ▼	Dubai-UAE	476 ▼
Lithuania[2,4]	528 ▼	Maltese-MLT	457 ▼
Australia	527 ▼	Abu Dhabi-UAE	424 ▼
Poland	526 ▼		

▲ Average score is higher than U.S. average score.
▼ Average score is lower than U.S. average score.
[1] National Defined Population covers less than 90 percent of National Target Population defined by PIRLS.
[2] National Defined Population covers 90 percent to 95 percent of National Target Population defined by PIRLS.
[3] Met guidelines for sample participation rates only after replacement schools were included.
[4] National Target Population does not include all of the International Target Population defined by PIRLS.
[5] Nearly satisfied guidelines for sample participation rates after replacement schools were included.
[6] Exclusion rates for Azerbaijan and Georgia are slightly underestimated as some conflict zones were not covered and no official statistics were available.
[7] The PIRLS International Study Center has reservations about the reliability of the average achievement score because the percentage of students with achievement too low for estimation exceeds 15 percent, though it is less than 25 percent.
[8] The PIRLS International Study Center has reservations about the reliability of the average achievement score because the percentage of students with achievement too low for estimation exceeds 25 percent.
NOTE: Education systems are ordered by 2011 average score. Italics indicate participants identified and counted in this report as an education system and not as a separate country. The Progress in International Reading Literacy Study (PIRLS) scores are reported on a scale from 0 to 1,000, with the scale average set at 500 and the standard deviation set at 100. The PIRLS average includes only education systems that are members of the International Association for the Evaluation of Educational Achievement (IEA), which develops and implements PIRLS at the international level. "Benchmarking" education systems are not members of the IEA and are therefore not included in the average. All U.S. state data are based on public school students only.
SOURCE: Thompson, S., Provasnik, S., Kastberg, D., Ferraro, D., Lemanski, N., Roey, S., and Jenkins, F. (2012). *Highlights From PIRLS 2011: Reading Achievement of U.S. Fourth-Grade Students in an International Context* (NCES 2013-010), table 3, data from the International Association for the Evaluation of Educational Achievement (IEA), Progress in International Reading Literacy Study (PIRLS), 2011. See *Digest of Education Statistics 2012*, table 462.

In 2011, there were 53 education systems that had PIRLS reading literacy data at grade 4. These 53 education systems included both countries and other benchmarking education systems. In addition to participating in the U.S. national sample, Florida-USA participated individually and was included as an education system. In 2011, the U.S. average 4th-grade reading literacy score (556) was higher than the PIRLS scale average (500). The United States was among the top 13 education systems in reading literacy (5 education systems had higher average scores, and 7 had scores that were not measurably different).

The United States scored higher, on average, than 40 education systems.

The five education systems with average reading scores above the U.S. score were Finland, Hong Kong-CHN, the Russian Federation, Singapore, and, within the United States, Florida-USA. Additionally, Florida-USA's average score (569) was higher than the PIRLS scale average. No education system scored higher than Florida-USA, although four had scores that were not measurably different. Forty-eight education systems scored lower than Florida-USA.

Reference tables: *Digest of Education Statistics 2012*, tables 460, 461, 462

For more information, see the Reader's Guide and the Guide to Sources.

Indicator 27
High School Coursetaking

Chapter: 3/Elementary and Secondary Education
Section: Student Effort, Persistence, and Progress

The percentages of high school graduates who had taken mathematics courses in algebra I, geometry, algebra II/trigonometry, analysis/precalculus, statistics/probability, and calculus increased from 1990 to 2009. The percentages of high school graduates who had taken science courses in chemistry and physics also increased between 1990 and 2009.

In addition to administering students' assessments, the National Assessment of Educational Progress (NAEP) periodically collects data on the transcripts of high school graduates. The transcript survey gathers information about the types of courses that graduates from regular and honors programs take, how many credits they earn, their grade point averages, and the relationship between coursetaking patterns and achievement. The transcript data include only information about the coursework that graduates completed while they were enrolled in grades 9 through 12.

Figure 1. Percentage of high school graduates who completed selected mathematics and science courses in high school: 1990 and 2009

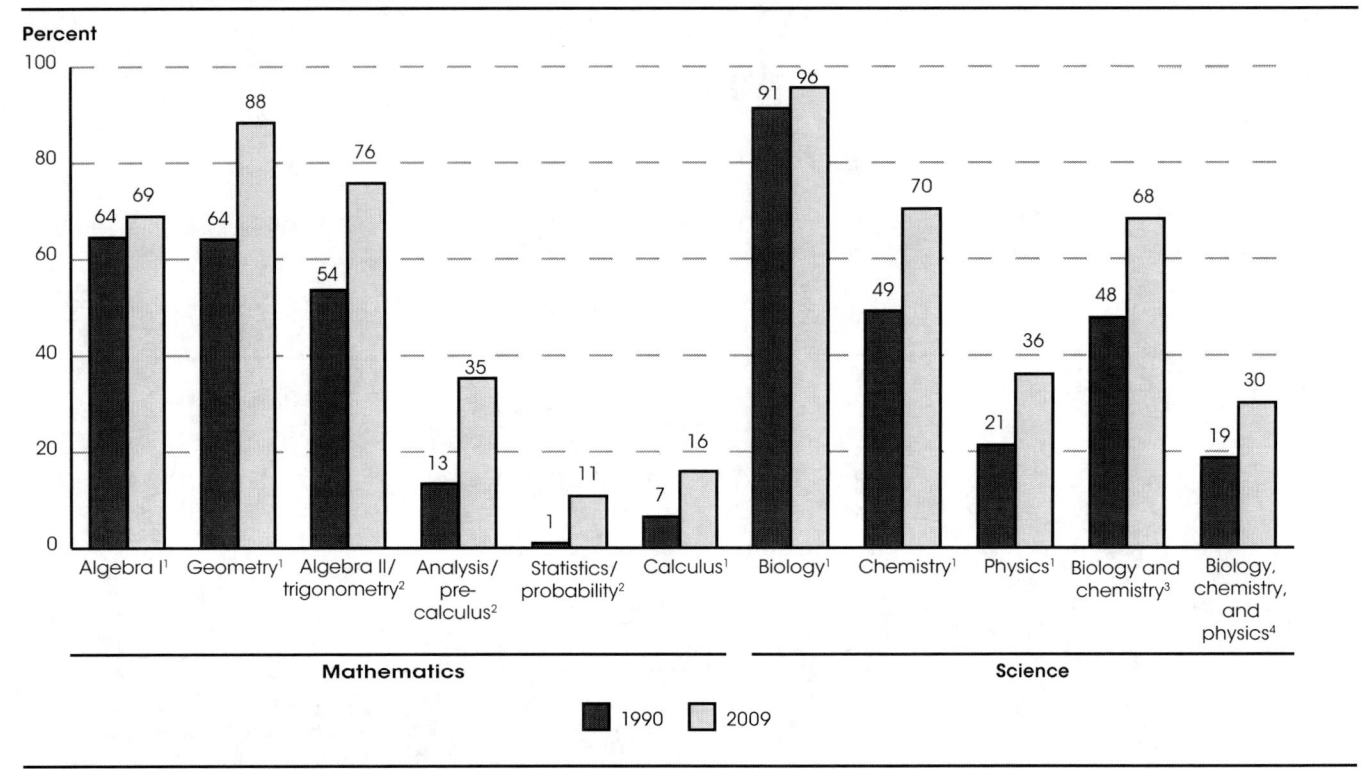

Course	1990	2009
Algebra I[1]	64	69
Geometry[1]	64	88
Algebra II/trigonometry[2]	54	76
Analysis/pre-calculus[2]	13	35
Statistics/probability[2]	1	11
Calculus[1]	7	16
Biology[1]	91	96
Chemistry[1]	49	70
Physics[1]	21	36
Biology and chemistry[3]	48	68
Biology, chemistry, and physics[4]	19	30

[1] Percentages are for students who earned at least one Carnegie credit.
[2] Percentages are for students who earned at least one-half of a Carnegie credit.
[3] Percentages are for students who earned at least one Carnegie credit each in biology and chemistry.
[4] Percentages are for students who earned at least one Carnegie credit each in biology, chemistry, and physics.
NOTE: For a transcript to be included in the analyses, the graduate had to receive either a standard or honors diploma.
SOURCE: U.S. Department of Education, National Center for Education Statistics, High School Transcript Study (HSTS), 1990 and 2009. See *Digest of Education Statistics 2012*, table 180.

The percentages of high school graduates who had completed mathematics courses in algebra I, geometry, algebra II/trigonometry, analysis/precalculus, statistics/probability, and calculus increased between 1990 and 2009. For example, the percentage of graduates who had completed calculus increased from 7 percent to 16 percent between 1990 and 2009. Similarly, the percentage of graduates who had completed algebra II/trigonometry increased from 54 percent to 76 percent.

For more information, see the Reader's Guide and the Guide to Sources.

Chapter: 3/Elementary and Secondary Education
Section: Student Effort, Persistence, and Progress

Figure 2. Average National Assessment of Educational Progress (NAEP) 12th-grade mathematics scale scores of high school graduates, by highest mathematics course taken and race/ethnicity: 2009

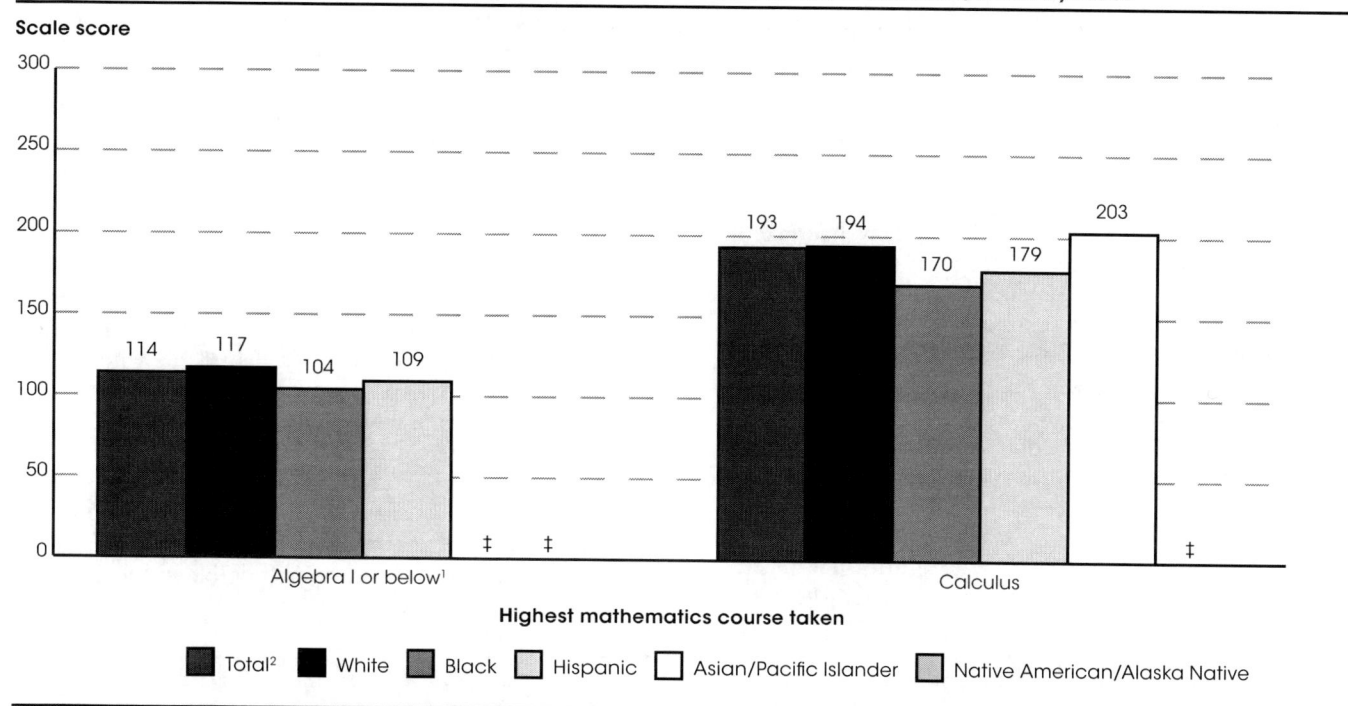

‡ Reporting standards not met (too few cases for a reliable estimate).
[1] Includes basic math, general math, applied math, pre-algebra, and algebra I.
[2] Includes other racial/ethnic groups not shown separately and cases that were missing information on race/ethnicity and/or sex of student.
NOTE: The scale of the NAEP mathematics assessment for grade 12 ranges from 0 to 300. For a transcript to be included in the analyses, the graduate had to receive either a standard or honors diploma. Race categories exclude persons of Hispanic ethnicity. Reporting standards were not met for American Indian/Alaska Native estimates, therefore, data for this racial group are not shown in the figure.
SOURCE: U.S. Department of Education, National Center for Education Statistics, National Assessment of Educational Progress (NAEP), 2009 Mathematics Assessment; and High School Transcript Study (HSTS), 2009. See *Digest of Education Statistics 2012*, table 163.

Between 1990 and 2009, the percentages of high school graduates who had taken various mathematics courses generally increased across subgroups. For example, the percentage of Hispanic graduates completing calculus increased from 4 percent in 1990 to 9 percent in 2009. Also, the percentage of Hispanic graduates completing algebra II/trigonometry increased from 40 percent to 71 percent. Similarly, the percentage of Black graduates completing calculus during this period increased from 3 to 6 percent, and the percentage completing algebra II/trigonometry increased from 44 to 71 percent. Although there were increases in mathematics coursetaking across racial/ethnic groups during this period, gaps between groups remained in terms of the percentages of graduates completing courses. For example, in 2009 higher percentages of Asian/Pacific Islander (42 percent) and White graduates (18 percent) had taken calculus than had their Black (6 percent) and Hispanic peers (9 percent). In 2009, there was no measurable difference between the percentages of males and females who had taken calculus (16 percent each). However, the percentage of females who had taken algebra II/trigonometry (78 percent) was higher than that of male graduates (74 percent).

The percentages of high school graduates who had taken science courses in chemistry and physics also increased between 1990 and 2009. The percentage of graduates who had taken chemistry increased from 49 to 70 percent, and the percentage of graduates who had completed physics courses increased from 21 to 36 percent. The percentage of graduates who earned at least one credit in biology, chemistry, and physics increased from 19 percent in 1990 to 30 percent in 2009.

The general increases in science coursetaking in biology, chemistry, and physics between 1990 and 2009 were reflected by increases for students of most racial/ethnic groups. For instance, the percentage of Hispanic graduates who had completed a chemistry course increased from 38 to 66 percent, and the percentage of Hispanic graduates who had completed at least one credit in biology, chemistry, and physics increased from 10 to 23 percent. Similarly, the percentage of Black graduates who had completed a chemistry course increased from 40 to 65 percent, and the percentage of Black graduates who had completed at least one credit in biology, chemistry, and physics increased from 12 to 22 percent. Although there were increases in coursetaking among student groups from 1990 to 2009, gaps between different subgroups in coursetaking remained unchanged. In 2009, a higher percentage of Asian (54 percent) and White (31 percent) graduates had completed the combination of biology, chemistry, and physics courses than had their Black and Hispanic peers (22 percent and 23 percent, respectively). A higher percentage of males (39 percent) than of females (33 percent) had completed a physics

For more information, see the Reader's Guide and the Guide to Sources.

Elementary and Secondary Education 121

Chapter: 3/Elementary and Secondary Education
Section: Student Effort, Persistence, and Progress

class in 2009; however, a higher percentage of females (73 percent) than of males (67 percent) had taken chemistry, and a higher percentage of females (96 percent) than of males (95 percent) had taken a biology class.

A higher percentage of 2009 graduates from private schools (85 percent) had taken courses in algebra II/trigonometry than had graduates from traditional public schools (75 percent), and a higher percentage of graduates from private schools (23 percent) had taken courses in calculus than had graduates from public schools (15 percent). Also, a higher percentage of private high school graduates (44 percent) had taken at least one credit in biology, chemistry, and physics than had graduates from traditional public schools (29 percent). A higher percentage of graduates from city (32 percent) and suburban (39 percent) schools had taken courses in biology, chemistry, and physics than had graduates from schools in towns (19 percent) or rural areas (20 percent).

In 2009, higher average scale scores on the National Assessment of Educational Progress (NAEP) 12th-grade mathematics assessment were associated with higher levels of high school mathematics coursetaking. For example, graduates who had taken only algebra I or below had an average scale score of 114 (on a scale of 0–300), whereas graduates who had taken calculus had an average scale score of 193. In addition, among those students who had completed specific mathematics courses, there were differences across demographic subgroups. For graduates who had taken calculus, the average scale score was higher for males than for females (197 vs. 190). Average scale scores were also higher for students who had taken calculus who were Asian/Pacific Islander (203) and White (194) than for their Hispanic (179) and Black (170) peers. Among students who had taken calculus, the average scale score for those who had attended low-poverty schools (schools in which 0 to 25 percent of students receive, or are eligible to receive, free or reduced-price lunch under the National School Lunch Program) was 199, compared with a score of 163 for their peers at high-poverty schools (schools in which 75 to 100 percent of students receive, or are eligible to receive, free or reduced-price lunch).

Reference tables: *Digest of Education Statistics 2012,* tables 163, 180

Glossary: Free or reduced-price lunch, Private school, Public school

For more information, see the Reader's Guide and the Guide to Sources.

This page intentionally left blank.

Chapter: 3/Elementary and Secondary Education
Section: Student Effort, Persistence, and Progress

Indicator 28
Public High School Graduation Rates

In school year 2009–10, some 3.1 million public high school students, or 78.2 percent, graduated on time with a regular diploma. Among all public high school students, Asian/Pacific Islanders had the highest graduation rate (93.5 percent), followed by Whites (83.0 percent), Hispanics (71.4 percent), American Indian/ Alaska Natives (69.1 percent), and Blacks (66.1 percent).

Figure 1. Averaged Freshman Graduation Rate (AFGR) for public high school students: School years 1990–91 through 2009–10

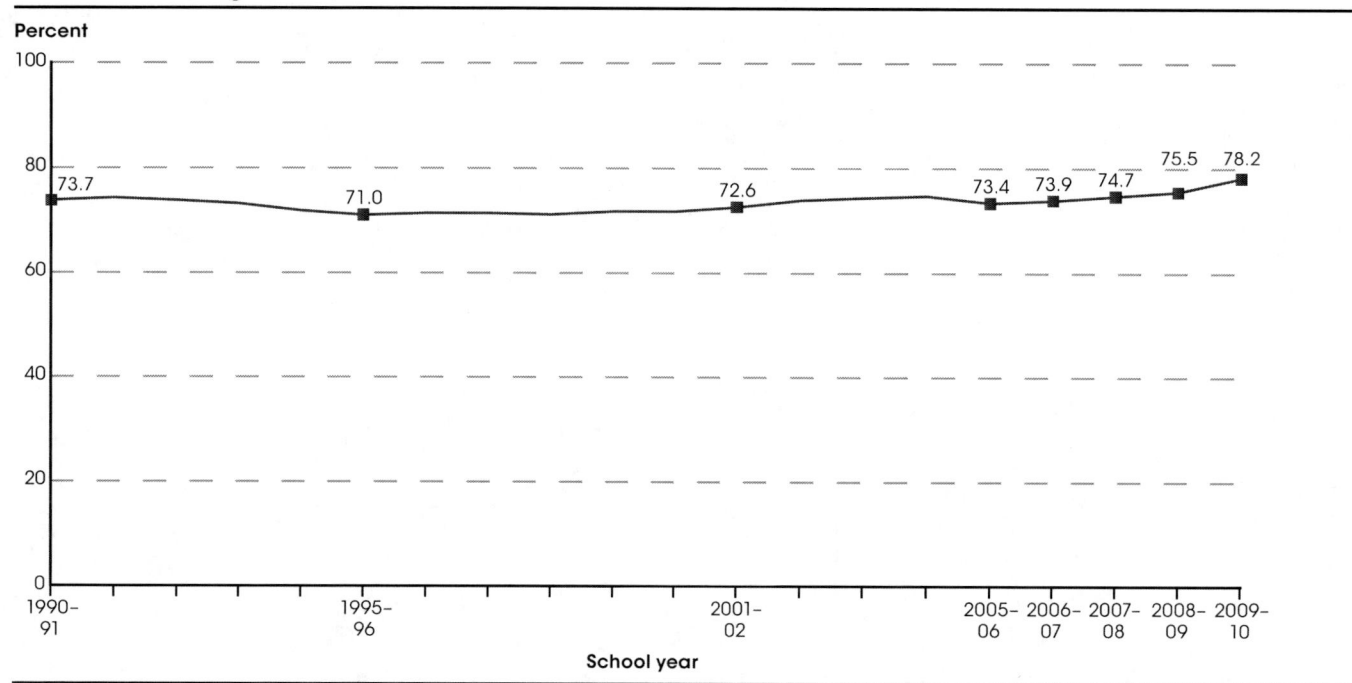

NOTE: The Averaged Freshman Graduation Rate is the number of graduates divided by the estimated freshman enrollment count 4 years earlier. This count is the sum of the number of 8th-graders 5 years earlier, the number of 9th-graders 4 years earlier, and the number of 10th-graders 3 years earlier, divided by 3. Ungraded students are allocated to individual grades proportional to each state's enrollment in those grades. Graduates include only those who earned regular diplomas or diplomas for advanced academic achievement (e.g., honors diploma) as defined by the state or jurisdiction. The 2005–06 national estimates include imputed data for the District of Columbia, Pennsylvania, and South Carolina. The 2007–08 and 2008–09 estimates for Maine include graduates from semiprivate schools. The 2008–09 national estimate includes imputed data for California and Nevada. The 2009–10 estimate includes fall 2006 ninth-graders from publicly funded private schools in the data for Maine. The 2009–10 national estimate includes imputed data for Connecticut and Nevada.
SOURCE: U.S. Department of Education, National Center for Education Statistics, Common Core of Data (CCD), "State Nonfiscal Survey of Public Elementary/Secondary Education," 1986–87 through 2007–08; "State Dropout and Completion Data File," 2005–06 through 2009–10; The Averaged Freshman Graduation Rate for Public High Schools From the CCD: School Years 2002–03 and 2003–04; and Public School Graduates and Dropouts from the CCD, 2007–08 and 2008–09. See *Digest of Education Statistics 2012*, table 124.

This indicator examines the percentage of public high school students who graduate on time with a regular diploma. To do so, it uses the *Averaged Freshman Graduation Rate* (AFGR), which is the number of high school diplomas expressed as a percentage of the estimated freshman class 4 years earlier. In school year 2009–10, the AFGR was 78.2 percent, and some 3.1 million public high school students graduated on time with a regular diploma. The overall AFGR was higher for the graduating class of 2009–10 than it was for the class of 1990–91 (73.7 percent). However, during the earlier part of the period from 1990–91 to 1995–96, the graduation rate decreased from 73.7 to 71.0 percent. The rate fluctuated from a low of 71.1 to a high of 74.7 percent from 1997–98 to 2004–05. Since 2005–06, the graduation rate has increased by nearly 5 percentage points from 73.4 to 78.2 percent.

For more information, see the Reader's Guide and the Guide to Sources.

Chapter: 3/Elementary and Secondary Education
Section: Student Effort, Persistence, and Progress

Figure 2. Averaged Freshman Graduation Rate (AFGR) for public high school students, by race/ethnicity: School year 2009–10

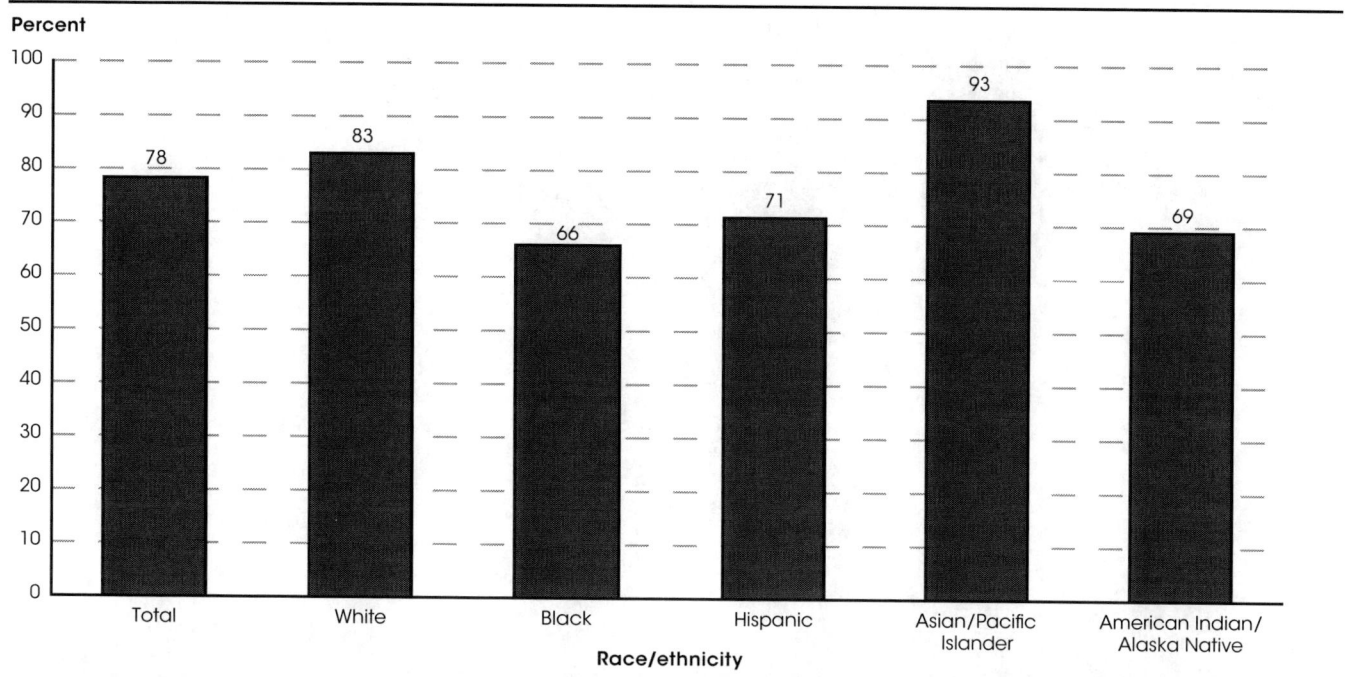

Race/ethnicity	Percent
Total	78
White	83
Black	66
Hispanic	71
Asian/Pacific Islander	93
American Indian/Alaska Native	69

NOTE: The Averaged Freshman Graduation Rate is the number of graduates divided by the estimated freshman enrollment count 4 years earlier. This count is the sum of the number of 8th-graders 5 years earlier, the number of 9th-graders 4 years earlier, and the number of 10th-graders 3 years earlier, divided by 3. Ungraded students are allocated to individual grades proportional to each state's enrollment in those grades. Graduates include only those who earned regular diplomas or diplomas for advanced academic achievement (e.g., honors diploma) as defined by the state or jurisdiction. Includes fall 2006 ninth-graders from publicly funded private schools in the data for Maine. Includes only graduates for whom race/ethnicity was reported. Race categories exclude persons of Hispanic ethnicity.
SOURCE: U.S. Department of Education, National Center for Education Statistics, Common Core of Data (CCD), "State Dropout and Completion Data File," 2009–10. See *Digest of Education Statistics 2012*, table 125.

Averaged Freshman Graduation Rates varied by race/ethnicity in 2009–10. Asian/Pacific Islander students had the highest graduation rate (93.5 percent), followed by White (83.0 percent), Hispanic (71.4 percent), American Indian/Alaska Native (69.1 percent), and Black students (66.1 percent).

For more information, see the Reader's Guide and the Guide to Sources.

Chapter: 3/Elementary and Secondary Education
Section: Student Effort, Persistence, and Progress

Figure 3. Averaged Freshman Graduation Rate (AFGR) for public high school students, by state or jurisdiction: School year 2009–10

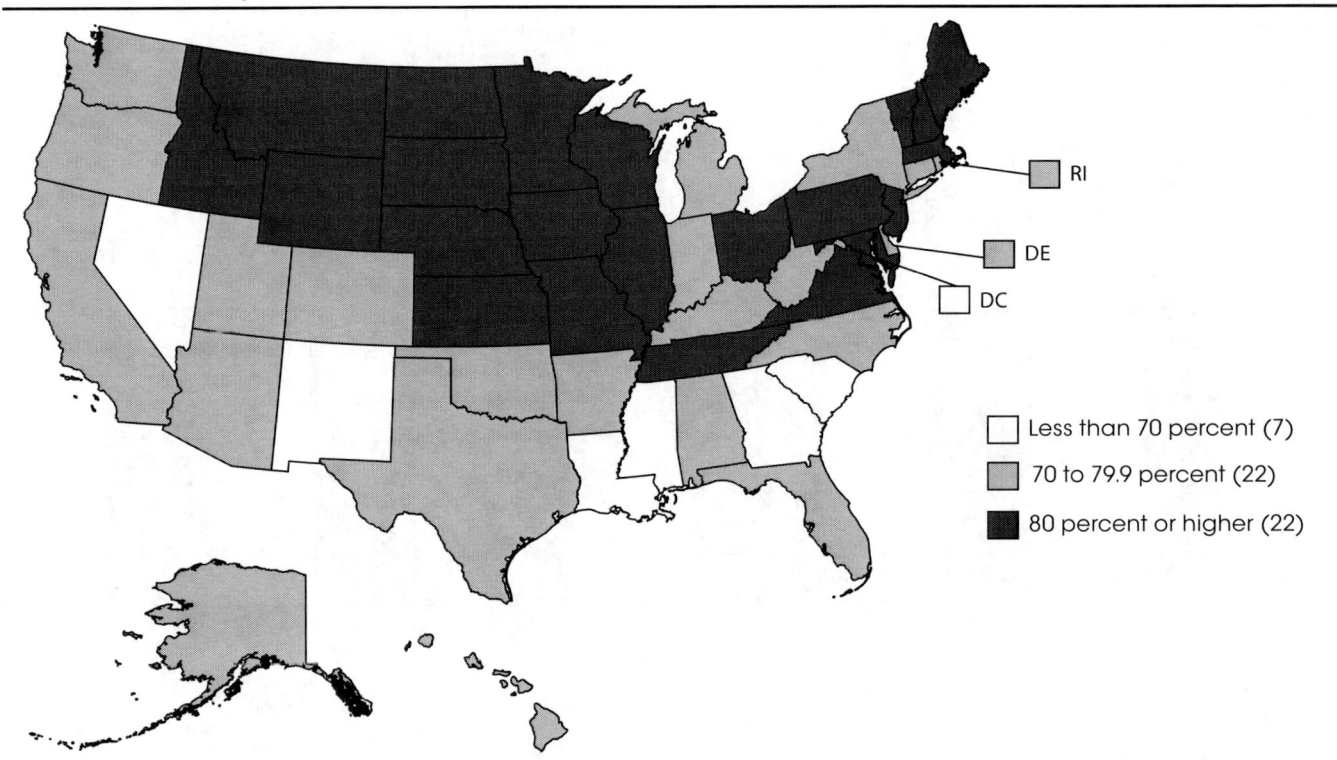

☐ Less than 70 percent (7)
▨ 70 to 79.9 percent (22)
■ 80 percent or higher (22)

NOTE: The Averaged Freshman Graduation Rate is the number of graduates divided by the estimated freshman enrollment count 4 years earlier. This count is the sum of the number of 8th-graders 5 years earlier, the number of 9th-graders 4 years earlier, and the number of 10th-graders 3 years earlier, divided by 3. Ungraded students are allocated to individual grades proportional to each state's enrollment in those grades. Graduates include only those who earned regular diplomas or diplomas for advanced academic achievement (e.g., honors diploma) as defined by the state or jurisdiction. Data for Maine included fall 2006 ninth-graders from publicly funded private schools. Data for Connecticut and Nevada were imputed.
SOURCE: U.S. Department of Education, National Center for Education Statistics, Common Core of Data (CCD), "State Dropout and Completion Data File," 2009–10. See *Digest of Education Statistics 2012,* table 124.

In school year 2009–10, the AFGR ranged by more than 30 percentage points among the states. Vermont had the highest graduation rate, at 91.4 percent. Twenty-one other states had graduation rates of 80 percent or more (ordered from high to low): Wisconsin, North Dakota, Minnesota, Iowa, New Jersey, New Hampshire, Kansas, Pennsylvania, Idaho, Nebraska, Missouri, Maine, Massachusetts, Maryland, Illinois, Montana, South Dakota, Ohio, Virginia, Tennessee, and Wyoming. Nevada had the lowest rate, at 57.8 percent. Five other states and the District of Columbia had graduation rates below 70 percent (ordered from high to low): Georgia, Louisiana, South Carolina, New Mexico, Mississippi, and the District of Columbia.

In terms of changes by state, there was an increase in the AFGR in 43 states from school year 2005–06 to 2009–10. In 3 states (Tennessee, Louisiana, and Vermont), the rate increased by between 9 and 10 percentage points; in 14 others (Alaska, California, New York, Georgia, Florida, South Carolina, Kansas, Virginia, Maine, Texas, North Dakota, Alabama, New Hampshire, and North Carolina), rates increased by more than 5 percentage points but less than 9 percentage points. The graduation rate decreased from 2005–06 to 2009–10 in the District of Columbia and 7 states (Hawaii, Delaware, Rhode Island, South Dakota, Nebraska, Arkansas, and Connecticut) with decreases of more than 5 percentage points occurring in Arkansas (5.4 percent), the District of Columbia (5.5 percent), and Connecticut (5.8 percent).

Reference tables: *Digest of Education Statistics 2012,* tables 122, 124, 125

Glossary: High school diploma, Public school or institution

For more information, see the Reader's Guide and the Guide to Sources.

This page intentionally left blank.

Indicator 29
Status Dropout Rates

Chapter: 3/Elementary and Secondary Education
Section: Student Effort, Persistence, and Progress

The gap in the status dropout rate between high-income and low-income families narrowed between 1970 and 2011, particularly during the past two decades, when the gap narrowed from 21 percentage points in 1990 to 11 percentage points in 2011.

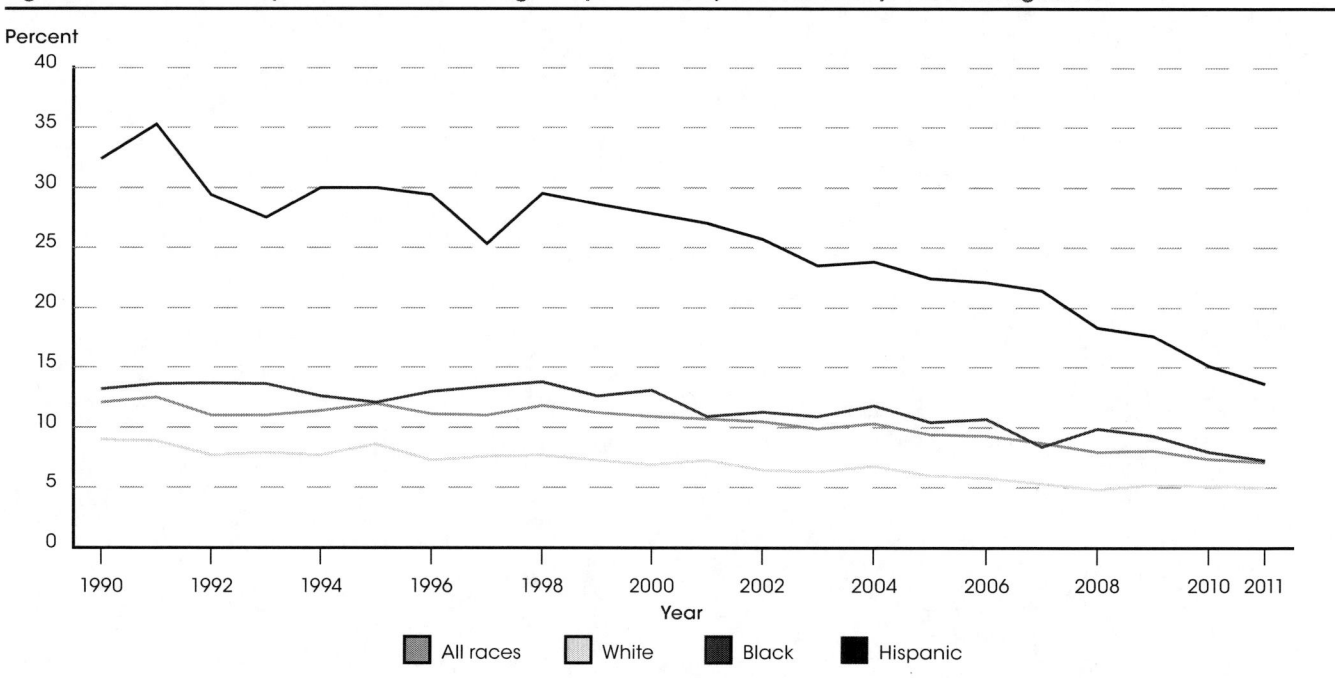

The *status dropout rate* represents the percentage of 16- through 24-year-olds who are not enrolled in school and have not earned a high school credential (either a diploma or an equivalency credential such as a General Educational Development [GED] certificate). In this indicator, status dropout rates are estimated using both the Current Population Survey (CPS) and the American Community Survey (ACS). Data for the CPS have been collected annually for decades, allowing for detailed long term trends for the civilian, noninstitutionalized population. Young adults in the military or those who are incarcerated are not included in the CPS measure. National-level data from the ACS are available from 2000 onward. Data for those living in group quarters, including those in institutionalized and noninstitutionalized settings, from the ACS are available from 2006 onward. The 2010 ACS has larger sample sizes than the CPS, which allows for more detailed comparisons of status dropout rates by sex, race/ethnicity, and nativity.

Based on the CPS, the status dropout rate declined from 12 percent in 1990 to 7 percent in 2011. Reflecting the overall decline, the status dropout rate also declined for young adults in all but the highest family income category during this period. The status dropout rates declined for low-income families (the bottom 25 percent of all family incomes) from 24 percent to 13 percent, middle-low income families from 15 percent to 9 percent, and middle-high income families from 9 percent to 5 percent. There was no measurable change for high income families (the top 25 percent of all family incomes). Over this period, the dropout rate for young adults in the highest income families was consistently lower than the rates for those in lower income families. While differences remained, the gap in the status dropout rate between high-income and low-income families narrowed between 1970 and 2011, particularly during the past two decades, when the gap narrowed from 21 percentage points in 1990 to 11 percentage points in 2011.

Figure 1. Status dropout rates of 16- through 24-year-olds, by race/ethnicity: 1990 through 2011

NOTE: The "status dropout rate" represents the percentage of 16- through 24-year-olds who are not enrolled in school and have not earned a high school credential (either a diploma or an equivalency credential such as a General Educational Development [GED] certificate). Data are based on sample surveys of the civilian noninstitutionalized population, which excludes persons in prisons, persons in the military, and other persons not living in households. Data for all races include other racial/ethnic categories not separately shown. Race categories exclude persons of Hispanic ethnicity.
SOURCE: U.S. Department of Commerce, Census Bureau, Current Population Survey (CPS), October 1990 through 2011. See *Digest of Education Statistics 2012*, table 128.

For more information, see the Reader's Guide and the Guide to Sources.

Reflecting the overall decline in the status dropout rate between 1990 and 2011, the rates also declined for Whites (from 9 percent to 5 percent), Blacks (from 13 percent to 7 percent), and Hispanics (from 32 percent to 14 percent). Over this period, the status dropout rate was lowest for Whites, followed by Blacks and Hispanics. For example, in 2011, the status dropout rate for Whites (5 percent) was lower than the status dropout rates for Blacks (7 percent) and Hispanics (14 percent). The gap between Whites and Hispanics narrowed from 23 percentage points in 1990 to 9 percentage points in 2011; the gaps between Whites and Blacks in these two years were not measurably different.

Figure 2. Status dropout rates of 16- through 24-year-olds, by number of years of school completed: Selected years, 1990 through 2011

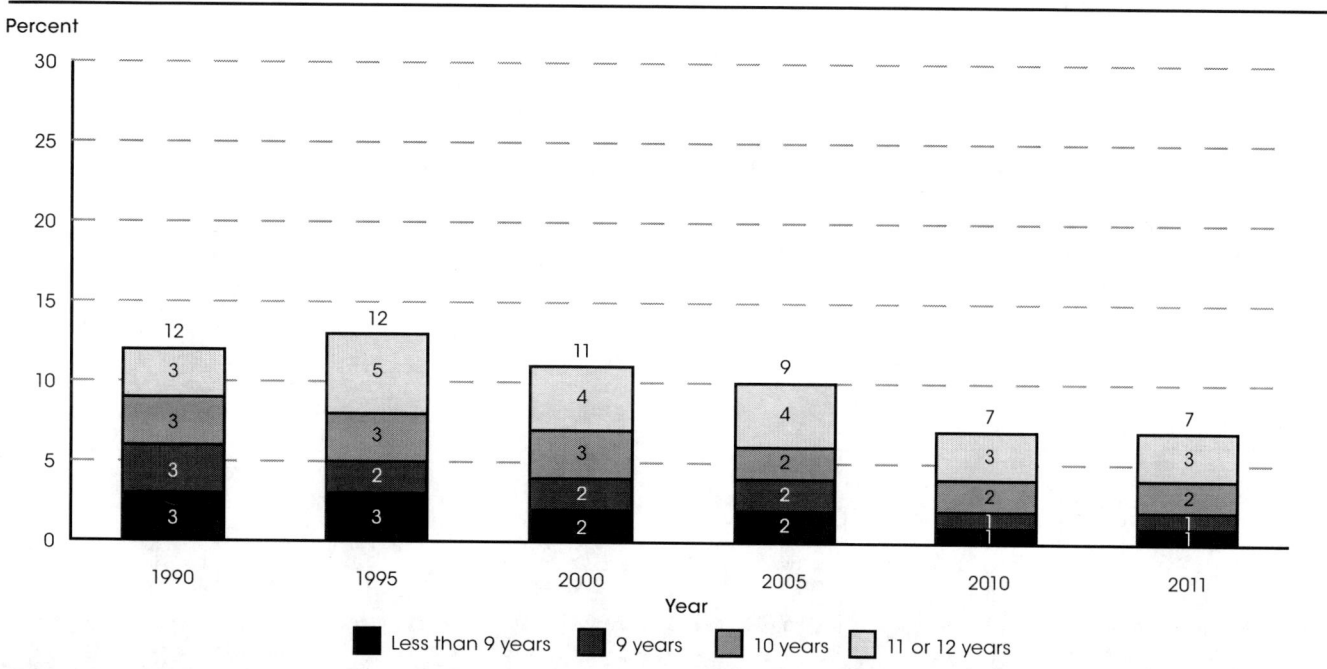

NOTE: "Status dropouts" are persons 16 through 24 years old who are not enrolled in school and have not earned a high school credential (either a diploma or an equivalency credential such as a General Educational Development [GED] certificate). Data are based on sample surveys of the civilian noninstitutionalized population, which excludes persons in prisons, persons in the military, and other persons not living in households. Detail may not sum to totals because of rounding.
SOURCE: U.S. Department of Commerce, Census Bureau, Current Population Survey (CPS), October 1990 through 2011. See *Digest of Education Statistics 2012*, table 129.

The level of schooling completed by high school dropouts has increased over the past few decades. Reflecting both the decline in the dropout rate and the decrease in the percentage of dropouts with low levels of education, the overall percentage of the young adult population with less than 9 years of schooling decreased from 3 percent in 1990 to 1 percent in 2011. This group, which had essentially not attended high school, accounted for 29 percent of status dropouts in 1990, compared with 18 percent in 2011. The percentage of dropouts who had completed 11–12 years of school was 3 percent in 1990 and 3 percent in 2011. In 2011, however, this group was a larger proportion of high school status dropouts (48 percent) than they were in 1990 (26 percent).

For more information, see the Reader's Guide and the Guide to Sources.

Chapter: 3/Elementary and Secondary Education
Section: Student Effort, Persistence, and Progress

Figure 3. Status dropout rates of 16- through 24-year-olds in the noninstitutionalized group quarters and household population, by nativity and race/ethnicity: American Community Survey (ACS) 2010

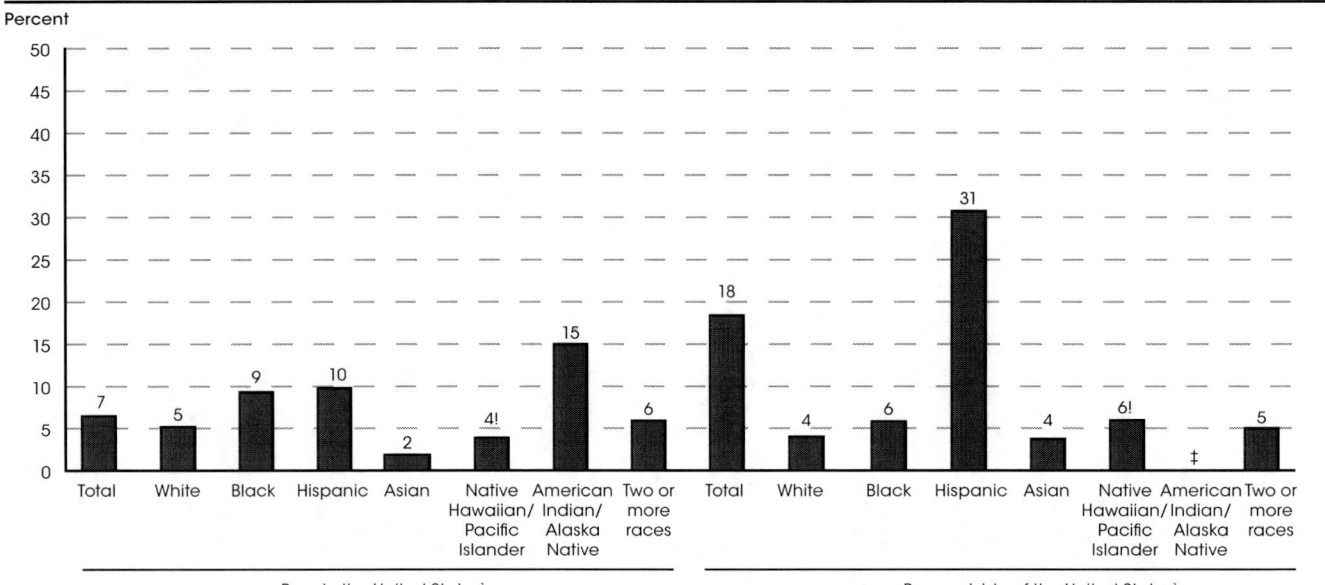

Race/ethnicity	Born in the United States[1]	Born outside of the United States[1]
Total	7	18
White	5	4
Black	9	6
Hispanic	10	31
Asian	2	4
Native Hawaiian/Pacific Islander	4!	6!
American Indian/Alaska Native	15	‡
Two or more races	6	5

! Interpret data with caution.
‡ Reporting standards not met (too few cases).
[1] United States refers to the 50 states and the District of Columbia.
NOTE: This figure uses a different data source than figure 1; therefore, estimates are not directly comparable to the 2010 estimates in figure 1. Noninstitutionalized group quarters include college and university housing, military quarters, facilities for workers and religious groups, and temporary shelters for the homeless. Among those counted in noninstitutionalized group quarters in the American Community Survey (ACS), only the residents of military barracks are not included in the civilian noninstitutionalized population in the Current Population Survey. Race categories exclude persons of Hispanic ethnicity.
SOURCE: U.S. Department of Commerce, Census Bureau, American Community Survey (ACS), 2010. See *Digest of Education Statistics 2012,* table 130.

The ACS allows for comparisons of status dropout rates for 16- through 24-year-olds residing in households, as well as those in noninstitutionalized group quarters (such as military quarters), and institutionalized group quarters (such as adult and juvenile correctional facilities and nursing facilities). Among those living in households and noninstitutionalized group quarters, the status dropout rate was 8 percent in 2010. A higher percentage of males than females were status dropouts (9 vs. 7 percent). Differences between males and females overall were reflected in each racial/ethnic group except for Native Hawaiians/Pacific Islanders. Data for 16- through 24-year-olds living in institutionalized group quarters also showed a higher dropout rate for males than females. However, the rates were notably higher than for those in households and noninstitutionalized group quarters. In 2010, the status dropout rate for those in institutionalized group quarters was 37.4 percent.

In 2010, Hispanics and Asians born in the United States had lower status dropout rates than did their counterparts born outside of the United States, whereas U.S.-born Whites and Blacks had higher status dropout rates than did their foreign-born counterparts. A higher dropout rate among Hispanics who were foreign born (31 percent) versus those who were native born (10 percent) partially accounts for the relatively high overall Hispanic dropout rate (16 percent).

Reference tables: *Digest of Education Statistics 2012,* tables 128, 129, 130

Glossary: Dropout, GED certificate, High school diploma, High school equivalent certificate

For more information, see the Reader's Guide and the Guide to Sources.

The Condition of Education 2013

This page intentionally left blank.

Indicator 30
Immediate Transition to College

Chapter: 3/Elementary and Secondary Education
Section: Student Effort, Persistence, and Progress

Between 1975 and 2011, the immediate college enrollment rate increased from 51 percent to 68 percent. In 2011, the immediate enrollment rate for high school completers from low-income families (52 percent) was 30 percentage points lower than the rate for completers from high-income families (82 percent, based on a 3-year moving average).

The *immediate college enrollment rate* in this indicator is defined as the annual percentage of high school completers (including GED recipients) of a given year who enroll in 2- or 4-year colleges in the fall immediately after completing high school. Between 1975 and 2011, the immediate college enrollment rate increased from 51 percent to 68 percent. This rate increased from 1975 to 1997 (51 to 67 percent), declined from 1997 to 2001 (to 62 percent), then increased from 2001 to 2011 (to 68 percent). The immediate college enrollment rates for both males and females increased between 1975 and 2011: the rate for males increased from 53 to 65 percent and the rate for females from 49 to 72 percent. Thus, the enrollment pattern has shifted over time to higher enrollment rates for females than for males.

In each year between 1975 and 2011, the immediate college enrollment rates for high school completers from low- and middle-income families were lower than that of high school completers from high-income families. Due to some short-term data fluctuations associated with small sample sizes, estimates for the income groups were calculated based on 3-year moving averages, except in 1975 and 2011 when estimates were calculated on 2-year moving averages. Low income refers to the bottom 20 percent of all family incomes, high income refers to the top 20 percent of all family incomes, and middle income refers to the 60 percent in between. In 2011, the immediate college enrollment rate for high school completers from low-income families was 52 percent, 30 percentage points lower than the rate for completers from high-income families (82 percent). The immediate college enrollment rate for completers from middle-income families (66 percent) was 16 percentage points lower than the rate for their peers from high-income families.

Figure 1. Percentage of high school completers who were enrolled in 2- or 4-year colleges by the October immediately following high school completion, by family income: 1975–2011

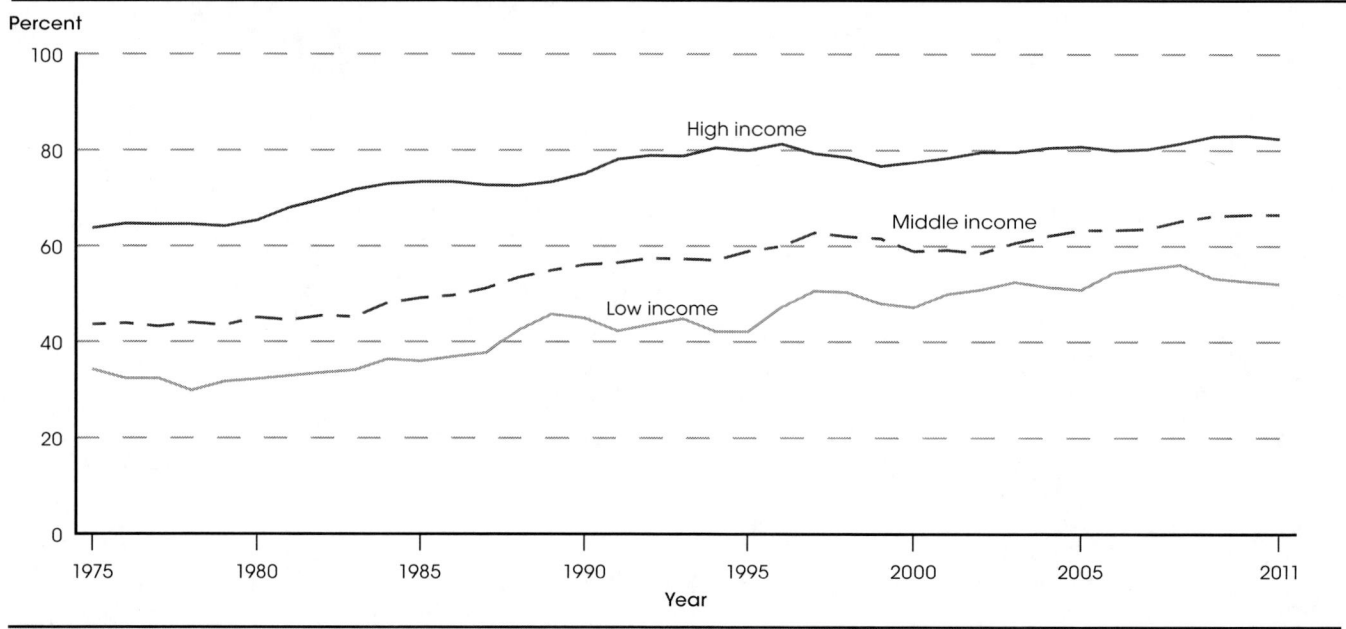

NOTE: Due to some short-term data fluctuations associated with small sample sizes, percentages for the income groups were calculated based on 3-year moving averages. High school completers include GED recipients.
SOURCE: U.S. Department of Commerce, Census Bureau, Current Population Survey (CPS), October Supplement, 1975–2011. See *Digest of Education Statistics 2012*, table 236.

For more information, see the Reader's Guide and the Guide to Sources.

Chapter: 3/Elementary and Secondary Education
Section: Student Effort, Persistence, and Progress

The 30 percentage point gap between the immediate enrollment rates of high school completers from high-income families and from low-income families in 2011 was not measurably different from the gap in 1975. There were patterns of increases and decreases in the gap during this period. This gap increased from 1975 to 1983 (from 29 to 38 percentage points), declined from 1983 to 1989 (to 28 percentage points), did not measurably change from 1990 to 1993 (ranging from 30 to 36 percentage points), and then narrowed from 1994 to 2011 (from 38 to 30 percentage points). Between 1975 and 2011, the gap between immediate college enrollment rates of high school completers from middle-income families and low-income families ranged from 8 to 17 percentage points. The low-income to middle-income gap in 2011 (14 percentage points) was not measurably different from the gap in 1975 (9 percentage points).

Between 1995 and 2011, immediate college enrollment rates increased for White (65 to 69 percent), Black (53 to 65 percent), and Hispanic (52 to 63 percent) high school completers. The estimates for racial/ethnic groups are also based on 2- or 3-year moving averages. Separate data on Asian high school completers have been collected since 2003. In each year between 2003 and 2011, the immediate college enrollment rate for Asians was higher than the rates for Whites, Blacks, and Hispanics. Between 2003 and 2011, the immediate college enrollment rate for Asian completers did not measurably change, ranging from 80 to 90 percent. The immediate college enrollment rate for Whites was also higher than the rate for Hispanics in every year during this period and higher than the rate for Blacks in every year from 2003 to 2009. In 2010 and 2011, there was no measurable difference between the rates for Whites and for Blacks.

Figure 2. Percentage of high school completers who were enrolled in 2- or 4-year colleges by the October immediately following high school completion, by level of institution: 1975–2011

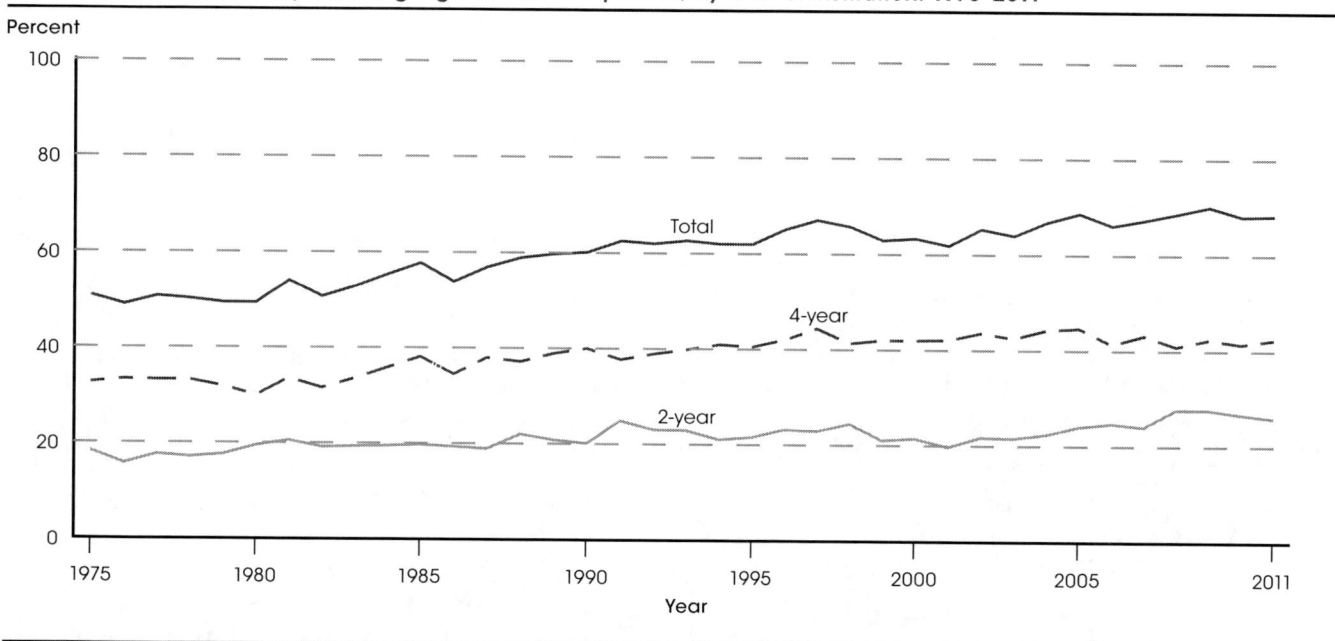

NOTE: High school completers include GED recipients.
SOURCE: U.S. Department of Commerce, Census Bureau, Current Population Survey (CPS), October Supplement, 1975-2011. See *Digest of Education Statistics 2012*, table 234.

Overall, the immediate college enrollment rates of high school completers going to both 2- and 4-year colleges increased between 1975 and 2011. In 1975, about 18 percent of high school completers enrolled at a 2-year college immediately after high school, while 26 percent did so in 2011. Similarly, in 1975 some 33 percent of high school completers enrolled at a 4-year college immediately after high school, compared with 42 percent in 2011. In each year during this period, the immediate college enrollment rate at 4-year colleges was higher than that at 2-year colleges. For example, in 2011 the immediate college enrollment rate at 4-year colleges was 60 percent higher than that at 2-year colleges.

Reference table: *Digest of Education Statistics 2012,* tables 234, 235, 236

Glossary: Educational attainment, High school completer

For more information, see the Reader's Guide and the Guide to Sources.

Elementary and Secondary Education

The indicators in this section of *The Condition of Education* examine features of postsecondary education, many of which parallel those presented in the previous section on elementary and secondary education. The indicators examine the characteristics of postsecondary students; postsecondary programs and courses of study; finance and resources; postsecondary completions; and economic outcomes, both for postsecondary graduates and the general population.

Postsecondary education is characterized by diversity both in the types of institutions and in the characteristics of students. Postsecondary institutions vary by the types of degrees awarded, control (public or private), and whether they are operated on a not-for-profit or for-profit basis. Beyond these basic differences, postsecondary institutions have distinctly different missions and provide students with a wide range of learning environments.

Indicators on postsecondary education and outcomes from previous editions of *The Condition of Education* not included in this volume are available at http://nces.ed.gov/programs/coe.

Chapter 4

Postsecondary Education

Spotlight on Finance and Resources
Financing Postsecondary Education in the United States 136

Characteristics of Postsecondary Students
Indicator 31. Characteristics of Postsecondary Institutions 142
Indicator 32. Characteristics of Postsecondary Students 146

Programs and Courses
Indicator 33. Undergraduate Fields of Study 152
Indicator 34. Graduate Fields of Study 154

Finance and Resources
Indicator 35. Price of Attending an Undergraduate Institution 156
Indicator 36. Grants and Loan Aid to Undergraduate Students 160
Indicator 37. Postsecondary Revenues by Source 166
Indicator 38. Expenses of Postsecondary Institutions 170
Indicator 39. Characteristics of Postsecondary Faculty 174
Indicator 40. Student Loan Volume and Default Rates 178

Completions
Indicator 41. Institutional Retention and Graduation Rates for Undergraduate Students ... 182
Indicator 42. Degrees Conferred by Public and Private Institutions 186

Spotlight

Financing Postsecondary Education in the United States

Chapter: 4/Postsecondary Education
Section: Spotlight

In 2011, the federal government provided $146 billion in student financial aid in grants and loans. The total amount, in constant 2011 dollars, disbursed in grant aid increased almost fourfold, from $10 billion in 2000 to $38 billion in 2010. The total annual amount disbursed to students as loans (Direct and Federal Family Education Loans) increased 2 1/2 times—from $43 billion in 2000 to $109 billion in 2010.

Postsecondary education in the United States includes academic, career and technical, and continuing professional education programs after high school. American colleges and universities and technical and vocational institutions offer a diverse array of postsecondary education experiences. Participation in postsecondary education in the United States has expanded over the last decade, as has the total financing for this growing sector of the U.S. economy. Students are increasingly relying on loans as a funding source, affecting the balance sheets of current students, prior students, and those who loan money to them, including the federal government.

In 2000, some 45 percent of 18- and 19-year-olds and 32 percent of 20- to 24-year-olds were enrolled in postsecondary education (see *Digest of Education Statistics 2012*, table 7). By 2011, these numbers had increased to 50 percent of 18- and 19-year-olds and 40 percent of 20- to 24-year-olds. In addition, in 2011, some 15 percent of 25- to 29-year-olds and 8 percent of 30- to 34-year-olds were enrolled in school.

Figure 1. Total fall enrollment in degree-granting postsecondary institutions: Academic years 2000–01 through 2010–11

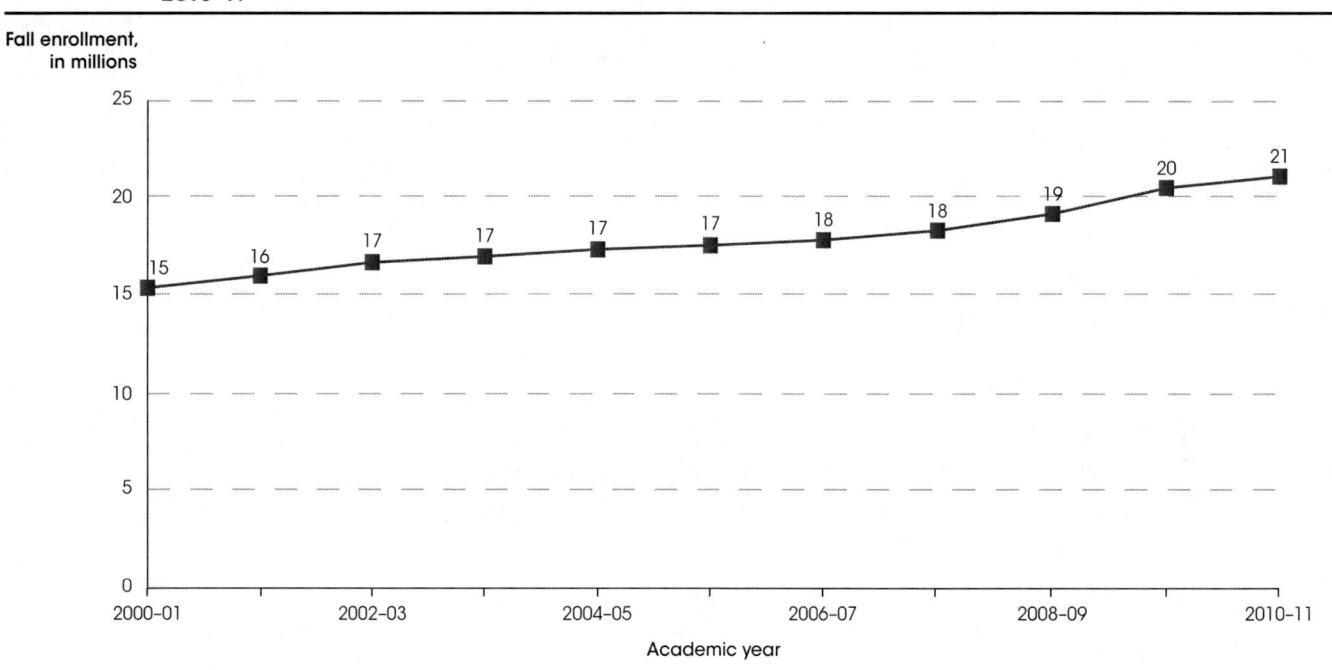

NOTE: Degree-granting institutions grant associate's or higher degrees and participate in Title IV federal financial aid programs. Some data have been revised from previously published figures.
SOURCE: U.S. Department of Education, National Center for Education Statistics, Integrated Postsecondary Education Data System (IPEDS), Spring 2001 through Spring 2011, Fall Enrollment component. See *Digest of Education Statistics 2012*, table 222.

For more information, see the Reader's Guide and the Guide to Sources.

Chapter: 4/Postsecondary Education
Section: Spotlight

Overall, between 2000 and 2010, fall enrollment in degree-granting institutions increased by 37 percent, from 15 million students to 21 million students (see *Digest of Education Statistics 2012,* table 222). Of these 21 million students in 2010, about 18 million were in undergraduate programs and 3 million were in graduate, or postbaccalaureate, programs (see *Digest of Education Statistics 2012,* table 228).

Figure 2. Total expenditures of postsecondary degree-granting institutions in constant 2011-12 dollars: Fiscal years 2000-01 through 2011-12

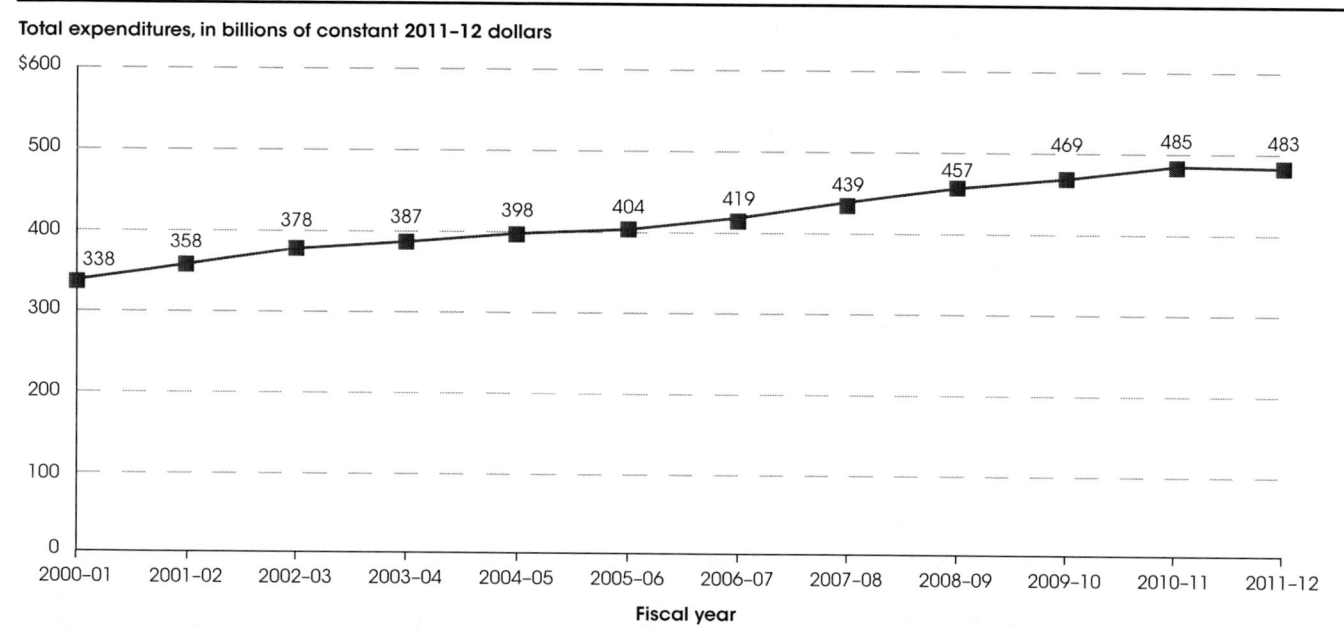

NOTE: Degree-granting institutions grant associate's or higher degrees and participate in Title IV federal financial aid programs.
SOURCE: U.S. Department of Education, National Center for Education Statistics, Integrated Postsecondary Education Data System (IPEDS), Spring 2001 through Spring 2012, Finance component; and unpublished tabulations. See *Digest of Education Statistics 2012,* table 29.

Reflecting the growth in enrollment, postsecondary education has grown as an economic sector. In 2010, expenditures by postsecondary institutions accounted for 3.2 percent of the gross domestic product (GDP) in the United States, compared to 2.6 percent in 2000 (see *Digest of Education Statistics 2012,* table 28). This is evidenced by the fact that total expenditures by postsecondary institutions increased, in constant 2011–12 dollars, from $338 billion in 2000 to $483 billion in 2011, an increase of 43 percent (see *Digest of Education Statistics 2012,* table 29).

One-third of the total expenditures on postsecondary education in 2011, or $181 billion, was provided by the federal government (see *Digest of Education Statistics 2012,* table 419). Of this amount, $146 billion was in the form of student financial aid. The federal government offers students several financial aid programs, including grants (which do not have to be repaid), student loans (which do have to be repaid), and work-study (which allows students with demonstrated financial need to earn money to pay for school).

For more information, see the Reader's Guide and the Guide to Sources.

Chapter: 4/Postsecondary Education
Section: Spotlight

Figure 3. Total annual disbursements of grants and student loans by the federal government, in constant 2011–12 dollars: Fiscal years 2000–01 through 2010–11

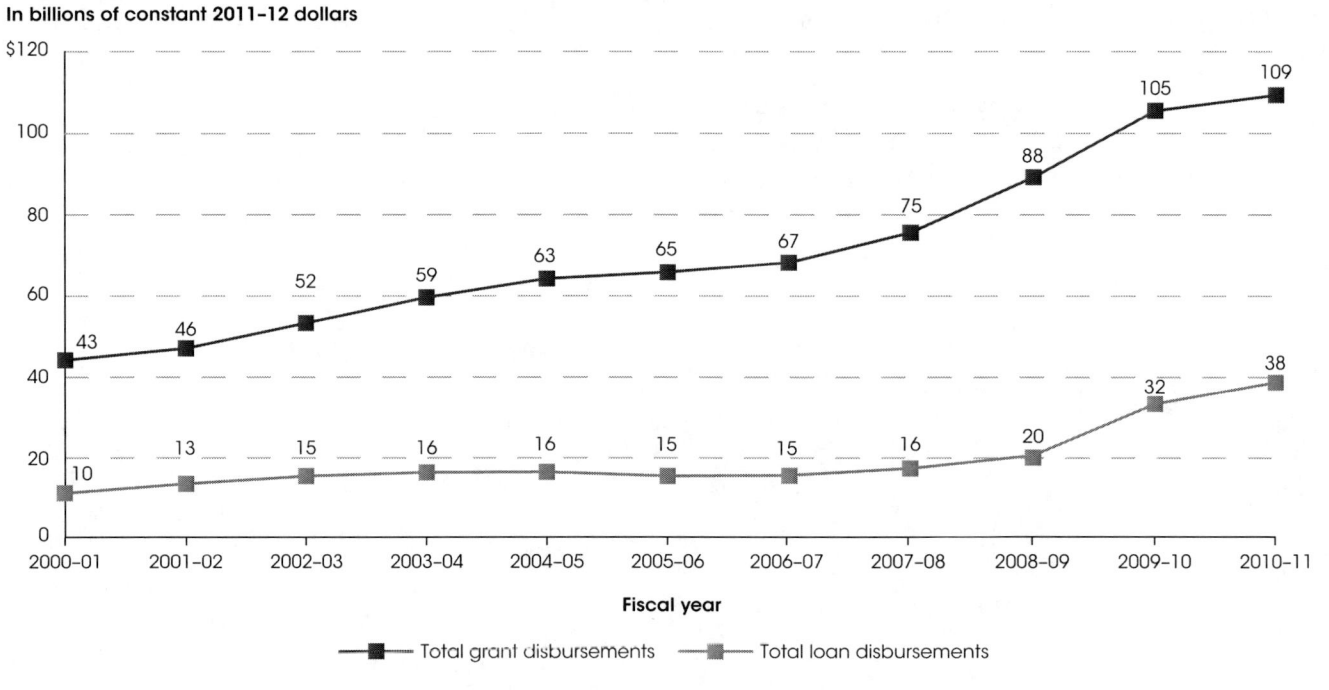

In billions of constant 2011–12 dollars

	2000–01	2001–02	2002–03	2003–04	2004–05	2005–06	2006–07	2007–08	2008–09	2009–10	2010–11
Grant recipients, in thousands	4,059	4,528	4,977	5,365	5,548	5,415	5,658	6,152	6,840	9,123	10,517
Grant disbursements, in billions	$10.4	$12.7	$14.6	$15.5	$15.6	$14.6	$14.8	$16.5	$19.7	$32.4	$37.8
Loan recipients, in thousands	7,544	8,181	9,152	10,234	11,038	11,459	11,846	12,589	15,303	18,783	19,174
Loan disbursement, in billions	$43.3	$46.2	$52.4	$58.7	$63.3	$64.9	$67.3	$74.7	$88.3	$104.7	$108.6

NOTE: Data for federal work-study programs are not included as they are a much smaller component of federal student aid and are not directly funded to the student.
SOURCE: U.S. Department of Education, Federal Student Aid, *Title IV Program Volume Reports*, Direct Loan Program, Federal Family Education Loan Program, Grant Programs. Retrieved February 11, 2013, from http://studentaid.ed.gov/about/data-center/student/title-iv.

The primary federal grant program is the Pell Grant Program. These grants are needs based and are usually only awarded to undergraduate students who have not yet earned a bachelor's degree. In the last decade, the total annual amount, in constant 2011–12 dollars, that was disbursed by the federal government in grant aid increased almost fourfold, from $10 billion in 2000 (when 100 percent of federal grants were Pell Grants) to nearly $38 billion in 2010 (when 97 percent of federal grants were Pell Grants). During this same time period, the number of recipients of federal grants increased from 4 million students to 11 million students.

The William D. Ford Federal Direct Loan (Direct Loan) Program is the largest federal student loan program. Direct Loans can be awarded to undergraduate students, either with the interest subsidized (DL Subsidized) or unsubsidized (DL Unsubsidized); to parents of undergraduate students (DL PLUS); or to graduate students (DL GRAD PLUS). The U.S. Department of Education is the lender for these loans. Prior to 2010, the federal government also offered the Federal Family Education Loan (FFEL) Program. Under this program, private lenders loaned money to students and the federal government insured the loans. In 2010, it was decided that the U.S. Department of Education would become the lender for all federal student loans, and the FFEL program was ended. As a result, no new FFEL loans have been made since July 2010. The total annual amount disbursed to students as loans (Direct and FFEL) increased by 150 percent (in constant 2011–12 dollars) in the last decade, from $43 billion in 2000 to $109 billion in 2010. The number of loan recipients increased from 8 million students to 19 million students. However, it is possible for a student to be the recipient of multiple loans in a given year.

For more information, see the Reader's Guide and the Guide to Sources.

Chapter: 4/Postsecondary Education
Section: Spotlight

Figure 4. Total outstanding balance of student loans owned by the federal government, in constant 2011 dollars: October 2000 through October 2012

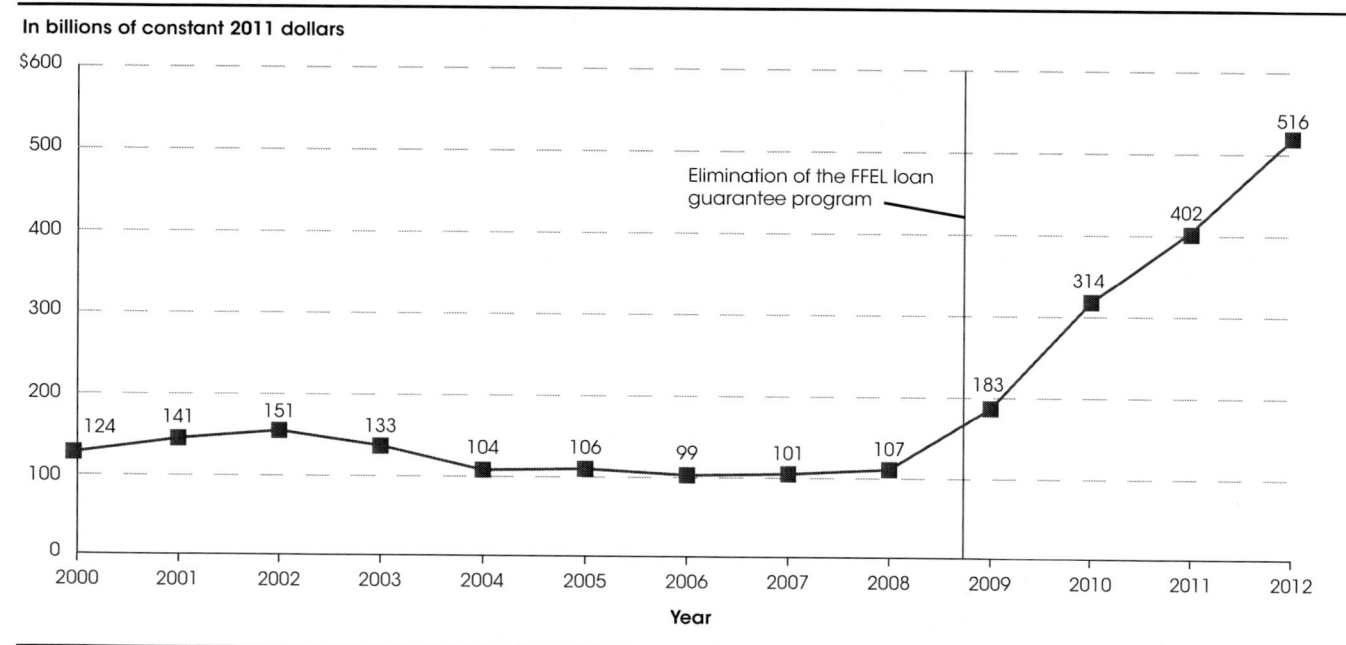

In billions of constant 2011 dollars

Year	Amount
2000	124
2001	141
2002	151
2003	133
2004	104
2005	106
2006	99
2007	101
2008	107
2009	183
2010	314
2011	402
2012	516

Elimination of the FFEL loan guarantee program (between 2008 and 2009)

NOTE: Under the Federal Family Education Loan Program (FFEL) the federal government insured student loans, but did not provide the financing. As of July 2010, no new FFEL loans have been issued.
SOURCE: Board of Governors of the Federal Reserve System, G-19 Statistical Release, "Consumer Credit," December 2012. Retrieved February 11, 2013, from http://www.federalreserve.gov/releases/g19/current/default.htm.

In its monthly G-19 statistical report on consumer credit, the Federal Reserve Bank provides data on the total amount of student loans owned by the federal government. According to the report, the federal government originates consumer credit solely in the form of nonrevolving student loans through the Department of Education. The G-19 quarterly report includes data on federal government balances on loans issued through the Direct Loan Program, as well as the FFEL program loans purchased from depository institutions and finance companies. Between October 2000 and October 2009, the total outstanding amount of student loans owned by the federal government, in constant 2011 dollars, remained between approximately $100 and $150 billion. A combination of the federal student loan policy change and a growing demand for student loans resulted in a balance of over $500 billion by October of 2012.

Figure 5. Total outstanding student loan debt held by consumers, in constant 2011 dollars: Third quarter 2003 through third quarter 2012

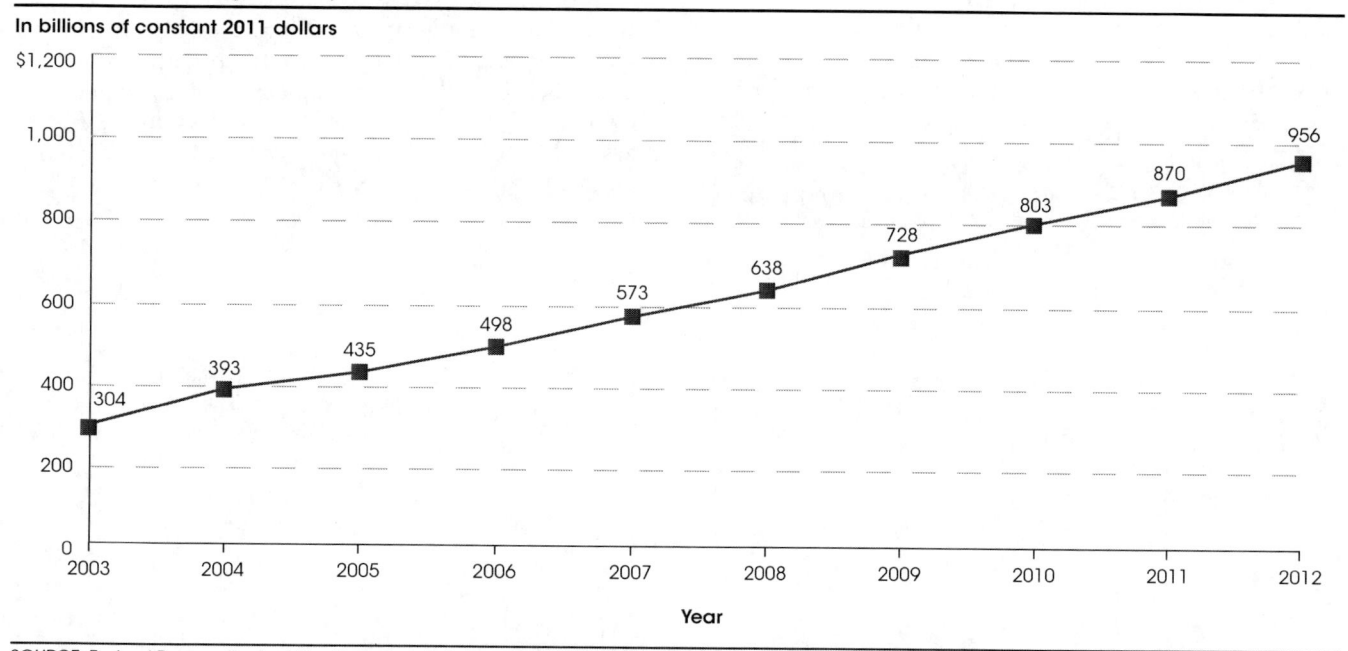

In billions of constant 2011 dollars

Year	Amount
2003	304
2004	393
2005	435
2006	498
2007	573
2008	638
2009	728
2010	803
2011	870
2012	956

SOURCE: Federal Reserve Bank of New York, *Quarterly Report on Household Debt and Credit*, 2012 Q3. Retrieved February 11, 2013, from http://www.newyorkfed.org/householdcredit/.

For more information, see the Reader's Guide and the Guide to Sources.

In addition to loans originated by the federal government, students can obtain private student loans from financial institutions, nonprofit lenders, and certain schools that elect to fund or guarantee loans. According to the Federal Reserve Bank of New York's *Quarterly Report on Household Debt and Credit,* total student loan debt, across all age groups, stood at nearly $1 trillion ($956 billion) in the fall of 2012. By comparison, in fall 2003, total student loan debt outstanding was $304 billion (in constant 2011 dollars), meaning that it has more than tripled in the last 9 years. Further, student loan debt is the only form of consumer debt that has grown since the peak of consumer debt in 2008, and balances of student loans have eclipsed both auto loans and credit cards, making student loan debt the largest form of consumer debt outside of mortgages.[5]

Figure 6. Postsecondary federal student loan 2-year cohort default rates: Fiscal years 2000 through 2010

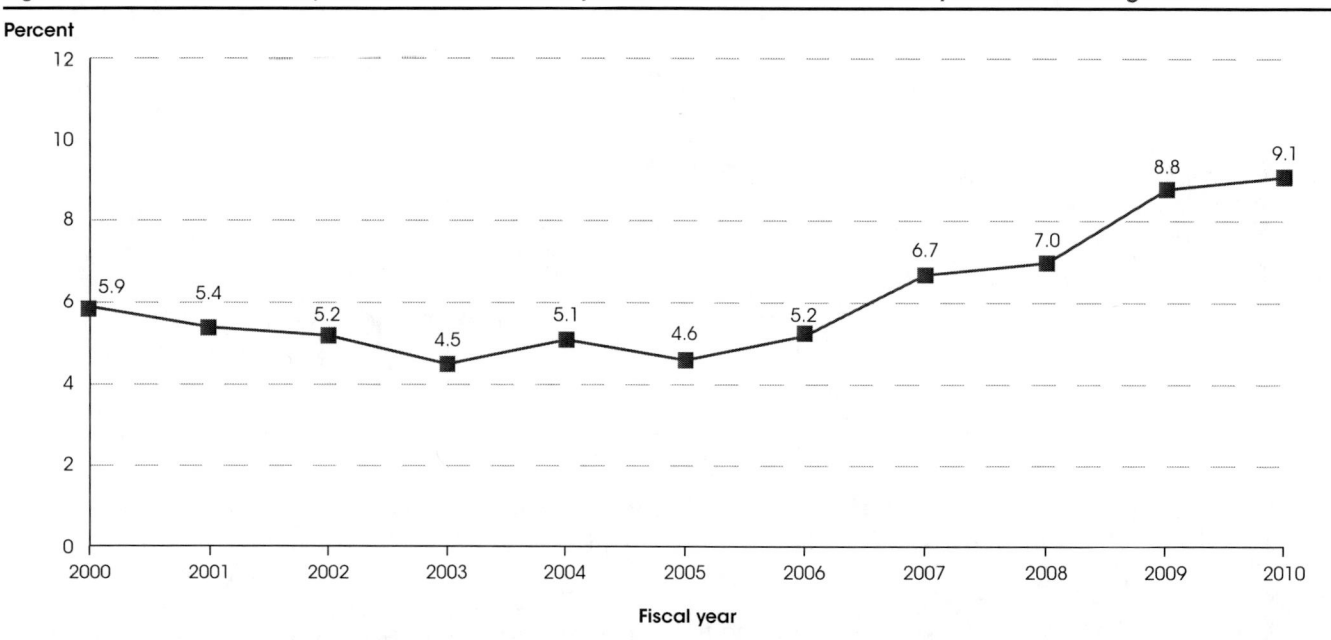

NOTE: The Department of Education issues default rates according to the fiscal year that borrowers entered repayment. For example, the fiscal year 2010 default rate is based on students who entered repayment between October 1, 2009, and September 30, 2010. The Department publishes default rates approximately 2 years after the fiscal year in which students enter repayment.
SOURCE: U.S. Department of Education, Federal Student Aid. Retrieved February 11, 2013, from http://www2.ed.gov/offices/OSFAP/defaultmanagement/defaultrates.html.

According to the federal government, a federal student loan is in default if there has been no payment on the loan in 270 days. The Department of Education calculates a 2-year cohort default rate, which is the percentage of students who entered repayment in a given fiscal year (from October 1 to September 30) and then defaulted within the following 2 fiscal years. In 2010, the national 2-year cohort default rate was 9.1 percent, meaning that of those students who entered repayment during fiscal year 2008, some 9.1 percent had not made a payment on their loans for at least 270 consecutive days during fiscal years 2009 and 2010. The 2-year cohort default rate has been increasing since 2005, when it was 4.6 percent.

---
[5] Federal Reserve Bank of New York, Research and Statistics Group. (November 2012). *Quarterly Report on Household Debt and Credit,* p. 1. Retrieved February 11, 2013, from http://www.newyorkfed.org/research/national_economy/householdcredit/DistrictReport_Q32012.pdf.

For more information, see the Reader's Guide and the Guide to Sources.

Chapter: 4/Postsecondary Education
Section: Spotlight

Figure 7. Percentage of total outstanding student loan debt held by consumers that is **90 or more days delinquent**: First quarter 2003 though third quarter 2012

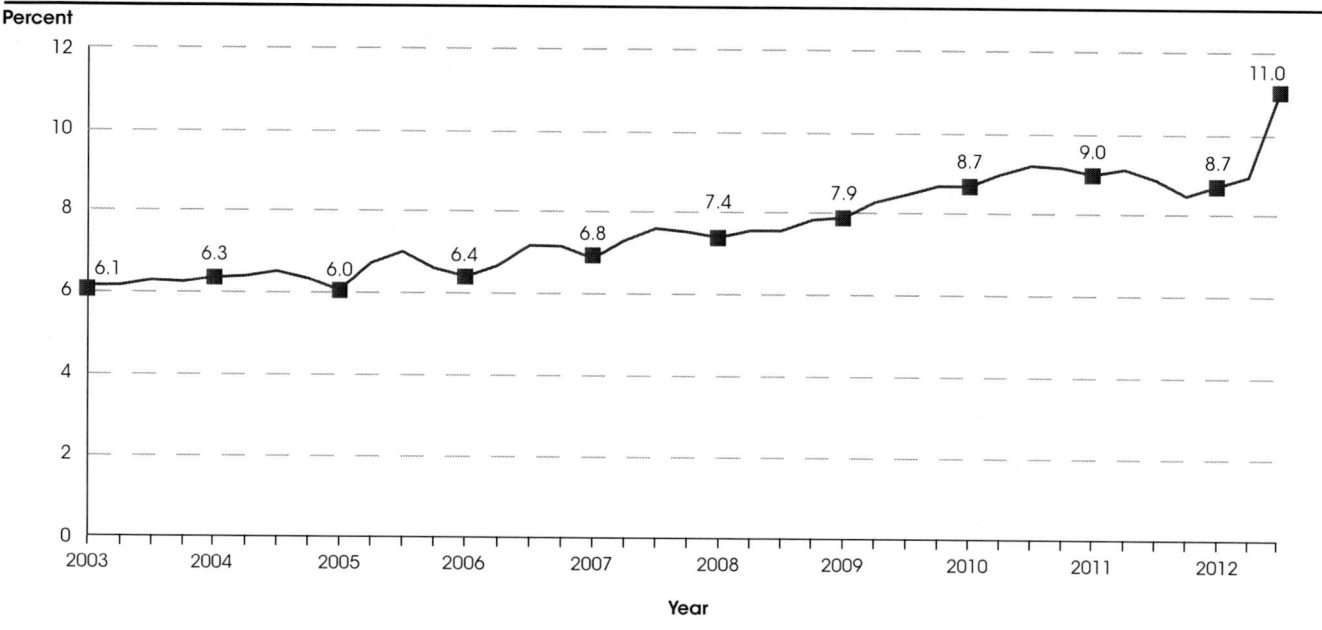

SOURCE: Federal Reserve Bank of New York, *Quarterly Report on Household Debt and Credit*, 2012 Q3. Retrieved on February 11, 2013, from http://www.newyorkfed.org/householdcredit/.

In addition to providing data on the total student loan debt outstanding, the Federal Reserve Bank of New York's *Quarterly Report on Household Debt and Credit* contains data on those student loans that are delinquent in a given month, meaning that they are at least 30 days past due, as well as those that are "seriously" delinquent, meaning that they are at least 90 days past due. In the first quarter of 2003, approximately 6 percent of all outstanding student loans were at least 90 days delinquent. By the third quarter of 2012, that rate had increased to 11 percent.

Reference tables: *Digest of Education Statistics 2012,* tables 7, 28, 29, 222, 228, 419

Glossary: Private institution, Public institution

For more information, see the Reader's Guide and the Guide to Sources.

Indicator 31
Characteristics of Postsecondary Institutions

Chapter: 4/Postsecondary Education
Section: Characteristics of Postsecondary Students

In 2011–12, some 25 percent of 4-year institutions had open admissions policies, 25 percent accepted three-quarters or more of their applicants, 35 percent accepted one-half to less than three-quarters of their applicants, and the remaining 15 percent accepted less than one-half of their applicants.

Figure 1. Number of degree-granting institutions with first-year undergraduates, by level and control of institution: 2000–01 and 2011–12

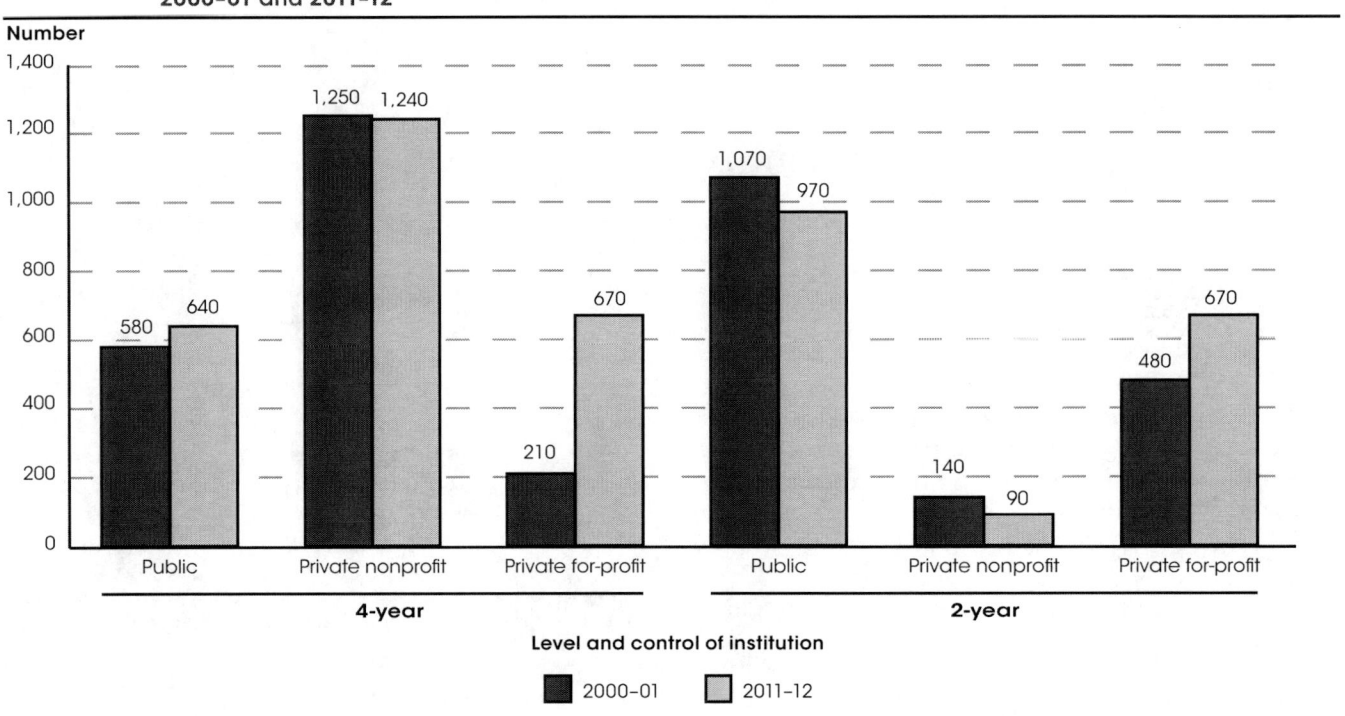

Level and control of institution	2000–01	2011–12
4-year Public	580	640
4-year Private nonprofit	1,250	1,240
4-year Private for-profit	210	670
2-year Public	1,070	970
2-year Private nonprofit	140	90
2-year Private for-profit	480	670

NOTE: Detail may not sum to totals because of rounding.
SOURCE: U.S. Department of Education, National Center for Education Statistics, Integrated Postsecondary Education Data System (IPEDS), Fall 2011, Institutional Characteristics component. See *Digest of Education Statistics 2012*, table 373.

In 2011–12, there were 4,280 degree-granting institutions, including 2,560 4-year institutions offering programs at the bachelor's or higher degree level and 1,730 2-year institutions offering associate's degrees. These institutions may be governed by publicly appointed or elected officials, with major support from public funds (publicly controlled), or by privately elected or appointed officials, with major support from private sources (private control). Privately controlled institutions may be operated on a nonprofit or for-profit basis. The number of private nonprofit institutions in 2011–12 (1,340) was 3 percent lower than in 2000–01 (1,380), and the number of public institutions in 2011–12 (1,610) was 2 percent lower than in 2000–01 (1,650). In contrast, the number of private for-profit institutions increased by 95 percent between 2000–01 and 2011–12 (from 690 to 1,340).

For more information, see the Reader's Guide and the Guide to Sources.

Chapter: 4/Postsecondary Education
Section: Characteristics of Postsecondary Students

Figure 2. Percentage distribution of 4-year degree-granting institutions with first-year undergraduates, by application acceptance rate and control of institution: 2011-12

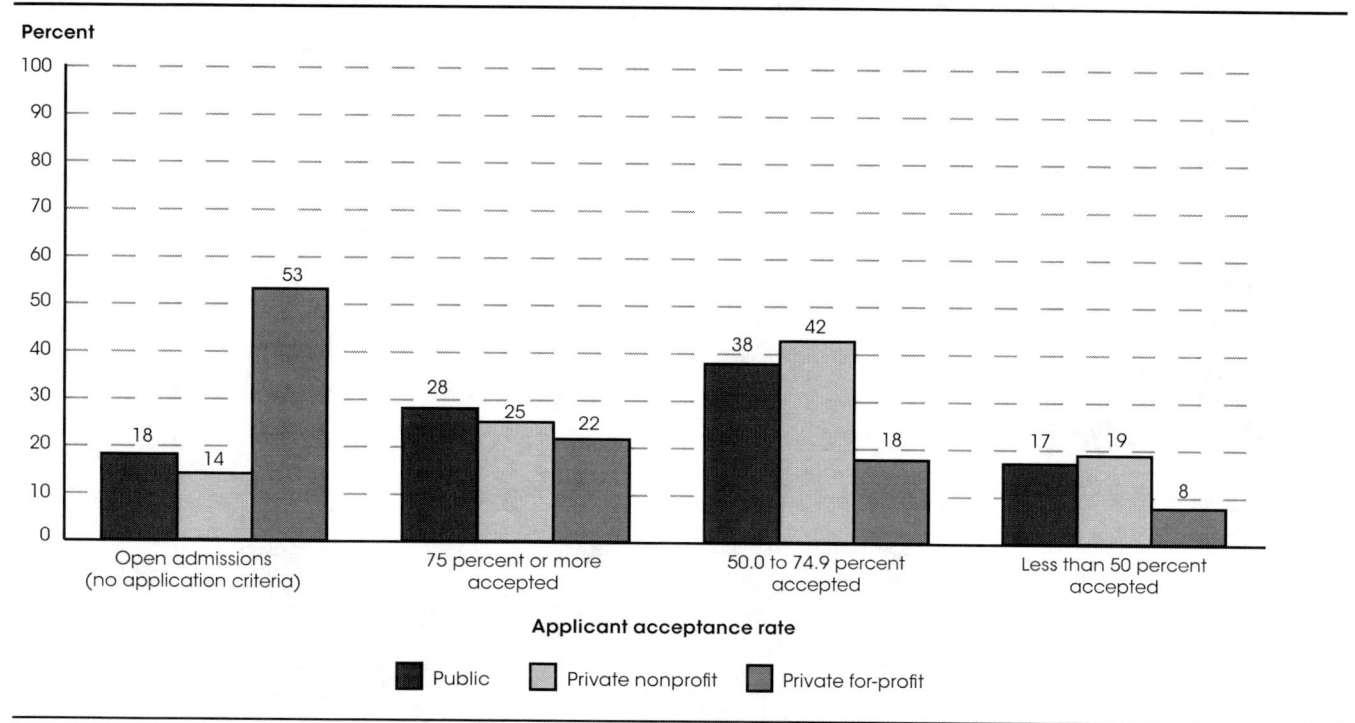

Applicant acceptance rate	Public	Private nonprofit	Private for-profit
Open admissions (no application criteria)	18	14	53
75 percent or more accepted	28	25	22
50.0 to 74.9 percent accepted	38	42	18
Less than 50 percent accepted	17	19	8

NOTE: Detail may not sum to totals because of rounding.
SOURCE: U.S. Department of Education, National Center for Education Statistics, Integrated Postsecondary Education Data System (IPEDS), Fall 2011, Institutional Characteristics component. See *Digest of Education Statistics 2012*, table 374.

In 2011–12, some 25 percent of 4-year institutions had open admissions policies (accepted all applicants), 25 percent accepted three-quarters or more of their applicants, 35 percent accepted one-half to less than three-quarters of their applicants, and 15 percent accepted less than one-half of their applicants. Among 4-year institutions, a higher percentage of private for-profit institutions (53 percent) than public (18 percent) and private nonprofit institutions (14 percent) had open admissions policies in 2011–12. Some 22 percent of private for-profit 4-year institutions accepted three-quarters or more of their applicants, whereas 28 percent of public 4-year institutions and 25 percent of private 4-year nonprofit institutions did so.

For more information, see the Reader's Guide and the Guide to Sources.

Chapter: 4/Postsecondary Education
Section: Characteristics of Postsecondary Students

Figure 3. Percentage distribution of 2-year degree-granting institutions with first-year undergraduates, by application acceptance rate and control of institution: 2011–12

Applicant acceptance rate	Public	Private nonprofit	Private for-profit
Open admissions (no application criteria)	97	50	80
75 percent or more accepted	1	17	15
50.0 to 74.9 percent accepted	1	24	4
Less than 50 percent accepted	#	9	1

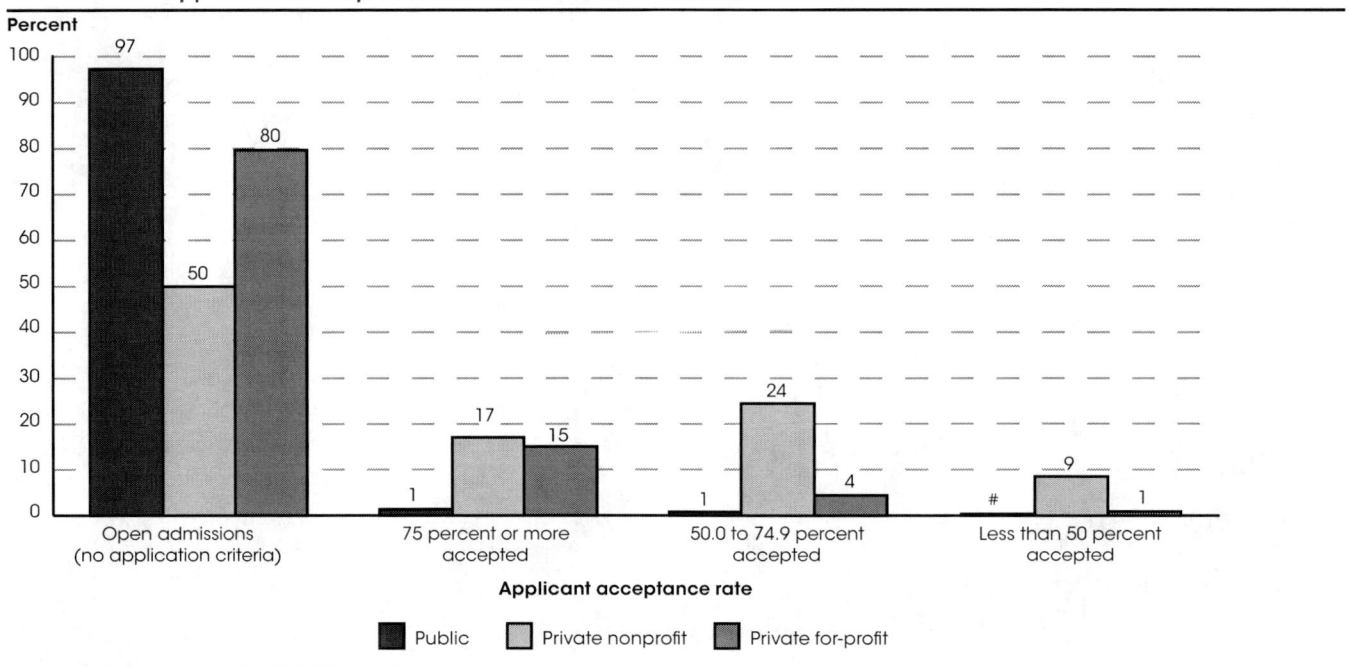

Rounds to zero.
NOTE: Detail may not sum to totals because of rounding.
SOURCE: U.S. Department of Education, National Center for Education Statistics, Integrated Postsecondary Education Data System (IPEDS), Fall 2011, Institutional Characteristics component. See *Digest of Education Statistics 2012*, table 374.

In 2011–12 some 88 percent of 2-year institutions had open admissions, 8 percent accepted three-quarters or more of their applicants, 3 percent accepted one-half to less than three-quarters of applicants, and 1 percent accepted less than one-half of their applicants. Among 2-year institutions, almost all public institutions had open admissions (97 percent), while 79 percent of private for-profit institutions and 50 percent of private nonprofit ones had open admissions.

Figure 4. Percentage of 4-year degree-granting institutions with first-year undergraduates, by admissions requirement and control of institution: 2011–12

Admissions requirement	Public	Private nonprofit	Private for-profit
Secondary school record	79	79	40
TOEFL scores[1]	71	69	35
Secondary grades	68	69	14
Test scores[2]	75	63	1
College preparatory program	46	25	0
Secondary class rank	22	15	5
Recommendations	9	53	2
Demonstration of competencies[3]	4	9	6

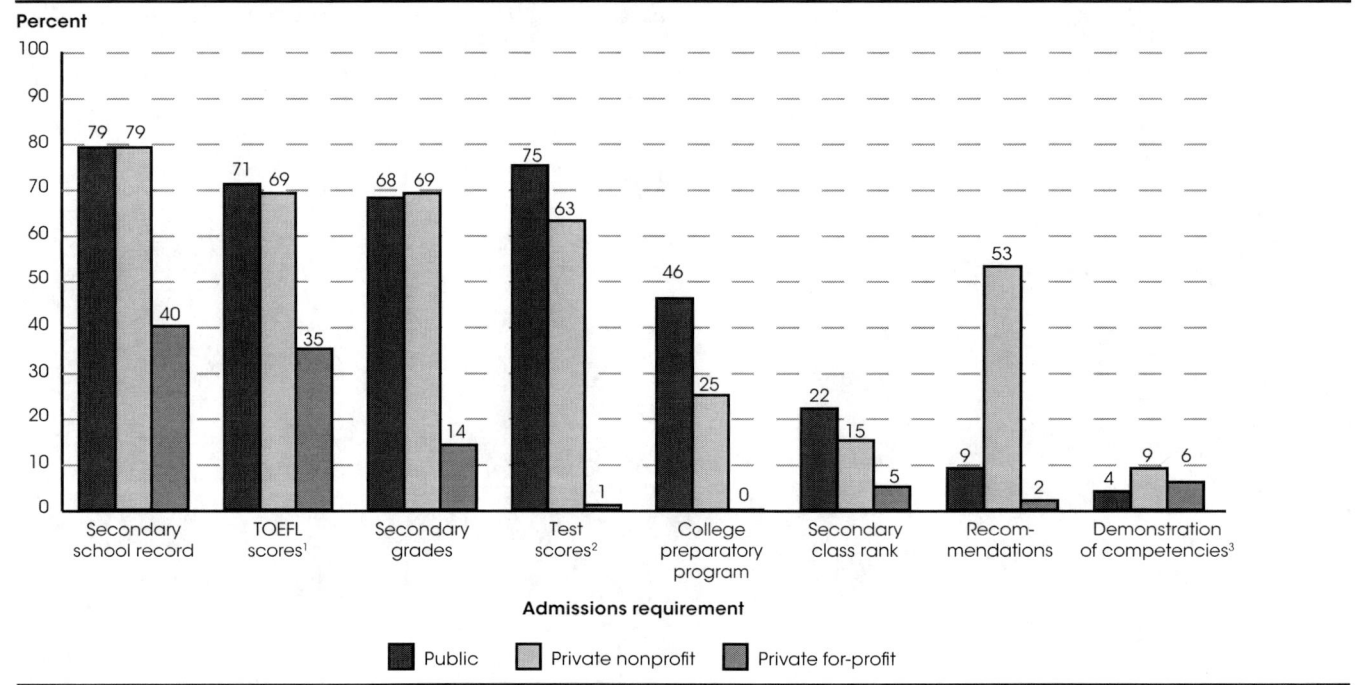

[1] Test of English as a Foreign Language.
[2] Includes SAT, ACT, or other admission tests.
[3] Formal demonstration of competencies (e.g., portfolios, certificates of mastery, assessment instruments).
NOTE: Detail may not sum to totals because of rounding.
SOURCE: U.S. Department of Education, National Center for Education Statistics, Integrated Postsecondary Education Data System (IPEDS), Fall 2011, Institutional Characteristics component. See *Digest of Education Statistics 2012*, table 373.

For more information, see the Reader's Guide and the Guide to Sources.

Chapter: 4/Postsecondary Education
Section: Characteristics of Postsecondary Students

Figure 5. Percentage of 2-year degree-granting institutions with first-year undergraduates, by admissions requirement and control of institution: 2011–12

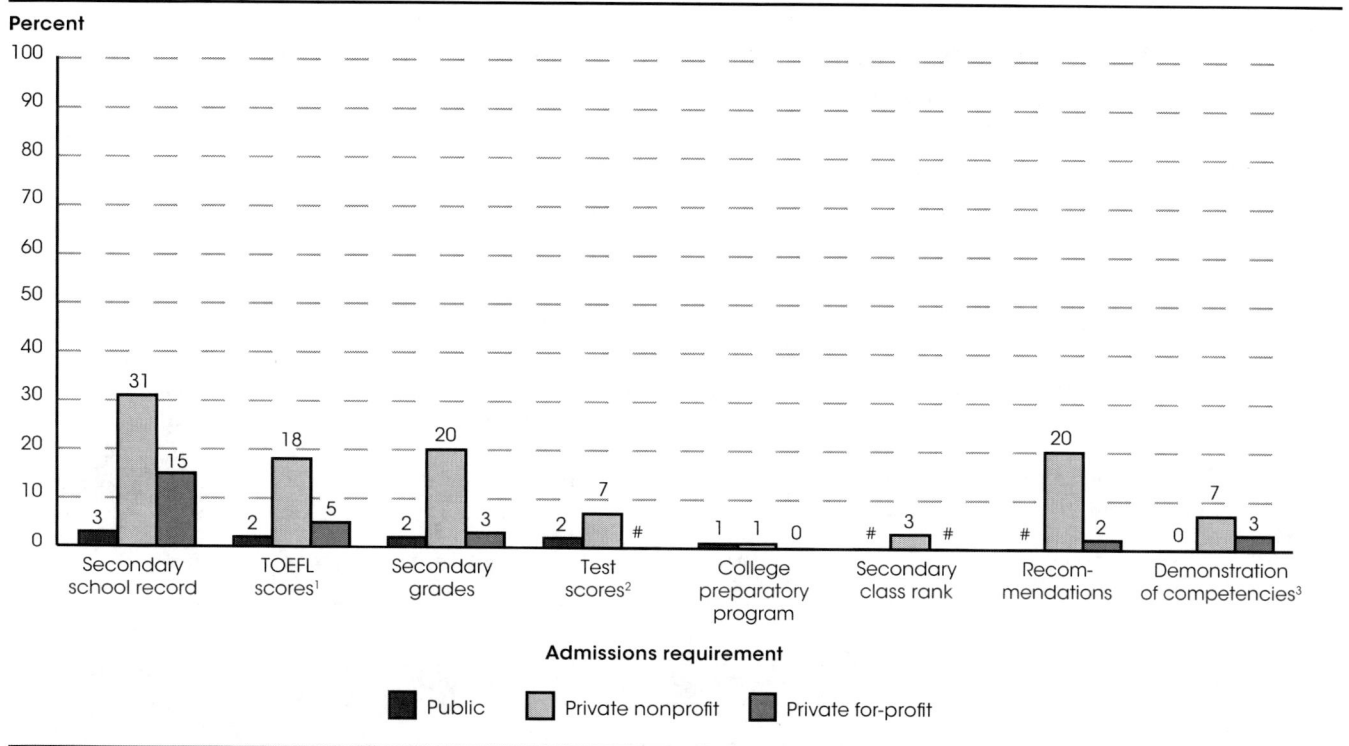

Admissions requirement	Public	Private nonprofit	Private for-profit
Secondary school record	3	31	15
TOEFL scores[1]	2	18	5
Secondary grades	2	20	3
Test scores[2]	2	7	#
College preparatory program	1	1	0
Secondary class rank	#	3	#
Recommendations	#	20	2
Demonstration of competencies[3]	0	7	3

\# Rounds to zero.
[1] Test of English as a Foreign Language.
[2] Includes SAT, ACT, or other admission tests.
[3] Formal demonstration of competencies (e.g., portfolios, certificates of mastery, assessment instruments).
NOTE: Detail may not sum to totals because of rounding.
SOURCE: U.S. Department of Education, National Center for Education Statistics, Integrated Postsecondary Education Data System (IPEDS), Fall 2011, Institutional Characteristics component. See *Digest of Education Statistics 2012*, table 373.

In 2011–12, some 74 percent of 4-year and 11 percent of 2-year institutions had admissions criteria for their applicants. A small percentage of 4-year (1 percent) and 2-year institutions (2 percent) had no admissions requirements, only suggested admissions criteria. Admissions criteria are requirements for all applicants to an institution to submit specific information, such as secondary school administrative records, Test of English as a Foreign Language (TOEFL) scores, secondary school grades, admission tests (such as the SAT or ACT), recommendations, and college preparatory programs (i.e., International Baccalaureate). Among 4-year institutions, 75 percent of public institutions had a requirement for admission tests such as the SAT or ACT, compared with 63 percent of private nonprofit and 1 percent of private for-profit institutions. The percentage of 4-year private nonprofit institutions (53 percent) that required recommendations for admission was higher than the percentages for public (9 percent) and private for-profit 4-year institutions (2 percent). The percentage of 4-year public and private nonprofit institutions requiring TOEFL scores (71 percent and 69 percent, respectively) was higher than the percentage for 4-year private for-profit institutions (35 percent). Among 2-year institutions, 31 percent of private nonprofit and 15 percent of private for-profit institutions had a requirement for secondary school records, compared with 3 percent of public institutions.

Reference tables: *Digest of Education Statistics 2012*, tables 373, 374

Glossary: Degree-granting institution, For-profit institution, Nonprofit institution

For more information, see the Reader's Guide and the Guide to Sources.

Indicator 32
Characteristics of Postsecondary Students

Some 10.6 million undergraduate students attended 4-year institutions in 2011, while 7.5 million attended 2-year institutions. At 4-year institutions in 2011, some 78 percent of undergraduate students attended full time, compared with 42 percent of undergraduate students at 2-year institutions.

In fall 2011, there were 18.1 million undergraduate students and 2.9 million postbaccalaureate students attending degree-granting postsecondary institutions in the United States. Undergraduate students can attend either 4-year institutions that can award a bachelor's or higher degree or 2-year institutions that can award associate's degrees but may also award certificates in 2-year and less than 2-year programs. Some 10.6 million undergraduate students (58 percent of the total) attended 4-year institutions in fall 2011, while 7.5 million (42 percent of the total) attended 2-year institutions. Of undergraduate students at 4-year institutions that year, 8.2 million, or 78 percent, attended full time. Of undergraduate students at 2-year institutions that year, 3.2 million (42 percent) were full-time students and 4.3 million (58 percent) were part-time students.

Figure 1. Percentage distribution of full-time undergraduate enrollment in degree-granting institutions, by institutional level and control and student age: Fall 2011

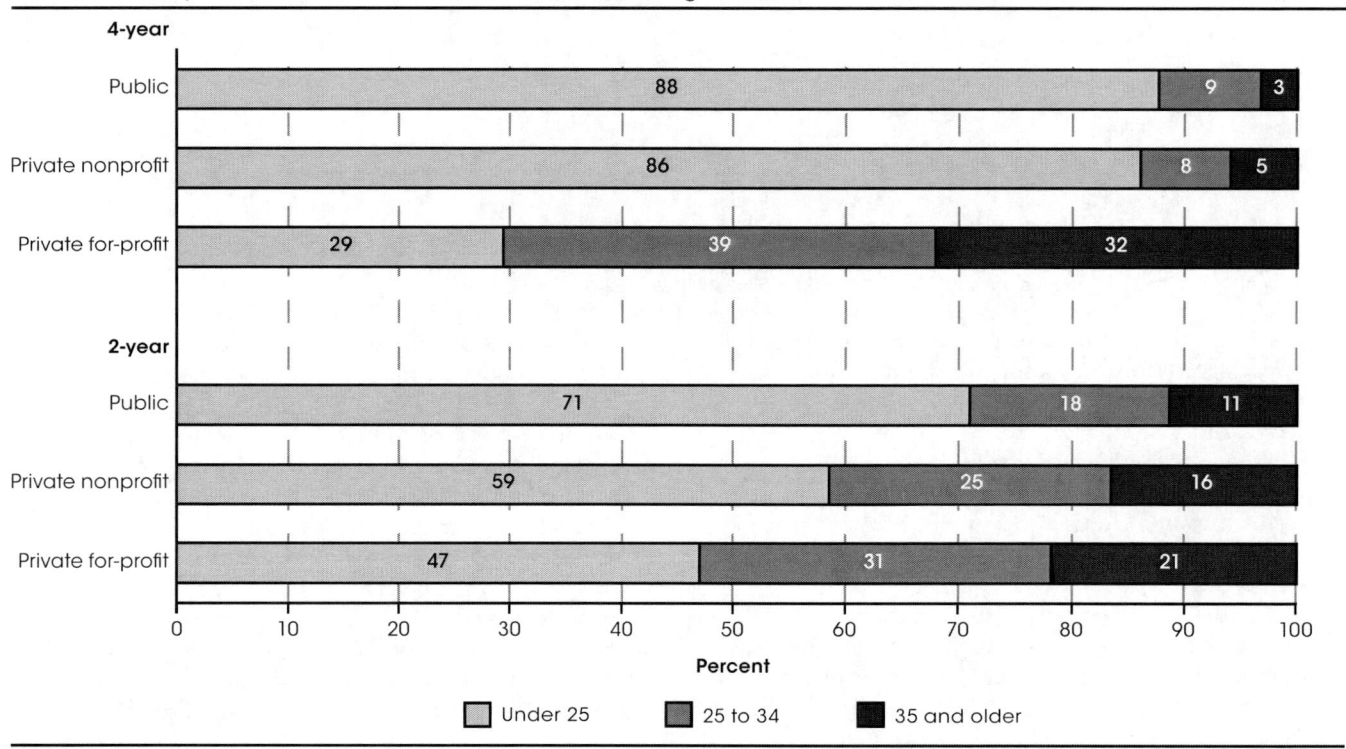

Institution	Under 25	25 to 34	35 and older
4-year			
Public	88	9	3
Private nonprofit	86	8	5
Private for-profit	29	39	32
2-year			
Public	71	18	11
Private nonprofit	59	25	16
Private for-profit	47	31	21

NOTE: Degree-granting institutions grant associate's or higher degrees and participate in Title IV federal financial aid programs. Detail may not sum to totals because of rounding and the absence of "age unknown" students.
SOURCE: U.S. Department of Education, National Center for Education Statistics, Integrated Postsecondary Education Data System (IPEDS), Spring 2012, Enrollment component. See *Digest of Education Statistics 2012*, table 226.

At public and private nonprofit 4-year institutions in 2011, most of the full-time students (88 percent and 86 percent, respectively) were young adults under the age of 25. However, at private for-profit 4-year institutions in 2011 just 29 percent of full-time students were young adults; 39 percent were between the ages of 25 and 34, and 32 percent were age 35 and older.

Of full-time students at 2-year institutions in 2011, young adults accounted for 71 percent of enrollment at public institutions, 59 percent of enrollment at private nonprofit institutions, and 47 percent of enrollment at private for-profit institutions. Regarding the remaining age groups of full-time students in 2011, at public 2-year institutions some 18 percent were between 25 and 34 years old, and 11 percent were 35 and older; at private nonprofit institutions 25 percent were between 25 and 34, and 16 percent were 35 and older; and at private for-profit institutions 31 percent were between 25 and 34, and 21 percent were 35 and older.

For more information, see the Reader's Guide and the Guide to Sources.

Chapter: 4/Postsecondary Education
Section: Characteristics of Postsecondary Students

Figure 2. Percentage distribution of part-time undergraduate enrollment in degree-granting institutions, by institutional level and control and student age: Fall 2011

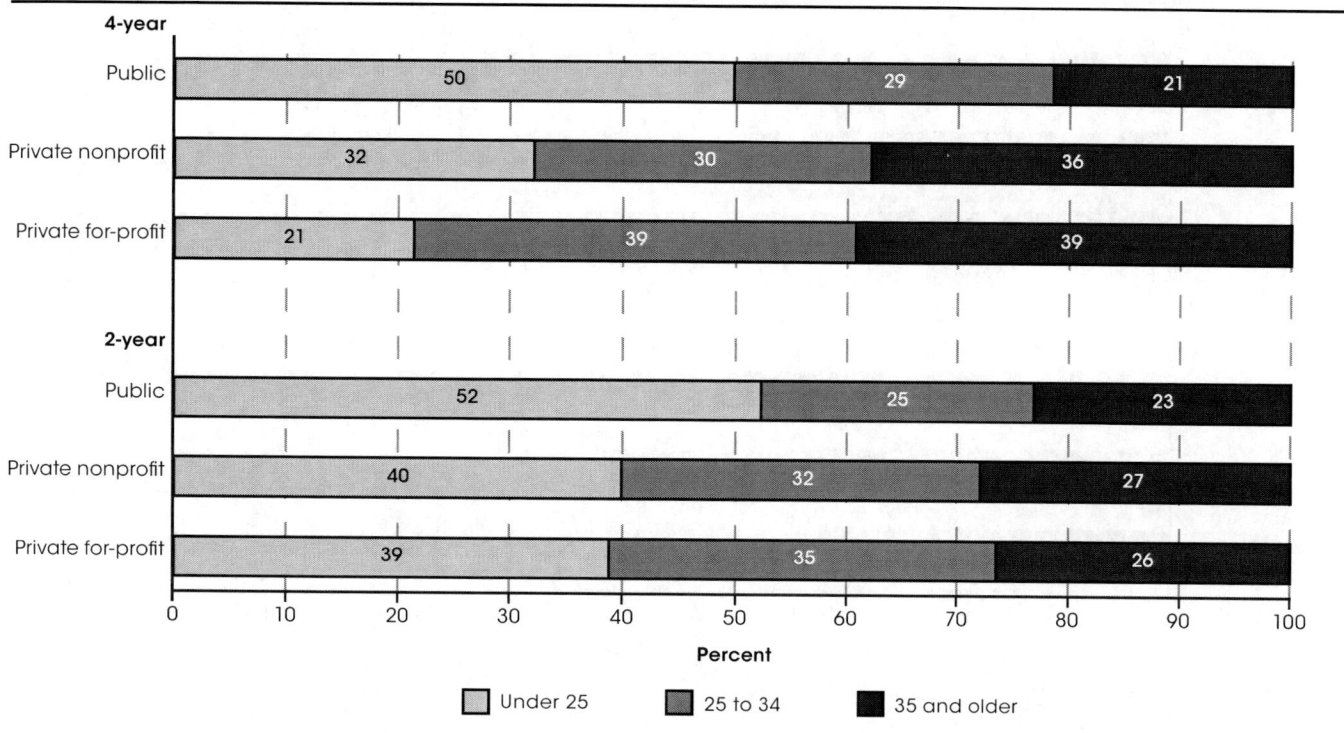

Institution	Under 25	25 to 34	35 and older
4-year			
Public	50	29	21
Private nonprofit	32	30	36
Private for-profit	21	39	39
2-year			
Public	52	25	23
Private nonprofit	40	32	27
Private for-profit	39	35	26

NOTE: Degree-granting institutions grant associate's or higher degrees and participate in Title IV federal financial aid programs. Detail may not sum to totals because of rounding and the absence of "age unknown" students.
SOURCE: U.S. Department of Education, National Center for Education Statistics, Integrated Postsecondary Education Data System (IPEDS), Spring 2012, Enrollment component. See *Digest of Education Statistics 2012*, table 226.

Of undergraduate students enrolled part time in 4-year institutions in 2011, young adults made up 50 percent of the enrollment at public institutions, 32 percent of the enrollment at private nonprofit institutions, and 21 percent of the enrollment at private for-profit institutions. Thus, students ages 25–34 and 35 and older accounted for the other half of the part-time enrollment at public 4-year institutions (29 percent and 21 percent, respectively), two-thirds of the part-time enrollment at private nonprofit 4-year institutions (30 percent and 36 percent, respectively), and over three-quarters of the part-time enrollment at private for-profit 4-year institutions (39 percent each).

In 2011, some 52 percent of part-time students at public 2-year institutions were young adults, while 25 percent were between the ages of 25 and 34, and 23 percent were 35 and older. At private nonprofit 2-year institutions, some 40 percent of part-time students were young adults, 32 percent were between the ages of 25 and 34, and 27 percent were 35 and older. At private for-profit 2-year institutions, 39 percent of part-time students were young adults, 35 percent were between the ages of 25 and 34, and 26 percent were age 35 and older.

For more information, see the Reader's Guide and the Guide to Sources.

Chapter: 4/Postsecondary Education
Section: Characteristics of Postsecondary Students

Figure 3. Percentage distribution of total undergraduate enrollment in degree-granting institutions, by institutional level and control and race/ethnicity of student: Fall 2011

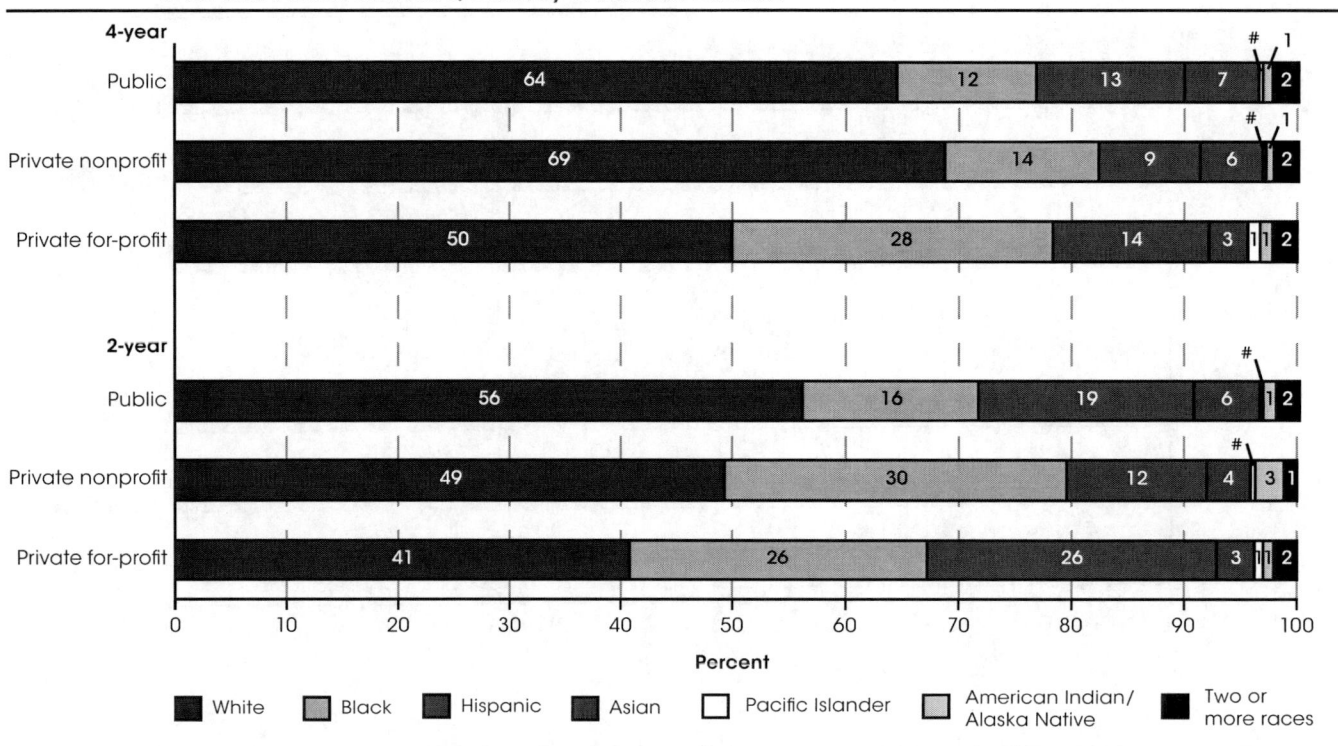

4-year
- Public: 64, 12, 13, 7, #, 1, 2
- Private nonprofit: 69, 14, 9, 6, #, 1, 2
- Private for-profit: 50, 28, 14, 3, 1, 1, 2

2-year
- Public: 56, 16, 19, 6, #, 1, 2
- Private nonprofit: 49, 30, 12, 4, #, 3, 1
- Private for-profit: 41, 26, 26, 3, 1, 1, 2

Legend: White, Black, Hispanic, Asian, Pacific Islander, American Indian/Alaska Native, Two or more races

Rounds to zero.
NOTE: Degree-granting institutions grant associate's or higher degrees and participate in Title IV federal financial aid programs. Race categories exclude persons of Hispanic ethnicity. Detail may not sum to totals because of rounding.
SOURCE: U.S. Department of Education, National Center for Education Statistics, Integrated Postsecondary Education Data System (IPEDS), Spring 2012, Enrollment component. See *Digest of Education Statistics 2012*, table 268.

Sixty-nine percent of all undergraduate students (full-time and part-time) at private nonprofit 4-year institutions in 2011 were White, which was higher than the percentage of White students at either public or private for-profit 4-year institutions. For Asian undergraduate students at 4-year institutions that year, the highest percentage was at public institutions (7 percent). Higher percentages of Black (28 percent) and Hispanic (14 percent) undergraduates attended private for-profit 4-year institutions than public (12 percent and 13 percent, respectively) and private nonprofit (14 and 9 percent, respectively) 4-year institutions.

At 2-year institutions in 2011, the highest percentages of White and Asian undergraduate students were at public institutions, at 56 percent and 6 percent, respectively, and the highest percentage of Black students was at private nonprofit institutions, at 30 percent. The highest percentage of Hispanic students at 2-year institutions in 2011 was at private for-profit institutions, at 26 percent.

For more information, see the Reader's Guide and the Guide to Sources.

148 *The Condition of Education 2013*

Chapter: 4/Postsecondary Education
Section: Characteristics of Postsecondary Students

Figure 4. Percentage distribution of total postbaccalaureate enrollment in degree-granting institutions, by institutional control and race/ethnicity of student: Fall 2011

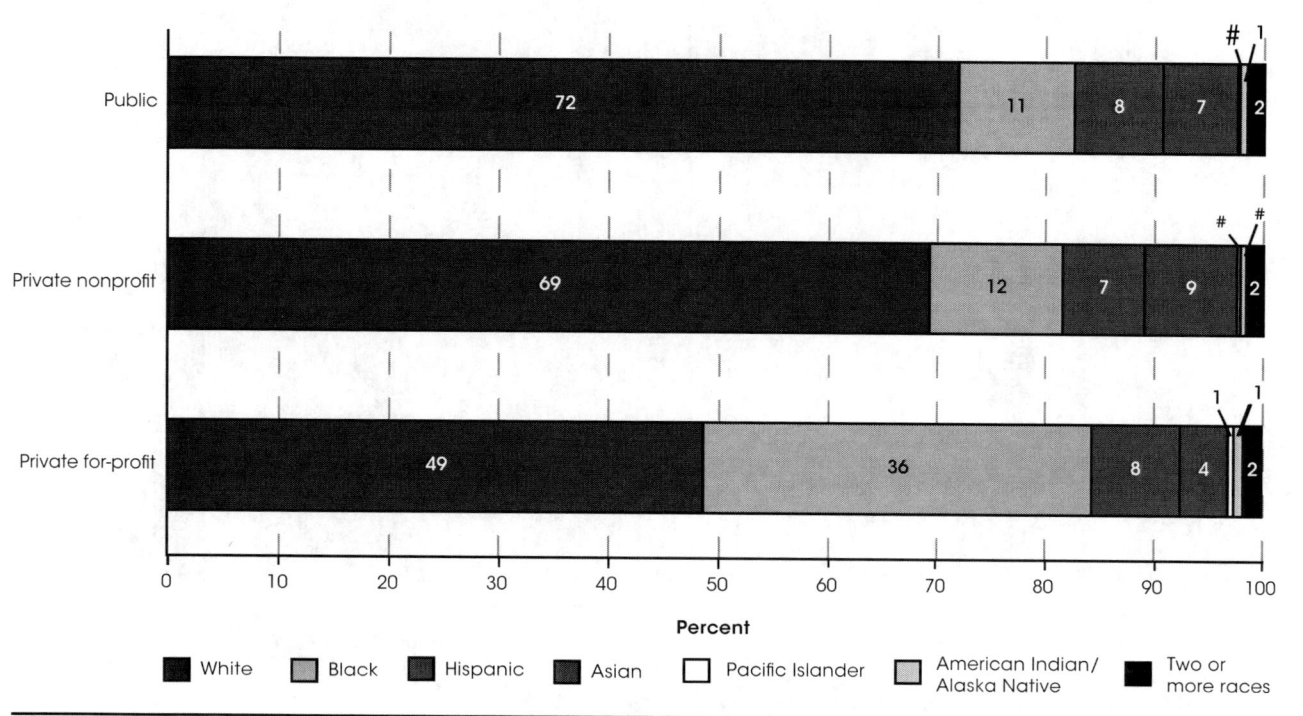

Institution	White	Black	Hispanic	Asian	Pacific Islander	American Indian/Alaska Native	Two or more races
Public	72	11	8	7	#	1	2
Private nonprofit	69	12	7	9	#	#	2
Private for-profit	49	36	8	4	1	1	2

Rounds to zero.
NOTE: Degree-granting institutions grant associate's or higher degrees and participate in Title IV federal financial aid programs. Race categories exclude persons of Hispanic ethnicity. Detail may not sum to totals because of rounding.
SOURCE: U.S. Department of Education, National Center for Education Statistics, Integrated Postsecondary Education Data System (IPEDS), Spring 2012, Enrollment component. See *Digest of Education Statistics 2012*, table 268.

In 2011, some 48 percent of postbaccalaureate (graduate) students attended public institutions, 41 percent attended private nonprofit institutions, and 10 percent attended private for-profit institutions. There were differences in attendance patterns by race/ethnicity, however. At public institutions in 2011, some 72 percent of graduate students were White, compared with 69 percent at private nonprofit institutions and 49 percent at private for-profit institutions. Thirty-six percent of graduate students at private for-profit institutions were Black, compared with 12 percent of students at private nonprofit institutions and 11 percent of students at public institutions. Hispanics accounted for 8 percent of graduate enrollment at public and private for-profit institutions and 7 percent of graduate enrollment at private nonprofit institutions, while Asians accounted for 9 percent of graduate enrollment at private nonprofit institutions, 7 percent of graduate enrollment at public institutions, and 4 percent of graduate enrollment at private for-profit institutions.

For more information, see the Reader's Guide and the Guide to Sources.

Chapter: 4/Postsecondary Education
Section: Characteristics of Postsecondary Students

Figure 5. Percentage of undergraduate college students 16 to 24 years old who were employed, by attendance status, hours worked per week, and institutional level: October 2011

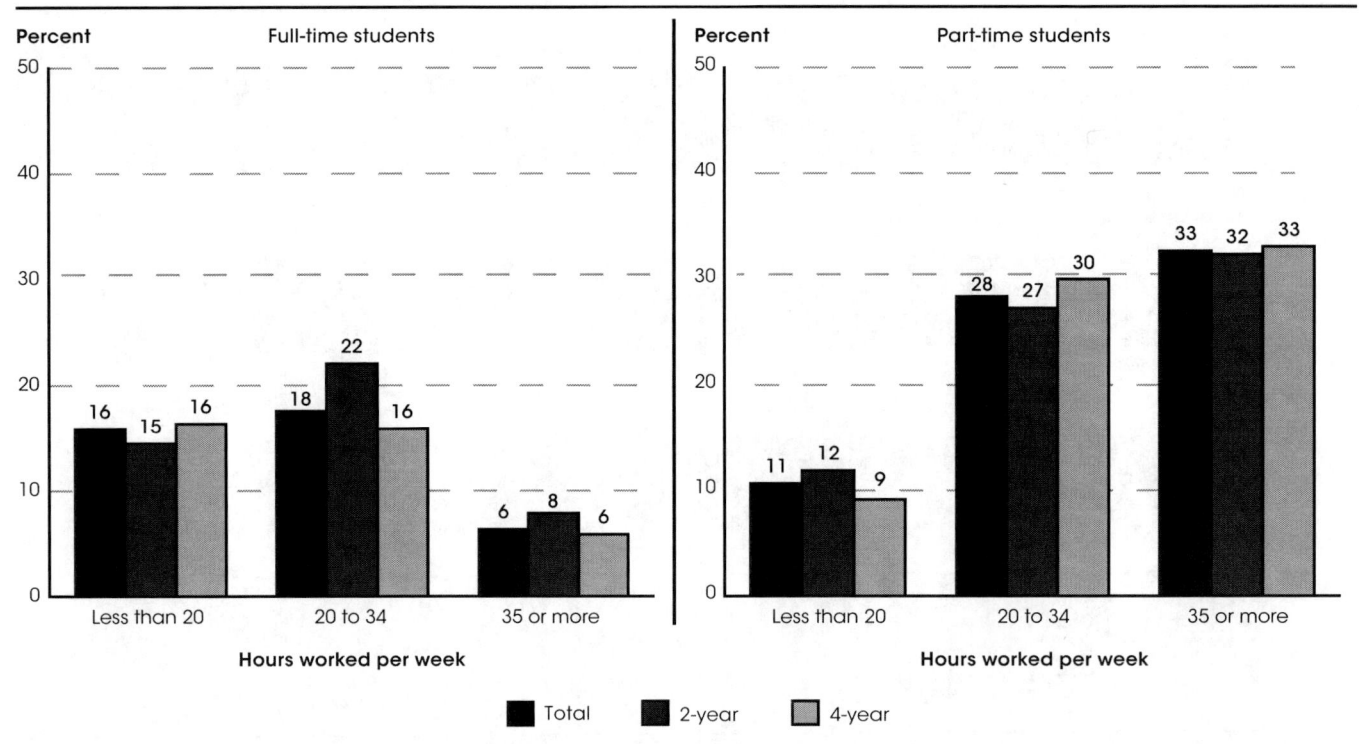

Full-time students

Hours worked per week	Total	2-year	4-year
Less than 20	16	15	16
20 to 34	18	22	16
35 or more	6	8	6

Part-time students

Hours worked per week	Total	2-year	4-year
Less than 20	11	12	9
20 to 34	28	27	30
35 or more	33	32	33

NOTE: Students were classified as full time if they were taking at least 12 hours of classes (or at least 9 hours of graduate classes) during an average school week and as part time if they were taking fewer hours.
SOURCE: U.S. Department of Commerce, Census Bureau, Current Population Survey (CPS), October, 2011. See *Digest of Education Statistics 2012*, table 443.

According to the Current Population Survey (CPS), in 2011 about 41 percent of full-time undergraduate students and 74 percent of part-time undergraduate students ages 16 to 24 years old worked in addition to being enrolled in a postsecondary institution. Of full-time undergraduate students, 16 percent of college students who were employed reported working less than 20 hours per week, 18 percent reported working 20 to 34 hours per week, and 6 percent reported working 35 hours or more per week. By comparison, 11 percent of part-time undergraduate students who were employed reported working less than 20 hours per week while they attended school, another 28 percent reported working 20 to 34 hours per week, and 33 percent reported working 35 or more hours per week.

For more information, see the Reader's Guide and the Guide to Sources.

Chapter: 4/Postsecondary Education
Section: Characteristics of Postsecondary Students

Figure 6. Percentage of college students 16 to 24 years old who were employed, by attendance status and hours worked per week: October 2000 through 2011

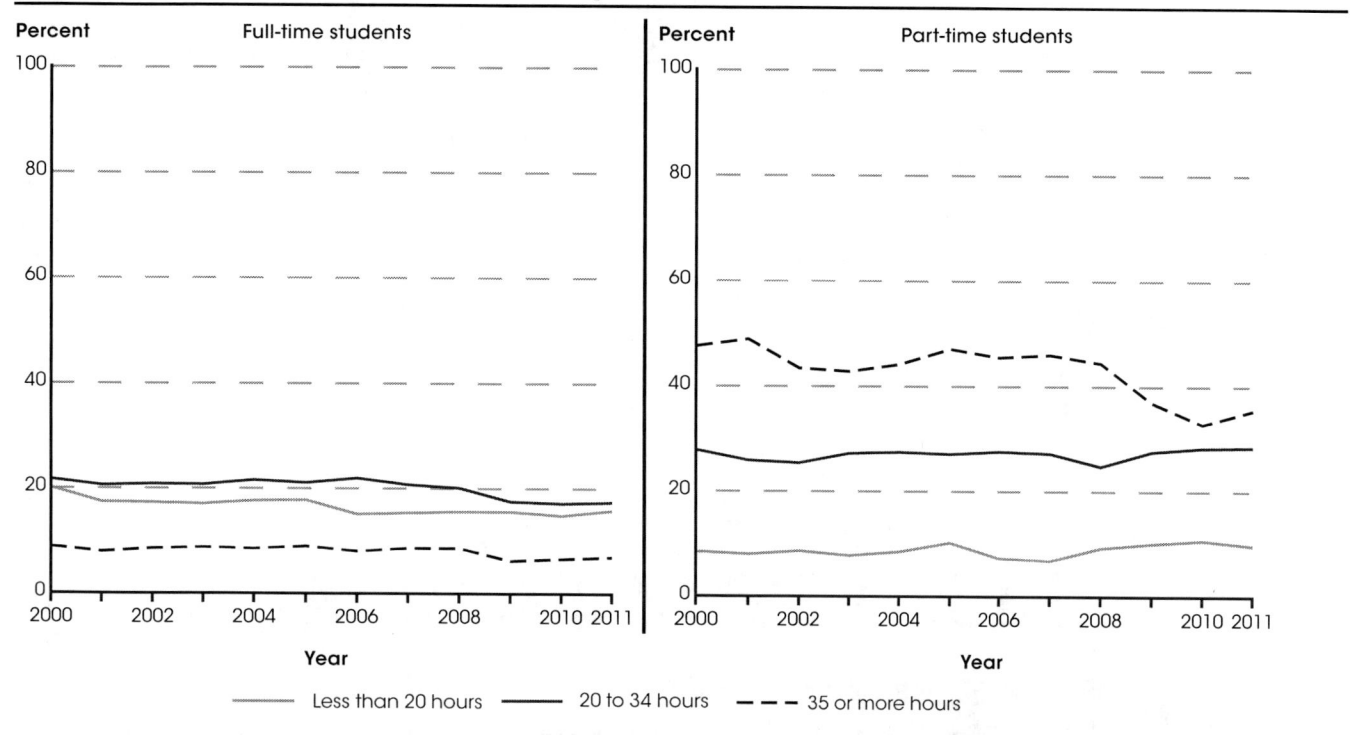

——— Less than 20 hours   ——— 20 to 34 hours   – – – 35 or more hours

NOTE: Students were classified as full time if they were taking at least 12 hours of classes (or at least 9 hours of graduate classes) during an average school week and as part time if they were taking fewer hours.
SOURCE: U.S. Department of Commerce, Census Bureau, Current Population Survey (CPS), October 2000 through October 2011. See *Digest of Education Statistics 2012*, table 442.

In general, smaller percentages of all postsecondary students ages 16 to 24 years old were working in 2011 than had been working a decade prior. For full-time students, the decline in the percentage of all students who worked was from 52 percent in 2000 to 41 percent in 2011. For part-time students, the decline was from 85 percent to 75 percent. Further, for full-time students who were employed, the percentage of all students who worked less than 20 hours per week decreased from 20 percent in 2000 to 16 percent in 2011. Those full-time students who were working 20 to 34 hours per week decreased from 22 percent to 17 percent, and those who were working 35 or more hours per week decreased from 9 percent to 7 percent over the same period.

Meanwhile, nearly half (47 percent) of all part-time students worked 35 hours or more per week in 2000, while in 2011 just 35 percent did. The percentages of part-time students who worked less than 20 hours per week or between 20 and 34 hours per week did not change measurably between 2000 and 2011.

Reference tables: *Digest of Education Statistics 2012*, tables 226, 228, 268, 442, 443

Glossary: Degree-granting institutions, Full-time enrollment, Part-time enrollment, Postbaccalaureate enrollment, Private for-profit institution, Private nonprofit institution, Public school or institution, Undergraduate students

For more information, see the Reader's Guide and the Guide to Sources.

Postsecondary Education

Chapter: 4/Postsecondary Education
Section: Programs and Courses

Indicator 33
Undergraduate Fields of Study

From academic year 2000–01 to 2010–11, the number of associate's degrees awarded increased by 63 percent to 0.9 million, and the number of bachelor's degrees awarded increased by 38 percent to 1.7 million.

About two-thirds of the 942,000 associate's degrees awarded by degree-granting institutions in academic year 2010–11 were in three broad fields of study: liberal arts and sciences, general studies, and humanities (33 percent); health professions and related programs (21 percent); and business, management, marketing, and support services (13 percent). These are the same three fields in which the largest numbers of associate's degrees were awarded in 2000–01.

Figure 1. Number of associate's degrees awarded by degree-granting institutions in selected fields of study: Academic years 2000–01 and 2010–11

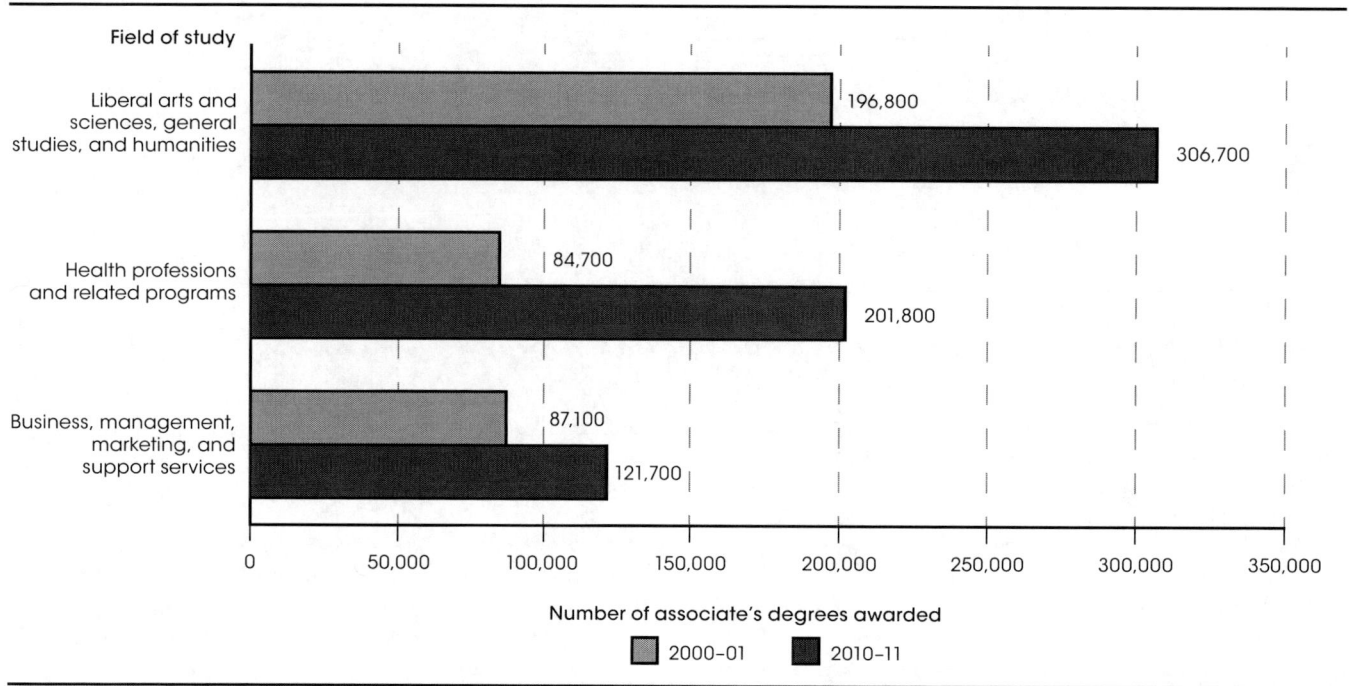

Field of study	2000–01	2010–11
Liberal arts and sciences, general studies, and humanities	196,800	306,700
Health professions and related programs	84,700	201,800
Business, management, marketing, and support services	87,100	121,700

NOTE: These three fields were selected because they were the top fields in which associate's degrees were awarded in 2010–11. Includes only institutions that participated in Title IV federal financial aid programs. The new Classification of Instructional Programs was initiated in 2009–10. The estimates for 2000–01 have been reclassified when necessary to make them conform to the new taxonomy.
SOURCE: U.S. Department of Education, National Center for Education Statistics, Integrated Postsecondary Education Data System (IPEDS), Fall 2001 and Fall 2011, Completions component. See *Digest of Education Statistics 2012*, table 312.

Overall, the number of associate's degrees awarded from academic year 2000–01 to 2010–11 increased by 363,000 degrees, or 63 percent. Of the 20 major fields of study in which the most associate's degrees were awarded in 2010–11, the field of homeland security, law enforcement, and firefighting had the largest percentage increase (174 percent, from 16,400 to 44,900 degrees). Additionally, the number of associate's degrees awarded more than doubled in the following fields: psychology (it increased 149 percent), social sciences and history (it increased 149 percent), health professions and related programs (138 percent), multi/interdisciplinary studies (127 percent), public administration and social service professions (124 percent), physical sciences and science technologies (116 percent), education (115 percent), and construction trades (101 percent). In contrast, the number of degrees conferred declined in two fields from 2000–01 to 2010–11: Some 6,800 fewer associate's degrees were awarded in engineering technologies and engineering-related fields (a decrease of 16 percent), and 220 fewer degrees were awarded in agriculture and natural resources (a decrease of 3 percent).

For more information, see the Reader's Guide and the Guide to Sources.

Chapter: 4/Postsecondary Education
Section: Programs and Courses

Of the 1.7 million bachelor's degrees awarded in academic year 2010–11, almost one-third were concentrated in two fields: business (21 percent) and social sciences and history (10 percent). Five other fields each accounted for 5 percent or more of all bachelor's degrees awarded. These were health professions and related programs, education, psychology, visual and performing arts, and biological and biomedical sciences. These are the same seven fields in which the largest numbers of bachelor's degrees were awarded in 2000–01.

Overall, the number of bachelor's degrees awarded increased by 472,000 degrees from academic year 2000–01 to 2010–11, reflecting an increase of 38 percent.

During this period, the two largest fields of study, business and social sciences, had increases of 39 percent and 38 percent, respectively. Of the 20 major fields of study in which the most bachelor's degrees were awarded in 2010–11, the largest percentage increase in the number of bachelor's degrees awarded occurred in the field of parks, recreation, leisure, and fitness studies (from 17,900 to 35,900 degrees, an increase of more than 100 percent). In contrast, the number of degrees conferred declined in two fields from 2000–01 to 2010–11: Some 1,500 fewer bachelor's degrees were awarded in education (a decrease of 1 percent), and 1,100 fewer degrees were awarded in computer and information sciences (a decrease of 2 percent).

Figure 2. Number of bachelor's degrees awarded by degree-granting institutions in selected fields of study: Academic years 2000-01 and 2010-11

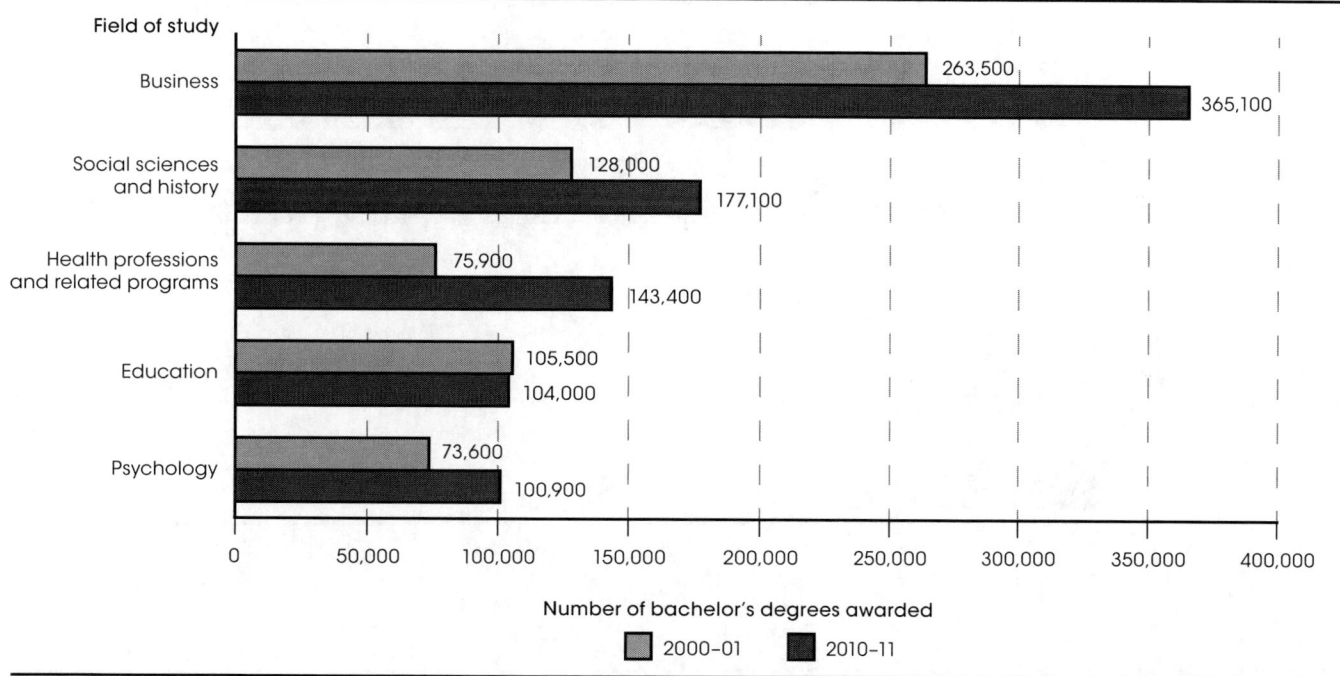

Field of study	2000-01	2010-11
Business	263,500	365,100
Social sciences and history	128,000	177,100
Health professions and related programs	75,900	143,400
Education	105,500	104,000
Psychology	73,600	100,900

NOTE: These five fields were selected because they were the top fields in which bachelor's degrees were awarded in 2010-11. Includes only institutions that participated in Title IV federal financial aid programs. The new Classification of Instructional Programs was initiated in 2009-10. The estimates for 2000-01 have been reclassified when necessary to make them conform to the new taxonomy. "Business" includes Business, management, marketing, and related support services and Personal and culinary services.
SOURCE: U.S. Department of Education, National Center for Education Statistics, Integrated Postsecondary Education Data System (IPEDS), Fall 2001 and Fall 2011, Completions component. See *Digest of Education Statistics 2012*, table 313.

Reference tables: *Digest of Education Statistics 2012*, tables 312, 313

Glossary: Associate's degree, Bachelor's degree, Classification of Instructional Programs (CIP)

For more information, see the Reader's Guide and the Guide to Sources.

Indicator 34
Graduate Fields of Study

Chapter: 4/Postsecondary Education
Section: Programs and Courses

Between academic years 2000–01 and 2010–11, the number of master's degrees awarded increased by 54 percent to 731,000, and the number of doctor's degrees awarded increased by 37 percent to 164,000.

Of the 731,000 master's degrees awarded by degree-granting institutions in academic year 2010–11, over 50 percent were concentrated in two fields: business (26 percent) and education (25 percent). Three other fields each accounted for 5 percent or more of all master's degrees awarded. These were health professions and related programs, engineering, and public administration and social services. These are the same five fields in which the largest numbers of master's degrees were awarded in 2000–01.

Figure 1.   Number of master's degrees awarded by degree-granting institutions in selected fields of study: Academic years 2000–01 and 2010–11

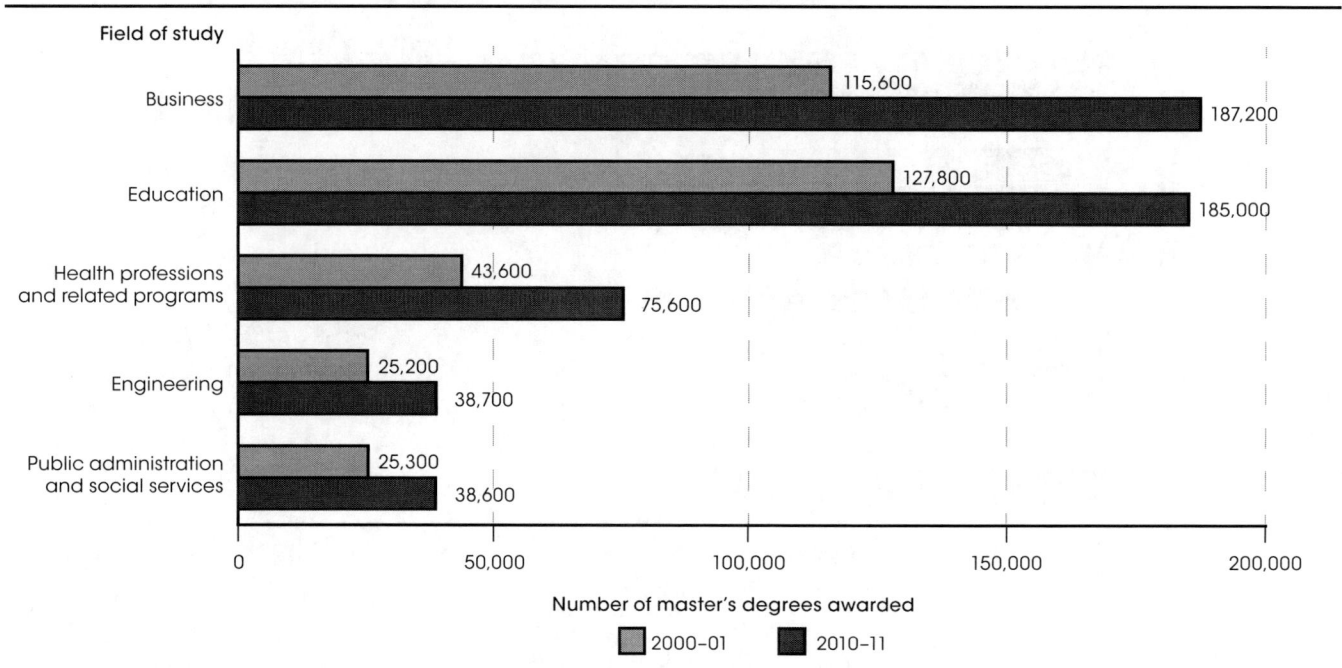

Field of study	2000–01	2010–11
Business	115,600	187,200
Education	127,800	185,000
Health professions and related programs	43,600	75,600
Engineering	25,200	38,700
Public administration and social services	25,300	38,600

NOTE: These five fields were selected because they were the top fields in which master's degrees were awarded in 2010–11. Includes only institutions that participated in Title IV federal financial aid programs. The new Classification of Instructional Programs was initiated in 2009–10. The estimates for 2000–01 have been reclassified when necessary to make them conform to the new taxonomy.
SOURCE: U.S. Department of Education, National Center for Education Statistics, Integrated Postsecondary Education Data System (IPEDS), Fall 2001 and Fall 2011, Completions component. See *Digest of Education Statistics 2012*, table 314.

Overall, the number of master's degrees awarded increased by 257,000 degrees between academic years 2000–01 and 2010–11, reflecting an increase of 54 percent. During this period, the two largest fields of study, business and education, had increases of 62 percent and 45 percent, respectively. In each of the 20 major fields of study in which the most master's degrees were awarded in 2010–11, the number of master's degrees awarded was higher in 2010–11 than in 2000–01. Master's degrees awarded in the field of homeland security, law enforcement, and firefighting exhibited the largest percentage increase of all fields (from 2,500 to 7,400 degrees, a 196 percent increase). The next largest percentage increase was in the field of parks, recreation, leisure, and fitness studies (from 2,400 to 6,600 degrees, a 178 percent increase). The field of computer and information sciences saw the smallest percentage increase (15 percent) in the number of master's degrees awarded over this period (from 16,900 to 19,400 degrees).

For more information, see the Reader's Guide and the Guide to Sources.

Chapter: 4/Postsecondary Education
Section: Programs and Courses

Almost two-thirds of the 164,000 doctor's degrees awarded in academic year 2010–11 were awarded in health professions and related programs degrees (37 percent) and legal professions and studies degrees (27 percent). Three other fields each accounted for 4 percent or more of all doctor's degrees awarded. These were education, engineering, and biological and biomedical sciences. These are the same five fields in which the largest numbers of doctor's degrees were awarded in 2000–01.

Figure 2. Number of doctor's degrees awarded by degree-granting institutions in selected fields of study: Academic years 2000–01 and 2010–11

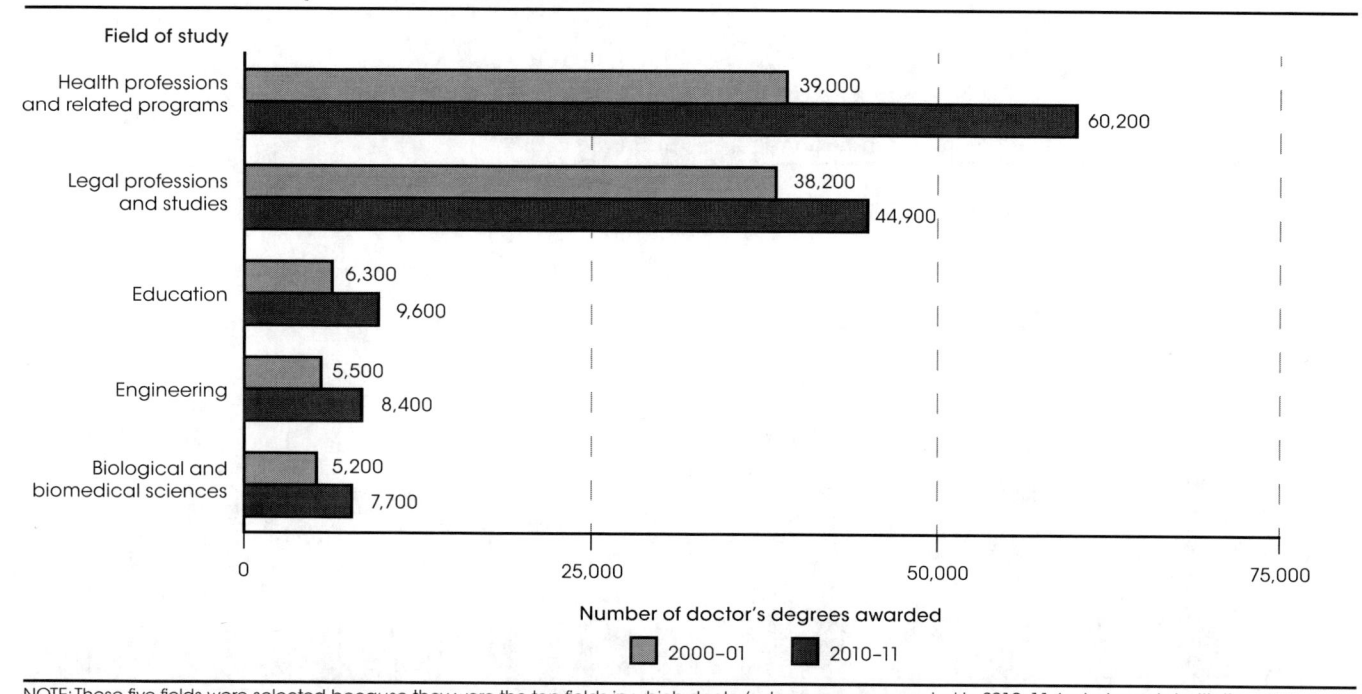

Field of study	2000–01	2010–11
Health professions and related programs	39,000	60,200
Legal professions and studies	38,200	44,900
Education	6,300	9,600
Engineering	5,500	8,400
Biological and biomedical sciences	5,200	7,700

NOTE: These five fields were selected because they were the top fields in which doctor's degrees were awarded in 2010–11. Includes only institutions that participated in Title IV federal financial aid programs. The new Classification of Instructional Programs was initiated in 2009–10. The estimates for 2000–01 have been reclassified when necessary to make them conform to the new taxonomy.
SOURCE: U.S. Department of Education, National Center for Education Statistics, Integrated Postsecondary Education Data System (IPEDS), Fall 2001 and Fall 2011, Completions component. See *Digest of Education Statistics 2012*, table 315.

Overall, the number of doctor's degrees awarded from academic year 2000–01 to 2010–11 increased by 44,200 degrees, or 37 percent. During this period, the two largest fields of study, health professions and related programs and legal professions and studies, had increases of 54 percent and 18 percent, respectively. In all of the 20 major fields of study in which the most doctor's degrees were awarded in 2010–11, the numbers of doctor's degrees awarded increased from 2000–01 to 2010–11. The field of computer and information sciences had the largest percentage increase (107 percent) in the numbers of doctor's degrees awarded (from 770 to 1,600 degrees). The field of English language and literature/letters had the smallest percentage increase (1 percent) in the number of doctor's degrees awarded (about 1,300 degrees in both years).

Reference tables: *Digest of Education Statistics 2012*, tables 314, 315

Glossary: Classification of Instructional Programs (CIP), Doctor's degree, Master's degree

For more information, see the Reader's Guide and the Guide to Sources.

Chapter: 4/Postsecondary Education
Section: Finance and Resources

Indicator 35
Price of Attending an Undergraduate Institution

The average total cost of attendance in 2011–12 for first-time, full-time students living on campus and paying in-state tuition was $21,000 at public 4-year institutions, $41,420 at private nonprofit 4-year institutions, and $30,840 at private for-profit 4-year institutions.

Figure 1. Average total cost of attending degree-granting institutions for first-time, full-time students, by level and control of institution and living arrangement: Academic year 2011–12

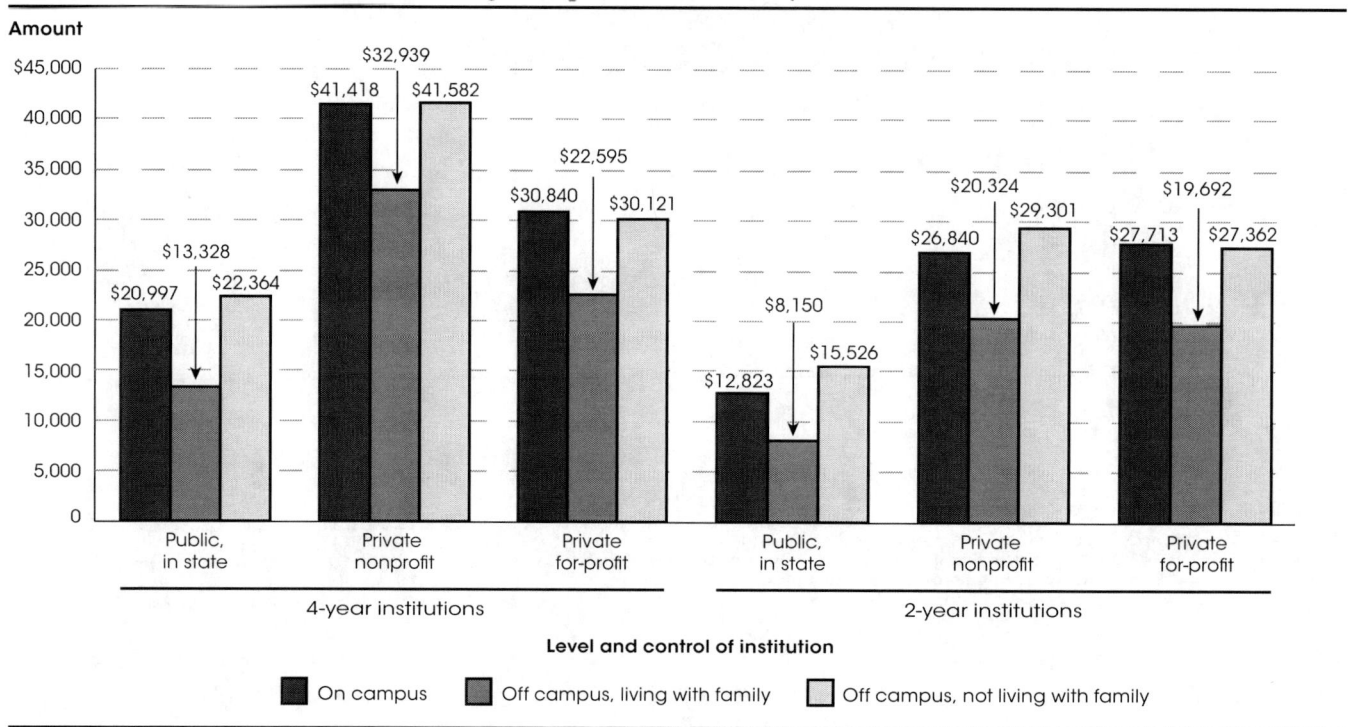

[Bar chart showing average total cost of attendance by institution type and living arrangement. Values shown:

4-year institutions:
- Public, in state: On campus $20,997; Off campus, living with family $13,328; Off campus, not living with family $22,364
- Private nonprofit: On campus $41,418; Off campus, living with family $32,939; Off campus, not living with family $41,582
- Private for-profit: On campus $30,840; Off campus, living with family $22,595; Off campus, not living with family $30,121

2-year institutions:
- Public, in state: On campus $12,823; Off campus, living with family $8,150; Off campus, not living with family $15,526
- Private nonprofit: On campus $26,840; Off campus, living with family $20,324; Off campus, not living with family $29,301
- Private for-profit: On campus $27,713; Off campus, living with family $19,692; Off campus, not living with family $27,362]

NOTE: Excludes students who have already attended another postsecondary institution or who began their studies on a part-time basis. Data illustrating the average total cost of attendance for all students are weighted by the number of students at the institution receiving Title IV aid.
SOURCE: U.S. Department of Education, National Center for Education Statistics, Integrated Postsecondary Education Data System (IPEDS), Fall 2011, Institutional Characteristics component. See *Digest of Education Statistics 2012*, table 384.

The total cost of attending a postsecondary institution is the sum of published tuition and required fees, books and supplies, and the weighted average for room, board, and other expenses. In 2011–12, the total cost of attendance differed by institution level and control and by student living arrangements. At 4-year institutions, the average total cost of attendance for first-time, full-time students living on campus and paying in-state tuition was $21,000 at public institutions, $41,420 at private nonprofit institutions, and $30,840 at private for-profit institutions. All averages are weighted by the number of students at the institution receiving Title IV aid including grant aid, work-study aid, and loan aid. At 2-year institutions, the average total cost of attendance for first-time, full-time students living on campus and paying in-state tuition was $12,820 at public institutions, $26,840 at private nonprofit institutions, and $27,710 at private for-profit institutions. Across institution levels and controls, the average total cost of attendance was lowest for students living with family. For example, the average total cost of attendance for students paying in-state tuition at public 2-year institutions and living with family was $8,150, compared with $12,820 for students living on campus and $15,530 for students living off campus but not with family.

Out of these total costs, the cost of room and board differed by institution level and control and by student living arrangements. In 2011–12, the average cost of room and board was higher for students at 4-year institutions than for students at 2-year institutions. For example, the average cost of room and board for students living on campus and paying in-state tuition at public institutions was $8,830 at 4-year institutions, compared with $5,550 at 2-year institutions; the average cost for students living off campus but not with family was $9,260 at 4-year institutions, compared with $7,470 at 2-year institutions. The average cost of room and board was also lower for students paying in-state tuition at public institutions than for students at private nonprofit and private for-profit

For more information, see the Reader's Guide and the Guide to Sources.

institutions. For example, the average cost of room and board for students living on campus and paying in-state tuition at 4-year public institutions was $8,830, compared with $9,850 at private nonprofit institutions and $9,530 at private for-profit institutions.

The cost of books and supplies also varied by institution level and control. The average cost of books and supplies ranged from $1,230 for students paying in-state tuition at public 4-year institutions to $1,420 at private for-profit 4-year institutions.

Many students and their families do not pay the full price of attendance because they receive financial aid to help cover their expenses. The primary types of financial aid are grants, which do not have to be repaid, and loans, which must be repaid. Grants, which include scholarships, may be awarded on the basis of financial need, merit, or both and may include tuition aid from employers. In 2010–11, first-time, full-time students who received grants received an average of $9,660 at 4-year institutions and $4,630 at 2-year institutions.

The net price is the estimate of the actual amount of money that students and their families need to pay in a given year to cover educational expenses. Net price is calculated here as the total cost of attendance minus grants. Net price provides an indication of what the actual financial burden is upon students and their families. In 2010–11, first-time, full-time students paid an average net price of $16,820 at 4-year institutions and $9,370 at 2-year institutions.

Figure 2. Average total price, net price, and grants and scholarship aid for first-time, full-time students paying in-state tuition and receiving aid at public 4-year institutions, by income level: Academic year 2010–11

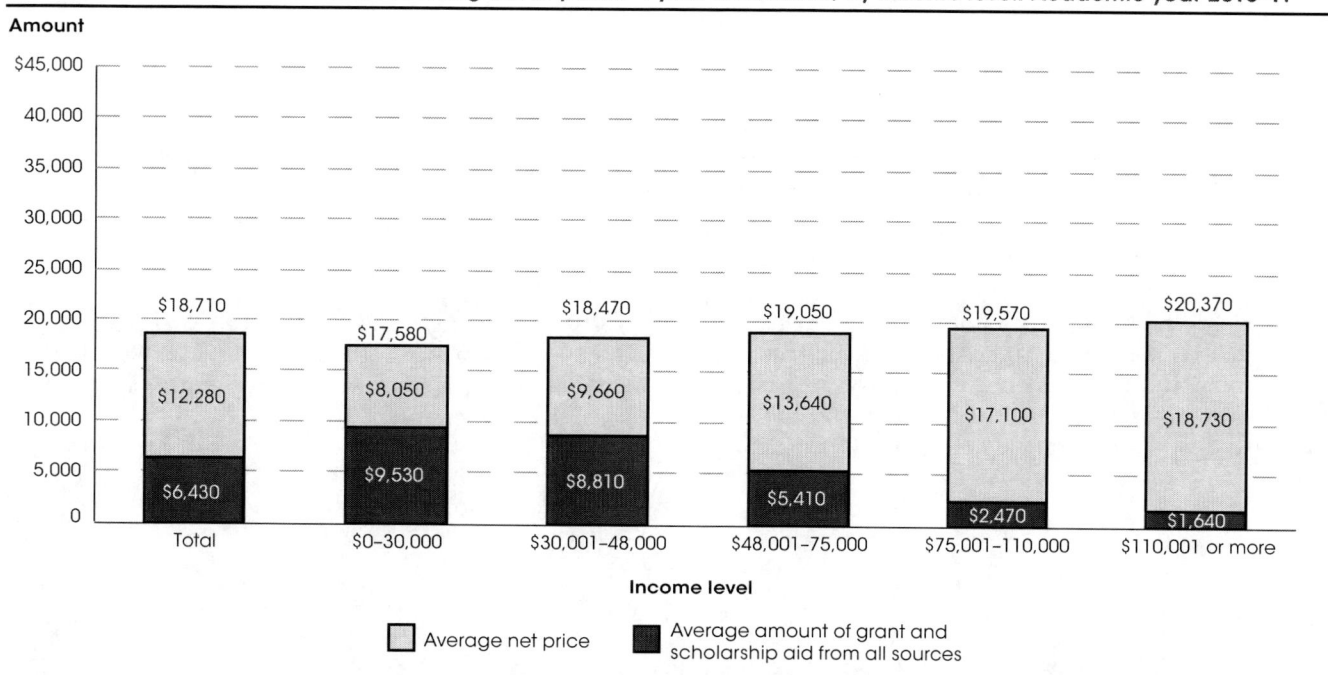

Income level	Average net price	Average grant/scholarship aid	Total
Total	$12,280	$6,430	$18,710
$0–30,000	$8,050	$9,530	$17,580
$30,001–48,000	$9,660	$8,810	$18,470
$48,001–75,000	$13,640	$5,410	$19,050
$75,001–110,000	$17,100	$2,470	$19,570
$110,001 or more	$18,730	$1,640	$20,370

NOTE: Excludes students who previously attended another postsecondary institution or who began their studies on a part-time basis. Includes only first-time, full-time students who paid the in-state or in-district tuition rate and who received Title IV aid. Excludes the 17.7 percent of students who did not receive any Title IV aid. Title IV aid includes grant aid, work-study aid, and loan aid. Data are weighted by the number of students at the institution receiving Title IV aid.
SOURCE: U.S. Department of Education, National Center for Education Statistics, Integrated Postsecondary Education Data System (IPEDS), Spring 2012, Student Financial Aid component. See *Digest of Education Statistics 2012*, table 388.

The average amount of grant aid received and net price paid differed by family income level. In general, the lower the income, the greater the total amount of grant aid received. At public 4-year institutions, the average amount of grant aid received by first-time, full-time students paying in-state tuition was highest for those with incomes of $30,000 or less ($9,530 in 2010–11) and lowest for those with incomes of $110,001 or more ($1,640). Accordingly, the lowest average net price was for those with incomes of $30,000 or less ($8,050), and the highest average net price was for those with incomes of $110,001 or more ($18,730).

For more information, see the Reader's Guide and the Guide to Sources.

Chapter: 4/Postsecondary Education
Section: Finance and Resources

Figure 3. Average total price, net price, and grants and scholarship aid for first-time, full-time students receiving aid at private for-profit 4-year institutions, by income level: Academic year 2010–11

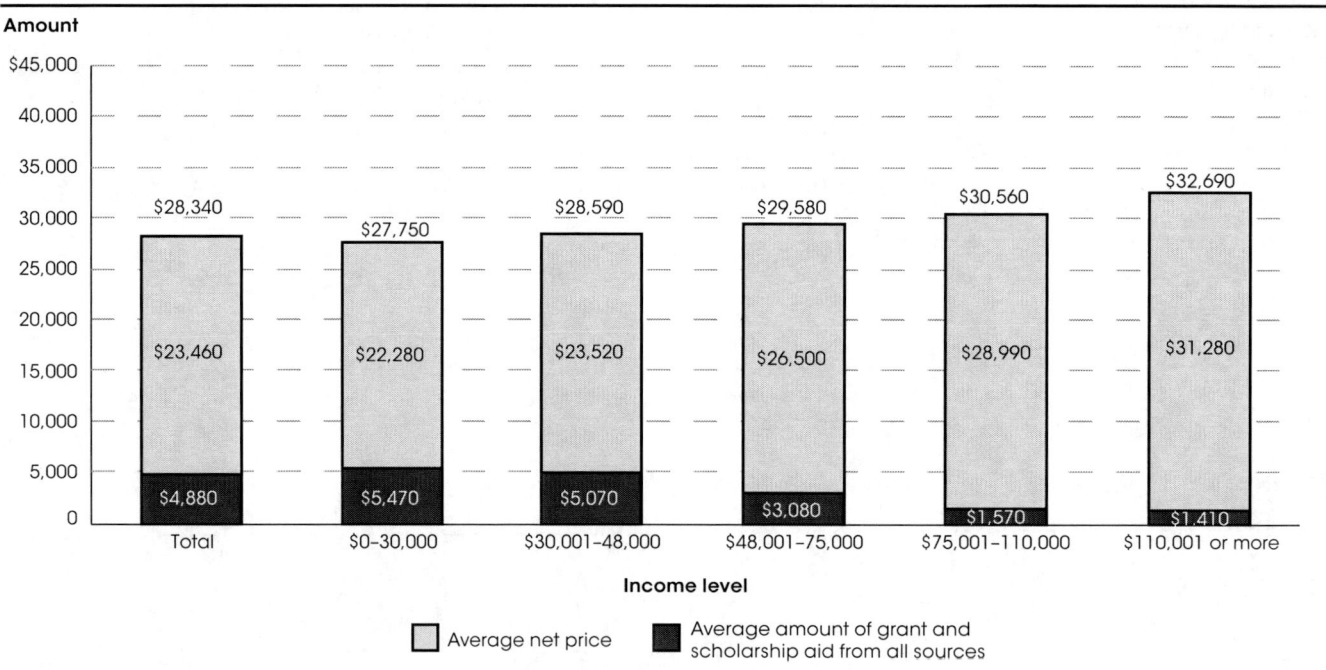

Income level	Total price	Average net price	Average grant and scholarship aid
Total	$28,340	$23,460	$4,880
$0–30,000	$27,750	$22,280	$5,470
$30,001–48,000	$28,590	$23,520	$5,070
$48,001–75,000	$29,580	$26,500	$3,080
$75,001–110,000	$30,560	$28,990	$1,570
$110,001 or more	$32,690	$31,280	$1,410

NOTE: Excludes students who previously attended another postsecondary institution or who began their studies on a part-time basis. Includes only first-time, full-time students who received Title IV aid. Excludes the 17.7 percent of students who did not receive any Title IV aid. Title IV aid includes grant aid, work-study aid, and loan aid. Data are weighted by the number of students at the institution receiving Title IV aid.
SOURCE: U.S. Department of Education, National Center for Education Statistics, Integrated Postsecondary Education Data System (IPEDS), Spring 2012, Student Financial Aid component. See *Digest of Education Statistics 2012*, table 388.

At private for-profit 4-year institutions, the same pattern was observed. The average amount of grant aid received by first-time, full-time students was highest for those with family incomes of $30,000 or less ($5,470 in 2010–11) and lowest for those with incomes of $110,001 or more ($1,410). Accordingly, the lowest average net price was for those with incomes of $30,000 or less ($22,280), and the highest average net price was for those with incomes of $110,001 or more ($31,280).

For more information, see the Reader's Guide and the Guide to Sources.

Chapter: 4/Postsecondary Education
Section: Finance and Resources

Figure 4. Average total price, net price, and grants and scholarship aid for first-time, full-time students receiving aid at private nonprofit 4-year institutions, by income level: Academic year 2010–11

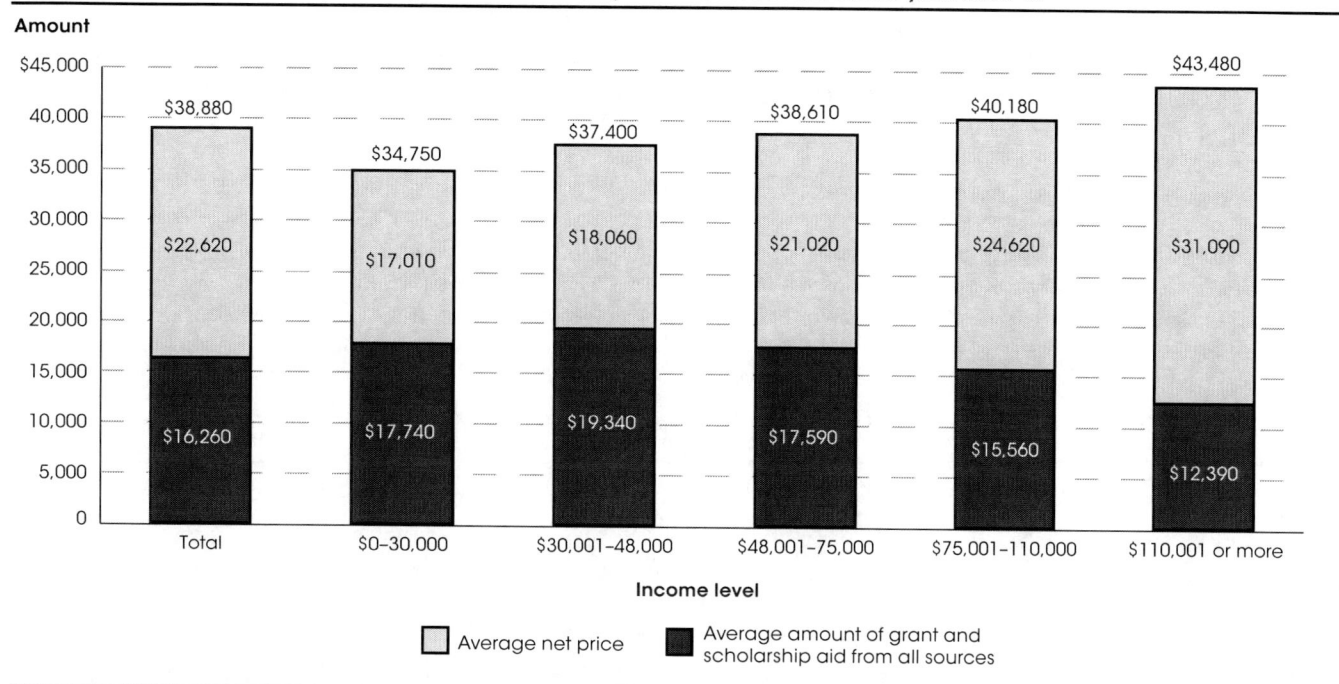

Income level	Average net price	Average amount of grant and scholarship aid from all sources	Total
Total	$22,620	$16,260	$38,880
$0–30,000	$17,010	$17,740	$34,750
$30,001–48,000	$18,060	$19,340	$37,400
$48,001–75,000	$21,020	$17,590	$38,610
$75,001–110,000	$24,620	$15,560	$40,180
$110,001 or more	$31,090	$12,390	$43,480

NOTE: Excludes students who previously attended another postsecondary institution or who began their studies on a part-time basis. Includes only first-time, full-time students who received Title IV aid. Excludes the 17.7 percent of students who did not receive any Title IV aid. Title IV aid includes grant aid, work-study aid, and loan aid. Data are weighted by the number of students at the institution receiving Title IV aid.
SOURCE: U.S. Department of Education, National Center for Education Statistics, Integrated Postsecondary Education Data System (IPEDS), Spring 2012, Student Financial Aid component. See *Digest of Education Statistics 2012*, table 388.

The pattern of average net price increasing with family income was also observed for private nonprofit 4-year institutions. However, the average amount of grant aid received was highest for those with incomes between $30,001 and $48,000 ($19,340 in 2010–11), followed by those with incomes of $30,000 or less ($17,740), those with incomes between $48,001 and $75,000 ($17,590), those with incomes between $75,001 and $110,000 ($15,560), and those with incomes of $110,001 or more ($12,390).

The average amount of grant aid received and average net price of attendance also varied by institution control. Across family income levels, the average amount of grant aid was generally highest for students at private nonprofit institutions and lowest for students at private for-profit institutions; the average net price was highest for students at private for-profit institutions and lowest for students paying in-state tuition at public institutions. For example, the average amount of grant aid received by students with family incomes between $30,001 and $48,000 at private for-profit 4-year institutions was $5,070, compared with $8,810 for students paying in-state tuition at public 4-year institutions; the average net price of attendance was $23,520 for students at this income level attending private for-profit institutions, compared with $9,660 for students paying in-state tuition at public institutions.

Reference tables: *Digest of Education Statistics 2012*, tables 384, 388

Glossary: Financial aid, Private institution, Public school or institution, Tuition and fees

For more information, see the Reader's Guide and the Guide to Sources.

Chapter: 4/Postsecondary Education
Section: Finance and Resources

Indicator 36

Grants and Loan Aid to Undergraduate Students

From academic years 2006–07 to 2010–11, the percentage of first-time, full-time undergraduate students at 4-year degree-granting institutions receiving any financial aid increased from 75 to 85 percent.

Grants and loans are the major forms of federal financial aid for degree-seeking undergraduate students. The largest federal grant program available to undergraduate students is the Pell Grant program. In order to qualify for a Pell Grant, a student must demonstrate financial need. Federal loans, on the other hand, are available to all students. In addition to federal financial aid, there are also grants from state and local governments, institutions, and private sources, as well as private loans.

Figure 1. Percentage of first-time, full-time undergraduate students in degree-granting institutions receiving any financial aid, by level and control of institution: Academic years 2006–07 through 2010–11

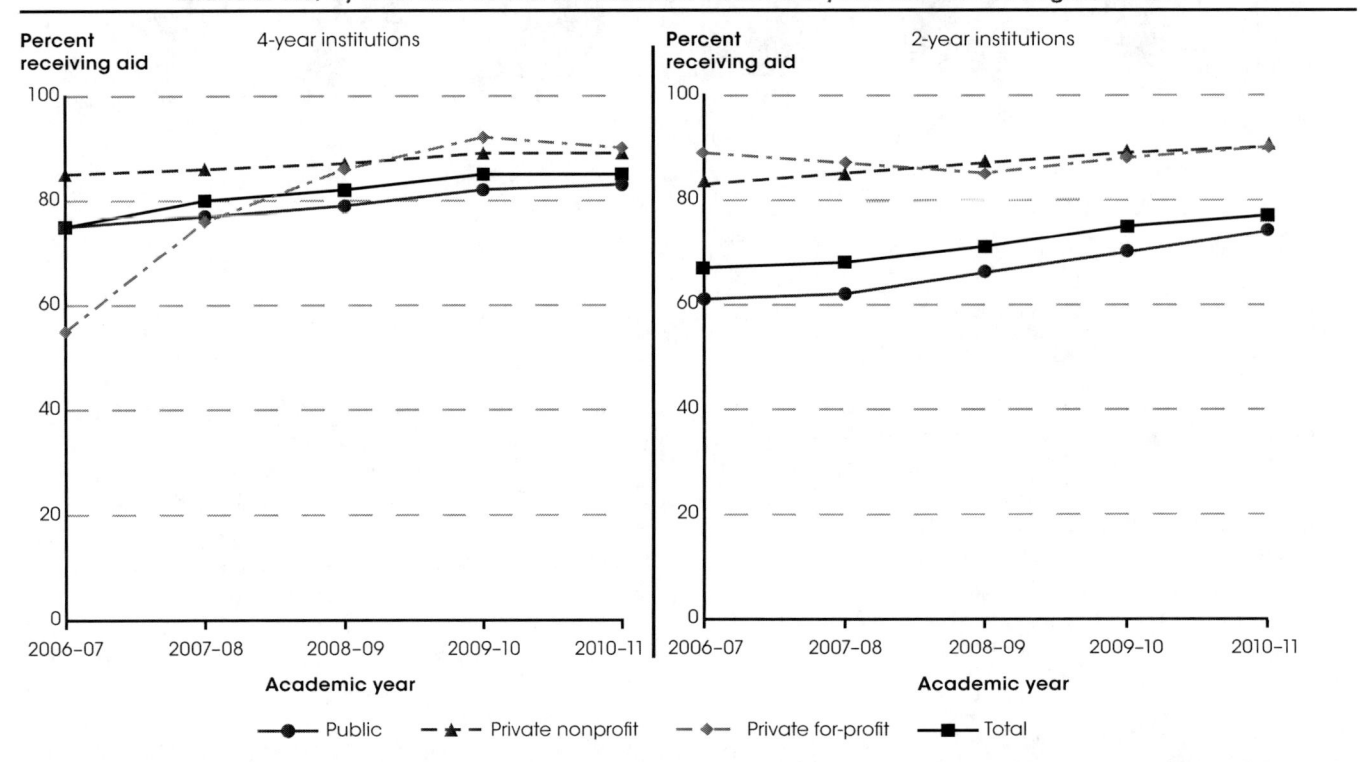

NOTE: Degree-granting institutions grant associate's or higher degrees and participate in Title IV federal financial aid programs. Any student financial aid includes any Federal Work-Study, loans to students, or grant or scholarship aid from the federal government, state/local government, the institution, or other sources known to the institution. Includes only loans made directly to students. Does not include Parent Loans for Undergraduate Students (PLUS) and other loans made directly to parents.
SOURCE: U.S. Department of Education, National Center for Education Statistics, Integrated Postsecondary Education Data System (IPEDS), Spring 2008 through Spring 2012, Student Financial Aid component. See *Digest of Education Statistics 2012*, table 387.

From academic years 2006–07 to 2010–11, the percentage of first-time, full-time undergraduate students at 4-year degree-granting institutions receiving any financial aid increased from 75 to 85 percent. During this time, the largest percentage increase in first-time, full-time students receiving aid was at private for-profit institutions, from 55 to 90 percent. The percentage of students receiving aid at 4-year public institutions increased from 75 to 83 percent, while the percentage of students at private nonprofit institutions had the smallest increase, from 85 to 89 percent. For 2-year institutions, the percentage of first-time, full-time undergraduate students receiving aid increased from 67 percent in 2006–07 to 77 percent in 2010–11. For 2-year institutions, the largest percentage increase in first-time, full-time students receiving aid was at public institutions, from 61 to 74 percent. The percentage of students receiving aid at private nonprofit institutions increased from 83 to 90 percent. For students attending private for-profit institutions, the percentage receiving any financial aid was higher in 2010–11 than in 2006–07 (90 vs. 89 percent).

For more information, see the Reader's Guide and the Guide to Sources.

Chapter: 4/Postsecondary Education
Section: Finance and Resources

Figure 2. Percentage of first-time, full-time undergraduate students receiving financial aid at 4-year degree-granting institutions, by type of aid and institutional control: Academic year 2010–11

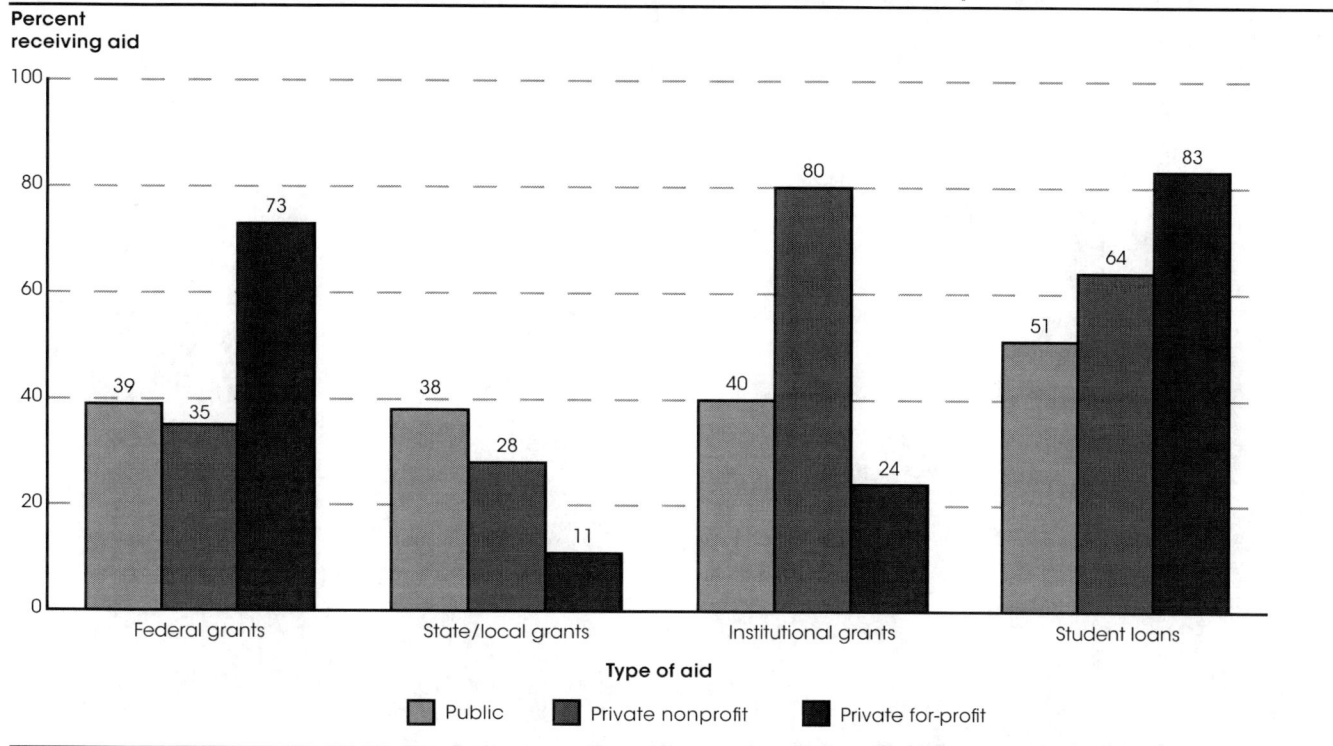

Type of aid	Public	Private nonprofit	Private for-profit
Federal grants	39	35	73
State/local grants	38	28	11
Institutional grants	40	80	24
Student loans	51	64	83

NOTE: Degree-granting institutions grant associate's or higher degrees and participate in Title IV federal financial aid programs. Any student financial aid includes any Federal Work-Study, loans to students, or grant or scholarship aid from the federal government, state/local government, the institution, or other sources known to the institution. Includes only loans made directly to students. Does not include Parent Loans for Undergraduate Students (PLUS) and other loans made directly to parents.
SOURCE: U.S. Department of Education, National Center for Education Statistics, Integrated Postsecondary Education Data System (IPEDS), Spring 2012, Student Financial Aid component. See *Digest of Education Statistics 2012*, table 387.

In 2010–11, the percentage of first-time, full-time undergraduate students receiving federal grants at 4-year institutions was highest at private for-profit institutions (73 percent), followed by 39 percent of students at public institutions and 35 percent at private nonprofit institutions. In the same year, the percentage of students at 4-year institutions receiving state or local grants was highest at public institutions (38 percent), followed by 28 percent at private nonprofit institutions and 11 percent at private for-profit institutions. The percentage of students receiving institutional grants was highest at 4-year private nonprofit institutions (80 percent), followed by 40 percent at public institutions and 24 percent at private for-profit institutions. The percentage of first-time, full-time undergraduate students at 4-year institutions receiving student loan aid was highest at private for-profit institutions (83 percent). In comparison, 64 percent of students at 4-year private nonprofit institutions and 51 percent of students at public institutions received student loan aid.

For more information, see the Reader's Guide and the Guide to Sources.

Chapter: 4/Postsecondary Education
Section: Finance and Resources

Figure 3. Percentage of first-time, full-time undergraduate students receiving financial aid at 2-year degree-granting institutions, by type of aid and institutional control: Academic year 2010–11

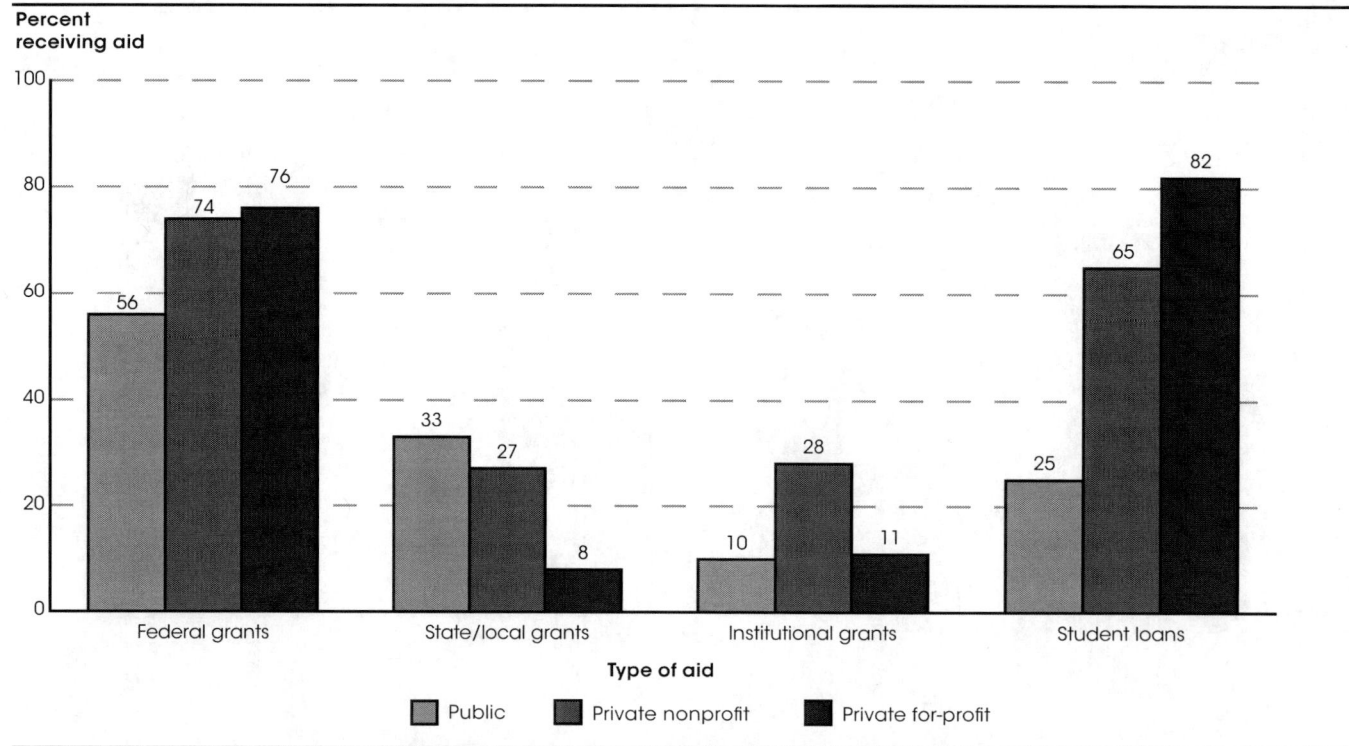

[Bar chart showing percent receiving aid by type of aid and institutional control:

Federal grants: Public 56, Private nonprofit 74, Private for-profit 76
State/local grants: Public 33, Private nonprofit 27, Private for-profit 8
Institutional grants: Public 10, Private nonprofit 28, Private for-profit 11
Student loans: Public 25, Private nonprofit 65, Private for-profit 82]

NOTE: Degree-granting institutions grant associate's or higher degrees and participate in Title IV federal financial aid programs. Any student financial aid includes any Federal Work-Study, loans to students, or grant or scholarship aid from the federal government, state/local government, the institution, or other sources known to the institution. Includes only loans made directly to students. Does not include Parent Loans for Undergraduate Students (PLUS) and other loans made directly to parents.
SOURCE: U.S. Department of Education, National Center for Education Statistics, Integrated Postsecondary Education Data System (IPEDS), Spring 2012, Student Financial Aid component. See *Digest of Education Statistics 2012*, table 387.

For 2-year institutions in 2010–11, the percentage of first-time, full-time undergraduate students receiving federal grants was highest at private for-profit institutions (76 percent), compared with 74 percent at private non-profit institutions and 56 percent of students at public institutions. In the same year, 33 percent of students at 2-year public institutions received state or local grants, compared with 27 percent at private nonprofit institutions and 8 percent at private for-profit institutions. About 28 percent of first-time, full-time undergraduate students at 2-year private nonprofit institutions received institutional grants, compared with 11 percent at private for-profit institutions and 10 percent at public institutions. The percentage of first-time, full-time undergraduate students at 2-year institutions receiving student loan aid was highest at private for-profit institutions (82 percent), compared with 65 percent of students at private nonprofit institutions and 25 percent of students at public institutions.

For more information, see the Reader's Guide and the Guide to Sources.

Chapter: 4/Postsecondary Education
Section: Finance and Resources

Figure 4. Average amount of student aid awarded to first-time, full-time undergraduate students receiving aid at 4-year degree-granting institutions, by institutional control and type of financial aid: Academic year 2010–11

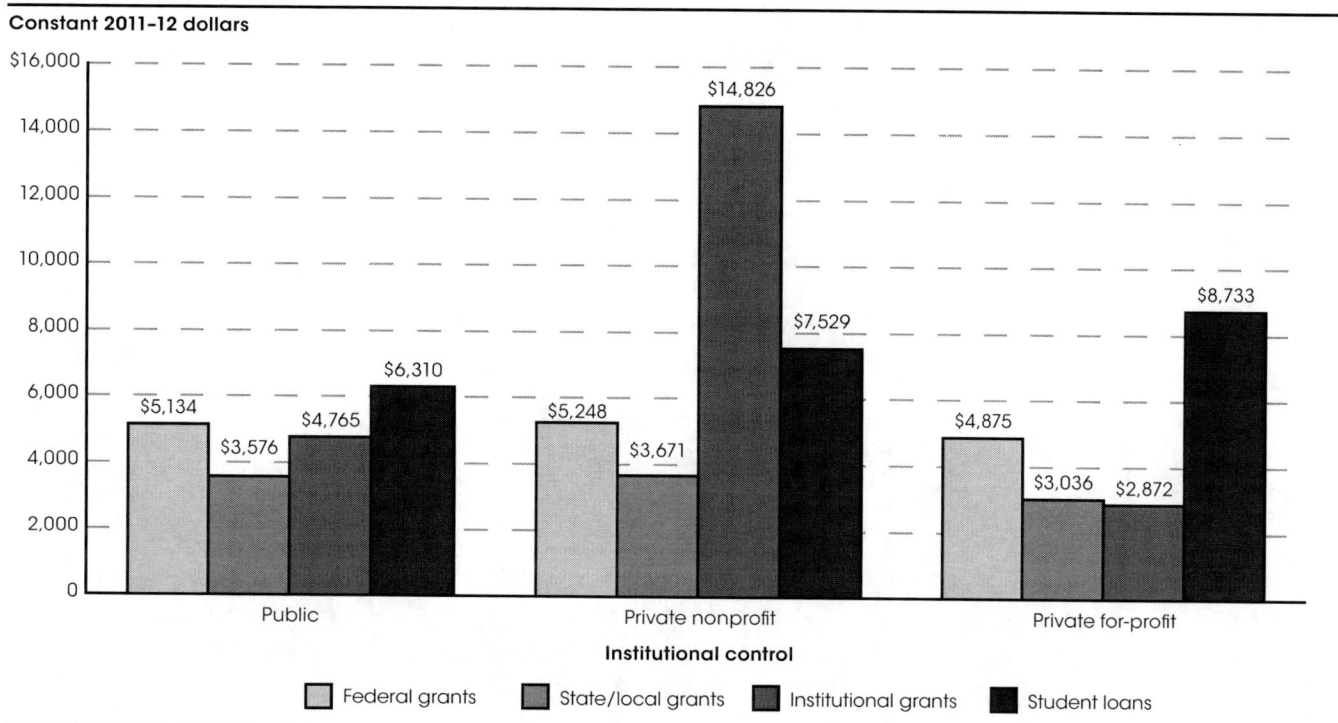

Constant 2011–12 dollars

Institutional control	Federal grants	State/local grants	Institutional grants	Student loans
Public	$5,134	$3,576	$4,765	$6,310
Private nonprofit	$5,248	$3,671	$14,826	$7,529
Private for-profit	$4,875	$3,036	$2,872	$8,733

NOTE: Degree-granting institutions grant associate's or higher degrees and participate in Title IV federal financial aid programs. Grant award amounts are in constant 2011–12 dollars, based on the Consumer Price Index (CPI).
SOURCE: U.S. Department of Education, National Center for Education Statistics, Integrated Postsecondary Education Data System (IPEDS), Spring 2012, Student Financial Aid component. See *Digest of Education Statistics 2012*, table 387.

Average grant amounts are reported in constant 2011–12 dollars. The average institutional grant award for students receiving institutional grants at 4-year institutions was highest at private nonprofit institutions ($14,826), compared with the average institutional grant award for those at public institutions ($4,765) and for those at private for-profit institutions ($2,872). The average federal grant award for students receiving federal grants at 4-year institutions was higher for students attending private nonprofit institutions ($5,248) than for students attending public institutions ($5,134) and for students attending private for-profit institutions ($4,875).

For more information, see the Reader's Guide and the Guide to Sources.

Chapter: 4/Postsecondary Education
Section: Finance and Resources

Figure 5. Average amount of student aid awarded to first-time, full-time undergraduate students receiving aid at 2-year degree-granting institutions, by institutional control and type of financial aid: Academic year 2010–11

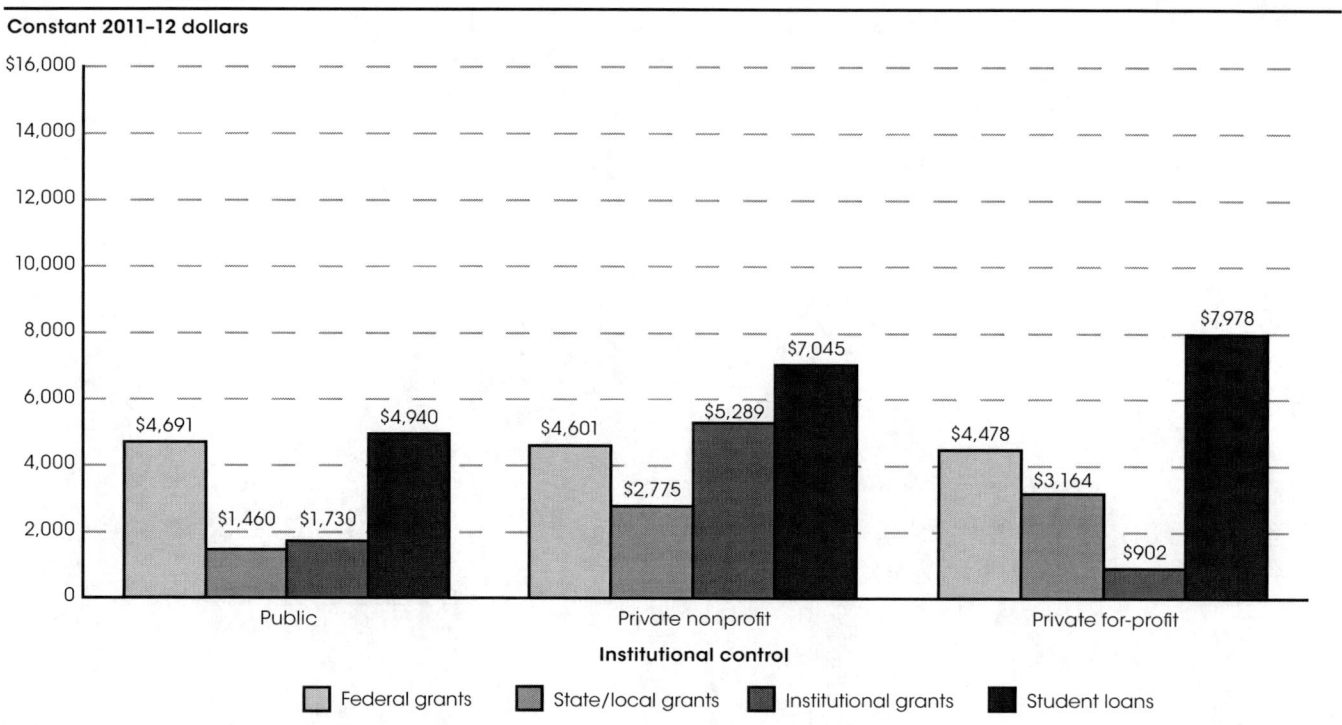

Constant 2011–12 dollars

Institutional control	Federal grants	State/local grants	Institutional grants	Student loans
Public	$4,691	$1,460	$1,730	$4,940
Private nonprofit	$4,601	$2,775	$5,289	$7,045
Private for-profit	$4,478	$3,164	$902	$7,978

NOTE: Degree-granting institutions grant associate's or higher degrees and participate in Title IV federal financial aid programs. Grant award amounts are in constant 2011–12 dollars, based on the Consumer Price Index (CPI).
SOURCE: U.S. Department of Education, National Center for Education Statistics, Integrated Postsecondary Education Data System (IPEDS), Spring 2012, Student Financial Aid component. See *Digest of Education Statistics 2012*, table 387.

Among 2-year institutions, the average institutional grant award for students receiving institutional grants was highest at private nonprofit institutions ($5,289), compared with the average institutional grant amount awarded to those at public institutions ($1,730) and to those at private for-profit institutions ($902). The average federal grant award for first-time, full-time undergraduate students receiving federal grants in 2010–11 was higher for students attending public institutions ($4,691) than for those attending private nonprofit institutions ($4,601) and for those attending private for-profit institutions ($4,478).

Reference tables: *Digest of Education Statistics 2012*, table 387

Glossary: 2-year institution, 4-year institution, Financial aid, Higher education institutions, Private institution, Public school or institution, Undergraduate students

For more information, see the Reader's Guide and the Guide to Sources.

This page intentionally left blank.

Chapter: 4/Postsecondary Education
Section: Finance and Resources

Indicator 37
Postsecondary Revenues by Source

From 2005–06 to 2010–11, revenues per full-time-equivalent (FTE) student from tuition and fees increased by 16 percent (from $5,087 to $5,884, in constant 2011–12 dollars) at public institutions, by 8 percent (from $17,400 to $18,812) at private nonprofit institutions, and were 12 percent higher ($13,990 vs. $15,716) at private for-profit institutions.

In 2010–11, total revenues, in current dollars, at postsecondary degree-granting institutions were $324 billion at public institutions, $207 billion at private nonprofit institutions, and $28 billion at private for-profit institutions. At private nonprofit institutions and private for-profit institutions, student tuition and fees constituted the largest percentage of total revenues (29 and 89 percent, respectively). At public institutions, the largest revenue sources were student tuition and fees (19 percent) and state appropriations (19 percent). It is important to note that revenue data are not comparable across institutional control categories because Pell grants are included in the federal grant revenues at public institutions but tend to be included in tuition and fees and auxiliary enterprise revenues at private nonprofit and private for-profit institutions.

Figure 1. Percentage distribution of total revenues at postsecondary degree-granting institutions, by institution level, institution control, and source of funds: 2010–11

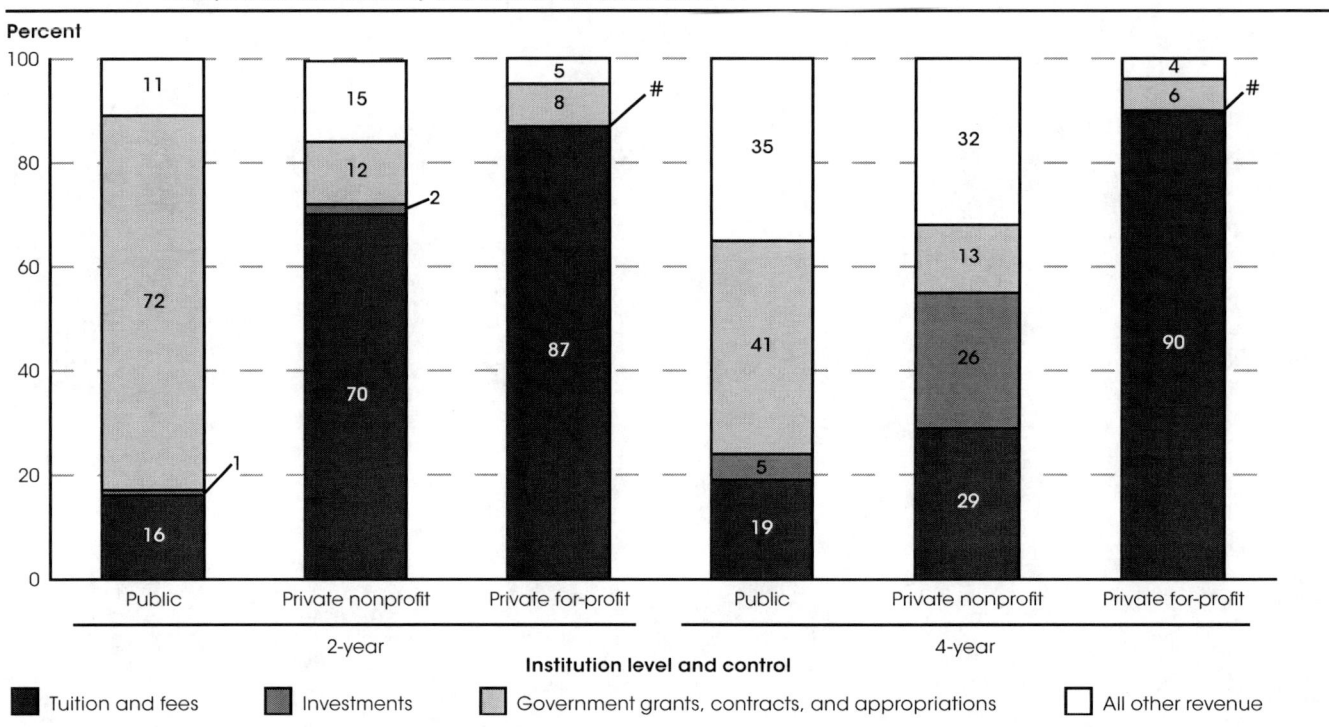

Institution level and control	Tuition and fees	Investments	Government grants, contracts, and appropriations	All other revenue
2-year Public	16	1	72	11
2-year Private nonprofit	70	2	12	15
2-year Private for-profit	87	#	8	5
4-year Public	19	5	41	35
4-year Private nonprofit	29	26	13	32
4-year Private for-profit	90	#	6	4

Rounds to zero.
NOTE: Percentages are based on current 2010–11 dollars. Government grants, contracts, and appropriations include revenue from federal, state, and local governments. All other revenue includes gifts, grants, contracts, auxiliary enterprises, and other revenue. Revenue data are not comparable across institutional control categories because Pell grants are included in the federal grant revenues at public institutions but tend to be included in tuition and auxiliary enterprise revenues at private nonprofit and private for-profit institutions. Degree-granting institutions grant associate's or higher degrees and participate in Title IV federal financial aid programs. Detail may not sum to totals because of rounding.
SOURCE: U.S. Department of Education, National Center for Education Statistics, Integrated Postsecondary Education Data System (IPEDS), Spring 2012, Finance component. See *Digest of Education Statistics 2012*, tables 401, 405, and 407.

Revenues from tuition and fees made up over three-quarters of all revenues for both 2-year and 4-year private for-profit institutions (87 and 90 percent, respectively) and 70 percent at 2-year private nonprofit institutions. Revenues from government sources (which include federal, state, and local government grants, contracts, and appropriations) constituted 41 percent of total revenues at 4-year public institutions and 72 percent at 2-year public institutions. Investment returns or investment income accounted for 26 percent of total revenues at 4-year private nonprofit institutions and 5 percent of total revenues at 4-year public institutions; this source accounted for less than 5 percent of total revenues for all other 4-year and 2-year postsecondary institutions.

For more information, see the Reader's Guide and the Guide to Sources.

Chapter: 4/Postsecondary Education
Section: Finance and Resources

Figure 2. Revenues per full-time-equivalent (FTE) student from tuition and fees for postsecondary degree-granting institutions, by institution control and level: 2005-06 and 2010-11
[In constant 2011-12 dollars]

Institution control and level

Public
- 4-year: $6,889 (2005-06); $8,302 (2010-11)
- 2-year: $2,269 (2005-06); $2,253 (2010-11)

Private nonprofit
- 4-year: $17,463 (2005-06); $18,867 (2010-11)
- 2-year: $11,642 (2005-06); $13,718 (2010-11)

Private for-profit
- 4-year: $14,200 (2005-06); $15,987 (2010-11)
- 2-year: $13,406 (2005-06); $14,854 (2010-11)

Revenues per FTE student

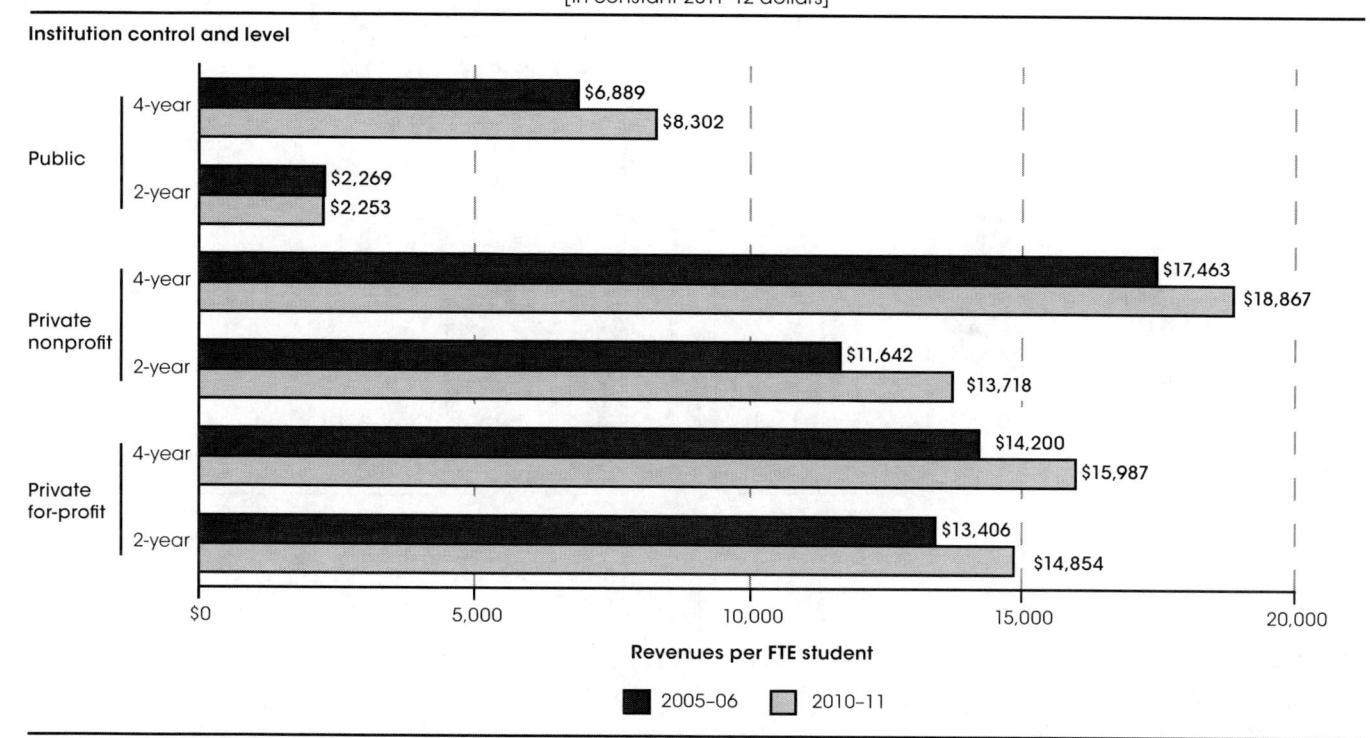

■ 2005-06   □ 2010-11

NOTE: Full-time-equivalent (FTE) student includes full-time students plus the full-time equivalent of part-time students. Revenues per FTE student are reported in constant 2011-12 dollars, based on the Consumer Price Index (CPI) adjusted to a school-year basis. Revenue data are not comparable across institutional control categories because Pell grants are included in the federal grant revenues at public institutions but tend to be included in tuition and auxiliary enterprise revenues at private nonprofit and private for-profit institutions. Degree-granting institutions grant associate's or higher degrees and participate in Title IV federal financial aid programs.
SOURCE: U.S. Department of Education, National Center for Education Statistics, Integrated Postsecondary Education Data System (IPEDS), Spring 2006 and 2011, Finance and Enrollment components. See *Digest of Education Statistics 2012*, tables 401, 405, and 407.

Between 2005–06 and 2010–11, the percentage change of revenues per full-time-equivalent (FTE) student varied by institutional control and level. Revenues per FTE student are reported in constant 2011–12 dollars, based on the Consumer Price Index (CPI). During this period, revenues from tuition and fees per FTE student increased by 16 percent at public institutions (from $5,087 to $5,884), by 8 percent at private nonprofit institutions (from $17,400 to $18,812), and were 12 percent higher at private for-profit institutions ($13,990 vs. $15,716). Between 2005–06 and 2010–11, across levels of public institutions, revenues from tuition and fees per FTE student increased by 21 percent at 4-year institutions (from $6,889 to $8,302), while at 2-year institutions revenues were 1 percent lower ($2,269 vs. $2,253). At private nonprofit institutions, revenues from tuition and fees per FTE student increased by 8 percent at 4-year institutions (from $17,463 to $18,867) and by 18 percent at 2-year institutions (from $11,642 to $13,718). At private for-profit institutions, revenues from tuition and fees per FTE student at 4-year institutions were 13 percent higher in 2010–11 than they were in 2005–06 ($15,987 vs. $14,200), while at 2-year institutions they were 11 percent higher ($14,854 vs. $13,406).

The revenues from tuition and fees at public institutions rose more rapidly than did government revenues between 2005–06 and 2010–11. As a result, the percentage distribution of revenues from tuition and fees was higher in 2010–11 (19 percent) than in 2005–06 (17 percent), and the percentage distribution of revenues from government sources was lower in 2010–11 (46 percent) than in 2005–06 (48 percent).

For more information, see the Reader's Guide and the Guide to Sources.

Chapter: 4/Postsecondary Education
Section: Finance and Resources

Figure 3. Revenue per full-time-equivalent (FTE) student from government grants, contracts, and appropriations for postsecondary degree-granting institutions, by type of revenue and institution control and level: 2005–06 and 2010–11

[In constant 2011–12 dollars]

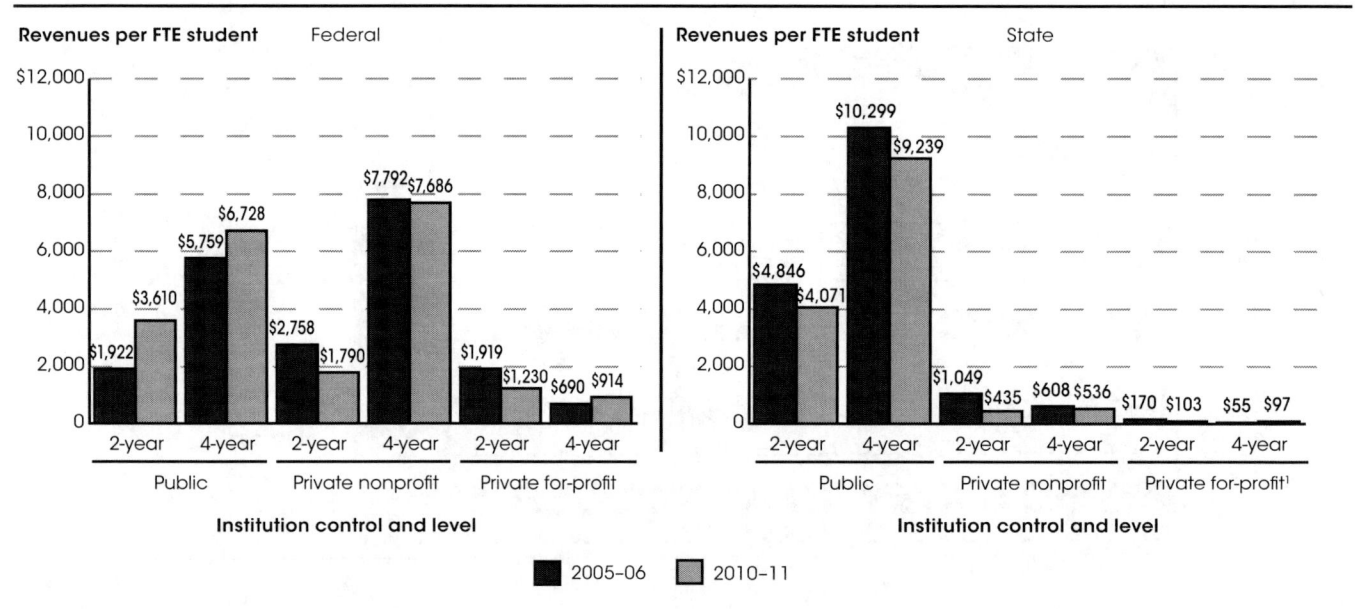

[1] The funding data for private for-profit institutions are not differentiated between state and local sources.
NOTE: Full-time-equivalent (FTE) student includes full-time students plus the full-time equivalent of part-time students. Revenues per FTE student are reported in constant 2011–12 dollars, based on the Consumer Price Index (CPI) adjusted to a school-year basis. Revenue data are not comparable across institutional control categories because Pell grants are included in the federal grant revenues at public institutions but tend to be included in tuition and auxiliary enterprise revenues at private nonprofit and private for-profit institutions. Degree-granting institutions grant associate's or higher degrees and participate in Title IV federal financial aid programs.
SOURCE: U.S. Department of Education, National Center for Education Statistics, Integrated Postsecondary Education Data System (IPEDS), Spring 2006 and 2011, Finance and Enrollment components. See *Digest of Education Statistics 2012*, tables 401, 405, and 407.

Actual revenues per full-time-equivalent (FTE) student, in constant 2011–12 dollars, from government sources at public institutions were 2 percent higher in 2010–11 than in 2005–06 ($14,638 vs. $14,379), 3 percent lower at private nonprofit institutions ($8,302 vs. $8,554), and 1 percent lower at private for-profit institutions ($1,087 vs. $1,100).

Among types of government funding, state revenues per FTE student were generally lower in 2010–11 than in 2005–06 across postsecondary institutions. Compared with 2005–06, revenues per FTE student from state sources in 2010–11 were 10 percent lower at 4-year public institutions, 12 percent lower at 4-year private nonprofit institutions, 16 percent lower at 2-year public institutions, and 59 percent lower at 2-year private nonprofit institutions.

Across postsecondary degree-granting institutions, revenues from federal sources were higher at public institutions and generally lower at private nonprofit and private for-profit institutions in 2010–11 than in 2005–06. At public institutions, there was a 29 percent increase in federal revenues per FTE student, whereas the state revenues were 12 percent lower in 2010–11 than in 2005–06. Additionally, federal funding per FTE student, in constant 2011–12 dollars, was 17 percent higher at 4-year public institutions ($6,728 vs. $5,759) and increased by 88 percent (from $1,922 to $3,610) at 2-year public institutions. Compared with 2005–06, revenues per FTE student from federal sources in 2010–11 were 1 percent lower at private nonprofit institutions ($7,738 vs. $7,624). At 4-year private nonprofit institutions, federal revenues were also 1 percent lower in 2010–11 than in 2005–06 (7,686 vs. $7,792), and at 2-year private nonprofit institutions federal revenues were 35 percent lower ($1,790 vs. $2,758). Revenues per FTE student from federal sources at private for-profit institutions were 3 percent lower in 2010–11 than in 2005–06 ($989 vs. $1,015). Additionally, federal funding was 32 percent higher at 4-year private for-profit institutions ($914 vs. $690) and 36 percent lower at 2-year private for-profit institutions ($1,230 vs. $1,919) in 2010–11 than in 2005–06.

Reference tables: *Digest of Education Statistics 2012*, tables 401, 405, 407

Glossary: Consumer Price Index (CPI), Full-time-equivalent (FTE) enrollment, Private for-profit institution, Private institution, Private nonprofit institution, Public school or institution, Revenue, Tuition and fees

For more information, see the Reader's Guide and the Guide to Sources.

This page intentionally left blank.

Chapter: 4/Postsecondary Education
Section: Finance and Resources

Indicator 38

Expenses of Postsecondary Institutions

In 2010–11, instruction expense per full-time-equivalent (FTE) student, in constant 2011–12 dollars, was the largest expense category at public ($7,413) and private nonprofit institutions ($15,568). At private for-profit institutions, instruction expense was the second largest expense category, at $3,534 per student; expense on student services, academic support, and institutional support was the largest expense category, at $9,279 per student.

In 2010–11, total expenses were $296 billion (in current dollars) at public postsecondary institutions, $153 billion at private nonprofit institutions, and $23 billion at private for-profit institutions. Some financial data may not be comparable across institutions by control categories because of differences in accounting standards. Comparisons by institutional level (i.e., between 2-year and 4-year institutions) may also be limited because of different institutional missions.

Figure 1. Percentage of total expenses at degree-granting postsecondary institutions, by purpose of expenses and control of institution: 2010–11

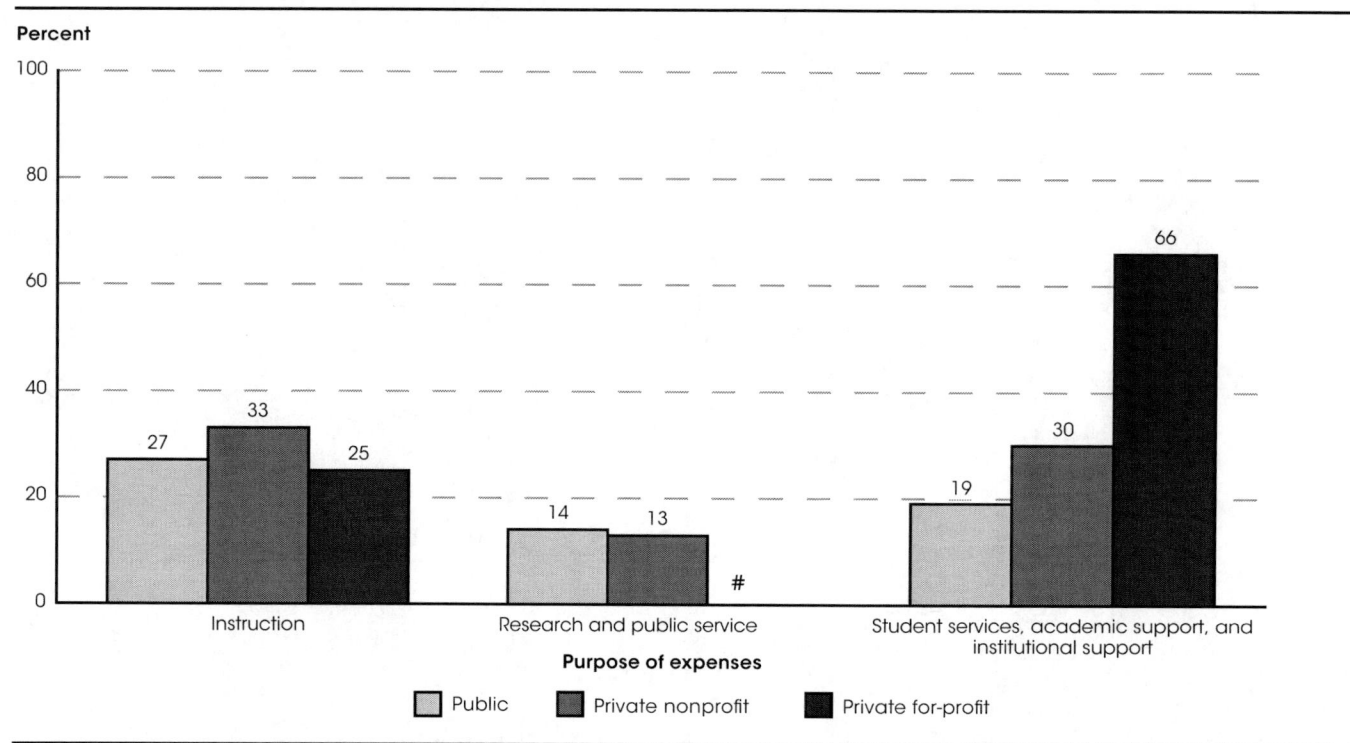

[Bar chart showing:
- Instruction: Public 27, Private nonprofit 33, Private for-profit 25
- Research and public service: Public 14, Private nonprofit 13, Private for-profit #
- Student services, academic support, and institutional support: Public 19, Private nonprofit 30, Private for-profit 66]

Rounds to zero.
SOURCE: U.S. Department of Education, National Center for Education Statistics, Integrated Postsecondary Education Data System (IPEDS), Spring 2012, Finance component. See *Digest of Education Statistics 2012*, tables 412, 414, and 416.

Instruction, including faculty salaries and benefits, is the largest expense category at public and private nonprofit postsecondary institutions and the second largest category at private for-profit institutions. In 2010–11, the percentage of total expenses spent on instruction was 27 percent at public institutions and 33 percent at private nonprofit institutions. At private for-profit institutions, instruction constituted 25 percent of total expenses; but student services, academic support, and institutional support, which includes expenses associated with admissions, student activities, libraries, and administrative and executive activities, was the largest category, at 66 percent. At public and private nonprofit institutions, expenses on student services, academic support, and institutional support are available as separate categories. Combined expenses on student services, academic support, and institutional support made up 19 percent of total expenses at public institutions and 30 percent at private nonprofit institutions. Other relatively large categories at public institutions (i.e., those accounting for 8–10 percent of expenses) were research, hospitals, and institutional support. At private

For more information, see the Reader's Guide and the Guide to Sources.

Chapter: 4/Postsecondary Education
Section: Finance and Resources

nonprofit institutions, some of the other large categories (i.e., those accounting for 8–13 percent of expenses) were institutional support, research, auxiliary enterprises (i.e., self-supporting operations, such as residence halls), hospitals, academic support, and student services.

In 2010–11, across all levels of postsecondary institutional control, 2-year institutions spent a greater share of their total expenses on instruction than 4-year institutions did.

The percentage of total expenses at public institutions for instruction was 35 percent at 2-year institutions, compared with 25 percent at 4-year institutions. At private nonprofit institutions, instruction accounted for 34 percent of total expenses at 2-year institutions and 33 percent at 4-year institutions; at private for-profit institutions, the percentage of total expenses on instruction at 2-year and 4-year institutions were 32 and 23 percent, respectively.

Figure 2. Expenses per full-time-equivalent (FTE) student at degree-granting postsecondary institutions, by purpose of expenses and control of institution: 2010–11
[In constant 2011–12 dollars]

Purpose of expenses	Public	Private nonprofit	Private for-profit
Instruction	$7,413	$15,568	$3,534
Research and public service	$3,850	$6,151	$12
Student services, academic support, and institutional support	$5,302	$14,437	$9,279

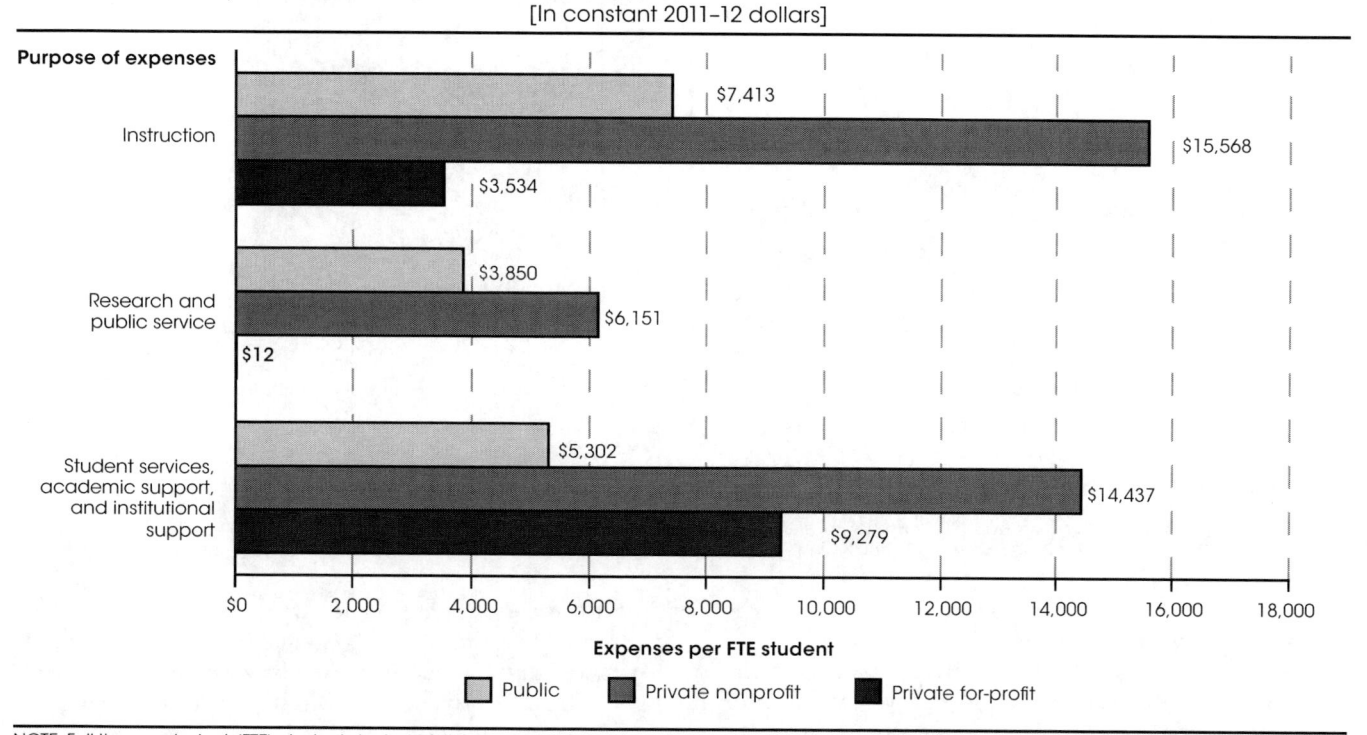

NOTE: Full-time-equivalent (FTE) students include full-time students plus the full-time equivalent of part-time students. Expenses per FTE student are reported in constant 2011–12 dollars, based on the Consumer Price Index (CPI).
SOURCE: U.S. Department of Education, National Center for Education Statistics, Integrated Postsecondary Education Data System (IPEDS), Spring 2011, Enrollment component; and Spring 2012, Finance component. See *Digest of Education Statistics 2012*, tables 412, 414, and 416.

In 2010–11, total expenses per full-time-equivalent (FTE) student were much higher at private nonprofit postsecondary institutions ($47,779) than at public institutions ($27,656) and private for-profit institutions ($14,111). Expenses per FTE student are reported in constant 2011–12 dollars, based on the Consumer Price Index (CPI). Private nonprofit institutions spent more than twice as much per student on instruction ($15,568) as public institutions did ($7,413). A similar pattern was found for most other expense classifications, such as student services, academic support, and institutional support (a total of $14,437 for private nonprofit institutions vs. $5,302 for public institutions). Expenses per FTE student for public service, such as expenses for public broadcasting and community services, were an exception to this pattern, with public institutions spending more than private nonprofit institutions ($1,108 vs. $706). Expenses per student for instruction were more than twice as high at public institutions as at private for-profit institutions ($7,413 vs. $3,534), but expenses per student for student services, academic support, and institutional support were higher at private for-profit institutions ($9,279) than at public institutions ($5,302).

For more information, see the Reader's Guide and the Guide to Sources.

Chapter: 4/Postsecondary Education
Section: Finance and Resources

Figure 3. Instructional expenses per full-time-equivalent (FTE) student for instruction at 2-year and 4-year degree-granting postsecondary institutions, by control of institution: 2005–06 and 2010–11
[In constant 2011–12 dollars]

Instruction expense per FTE student — 2-year institutions

Control of institution	2005–06	2010–11
Public	$4,904	$4,405
Private nonprofit	$7,894	$6,177
Private for-profit	$4,353	$4,529

Instruction expense per FTE student — 4-year institutions

Control of institution	2005–06	2010–11
Public	$9,440	$9,401
Private nonprofit	$15,199	$15,669
Private for-profit	$2,901	$3,222

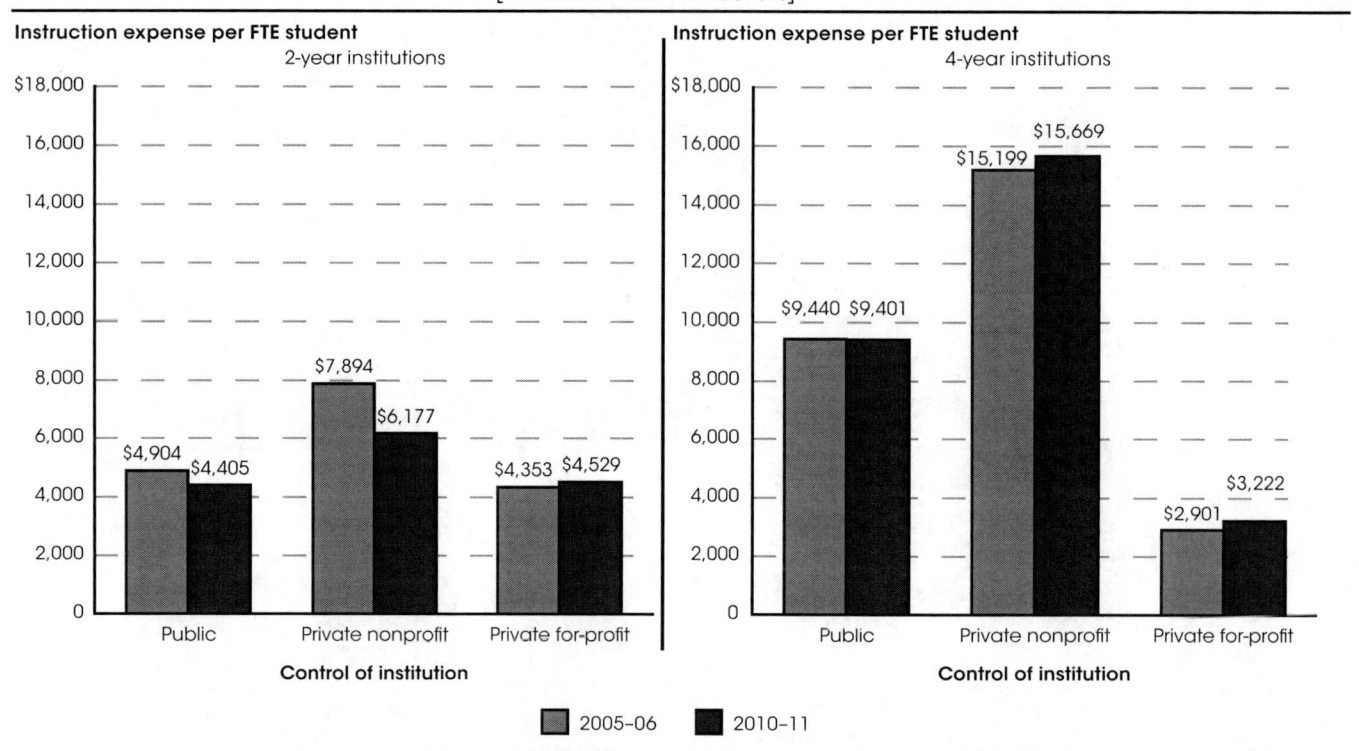

NOTE: Full-time-equivalent (FTE) students include full-time students plus the full-time equivalent of part-time students. Expenses per FTE student are reported in constant 2011–12 dollars, based on the Consumer Price Index (CPI).
SOURCE: U.S. Department of Education, National Center for Education Statistics, Integrated Postsecondary Education Data System (IPEDS), Spring 2006 and Spring 2011, Enrollment component; and Spring 2007 and Spring 2012, Finance component. See *Digest of Education Statistics 2012*, tables 412, 414, and 416.

Expenses per FTE student for instruction have shown varying patterns of change between 2005–06 and 2010–11 at the different postsecondary institution types, after adjusting for inflation. At public 4-year institutions, instruction expenses per FTE student were less than 1 percent lower in 2010–11 than they were in 2005–06, and these expenses were 10 percent lower at public 2-year institutions. At private nonprofit institutions, instruction expenses per FTE increased by 3 percent at 4-year institutions but decreased by 22 percent at 2-year institutions. At private for-profit institutions, expenses per FTE student for instruction in 2010–11 were higher than they were in 2005–06 for both 4-year and 2-year institutions (11 and 4 percent higher, respectively).

Reference tables: *Digest of Education Statistics 2012*, tables 412, 414, 416

Glossary: Consumer Price Index (CPI), Full-time-equivalent (FTE) enrollment, Private institution, Public school or institution, Revenue, Tuition and fees

For more information, see the Reader's Guide and the Guide to Sources.

This page intentionally left blank.

Chapter: 4/Postsecondary Education
Section: Finance and Resources

Indicator 39
Characteristics of Postsecondary Faculty

The number of full-time faculty in degree-granting institutions increased by 42 percent from fall 1991 to fall 2011, compared with an increase of 162 percent in the number of part-time faculty. As a result of the faster increase in the number of part-time faculty, the percentage of faculty who were part time increased from 35 percent to 50 percent during this period.

In fall 2011, there were 1.5 million faculty in degree-granting institutions—approximately half were full time and half were part time. Full-time faculty include professors, associate professors, assistant professors, instructors, lecturers, assisting professors, adjunct professors, or interim professors (or the equivalent). From fall 1991 to fall 2011, the number of faculty in degree-granting institutions increased by 84 percent. The number of full-time faculty in degree-granting institutions increased by 42 percent from fall 1991 to fall 2011, compared with an increase of 162 percent in the number of part-time faculty. As a result of the faster increase in the number of part-time faculty, the percentage of faculty who were part time increased from 35 percent to 50 percent during this period. Additionally, the percentage of all faculty who were female increased from 36 percent in 1991 to 48 percent in 2011.

Figure 1. Number of faculty in degree-granting institutions, by employment status: Selected years, fall 1991 through fall 2011

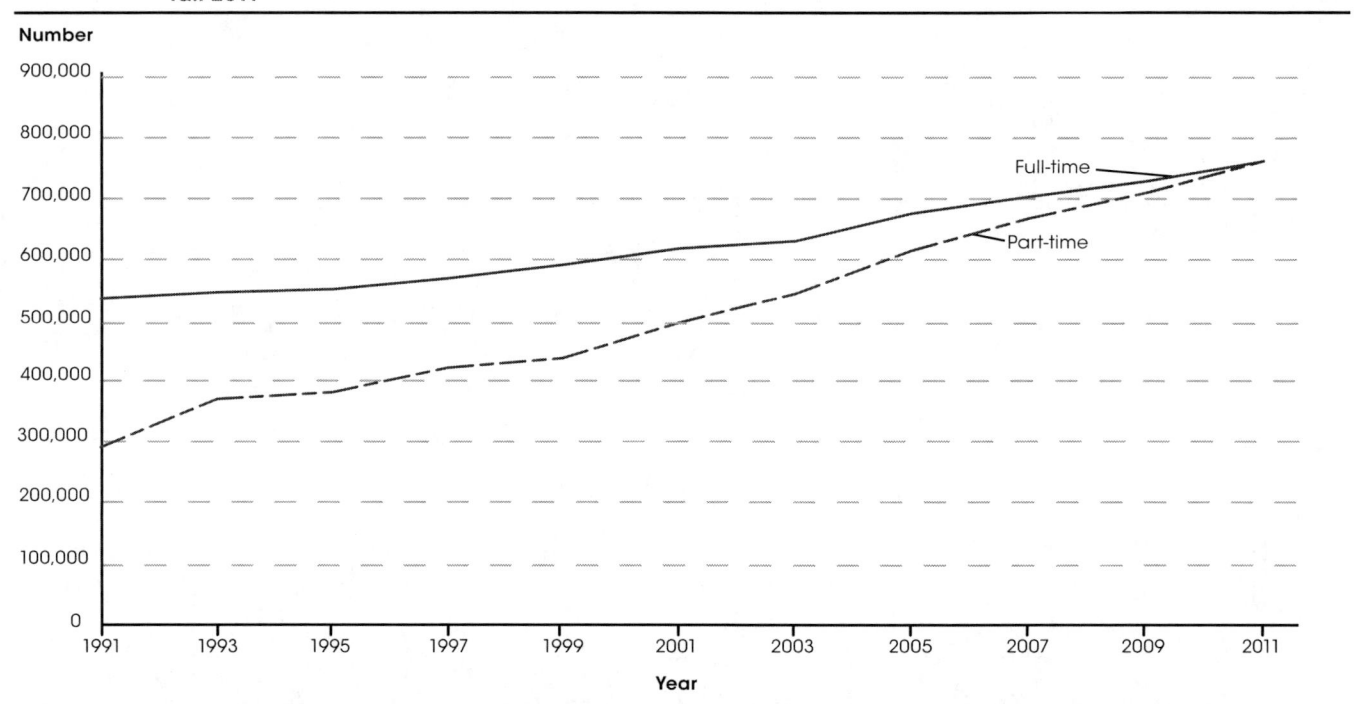

NOTE: Graduate students with titles such as graduate or teaching fellow who assist senior faculty are excluded. Degree-granting institutions grant associate's degrees or higher and participate in Title IV federal financial aid programs. Beginning in 2007, includes institutions with fewer than 15 full-time employees; these institutions did not report staff data prior to 2007.
SOURCE: U.S. Department of Education, National Center for Education Statistics, Integrated Postsecondary Education Data System (IPEDS), "Fall Staff Survey" (IPEDS-S:91–99); and IPEDS Winter 2001–02 through Winter 2011–12, Human Resources component, Fall Staff section. See *Digest of Education Statistics 2012*, table 290.

The number of faculty increased at institutions of each control type during this period; the percentage increases in faculty were smaller for public and private nonprofit institutions than for private for-profit institutions. From fall 1991 to fall 2011, the number of faculty increased by 64 percent at public institutions, by 83 percent at private nonprofit institutions, and by almost 1,400 percent at private for-profit institutions. Despite the faster growth in the number of faculty at private for-profit institutions over this period, approximately 9 percent of all faculty were employed by private for-profit institutions in fall 2011, while 63 percent were employed by public institutions and 28 percent by private nonprofit institutions.

For more information, see the Reader's Guide and the Guide to Sources.

Chapter: 4/Postsecondary Education
Section: Finance and Resources

Figure 2. Percentage of full-time faculty whose race/ethnicity was known, in degree-granting institutions, by academic rank, selected race/ethnicity, and sex: Fall 2011

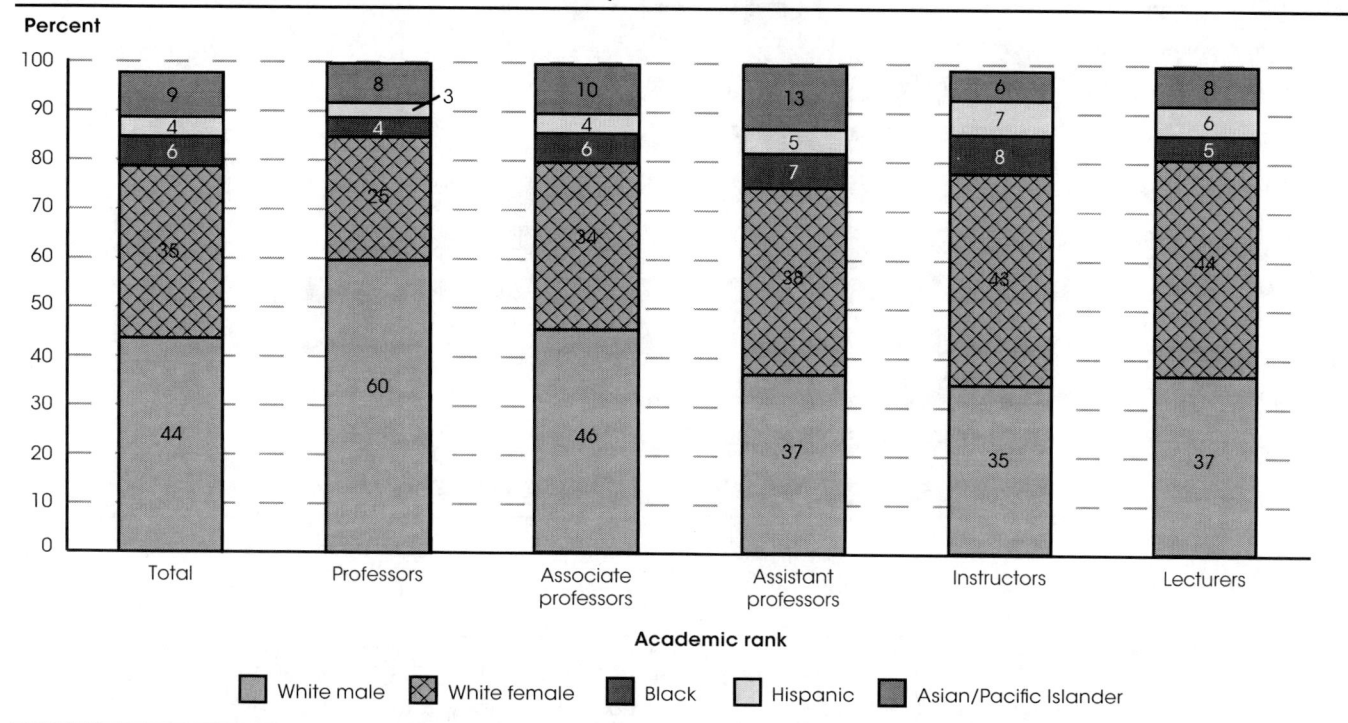

Academic rank	White male	White female	Black	Hispanic	Asian/Pacific Islander
Total	44	35	6	4	9
Professors	60	25	4	3	8
Associate professors	46	34	6	4	10
Assistant professors	37	38	7	5	13
Instructors	35	43	8	7	6
Lecturers	37	44	5	6	8

NOTE: Degree-granting institutions grant associate's degrees or higher and participate in Title IV federal financial aid programs. Race categories exclude persons of Hispanic ethnicity. Estimates are based on full-time faculty whose race/ethnicity was known. Detail may not sum to 100 percent because data on some racial/ethnic groups are not shown.
SOURCE: U.S. Department of Education, National Center for Education Statistics, Integrated Postsecondary Education Data System (IPEDS), Winter 2011-12, Human Resources component, Fall Staff section. See *Digest of Education Statistics 2012*, table 291.

In 2011, of those full-time faculty whose race/ethnicity was known, 79 percent were White (44 percent were White males and 35 percent were White females), 6 percent were Black, 4 percent were Hispanic, 9 percent were Asian/Pacific Islander, and less than 1 percent were American Indian/Alaska Native or two or more races. Among full-time professors, 84 percent were White (60 percent were White males and 25 percent were White females), 4 percent were Black, 3 percent were Hispanic, 8 percent were Asian/Pacific Islander, and less than 1 percent were American Indian/Alaska Native.

In academic year 2011–12, the average salary for full-time instructional faculty on 9- and 10-month contracts at degree-granting institutions was $76,600; average salaries ranged from $53,400 for lecturers to $107,100 for professors. The average salary (adjusted for inflation) for all full-time instructional faculty on 9- and 10-month contracts increased by 9 percent from 1991–92 to 2009–10, but decreased by 2 percent from 2009–10 to 2011–12. Average salaries for specific academic ranks also increased between 1991–92 and 2009–10: Average salary increases were 15 percent for professors, 10 percent for associate professors, 11 percent for assistant professors, 19 percent for instructors, and 9 percent for lecturers. From 2009–10 to 2011–12, however, average salaries across academic ranks decreased: the decreases ranged from 2 percent to 4 percent.

The average salary for all full-time instructional faculty was higher for males than for females in all years for which data were available. In academic year 2011–12, the average salary was 21 percent higher for males than for females ($83,200 versus $68,500 in current dollars). Between 1991–92 and 2011–12, the average salary increased by 8 percent for males and by 11 percent for females, after adjusting for inflation. Due to the faster increase in salary for females, the salary gap between male and female instructional faculty overall decreased from $15,300 in 1991–92 to $14,700 in 2011–12. However, the gender gap in salary for professors increased from $11,300 to $16,200 during this period.

For more information, see the Reader's Guide and the Guide to Sources.

Chapter: 4/Postsecondary Education
Section: Finance and Resources

Figure 3. Average salary of full-time instructional faculty on 9-month contracts in degree-granting institutions, by control and level of institution: 2011–12

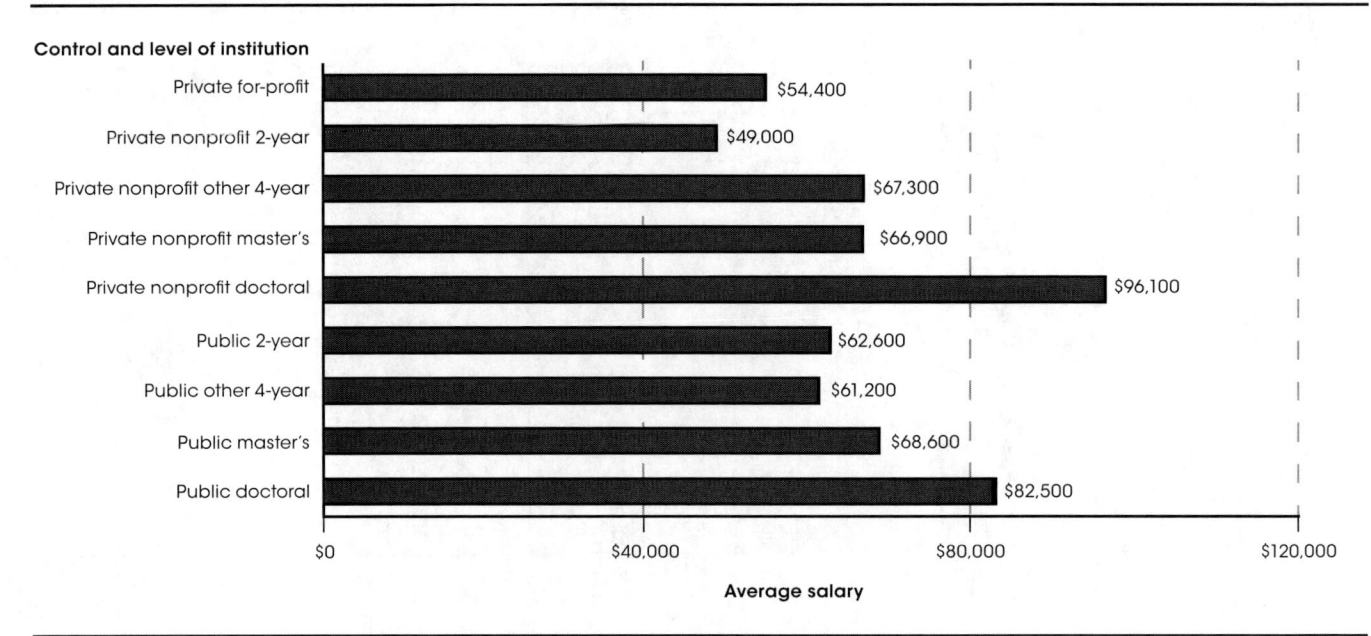

Control and level of institution	Average salary
Private for-profit	$54,400
Private nonprofit 2-year	$49,000
Private nonprofit other 4-year	$67,300
Private nonprofit master's	$66,900
Private nonprofit doctoral	$96,100
Public 2-year	$62,600
Public other 4-year	$61,200
Public master's	$68,600
Public doctoral	$82,500

NOTE: Degree-granting institutions grant associate's degrees or higher and participate in Title IV federal financial aid programs. Salaries reflect an average of all faculty on 9-month contracts rather than a weighted average based on contract length that appears in some other reports of the National Center for Education Statistics.
SOURCE: U.S. Department of Education, National Center for Education Statistics, Integrated Postsecondary Education Data System (IPEDS), Winter 2011–12, Human Resources component, Salaries section. See *Digest of Education Statistics 2012*, table 299.

In academic year 2011–12, the average salary for full-time instructional faculty at private nonprofit institutions ($83,800) was higher than for instructional faculty at public institutions ($73,500) or private for-profit institutions ($54,400). Among the specific institutional types, average instructional faculty salaries were highest at private nonprofit doctoral institutions ($96,100) and public doctoral institutions ($82,500). The average salaries were lowest for instructional faculty at private nonprofit 2-year institutions ($49,000) and private for-profit institutions ($54,400). From 1999–2000 to 2011–12, average instructional faculty salaries decreased by 1 percent at public institutions, but increased by 7 percent at private nonprofit institutions and by 37 percent at private for-profit institutions, after adjusting for inflation.

In academic year 2011–12, approximately 45 percent of institutions had tenure systems. The percentage of institutions with tenure systems ranged from 1 percent at private for-profit institutions to almost 100 percent at public doctoral institutions. Of those faculty at institutions with tenure systems, 49 percent of full-time faculty had tenure in 2011–12, compared with 54 percent in 1999–2000. From 1999–2000 to 2011–12, the percentage of full-time faculty having tenure decreased 5 percentage points at public institutions, 4 percentage points at private nonprofit institutions, and 46 percentage points at private for-profit institutions. At institutions with tenure systems, the percentage of full-time faculty having tenure was generally higher for males than for females. In 2011–12, some 54 percent of males had tenure, compared with 41 percent of females.

Reference tables: *Digest of Education Statistics 2012*, tables 290, 291, 298, 299, 305

Glossary: Private institution, Public institution

For more information, see the Reader's Guide and the Guide to Sources.

This page intentionally left blank.

Indicator 40
Student Loan Volume and Default Rates

Chapter: 4/Postsecondary Education
Section: Finance and Resources

In 2010–11, the average student loan amount, in constant 2011–12 dollars, was $6,800, which was a 39 percent increase from 2000–01, when the average student loan amount was $4,900. Of the 4.1 million students who entered the repayment phase on their student loans in fiscal year (FY) 2010, some 375,000, or 9 percent, had defaulted before FY 2011.

Title IV of the Higher Education Act of 1965 authorized several student financial assistance programs—including federal grants, loans, and work study—to help offset the cost of attending a postsecondary institution. The largest federal loan program is the William D. Ford Federal Direct Loan program, in which the federal government is the lender. Interest on the loans made under the Direct Loan program may be subsidized, based on need, by the federal government while the student is in school. Most loans are payable over 10 years, beginning 6 months after the student leaves the institution, either by completing the program or by leaving prior to completion.

In 2010–11, average undergraduate tuition and fees for full-time students across all postsecondary degree-granting institutions were $9,900, in constant 2011–12 dollars—a 41 percent increase over the constant-dollar amount from 10 years earlier ($7,000). Average annual student loan amounts for first-time, full-time students have kept pace with this increase. In 2010–11, the average student loan amount, in constant 2011–12 dollars, was $6,800, which was a 39 percent increase from 2000–01 ($4,900).

Figure 1. Average tuition and fees and average loan amounts for first-time, full-time students with loans at postsecondary degree-granting institutions, by level and control of institution: 2010–11

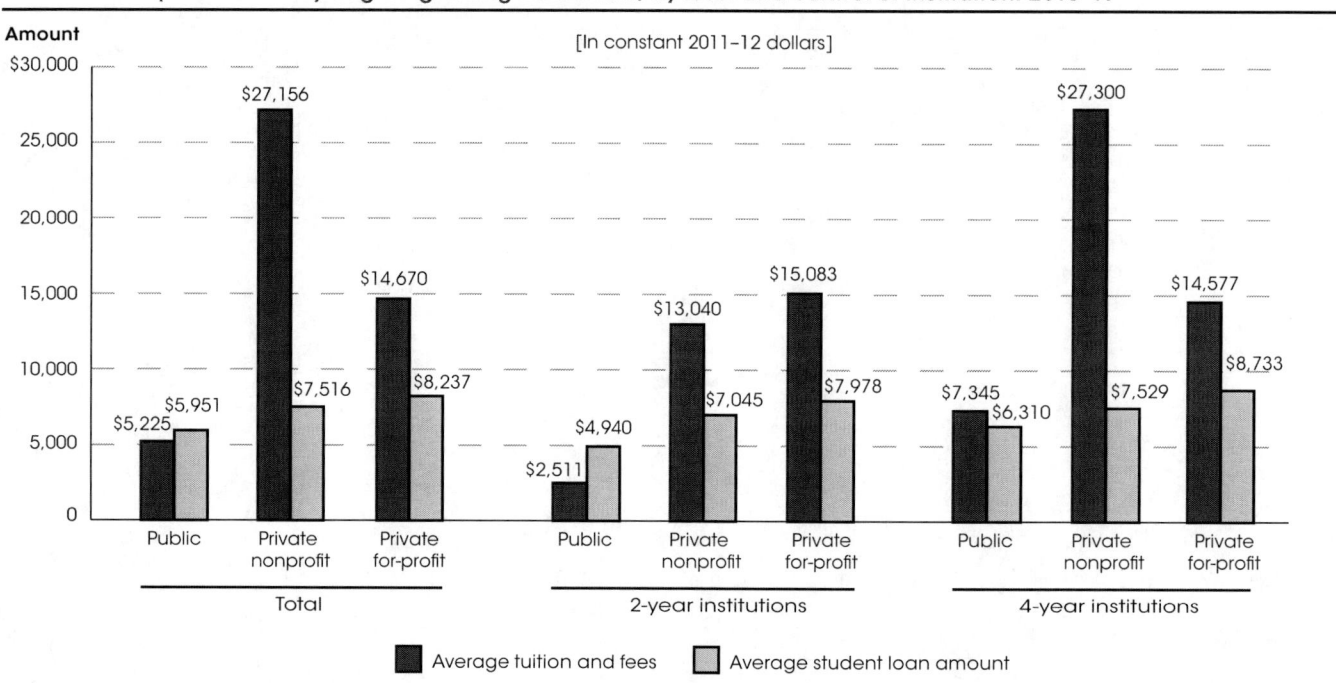

[In constant 2011–12 dollars]

	Public	Private nonprofit	Private for-profit
Total — Average tuition and fees	$5,225	$27,156	$14,670
Total — Average student loan amount	$5,951	$7,516	$8,237
2-year institutions — Average tuition and fees	$2,511	$13,040	$15,083
2-year institutions — Average student loan amount	$4,940	$7,045	$7,978
4-year institutions — Average tuition and fees	$7,345	$27,300	$14,577
4-year institutions — Average student loan amount	$6,310	$7,529	$8,733

NOTE: Degree-granting institutions grant associate's or higher degrees and participate in Title IV federal financial aid programs. Tuition and fee data for public institutions are for in-state students only. Tuition and fee data are collected in the fall, and loan data are collected in the spring.
SOURCE: U.S. Department of Education, National Center for Education Statistics, Integrated Postsecondary Education Data System (IPEDS) Spring 2011, Student Financial Aid component; Fall 2011, Institutional Characteristics component. See *Digest of Education Statistics 2012*, tables 381 and 387.

For more information, see the Reader's Guide and the Guide to Sources.

Chapter: 4/Postsecondary Education
Section: Finance and Resources

At 2-year postsecondary degree-granting institutions, average tuition and fees (in constant 2011–12 dollars) were $3,200 in 2010–11. At public 2-year institutions, average in-state tuition and fees were $2,500; at private nonprofit 2-year institutions, average tuition and fees were $13,000; and at private for-profit 2-year institutions, average tuition and fees were $15,100. Some 25 percent of first-time, full-time students attending public 2-year institutions had student loans, with an average loan amount of $4,900. At private nonprofit 2-year institutions, 65 percent of students had student loans, with an average loan amount of $7,000. At private for-profit 2-year institutions, 82 percent of students had student loans, with an average amount of $8,000.

At 4-year postsecondary degree-granting institutions, average tuition and fees (in constant 2011–12 dollars) were $13,300 in 2010–11. At public 4-year institutions, average in-state tuition and fees were $7,300, compared with $14,600 at private for-profit institutions and $27,300 at private nonprofit institutions. In 2010–11, average annual student loan amounts, in constant 2011–12 dollars, were highest at private for-profit 4-year institutions ($8,700), and 83 percent of students had student loans. At private nonprofit 4-year institutions, the average student loan amount was $7,500, and 64 percent of students had student loans. At public 4-year institutions, the average student loan amount was $6,300, and 51 percent of students had student loans.

Approximately 4.1 million students entered the repayment phase of their student loans in fiscal year (FY) 2010, meaning their student loans became due between October 1, 2009, and September 30, 2010. The percentage of students who entered repayment on their loans in FY 2010 and defaulted prior to the end of the next fiscal year is the 2-year cohort default rate. Of the 4.1 million students who entered repayment in FY 2010, some 375,000, or 9.2 percent, had defaulted on the payments before FY 2011 ended on September 30, 2011. For students in the Direct Loan Program or the Federal Family Education Loan (FFEL) program, default occurs when a payment has not been made for 270 days.

Figure 2. Two-year student loan cohort default rates at postsecondary degree-granting institutions, by level and control of institution: Fiscal years (FY) 2007 through 2010

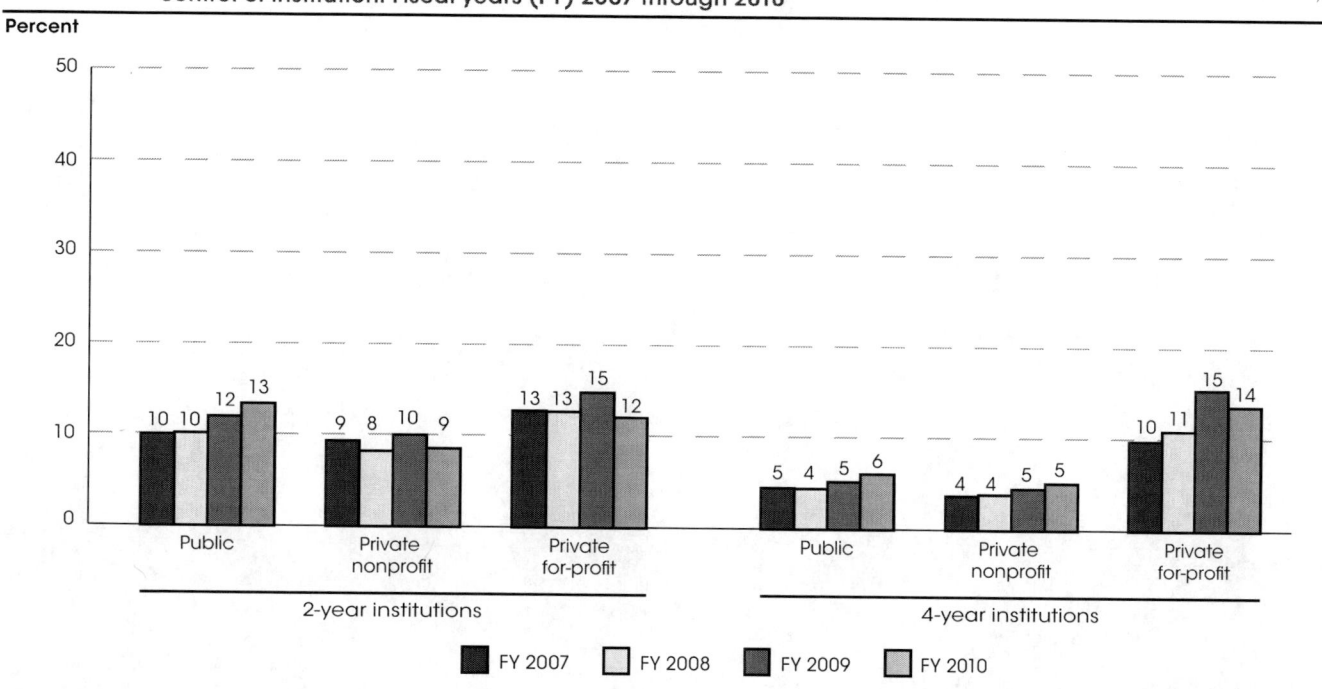

Institution	FY 2007	FY 2008	FY 2009	FY 2010
2-year Public	10	10	12	13
2-year Private nonprofit	9	8	10	9
2-year Private for-profit	13	13	15	12
4-year Public	5	4	5	6
4-year Private nonprofit	4	4	5	5
4-year Private for-profit	10	11	15	14

NOTE: Does not include foreign or unclassified institutions. Default rates were calculated using student counts by institution from the Federal Student Aid Cohort Default Rate Database and the Integrated Postsecondary Education Data System (IPEDS) classification of institutions. The repayment phase is the period when student loans must be repaid and generally begins 6 months after a student leaves an institution. Default occurs when a borrower fails to make a payment for 270 days. The 2-year cohort default rate is the percentage of students who entered repayment during a given fiscal year and defaulted within the two following fiscal years. Degree-granting institutions grant associate's or higher degrees and participate in federal Title IV programs.
SOURCE: U.S. Department of Education, Federal Student Aid, Direct Loan and Federal Family Education Loan Programs, Cohort Default Rate Database retrieved December 15, 2012, from http://www2.ed.gov/offices/OSFAP/defaultmanagement/cdr.html. See *Digest of Education Statistics 2012*, table 400.

For more information, see the Reader's Guide and the Guide to Sources.

Chapter: 4/Postsecondary Education
Section: Finance and Resources

The default rate for students in the FY 2010 cohort was 7.8 percent at 4-year degree-granting institutions and 12.8 percent at 2-year degree-granting institutions. Default rates for the FY 2010 cohort were highest at private for-profit 4-year institutions (13.6 percent) and public 2-year institutions (13.4 percent). The lowest default rate was for students at private nonprofit 4-year institutions (5.2 percent).

The 9.2 percent rate of default across all institutions for the FY 2010 cohort was higher than rates for FY 2009 (8.8 percent), FY 2008 (7.1 percent), and FY 2007 (6.7 percent) cohorts. The percentage point increase in default rates from FY 2007 to FY 2010 was greatest at private for-profit 4-year institutions (from 9.8 percent to 13.6 percent). At private nonprofit and private for-profit 2-year institutions, default rates declined by less than 1 percentage point between FY 2007 and FY 2010.

Reference tables: *Digest of Education Statistics 2012,* tables 381, 387, 400

Glossary: Default rate, Degree-granting institutions, Postsecondary education

This page intentionally left blank.

Indicator 41

Chapter: 4/Postsecondary Education
Section: Completions

Institutional Retention and Graduation Rates for Undergraduate Students

About 59 percent of full-time, first-time students who began seeking a bachelor's degree at a 4-year institution in fall 2005 completed that degree within 6 years. The graduation rate for females (61 percent) was higher than the rate for males (56 percent).

The 2011 graduation rate for full-time, first-time undergraduate students who began their pursuit of a bachelor's degree at a 4-year degree-granting institution in fall 2005 was 59 percent. That is, 59 percent of full-time, first-time students who began seeking a bachelor's degree at a 4-year institution in fall 2005 completed the degree at that institution within 6 years. Graduation rates are calculated to meet requirements of the 1990 Student Right to Know Act, which directed postsecondary institutions to report the percentage of students that complete their program within 150 percent of the normal time for completion (that is, within 6 years for students pursuing a bachelor's degree). Students who transfer and complete a degree at another institution are not included as completers in these rates.

Figure 1. Percentage of students seeking a bachelor's degree at 4-year degree-granting institutions who completed a bachelor's degree within 6 years, by control of institution and sex: Starting cohort year 2005

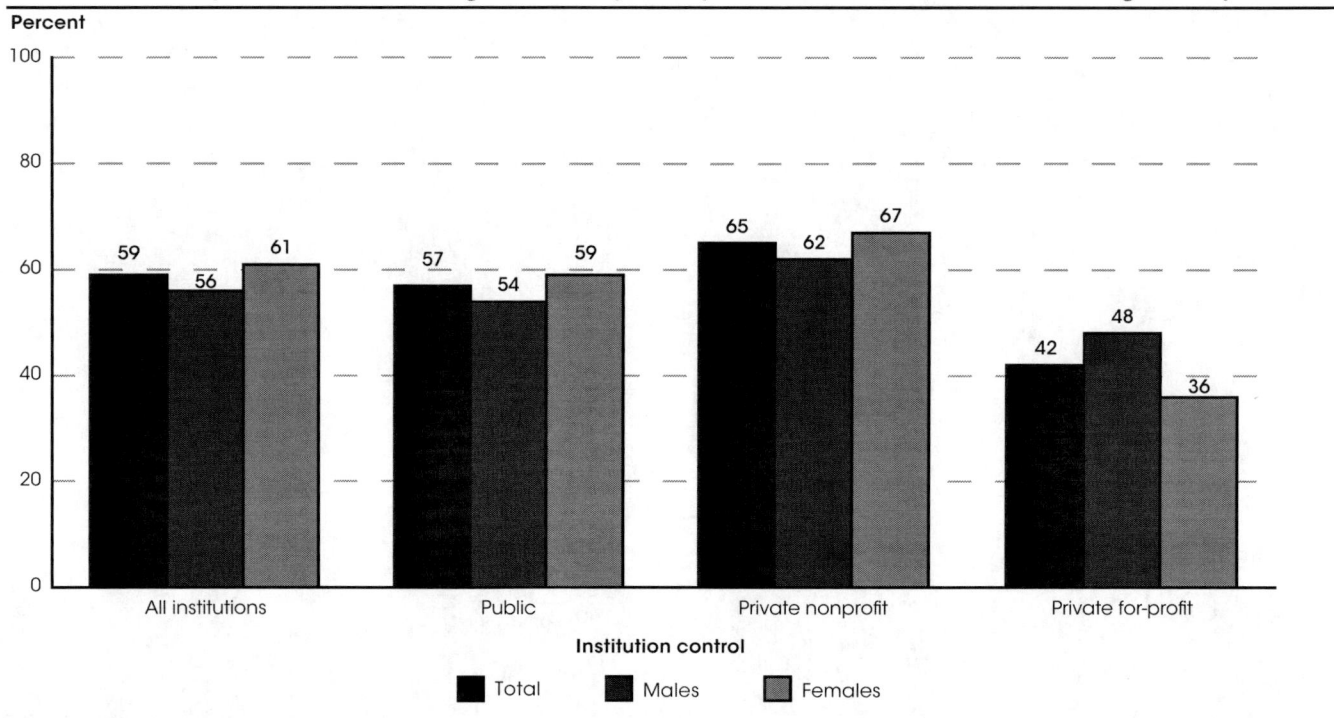

Institution control	Total	Males	Females
All institutions	59	56	61
Public	57	54	59
Private nonprofit	65	62	67
Private for-profit	42	48	36

NOTE: Degree-granting institutions grant associate's or higher degrees and participate in Title IV federal financial aid programs. Graduation rates apply to full-time, first-time undergraduates seeking a bachelor's or equivalent degree. Students who transferred to another institution and graduated are not counted as completers at their initial institution.
SOURCE: U.S. Department of Education, National Center for Education Statistics, Integrated Postsecondary Education Data System (IPEDS), Spring 2012, Graduation Rates component. See *Digest of Education Statistics 2012*, table 376.

Among full-time, first-time undergraduate students who began seeking a bachelor's degree at a 4-year degree-granting institution in fall 2005, the 6-year graduation rate was 57 percent at public institutions, 65 percent at private nonprofit institutions, and 42 percent at private for-profit institutions. This graduation rate was 56 percent for males and 61 percent for females; it was higher for females than for males at both public (59 percent vs. 54 percent) and private nonprofit institutions (67 percent vs. 62 percent). At private for-profit institutions, however, males had a higher graduation rate than females; the rate was 48 percent for males and 36 percent for females.

For more information, see the Reader's Guide and the Guide to Sources.

Chapter: 4/Postsecondary Education
Section: Completions

Figure 2. Percentage of students seeking a certificate or degree at 2-year degree-granting institutions who completed a credential within 150 percent of the normal time required to do so (for example, 3 years for a 2-year degree), by control of institution and sex: Starting cohort year 2008

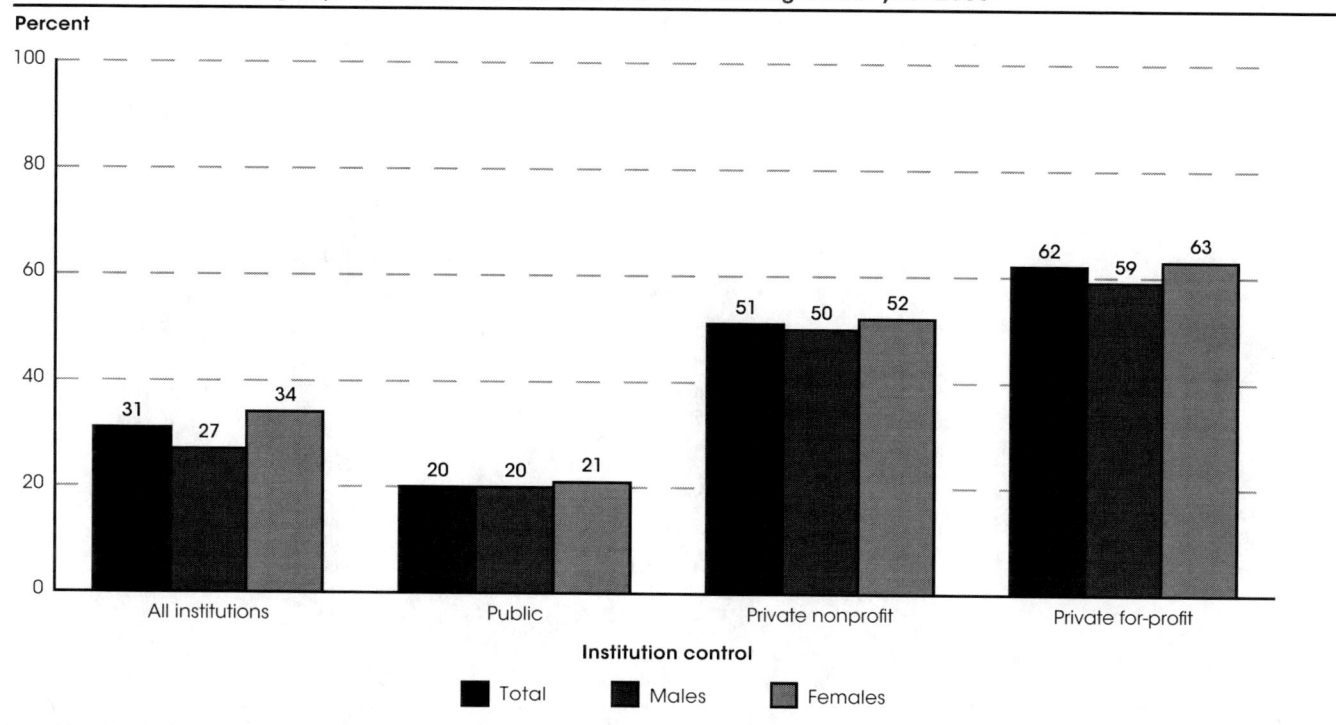

Institution control	Total	Males	Females
All institutions	31	27	34
Public	20	20	21
Private nonprofit	51	50	52
Private for-profit	62	59	63

NOTE: Degree-granting institutions grant associate's or higher degrees and participate in Title IV federal financial aid programs. Completion rates refer to full-time, first-time students receiving associate's degrees or certificates from their initial institutions of attendance only. Students who transferred to another institution and graduated are not counted as completers at their initial institution.
SOURCE: U.S. Department of Education, National Center for Education Statistics, Integrated Postsecondary Education Data System (IPEDS), Spring 2012, Graduation Rates component. See *Digest of Education Statistics 2012*, table 377.

At 2-year degree-granting institutions, 31 percent of full-time, first-time undergraduate students who began their pursuit of a certificate or associate's degree in fall 2008 attained it within 150 percent of the normal time required to do so. For example, this measure refers to students who were seeking a 2-year associate's degree and completed the degree within 3 years. This graduation rate was 20 percent at public 2-year institutions, 51 percent at private nonprofit 2-year institutions, and 62 percent at private for-profit 2-year institutions. At 2-year institutions overall, as well as at each type of 2-year institution, the completion rate was higher for females than for males. At 2-year private for-profit institutions, for example, 63 percent of females versus 59 percent of males completed a certificate or associate's degree within 150 percent of the normal time required.

For more information, see the Reader's Guide and the Guide to Sources.

Chapter: 4/Postsecondary Education
Section: Completions

Figure 3. Percentage of students seeking a bachelor's degree at 4-year degree-granting institutions who completed a bachelor's degree within 6 years, by applicant acceptance rate: Starting cohort year 2005

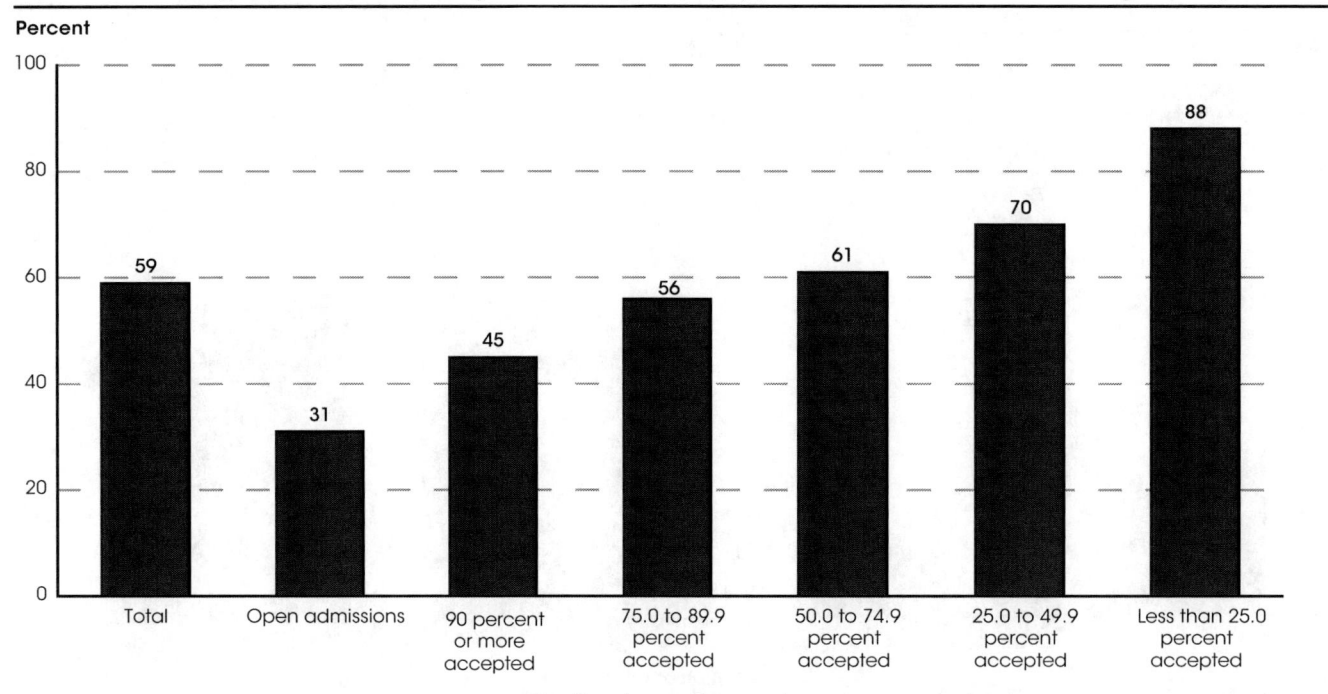

Applicant acceptance rate	Percent
Total	59
Open admissions	31
90 percent or more accepted	45
75.0 to 89.9 percent accepted	56
50.0 to 74.9 percent accepted	61
25.0 to 49.9 percent accepted	70
Less than 25.0 percent accepted	88

NOTE: Degree-granting institutions grant associate's or higher degrees and participate in Title IV federal financial aid programs. The graduation rate is the percentage of full-time, first-time bachelor's degree-seeking students who completed their degree from their initial institution within 6 years. Students who transferred to another institution and graduated are not counted as completers at their initial institution.
SOURCE: U.S. Department of Education, National Center for Education Statistics, Integrated Postsecondary Education Data System (IPEDS), Spring 2012, Graduation Rates component. See *Digest of Education Statistics 2012*, table 376.

Differences in 6-year graduation rates for full-time, first-time students who began seeking a bachelor's degree in fall 2005 varied according to institutions' level of selectivity. In particular, graduation rates were highest at postsecondary degree-granting institutions that were the most selective (i.e., had the lowest admissions acceptance rates). For example, at 4-year institutions with open admissions policies, 31 percent of students completed a bachelor's degree within 6 years. At 4-year institutions where the acceptance rate was less than 25 percent of applicants, the 6-year graduation rate was 88 percent.

For more information, see the Reader's Guide and the Guide to Sources.

Chapter: 4/Postsecondary Education
Section: Completions

Figure 4. Annual full-time student retention rates at 2- and 4-year degree-granting institutions, by institution level, acceptance rate, and institution control: 2011

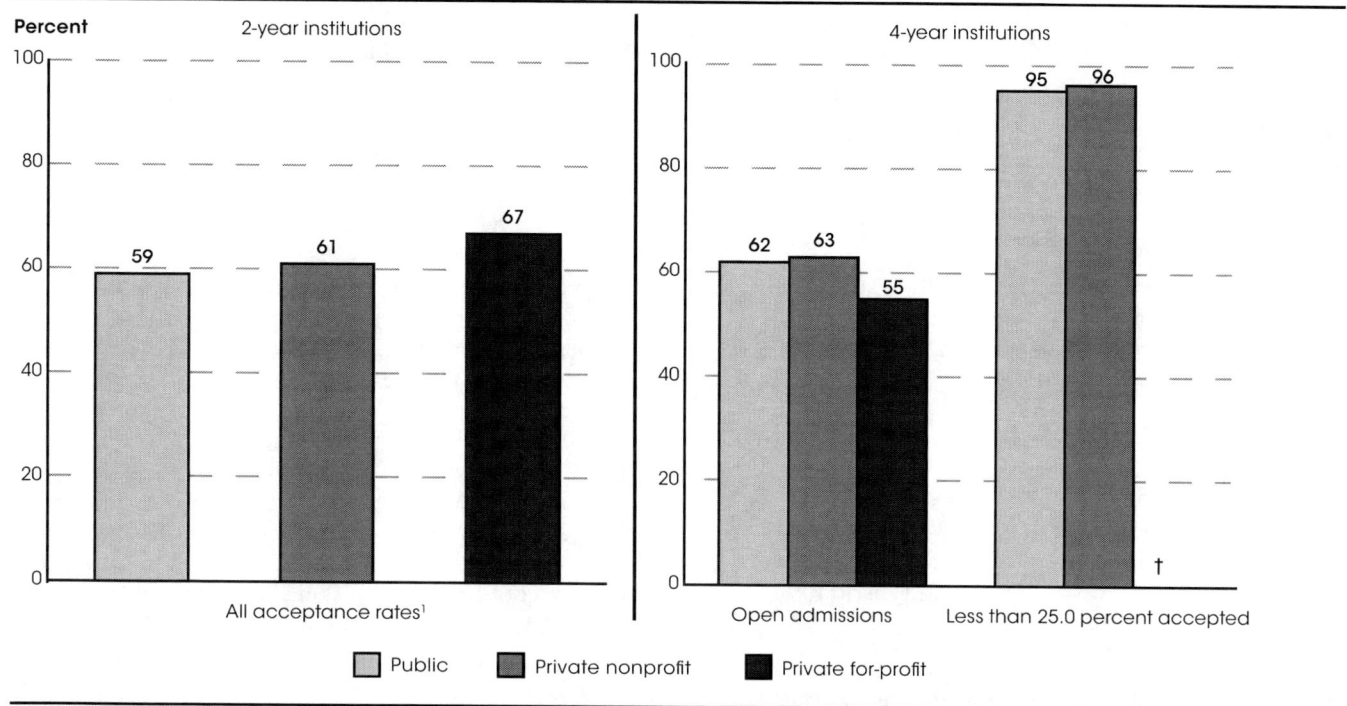

2-year institutions (All acceptance rates[1])
- Public: 59
- Private nonprofit: 61
- Private for-profit: 67

4-year institutions

Open admissions:
- Public: 62
- Private nonprofit: 63
- Private for-profit: 55

Less than 25.0 percent accepted:
- Public: 95
- Private nonprofit: 96
- Private for-profit: †

† Not applicable.
[1] All acceptance rates includes open admissions, all percentages of applications accepted, and information not available.
NOTE: Degree-granting institutions grant associate's or higher degrees and participate in Title IV federal financial aid programs. The retention rate is the percentage of first-time degree-seeking students who return to the institution to continue their studies the following fall.
SOURCE: U.S. Department of Education, National Center for Education Statistics, Integrated Postsecondary Education Data System (IPEDS), Spring 2011, Enrollment component. See *Digest of Education Statistics 2012*, table 378.

In terms of student retention, among full-time, first-time students who enrolled in a postsecondary degree-granting institution in 2010, about 79 percent returned to 4-year institutions and 60 percent to 2-year institutions in the following fall. At public 4-year institutions, the retention rate was 79 percent, with a range of 62 percent at the least selective institutions (those with open admissions) to 95 percent at the most selective institutions (those where less than 25 percent of students are accepted). Retention rates for private nonprofit 4-year institutions followed a similar pattern: the overall retention rate was 80 percent, ranging from 63 percent at the least selective institutions to 96 percent at the most selective. The retention rate at private for-profit institutions was 54 percent; it differed little (2 percent or less) in terms of institution selectivity level. At 2-year institutions overall, the retention rate was 60 percent. The retention rate for 2-year institutions was highest at private for-profit institutions (67 percent), followed by private nonprofit institutions (61 percent) and public institutions (59 percent).

Reference tables: *Digest of Education Statistics 2012*, tables 376, 377, 378

Glossary: Associate's degree, Bachelor's degree, Doctor's degree, Master's degree, Private institution, Public school or institution

For more information, see the Reader's Guide and the Guide to Sources.

Indicator 42

Chapter: 4/Postsecondary Education
Section: Completions

Degrees Conferred by Public and Private Institutions

From academic year 2000–01 to 2010–11, the number of postsecondary degrees conferred by private for-profit institutions increased by a larger percentage than the number conferred by public institutions and private nonprofit institutions; this was true for all levels of degrees.

From academic year 2000–01 to 2010–11, the number of postsecondary degrees conferred by public, private for-profit, and private nonprofit institutions increased for each level of degree. For all Title IV institutions, the total number of certificates awarded increased by 86 percent, associate's degrees increased by 63 percent, bachelor's degrees increased by 38 percent, master's degrees increased by 54 percent, and doctor's degrees increased by 37 percent. For all postsecondary degree levels, the percentage increases from 2000–01 to 2010–11 were smaller for public and private nonprofit institutions than for private for-profit institutions.

From academic year 2000–01 to 2010–11, the number of certificates awarded by public institutions increased by 68 percent (from 310,000 to 520,000 certificates), by 24 percent for private nonprofit institutions (from 29,300 to 36,500 certificates), and by 122 percent for private for-profit institutions (from 214,000 to 473,000 certificates). As a result of these changes, the share of all certificates awarded by private for-profit institutions increased from 39 percent in academic year 2000–01 to 46 percent in 2010–11 while the share conferred by public and private nonprofit institutions decreased during this period (from 56 to 50 percent and from 5 to 4 percent, respectively).

Table 1. Number of degrees conferred by Title IV institutions and percent change, by control of institution and level of degree: Academic years 2000–01 and 2010–11

Level of degree and academic year	Total	Public	Private Total	Private Nonprofit	Private For-profit
Certificate					
2000–01	552,503	309,624	242,879	29,336	213,543
2010–11	1,029,557	519,670	509,887	36,513	473,374
Percent change	86.3	67.8	109.9	24.5	121.7
Associate's					
2000–01	578,865	456,487	122,378	45,711	76,667
2010–11	942,327	696,788	245,539	51,969	193,570
Percent change	62.8	52.6	100.6	13.7	152.5
Bachelor's					
2000–01	1,244,171	812,438	431,733	408,701	23,032
2010–11	1,715,913	1,088,297	627,616	513,106	114,510
Percent change	37.9	34.0	45.4	25.5	397.2
Master's					
2000–01	473,502	246,054	227,448	215,815	11,633
2010–11	730,635	339,250	391,385	313,200	78,185
Percent change	54.3	37.9	72.1	45.1	572.1
Doctor's[1]					
2000–01	119,585	60,820	58,765	57,722	1,043
2010–11	163,765	81,938	81,827	76,608	5,219
Percent change	36.9	34.7	39.2	32.7	400.4

[1] Includes Ph.D., Ed.D., and comparable degrees at the doctoral level. Includes most degrees formerly classified as first-professional, such as M.D., D.D.S., and law degrees.
NOTE: Includes only postsecondary institutions that participated in Title IV federal financial aid programs.
SOURCE: U.S. Department of Education, National Center for Education Statistics, Integrated Postsecondary Education Data System (IPEDS), Fall 2001 and Fall 2011, Completions component. See *Digest of Education Statistics 2002,* table 170 and *Digest of Education Statistics 2012,* tables 318 and 323.

The number of associate's degrees awarded from academic year 2000–01 to 2010–11 increased by 53 percent for public institutions (from 456,000 to 697,000 degrees), by 14 percent for private nonprofit institutions (from 45,700 to 52,000 degrees), and by 152 percent for private for-profit institutions (from 76,700 to 194,000 degrees). Due to these changes, the share of all associate's degrees conferred by private for-profit institutions increased from 13 percent in 2000–01 to 21 percent in 2010–11, while the share conferred by public and private nonprofit institutions decreased during this period (from 79 to 74 percent and from 8 to 6 percent, respectively).

For more information, see the Reader's Guide and the Guide to Sources.

Chapter: 4/Postsecondary Education
Section: Completions

Figure 1. Number of certificates and associate's degrees conferred by Title IV institutions: Academic years 2000–01, 2005–06, and 2010–11

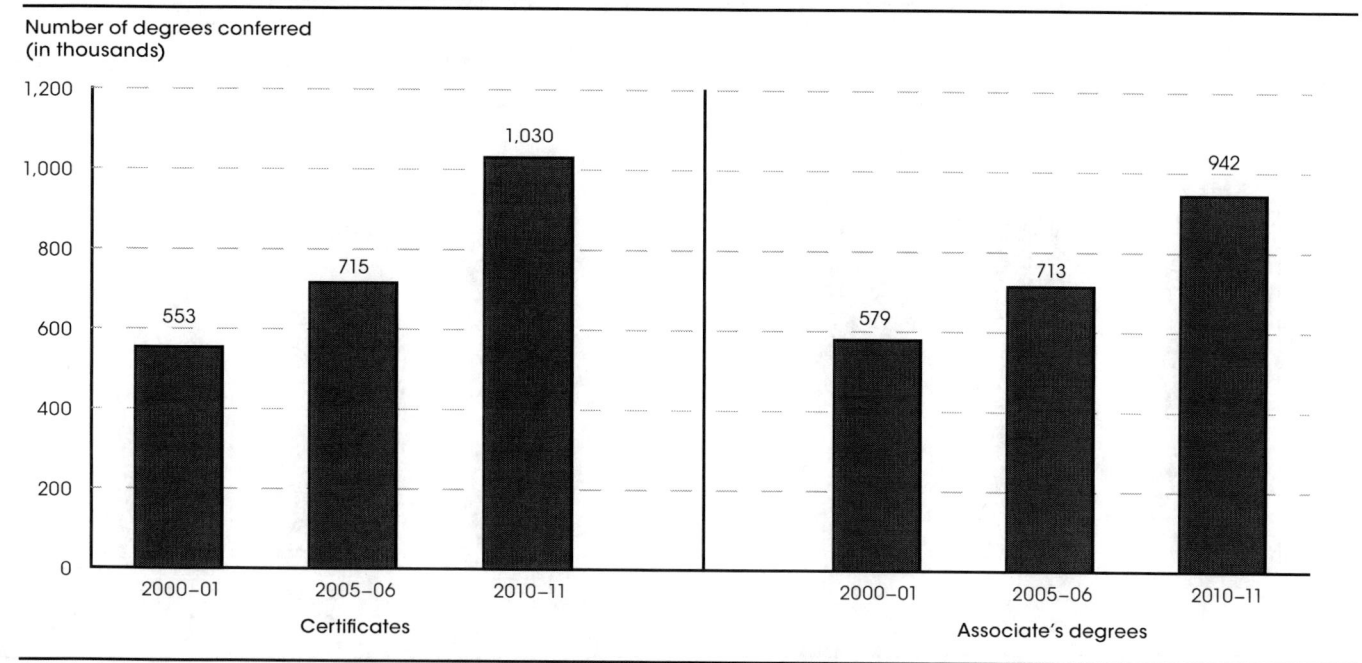

Number of degrees conferred (in thousands)

Certificates:
- 2000–01: 553
- 2005–06: 715
- 2010–11: 1,030

Associate's degrees:
- 2000–01: 579
- 2005–06: 713
- 2010–11: 942

NOTE: Includes only postsecondary institutions that participated in Title IV federal financial aid programs.
SOURCE: U.S. Department of Education, National Center for Education Statistics, Integrated Postsecondary Education Data System (IPEDS), Fall 2001, Fall 2006, and Fall 2011, Completions component. See *Digest of Education Statistics 2012*, tables 318 and 323.

From academic year 2000–01 to 2010–11, the number of bachelor's degrees awarded by public institutions increased by 34 percent (from 812,000 to 1.1 million degrees), the number awarded by private nonprofit institutions increased by 26 percent (from 409,000 to 513,000 degrees), and the number awarded by private for-profit institutions increased by 397 percent (from 23,000 to 115,000 degrees). Despite the gain made by private for-profit institutions, they awarded 7 percent of all bachelor's degrees conferred in 2010–11, while public institutions awarded 63 percent and private nonprofit institutions awarded 30 percent.

The number of master's degrees awarded by public institutions increased 38 percent (from 246,000 to 339,000 degrees) from academic year 2000–01 to 2010–11, yet the percentage of all master's degrees conferred by these institutions declined from 52 to 46 percent. The number of master's degrees conferred by private nonprofit institutions increased 45 percent (from 216,000 to 313,000 degrees) from 2000–01 to 2010–11, resulting in a decrease in their share of all master's degrees (from 46 to 43 percent). In contrast, the number of master's degrees conferred by private for-profit institutions increased by 572 percent (from 11,600 to 78,200 degrees) from 2000–01 to 2010–11, resulting in an increase in their share of total master's degrees conferred. The percentage of all master's degrees conferred by private for-profit colleges increased from 2 percent to 11 percent between 2000–01 and 2010–11.

For more information, see the Reader's Guide and the Guide to Sources.

Chapter: 4/Postsecondary Education
Section: Completions

Figure 2. Number of bachelor's and master's degrees conferred by Title IV institutions, by level of degree: Academic years 2000–01, 2005–06, and 2010–11

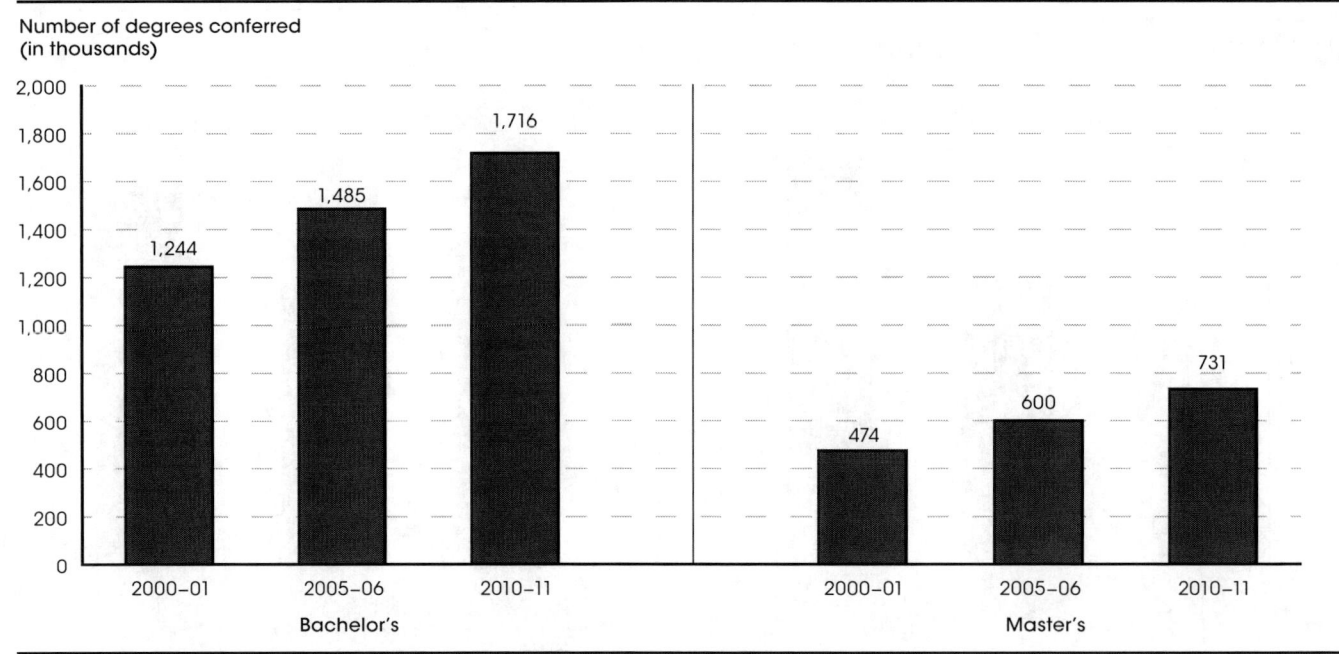

Number of degrees conferred (in thousands)

Bachelor's: 2000–01: 1,244; 2005–06: 1,485; 2010–11: 1,716
Master's: 2000–01: 474; 2005–06: 600; 2010–11: 731

SOURCE: U.S. Department of Education, National Center for Education Statistics, Integrated Postsecondary Education Data System (IPEDS), Fall 2001, Fall 2006, and Fall 2011, Completions component. See *Digest of Education Statistics 2012*, table 318.

From academic year 2000–01 to 2010–11, the number of doctor's degrees conferred increased by 35 percent at public institutions (from 60,800 to 81,900 degrees), by 33 percent at private nonprofit institutions (from 57,700 to 76,600 degrees), and by 400 percent at private for-profit institutions (from 1,000 to 5,200 degrees). In 2010–11, public institutions awarded 50 percent of all doctor's degrees, private nonprofit institutions awarded 47 percent, and private for-profit institutions awarded 3 percent.

Reference tables: *Digest of Education Statistics 2012,* tables 219, 318, 323; and *Digest of Education Statistics 2002,* table 170

Glossary: Associate's degree, Bachelor's degree, Doctor's degree, Master's degree, Private institution, Public institution

For more information, see the Reader's Guide and the Guide to Sources.

This page intentionally left blank.

Guide to Sources

National Center for Education Statistics (NCES)

Common Core of Data

The Common Core of Data (CCD) is NCES's primary database on public elementary and secondary education in the United States. It is a comprehensive, annual, national statistical database of all public elementary and secondary schools and school districts containing data designed to be comparable across all states. This database can be used to select samples for other NCES surveys and provide basic information and descriptive statistics on public elementary and secondary schools and schooling in general.

The CCD collects statistical information annually from approximately 100,000 public elementary and secondary schools and approximately 18,000 public school districts (including supervisory unions and regional education service agencies) in the 50 states, the District of Columbia, Department of Defense (DoD) dependents schools, the Bureau of Indian Education, Puerto Rico, American Samoa, Guam, the Northern Mariana Islands, and the U.S. Virgin Islands. Three categories of information are collected in the CCD survey: general descriptive information on schools and school districts; data on students and staff; and fiscal data. The general descriptive information includes name, address, phone number, and type of locale; the data on students and staff include selected demographic characteristics; and the fiscal data pertain to revenues and current expenditures.

The EDFacts data collection system is the primary collection tool for the CCD. NCES works collaboratively with the Department of Education's Performance Information Management Service to develop the CCD collection procedures and data definitions. Coordinators from State Education Agencies (SEAs) submit the CCD data at different levels (school, agency, and state) to the EDFacts collection system. Prior to submitting CCD files to EDFacts, SEAs must collect and compile information from their respective Local Education Agencies (LEAs) through established administrative records systems within their state or jurisdiction.

Once SEAs have completed their submissions, the CCD survey staff analyzes and verifies the data for quality assurance. Even though the CCD is a universe collection and thus not subject to sampling errors, nonsampling errors can occur. The two potential sources of nonsampling errors are nonresponse and inaccurate reporting. NCES attempts to minimize nonsampling errors through the use of annual training of SEA coordinators, extensive quality reviews, and survey editing procedures. In addition, each year, SEAs are given the opportunity to revise their state-level aggregates from the previous survey cycle.

The CCD survey consists of six components: The Public Elementary/Secondary School Universe Survey, the Local Education Agency (School District) Universe Survey, the State Nonfiscal Survey of Public Elementary/Secondary Education, the National Public Education Financial Survey (NPEFS), the School District Fiscal Data Survey (F-33), and the Teacher Compensation Survey.

Public Elementary/Secondary School Universe Survey

The Public Elementary/Secondary School Universe Survey includes all public schools providing education services to prekindergarten, kindergarten, grade 1–12, and ungraded students. The CCD Public Elementary/Secondary School Universe Survey includes records for each public elementary and secondary school in the 50 states, the District of Columbia, Puerto Rico, the Commonwealth of the Northern Mariana Islands, the U.S. Virgin Islands, the Bureau of Indian Education, and the DoD dependents schools (overseas and domestic).

The Public Elementary/Secondary School Universe Survey includes data for the following variables: NCES school ID number, state school ID number, name of the school, name of the agency that operates the school, mailing address, physical location address, phone number, school type, operational status, locale code, latitude, longitude, county number, county name, full-time-equivalent (FTE) classroom teacher count, low/high grade span offered, congressional district code, school level, free lunch eligible students, reduced-price lunch eligible students, total free and reduced-price lunch eligible students, and student totals and detail (by grade, by race/ethnicity, and by sex). The survey also contains flags indicating whether a school is Title I eligible, schoolwide Title I eligible, a magnet school, a charter school, a shared-time school, or a BIE school; which grades are offered at the school; and if the school was reconstituted due to Annual Yearly Progress (AYP) reasons.

Local Education Agency (School District) Universe

The coverage of the Local Education Agency Universe Survey includes all school districts and administrative units providing education services to prekindergarten, kindergarten, grade 1–12, and ungraded students. The CCD Local Education Agency Universe Survey includes records for the 50 states, the District of Columbia, Puerto Rico, the Bureau of Indian Education, American Samoa, Guam, the Commonwealth of the Northern Mariana Islands, the U.S. Virgin Islands, and the DoD dependents schools (overseas and domestic).

The Local Education Agency Universe Survey includes the following variables: NCES agency ID number, state agency ID number, agency name, phone number, mailing address, physical location address, agency type code, supervisory union number, American National Standards Institute (ANSI) state and county code, county name, core based statistical area (CBSA) code, metropolitan/micropolitan code, metropolitan status code, district locale code, congressional district code, operational status code, BIE agency status, low/high grade span offered, agency charter status, number of schools, number of full-time-equivalent (FTE) teachers, number of ungraded students, number of PK–12 students, number of special education/Individualized Education Program (IEP) students, number of English language learner (ELL) students, instructional staff fields, support staff fields, and a flag indicating whether student counts by race/ethnicity were reported by five or seven racial/ethnic categories.

State Nonfiscal Survey of Public Elementary/Secondary Education

The State Nonfiscal Survey of Public Elementary/Secondary Education for the 2010–11 school year provides state-level, aggregate information about students and staff in public elementary and secondary education. It includes 58 responding units: the 50 states, the District of Columbia, Puerto Rico, American Samoa, Guam, the Commonwealth of the Northern Mariana Islands, the U.S. Virgin Islands, the DoD dependents schools (overseas and domestic), and the Bureau of Indian Education. This survey covers public school student membership by grade, race/ethnicity, and state or jurisdiction and covers number of staff in public schools by category and state or jurisdiction. Beginning with the 2006–07 school year, the number of diploma recipients and other high school completers are no longer included in the State Nonfiscal Survey of Public Elementary/Secondary Education file. These data are now published in the public-use Common Core of Data State Dropout and Completion Data File.

National Public Education Financial Survey

The purpose of the National Public Education Financial Survey (NPEFS) is to provide district, state, and federal policymakers, researchers, and other interested users with descriptive information about revenues and expenditures for public elementary and secondary education. The data collected are useful to (1) chief officers of state education agencies; (2) policymakers in the executive and legislative branches of federal and state governments; (3) education policy and public policy researchers; and (4) the public, journalists, and others.

Data for NPEFS are collected from SEAs in the 50 states, the District of Columbia, Puerto Rico, and four other jurisdictions (American Samoa, Guam, the Commonwealth of the Northern Mariana Islands, and the U.S. Virgin Islands). The data file is organized by state or jurisdiction and contains revenue data by source and expenditure data by source (e.g., local, state, federal), function (the activity being supported by the expenditure), and object (the category of expenditure). The data file also contains average daily attendance data, as well as total student membership data from the CCD State Nonfiscal Survey of Public Elementary/Secondary Education.

School District Finance Survey

The purpose of the School District Finance Survey (F-33) is to provide finance data for all local education agencies (LEAs) that provide free public elementary and secondary education in the United States. National and state totals are not included (national- and state-level figures are presented, however, in the National Public Education Financial Survey [NPEFS]).

Both NCES and the Governments Division of the U.S. Census Bureau collect public school system finance data, and they collaborate in their efforts to gather these data. The Census Bureau acts as the primary collection agent and produces two data files: one for distribution and reporting by the Census Bureau and the other for distribution and reporting by NCES.

The data file for the FY 09 CCD School District Finance Survey (F-33) contains 16,563 records representing the public elementary and secondary education agencies in the 50 states and the District of Columbia. The F-33 file includes variables for revenues by source, expenditures by function, indebtedness, assets, student membership counts, as well as identification variables.

Teacher Compensation Survey

The Teacher Compensation Survey (TCS) collects total compensation, teacher status, and demographic data about individual teachers from multiple states. Twenty-three (23) states participated in the TCS for SY 2008–09. Participating states provided data on salaries, years of teaching experience, highest degree earned, race/ethnicity, and gender for each public school teacher.

Further information on the nonfiscal CCD data may be obtained from

Patrick Keaton
Elementary/Secondary and Library Studies Division
Elementary/Secondary Cooperative System and
  Institutional Studies Program
National Center for Education Statistics
1990 K Street NW
Washington, DC 20006
patrick.keaton@ed.gov
http://nces.ed.gov/ccd

Further information on the fiscal CCD data may be obtained from

Stephen Cornman
Elementary/Secondary and Library Studies Division
Elementary/Secondary Cooperative System and
  Institutional Studies Program
National Center for Education Statistics
1990 K Street NW
Washington, DC 20006
stephen.cornman@ed.gov
http://nces.ed.gov/ccd

Early Childhood Longitudinal Study, Kindergarten Class of 2010–11 (ECLS-K:2011)

The Early Childhood Longitudinal Study, Kindergarten Class of 2010–11 (ECLS-K:2011) is sponsored by the National Center for Education Statistics (NCES) in the Institute of Education Sciences of the U.S. Department of Education to provide detailed information on the school achievement and experiences of students throughout their elementary school years. The students participating in ECLS-K:2011 are being followed longitudinally from the kindergarten year (the 2010–11 school year) through the spring of 2016, when most of them are expected to be in fifth grade. This sample of students is designed to be nationally representative of all students who were enrolled in kindergarten or who were of kindergarten age and being educated in an ungraded classroom or school in the United States in the 2010–11 school year, including those in public and private schools, those who attended full-day and part-day programs, those who were in kindergarten for the first time, and those who were kindergarten repeaters. Students who attended early learning centers or institutions that offered education only through kindergarten are included in the study sample and represented in the cohort.

The ECLS-K:2011 places emphasis on measuring students' experiences within multiple contexts and development in multiple domains. The design of the study includes the collection of information from the students, their parents/guardians, their teachers, their schools, and their before- and after-school care providers.

A nationally representative sample of approximately 18,200 children enrolled in 970 schools during the 2010–11 school year participated in the base year of ECLS-K:2011. The sample includes children from different racial/ethnic and socioeconomic backgrounds. Asian/Pacific Islander students were oversampled to assure that the sample included enough students of this race/ethnicity to be able to make accurate estimates for these students as a group. Two data collections were conducted in the 2010–11 school year, one in the fall and one in the spring. A total of approximately 780 of the 1,320 originally sampled schools participated during the base year of the study. This translates into a weighted unit response rate (weighted by the base weight) of 63 percent for the base year.

Further information on the ECLS-K may be obtained from

Gail Mulligan
Early Childhood, International, and Crosscutting Studies Division
Early Childhood and Household Studies Program
National Center for Education Statistics
1990 K Street NW
Washington, DC 20006
ecls@ed.gov
http://nces.ed.gov/ecls/birth.asp

Integrated Postsecondary Education Data System

The Integrated Postsecondary Education Data System (IPEDS) surveys approximately 7,500 postsecondary institutions, including universities and colleges, as well as institutions offering technical and vocational education beyond the high school level. IPEDS, an annual universe collection that began in 1986, replaced the Higher Education General Information Survey (HEGIS).

IPEDS consists of eight interrelated components that are collected over three collection periods (fall, winter, and spring) each year. These components obtain information on who provides postsecondary education (institutions), who participates in it and completes it (students), what programs are offered and what programs are completed, and both the human and financial resources involved in the provision of institutionally based postsecondary education. Until 2000, these components were institutional characteristics, fall enrollment, completions, salaries, finance, and fall staff. Beginning in 2000, data were collected in the fall for institutional characteristics and completions; in the winter for employees by assigned position (EAP), salaries, and fall staff; and in the spring for enrollment, student financial aid, finances, and graduation rates. With the winter 2005–06 survey, the employees by assigned position, fall staff, and salaries components were merged into the human resources component. In 2007–08, the enrollment component was broken into two separate components: 12-month enrollment (collected in the fall) and fall enrollment (collected in the spring). In the 2011–12 IPEDS data collection year, the student financial aid component was moved to the winter data collection to aid in the timing of the net price of attendance calculations displayed on College Navigator (http://nces.ed.gov/collegenavigator).

Beginning in 2008–09, the first-professional degree category was combined with the post-master's certificate category. Some degrees formerly identified as first-professional that take more than two full-time-equivalent academic years to complete, such as those in Theology (M.Div, M.H.L./Rav), are included in the Master's degree category. Doctor's degrees were broken out into three distinct categories: research/scholarship, professional practice, and other doctor's degrees.

IPEDS race/ethnicity data collection also changed in 2008–09. The "Asian" race category is now separate from a "Native Hawaiian or Other Pacific Islander" category. Survey takers also have the option of identifying themselves as being of "Two or more races." To reflect the recognition that "Hispanic" refers to ethnicity, not race, the new Hispanic category reads "Hispanics of any race."

The degree-granting institutions portion of IPEDS is a census of colleges that award associate's or higher degrees and are eligible to participate in Title IV financial aid programs. Prior to 1993, data from technical and vocational institutions were collected through a sample survey. Beginning in 1993, all data are gathered in a census of all postsecondary institutions. The tabulations on "institutional characteristics" from 1993 forward are based on lists of all institutions and are not subject to sampling errors.

The classification of institutions offering college and university education changed as of 1996. Prior to 1996, institutions that had courses leading to an associate's or higher degree or that had courses accepted for credit toward those degrees were considered higher education institutions. Higher education institutions were accredited by an agency or association that was recognized by the U.S. Department of Education or were recognized directly by the Secretary of Education. Tables, or portions of tables, that use only this standard are noted as "higher education." The newer standard includes institutions that award associate's or higher degrees and that are eligible to participate in Title IV federal financial aid programs. Tables that contain any data according to this standard are titled "degree-granting" institutions. Time-series tables may contain data from both series, and they are noted accordingly. The impact of this change on data collected in 1996 was not large. For example, tables on faculty salaries and benefits were only affected to a very small extent. Also, degrees awarded at the bachelor's level or higher were not heavily affected. The largest impact was on private 2-year college enrollment. In contrast, most of the data on public 4-year colleges were affected to a minimal extent. The impact on enrollment in public 2-year colleges was noticeable in certain states, but was relatively small at the national level. Overall, total enrollment for all institutions was about one-half of a percent higher in 1996 for degree-granting institutions than for higher education institutions.

Prior to the establishment of IPEDS in 1986, HEGIS acquired and maintained statistical data on the characteristics and operations of institutions of higher education. Implemented in 1966, HEGIS was an annual universe survey of institutions accredited at the college level by an agency recognized by the Secretary of the U.S. Department of Education. These institutions were listed in NCES's Education Directory, Colleges and Universities.

HEGIS surveys collected information on institutional characteristics, faculty salaries, finances, enrollment, and degrees. Since these surveys, like IPEDS, were distributed to all higher education institutions, the data presented are not subject to sampling error. However, they are subject to nonsampling error, the sources of which varied with the survey instrument.

The NCES Taskforce for IPEDS Redesign recognized that there were issues related to the consistency of data definitions as well as the accuracy, reliability, and validity of other quality measures within and across surveys. The IPEDS redesign in 2000 provided institution-specific web-based data forms. While the new system shortened data processing time and provided better data consistency, it did not address the accuracy of the data provided by institutions.

Beginning in 2003–04 with the Prior Year Data Revision System, prior-year data have been available to institutions entering current data. This allows institutions to make changes to their prior-year entries either by adjusting the data or by providing missing data. These revisions allow the evaluation of the data's accuracy by looking at the changes made.

NCES conducted a study (NCES 2005-175) of the 2002–03 data that were revised in 2003–04 to determine the accuracy of the imputations, track the institutions that submitted revised data, and analyze the revised data they submitted. When institutions made changes to their data, it was assumed that the revised data were the "true" data. The data were analyzed for the number and type of institutions making changes, the type of changes, the magnitude of the changes, and the impact on published data.

Because NCES imputes missing data, imputation procedures were also addressed by the Redesign Taskforce. For the 2003–04 assessment, differences between revised values and values that were imputed in the original files were compared (i.e., revised value minus imputed value). These differences were then used to provide an assessment of the effectiveness of imputation procedures. The size of the differences also provides an indication of the accuracy of imputation procedures. To assess the overall impact of changes on aggregate IPEDS estimates, published tables for each component were reconstructed using the revised 2002–03 data. These reconstructed tables were then compared to the published tables to determine the magnitude of aggregate bias and the direction of this bias.

The fall 2011 and spring 2012 data collections were entirely web-based. Data were provided by "keyholders," institutional representatives appointed by campus chief executives, who were responsible for ensuring that survey data submitted by the institution were correct and complete. Because Title IV institutions are the primary focus of IPEDS and because these institutions are required to respond to the survey, response rates for Title IV institutions in the fall 2011 IPEDS collection were high. The Institutional Characteristics (IC) component response rate among all Title IV entities was 100.0 percent (all 7,479 Title IV entities responded). In addition, the response rates for the Completions and 12-Month Enrollment components were also 100.0 percent.

NCES statistical standards require that the potential for nonresponse bias for all institutions (including those in other U.S. jurisdictions) be analyzed for sectors for which the response rate is less than 85 percent. Due to response rates of 100.0 percent at the unit level for all three of the survey components, analysis for nonresponse bias was not necessary for the fall 2011 collection. However, data from four institutions that responded to the IC component contained item nonresponse. Price of attendance data collected during fall 2011 but covering prior academic years were imputed for these institutions.

Although IPEDS provides the most comprehensive data system for postsecondary education, there are 100 or more entities that collect their own information from postsecondary institutions. This raises the issue of how valid IPEDS data are when compared to education data collected by non-IPEDS sources. In the Data Quality Study, Thomson Peterson data were chosen to assess the validity of IPEDS data because Thomson Peterson is one of the largest and most comprehensive sources of postsecondary data available.

Not all IPEDS components could be compared to Thomson Peterson. Either Thomson Peterson did not collect data related to a particular IPEDS component, or the data items collected by Thomson Peterson were not comparable to the IPEDS items (i.e., the data items were defined differently). Comparisons were made for a selected number of data items in five areas—tuition and price, employees by assigned position, enrollment, student financial aid, and finance. More details on the accuracy and reliability of IPEDS data can be found in the Integrated Postsecondary Education Data System Data Quality Study (NCES 2005-175).

Further information on IPEDS may be obtained from

Jessica Shedd
Postsecondary, Adult, and Career Education Division
Postsecondary Institutional Studies Program
National Center for Education Statistics
1990 K Street NW
Washington, DC 20006
jessica.shedd@ed.gov
http://nces.ed.gov/ipeds

Fall (12-Month Enrollment)

Data on 12-month enrollment are collected for award levels ranging from postsecondary certificates of less than 1 year to doctoral degrees. The 12-month period during which data are collected is selected by the institution and can be either July 1 through June 30 or September 1 through August 31. Data are collected by race/ethnicity and gender and include unduplicated headcounts and instructional activity (contact or credit hours). These data are also used to calculate a full-time-equivalent (FTE) enrollment based on instructional activity. FTE enrollment is useful for gauging the size of the educational enterprise at the institution. Prior to the 2007–08 IPEDS data collection, the data collected in the 12-Month Enrollment component were part of the Fall Enrollment component, which is conducted during the Spring data collection period. However, to improve the timeliness of the data, a separate 12-Month Enrollment survey component was developed in 2007. These data are now collected in the fall for the previous academic year. Of the 7,479 Title IV entities eligible for the 12-Month Enrollment component of the fall 2011 data collection, 7,479 responded, for an approximate response rate of 100.0 percent.

Further information on the IPEDS 12-Month Enrollment component may be obtained from

Allison Bell
Postsecondary, Adult, and Career Education Division
Postsecondary Institutional Studies Program
National Center for Education Statistics
1990 K Street NW
Washington, DC 20006
allison.bell@ed.gov
http://nces.ed.gov/ipeds

Fall (Completions)

This survey was part of the HEGIS series throughout its existence. However, the degree classification taxonomy was revised in 1970–71, 1982–83, 1991–92, and 2002–03. Collection of degree data has been maintained through IPEDS.

Degrees-conferred trend tables arranged by the 2002–03 classification are included to provide consistent data from 1970–71 through the most recent year. Data on associate's and other formal awards below the baccalaureate degree, by field of study, cannot be made comparable with figures from years prior to 1982–83. The nonresponse rate does not appear to be a significant source of nonsampling error for this survey. The unweighted response rate over the years has been high, with the degree-granting institution response rate at 100.0 percent and the overall unweighted response rate for non-degree-granting institutions at 99.9 percent in fall 2010. Because of the high response rate for degree-granting institutions, nonsampling error caused by imputation is also minimal. Imputation methods and the response bias analysis for the fall 2010 Completions component are discussed in *Postsecondary Institutions and Price of Attendance in the United States: 2010–11, Degrees and Other Awards Conferred: 2009–10, and 12-Month Enrollment: 2009–10* (NCES 2011-250).

The *Integrated Postsecondary Education Data System Data Quality Study* (NCES 2005-175) indicated that most Title IV institutions supplying revised data on completions in 2003–04 were able to supply missing data for the prior year. The small differences between imputed data for the prior year and the revised actual data supplied by the institution indicated that the imputed values produced by NCES were acceptable.

Further information on the IPEDS Completions survey may be obtained from

Allison Bell
Postsecondary, Adult, and Career Education Division
Postsecondary Institutional Studies Program
National Center for Education Statistics
1990 K Street NW
Washington, DC 20006
allison.bell@ed.gov
http://nces.ed.gov/ipeds

Fall (Institutional Characteristics)

This survey collects the basic information necessary to classify institutions, including control, level, and types of programs offered, as well as information on tuition, fees, and room and board charges. Beginning in 2000, the survey collected institutional pricing data from institutions with first-time, full-time, degree/certificate-seeking undergraduate students. Unduplicated full-year enrollment counts and instructional activity are now collected in the Fall Enrollment survey. Beginning in 2008–09, student financial aid data collected includes greater detail. The overall unweighted response rate was 100.0 percent for Title IV degree-granting institutions for 2009 data.

The response rate for the Institutional Characteristics (IC) component among all Title IV entities was 100.0 percent (all 7,479 Title IV entities responded). Imputation methods for the fall 2011 Institutional Characteristics component are discussed in the 2011–12 *Integrated Postsecondary Education Data System (IPEDS) Methodology Report* (NCES 2012-293).

The *Integrated Postsecondary Education Data System Data Quality Study* (NCES 2005-175) looked at tuition and price in Title IV institutions. Only 8 percent of institutions in 2002–03 and 2003–04 reported the same data to IPEDS and Thomson Peterson consistently across all selected data items. Differences in wordings or survey items may account for some of these inconsistencies.

Further information on the IPEDS Institutional Characteristics survey may be obtained from

Tara Lawley
Postsecondary, Adult, and Career Education Division
Postsecondary Institutional Studies Program
National Center for Education Statistics
1990 K Street NW
Washington, DC 20006
tara.lawley@ed.gov
http://nces.ed.gov/ipeds

Winter (Human Resources)

The IPEDS Human Resources (HR) component comprises three sections: Employees by Assigned Position (EAP), Fall Staff, and Salaries.

Employees by Assigned Position

Data gathered by the Employees by Assigned Position (EAP) section categorizes all employees by full- or part-time status, faculty status, and primary function/occupational activity. Institutions with M.D. or D.O. programs are required to report their medical school employees separately. A response to the EAP was required of all 6,858 Title IV institutions and administrative offices in the United States and other jurisdictions for winter 2008–09, and 6,845, or 99.8 percent unweighted, responded. Of the 6,970 Title IV institutions and administrative offices required to respond to the winter 2009–10 EAP, 6,964, or 99.9 percent, responded. And of the 7,256 Title IV institutions and administrative offices expected to respond to the EAP for winter 2010–11, 7,252, or 99.9 percent, responded.

The primary functions/occupational activities of the EAP section are primarily instruction, instruction combined with research and/or public service, primarily research, primarily public service, executive/administrative/managerial, other professionals (support/service), graduate assistants, technical and paraprofessionals, clerical and secretarial, skilled crafts, and service/maintenance.

All full-time instructional faculty classified in the EAP full-time non-medical school part as either (1) primarily instruction or (2) instruction combined with research and/or public service are included in the Salaries section, unless they are exempt.

Fall Staff

The section categorizes all staff on the institution's payroll as of November 1 of the collection year, by employment status (full time or part time), primary function/occupational activity, gender, and race/ethnicity. These data elements are collected from degree-granting and non-degree-granting institutions; however, additional data elements are collected from degree-granting institutions and related administrative offices with 15 or more full-time staff. These elements include faculty status, contract length/teaching period, academic rank, salary class intervals, and newly hired full-time permanent staff.

The Fall Staff section, which is required only in odd-numbered reporting years, was not required during the 2008–09 HR data collection. However, of the 6,858 Title IV institutions and administrative offices in the United States and other jurisdictions, 3,295, or 48.0 percent unweighted, did provide data in the Fall Staff section that year. During the 2009–10 HR data collection, when all 6,970 Title IV institutions and administrative offices were required to respond to the Fall Staff section, 6,964, or 99.9 percent, did so. A response to the Fall Staff section of the 2010–11 HR collection was optional, and 3,364 Title IV institutions and administrative offices responded that year (a response rate of 46.3 percent).

The data quality study *Integrated Postsecondary Education Data System Data Quality Study* (NCES 2005-175) found that for 2003–04 employee data items, changes were made by 1.2 percent (77) of the institutions that responded. All who made changes made changes that resulted in different employee counts. For both institutional and aggregate differences, the changes had little impact on the original employee count submissions. A large number of institutions reported different staff data to IPEDS and Thomson Peterson; however, the magnitude of the differences was small—usually no more than 17 faculty members for any faculty variable.

Salaries

This section collects data for full-time instructional faculty on the institution's payroll as of November 1 of the collection year (except those in medical schools of the EAP section, as described above), by contract length/teaching period, gender, and academic rank. The reporting of data by faculty status in the Salaries section is required from 4-year degree-granting institutions and above only. Salary outlays and fringe benefits are also collected for full-time instructional staff on 9/10- and 11/12-month contracts/teaching periods. This section is applicable to degree-granting institutions unless exempt.

This institutional survey was conducted for most years from 1966–67 to 1987–88; it has been conducted annually since 1989–90, except for 2000–01. Although the survey form has changed a number of times during these years, only comparable data are presented.

Between 1966–67 and 1985–86, this survey differed from other HEGIS surveys in that imputations were not made for nonrespondents. Thus, there is some possibility that the salary averages presented may differ from the results of a complete enumeration of all colleges and universities. Beginning with the surveys for 1987–88, the IPEDS data tabulation procedures included imputations for survey nonrespondents. The unweighted response rate for the 2008–09 Salaries survey section was 99.9 percent. The response rate for the 2009–10 Salaries section was 100.0 percent (4,453 of the 4,455 required institutions responded), and the response rate for 2010–11 was 99.9 percent (4,561 of the 4,565 required institutions responded). Imputation methods for the 2010–11 Salaries survey section are discussed in *Employees in Postsecondary Institutions, Fall 2010, and Salaries of Full-Time Instructional Staff, 2010–11* (NCES 2012-276).

Although data from this survey are not subject to sampling error, sources of nonsampling error may include computational errors and misclassification in reporting and processing. The electronic reporting system does allow corrections to prior-year reported or missing data, and this should help with these problems. Also, NCES reviews individual institutions' data for internal and longitudinal consistency and contacts institutions to check inconsistent data.

The *Integrated Postsecondary Education Data System Data Quality Study* (NCES 2005-175) found that only 1.3 percent of the responding Title IV institutions in 2003–04 made changes to their salaries data. The differences between the imputed data and the revised data were small and found to have little impact on the published data.

Further information on the Human Resources component may be obtained from

IPEDS Staff
Postsecondary, Adult, and Career Education Division
Postsecondary Institutional Studies Program
National Center for Education Statistics
1990 K Street NW
Washington, DC 20006
http://nces.ed.gov/ncestaff/SurvDet1.asp?surveyID=010

Winter (Student Financial Aid)

This component was part of the spring data collection from IPEDS data collection years 2000–01 to 2010–11, but it moved to the winter data collection starting with the 2011–12 IPEDS data collection year. This move will aid in the timing of the net price of attendance calculations displayed on College Navigator (http://nces.ed.gov/collegenavigator).

Financial aid data are collected for undergraduate students. Data are collected regarding federal grants, state and local government grants, institutional grants, and loans. The collected data include the number of students receiving each type of financial assistance and the average amount of aid received by type of aid. Beginning in 2008–09, student financial aid data collected includes greater detail on types of aid offered.

In the winter 2011–12 data collection, the Student Financial Aid component presented data on the number of full-time, first-time degree- and certificate-seeking undergraduate financial aid recipients for the 2010–11 academic year. The response rate for this component was 99.8 percent for degree-granting institutions overall.

Further information on the IPEDS Student Financial Aid survey may be obtained from

Tara Lawley
Postsecondary, Adult, and Career Education Division
Postsecondary Institutional Studies Program
National Center for Education Statistics
1990 K Street NW
Washington, DC 20006
tara.lawley@ed.gov
http://nces.ed.gov/ipeds

Spring (Fall Enrollment)

This survey has been part of the HEGIS and IPEDS series since 1966. Response rates for this survey have been relatively high, generally exceeding 85 percent. Beginning in 2000, with web-based data collection, higher response rates were attained. In the Spring data collection, where the Fall Enrollment component covered fall 2009, the overall response rate was 100.0 percent for degree-granting institutions. The response rate for 4-year private not-for-profit institutions was 99.9 percent, while 4-year public, 4-year private-for-profit, 2-year public, 2-year private not-for-profit, and 2-year private for-profit institutions had response rates of 100.0 percent. Imputation methods for the Fall Enrollment component of the Spring 2010 data collection are discussed in *Enrollment in Postsecondary Institutions, Fall 2009; Graduation Rates, 2003 and 2006 Cohorts; and Financial Statistics, Fiscal Year 2009* (NCES 2011-230).

In the spring 2011 data collection, where the Fall Enrollment component covered fall 2010, the response rate was 100.0 percent for degree-granting institutions overall. (The response rates were also 100.0 percent for 4-year and 2-year public, private nonprofit, and private for-profit degree-granting institutions). Imputation procedures for the Fall Enrollment component of the spring 2011 data collection are presented in *Enrollment in Postsecondary Institutions, Fall 2010; Financial Statistics, Fiscal Year 2010; and Graduation Rates, Selected Cohorts, 2002–07* (NCES 2012-280).

Beginning with the fall 1986 survey and the introduction of IPEDS (see above), the survey was redesigned. The survey allows (in alternating years) for the collection of age and residence data. Beginning in 2000, the survey collected instructional activity and unduplicated headcount data, which are needed to compute a standardized, full-time-equivalent (FTE) enrollment statistic for the entire academic year.

The *Integrated Postsecondary Education Data System Data Quality Study* (NCES 2005-175) showed that public institutions made the majority of changes to enrollment data during the 2004 revision period. The majority of changes were made to unduplicated headcount data, with the net differences between the original data and the revised data at about 1 percent. Part-time students in general and enrollment in private not-for-profit institutions were often underestimated. The fewest changes by institutions were to Classification of Instructional Programs (CIP) code data. (The CIP is a taxonomic coding scheme that contains titles and descriptions of primarily postsecondary instructional programs.) More institutions provided enrollment data to IPEDS than to Thomson Peterson. A fairly high percentage of institutions that provided data to both provided the same data, and among those that did not, the difference in magnitude was less than 10 percent.

Further information on the IPEDS Fall Enrollment survey may be obtained from

Allison Bell
Postsecondary, Adult, and Career Education Division
Postsecondary Institutional Studies Program
National Center for Education Statistics
1990 K Street NW
Washington, DC 20006
allison.bell@ed.gov
http://nces.ed.gov/ipeds

Spring (Finance)

This survey was part of the HEGIS series and has been continued under IPEDS. Substantial changes were made in the financial survey instruments in fiscal year (FY) 1976, FY 82, FY 87, FY 97, and FY 02. While these changes were significant, considerable effort has been made to present only comparable information on trends and to note inconsistencies. The FY 76 survey instrument contained numerous revisions to earlier survey forms, which made direct comparisons of line items very difficult. Beginning in FY 82, Pell Grant data were collected in the categories of federal restricted grant and contract revenues and restricted scholarship and fellowship expenditures. Finance tables including data prior to 2000 have been adjusted by subtracting the largely duplicative Pell Grant amounts from the later data to maintain comparability with pre-FY 82 data. The introduction of IPEDS in the FY 87 survey included several important changes to the survey instrument and data processing procedures. Beginning in FY 97, data for private institutions were collected using new financial concepts consistent with Financial Accounting Standards Board (FASB) reporting standards, which provide a more comprehensive view of college finance activities. The data for public institutions continued to be collected using the older survey form. The data for public and private institutions were no longer comparable and, as a result, no longer presented together in analysis tables. In FY 01, public institutions had the option of either continuing to report using Government Accounting Standards Board (GASB) standards or using the new FASB reporting standards. Beginning in FY 02, public institutions had three options: the original GASB standards, the FASB standards, or the new GASB Statement 35 standards (GASB35). Because of the complexity of the multiple forms used by public institutions, finance data for public institutions for some recent years are not available.

Possible sources of nonsampling error in the financial statistics include nonresponse, imputation, and misclassification. The unweighted response rate has been about 85 to 90 percent for most of the historic years; however, in more recent years, response rates have been much higher because Title IV institutions are required to respond. The 2002 IPEDS data collection was a full-scale web-based collection, which offered features that improved the quality and timeliness of the data. The ability of IPEDS to tailor online data entry forms for each institution based on characteristics such as institutional control, level of institution, and calendar system, and the institutions' ability to submit their data online, were two such features that improved response. The response rate for the FY 2010 Finance survey component was 99.8 percent for Title IV degree-granting institutions. Data collection procedures for the FY 2010 survey are discussed in *Enrollment in Postsecondary Institutions, Fall 2011; Financial Statistics, Fiscal Year 2011; and Graduation Rates, Selected Cohorts, 2003–2008: First Look (Provisional Data)* (NCES 2012-174REV). Two general methods of imputation were used in HEGIS. If prior-year data were available for a nonresponding institution, they were inflated using the Higher Education Price Index and adjusted according to changes in enrollments. If prior-year data were not available, current data were used from peer institutions selected for location (state or region), control, level, and enrollment size of institution. In most cases, estimates for nonreporting institutions in HEGIS were made using data from peer institutions.

Beginning with FY 87, IPEDS included all postsecondary institutions, but maintained comparability with earlier surveys by allowing 2- and 4-year institutions to be tabulated separately. For FY 87 through FY 91, in order to maintain comparability with the historical time series of HEGIS institutions, data were combined from two of the three different survey forms that make up IPEDS. The vast majority of the data were tabulated from form 1, which was used to collect information from public and private not-for-profit 2- and 4-year colleges. Form 2, a condensed form, was used to gather data for 2-year for-profit institutions. Because of the differences in the data requested on the two forms, several assumptions were made about the form 2 reports so that their figures could be included in the degree-granting institution totals.

In IPEDS, the form 2 institutions were not asked to separate appropriations from grants and contracts, nor were they asked to separate state from local sources of funding. For the form 2 institutions, all federal revenues were assumed to be federal grants and contracts, and all state and local revenues were assumed to be restricted state grants and contracts. All other form 2 sources of revenue, except for tuition and fees and sales and services of educational activities, were included under "other." Similar adjustments were made to the expenditure accounts. The form 2 institutions reported instruction and scholarship and fellowship expenditures only. All other educational and general expenditures were allocated to academic support.

The *Integrated Postsecondary Education Data System Data Quality Study* (NCES 2005-175) found that only a small percentage (2.9 percent, or 168) of postsecondary institutions either revised 2002–03 data or submitted data for items they previously left unreported. Though relatively few institutions made changes, the changes made were relatively large—greater than 10 percent of the original data. With a few exceptions, these changes, large as they were, did not greatly affect the aggregate totals.

Again, institutions were more likely to report data to IPEDS than to Thomson Peterson, and there was a higher percentage reporting different values among those reporting to both. The magnitude of the difference was generally greater for research expenditures. It is likely that the large differences are a function of the way institutions report these data to both entities.

Further information on the IPEDS Finance survey may be obtained from

Colleen Lenihan
Postsecondary, Adult, and Career Education Division
Postsecondary Institutional Studies Program
National Center for Education Statistics
1990 K Street NW
Washington, DC 20006
colleen.lenihan@ed.gov
http://nces.ed.gov/ipeds

Spring (Graduation Rates and Graduation Rates 200 Percent)

Graduation rates data are collected for full-time, first-time degree- and certificate-seeking undergraduate students. Data included are the number of students entering the institution as full-time, first-time degree- or certificate-seeking students in a particular year (cohort), by race/ethnicity and gender; the number of students completing their program within a time period equal to 1½ times (150 percent) the normal period of time; and the number of students who transferred to other institutions.

In the spring 2012 data collection, the Graduation Rates component collected counts of full-time, first-time degree- and certificate-seeking undergraduate students entering an institution in the cohort year (4-year institutions used the cohort year 2005; less-than-4-year institutions used the cohort year 2008), and their completion status as of August 31, 2011 (150 percent of normal program completion time) at the institution initially entered. The response rate for this component was 99.8 percent.

The 200 Percent Graduation Rates component collected counts of full-time, first-time degree- and certificate-seeking undergraduate students beginning their post-secondary education in the reference period and their completion status as of August 31, 2011 (200 percent of normal program completion time) at the same institution where the students started. Four-year institutions report on bachelor's or equivalent degree-seeking students and use cohort year 2003 as the reference period, while less-than-4-year institutions report on all students in the cohort and use cohort year 2007 as the reference period. The response rate for this component was 99.8 percent.

Further information on the IPEDS Graduation surveys may be obtained from

Allison Bell
Postsecondary, Adult, and Career Education Division
Postsecondary Institutional Studies Program
National Center for Education Statistics
1990 K Street NW
Washington, DC 20006
allison.bell@ed.gov
http://nces.ed.gov/ipeds

National Assessment of Educational Progress

The National Assessment of Educational Progress (NAEP) is a series of cross-sectional studies initially implemented in 1969 to assess the educational achievement of U.S. students and monitor changes in those achievements. In the main national NAEP, a nationally representative sample of students is assessed at grades 4, 8, and 12 in various academic subjects.

The assessments are based on frameworks developed by the National Assessment Governing Board (NAGB). Items include both multiple-choice and constructed-response (requiring written answers) items. Results are reported in two ways: by average score and by achievement level. Average scores are reported for the nation, for participating states and jurisdictions, and for subgroups of the population. Percentages of students meeting certain achievement levels are also reported for these groups. The achievement levels, developed by NAGB, are at or above *Basic*, at or above *Proficient*, and at or above *Advanced*.

From 1990 until 2001, main NAEP was conducted for states and other jurisdictions that chose to participate. In 2002, under the provisions of the No Child Left Behind Act of 2001, all states began to participate in main NAEP and an aggregate of all state samples replaced the separate national sample.

Mathematics assessments were administered in 2000, 2003, 2005, 2007, 2009, and 2011. In 2005, NAGB called for the development of a new mathematics framework. The revisions made to the mathematics framework for the 2005 assessment were intended to reflect recent curricular emphases and better assess the specific objectives for students at each grade level.

The revised mathematics framework focuses on two dimensions: mathematical content and cognitive demand. By considering these two dimensions for each item in the assessment, the framework ensures that NAEP assesses an appropriate balance of content, as well as a variety of ways of knowing and doing mathematics.

For grades 4 and 8, comparisons over time can be made among the assessments prior to and after the implementation of the 2005 framework. The changes to the grade 12 assessment were too drastic to allow the results to be directly compared with previous years. The changes to the grade 12 assessment included adding more questions on algebra, data analysis, and probability to reflect changes in high school mathematics standards and coursework, as well as the merging of the measurement and geometry content areas. The reporting scale for grade 12 mathematics was changed from 0–500 to 0–300. For more information regarding the 2005 mathematics framework revisions, see http://nces.ed.gov/nationsreportcard/mathematics/frameworkcomparison.asp.

Reading assessments were administered in 2000, 2002, 2003, 2005, 2007, 2009, and 2011. In 2009, a new framework was developed for the 4th-, 8th-, and 12th-grade NAEP reading assessments.

Both a content alignment study and a reading trend or bridge study were conducted to determine if the "new" assessment was comparable to the "old" assessment. Overall, the results of the special analyses suggested that the old and new assessments were similar in terms of their item and scale characteristics and the results they produced for important demographic groups of students. Thus, it was determined that the results of the 2009 reading assessment could still be compared to those from earlier assessment years, thereby maintaining the trend lines first established in 1992. For more information regarding the 2009 reading framework revisions, see http://nces.ed.gov/nationsreportcard/reading/whatmeasure.asp.

Further information on NAEP may be obtained from

Arnold Goldstein
Assessment Division
State Support and Constituency Outreach
National Center for Education Statistics
1990 K Street NW
Washington, DC 20006
arnold.goldstein@ed.gov
http://nces.ed.gov/nationsreportcard

Private School Universe Survey

The purposes of the Private School Universe Survey (PSS) data collection activities are (1) to build an accurate and complete list of private schools to serve as a sampling frame for NCES sample surveys of private schools and (2) to report data on the total number of private schools, teachers, and students in the survey universe. Begun in 1989 under the U.S. Census Bureau, the PSS has been conducted every 2 years, and data for the 1989–90, 1991–92, 1993–94, 1995–96, 1997–98, 1999–2000, 2001–02, 2003–04, 2005–06, 2007–08, and 2009–10 school years have been released. A First Look report of the 2009–10 PSS data was released in May 2011.

The PSS produces data similar to that of the CCD for public schools, and can be used for public-private comparisons. The data are useful for a variety of policy-

and research-relevant issues, such as the growth of religiously affiliated schools, the number of private high school graduates, the length of the school year for various private schools, and the number of private school students and teachers.

The target population for this universe survey is all private schools in the United States that meet the PSS criteria of a private school (i.e., the private school is an institution that provides instruction for any of grades K through 12, has one or more teachers to give instruction, is not administered by a public agency, and is not operated in a private home). The survey universe is composed of schools identified from a variety of sources. The main source is a list frame initially developed for the 1989–90 PSS. The list is updated regularly by matching it with lists provided by nationwide private school associations, state departments of education, and other national guides and sources that list private schools. The other source is an area frame search in approximately 124 geographic areas, conducted by the U.S. Census Bureau.

Of the 40,302 schools included in the 2009–10 sample, 10,229 were found ineligible for the survey. Those not responding numbered 1,856, and those responding numbered 28,217. The unweighted response rate for the 2009–10 PSS survey was 93.8 percent.

Further information on the PSS may be obtained from

Steve Broughman
Elementary/Secondary and Libraries Studies Division
Elementary/Secondary Sample Survey Studies Program
National Center for Education Statistics
1990 K Street NW
Washington, DC 20006
stephen.broughman@ed.gov
http://nces.ed.gov/surveys/pss

Projections of Education Statistics

Since 1964, NCES has published projections of key statistics for elementary and secondary schools and institutions of higher education. The latest report is titled *Projections of Education Statistics to 2021* (NCES 2013-008). These projections include statistics for enrollments, instructional staff, graduates, earned degrees, and expenditures. These reports include several alternative projection series and a methodology section describing the techniques and assumptions used to prepare them.

Differences between the reported and projected values are, of course, almost inevitable. An evaluation of past projections revealed that, at the elementary and secondary level, projections of enrollments have been quite accurate: mean absolute percentage differences for enrollment ranged from 0.3 to 1.3 percent for projections from 1 to 5 years in the future, while those for teachers were less than 3 percent. At the higher education level, projections of enrollment have been fairly accurate: mean absolute percentage differences were 5 percent or less for projections from 1 to 5 years into the future.

Further information on *Projections of Education Statistics* may be obtained from

William Hussar
Early Childhood, International, and Crosscutting Studies Division
Annual Reports Program
National Center for Education Statistics
1990 K Street NW
Washington, DC 20006
william.hussar@ed.gov
http://nces.ed.gov/annuals

Other Department of Education Agencies

Office of Special Education Programs

Annual Report to Congress on the Implementation of the Individuals with Disabilities Education Act

The Individuals with Disabilities Education Act (IDEA) is a law ensuring services to children with disabilities throughout the nation. IDEA governs how states and public agencies provide early intervention, special education, and related services to more than 6.5 million eligible infants, toddlers, children, and youth with disabilities.

The Individuals with Disabilities Education Act (IDEA), formerly the Education of the Handicapped Act (EHA), requires the Secretary of Education to transmit to Congress annually a report describing the progress made in serving the nation's children with disabilities. This annual report contains information on children served by public schools under the provisions of Part B of the IDEA and on children served in state-operated programs for the disabled under Chapter I of the Elementary and Secondary Education Act.

Statistics on children receiving special education and related services in various settings and school personnel providing such services are reported in an annual submission of data to the Office of Special Education Programs (OSEP) by the 50 states, the District of Columbia, and the outlying areas. The child count information is based on the number of children with disabilities receiving special education and related services on December 1 of each year. Count information is available from http://www.ideadata.org.

Since each participant in programs for the disabled is reported to OSEP, the data are not subject to sampling error. However, nonsampling error can arise from a variety of sources. Some states follow a noncategorical approach to the delivery of special education services, but produce counts of students by disabling condition because Part B of the EHA requires it. In those states that do categorize their disabled students, definitions and labeling practices vary.

Further information on this annual report to Congress may be obtained from

Office of Special Education Programs
Office of Special Education and Rehabilitative Services
U.S. Department of Education
400 Maryland Avenue SW
Washington, DC 20202-7100
http://www.ed.gov/about/reports/annual/osep/index.html
http://idea.ed.gov/
http://www.ideadata.org

Other Governmental Agencies

Bureau of Justice Statistics

National Crime Victimization Survey (NCVS)

The National Crime Victimization Survey (NCVS), administered for the U.S. Bureau of Justice Statistics by the U.S. Census Bureau, is the nation's primary source of information on crime and the victims of crime. Initiated in 1972 and redesigned in 1992, the NCVS collects detailed information on the frequency and nature of the crimes of rape, sexual assault, robbery, aggravated and simple assault, theft, household burglary, and motor vehicle theft experienced by Americans and their households each year. The survey measures both crimes reported to police and crimes not reported to the police.

NCVS estimates presented may differ from those in previous published reports. This is because a small number of victimizations, referred to as series victimizations, are included using a new counting strategy. High-frequency repeat victimizations, or series victimizations, are six or more similar but separate victimizations that occur with such frequency that the victim is unable to recall each individual event or describe each event in detail. As part of ongoing research efforts associated with the redesign of the NCVS, BJS investigated ways to include high-frequency repeat victimizations, or series victimizations, in estimates of criminal victimization. Including series victimizations would obtain a more accurate estimate of victimization. BJS has decided to include series victimizations using the victim's estimates of the number of times the victimizations occurred over the past 6 months, capping the number of victimizations within each series at a maximum of 10. This strategy for counting series victimizations balances the desire to estimate national rates and account for the experiences of persons with repeat victimizations while noting that some estimation errors exist in the number of times these victimizations occurred. Including series victimizations in national rates results in rather large increases in the level of violent victimization; however, trends in violence are generally similar regardless of whether series victimizations are included. For more information on the new counting strategy and supporting research, see *Methods for Counting High-Frequency Repeat Victimizations in the National Crime Victimization Survey* at http://bjs.ojp.usdoj.gov/content/pub/pdf/mchfrv.pdf.

Readers should note that in 2003, in accordance with changes to the Office of Management and Budget's standards for the classification of federal data on race and ethnicity, the NCVS item on race/ethnicity was modified. A question on Hispanic origin is followed by a question on race. The new question about race allows the respondent to choose more than one race and delineates Asian as a separate category from Native Hawaiian or Other Pacific Islander. Analysis conducted by the Demographic Surveys Division at the U.S. Census Bureau showed that the new question had very little impact on the aggregate racial distribution of the NCVS respondents, with one exception: There was a 1.6 percentage point decrease in the percentage of respondents who reported themselves as White. Due to changes in race/ethnicity categories, comparisons of race/ethnicity across years should be made with caution.

There were changes in the sample design and survey methodology in the 2006 NCVS that may have affected survey estimates. Caution should be used when comparing the 2006 estimates to those of other years. Data from 2007 onward are comparable to earlier years. Analyses of the 2007 estimates indicate that the program changes made in 2006 had relatively small effects on NCVS changes. For more information on the 2006 NCVS data, see *Criminal Victimization, 2006,* at http://bjs.ojp.usdoj.gov/content/pub/pdf/cv06.pdf, the technical notes at http://bjs.ojp.usdoj.gov/content/pub/pdf/cv06tn.pdf, and *Criminal Victimization, 2007,* at http://bjs.ojp.usdoj.gov/content/pub/pdf/cv07.pdf.

The number of NCVS-eligible households in the sample in 2011 was about 89,000. They were selected using a stratified, multistage cluster design. In the first stage, the primary sampling units (PSUs), consisting of counties or groups of counties, were selected. In the second stage, smaller areas, called Enumeration Districts (EDs), were selected from each sampled PSU. Finally, from selected EDs, clusters of four households, called segments, were selected for interview. At each stage, the selection was done proportionate to population size in order to create a self-weighting sample. The final sample was augmented to account for households constructed after the decennial Census. Within each sampled household, U.S. Census Bureau personnel attempt to interview all household members age 12 and older to determine whether they had been victimized by the measured crimes during the 6 months preceding the interview.

The first NCVS interview with a housing unit is conducted in person. Subsequent interviews are conducted by telephone, if possible. About 72,000 persons age 12 and older are interviewed each 6 months. Households remain in the sample for 3 years and are interviewed seven times at 6-month intervals. Since the survey's inception, the initial interview at each sample unit has been used only to bound future interviews to establish a time frame to avoid duplication of crimes uncovered in these subsequent interviews. Beginning in 2006, data from the initial interview have been adjusted to account for the effects of bounding and included in the survey estimates. After their seventh interview, households are replaced by new sample households. The NCVS has consistently obtained a response rate of over 90 percent at the household level. The completion rates for persons within households in 2011 were about 88 percent. Weights were developed to permit estimates for the total U.S. population 12 years and older.

Further information on the NCVS may be obtained from

Jennifer Truman
Victimization Statistics Branch
Bureau of Justice Statistics
810 Seventh Street NW
Washington, DC 20531
jennifer.truman@usdoj.gov

Bureau of Labor Statistics

Consumer Price Indexes

The Consumer Price Index (CPI) represents changes in prices of all goods and services purchased for consumption by urban households. Indexes are available for two population groups: a CPI for All Urban Consumers (CPI-U) and a CPI for Urban Wage Earners and Clerical Workers (CPI-W). Unless otherwise specified, data are adjusted for inflation using the CPI-U. These values are frequently adjusted to a school-year basis by averaging the July through June figures. Price indexes are available for the United States, the four Census regions, size of city, cross-classifications of regions and size classes, and 26 local areas. The major uses of the CPI include as an economic indicator, as a deflator of other economic series, and as a means of adjusting income.

Also available is the Consumer Price Index research series using current methods (CPI-U-RS), which presents an estimate of the CPI-U from 1978 to the present that incorporates most of the improvements that the Bureau of Labor Statistics has made over that time span into the entire series. The historical price index series of the CPI-U does not reflect these changes, though these changes do make the present and future CPI more accurate. The limitations of the CPI-U-RS include considerable uncertainty surrounding the magnitude of the adjustments and the several improvements in the CPI that have not been incorporated into the CPI-U-RS for

various reasons. Nonetheless, the CPI-U-RS can serve as a valuable proxy for researchers needing a historical estimate of inflation using current methods.

Further information on consumer price indexes may be obtained from

Bureau of Labor Statistics
U.S. Department of Labor
2 Massachusetts Avenue NE
Washington, DC 20212
http://www.bls.gov/cpi

Employment and Unemployment Surveys

Statistics on the employment and unemployment status of the population and related data are compiled by the Bureau of Labor Statistics (BLS) using data from the Current Population Survey (CPS) (see below) and other surveys. The Current Population Survey, a monthly household survey conducted by the U.S. Census Bureau for the Bureau of Labor Statistics, provides a comprehensive body of information on the employment and unemployment experience of the nation's population, classified by age, sex, race, and various other characteristics.

Further information on unemployment surveys may be obtained from

Bureau of Labor Statistics
U.S. Department of Labor
2 Massachusetts Avenue NE
Washington, DC 20212
cpsinfo@bls.gov
http://www.bls.gov/bls/employment.htm

Census Bureau

American Community Survey (ACS)

The Census Bureau introduced the American Community Survey (ACS) in 1996. Fully implemented in 2005, it provides a large monthly sample of demographic, socioeconomic, and housing data comparable in content to the Long Forms of the Decennial Census up to and including the 2000 long form. Aggregated over time, these data will serve as a replacement for the Long Form of the Decennial Census. The survey includes questions mandated by federal law, federal regulations, and court decisions.

Since 2005, the survey has been mailed to approximately 250,000 addresses in the United States and Puerto Rico each month, or about 2.5 percent of the population annually. A larger proportion of addresses in small governmental units (e.g., American Indian reservations, small counties, and towns) also receive the survey. The monthly sample size is designed to approximate the ratio used in the 2000 Census, which requires more intensive distribution in these areas. The ACS covers the U.S. resident population, which includes the entire civilian, noninstitutionalized population; incarcerated persons; institutionalized persons; and the active duty military who are in the United States. In 2006, the ACS began interviewing residents in group quarter facilities. Institutionalized group quarters include adult and juvenile correctional facilities, nursing facilities, and other health care facilities. Noninstitutionalized group quarters include college and university housing, military barracks, and other noninstitutional facilities such as workers and religious group quarters and temporary shelters for the homeless.

National-level data from the ACS are available from 2000 onward. The ACS produces 1-year estimates for populations of 65,000 and over, 3-year estimates for populations of 20,000 or over, and 5-year estimates for populations of almost any size. To illustrate, 2011 ACS 1-year estimates represented data collected between January 1, 2011, and December 31, 2011; 2009–11 ACS 3-year estimates represented data collected between January 1, 2009, and December 31, 2011; and the 2007–11 ACS 5-year estimates represented data collected between January 1, 2007, and December 31, 2011.

Further information about the ACS is available at http://www.census.gov/acs/www/.

Current Population Survey

The Current Population Survey (CPS) is a monthly survey of about 60,000 households conducted by the U.S. Census Bureau for the Bureau of Labor Statistics. The CPS is the primary source of information of labor force statistics for the U.S. noninstitutionalized population (e.g., excludes military personnel and their families living on bases and inmates of correctional institutions). In addition, supplemental questionnaires are used to provide further information about the U.S. population. Specifically, in October, detailed questions regarding school enrollment and school characteristics are asked. In March, detailed questions regarding income are asked.

The current sample design, introduced in July 2001, includes about 72,000 households. Each month about 58,900 of the 72,000 households are eligible for interview, and of those, 7 to 10 percent are not interviewed because of temporary absence or unavailability. Information is obtained each month from those in the household who are 15 years of age and older, and demographic data are collected for children 0–14 years of age. In addition, supplemental questions regarding school enrollment are asked about eligible household members ages 3 and older. Prior to July 2001, data were collected in the CPS from about 50,000 dwelling units. The samples are initially selected based on the decennial census files and are periodically updated to reflect new housing construction.

A major redesign of the CPS was implemented in January 1994 to improve the quality of the data collected. Survey questions were revised, new questions were added, and computer-assisted interviewing methods were used for the survey data collection. Further information about the redesign is available in *Current Population Survey, October 1995: (School Enrollment Supplement) Technical Documentation*.

Caution should be used when comparing data from 1994 through 2001 with data from 1993 and earlier. Data from 1994 through 2001 reflect 1990 census-based population controls, while data from 1993 and earlier reflect 1980 or earlier census-based population controls. Also use caution when comparing data from 1994 through 2001 with data from 2002 onward, as data from 2002 reflect 2000 census-based controls. Changes in population controls generally have relatively little impact on summary measures such as means, medians, and percentage distributions. They can have a significant impact on population counts. For example, use of the 1990 census-based population control resulted in about a 1 percent increase in the civilian noninstitutional population and in the number of families and households. Thus, estimates of levels for data collected in 1994 and later years will differ from those for earlier years by more than what could be attributed to actual changes in the population. These differences could be disproportionately greater for certain subpopulation groups than for the total population.

Beginning in 2003, race/ethnicity questions expanded to include information on people of two or more races. Native Hawaiian/Pacific Islander data are collected separately from Asian data. The questions have also been worded to make it clear that self-reported data on race/ethnicity should reflect the race/ethnicity with which the responder identifies, rather than what may be written in official documentation.

The estimation procedure employed for monthly CPS data involves inflating weighted sample results to independent estimates of characteristics of the civilian noninstitutional population in the United States by age, sex, and race. These independent estimates are based on statistics from decennial censuses; statistics on births, deaths, immigration, and emigration; and statistics on the population in the armed services. Generalized standard error tables are provided in the Current Population Reports; methods for deriving standard errors can be found within the CPS technical documentation at http://www.census.gov/cps/methodology/techdocs.html. The CPS data are subject to both nonsampling and sampling errors.

Prior to 2009, standard errors were estimated using the generalized variance function. The generalized variance function is a simple model that expressed the variance as a function of the expected value of a survey estimate. Beginning with March 2009 CPS data, standard errors were estimated using replicate weight methodology. Those interested in using CPS household-level supplement replicate weights to calculate variances may refer to *Estimating Current Population Survey (CPS) Household-Level Supplement Variances Using Replicate Weights* at http://smpbff2.dsd.census.gov/pub/cps/supps/HH-level_Use_of_the_Public_Use_Replicate_Weight_File.doc.

Further information on CPS may be obtained from

Education and Social Stratification Branch
Population Division
Census Bureau
U.S. Department of Commerce
4600 Silver Hill Road
Washington, DC 20233
http://www.census.gov/cps

Dropouts

Each October, the Current Population Survey (CPS) includes supplemental questions on the enrollment status of the population ages 3 years and over as part of the monthly basic survey on labor force participation. In addition to gathering the information on school enrollment, with the limitations on accuracy as noted below under "School Enrollment," the survey data permit calculations of dropout rates. Both status and event dropout rates are tabulated from the October CPS. Event rates describe the proportion of students who leave school each year without completing a high school program. Status rates provide cumulative data on dropouts among all young adults within a specified age range. Status rates are higher than event rates because they include all dropouts ages 16 through 24, regardless of when they last attended school.

In addition to other survey limitations, dropout rates may be affected by survey coverage and exclusion of the institutionalized population. The incarcerated population has grown more rapidly and has a higher dropout rate than the general population. Dropout rates for the total population might be higher than those for the noninstitutionalized population if the prison and jail populations were included in the dropout rate calculations. On the other hand, if military personnel, who tend to be high school graduates, were included, it might offset some or all of the impact from the theoretical inclusion of the jail and prison population.

Another area of concern with tabulations involving young people in household surveys is the relatively low coverage ratio compared to older age groups. CPS undercoverage results from missed housing units and missed people within sample households. Overall CPS undercoverage for March 2008 is estimated to be about 12 percent. CPS undercoverage varies with age, sex, and race. Generally, undercoverage is larger for males than for females and larger for Blacks than for non-Blacks. For example, in 2008 the undercoverage ratio for Black 20- to 24-year-old males is 30 percent. The CPS weighting procedure partially corrects for the bias due to undercoverage. Further information on CPS methodology may be obtained from http://www.census.gov/cps.

Further information on the calculation of dropouts and dropout rates may be obtained from *High School Dropout and Completion Rates in the United States: 2007* at http://nces.ed.gov/pubsearch/pubsinfo.asp?pubid=2009064 or by contacting

Chris Chapman
Early Childhood, International, and Crosscutting Studies Division
Early Childhood and Household Studies Program
National Center for Education Statistics
1990 K Street NW
Washington, DC 20006
chris.chapman@ed.gov

Educational Attainment

Reports documenting educational attainment are produced by the Census Bureau using March CPS supplement (Annual Social and Economic Supplement [ASEC]) results. The sample size for the 2012 ASEC supplement (including basic CPS) was about 99,000 households. The latest release is *Educational Attainment in the United States: 2012*; the tables may be downloaded at http://www.census.gov/hhes/socdemo/education/data/cps/2012/tables.html.

In addition to the general constraints of CPS, some data indicate that the respondents have a tendency to overestimate the educational level of members of their household. Some inaccuracy is due to a lack of the respondent's knowledge of the exact educational attainment of each household member and the hesitancy to acknowledge anything less than a high school education. Another cause of nonsampling variability is the change in the numbers in the armed services over the years.

Further information on CPS's educational attainment may be obtained from the CPS website at http://www.census.gov/cps.

Further information on CPS's educational attainment data may be obtained from

Education and Social Stratification Branch
Census Bureau
U.S. Department of Commerce
4600 Silver Hill Road
Washington, DC 20233
http://www.census.gov/hhes/socdemo/education

School Enrollment

Each October, the Current Population Survey (CPS) includes supplemental questions on the enrollment status of the population ages 3 years and over. Prior to 2001, the October supplement consisted of approximately 47,000 interviewed households. Beginning with the October 2001 supplement, the sample was expanded by 9,000 to a total of approximately 56,000 interviewed households. The main sources of nonsampling variability in the responses to the supplement are those inherent in the survey instrument. The question of current enrollment may not be answered accurately for various reasons. Some respondents may not know current grade information for every student in the household, a problem especially prevalent for households with members in college or in nursery school. Confusion over college credits or hours taken by a student may make it difficult to determine the year in which the student is enrolled. Problems may occur with the definition of nursery school (a group or class organized to provide educational experiences for children) where respondents' interpretations of "educational experiences" vary.

For the October 2011 basic CPS, the household-level nonresponse rate was 8.71 percent. The person-level nonresponse rate for the school enrollment supplement was an additional 6.9 percent. Since the basic CPS nonresponse rate is a household-level rate and the school enrollment supplement nonresponse rate is a person-level rate, these rates cannot be combined to derive an overall nonresponse rate. Nonresponding households may have fewer persons than interviewed ones, so combining these rates may lead to an overestimate of the true overall nonresponse rate for persons for the school enrollment supplement.

Further information on CPS methodology may be obtained from http://www.census.gov/cps.

Further information on the CPS School Enrollment Supplement may be obtained from

Education and Social Stratification Branch
Census Bureau
U.S. Department of Commerce
4600 Silver Hill Road
Washington, DC 20233
http://www.census.gov/hhes/school/index.html

Decennial Census, Population Estimates, and Population Projections

The Decennial Census is a universe survey mandated by the U.S. Constitution. It is a questionnaire sent to every household in the country, and it is composed of seven questions about the household and its members (name, sex, age, relationship, Hispanic origin, race, and whether the housing unit is owned or rented). The Census Bureau also produces annual estimates of the resident population by demographic characteristics (age, sex, race, and Hispanic origin) for the nation, states, and counties, as well as national and state projections for the resident population. The reference date for population estimates is July 1 of the given year. With each new issue of July 1 estimates, the Census Bureau revises estimates for each year back to the last census. Previously published estimates are superseded and archived.

Census respondents self-report race and ethnicity. In the 2000 Census, they were first asked, "Is this person Spanish/Hispanic/Latino?" and then given the following options: No, not Spanish/Hispanic/Latino; Yes, Puerto Rican; Yes, Mexican, Mexican American, Chicano; Yes, Cuban; and Yes, other Spanish/Hispanic/Latino (with space to print the specific group). The next question was "What is this person's race?" The options were White; Black, African American, or Negro; American Indian or Alaska Native (with space to print the name of enrolled or principal tribe); Asian Indian; Japanese; Native Hawaiian; Chinese; Korean; Guamanian or Chamorro; Filipino; Vietnamese; Samoan; Other Asian; Other Pacific Islander; and Some other race. The last three options included space to print the specific race. The 2000 Census was also the first time that respondents were given the option of choosing more than one race. The Census population estimates program modified the enumerated population from the 2000 Census to produce the population estimates base for 2000 and onward. As part of the modification, the Census Bureau recoded the "Some other race" responses from the 2000 Census to one or more of the five OMB race categories used in the estimates program (for more information, see http://www.census.gov/popest/methodology/2008-nat-meth.pdf). Prior to 2000, the Census Bureau combined the categories Asian and Native Hawaiian or Other Pacific Islander. For all years, all persons of Hispanic origin were included in the Hispanic category regardless of the race option(s) chosen. Therefore, persons of Hispanic origin may be of any race.

Further information on the Decennial Census may be obtained from http://www.census.gov.

Survey of Income and Program Participation

The main objective of the Survey of Income and Program Participation (SIPP) is to provide accurate and comprehensive information about the income and program participation of individuals and households in the United States and about the principal determinants of income and program participation. SIPP offers detailed information on cash and noncash income on a subannual basis. The survey also collects data on taxes, assets, liabilities, and participation in government transfer programs. SIPP data allow the government to evaluate the effectiveness of federal, state, and local programs.

The survey design is a continuous series of national panels, with sample size ranging from approximately 14,000 to 36,700 interviewed households. The duration of each panel ranges from 2½ to 4 years. The SIPP sample is a multistage-stratified sample of the U.S. civilian noninstitutionalized population. For the 1984–93 panels, a new panel of households was introduced each year in February. A 4-year panel was introduced in April 1996. A 2000 panel was introduced in February 2000 for two waves, but was cancelled after 8 months. A 2½-year panel was introduced in February 2004 and is the first SIPP panel to use the 2000 decennial-based redesign of the sample. All household members ages 15 years and over are interviewed by self-response, if possible. Proxy response is permitted when household members are not available for interviewing. The latest panel was selected in September 2008.

The SIPP content is built around a "core" of labor force, program participation, and income questions designed to measure the economic situation of people in the United States. These questions expand the data currently available on the distribution of cash and noncash income and are repeated at each interviewing wave. The survey uses a 4-month recall period, with approximately the same number of interviews being conducted in each month of the 4-month period for each wave. Interviews are conducted by personal visit and by decentralized telephone.

The survey has been designed to also provide a broader context for analysis by adding questions on a variety of topics not covered in the core section. These questions are labeled "topical modules" and are assigned to particular interviewing waves of the survey. Topics covered by the modules include personal history, child care, wealth, program eligibility, child support, utilization and cost of healthcare, disability, school enrollment, taxes, and annual income.

Further information on the SIPP may be obtained from

Economics and Statistics Administration
Census Bureau
U.S. Department of Commerce
4600 Silver Hill Road
Washington, DC 20233
http://www.census.gov/sipp/intro.html

International Association for the Evaluation of Educational Achievement

The International Association for the Evaluation of Educational Achievement (IEA) is composed of governmental research centers and national research institutions around the world whose aim is to investigate education problems common among countries. Since its inception in 1958, the IEA has conducted more than 30 research studies of cross-national achievement. The regular cycle of studies encompasses learning in basic school subjects. Examples are the Trends in International Mathematics and Science Study (TIMSS) and the Progress in International Reading Literacy Study (PIRLS). IEA projects also include studies of particular interest to IEA members, such as the TIMSS 1999 Video Study of Mathematics and Science Teaching, the Civic Education Study, and studies on information technology in education.

The international bodies that coordinate international assessments vary in the labels they apply to participating education systems, most of which are countries. IEA differentiates between IEA members, which IEA refers to as "countries" in all cases, and "benchmarking participants." IEA members include countries such as the United States and Ireland, as well as subnational entities such as England and Scotland (which are both part of the United Kingdom), the Flemish community of Belgium, and Hong Kong-CHN (which is a Special Administrative Region of China). IEA benchmarking participants are all subnational entities and include Canadian provinces, U.S. states, and Dubai in the United Arab Emirates (among others). Benchmarking participants, like the participating countries, are given the opportunity to assess the comparative international standing of their students' achievement and to view their curriculum and instruction in an international context. Subnational entities that participated as benchmarking participants are excluded from this indicator's analysis.

Some IEA studies, such as TIMSS and PIRLS, include an assessment portion as well as contextual questionnaires to collect information about students' home and school experiences. The TIMSS and PIRLS scales, including the scale averages and standard deviations, are designed to remain constant from assessment to assessment so that education systems (including countries and subnational education systems) can compare their scores over time, as well as compare their scores directly with the scores of other education systems. Although each scale was created to have a mean of 500 and a standard deviation of 100, the subject matter and the level of difficulty of items necessarily differ by grade, subject, and domain/dimension. Therefore, direct comparisons between scores across grades, subjects, and different domain/dimension types should not be made.

Further information on the International Association for the Evaluation of Educational Achievement may be obtained from http://www.iea.nl.

Trends in International Mathematics and Science Study

The Trends in International Mathematics and Science Study (TIMSS, formerly known as the Third International Mathematics and Science Study) provides reliable and timely data on the mathematics and science achievement of U.S. fourth- and eighth-graders compared with that of their peers in other countries. TIMSS is on a 4-year cycle, with data collection occurring in 1995, 1999 (eighth grade only), 2003, 2007, and 2011. In 2011, a total of 77 education systems, including 63 IEA members and 14 benchmarking participants, participated in TIMSS. The next TIMSS data collection is scheduled for 2015. TIMSS collects information through mathematics and science assessments and questionnaires. The questionnaires request information to help provide a context for student performance, focusing on such topics as students' attitudes and beliefs about learning mathematics and science, what students do as part of their mathematics and science lessons, students' completion of homework, and their lives both in and outside of school; teachers' perceptions of their preparedness for teaching mathematics and science topics, teaching assignments, class size and organization, instructional content and practices, and participation in professional development activities; and principals' viewpoints on policy and budget responsibilities, curriculum and instruction issues, and student behavior, as well as descriptions of the organization of schools and courses. The assessments and questionnaires are designed to specifications in a guiding framework. The TIMSS framework describes the mathematics and science content to be assessed and provides grade-specific objectives, an overview of the assessment design, and guidelines for item development.

Progress in International Reading Literacy Study

The Progress in International Reading Literacy Study (PIRLS) provides reliable and timely data on the reading literacy of U.S. fourth-graders compared with that of their peers in other countries. PIRLS is on a 5-year cycle, with data having been collected in 2001, 2006, and 2011. In 2011, a total of 57 education systems, including 48 IEA members and 9 benchmarking participants, participated in PIRLS. The next PIRLS data collection is scheduled for 2016. PIRLS collects information through a reading literacy assessment and questionnaires that help to provide a context for student performance. Questionnaires are administered to collect information about students' home and school experiences in learning to read. A student questionnaire addresses students' attitudes towards reading and their reading habits. In addition, questionnaires are given to students' teachers and school principals to gather information about students' school experiences in developing reading literacy. In countries other than the United States, a parent questionnaire is also administered. The assessments and questionnaires are designed to specifications in a guiding framework. The PIRLS framework describes the reading content to be assessed and provides objectives specific to fourth grade, an overview of the assessment design, and guidelines for item development.

TIMSS and PIRLS Sampling and Response Rates

It is not feasible to assess every fourth- or eighth-grade student in the United States. As is done in all participating countries and other education systems, representative samples of students are selected. The sample design employed by TIMSS and PIRLS in 2011 is generally referred to as a two-stage stratified cluster sample. In the first stage of sampling, individual schools were selected with a probability proportionate to size (PPS) approach, which means that the probability is proportional to the estimated number of students enrolled in the target grade. In the second stage of sampling, intact classrooms were selected within sampled schools.

TIMSS and PIRLS guidelines call for a minimum of 150 schools to be sampled, with a minimum of 4,000 students assessed. The basic sample design of one classroom per school was designed to yield a total sample of approximately 4,500 students per population.

About 23,000 students in almost 900 schools across the United States participated in the 2011 TIMSS, joining 600,000 other student participants around the world. Because the Progress in International Reading Literacy Study (PIRLS) was also administered at grade 4 in spring 2011, TIMSS and PIRLS in the United States were administered in the same schools to the extent feasible. Students took either TIMSS or PIRLS on the day of the assessments. About 13,000 U.S. students participated in PIRLS in 2011, joining 300,000 other student participants around the world. Accommodations were not provided for students with disabilities or students who were unable to read or speak the language of the test. These students were excluded from the sample. The IEA requirement is that the overall exclusion rate, which is composed of exclusions of schools and students, should not exceed more than 5 percent of the national desired target population.

In order to minimize the potential for response biases, the IEA developed participation or response rate standards that apply to all participating education systems and govern whether or not an education system's data are included in the TIMSS or PIRLS international datasets and the way in which its statistics are presented in the international reports. These standards were set using composites of response rates at the school, classroom, and student and teacher levels. Response rates were calculated with and without the inclusion of substitute schools that were selected to replace schools refusing to participate. In TIMSS 2011 at grade 4 in the United States, the weighted school participation rate was 79 percent before the use of substitute schools and 84 percent after the use of replacement schools; the weighted student response rate was 95 percent. In TIMSS 2011 at grade 8 in the United States, the weighted school participation rate was 87 percent before the use of substitute schools and 87 percent after the use of replacement schools; the weighted student response rate was 94 percent. In the 2011 PIRLS administered in the United States, the weighted school participation rate was 80 percent before the use of substitute schools and 85 percent after the use of replacement schools; the weighted student response rate was 96 percent.

Further information on the TIMSS study may be obtained from

Stephen Provasnik
International Activities Program
National Center for Education Statistics
1990 K Street NW, Room 9034
Washington, DC 20006
(202) 502-7480
stephen.provasnik@ed.gov
http://nces.ed.gov/timss
http://www.iea.nl/timss_2011.html

Further information on the PIRLS study may be obtained from

Sheila Thompson
International Activities Program
National Center for Education Statistics
1990 K Street NW, Room 9031
Washington, DC 20006
(202) 502-7425
sheila.thompson@ed.gov
http://nces.ed.gov/surveys/pirls/
http://www.iea.nl/pirls_2011.html

Organization for Economic Cooperation and Development

The Organization for Economic Cooperation and Development (OECD) publishes analyses of national policies and survey data in education, training, and economics in OECD and partner countries. Newer studies include student survey data on financial literacy and on digital literacy.

Education at a Glance (EAG)

To highlight current education issues and create a set of comparative education indicators that represent key features of education systems, OECD initiated the Indicators of Education Systems (INES) project and charged the Centre for Educational Research and Innovation (CERI) with developing the cross-national indicators for it. The development of these indicators involved representatives of the OECD countries and the OECD Secretariat. Improvements in data quality and comparability among OECD countries have resulted from the country-to-country interaction sponsored through the INES project. The most recent publication in this series is *Education at a Glance 2012: OECD Indicators*.

The 2012 EAG featured the following 34 OECD countries: Australia, Austria, Belgium, Canada, Chile, the Czech Republic, Denmark, Estonia, Finland, France, Germany, Greece, Hungary, Iceland, Ireland, Israel, Italy, Japan, the Republic of Korea, Luxembourg, Mexico, the Netherlands, New Zealand, Norway, Poland, Portugal, the Slovak Republic, Slovenia, Spain, Sweden, Switzerland, Turkey, the United Kingdom, and the United States. In addition to these OECD countries, two non-OECD countries that participated in OECD's Indicators of Education Systems (INES) program, Brazil and the Russian Federation, were often included, along with six other G20 countries that did not participate in INES (Argentina, China, India, Indonesia, Saudi Arabia, and South Africa).

The *OECD Handbook for Internationally Comparative Education Statistics: Concepts, Standards, Definitions, and Classifications* provides countries with specific guidance on how to prepare information for OECD education surveys; facilitates countries' understanding of OECD indicators and their use in policy analysis; and provides a reference for collecting and assimilating educational data. Chapter 7 of the *OECD Handbook for Internationally Comparative Education Statistics* contains a discussion of data quality issues. Users should examine footnotes carefully to recognize some of the data limitations.

Further information on international education statistics may be obtained from

Andreas Schleicher
Indicators & Analysis Division
OECD Directorate for Education
2, rue André Pascal
75775 Paris CEDEX 16
France
andreas.schleicher@oecd.org
http://www.oecd.org

Program for International Student Assessment

The Program for International Student Assessment (PISA) is a system of international assessments that focuses on 15-year-olds' capabilities in reading literacy, mathematics literacy, and science literacy. PISA also includes measures of general, or cross-curricular, competencies such as learning strategies. PISA emphasizes functional skills that students have acquired as they near the end of mandatory schooling. PISA is organized by the Organization for Economic Cooperation and Development (OECD), an intergovernmental organization of industrialized countries, and was administered for the first time in 2000, when 43 education systems participated. In 2003, 41 education systems participated in the assessment; in

2006, 57 education systems (30 OECD member countries and 27 nonmember countries or education systems) participated; and in 2009, 65 education systems (34 OECD member countries and 31 nonmember countries or education systems) participated. An additional 9 education systems administered PISA 2009 in 2010.

PISA is a 2-hour paper-and-pencil exam. Assessment items include a combination of multiple-choice and open-ended questions, which require students to come up with their own response. PISA scores are reported on a scale that ranges from 0 to 1,000, with the OECD mean set at 500 and a standard deviation set at 100.

PISA is implemented on a 3-year cycle that began in 2000. Each PISA assessment cycle focuses on one subject in particular, although all three subjects are assessed every 3 years. In the first cycle, PISA 2000, reading literacy was the major focus, occupying roughly two-thirds of assessment time. For 2003, PISA focused on mathematics literacy as well as the ability of students to solve problems in real-life settings. In 2006, PISA focused on science literacy. In 2009, PISA focused on reading literacy again.

The intent of PISA reporting is to provide an overall description of performance in reading literacy, mathematics literacy, and science literacy every 3 years, and to provide a more detailed look at each domain in the years when it is the major focus. These cycles will allow education systems to compare changes in trends for each of the three subject areas over time.

To implement PISA, each of the participating education systems scientifically draws a nationally representative sample of 15-year-olds, regardless of grade level. In the United States, about 5,200 students from 165 public and private schools took the PISA 2009 assessment.

In each education system, the assessment is translated into the primary language of instruction; in the United States, all materials are written in English.

Further information on PISA may be obtained from

Holly Xie
Dana Kelly
Early Childhood, International, and Crosscutting Studies Division
International Activities Program
National Center for Education Statistics
1990 K Street NW
Washington, DC 20006
holly.xie@ed.gov
dana.kelly@ed.gov
http://nces.ed.gov/surveys/pisa

Glossary

A

Achievement gap Occurs when one group of students outperforms another group, and the difference in average scores for the two groups is statistically significant (that is, larger than the margin of error).

Achievement levels, NAEP Specific achievement levels for each subject area and grade to provide a context for interpreting student performance. At this time they are being used on a trial basis.

>   *Basic*—denotes partial mastery of the knowledge and skills that are fundamental for *proficient* work at a given grade.
>
>   *Proficient*—represents solid academic performance. Students reaching this level have demonstrated competency over challenging subject matter.
>
>   *Advanced*—signifies superior performance.

Associate's degree A degree granted for the successful completion of a sub-baccalaureate program of studies, usually requiring at least 2 years (or equivalent) of full-time college-level study. This includes degrees granted in a cooperative or work-study program.

Averaged freshman graduation rate (AFGR) A measure of the percentage of the incoming high school freshman class that graduates 4 years later. It is calculated by taking the number of graduates with a regular diploma and dividing that number by the estimated count of incoming freshman 4 years earlier, as reported through the NCES Common Core of Data (CCD). The estimated count of incoming freshman is the sum of the number of 8th-graders 5 years earlier, the number of 9th-graders 4 years earlier (when current seniors were freshman), and the number of 10th-graders 3 years earlier, divided by 3. The purpose of this averaging is to account for the high rate of grade retention in the freshman year, which adds 9th-grade repeaters from the previous year to the number of students in the incoming freshman class each year. Ungraded students are allocated to individual grades proportional to each state's enrollment in those grades. The AFGR treats students who transfer out of a school or district in the same way as it treats students from that school or district who drop out.

B

Bachelor's degree A degree granted for the successful completion of a baccalaureate program of studies, usually requiring at least 4 years (or equivalent) of full-time college-level study. This includes degrees granted in a cooperative or work-study program.

C

Charter school A school providing free public elementary and/or secondary education to eligible students under a specific charter granted by the state legislature or other appropriate authority, and designated by such authority to be a charter school.

Classification of Instructional Programs (CIP) The CIP is a taxonomic coding scheme that contains titles and descriptions of primarily postsecondary instructional programs. It was developed to facilitate NCES' collection and reporting of postsecondary degree completions by major field of study using standard classifications that capture the majority of reportable program activity. It was originally published in 1980 and was revised in 1985, 1990, 2000, and 2010.

College A postsecondary school which offers general, or liberal arts education, usually leading to an associate's, bachelor's, master's, doctor's, or first-professional degree. Junior colleges and community colleges are included under this terminology.

Combined school A school that encompasses instruction at both the elementary and the secondary levels; includes schools starting with grade 6 or below and ending with grade 9 or above.

Constant dollars Dollar amounts that have been adjusted by means of price and cost indexes to eliminate inflationary factors and allow direct comparison across years.

Consumer Price Index (CPI) This price index measures the average change in the cost of a fixed market basket of goods and services purchased by consumers. Indexes vary for specific areas or regions, periods of time, major groups of consumer expenditures, and population groups. The CPI reflects spending patterns for two population groups: (1) all urban consumers and urban wage earners and (2) clerical workers. CPIs are calculated for both the calendar year and the school year using the U.S. All Items CPI for All Urban Consumers (CPI-U). The calendar year CPI is the same as the annual CPI-U. The school year CPI is calculated by adding the monthly CPI-U figures, beginning with July of the first year and ending with June of the following year, and then dividing that figure by 12.

Current expenditures (elementary/secondary) The expenditures for operating local public schools, excluding capital outlay and interest on school debt. These expenditures include such items as salaries for school personnel, benefits, student transportation, school books and materials, and energy costs. Beginning in 1980–81, expenditures for state administration are excluded.

>   *Instruction expenditures* Includes expenditures for activities related to the interaction between teacher and students. Includes salaries and benefits for teachers and

instructional aides, textbooks, supplies, and purchased services such as instruction via television. Also included are tuition expenditures to other local education agencies.

Administration expenditures Includes expenditures for school administration (i.e., the office of the principal, full-time department chairpersons, and graduation expenses), general administration (the superintendent and board of education and their immediate staff), and other support services expenditures.

Transportation Includes expenditures for vehicle operation, monitoring, and vehicle servicing and maintenance.

Food services Includes all expenditures associated with providing food to students and staff in a school or school district. The services include preparing and serving regular and incidental meals or snacks in connection with school activities, as well as the delivery of food to schools.

Enterprise operations Includes expenditures for activities that are financed, at least in part, by user charges, similar to a private business. These include operations funded by sales of products or services, together with amounts for direct program support made by state education agencies for local school districts.

D

Default rate The percentage of loans that are in delinquency and have not been repaid according to the terms of the loan. According to the federal government, a federal student loan is in default if there has been no payment on the loan in 270 days. The Department of Education calculates a *2-year cohort* default rate, which is the percentage of students who entered repayment in a given fiscal year (from October 1 to September 30) and then defaulted within the following two fiscal years.

Degree-granting institutions Postsecondary institutions that are eligible for Title IV federal financial aid programs and grant an associate's or higher degree. For an institution to be eligible to participate in Title IV financial aid programs it must offer a program of at least 300 clock hours in length, have accreditation recognized by the U.S. Department of Education, have been in business for at least 2 years, and have signed a participation agreement with the Department.

Disabilities, children with Those children evaluated as having any of the following impairments and needing special education and related services because of these impairments. (These definitions apply specifically to data from the U.S. Office of Special Education and Rehabilitative Services presented in this publication.)

Deaf-blindness Having concomitant hearing and visual impairments which cause such severe communication and other developmental and educational problems that the student cannot be accommodated in special education programs solely for deaf or blind students.

Deafness Having a hearing impairment which is so severe that the student is impaired in processing linguistic information through hearing (with or without amplification) and which adversely affects educational performance.

Hearing impairment Having a hearing impairment, whether permanent or fluctuating, which adversely affects the student's educational performance, but which is not included under the definition of "deaf" in this section.

Intellectual disability Having significantly subaverage general intellectual functioning, existing concurrently with defects in adaptive behavior and manifested during the developmental period, which adversely affects the child's educational performance.

Multiple disabilities Having concomitant impairments (such as intellectually disabled-blind, intellectually disabled-orthopedically impaired, etc.), the combination of which causes such severe educational problems that the student cannot be accommodated in special education programs solely for one of the impairments. Term does not include deaf-blind students.

Orthopedic impairment Having a severe orthopedic impairment which adversely affects a student's educational performance. The term includes impairment resulting from congenital anomaly, disease, or other causes.

Other health impairment Having limited strength, vitality, or alertness due to chronic or acute health problems, such as a heart condition, tuberculosis, rheumatic fever, nephritis, asthma, sickle cell anemia, hemophilia, epilepsy, lead poisoning, leukemia, or diabetes, which adversely affect the student's educational performance.

Serious emotional disturbance Exhibiting one or more of the following characteristics over a long period of time, to a marked degree, and adversely affecting educational performance: an inability to learn which cannot be explained by intellectual, sensory, or health factors; an inability to build or maintain satisfactory interpersonal relationships with peers and teachers; inappropriate types of behavior or feelings under normal circumstances; a general pervasive mood of unhappiness or depression; or a tendency to develop physical symptoms or fears associated with personal or school problems. This term does not include children who are socially maladjusted, unless they also display one or more of the listed characteristics.

Specific learning disability Having a disorder in one or more of the basic psychological processes involved in understanding or in using spoken or written language, which may manifest itself in an imperfect ability to listen, think, speak, read, write, spell, or do mathematical calculations. The term includes such conditions as perceptual disabilities, brain injury, minimal brain dysfunction, dyslexia, and developmental aphasia. The term does not include children who have learning problems which are primarily the result of visual, hearing, or environmental, cultural, or economic disadvantage.

Speech/language impairment Having a communication disorder, such as stuttering, impaired articulation, language impairment, or voice impairment, which adversely affects the student's educational performance.

Visual impairment Having a visual impairment which, even with correction, adversely affects the student's educational performance. The term includes partially seeing and blind children.

Doctor's degree An earned degree that generally carries the title of Doctor. The Doctor of Philosophy degree (Ph.D.) is the highest academic degree and requires mastery within a field of knowledge and demonstrated ability to perform scholarly research. Other doctor's degrees are awarded for fulfilling specialized requirements in professional fields, such as education (Ed.D.), musical arts (D.M.A.), business administration (D.B.A.), and engineering (D.Eng. or D.E.S.). Many doctor's degrees in academic and professional fields require an earned master's degree as a prerequisite. The doctor's degree classification includes most degrees that NCES formerly classified as first-professional degrees. Such degrees are awarded in the fields of dentistry (D.D.S. or D.M.D.), medicine (M.D.), optometry (O.D.), osteopathic medicine (D.O.), pharmacy (Pharm.D.), podiatry (D.P.M., Pod.D., or D.P.), veterinary medicine (D.V.M.), chiropractic (D.C. or D.C.M.), and law (L.L.B. or J.D.).

Dropout The term is used to describe both the event of leaving school before completing high school and the status of an individual who is not in school and who is not a high school completer. High school completers include both graduates of school programs as well as those completing high school through equivalency programs such as the General Educational Development (GED) program. Transferring from a public school to a private school, for example, is not regarded as a dropout event. A person who drops out of school may later return and graduate but is called a "dropout" at the time he or she leaves school. Measures to describe these behaviors include the event dropout rate (or the closely related school persistence rate), the status dropout rate, and the high school completion rate.

E

Educational attainment The highest grade of regular school attended and completed.

Educational attainment (Current Population Survey) This measure uses March CPS data to estimate the percentage of civilian, noninstitutionalized people ages 25 through 29 who have achieved certain levels of educational attainment. Estimates of educational attainment do not differentiate between those who graduated from public schools, those who graduated from private schools, and those who earned a GED; these estimates also include individuals who earned their credential or completed their highest level of education outside of the United States.

1972–1991 During this period, an individual's educational attainment was considered to be his or her last fully completed year of school. Individuals who completed 12 years of schooling were deemed to be high school graduates, as were those who began but did not complete the first year of college. Respondents who completed 16 or more years of schooling were counted as college graduates.

1992–present Beginning in 1992, CPS asked respondents to report their highest level of school completed or their highest degree received. This change means that some data collected before 1992 are not strictly comparable with data collected from 1992 onward and that care must be taken when making comparisons across years. The revised survey question emphasizes credentials received rather than the last grade level attended or completed. The new categories include the following:

- High school graduate, high school diploma, or the equivalent (e.g., GED)
- Some college but no degree
- Associate's degree in college, occupational/vocational program
- Associate's degree in college, academic program (e.g., A.A., A.S., A.A.S.)
- Bachelor's degree (e.g., B.A., A.B., B.S.)
- Master's degree (e.g., M.A., M.S., M.Eng., M.Ed., M.S.W., M.B.A.)
- Professional school degree (e.g., M.D., D.D.S., D.V.M., LL.B., J.D.)
- Doctor's degree (e.g., Ph.D., Ed.D.)

Elementary school A school classified as elementary by state and local practice and composed of any span of grades not above grade 8.

English language learner (ELL) An individual who, due to any of the reasons listed below, has sufficient difficulty speaking, reading, writing, or understanding the English language to be denied the opportunity to learn successfully in classrooms where the language of instruction is English or to participate fully in the larger U.S. society. Such an individual (1) was not born in the United States or has a native language other than English; (2) comes from environments where a language other than English is dominant; or (3) is an American Indian or Alaska Native and comes from environments where a language other than English has had a significant impact on the individual's level of English language proficiency.

Expenditures, Total For elementary/secondary schools, these include all charges for current outlays plus capital outlays and interest on school debt. For degree-granting institutions, these include current outlays plus capital outlays. For government, these include charges net of recoveries and other correcting transactions other than for retirement of debt, investment in securities, extension of credit, or as agency transactions. Government expenditures include only external transactions, such as the provision of perquisites or other payments in kind. Aggregates for groups of governments exclude intergovernmental transactions among the governments.

Expenditures per pupil Charges incurred for a particular period of time divided by a student unit of measure, such as average daily attendance or fall enrollment.

F

Financial aid Grants, loans, assistantships, scholarships, fellowships, tuition waivers, tuition discounts, veteran's benefits, employer aid (tuition reimbursement), and other monies (other than from relatives or friends) provided to students to help them meet expenses. Except where designated, includes Title IV subsidized and unsubsidized loans made directly to students.

For-profit institution A private institution in which the individual(s) or agency in control receives compensation other than wages, rent, or other expenses for the assumption of risk.

Free or reduced-price lunch See National School Lunch Program.

Full-time enrollment The number of students enrolled in higher education courses with total credit load equal to at least 75 percent of the normal full-time course load. At the undergraduate level, full-time enrollment includes students who have a credit load of 12 or more semester or quarter credits. At the postbaccalaureate level, full-time enrollment includes students who have a credit load of 9 or more semester or quarter credits, as well as other students who are considered full time by their institutions.

Full-time-equivalent (FTE) enrollment For institutions of higher education, enrollment of full-time students, plus the full-time equivalent of part-time students. The full-time equivalent of the part-time students is estimated using different factors depending on the type and control of institution and level of student.

G

GED certificate This award is received following successful completion of the General Educational Development (GED) test. The GED program, sponsored by the American Council on Education, enables individuals to demonstrate that they have acquired a level of learning comparable to that of high school graduates. See also High school equivalency certificate.

Graduate enrollment The number of students who are working towards a master's or doctor's degree. These enrollment data measure those students who are registered at a particular time during the fall. At some institutions, graduate enrollment also includes students who are in postbaccalaureate classes but not in degree programs. In most tables, graduate enrollment includes all students in regular graduate programs and all students in postbaccalaureate classes but not in degree programs (unclassified postbaccalaureate students).

Gross domestic product (GDP) The total national output of goods and services valued at market prices. GDP can be viewed in terms of expenditure categories which include purchases of goods and services by consumers and government, gross private domestic investment, and net exports of goods and services. The goods and services included are largely those bought for final use (excluding illegal transactions) in the market economy. A number of inclusions, however, represent imputed values, the most important of which is rental value of owner-occupied housing. GDP, in this broad context, measures the output attributable to the factors of production—labor and property—supplied by U.S. residents.

H

High school completer An individual who has been awarded a high school diploma or an equivalent credential, including a General Educational Development (GED) certificate.

High school diploma A formal document regulated by the state certifying the successful completion of a prescribed secondary school program of studies. In some states or communities, high school diplomas are differentiated by type, such as an academic diploma, a general diploma, or a vocational diploma.

High school equivalency certificate A formal document certifying that an individual has met the state requirements for high school graduation equivalency by obtaining satisfactory scores on an approved examination and meeting other performance requirements (if any) set by a state education agency or other appropriate body. One particular version of this certificate is the General Educational Development (GED) test. The GED test is a comprehensive test used primarily to appraise the educational development of students who have not completed their formal high school education and who may earn a high school equivalency certificate by achieving satisfactory scores. GEDs are awarded by the states or other agencies, and the test is developed and distributed by the GED Testing Service of the American Council on Education.

Higher education institutions (basic classification)

4-year institution An institution legally authorized to offer and offering at least a 4-year program of college-level studies wholly or principally creditable toward a baccalaureate degree. In some tables, a further division between universities and other 4-year institutions is made. A "university" is a postsecondary institution which typically comprises one or more graduate professional schools. For purposes of trend comparisons in this volume, the selection of universities has been held constant for all tabulations after 1982. "Other 4-year institutions" would include the rest of the nonuniversity 4-year institutions.

2-year institution An institution legally authorized to offer and offering at least a 2-year program of college-level studies which terminates in an associate degree or is principally creditable toward a baccalaureate degree. Also includes some institutions that have a less than 2-year program but were designated as institutions of higher education in the Higher Education General Information Survey.

Less-than-2-year institution An institution that offers programs of less than 2 years' duration below the baccalaureate level. Includes occupational and vocational schools with programs that do not exceed 1,800 contact hours.

I

Individuals with Disabilities Education Act (IDEA) IDEA is a federal law requiring services to children with disabilities throughout the nation. IDEA governs how states and public agencies provide early intervention, special education, and related services to more than 6.8 million eligible infants, toddlers, children, and youth with disabilities. Infants and toddlers with disabilities (birth–age 2) and their families receive early intervention services under IDEA, Part C. Children and youth (ages 3–21) receive special education and related services under IDEA, Part B.

International Standard Classification of Education (ISCED) Used to compare educational systems in different countries. ISCED is the standard used by many countries to report education statistics to the United Nations Educational, Scientific, and Cultural Organization (UNESCO) and the Organisation for Economic Co-operation and Development (OECD). ISCED divides educational systems into the following seven categories, based on six levels of education.

ISCED Level 0 Education preceding the first level (early childhood education) usually begins at age 3, 4, or 5 (sometimes earlier) and lasts from 1 to 3 years, when it is provided. In the United States, this level includes nursery school and kindergarten.

ISCED Level 1 Education at the first level (primary or elementary education) usually begins at age 5, 6, or 7 and continues for about 4 to 6 years. For the United States, the first level starts with 1st grade and ends with 6th grade.

ISCED Level 2 Education at the second level (lower secondary education) typically begins at about age 11 or 12 and continues for about 2 to 6 years. For the United States, the second level starts with 7th grade and typically ends with 9th grade. Education at the lower secondary level continues the basic programs of the first level, although teaching is typically more subject focused, often using more specialized teachers who conduct classes in their field of specialization. The main criterion for distinguishing lower secondary education from primary education is whether programs begin to be organized in a more subject-oriented pattern, using more specialized teachers conducting classes in their field of specialization. If there is no clear breakpoint for this organizational change, lower secondary education is considered to begin at the end of 6 years of primary education. In countries with no clear division between lower secondary and upper secondary education, and where lower secondary education lasts for more than 3 years, only the first 3 years following primary education are counted as lower secondary education.

ISCED Level 3 Education at the third level (upper secondary education) typically begins at age 15 or 16 and lasts for approximately 3 years. In the United States, the third level starts with 10th grade and ends with 12th grade. Upper secondary education is the final stage of secondary education in most OECD countries. Instruction is often organized along subject-matter lines, in contrast to the lower secondary level, and teachers typically must have a higher level, or more subject-specific, qualification. There are substantial differences in the typical duration of programs both across and between countries, ranging from 2 to 5 years of schooling. The main criteria for classifications are (1) national boundaries between lower and upper secondary education and (2) admission into educational programs, which usually requires the completion of lower secondary education or a combination of basic education and life experience that demonstrates the ability to handle the subject matter in upper secondary schools.

ISCED Level 4 Education at the fourth level (postsecondary nontertiary education) straddles the boundary between secondary and postsecondary education. This program of study, which is primarily vocational in nature, is generally taken after the completion of secondary school and typically lasts from 6 months to 2 years. Although the content of these programs may not be significantly more advanced than upper secondary programs, these programs serve to broaden the knowledge of participants who have already gained an upper secondary qualification.

ISCED Level 5 Education at the fifth level (first stage of tertiary education) includes programs with more advanced content than those offered at the two previous levels. Entry into programs at the fifth level normally requires successful completion of either of the two previous levels.

ISCED Level 5A Tertiary-type A programs provide an education that is largely theoretical and is intended to provide sufficient qualifications for gaining entry into advanced research programs and professions with high skill requirements. Entry into these programs normally requires the successful completion of an upper secondary education; admission is competitive in most cases. The minimum cumulative theoretical duration at this level is 3 years of full-time enrollment. In the United States, tertiary-type A programs include first university programs that last approximately 4 years and lead to the award of a bachelor's degree and second university programs that lead to a master's degree.

ISCED Level 5B Tertiary-type B programs are typically shorter than tertiary-type A programs and focus on practical, technical, or occupational skills for direct entry into the labor market, although they may cover some theoretical foundations in the respective programs. They have a minimum duration of 2 years of full-time enrollment at the tertiary level. In the United States, such programs are often provided at community colleges and lead to an associate's degree.

ISCED Level 6 Education at the sixth level (advanced research qualification) is provided in graduate and professional schools that generally require a university degree or diploma as a minimum condition for admission. Programs at this level lead to the award of an advanced, postgraduate degree, such as a Ph.D. The theoretical duration of these programs is 3 years of full-time enrollment in most countries (for a cumulative total of at least 7 years at levels five and six), although the length of the actual enrollment is often longer. Programs at this level are devoted to advanced study and original research.

M

Master's degree A degree awarded for successful completion of a program generally requiring 1 or 2 years of full-time college-level study beyond the bachelor's degree. One type of master's degree, including the Master of Arts degree, or M.A., and the Master of Science degree, or M.S., is awarded in the liberal arts and sciences for advanced scholarship in a subject field or discipline and demonstrated ability to perform scholarly research. A second type of master's degree is awarded for the completion of a professionally oriented program, for example, an M.Ed. in education, an M.B.A. in business administration, an M.F.A. in fine arts, an M.M. in music, an M.S.W. in social work, and an M.P.A. in public administration. Some master's degrees—such as divinity degrees (M.Div. or M.H.L./Rav), which were formerly classified as "first-professional"—may require more than 2 years of full-time study beyond the bachelor's degree.

N

National School Lunch Program Established by President Truman in 1946, the program is a federally assisted meal program operated in public and private nonprofit schools and residential child care centers. To be eligible for free lunch, a student must be from a household with an income at or below 130 percent of the federal poverty guideline; to be eligible for reduced-price lunch, a student must be from a household with an income between 130 percent and 185 percent of the federal poverty guideline.

Nonprofit institution A private institution in which the individual(s) or agency in control receives no compensation other than wages, rent, or other expenses for the assumption of risk. Nonprofit institutions may be either independent nonprofit (i.e., having no religious affiliation) or religiously affiliated.

Nursery school An instructional program for groups of children during the year or years preceding kindergarten, which provides educational experiences under the direction of teachers. See also Prekindergarten.

O

Organisation for Economic Co-operation and Development (OECD) An intergovernmental organization of 34 industrialized countries that serves as a forum for member countries to cooperate in research and policy development on social and economic topics of common interest. These countries include: Australia, Austria, Belgium, Canada, Chile, the Czech Republic, Denmark, Estonia, Finland, France, Germany, Greece, Hungary, Iceland, Ireland, Israel, Italy, Japan, Korea, Luxembourg, Mexico, Netherlands, New Zealand, Norway, Poland, Portugal, Slovak Republic, Slovenia, Spain, Sweden, Switzerland, Turkey, United Kingdom, and United States. In addition to member countries, partner countries (Brazil, China, India, Indonesia, Russia, and South Africa) contribute to the OECD's work in a sustained and comprehensive manner.

P

Part-time enrollment The number of students enrolled in higher education courses with a total credit load less than 75 percent of the normal full-time credit load. At the undergraduate level, part-time enrollment includes students who have a credit load of less than 12 semester or quarter credits. At the postbaccalaureate level, full-time enrollment includes students who have a credit load of less than 9 semester or quarter credits.

Postbaccalaureate enrollment The number of students working towards advanced degrees and of students enrolled in graduate-level classes but not enrolled in degree programs. See also Graduate enrollment.

Postsecondary education The provision of formal instructional programs with a curriculum designed primarily for students who have completed the requirements for a high school diploma or equivalent. This includes programs of an academic, vocational, and continuing professional education purpose, and excludes avocational and adult basic education programs.

Poverty The U.S. Census Bureau uses a set of money income thresholds that vary by family size and composition. A family, along with each individual in it, is considered poor if the family's total income is less than that family's threshold. The poverty thresholds do not vary geographically and are adjusted annually for inflation using the Consumer Price Index. The official poverty definition counts money income before taxes and does not include capital gains and noncash benefits (such as public housing, Medicaid, and food stamps).

Prekindergarten Preprimary education for children typically ages 3–4 who have not yet entered kindergarten. It may offer a program of general education or special education and may be part of a collaborative effort with Head Start.

Private institution An institution that is controlled by an individual or agency other than a state, a subdivision of a state, or the federal government, which is usually supported primarily by other than public funds, and the operation of whose program rests with other than publicly elected or appointed officials.

Private nonprofit institution An institution in which the individual(s) or agency in control receives no compensation other than wages, rent, or other expenses for the assumption of risk. These include both independent nonprofit institutions and those affiliated with a religious organization.

Private for-profit institution An institution in which the individual(s) or agency in control receives compensation other than wages, rent, or other expenses for the assumption of risk (e.g., proprietary schools).

Private school Private elementary/secondary schools surveyed by the Private School Universe Survey (PSS) are assigned to one of three major categories (Catholic, other religious, or nonsectarian) and, within each major category, one of three subcategories based on the school's religious affiliation provided by respondents.

Catholic Schools categorized according to governance, provided by Catholic school respondents, into parochial, diocesan, and private schools.

Other religious Schools that have a religious orientation or purpose but are not Roman Catholic. Other religious schools are categorized according to religious association membership, provided by respondents, into Conservative Christian, other affiliated, and unaffiliated schools. Conservative Christian schools are those "Other religious" schools with membership in at least one of four associations: Accelerated Christian Education, American Association of Christian Schools, Association of Christian Schools International, and Oral Roberts University Education Fellowship. Affiliated schools are those "Other religious" schools not classified as Conservative Christian with membership in at least 1 of 11 associations—Association of Christian Teachers and Schools, Christian Schools International, Evangelical Lutheran Education Association, Friends Council on Education, General Conference of the Seventh-Day Adventist Church, Islamic School League of America, National Association of Episcopal Schools, National Christian School Association, National Society for Hebrew Day Schools, Solomon Schechter Day Schools, and Southern Baptist Association of Christian Schools—or indicating membership in "other religious school associations." Unaffiliated schools are those "Other religious" schools that have a religious orientation or purpose but are not classified as Conservative Christian or affiliated.

Nonsectarian Schools that do not have a religious orientation or purpose and are categorized according to program emphasis, provided by respondents, into regular, special emphasis, and special education schools. Regular schools are those that have a regular elementary/secondary or early childhood program emphasis. Special emphasis schools are those that have a Montessori, vocational/technical, alternative, or special program emphasis. Special education schools are those that have a special education program emphasis.

Property tax The sum of money collected from a tax levied against the value of property.

Public school or institution A school or institution controlled and operated by publicly elected or appointed officials and deriving its primary support from public funds.

Purchasing Power Parity (PPP) indexes PPP exchange rates, or indexes, are the currency exchange rates that equalize the purchasing power of different currencies, meaning that when a given sum of money is converted into different currencies at the PPP exchange rates, it will buy the same basket of goods and services in all countries. PPP indexes are the rates of currency conversion that eliminate the difference in price levels among countries. Thus, when expenditures on gross domestic product (GDP) for different countries are converted into a common currency by means of PPP indexes, they are expressed at the same set of international prices, so that comparisons among countries reflect only differences in the volume of goods and services purchased.

R

Racial/ethnic group Classification indicating general racial or ethnic heritage. Race/ethnicity data are based on the *Hispanic* ethnic category and the race categories listed below (five single-race categories, plus the *Two or more races* category). Race categories exclude persons of Hispanic ethnicity unless otherwise noted.

White A person having origins in any of the original peoples of Europe, the Middle East, or North Africa.

Black or African American A person having origins in any of the black racial groups of Africa. Used interchangeably with the shortened term *Black*.

Hispanic or Latino A person of Cuban, Mexican, Puerto Rican, South or Central American, or other Spanish culture or origin, regardless of race. Used interchangeably with the shortened term *Hispanic*.

Asian A person having origins in any of the original peoples of the Far East, Southeast Asia, or the Indian subcontinent, including, for example, Cambodia, China, India, Japan, Korea, Malaysia, Pakistan, the Philippine Islands, Thailand, and Vietnam. Prior to 2010–11, the Common Core of Data (CCD) combined Asian and Pacific Islander categories.

Native Hawaiian or Other Pacific Islander A person having origins in any of the original peoples of Hawaii, Guam, Samoa, or other Pacific Islands. Prior to 2010–11, the Common Core of Data (CCD) combined Asian and Pacific Islander categories.

American Indian or Alaska Native A person having origins in any of the original peoples of North and South America (including Central America), and who maintains tribal affiliation or community attachment.

Two or more races A person identifying himself or herself as of two or more of the following race groups: White, Black, Asian, Native Hawaiian or Other Pacific Islander, or American Indian or Alaska Native. Some, but not all, reporting districts use this category. "Two or more races" was introduced in the 2000 Census and became a regular category for data collection in the Current Population Survey (CPS) in 2003. The category is sometimes excluded from a historical series of data with constant categories. It is sometimes included within the category "Other."

Regular school A public elementary/secondary school providing instruction and education services that does not focus primarily on special education, vocational/technical education, or alternative education, or on any of the particular themes associated with magnet/special-program-emphasis schools.

Revenue All funds received from external sources, net of refunds, and correcting transactions. Noncash transactions, such as receipt of services, commodities, or other receipts in kind are excluded, as are funds received from the issuance of debt, liquidation of investments, and nonroutine sale of property.

S

Salary The total amount regularly paid or stipulated to be paid to an individual, before deductions, for personal services rendered while on the payroll of a business or organization.

Secondary school A school comprising any span of grades beginning with the next grade following an elementary or middle school (usually 7, 8, or 9) and ending with or below grade 12. Both junior high schools and senior high schools are included.

Student membership Student membership is an annual headcount of students enrolled in school on October 1 or the school day closest to that date. The Common Core of Data (CCD) allows a student to be reported for only a single school or agency. For example, a vocational school (identified as a "shared time" school) may provide classes for students from a number of districts and show no membership.

T

Traditional public school Publicly funded schools other than public charter schools. See also Public school or institution and Charter school.

Tuition and fees A payment or charge for instruction or compensation for services, privileges, or the use of equipment, books, or other goods. Tuition may be charged per term, per course, or per credit.

U

Undergraduate students Students registered at an institution of higher education who are working in a baccalaureate degree program or other formal program below the baccalaureate, such as an associate's degree, vocational, or technical program.